edited by **BURTON ONG**

INTELLECTUAL PROPERTY AND BIOLOGICAL RESOURCES

Marshall Cavendish Academic

Published 2004 by Marshall Cavendish Academic
An imprint of Marshall Cavendish International (Singapore) Private Limited
A member of Times Publishing Limited

Times Centre, 1 New Industrial Road,
Singapore 536196
Tel:(65) 6213 9288
Fax: (65) 6284 9772
E-mail: mca@sg.marshallcavendish.com
Website:
http://www.marshallcavendish.com/academic

ISBN: 981-210-371-6

A CIP catalogue record for this book is available from the National Library Board (Singapore).

Printed by Times Graphics Pte Ltd, Singapore
on non-acidic paper

London • New York • Beijing • Shanghai • Bangkok • Kuala Lumpur • Singapore

International Board of Advisors

Contents

Foreword

Not so long ago, biotechnology and, in particular, genetic engineering were heralded as exciting new sciences capable of solving mankind's most intractable problems. Disease was to be significantly reduced, and eventually eliminated; abundant and varied food supplies were to rescue the starving masses from their present wretched conditions; and the world would be well along the road to Valhalla.

Today, that image of biotechnology has changed. Its promise may be as great as ever, but the means of achieving these goals have become embroiled in many controversies, with intellectual property issues frequently at their centre. Access to, control over and ownership of biological resources and their products have been challenged by all kinds of interest groups: by environmentalists and others concerned with the long term protection of diminishing resources; by those concerned to protect the indigenous peoples who provide the essential traditional knowledge and materials to which our scientists add value; by developing countries who believe that their interests have been subjugated by the developed world; and by those concerned with the manifold ethical, religious, social, legal and political questions which the new technologies throw up.

The answer, as always in matters relating to intellectual property, is to find a proper balance between intellectual property rights and all these competing interests. As always, though, finding an acceptable balance is fraught with difficulty. Thus, the intellectual property/environmentalist battle features strict adherents to the TRIPS Agreement at one extreme versus beneficiaries of the Convention on Biological Diversity (and related Conventions) on the other. At first, there was little interest in addressing the critical issues affecting an appropriate relationship between these seemingly conflicting international agreements. Now, there is greater recognition that these must be addressed and some compromises made.

In December 2003, the Asia-Pacific Centre for Environmental Law (APCEL) of the Faculty of Law (National University of Singapore), the Singapore Academy of Law (SAL), the Intellectual Property Office of Singapore (IPOS) and the Intellectual Property Academy (Singapore) organised an international conference on "Intellectual Property and Biological Resources" to bring together academics, practitioners and policy makers to share their views on the controversies that the global biotechnology revolution have generated , with particular emphasis on the compatibility of intellectual property rights with the biological wealth that resides in the flora and fauna of developing countries.

Invited distinguished speakers presented papers on the legal, ethical, sociological and environmental implications of the expansion of traditional intellectual property rights, and the development of alternative models of legal protection, to encompass non-human biological products and all genetic resources extracted from nature.

This volume comprises the edited papers presented at the Conference. Chapter 1 by the editor of the volume, Burton Ong, provides an excellent account of the issues and a summary of the major themes tackled by the assembled experts. Their papers provide full and informed analyses of the current state of play and of various recommendations (including by the authors themselves) for reform. As with the biological resources with which they are concerned, these areas of activity cannot remain static. The debate is alive and developing rapidly. Nevertheless, to all those with an interest in these matters, this volume must rank highly as an authoritative and invaluable contribution to the literature on this subject.

It is appropriate to record thanks to those who partnered the organisers of the conference, namely the IUCN Commission on Environmental Law, IUCN Academy of Environmental Law, the Japan Bioindustry Association (JBA), the Macquarie University Centre for Environmental Law, the United Nations University Institute of Advanced Studies (UNU/IAS) and the World Intellectual Property Organisation; to the Lee Foundation and the Shaw Foundation Pte. who were sponsors of the conference; to all those involved in the organisation of the conference and of this volume; and, of course, to all those who presented these stimulating papers and otherwise attended and participated in the lively discussions.

In particular, the major contribution of Burton Ong in designing the programme must be acknowledged. His labour of love in editing the volume involved not only time, effort and "sweat of the brow" but also admirable intellectual creativity.

Gerald Dworkin
Director
IP Academy, Singapore
August 2004

Preface

The chapters in this book comprise the edited works of a broad range of leading academics, scholars and commentators with an interest in the myriad of contentious legal and policy issues which have emerged from the extension of intellectual property rights into the field of biotechnological innovations with non-human organic origins. These contributors, hailing from 10 countries across five continents, were invited to present papers at a conference held in Singapore from December 1–3, 2003: they were selected based on their individual expertise in different areas of intellectual property law or international environmental law, as well as their divergent perspectives on the multi-faceted character of the current controversies facing policy-makers around the world. To these contributors, I owe a debt of gratitude for contributing to the success of the conference and for collaborating with me on this publication project. Each of you has, in your respective chapters, presented critical strands of the key debates that remain unresolved by the global legal community, and I am grateful for your perceptive multi-disciplinary and geopolitical insights into the tapestry of interwoven issues that have driven, and will continue to drive, crucial legal developments in this sector of the legal universe.

I also need to thank a number of individuals for their varied contributions to the planning and running of the conference which brought together the contributors of this publication. To Professors Koh Kheng Lian and Lye Lin Heng, your energy and enthusiasm were largely responsible for the genesis of this project: thank you for your trust and for giving me the opportunity to engage in this intellectually satisfying endeavour. To Professors Gerald Dworkin, George Wei and Ng-Loy Wee Loon, your generosity of spirit, mentorship and friendship helped sustain me through the winding path that led to this publication: thank you for your unwavering moral support, and for sharing your wisdom and academic ebullience with me. To the student volunteers who worked diligently with me to organise the conference—Adeline, Alexandra, Ann Marie, Audrey, Berenice, Cheryl, Connie, Jane, Janice, Kelvin, Ming Yi, Sabrina, and Yi Lin—I would like to convey my appreciation for your dedication, professionalism and tireless efforts before, during and after the conference.

Finally, I wish to thank Joyce, my wife, for standing by me through the ups and downs of this editorial enterprise. I am grateful for the counsel, assistance and encouragement offered to me throughout the entire process.

Burton Ong
Faculty of Law,
National University of Singapore
August 2004

The 2003 Conference Organisers

ASIA-PACIFIC CENTRE FOR ENVIRONMENTAL LAW (APCEL)

The Asia-Pacific Centre for Environmental Law (APCEL) was established in February 1996 by the Faculty of Law, National University of Singapore, at the initiative of the Faculty and the World Conservation Union–Commission on Environmental Law (IUCN–CEL), and in collaboration with the United Nations Environment Programme (UNEP). It was launched on July 1 of the same year. The initiative was in response to the call in Agenda 21 to build capacity in environmental law and to promote awareness of environmental issues. One of APCEL's objectives is to develop itself as a centre of excellence in the region for capacity building in environmental law.

Some of the main objectives of APCEL include:

- Serving as a regional training centre for the teaching of environmental law;
- Organising conferences, seminars and other programmes on environmental issues;
- Serving as a regional centre for research, including multi-disciplinary research on international, regional and national environmental law and policy;
- Promoting the exchange of information on international, regional and national environmental law and policy;
- Cooperating and collaborating with law schools, institutes, centres and such other organisations to further its objectives.

Since its establishment, APCEL has organised numerous activities on its own as well as in collaboration with other international and local organisations such as the Asian Development Bank (ADB), IUCN–CEL,

UNEP, International Maritime Organisation (IMO), United Nations Development Programme (UNDP), United Nations Institute for Training and Research (UNITAR), United Nations University (UNU), United States–Asia Environmental Partnership (US–AEP), Pace University's Centre for Environmental Legal Studies, Southeast Asian Programme on Ocean Law Policy and Management (SEAPOL), Regional Institute of Environmental Technology (RIET), Singapore Ministry of the Environment and Water Resources, Maritime and Port Authority of Singapore, Singapore Ministry of Foreign Affairs, World Bank Institute, and Institute of Policy Studies, Singapore. These activities include conferences, seminars, forums, workshops, and training courses on various topics such as biodiversity, trade and environment, marine pollution, environmental legislation on sustainable development, and teaching environmental law at university level in the Asia-Pacific region.

For more information on APCEL, please visit http://law.nus.edu.sg/apcel/.

IPacademy
Empowering the Intellect

IP ACADEMY, SINGAPORE

The IP Academy was launched in January 2003, as the focal point for intellectual property (IP) education and training in Singapore. The IP Academy's mission is to promote education and training, research and scholarship in IP. With this in mind, the IP Academy has embarked upon two strategies; Education and Research.

The Education charter aims to provide continuing education and lifelong learning opportunities for IP professionals, businesses and research organisations. The IP Academy addresses the demands of the industry, academia and legal community, by designing courses that meet the need for cross-disciplinary knowledge and skill sets. Over the past year, the IP Academy has introduced a number of educational courses, which boost IP capabilities.

The Research charter aims to develop depth in IP competencies, enabling Singapore to keep at the forefront of IP developments. Various thought leadership programmes will be developed, including discussion fora, international conferences and research projects.

The IP Academy works strategically with both local and international partners, complementing each other's strengths, to better manage Singapore IP capabilities. Since its launch, the IP Academy has formed linkages with the Chicago Graduate School of Business, Intellectual Property Office of Singapore (IPOS), INSEAD, National University of Singapore, Nanyang Technological University, Singapore Management University, Intellectual Property Institute of Australia, Queen Mary Intellectual Property Research Institute, National Chiao Tung University, Sun Yat-sen Institute of Social Sciences and Philosophy, Academia Sinica, and University of Technology Sydney.

For more information on the IP Academy's courses and research projects, please visit http://www.ipacademy.edu.sg/.

IPOS

INTELLECTUAL PROPERTY
OFFICE OF SINGAPORE

INTELLECTUAL PROPERTY OFFICE OF SINGAPORE (IPOS)

Formerly known as the Registry of Trade Marks and Patents, the Intellectual Property Office of Singapore (IPOS) was established as a statutory board of the Ministry of Law on April 1, 2001. It is the lead government agency that advises on and administers intellectual property (IP) laws, promotes IP awareness and provides the infrastructure to facilitate the greater development of IP in Singapore. With IP fast becoming a critical resource in the new economy, IPOS' vision is to foster a creative Singapore where ideas and intellectual efforts are valued, developed and exploited.

To achieve this, IPOS has initiated several programmes targeted at the business sector, general public, and IP professionals.

Business

The initiatives for local business community are aimed towards building an IP-savvy business sector which is key in making Singapore a compelling intellectual property hub and a choice location for the conduct of IP business.

The latest initiative for the business sector is "Strategies for Creation, Ownership, Protection and Exploitation of Intellectual Property, " or SCOPE IP. This is a national IP Management programme designed for businesses in Singapore. It aims to help companies adopt best practices in IP management.

General Public

The *HIP Alliance* is IPOS' key public outreach and education programme aimed at raising public awareness on IP. *HIP* stands for Honour Intellectual Property. The *HIP Alliance* is a group of Government agencies, private organisations and industry associations with a common interest in reaching out to the public on the importance of respecting IP rights. Together, the Alliance is urging Singapore to "Saying NO! to Piracy," and encouraging people to "Be original, Be Creative, Be HIP and to Live for Real."

IP Professionals

Recognising that IP professionals need to keep tabs on the latest trends and developments in the law and establish best practices in IP, IPOS has put in place the necessary infrastructure and a series of programmes to grow the IP professional sector. Some of the initiatives include a series of regular IP Roundtable to spark discussion amongst the IP professional community; and the "Strategic Manpower Conversion Programme in Intellectual Property"—SMCP(IP), which aims to train non-IP executives and professionals for relevant IP roles.

For more information on IPOS' programmes, please visit http://www.ipos.gov.sg/.

SINGAPORE ACADEMY OF LAW

The Singapore Academy of Law ("SAL" or "the Academy") was established by the Singapore Academy of Law Act (Cap. 294A) in 1988. At the time of its inception, Parliament had envisaged an institution patterned after the English Inns of Court, to develop among the legal profession in Singapore "a collegiate spirit which is necessary for pride in the profession and in its honourable standards and practices.

Over the years, the Academy has evolved from a membership-based body to a service-based institution. It is now also the law reporting agency in Singapore; a continuing legal education provider; a legal publications body; an alternative dispute resolutions agency; an appointing body for Senior Counsel, commissioners for oaths and notaries public; a promoter of legal information technology and the keeper of stakeholding moneys in Singapore.

The Academy is a statutory body with a broad set of functions. Under the Academy is its subsidiary, the Singapore Mediation Centre, which plays a specialised and unique role in the promotion of mediation as alternative means for the resolution of civil, commercial and trade disputes.

The leadership of the Academy rests on the shoulders of The Honourable Chief Justice Yong Pung How, who is the President of the Academy and heads the Senate and the Executive Committee of the Academy. The Senate comprises all Supreme Court Judges and Judicial Commissioners, the Solicitor-Generals, and nine other distinguished members of the profession nominated by the Chief Justice. The Senate is the rule-making body, and the broad policy-making body of the Academy.

The main strategic policies, plans and day-to-day running of the Academy are led by the Executive Committee chaired by the Chief Justice, and assisted by the Director of the Academy, Ms Serene Wee, with the support of the Assistant Directors.

CHAPTER 1

Harnessing the Biological Bounty of Nature: Mapping the Wilderness of Legal, Socio-Cultural, Geo-Political and Environmental Issues

BURTON ONG*

1.1 THE ROOTS AND BRANCHES OF THE CONTROVERSY

At the heart of the legal and policy debates which have arisen from the intersection between the law of intellectual property and the world of biological resources are the rapid developments in the biotechnology industry over the last 20 years. The commercial exploitation of biotechnological innovations has fuelled industry efforts to fit organic subject matter—from modified living organisms to natural extracts and derivative substances—within the established intellectual property regimes, particularly the patent system, as well as to develop new legal frameworks to meet with the demands of these new technologies. The biological bounty of Nature has thus been increasingly viewed as a cornucopian repository of valuable, or at least potentially valuable, genetic resources[1] to be tapped by the industry for commercial profit. This has, in turn, led to various segments of industry[2] taking a much greater interest

* Assistant Professor, Faculty of Law, National University of Singapore

in those segments of the community which have traditionally enjoyed a close relationship with the natural world: traditional healers[3], herbalists, ethnobotanists, agriculturalists, farmers, plant and animal breeders. It is from these dealings between industry players and these other stakeholders[4], and the appropriations of biological resources and traditional know-how which characterise these dealings, that a number of complex and intertwined legal issues have germinated.[5]

From here, the controversies surrounding the relationship between intellectual property rights and biological resources branches off into two broad directions. On the one hand, there have been several debates largely internalised within the international intellectual property community—whether living things are patentable subject matter[6], whether distinctions should be drawn between "lower" life forms (including plants and micro-organisms) and "higher" life forms[7], how the standards of novelty and the inventive step should be applied in the context of organic innovations[8], whether *sui generis* systems of legal protection[9] are better suited to organic subject matter than the patent regime, and so forth. On the other hand, a large part of the global debate has been driven by parties from outside the intellectual property community: environmental activists, non-governmental organisations and lobby groups representing agrarian and indigenous communities, and other special interest coalitions. These parties have focused their attention on an even broader range of issues—sovereign control over access to genetic resources, the equitable treatment of providers of genetic resources, transfers of technology and capacity building, respect and protection for the cultural diversity of Indigenous Peoples, the North-South developmental divide and so forth.[10] These debates have spawned developments at the national, regional and international levels, leading to a flourish of legal and policy instruments introduced at all these levels to address these concerns.[11] The inextricable connections between the intellectual property issues, the environmental issues and the indigenous rights issues, have made it difficult to address any of these issues independently. Progress in this area at international fora has been slow and mired in disagreement.[12]

This chapter aims to outline the basic parameters of the debates which have arisen and will briefly introduce the identities and interests of the primary stakeholders, key concepts and issues, and the framework of international legal instruments which attempt to address the concerns which have arisen. Finally, an overview of the subject matter discussed in the other chapters of this book will be presented, highlighting the perspectives taken by the respective authors and their contributions to the broad recurrent themes which underlie the legal and policy dimensions of these debates.

1.2 THE DIFFERENT STAKEHOLDERS AND THEIR DIVERGENT INTERESTS: USERS AND PROVIDERS OF GENETIC RESOURCES

1.2.1 Users of genetic resources

The users of genetic resources are almost as diverse as the biological materials they extract from the natural world. Broadly speaking, we can divide them into commercial users, traditional users and academic users. As their labels suggest, the character of the uses to which these resources are put, and their objectives between, will vary considerably within and between each category of users.

Commercial users of genetic resources encompass the various researchers and scientists working for the various limbs of the biotechnology industry: the pharmaceutical companies (drug-discovery screening for bioactive compounds from germplasm), the agrotechnology business (cultivating crop hybrids with improved resistance or other desirable traits), chemical and petrochemical conglomerates (developing commercial applications from organic raw materials). These users seek to identify natural products with useful applications, either by drawing from the knowledge of traditional users of genetic resources or by independent throughput screening activities, and require access to physical samples of biological material for research, testing and product development purposes. The process of transforming these resources from their natural state into a commercially valuable end-product is long-drawn and fraught with uncertainty, with layers of rigorous experimentation, product viability studies, and regulatory approval to overcome before anything reaches the market, if at all.

Given the considerable financial risks undertaken by these commercial entities, which have to commit significant resources to each developmental project which may or may not bear fruit, it is not surprising that they have been especially keen on acquiring legal protection—utilising the existing intellectual property regimes—for their successful organic innovations. Without such protection to ward of imitators, there would be little incentive to make the sorts of investments necessary to generate new innovations. Arguments like these are central to the fundamental tenets which fuel the market-driven economies of the industrialised world. These utilitarian arguments are also used to justify having stronger and broader intellectual property rights to encourage the proliferation of intellectual products which are beneficial to the public at large.

Traditional users of genetic resources include local and indigenous communities whose lives are proximate to, and dependent on, the biological resources in their natural environment. These are communities which may rely on substances derived from plant and animal origins for food, or medicine, or some other purpose connected to their traditional ways of living. Each community develops its own body of traditional know-how and practices, related to the use of these biological resources, which are passed on to successive generations through the efforts of traditional healers or tribal elders. Village shamans may develop a system of herbal remedies and organic therapies, while local subsistence farmers may develop agricultural practices in response to the specific traits or characteristics of a particular crop variety. On occasion, these repositories of traditional knowledge[13] may be accessed by interested parties from outside these indigenous or local communities, including commercial and academic users. These traditional users of genetic resources may thus provide valuable information to these other categories of users which assists in their utilisation of living organisms and organic substances obtained from the wild.

The utilisation of local genetic resources by traditional users may constitute an integral part of their day-to-day existence. These users have learnt to adapt to their physical environment by making use of its biological components to sustain themselves. A close connection to their natural surroundings means that traditional users may develop practices to manage these genetic resources in a sustainable way, and to ensure that they are available for use by their descendants. Quite apart from the sustenance and curative properties which traditional users derive from the biological resources available to them, these resources may also have a cultural or spiritual significance to their respective communities.[14] These resources may also be used in ceremonial activities, or may be viewed as having talismanic qualities, or may serve some other purpose which contributes to the identities of these communities.[15] The intimate nature of the relationship between traditional users of genetic resources with the natural world around them often results in a heightened sensitivity towards any action taken by those outside these communities to commercially exploit their traditional practices, or to engage in any activity involving biological resources that they might interpret as disrespectful towards them.[16]

Academic users of genetic resources seek access to plant and animal specimens for variety of purposes, some of which may be more appropriately characterised as "commercial" (e.g., applied scientific research), while other uses are directed towards pure discoveries and the acquisition of new knowledge (e.g., taxonomic studies).[17] These users may serve as a bridge between commercial and traditional users of genetic resources, facilitating the transfer of traditional knowledge from the latter to the former, and are often collaborators in projects which may eventually yield commercially viable end-products. Where research into biological products is undertaken by an academic user within an institution of higher learning, there may be internal economic pressures to seek intellectual property rights in any organic innovations which emerge from such research activity as a means of generating revenue for, and enhancing the reputation of, the institution which employs the academic user.

1.2.2 Providers of genetic resources

The providers of genetic resources include both *in situ* and *ex situ* sources of biological material. The former category encompasses sovereign states, and smaller communities within those states, which are responsible for the plants and animals that are located in their natural habitats. The latter category of providers control repositories of biological specimens which have been removed from their original environment and housed in an artificially assembled collection: genebanks, seedbanks, botanical gardens, and other similar institutions which may or may not have conservation objectives, and which may or may not be engaged in commercial uses of the genetic resources under their stewardship. *Ex-situ* collections may be controlled by private entities (which might use the samples in its library for their screening programmes) or administered by public organisations[18], with correspondingly different objectives and policies regarding the provision of genetic resources to the users who request for access.

In most cases where controversies have emerged from the use of intellectual property rights to protect innovations developed from genetic resources, the providers involved are local or indigenous communities which have facilitated the process by which the genetic resource in question was identified and extracted, usually because these communities have had a long history of using the resource themselves for particular purposes, or in particular ways, that may not have been commonly known to those outside of these communities. These providers of genetic resources are, in other words, the traditional users who have learnt how to harness the organic materials found in their natural environment. In exchange for their assistance, these providers of genetic resources may be remunerated for their services, or given benefits in kind, by the outsiders seeking to learn from them. In these circumstances, the legal question which arises is this: given the contributions made by these local and indigenous communities, what *rights*, if any, should they have in respect of the economic returns generated by organic innovations that may eventually emerge in the market? If the commercial entities which make use of the genetic resources (and the traditional knowledge of the communities they collaborate with) develop products over which intellectual property rights may subsist, should the providers of those genetic resources (and traditional knowledge) be entitled to share in the economic benefits flowing from the exercise of those rights? Should intellectual property rights even subsist in these circumstances where there has been an appropriation of the traditional practices of local or indigenous communities by these commercial entities? These are some of the questions which some of the authors of the remaining chapters in this publication will seek to address.

Where the provider of genetic resources is an *ex-situ* repository, difficult questions relating to the legal status of these resources (which may or may not have been obtained through proper channels, or deposited by donors on the understanding that they are meant to be freely accessible to the public) further complicates the picture. These providers of genetic resources may, in addition, serve a variety of public interest functions—preserving the biological diversity of endangered species and preventing their extinction, educating the public at large, contributing to global efforts to promote food security and alleviating world hunger—which may have an impact on their relationships with users who wish to gain access to resources in these collections. Stringent qualifying criteria may be necessary, together with the relevant contractual restraints[19], to ensure that the genetic resources in these collections are not used in ways, or for purposes, which are inconsistent with the basic objectives of the institution responsible for the *ex-situ* collection.

1.3 KEY CONCEPTS, ISSUES, AND CONTROVERSIES

1.3.1 Differentiating between "bioprospecting" and "biopiracy"

Bioprospecting[20] expeditions, as the label suggests, are in some ways analogous to the conventional prospecting activities in which the objective of the exploration is to discover mineral deposits. However, instead of prospecting for oil, gold or gemstones, bioprospectors seek to identify and extract biological materials with useful properties that can be developed into products capable of commercial exploitation. Both types of activities carry with them considerable risks of failure, and both of them involve questions of ownership and control over the resources which are extracted from the land. Unlike mineral resources, however, genetic resources have the capacity for reproduction and cellular manipulation away from their place of extraction.

Advocates for providers of genetic resources challenge the legitimacy of bioprospecting activities which involve the participation of locals, who share their traditional knowledge and practices, but do not receive equitable compensation for their contributions. These activities have been characterised as episodes of "biopiracy," conveying the sentiment that a wrongdoing has been committed, bringing with it connotations of misappropriative and reprehensible behaviour. It should be pointed out, however, that "biopiracy" is not a term of art, nor does it have a specific legal meaning. Indeed, the notion of "biopiracy" evokes images of looting and plundering which may not be entirely appropriate given the nature of the subject matter involved. From whom have these "pirates" pillaged? What have they taken that they are not entitled to? Are the properties of the resources which they have harvested and the knowledge they have utilised in the public domain? Are commercial entities unjustly enriched when they secure intellectual property rights over innovations they have developed from genetic resources and traditional knowledge provided by other parties? Which parties should have rights of ownership or control over the genetic resources in question? Several of the chapters in this publication will address these issues.

Thus, the "biopiracy" label is part of the rhetoric used to communicate the injustice, or perceived inequity, which emerges from particular methods of exploiting genetic resources. Allegations of "biopiracy" require scrutiny into the details of the process by which the genetic resources were discovered, identified, extracted and developed into organic innovations. Close attention also needs to be paid to the issue of whether the parties who have made such use of these genetic resources should be legally entitled to obtain intellectual property rights over such subject matter, and to what extent the existence of proprietary rights will have an adverse impact on indigenous communities or other stakeholders with an interest in these biological resources.[21]

1.3.2 Intellectual Property Rights and *sui generis* systems of legal protection

The intangible products of intellectual effort may be protected by different categories of legal rights, depending on the nature of the subject matter for which protection is sought, and whether that subject matter satisfies the requisite qualifying criteria for the particular intellectual property regime. As far as biotechnological innovations are concerned, patent grants are the most sought after proprietary rights because of the scope of protection afforded to the holder of those rights: these include territorial protection for 20 years, protection from both copying and independent creation by third parties, and exclusive rights to make, sell and import the patented invention. To qualify for a patent, the inventor has to establish that the invention claimed is a patentable subject matter, that it is new and unanticipated by the prior art, that it involves an inventive step judged from the perspective of a hypothetical skilled person, and that it is capable of industrial application. With a patent in hand, the inventor is in a position to extract licence fees from others who wish to practise the invention or use the patented technology. Therein lies the economic value of these legal rights, the availability of which gives the various commercial users of genetic resources the incentive to invest in research and development activities that may generate further organic innovations and technologies.

Alternatively, other species of intellectual property have been developed to offer legal protection to intellectual products which, for one reason or other, are unable to qualify for patent protection. These *sui generis* legislative frameworks are developed with organic subject matter specifically in mind. These laws have been tailored to accommodate the concerns of the relevant stakeholders while looking out for the interests of the party seeking to protect his organic innovation. Plant variety protection rights are a classic example of a *sui generis* system of legal rights—they seek to protect new, distinct, uniform and stable varieties of plants and exist within a legal framework designed to protect plant breeders in the agrotechnological, botanical and horticultural industries. In response to the problems of "biopiracy" briefly described earlier, the World Intellectual Property Organization is also in the process of developing a new species of intellectual property rights to protect the traditional knowledge systems of indigenous communities.[22]

Given that intellectual property is territorial in nature—the legal protection enjoyed by a rights holder, if any, in a particular country is dependent on the features of the domestic legal framework adopted within that jurisdiction—while intellectual property owners might want to exploit their innovations in different countries around the world, multinational enterprises with significant intellectual property portfolios have lobbied for greater harmonisation between the legal standards adopted by the various jurisdictions in which they operate. This has translated into efforts at the international level to get nation states to agree to adopt common intellectual property standards in their respective national laws. International agreements such as the TRIPS Agreement (Trade Related Aspects of Intellectual Property Rights)[23], which is administered by the World Trade Organisation, have changed the international legal landscape, with signatory countries obliged to introduce, or modify, their own laws so that minimum standards of intellectual property protection are available in their respective territories.

1.3.3 Access and Benefit-Sharing regimes

In response to the increased awareness of *in-situ* biological resources as a potential source of economic wealth, there have been corresponding efforts by, and on behalf of, stakeholders involved (especially developing countries and communities of indigenous people) to regulate access to their genetic resources. This has resulted in the erection of legal obstacles which users of genetic resources have to overcome before they are allowed to harvest specimens from the field. Permits have to be obtained, disclosures of intent have to be made, undertakings have to be given, and various other regulatory requirements have to be complied with before access is granted to the bioprospecting party. One of the conditions on which access is usually granted is for the bioprospecting party to assume an obligation to share in any benefits generated, including any intellectual property rights subsequently acquired, from the genetic resources harvested. Unsurprisingly, these developments have not been particularly welcomed by commercial users of genetic resources, with some choosing to shift their bioprospecting activities to unregulated locations or turning to *ex-situ* collections[24] of genetic resources instead. Academic users of genetic resources also face similar regulatory obstacles which impede their fieldwork, thereby hampering their ability to collect and study plant and animal specimens from the wild.[25]

The international legal community has recognised the importance of having the use of genetic resources regulated by an effective access and benefit-sharing regime. This is reflected as one of the principal tenets of the Convention on Biological Diversity (CBD)[26] to which almost every country, with the notable exception of the United States, is a member state. The Convention recognises the close relationship between the conservation and sustainable use of genetic resources on the one hand, and the need to ensure that the indigenous people—under whose stewardship these resources have been prudently managed for generations—receive a fair and equitable[27] share of the benefits derived from the use of these resources. The Convention does not articulate a specific benefit-sharing mechanism or any details of how countries should implement its provisions. This international legal instrument merely provides an exhortatory framework of values which member states have to interpret and execute as they see fit. While the Convention makes it clear that any action taken pursuant to its Articles should not be inconsistent with established principles of intellectual property law[28], it does not discount the possibility of modifying the existing intellectual property regimes to accommodate the aspirations of the Convention. The conflict between the objectives of the CBD and the TRIPS Agreement has thus become an important battleground in the international legal arena and will feature prominently in several of the contributing chapters in this publication.

1.3.4 The North-South divide

An important feature of the international debate which has been sketched out thus far is the polarisation which has developed, whether actual or perceived, between the developed ("North") and developing ("South") countries. Most of the commercial users of genetic resources are private entities or conglomerates from the industrialised "North," whereas most of the providers of *in situ* genetic resources are from the biologically diverse "South." Products developed from organisms or biological substances harvested from the "South" are, more likely than not, commercially exploited in consumer markets in the "North." Intellectual property regimes in the "North" have also been more accommodating towards organic innovations and are more likely to confer legal protection on them as compared to their counterparts in the "South."

The lobby groups which represent stakeholders from both sides have campaigned actively to advance the interests of their sponsors, with significant efforts directed towards defending and strengthening, or criticising and challenging, the use of intellectual property systems to protect organic innovations.[29] Many of the well-documented cases involving allegations of "biopiracy," which are discussed by the authors in the other chapters, provide clear illustrations of these transnational tensions when the validity of U.S. patents over plant-based inventions have been challenged. Several of the commentators who have contributed to this publication will advance their arguments from a variety of perspectives.

1.4 CHAPTER SUMMARIES

In Chapter 2, Professor George Wei introduces the challenges facing policy-makers tasked with accommodating biological innovations within intellectual property legislative frameworks that were developed long before the biotechnological revolution. Approaching the issues from an intellectual property lawyer's perspective, this chapter provides a comprehensive overview of the legal issues that have arisen from the use of existing intellectual property regimes, especially the law of patents, to confer legal protection over modified living things, micro-organisms, organic substances, and commercially valuable intangibles with biological origins. Professor Wei examines several key aspects of patent law which have had an impact upon the broader question of whether exclusive rights should subsist over living things and their component parts. Should these innovations qualify as "inventions"? Should they be excluded from the patent system on broader public policy grounds? Do these inventions satisfy the formal requirements of "novelty" and "inventive step"? What is the proper scope of the "prior art base" against which these claimed inventions are assessed? These questions, and others related to the scope of liability for patent infringement and the defences available to third parties, are addressed by the author, who also provides a skeletal framework of the other types of intellectual property rights which may offer some form of legal protection.

This chapter provides a strong foundation of the approaches towards the patenting of biological inventions under leading international legal instruments—the Paris Convention for the Protection of Industrial Property of 1883, the European Patent Convention of 1973, the TRIPS Agreement of 1994, and the European Biotechnology Directive of 1998—mapping out the key provisions which have facilitated the entry of the natural world into the patent system. Against this backdrop of global developments in patent law, Professor Wei also briefly surveys the national approaches adopted in the United States, the United Kingdom, Australia, Canada, India and Singapore. Some of these jurisdictions were chosen partly because of their relatively mature patent jurisprudence, while others were included to illustrate their divergent attitudes towards biological resources as patentable subject matter. More significant, however, is the fact that these jurisdictions correspond with the nationalities of some of the authors who have contributed their works for inclusion in the other chapters of this book. The framework of intellectual property approaches presented by Professor Wei therefore sets the stage for the multi-national character of the discussion which follows in subsequent chapters by drawing attention towards the relevant national perspectives on the fundamentals of patent law.

In Chapter 3, Professor S. K. Verma explores the controversy surrounding the application of systems intellectual property protection to plant genetic resources from the perspective of a developing country with a significant agrarian sector in its economy. Examples of indigenous biological resources which have been commercially exploited are drawn from India, illustrating the interrelationships between the myriad of socio-legal issues involved: genetic resource conservation and sustainable use, access regulation and benefit sharing, investment in biotechnological research and development, traditional knowledge protection and management, biopiracy, bio-safety, food security, crop vulnerability, rural poverty, and so on. Professor Verma articulates the strong concerns of those opposed to the recognition of intellectual property rights over biological innovations, emphasising the inequitable character of bio-prospective practices which, while relying on the traditional wisdom of local and indigenous communities to identify and develop commercially valuable outputs, do not return an appropriate share of the resulting financial gains to the relevant stakeholders. The impact of such practices on those at the grassroots level, particularly tribal groups and farmers, is examined against a global setting that reflects a widening divide between economically wealthy North and the biologically wealthy South.

In this chapter, an effort is made to establish the connections between the TRIPS Agreement of 1994, the Convention on Biological Diversity of 1992 (CBD), and the International Treaty on Plant Genetic Resources for Food and Agriculture (ITPGRF) of 2001. Professor Verma argues that it is possible for these international legal documents to be interpreted and implemented consistently with each other, pointing to recent efforts in India to introduce three key legislative instruments: the *Patents (Amendment) Act* of 2002, the *Plant Variety Protection and Farmers' Rights Act* of 2001, and the *Biological Diversity Act* of 2002. The impact of these pieces of legislation on the relevant institutions is also discussed, along with the areas of overlap between the different executive administrative bodies responsible for executing their wide-ranging objectives. The Indian perspective in this chapter offers an account of the key issues from a viewpoint that is perhaps representative of major genetic resource providers around the world—states rich in biological diversity but lacking the technological means to exploit their full commercial potential. These insights provide a good counterpoint to the contrasting views taken in other chapters which address the issues from the standpoint of those who make commercial use of genetic resources.

In Chapter 4, Catherine Geci and Professor Bartha Maria Knoppers present a Canadian perspective on the patentability of higher life forms, contrasting the positions taken by the Canadian Biotechnology Advisory Committee (CBAC), the Canadian Intellectual Property Office and the Canadian Supreme Court. The CBAC's recommendations which support the patentability of plants, seeds and non-human animals are discussed, along with its proposals to balance the interests of other stakeholders by strengthening the farmer's privilege, enhancing the protection from infringement liability available to innocent bystanders, and clarifying the scope of the experimental use exception. These limitations to the exclusive rights of the patentee are viewed as sufficient checks to ensure that Canadian patent policy advances the public interest as a whole. Using the Canadian Supreme Court's recent decision, in which the Harvard Oncomouse was held to be non-patentable, as a point of reference, a comparative study is made of the approaches taken by the American and European patent offices towards the patentability of the same genetically modified animal. From here, issues of animal welfare and broader ethical considerations that were addressed by these agencies are introduced, leading on to a discussion of the CBAC's proposal to reconcile the patenting of higher life forms with an ethical framework of principles and values in the field of biotechnology.

The ethical aspects of the debate are further developed in this chapter by connecting the ethical concerns which have arisen in relation to the patenting of plants, seeds and non-human animals to the misgivings which have similarly surfaced in the area of biomedical law which relate to the patenting of human genes and cells. In arguing that the relevant ethical issues spill over naturally from the debate regarding human genetic resources to the debate involving non-human genetic resources, the authors draw broad parallels between the benefit-sharing provisions of the CBD with the Human Genome Organization (HUGO) Ethics Committee's Statement on Benefit Sharing of 2000 and UNESCO's International Declaration on Human Genetic Data of 2003. They conclude that the way forward is to move beyond the debate on patentability *per se*, focusing instead on developing more sophisticated mechanisms within the patent system—including public repositories and licensing "clearinghouses"—which are promote the values espoused by the international ethical framework that has emerged. The Canadian perspective presented in this chapter offers a glimpse into a developed country's attempts to balance, on the one hand, the interests of its biotechnology industry in having comprehensive intellectual property protection, against its desire to abide by an international framework of ethical principles governing the patentability of human and non-human genetic resources.

In Chapter 5, Professor Michael Jeffery attempts to tackle the issues arising from the incompatibilities between the TRIPS Agreement and the CBD, paying particular attention to the potential impact of the expanding global intellectual property regime on the conservation of biological diversity, the sustainable use of genetic resources, and the equitable sharing of benefits derived from such use. A broad survey of the key provisions of major international legal instruments relating to intellectual property rights is carried out, introducing the historical circumstances and geo-political forces surrounding the language that was adopted in these treaties and conventions. The practical problems which have arisen from the implementation of these provisions at the national level are also discussed, highlighting the inadequacies of conventional intellectual property rights which are unable, in their current shape and form, to effectively accommodate the CBD's objectives of safeguarding traditional knowledge systems connected to the use of biological resources by local and indigenous communities. The author also addresses other ground-level conflicts between the policies advanced by the CBD and those reflected in the TRIPS Agreement, such as the formulation of access and benefit-sharing systems that facilitate lawful bioprospecting activity, but without requiring the disclosure of details relating to the uses of the genetic resources that might prejudice the subsequent acquisition of patent rights over the final innovation that is developed.

This chapter identifies some of the points of intersection between the TRIPS Agreement and the CBD which have contributed to the conflict between them, offering a primer on basic issues and concepts that are essential to understanding the many facets of the contemporary controversy: "traditional ecological knowledge systems," "access and benefit-sharing," "prior informed consent and ownership," "transfer of technology," "*Ex-situ* conservation," and so forth. Navigating through a thicket of recent scholarly publications on the international interface between intellectual property rights and plant genetic resources, Professor Jeffery argues that the way forward is to adopt a pragmatic approach which builds on the existing intellectual property regimes by gradually integrating the principal objectives of the CBD into them.

In Chapter 6, Dr Jorge Caillaux and Susanna Clark give an overview of the measures taken by biodiversity-rich countries to regulate access to genetic resources within their jurisdictions, and to protect the traditional knowledge associated with the use of these resources which is held by their indigenous and local communities. Particular attention is paid to the regulatory initiatives introduced by the Andean Community in South America, as well as the specific legislative measures taken by Peru, where the authors hail from. A broad comparison between the key features of actual and proposed regulatory frameworks of the Megadiverse countries—including Brazil, China and Costa Rica—is carried out, as well as a summary of the field practices of private entities engaged in bio-prospecting activity in these countries. The authors argue that policy-makers designing regulatory frameworks should pay closer attention to the private codes of conduct and arrangements which have been voluntarily implemented by pharmaceutical corporations, research institutions, *ex-situ* centres and other entities involved in the acquisition, study and utilisation of biological resources.

The discussion in this chapter outlines some of the core issues which the Megadiverse countries have had to grapple with when formulating policies concerning access to, and use of, their respective plant and animal resources. The potential of the patent system being used defensively to prevent the misappropriation of traditional knowledge is discussed with reference to Decision 391 of the Andean Community on a Common Regime on Access to Genetic Resources, and Decision 486 on a Common Regime on Industrial Property of 2001. This is contrasted with the additional positive measures that can be taken to protect traditional knowledge, using the Peruvian legislation as an illustration, by giving indigenous communities rights which they can enforce against bio-prospectors who do not share the benefits derived from their bio-prospecting activities in a fair and equitable manner. This chapter offers insights into recent developments in Latin America to introduce comprehensive legislative frameworks regulating access to genetic resources which incorporate the protection of traditional knowledge through formal registers and licensing schemes, mandatory disclosure requirements in the patent system, and benefit-sharing mechanism to facilitate the transmission of monetary and non-monetary benefits to the relevant indigenous communities.

In Chapter 7, Professor Peter Drahos provides a compelling account of the international policy-making processes driving the development of bilateral and multilateral agreements which set benchmarks for domestic intellectual property laws, focusing on the role which private industrial and commercial entities play in influencing their governments' agendas at international standard-setting fora. Drawing from his extensive research on the economic and political impulses driving the foreign policy strategies of the United States of America in the international intellectual property arena, the author presents a vignette of the lobbying mechanisms—including national and international trade associations, chambers of commerce and advisory committees—utilised by the corporate leaders from the chemical, pharmaceutical and biotechnological industries to achieve higher standards of patent protection abroad via the TRIPS Agreement, regional treaties and bilateral free trade agreements. The intimate connection between the intellectual property rights debate and international trade negotiations is highlighted, with small but powerful business networks working behind the scenes to tie intellectual property protection issues to formal arrangements between the US and its trading partners, so as to bring the national intellectual property laws of developing countries in line with US domestic laws. Professor Drahos also sets out his theory of a global regulatory "ratchet"—a mechanism which permits incremental movement in one direction only—through which international intellectual property standards are progressively enhanced by the US strategy of alternating between bilateral agreements and occasional multilateral agreements, where the standard-setting process is shifted from forum to forum depending on the degree of resistance encountered. The end result for countries who participate in this process is a web of obligations to comply with multilateral standards in conventions to which they were not parties, as well as to amend their domestic laws to meet new standards based on US laws which may go beyond what they have agreed to under the TRIPS Agreement.

The issues addressed in this chapter offer critical insights into the role which industry plays in achieving the levels of patent protection it wants, while introduces an important dimension to the ongoing debates as to whether, and how, the TRIPS Agreement should be amended to reflect the conflicting objectives of the CBD. The extent of the influence of the bio-pharmaceutical and biotechnological users of genetic resources in guiding the direction of international intellectual property policy, as well as the strategies adopted by their governments to persuade developing countries to amend their national laws to reflect standards beyond what the TRIPS Agreement requires, may very well render these debates purely academic. Even the strongest arguments in favour of changing the way biological resources are treated under the patent regime, or any other *sui generis* system of legal protection proposed at the international level, are unlikely to have any practical effect if countries are bound by obligations under their bilateral trade agreements to observe specific intellectual property standards. Professor Drahos' cogent observations in this chapter are thus important to a comprehensive understanding of the powerful business interests and political forces which have shaped, and will continue to shape, the agenda of these debates.

In Chapter 8, Dr Steven King and his colleagues share their experiences working with indigenous communities to identify and develop commercial applications for natural substances used in traditional healing therapies. Drawing from their professional encounters with ethnomedicine and ethnobotany in African and South American countries, the authors provide concrete examples of bio-prospecting arrangements which have successfully integrated benefit-sharing programmes to benefit the communities who contribute their traditional knowledge of plant-based medicines, handed down from generation to generation, to the development therapeutic products with useful bio-active properties. These programmes include contributions to community-based infrastructure projects, upgraded health services, education and training initiatives, employment opportunities, as well as data and research output sharing with the scientific institutions of the host country. What is significant about the examples given by the authors is that all of them are ways in which the equitable benefit-sharing objectives of the CBD can be furthered independently of any legislative compulsion from the host country: the programmes described were pursued by researchers from private entities who implemented a self-imposed ethical code of conduct in their dealings with local and indigenous communities. Furthermore, these were successful benefit-sharing strategies which did not hinge on the availability of intellectual property rights, or any *sui generis* form of legal protection, to those who collaborated with the bio-prospecting researchers. This raises the interesting question of whether the perceived incompatibilities between the CBD and the TRIPs Agreement can be surmounted without necessarily making drastic changes to the global intellectual property landscape.

Unlike most of the other contributors to this book, Dr King and his colleagues are scientists and not legal scholars. This chapter is therefore written from a significantly different, but equally valuable, point of view: it provides an account of the issues of access to genetic resources, prior informed consent, traditional knowledge protection, and benefit-sharing programmes for indigenous peoples from a the perspective of someone actually participating in the bio-prospecting process—a hands-on "user" of genetic resources with an interest in commercially exploiting products derived from natural substances which have traditionally been used by indigenous communities for medicinal purposes. It offers a glimpse of some of the practical concerns and difficulties facing this category of stakeholders, who are often vilified for their inequitable conduct and questionable ethics when dealing with indigenous peoples who occupy weaker bargaining positions, while showcasing a laudable example of how a mutually beneficial partnership can be established within a co-operative framework of integrity, honesty, and reciprocity.

In Chapter 9, Professor Wang Xi and his associates present an overview of the legal framework protecting traditional Chinese medicines in China, while examining issues related to the overlapping rights that may be created through the concurrent operation of the patenting system under the *Patent Law* (2000), the administrative protection of "new" medicines under the *Pharmaceutical Administration Law* (2002), the protection of varieties of Chinese medicine under the *Regulations on Variety Protection of Chinese Medicine* (1993), the protection of plant varieties under the *Regulations on New Plant Variety Protection* (1997), the trademark system under the *Trademark Law* (1982), and the protection of commercial secrets under the *Anti-Unfair Competition Law* (1993). The authors compare the nature and scope of intellectual property, and quasi-intellectual property, protection available to those who seek to protect Chinese medicines—preparations made from herbal and other organic ingredients with biochemical compounds—while contrasting their respective advantages and disadvantages to the rights holder. Apart from the internal conflicts between these various systems of protection which have been introduced in China, the authors also identify provisions in the legislative instruments that are inconsistent with the obligations under the TRIPS Agreement to apply a "national treatment" principle to the protection of intellectual property rights. The authors conclude with a series of broad recommendations and strategies directed towards reforming the Chinese legal framework, and strengthening the legal infrastructure supporting the Chinese medicine industry.

The discussion in this chapter offers an insider's perspective of the approaches adopted in China to protect the traditional medicines which have been part of Chinese culture for centuries. It may be useful to contrast the subject matter which is protected in China—the composition of organic substances which comprise the medicines—with the attempts to protect traditional knowledge systems, a much broader body of information, of tribal groups in other developing countries. Unlike traditional Chinese medicines which have a deep-rooted cultural significance to billions of people, many of whom have emigrated from China but continue to develop these medicines, traditional knowledge systems are tied to specific indigenous or local communities within relatively insulated geographical confines. These differences may suggest that any new system of legal protection developed to protect traditional therapies based on natural substances may have to be modified to take into account the historical, sociological and cultural circumstances surrounding the existing uses of these biological resources.

In Chapter 10, Associate Professor Donna Craig examines the interface between intellectual property rights, biological resources and the human rights of indigenous communities. Recognising that these communities need to develop an economic base to sustain their continued existence as culturally distinct groups, the author explains the inadequacies of using conventional intellectual property rights to formulate legal strategies to protect their interests. The holistic concept of *Indigenous intellectual and cultural property* is introduced, emphasising the indivisible corpus of knowledge—relating to both the physical environment and the metaphysical aspects of a community's identity—that Western notions of intellectual property are unable to grapple with. Indeed, the very idea of "property" is argued to be inappropriate to traditional societies which view the intangible, and often spiritual, aspects of their knowledge systems as incapable of "belonging" to any human being. Darrell Posey's work in the area of *Traditional Resource Rights*—as an alternative platform for incorporating the broader bundle of environmental, cultural and economic interests that are important to Indigenous Peoples—is presented as a more constructive means of integrating human rights considerations into the broader debates.

This chapter gives consideration to the view of intellectual property rights as a fundamental human right of all individuals, under Article 27 of the *Universal Declaration of Human Rights* of 1948, while charting the progress made in other major international human rights instruments towards recognising the rights of Indigenous Peoples to manage their native lands, waters, resources, traditional ecological knowledge systems and so forth. The international legal terrain surveyed includes the International Labour Organisation's Convention (ILO) 169 Concerning Indigenous and Trial Peoples in Independent Countries of 1989, the United Nations' Draft Declaration of Principles on Human Rights and the Environment as well as its Draft Declaration on the Rights of Indigenous Peoples, the UNESCO Convention to Safeguard Intangible Cultural Heritage of 2003, and Article 8(j) of the CBD of 1992. The author also highlights the objections which indigenous communities have towards the basic premise of the CBD, which places their traditional knowledge systems and genetic resources under the ultimate control of Nation states, thereby usurping their fundamental rights of self-determination. Engaging the debate from the perspective of an international human rights advocate, Professor Craig addresses the political marginalisation of indigenous and local communities, whose stewardship and traditional practices have been responsible for many valuable ethnobotanical innovations, and the need for more importance to be placed on their rights of self-determination when shaping the international environmental and intellectual property legal landscapes.

In Chapter 11, Professor Michael Blakeney examines a number of recent cases in which allegations of "biopiracy" were levelled against private institutions which had sought to acquire intellectual property rights over plant-based innovations developed from food crops: chickpeas from the semi-arid tropics, blight-resistant rice from Mali, enola beans from Mexico, and yacon (a potato-like root vegetable), nuna beans, and maca (a high-altitude tuberous root from the mustard family) from the Andean region. Based on his extensive experience working with the Consultative Group on International Agricultural Research Group (CGIAR)—an association of sponsoring agencies which support a network of 16 international agricultural research centres and institutes, some of which were directly or indirectly connected to the germplasm used in the "biopiracy" cases discussed—the author provides a concise summary of the policy dilemmas faced by the CGIAR whose various *ex-situ* collections of genetic resources are "held in trust for the benefit of the international community, in particular developing countries" under the auspices of the Food and Agriculture Organisation (FAO). Given that the original mission of the CGIAR was to promote research which would help feed a growing world population—which translates to a policy in favour of germplasm being made freely available to researchers subject to standard material transfer agreements—to what extent should it permit its research centres to use the intellectual property systems to secure exclusive rights in respect of new and improved varieties of food crops and organic substances derived from them? The uncertainty over the legal status of the specimens in the germplasm collections complicates things further, as issues of ownership and other related rights were not matters which were carefully considered at the time the samples were accumulated. Also, as Professor Blakeney points out, the Group has yet to address the question of whether indigenous and traditional communities, from which seeds might have been collected by the various CGIAR institutes, should have any rights to the germplasm and their derivatives, including those varieties which have successfully obtained intellectual property protection.

The themes explored elsewhere by the other contributing authors are approached in this chapter with an emphasis placed on plant genetic resources used in modern commercial agriculture, and the contributions made by local and indigenous farming communities towards the cultivation and conservation of food crop varieties. The key provisions of the CBD, the ITPGRF, regional and national legislative frameworks, as well as current efforts by the World Intellectual Property Organization's (WIPO) Intergovernmental Committee on Intellectual Property and Genetic Resources, Traditional Knowledge and Folklore, are also briefly reviewed by the author to highlight their relevance to the protection of agricultural and biodiversity-related traditional knowledge, regulating access to genetic resources through bioprospecting contracts, and the equitable sharing of benefits derived from the commercial exploitation of those resources.

In Chapter 12, Professor Charles McManis critically evaluates current international efforts to develop a *sui generis* legal framework to protect the traditional knowledge of local and indigenous communities in developing countries, while proposing that existing intellectual property regimes can be employed, with fairly minor modifications, to achieve the same outcomes in a more practical, cost-efficient, and administratively straightforward manner. The author recommends, in particular, making two key changes to the patent and plant variety protection systems to facilitate the attainment of the benefit-sharing objectives of the CBD: by requiring, as a condition of enforcing a patent or other intellectual property right, that the rights holder disclose the origin of the genetic resources and the traditional knowledge relied upon in developing the invention for which protection is sought, as well as providing evidence of prior informed consent from the relevant source countries, communities and individuals. The underlying premise of these proposals is that having these legal requirements will give traditional knowledge holders, their communities, and the developing countries in which they are located, a measure of bargaining power to extract an equitable share of the benefits arising from the enforcement of these intellectual property rights. Unlike the *sui generis* systems of protection proposed by some policy-makers, which are beset by theoretical and practical difficulties, these modest proposals offer a pragmatic way forward which channels the protection of traditional knowledge into one or more of the existing intellectual property regimes.

This chapter revisits many of the prominent examples of biopiracy discussed in earlier chapters by the other contributors, addressing the specific intellectual property issues involved in each case and how they were resolved. Professor McManis carefully examines the legal challenges which were brought by various non-governmental organisations seeking to invalidate the US patents which had been granted over innovations derived from biological resources originating from developing countries, while systematically pointing out the factual inaccuracies these allegations of biopiracy, many of which were due to a flawed understanding of how the US patent system works, as well as exposing the misrepresentations made by these organisations in their campaigns to garner public support. The author draws a sharp distinction between biopiracy cases involving "bad patents" (which ought not have been granted because they failed to meet the relevant statutory requirements), and those cases involving validly issued patents where the allegations of biopiracy were based on arguments that the US standards of patentability were too low (such as the relative novelty standard in 35 U.S.C. §102(a) or the provision in 35 U.S.C. §102(f) which only prevents an inventor from making an application if the *complete* idea for the invention was taken from another source). In the latter category of cases, Professor McManis defends the public policy choices that were made when the US formulated these standards and argues that developing countries may stand to gain from adopting similar features in their respective domestic patent systems. Written from the perspective of a country which has been embroiled in some of the most contentious patent-related controversies involving biological resources, this chapter provides an articulate counterpoint to some of the criticisms which have been raised in earlier chapters, while offering constructive suggestions for reforming the patent system to address the legitimate demands of traditional knowledge holders and their supporters.

ENDNOTES

1 "Genetic resources" are defined in Article 2 of the Convention on Biological Diversity as "genetic material of actual or potential value," while "genetic material" is defined as "any material of plant, animal microbial or other origin containing functional units of heredity."

2 See, generally, Kerry ten Kate & Sarah A. Laird, *The Commercial Use of Biodiversity: Access to Genetic Resources and Benefit-Sharing* (UK: Earthscan Publications Ltd, 1999). The authors examine the commercial value of genetic resources to the Natural Products and Pharmaceutical industry,

the Botanical Medicine industry, the Seed industry, the Horticulture industry, the Natural Personal Care and Cosmetics industry and other Biotechnology industries. From their extensive studies and surveys, the authors estimate that the value of the combined global markets for products derived from these sectors lies between US$500 billion and US$800 billion.

3 Apart from shamans and tribal medicine men, traditional healers in this category would include Traditional Chinese Medicine practitioners, Ayurvedic physicians in India, and other individuals versed in botanical medicines. These botanical medicines may be commercialised as "dietary supplements," "nutraceuticals" (foods with health enhancing properties) or phytomedicines.

4 For a systematic account of the ways in which various industries identify and acquire natural products from these stakeholders, see Chapters 3 to 9 of note 2 above.

5 These issues are only briefly highlighted throughout this introductory chapter. They will be dealt with in a lot more detail by the authors of the other chapters of this publication.

6 A debate spawned by the landmark decision of the U.S. Supreme Court in *Diamond v. Chakrabarty* 447 US 303 (1980) which involved genetically modified bacteria.

7 See the Canadian Supreme Court's controversial decision in *President & Fellows of Harvard College v. Canada (Commissioner of Patents)* [2002] SCC 76 which rejected the Harvard Oncomouse, a mammalian "higher" life form, as patentable subject matter, while accepting that bacteria and plants were "lower" life forms which could be patented.

8 The "relative" novelty standard used by the U.S. patent system, for example, has been the subject of much criticism because it does not consider unpublished knowledge of traditional practices or undocumented public uses of genetic resources as part of the prior art for the purposes of assessing novelty. See 35 U.S.C. §102(a).

9 These include, for example, the Plant Variety Protection legislative framework found in the UPOV Convention for the Protection of New Varieties of Plants 1961 (revised most recently in 1991).

10 Major international non-governmental organisations campaigning in this area include the Action Group on Erosion, Technology and Concentration (ETC group, formerly known as RAFI—the Rural Advancement Foundation International) and Genetic Resources Action International (GRAIN). The projects and publications undertaken by these groups are available online: (http://www.etcgroup.org and http://www.grain.org).

11 The latest addition to the panoply of international treaties seeking to establish legal frameworks in this area is the International Treaty on Plant Genetic Resources for Food and Agriculture (ITPGRFA) which comes into force on June 29, 2004, a treaty signed by members of the Food and Agriculture Organisation (FAO) which aims to promote the objectives of the Convention on Biological Diversity (CBD) while facilitating sustainable

agriculture and food security. The text of the treaty is available online: (http://www.fao.org/ag/cgrfa/itpgr.htm).

12 For example, Article 27(3)(b) of the TRIPS Agreement, which allows for exemptions to patentable subject matter but requires member states to provide effective *sui generis* protection for plant varieties, was supposed to have been reviewed in 1999 but this has not been achieved as yet.

13 See, generally, Sarah A. Laird (ed.), *Biodiversity and Traditional Knowledge: Equitable Partnerships in Practice* (London: Earthscan Publications Ltd, 2002). Published as part of the "People and Plants Conservation Series," a joint initiative of the World Wildlife Fund, the United Nations Educational, Scientific and Cultural Organisation (UNESCO) and the Royal Botanic Gardens, Kew, the contributors to this book examine the nature of research and commercial partnerships involving studies of biodiversity and traditional knowledge. The contributions made by indigenous communities towards the biodiversity research and bioprospecting activities are identified in the course of illustrating how "equitable partnerships" may be achieved between the all the parties involved.

14 See, generally, Silke von Lewinski (ed.), *Indigenous Heritage and Intellectual Property: Genetic Resources, Traditional Knowledge and Folklore* (The Netherlands: Kluwer Law International, 2004). The contributors to this publication provide a comprehensive overview of the scope of legal protection required by, and available to, indigenous communities to ensure that their human rights are effectively safeguarded.

15 See, generally, Darrell A. Posey & Graham Dutfield, *Beyond Intellectual Property: Toward Traditional Resource Rights for Indigenous Peoples and Local Communities, International Development Research Centre*, (1996) Ottawa, Canada. The authors argue that conventional notions of intellectual property rights are too limited and incapable of accommodating the spiritual dimension of these resources, and that the very concept of "property" is inappropriate because indigenous people often saw these intangible aspects of property as inalienable and not capable of belonging to any human being. Instead, they argue that the term "traditional resource rights" be used in the debate to reflect the broader range of subject matter that is worthy of protection—including traditional practices, beliefs, customs, knowledge and cultural heritage—and necessary to achieve and maintain the dignity and well-being of these communities.

16 See, for example, the furore surrounding the acquisition of a plant patent over the particular breed of the Ayahuasca plant, native to South America, which was sacred to many tribal communities in the Amazon Basin. A discussion of the case can be found in David R. Downes, *How Intellectual Property Could be a Tool to Protect Traditional Knowledge* 25 Columbia J. Envtl. L. 253, 281 (2000).

17 For a further discussion of the difficulties involved in distinguishing between the academic users engaged in biodiversity *research*, and those engaged in biodiversity *prospecting* that may lead to some form of commercialisation, see above note 13 at Chapters 3 and 4.

18 The Consultative Group on International Agricultural Research (CGIAR), for example, maintains an *ex-situ* collection of crop germplasm and landraces "in trust" to benefit the public at large.

19 See, for example, the Common Policy Guidelines for Participating Botanic Gardens, a voluntary code developed by ex situ collections to give effect to the spirit and letter of the Convention on Biodiversity, discussed in Chapter 3 of Sarah A. Laird (ed.), above at note 13.

20 A shortened form of "biodiversity prospecting," a term first defined as "the exploration of biodiversity for commercially valuable genetic resources and biochemicals" in Reid, W. V., S. A. Laird, C. A. Meyer, R. Games, A. Sittenfeld, D. H. Janzen, M. A. Gollin and C. Juma (eds.), *Biodiversity Prospecting: Using Genetic Resources for Sustainable Development* (Washington DC: World Resources Institute, 1993).

21 For example, will the existence of intellectual property rights impede the ability of indigenous users to continue engaging in their traditional uses of the biological material? Will it foreclose markets abroad and prevent these users from reaping economic benefits of their own from dealings with the biological resources?

22 The ongoing work at the World Intellectual Property Organization (WIPO) in this area is spearheaded by the WIPO Intergovernmental Committee on Intellectual Property and Genetic Resources, Traditional Knowledge and Folklore—submissions to the Committee, published papers, updates and WIPO reports are available online: (http://www.wipo.int/tk/en/index.html).

23 The text of the agreement is available online: (http://www.wto.org/english/tratop_e/trips_e/wtowip_e.htm).

24 See note 2 above at Chapter 10.

25 See, for example, the Access and Benefit Sharing regime implemented in the Philippines which requires anyone seeking access to genetic resources to conclude either an *academic* research agreement, or a *commercial* research agreement, with the Philippines government: Executive Order 247 "Prescribing a Regulatory Framework for the Prospecting of Biological and Genetic Resources, Their By-Products and Derivatives, for Scientific and Commercial Purposes, and for Other Purposes" (1994). One of the pioneering regulatory frameworks introduced to implement the principles enshrined in the CBD, Executive Order 247 has been vilified for being unrealistic, cumbersome and unworkable.

26 The text of the Convention is available online: (http://www.biodiv.org/convention/articles.asp).

27 While the CBD has not defined the terms "fair" and "equitable" anywhere within its text, it has been argued by commentators that these concepts should be understood in the context of the *process* by which the benefits are calculated as well as the *outcome* of the sharing arrangement. A proper balance of the competing interests, rights and demands should be struck, with an outcome that that is "equitable" in light of the cultural, political, economic and social circumstances in which the research and development activities take place. See Bystrom, M., P. Einarsson and G. A. Nycander,

Fair and equitable: sharing the benefits from use of genetic resources and traditional knowledge, Report, September (1999), Swedish Scientific Council on Biological Diversity, Stockholm.

28 See Article 16(5) of the CBD.

29 See the papers posted online at the websites identified above at note 10.

CHAPTER 2

Fitting Biological Products within the Intellectual Property Framework: Challenges Facing the Policy Makers[1]

GEORGE WEI*

2.1 INTRODUCTION

By the end of year 2003, the world will have witnessed a number of significant anniversaries in the field of biotechnology and the life sciences. These include, the 50th anniversary of the publication by Dr James Watson and Francis Crick of the discovery of the structure of the DNA molecule in 1953[2]; the 40th anniversary of the development of new high yield wheat varieties in 1963[3]; the 30th anniversary of the production of the world's first transgenic bacterium by Stanley Cohen and Herbert Boyer in 1973[4]; the 20th anniversary of the isolation of the AIDS virus in 1983[5]; the 10th anniversary of the Nobel prize for the polymerase chain reaction in 1993[6]; the 9th anniversary of the first approval by the Food and Drug Administration (USA) of a genetically engineered plant in 1994[7]; the 8th anniversary of the first sequencing of the full genome of a living organism in 1995[8]; the 7th anniversary of the birth of the world's first cloned animal in 1996[9]; the 6th anniversary of the patenting of the world's first artificial chromosome in 1997[10]; the 5th anniversary of the

* Professor, Faculty of Law, National University of Singapore. The contents of this chapter are primarily based on materials available before November 2003.

sequencing of the nematode worm, *Caenorhabditis elegans*, in 1998[11]; the 4th anniversary of the complete sequencing of the first human chromosome in 1999[12]; the 3rd anniversary of the completion of the working draft of the human genome in 2000[13]; the 2nd anniversary of President George W. Bush's decision in 2001 to control the use of federal funds for stem cell research[14] and the 1st anniversary of the release of the draft genome of *Manaporthe grisea*, a fungus that causes rice blast disease and responsible for the loss of millions of tons of rice annually.[15]

The time-line for biotechnology, of course, goes back much further than a mere 50 years. Biotechnology at its heart encompasses the use of living organisms and living systems for industrial processes.[16] Defined in this way, the goals of the technology are not new. Humans have been trying to adapt nature from the dawn of civilisation. After all, the use of yeast in fermentation processes to make bread and beer dates back many thousands of years. In the area of agriculture and animal husbandry, the intervention of man is even older. Humans first started domesticating crops and livestock around 8,000 B.C. Selective breeding of animals and cross pollination techniques have also been used for a very long time to create new hybrids and varieties of plants and animals. In the area of health, humans have also long been using plants and their extracts to both treat and prevent disease.

Modern biotechnology has the same goals of biotechnology of yesteryear: to produce new drugs, new diagnostic and treatment therapies and new varieties of crops and animals that are better able to meet the food and other needs of human civilisation. The difference lies in the degree of control that humans have now acquired over life processes in achieving those goals. That control came from man's relatively recent and improved understanding of how life forms originated and evolved together with the knowledge of nature's means for storing and transmitting all the information essential to the replication of each and every life form across the generations. The key to unlocking the door to improved control was the discovery of the structure of the DNA molecule closely followed and accompanied by other pioneering work in the field of genetics and molecular biology.[17] In this way the seeds for modern biotechnology can be found in scientific discoveries of the 1950s with the technological fruition first beginning to appear in the 1970s. That technological fruition, for better or worse, has spawned a number of firsts, some of which have been mentioned already in the context of the anniversaries of 2003. They include: genetically engineered organisms from the tomato plant[18], to wheat[19], soy bean[20], mice[21] and beyond. It also includes artificial chromosomes[22], cloned animals with or without transgenes inserted[23], new drugs[24], new therapies and diagnostic test kits[25] and so on. Doubtless, there will be a host of further developments and more "firsts" to come. The world may or may not see the birth of the first human clone any time soon[26], but it will surely see many new transgenic animals and plants as well as drugs born out of the marriage of bioprospecting and biotechnology.

Bioprospecting, at its heart, involves searching nature and living systems for plants and animals that in one way or another are useful to mankind. In some cases, it may be a new plant species or plant variety that is useful as a food crop. In many other cases, it will be for a living organism (mostly plants, sometime animals) that has some medicinal or therapeutic value. The traditional knowledge of local and indigenous communities will often be critical in giving leads and pointing researchers towards plants and animals known to have useful medicinal and therapeutic effects. The knowledge that a plant produces a substance in its leaves that repels insects may be enough for indigenous peoples to develop numerous practical uses for the leaves from the plant. Indigenous peoples may even be able to extract or concentrate the active ingredients although they may not know what those ingredients are in terms of their "modern" chemical names or chemical formula.[27] What modern science does, in many cases, is to speed up the process of identifying the active ingredients. Often times, the active ingredient will be a protein. The protein can be isolated, extracted and purified and used in therapeutic treatments. Modern biotechnology techniques may even enable the identification of the gene that expresses the protein. It may then be possible to transfer the gene to other plants so as to confer the same advantage on the now transgenic plant. In other cases, armed with the knowledge of the amino acid sequence of the protein, the scientist may be able to synthesise the protein in the laboratory. Given these developments, it is not surprising that modern biotechnology, whilst always exciting, is sometimes frightening, sometimes uplifting, sometimes praiseworthy for creating solutions and sometimes worrisome for creating or exacerbating problems for society at large. The interface between biotechnology, law and society is therefore enormous. Looking at the interface from the perspective of the law and policy of intellectual property rights and biological resources, a number of large areas leap out. In the first place there will be the "hard" intellectual property law issues largely concerned with the extent to which current intellectual property rights such as patents protect "biological inventions." Second, there are the issues that have arisen concerning the relationship between intellectual property rights obligations set out in the Agreement on Trade-Related Aspects of Intellectual Property Rights (TRIPs) and the provisions of the Convention on Biological Diversity 1992 (CBD). Third, there are the issues concerned with the relationship between the various stakeholders in the bio-industry and how more equitable partnerships might develop between bio-pharmaceutical companies and indigenous communities. Finally, there are the numerous issues relating to the need to protect the biodiversity and traditional knowledge of developing countries and indigenous communities.[28] Whilst overlaps naturally arise between these four areas and whilst a holistic approach will need to be taken by the policy makers, this paper will focus largely on a broad overview of the first area.[29]

2.2 ACQUIRING RIGHTS IN MODIFIED LIVING THINGS AND OTHER BIOLOGICAL INVENTIONS: PATENT LAW

2.2.1 The policy of patent law

Given the enormous range of practical applications for biotechnology and the many different types of biological "invention" highlighted earlier, it is not surprising that the question of how these fit into the patent law requirement of "invention" is a frequently recurring problem. Indeed, the closer the alleged invention is to a natural product or living organism, the more acute the problem becomes. The inquiry as to what is an invention is perhaps best started with a discussion of the policy behind patent law. Patent law is concerned with providing limited protection for inventions that are useful (at least in the sense of being capable of industrial application), new and inventive (in the sense of being non-obvious). The protection conferred, like all intellectual property rights, involves the grant of exclusive rights to prevent others from making and exploiting the subject-matter of the invention. Having a patent does not mean that the patent owner has a positive right to exploit the invention—it simply confers a right of exclusion, leaving the question as to whether the patent owner should be allowed to exploit the invention to other regulatory bodies and mechanisms. Thus, the grant of a patent over a drug or a genetically modified organism does not mean that the owner is free to market the product. In both cases, approvals from food and drug licensing authorities are very likely to be needed. The grant of a patent in this way does not carry with it an endorsement or recommendation for use and exploitation. A patent is usually seen as a reward for the ingenuity and effort that goes into the making of the invention for the law generally recognises that it is wise to encourage creativity and innovation. The patent system implicitly recognises and accepts that creativity and industrial innovation can and will result in products and processes that will possess both advantages and disadvantages. In some cases, the disadvantages will be inherent within the technology itself as where a new drug slows a viral infection but increases the risk of cancer. In other cases, the disadvantage may lie in the danger of abuse by man, as where a mad man laces a nation's drinking supply with a patented pesticide. In some cases, however, the technology may be so destructive and inimical to public order, safety and morality that any conceivable benefit will be swamped by society's concern over the dangers and risks inherent in the invention such as land mines and weapons of mass destruction suitable for use by terrorists.[30] The patent system implicitly accepts that it will not be possible to limit individual creativity and innovation to areas of activity which are free of all risk and that the question of whether any invention is to be exploited, involves a cost/benefit/risk analysis that is better taken outside of the patent system. In this way, the grant of a patent over an invention is said to be a "neutral" act in that it does not confer any right or presumption that society must therefore allow the invention's free and unregulated use. The converse, it is said must also be true—namely that the fact that there are restrictions imposed by domestic law on the sale of the patented item does not mean that the item should have been treated as unpatentable in the first place.[31]

If the policy of modern day patent law is to encourage innovation and creativity in the field of industry, it is perhaps worth remembering that this has not always been the case. For example, in England, patent law dates back to the decision of the common law courts in the celebrated case of *Darcy v Allin*.[32] In this case, the Court of Queen's Bench ruled that the grant of patents by exercise of royal prerogative power would be invalid unless the following test was satisfied:

> Where any man by his own charge and industry, or by his own wit and invention doth bring any new trade into the realm or

> any engine tending to the furtherance of a trade that was never used before ...

What is significant about this decision is the fact that the common law was prepared to validate patents granted to individuals simply for the act of bringing into the realm inventions which had never been used before. Similarly, the Statute of Monopolies of 1624 validated patents granted to inventors of "any manner of new manufacture" within the realm—inventor being defined as including the person who first brought something new to the country. Grubb explains that:

> Many of the early patents granted before the Statute of Monopolies had been to inventors of this type; for example the first and second English patents for invention (in 1449 and 1552) both related to glass making techniques which were known in continental Europe, but not established in England. Here the consideration for the grant of the patent was the establishment of the new industry in England, or, in modern terms, the transfer of technology to a developing country. The basic objective was to improve the balance of trade by reducing imports and encouraging new industries which could generate exports.[33]

Another, more colourful and perhaps more provocative way of describing this type of patent will be "assimilation of the technology" of third countries.[34] This system of allowing first importers to be treated as inventors and the limitation of novelty to what was known in the United Kingdom continued right up to the coming into force of the *Patents Act* 1977. Thus, under the *Patents Act* 1949, section 32(1)(e) still defined novelty in terms of what was known or used at the priority date in the United Kingdom.[35] The passage of the *Patents Act* 1977[36] marked a major turning point in the development of English patent law. By then, the United Kingdom was part of the European Economic Community and a signatory to the European Patent Convention 1973 (EPC).[37] The *Patents Act* 1977 was enacted to bring United Kingdom patent law into line with the EPC 1973. As will be discussed in more detail later, the novelty requirement was changed to world-wide novelty and the concept of inventorship by being a first importer was abandoned.[38] The policy behind the grant of a patent had now changed. No longer did the consideration include what Grubb terms "transfer of technology to a developing country" (namely the United Kingdom). Instead, the goal now was solely to encourage creativity and innovation within the industrial sphere. The consideration for the grant of a patent that flowed from this was the technological and industrial progress that hopefully would result.[39]

The question that has now arisen as a result of rapid developments in biotechnology and bioprospecting is whether the patent system should take on a broader role than merely encouraging technological and cultural innovation. Should intellectual property rights in general and patents in particular acquire a role that extends beyond wealth creation and into wealth distribution? For example, Professor Drahos argues that whilst there is a strong and self evident connection between intellectual property and commerce and trade as is witnessed by the TRIPS Agreement, it is also clear that intellectual property is no longer just trade related as the WTO is not just a trade organisation. Professor Drahos comments that:

> The WTO has become a key meeting place in the global village. It is a place where environmental issues, labour standards and human rights issues are increasingly being linked to investment, competition and market access agendas...Intellectual property rights are being required to serve much broader regulatory agendas than they have in the past ... [and] the objectives of global intellectual property regulation have to be integrated with the regulatory objectives to be found in international regimes governing biodiversity, food and agriculture... In the past the main regulatory objective of intellectual property rights has been to promote the allocation of resources to technological and cultural innovation. The use of intellectual property solely for this purpose is being questioned from a variety of perspectives. Intellectual property rights as the literature on the Convention on Biological Diversity shows, are seen to be important in an equitable sharing of the benefits of the technological pie and not just in an increase in its size... Future intellectual property regulation may be called upon to play a much greater role in managing technological change as opposed to simply promoting it ...[40]

Whether patent law should take on such an expanded role is clearly an important matter of policy that needs to be addressed both within and outside of the patent system. If patent law is compelled to acquire a role in facilitating equitable wealth sharing and management of technology, numerous areas of patent law will be affected. These will include, the state of art relevant to novelty and inventive step enquiries, disclosure of source of biological materials and traditional knowledge used to make a biological based invention (whether as part of the patent application process or even as a new substantive condition for the grant) and evidence of prior informed consent of the source country for the biological materials and traditional knowledge as well as evidence of an equitable benefit sharing arrangement with biological material and traditional knowledge providers. Further, if patent law is to acquire an expanded role in managing technological change, a more aggressive application of *ordre public* and morality exclusions may be called for as well as a re-examination of the desirability of having lists of things which are declared to be unpatentable, whether because these are deemed not to be inventions or because they are said not to be *patentable* inventions.

2.2.2 The meaning of "invention"

2.2.2.1 Paris Convention for the protection of industrial property

The Paris Convention contains no definition of invention or indeed provision on what constitutes patentable subject-matter.[41] It does, however, give an indication of the direction of its thinking by setting out a general definition of industrial property. Thus, Article 1(3) states that industrial property is to be understood "in the broadest sense" and applies not just to "industry and commerce proper, but likewise to agricultural and extractive industries and to all manufactured or natural products, for example, wines, grain, tobacco leaf, cattle, mineral waters, beer, flowers and flour." Beyond this, Article 1(4) merely provides that patents are "to include the various kinds of patents recognised by the countries of the Union such as patents of importation, patents of improvement, patents and certificates of addition, etc." Thus, so long as the countries of the Union apply their patent law on a national treatment basis, the Paris Convention, by and large, leaves it to each member state to determine what might constitute patentable subject-matter. At best, what Article 1(3) suggests is that the countries of the Union should adopt a broad flexible approach in which the mere fact that the subject-matter involves a natural product or a living thing does not mean that it cannot be regarded as industrial property. This, of course, will tend to support the view that patentable subject-matter can and should cover biological inventions.

2.2.2.2 The TRIPS Agreement 1994

The TRIPS Agreement goes beyond the Paris Convention in that it sets out a general definition of patentable subject-matter in Article 27(1). This provides that:

> ...patents shall be available for any inventions, whether products or processes, in all fields of technology, provided that they are new, involve an inventive step and are capable of industrial application ...

What is conspicuously absent, however, is any definition of invention. It follows that whilst Member States must protect all inventions, in all fields of technology including biotechnology (whether the invention is a product or a process) on a national treatment and most favoured nation basis, that Member States retain the right to determine the scope of the concept of an invention. Does this mean that Member States have a completely free hand to adopt as restrictive an interpretation of invention as is desired? This seems unlikely. In the first place, TRIPS requires compliance with Article 1 of the Paris Convention, which as we have seen, requires a broad approach to the definition of industrial property of which patent law forms a part. Second, a strong argument can be made, that "invention" as understood in the context of technology (products or processes), at the very least, encompasses things which have some practical application in the field of industry. Third, if the intention behind Article 27(1) was to give a *carte blanc* to all Member States to adopt whatever definition of invention that they wanted, this could in extreme cases negate the express directive that patents were to be available to all products in all fields of technology. Thus, it seems that whilst Member States do have some room for flexibility in deciding what an invention is under their national patent laws, that the definition adopted must fall within the ball park area of things with practical or industrial utility. The problem, however, is that the ball park is large with indistinct boundaries. It begs the question as to what amounts to a sufficient practical or industrial utility such as to turn a mere discovery into an invention: a question that has been much debated in the context of the patenting of proteins, genes and gene fragments. In this context, some commentators have argued that because the TRIPS definition provides no definition of invention, TRIPS does not in principle prevent the exclusion of "naturally occurring substances, such as genes and cells, from patent protection."[42] Yet another commentator agrees and argues that:

> Nothing in the TRIPS Agreement ... obliges World Trade Organization (WTO) Member countries to follow an expansive approach in respect of patenting of substances existing in nature, such as genes, cells or plants as such. In effect, the TRIPS Agreement specifies the *requirements* that an invention must meet in order to be patentable, but it does not provide a definition of what an *invention* is. This leaves WTO Member countries free to determine what should be deemed an invention. Many laws in developing countries (e.g., Argentina, Brazil, the Andean Group) exclude the patentability of materials found in nature, even if isolated ... The exclusion may ban the patenting of genes, cells or any other sub cellular part found in nature, or isolated therefrom.[43]

The matter is further complicated, however, by the exclusions from patentability that are permitted under TRIPS. Article 27(3)(b) of TRIPS, in particular, expressly permits Member States to exclude from patentability animals, plants and essentially biological processes for the production of animals or plants. This exclusion, however, does not apply to micro-organisms and non-biological and microbiological processes. Putting it the other way round, Article 27(3)(b) demands that micro-organisms, non-biological and microbiological processes be treated as patentable subject-matter. This leads yet another commentator to query the position of genetic and biochemical resources as inventions under TRIPS and to conclude that:

> since these are not expressly excluded, patents must in principle be made available for these subject to the conditions that they be new, involve an inventive step and be capable of industrial application.[44]

What then about vectors used in genetic engineering processes to transfer and insert genes into foreign organisms? These vectors will include bacteriophages and plasmids. A bacteriophage is a virus that has the ability to infect bacteria and use the bacteria's DNA replication mechanism to make copies of its own genetic code. Plasmids are small bits of circular DNA found within bacterium and which have the ability to move from bacteria to bacteria. In principle, it would seem that even a conservative interpretation of Article 27(3)(b) will lead to the conclusion that bacteriophages are intended by TRIPS to be capable of constituting patentable material on the basis that these are "micro-organisms." Indeed, it has been pointed out that although "TRIPS Agreement requires that 'micro-organisms' be protected, nothing would prevent WTO Member countries applying the scientific definition of micro-organism" which covers viruses, algae, bacteria, fungi and protozoa.[45] What then is the position of plasmids and proteins? Correa argues that genes, cells or any other sub cellular part found or isolated from nature can be excluded simply on the basis that these are not inventions and are not within the TRIPS obligation to protect micro-organisms.[46] On the other hand, an opposing view might be that whilst these are not expressly mentioned by Article 27, it would be surprising if TRIPS did not intend these to be capable of forming the basis of patentable subject-matter. After all, TRIPS does requires patents to be made available for all inventions in all technologies and since there is no express exclusion of plasmids and proteins, these must in principle have been intended as being capable of forming the basis of patentable subject-matter.[47]

Ultimately, the issue of the patentability of micro-organisms, genes, proteins, viruses and bacterium under Article 27 of TRIPS is something that needs to be addressed by the WTO itself. How much flexibility do Member countries in fact have to shape the content of patentable subject-matter in this area by reference to the criterion of invention? For example, will a national definition of invention that excludes, *inter alia*, all micro-organisms, genes and proteins even when isolated from their natural environment be acceptable within the TRIPS framework? If not, will it be acceptable if the exclusion from invention was expressly limited to micro-organisms, genes, proteins as found in their natural environment on the basis that such a definition is consistent with the distinction between mere discovery and invention? Whilst there is much to be said for the second position, it is unlikely that the first position will find support within the European Union, the United States, Japan and other countries pushing the envelope of biotechnological research.[48]

2.2.2.3 The European Directive on Biotechnology

The European Directive on Biotechnology[49] like the TRIPS Agreement does not set out any statutory definition of invention. It does, on the other hand, contain detailed provisions which deal with many of the questions raised above in connection with TRIPS. Article 1 of the Directive sets out the general obligation to protect biotechnological inventions under national patent laws. Article 3(1) goes on to explain that inventions which are new, which involve an inventive step and which are susceptible of industrial application shall be patentable even if they concern a product consisting of or containing biological material[50] or a process by means of which biological material is produced, processed or used. Even more to the point is the express provision in Article 3(2) that "biological material which is isolated from its natural environment or produced by means of a technical process may be the subject of an invention even if it previously occurred in nature." Thus, even though there is no definition of invention, the Directive makes clear that material such as genes that have been isolated from the environment may form the basis of an invention. Synthesised biological material even if identical in terms of make up with their natural counterparts are also included. A similar position applies in the case of the human biological material. In the case of the human body and human genetic material, Article 5(1) accepts the basic distinction between discovery and invention by providing that the human body at all stages of formation and development as well as the simple discovery of one of its elements, including genes and gene sequences are not patentable inventions. What then is the difference between a "simple" discovery of a gene or a protein in the human body and an invention? The answer is, at least partially, to be found in Article 5(2) which states that

> an element isolated from the human body or otherwise produced by means of a technical process, including the sequence or partial sequence of a gene, may constitute a patentable invention, even if the structure of that element is identical to a natural element.

It follows that human proteins and genes, once isolated or synthesised artificially, can form the subject-matter of valid patent claims under the Directive.[51] This is subject, however, to the further requirement in Article 5.3 that the industrial application of the gene or gene sequence must be disclosed in the application. In this way, even though there is still no general definition of invention, the Directive puts that issue on the backburner as the specific provisions on biotechnological inventions deal with most of the invention related questions that might arise.[52] The approach adopted by the Directive to a large extent codifies that which was already the position in Europe under the European Patent Convention 1973 and is likely to commend itself to many countries actively involved in biotechnological research and development. Countries which provide the biological source materials and which are bio-diversity rich may beg to disagree. If the difference between discovery of a natural substance and an invention is nothing more than the process of isolation of the active ingredient—then some may question whether this is a sufficient step forward to warrant the grant of patent monopoly protection when the prior art may have already pointed to the existence of some ingredient possessing the therapeutic effects. But then again, perhaps this is not so much a question of whether the isolated active ingredient is an invention, as a question as to whether the prior art made that invention obvious.

2.2.2.4 The European Patent Convention 1973

The European Patent Convention 1973, like the Paris Convention, the TRIPS Agreement and the European Directive on Biotechnology, does not set out a general definition of invention.[53] The framers of the EPC 1973 had basically five options open to them on the question of invention. First, an attempt could have been made to craft a positive definition intended for general application by stating what the essential elements of any invention were to be. Second, the framers could have tried to set out a positive definition by reference to a list of things deemed to amount to an invention. Third, there could have been an attempt to fashion a definition by stating what in principle, invention did not cover. Fourth, it might be felt easier to come up with a list of things which were deemed not to be an invention rather than to craft some principle of general application. Fifth, the approach might have been taken to leave the definition to the courts to evolve on a case by case basis with the policy of patent law pointing the way forward. The framers of the EPC evidently decided to go for the fourth approach and to develop a non-exhaustive list of things which were to be deemed not to amount to invention. Thus, Article 52(2) states that the following are not inventions (as such):

(a) discoveries, scientific theories and mathematical methods;
(b) aesthetic creations;

(c) schemes, rules and methods for performing mental acts, playing games or doing business and programs for computers;
(d) presentations of information.

These bars to a large degree reflect the invention/discovery dichotomy in patent law as well European patent law's pre-occupation with things of practical/technical utility in the field of industry.[54] The bars are not absolute and are sufficiently flexible through the "as such" proviso to admit the enumerated items when some technical effect can be demonstrated.[55] Aside from this list of things declared not to be inventions "as such," Article 53 goes on to exclude certain items from patentability. These are first, "inventions the publication or exploitation of which would be contrary to *ordre public* or morality" and second, "plant or animal varieties or essentially biological processes for the production of plants or animals" (not being microbiological processes or the products thereof).[56]

The effect of these provisions in the case of gene sequences was considered by the European Patent Office in *Howard Florey/Relaxin Patent Application*.[57] This was a case that involved a biological invention concerning a human protein: "human H2-relaxin." The protein caused pelvic ligaments to relax in pregnant women. The patent claims were extensive and included claims to the gene and the protein. Numerous grounds of opposition were raised including an attack based on the argument that the claims offended the distinction between discovery and invention. For example, in the case of the gene sequences, the argument was made that sequences were merely discovered and could not be inventions for the purpose of patent law. The Opposition Division disagreed and in doing so adopted a broad approach to the question of invention. In the first place, it was pointed out that the gene claims were directed towards complementary DNA (cDNA) versions of the gene that were not found in nature. On this basis, the claims would be directed towards a version of the gene that was not found in nature and was made by man.[58] The breadth of the Opposition Division's approach to invention is even more apparent in its holding that even if the patent claims were directed towards genomic DNA, the claims would still be for inventions and not discoveries as such. In so holding the Opposition Division applied the Guidelines for Examination in the EPO.[59] Guideline C-IV, paragraph 2.3 (as it then existed) stated that:

> to find a substance freely occurring in nature is also a mere discovery and therefore unpatentable. However, if a substance found in nature has first to be isolated from its surroundings and a process for obtaining it is developed, that process is patentable. Moreover, if the substance can be properly characterised either by its structure, by the process by which it is obtained or by other parameters and it is new in the absolute sense of having no previously recognised existence, then the substance per se may be patentable.

Applying these guidelines, the Opposition Division found that the human H2 relaxin was new as it had no previously recognised existence. The applicants had developed a method of obtaining H2 relaxin and the DNA and had also managed to characterise the chemical structure of the products. The applicants had turned the discovery into an invention by finding a use for the protein. The Opposition Division was of the view that to amount to an invention, there had to be a "technical character" that is an industrially applicable solution to a technical problem that is reproducible without undue burden.[60] These requirements were satisfied on the facts.

This liberal approach taken by the Opposition Division of the EPO to the meaning of invention is now supported by the European Directive on Biotechnological Inventions. Indeed, amendments were made in 2001 to the guidelines for examination in the European Patent Office that strongly echo the principles and the requirements of the Directive. Thus, the new guideline C-IV 2a.1 states that "in principle, biotechnological inventions are patentable under the EPC." The new guideline C-IV 2a.2 also states "that biological material which is isolated from the natural environment or produced by means of a technical process is to be considered a patentable invention even if it already occurs in nature."[61]

2.2.2.5 The Australian approach

The Australian *Patents Act* 1990 (as amended) defines patentable invention as one which is a "manner of manufacture within the meaning of section 6 of Statute of Monopolies."[62] The meaning of this expression (rather than invention) was considered at length by the Australian High Court in *National Research and Development Corporation v Commissioner of Patents*[63] where the view was taken that it would be futile to try and carve out an exhaustive definition of manufacture. Instead, a flexible approach was to be adopted bearing in mind that the Act was passed to encourage national development. In *CCOM Pty Ltd v Jiejing Pty Ltd*, a case which concerned a Chinese language word processing program, the Federal Court of Australia accepted that the *NRDC* decision remained of considerable importance in Australia.[64] The *Patents Act* 1990 of Australia repealed and replaced the *Patents Act* 1952. This was said to have marked a point of departure with United Kingdom patent law which had in 1977 enacted the *Patents Act* 1977 based on the provisions of the European Patent Convention 1973. One major point of difference being that the Australian *Patent Act* of 1990 retained the linkage between invention and "manner of manufacture" and did not set out an extensive list of things deemed not to be inventions as such. Indeed, the Federal Court pointed out that the only bar was the express exclusion in section 18(2) against human beings and biological processes for their production.[65] It followed that the legislature in Australia had left the matter to be dealt with by the courts using the principles set out in the *Re NRDC* case.[66] On this basis, the court held that the right question was whether the subject-matter of the claims were a proper subject of letters patent according to the principles which have been developed out of the application of section 6 of the Statute of Monopolies. The *NRDC* case was interpreted broadly as requiring "a mode or manner of achieving an end result which is an artificially created state of affairs of utility in the field of economic endeavour."[67] On the facts, a relevant field of economic endeavour was held to be the use of word processing to assemble text in Chinese language characters. The utility was said to reside in the storage of data as to Chinese characters analysed by stroke-type categories, for search including flagging and selection.

Whilst the *NRDC/CCOM* decisions indicate that the Australian courts are likely to take a broad approach to biotechnological inventions, tricky questions are still likely to arise. For example, in *Rank Hovis McDougall Ltd's Application*, the Australian Patent Office accepted claims directed towards variants of a new strain of micro-organism said to be useful in generating edible proteins. Of this decision, Professor Ricketson writes that:

> The micro-organism itself was naturally occurring and was thus denied protection because of lack of novelty, although the process of isolating it may well have been patentable ... On the other hand, the specific variants of the organism ...

> did not occur in nature, but only as a result of the applicant's treatment. As these achieved a useful result, the Assistant Commissioner held that the fact that they were living organisms was no barrier to their patentability ...[68]

What then about claiming the naturally occurring micro-organism in an isolated form? The isolated form may be identical in structure to the natural organism and the utility may be the same or similar. Does this mean that the isolated form lacks novelty and invention? Whilst these are separate issues, they do tend to run into each other. Indeed, yet another line of attack will be to argue that the isolation even if it results in a new invention is obvious and lacking in inventive step. As we have seen, the position under both the European Patent Convention 1973 and the European Directive on Biotechnology is that claims may be directed towards isolated natural compounds that have technical effect or application. Others may beg to differ arguing that the mere process of isolating a natural compound cannot on its own confer novelty or amount to an invention. On this it is interesting to note that the Australian Patent Office has said of the *Rank Hovis* decision that:

> naturally occurring micro-organisms *per se* are not patentable as they represent a discovery and not an invention, but a claim to a pure culture, in the presence of some specified ingredients would satisfy the requirement of a technical intervention.[69]

Further, in what appears to closely follow the European practice, the Australian Patent Office has stated that:

> ... the discovery of a micro-organism, protein, enatiomer or antibiotic in nature can be claimed in its isolated form or as substantially free of (perhaps, specified) impurities. Also a gene can be claimed as a gene per se (as long as the claim does not include within its scope the native chromosome of which the gene forms part) or as the recombinant or isolated or purified gene.[70]

To reinforce the point, the Australian Patent Office has also stated that biological entities may be patentable so long as the technical intervention of man (manufacture) has resulted in an artificial state of affairs which does not exist in nature.[71] Further, it does not appear that the Australian Patent Office will draw any distinction between higher and lower life forms[72] although there is of course an express bar in Australia against the patenting of human beings and the biological processes for their production.[73] These statements are certainly helpful in revealing the thinking and current practice before the Australian Patent Office. What remains to be seen is whether the Australian courts will take a similar view in particular on the status of claims directed towards isolated (purified) natural substances and organisms and the requirement of manufacture (invention) and novelty.

2.2.2.6 The United States position

Under the United States Patents Act[74] as amended, the term invention is defined as meaning both "invention" as well as "discovery."[75] This, at first sight, seems to set US patent law far apart from the patent law of the rest of the common law world with the well-known distinction between discovery and invention proving to be almost as hard to pin down as the copyright distinction between expression and ideas and facts. But, in reality, this is not so since section 101 defines patentable inventions in terms of the invention or discovery of any "new useful process, machine, manufacture, or composition of matter, or any useful improvement therefor ..." Pure scientific discoveries are not patentable simply because of the need to show utility (usefulness) and that the discovery comprises some process, machine, manufacture or composition of matter.[76] The leading decision in the United States on the scope of patentable subject-matter remains the decision of the Supreme Court in *Diamond v Chakrabarty*.[77] The case concerned the patentability of a bacterium that had been "engineered" so that it could metabolise or break down crude oil—the practical application being its use to clean up oil spills. A challenge was brought on the basis that the engineered bacterium, being a life form, was not patentable. This was rejected by the Supreme Court. Chief Justice Burger for the majority explained that the Constitution provided Congress with a power to legislate so as to promote the progress of science and the useful arts.[78] Patent laws filled that role by offering inventors exclusive rights for a limited period as an incentive for their inventiveness and research efforts. The hope and expectation was that by so doing, society would benefit from the new products and processes of manufacture that would be introduced to the economy. Chief Justice Burger felt that the Patents Act embodied the philosophy of Thomas

Jefferson that "ingenuity should receive a liberal encouragement" and that "Congress intended statutory subject-matter to include anything under the sun that is made by man." [79] On this basis, the majority found that the micro-organism plainly qualified as patentable subject-matter. The claim was not for "some hitherto unknown natural phenomenon but to a non-naturally occurring manufacture or composition of matter—a product of human ingenuity ..."[80] The relevant distinction, according to the United States Supreme Court was not between living and inanimate things but between products of nature (whether living or not) and human made inventions.

The broad and flexible approach taken by the United States Supreme Court is clearly driven by the policy behind the grant of patent monopoly. It is an approach that had no difficulty supporting the grant of a patent for higher multi-cellular complex life forms such as genetically engineered mice and the like.[81] What then is the position of patent claims for natural substances and organisms that have been isolated or purified in some concrete manner and which have a useful purpose? Leaving aside problems of inventive step, we have seen that a favourable patent position has been taken by Australia and Europe. It is probable that the US courts will take a similar position under its broad flexible approach although there may still be some uncertainty where, no new (credible, specific and substantial) utility is achieved by the claimed invention.[82]

2.2.2.7 The Canadian position

The statutory provisions in Canadian legislation on patentable subject-matter bear a passing resemblance to both the Statute of Monopolies 1624 and the United States *Patents Act*. That this should be so is hardly surprising given the common intellectual property heritage of these three jurisdictions. In the recent landmark decision of the Canadian Supreme Court in *Commissioner of Patents* v *President and Fellows of Harvard College* [83], Binnie J (for the minority) points out that the expression "composition of matter" in the definition of invention first appeared in 1824 in the Lower Canada statute entitled "An Act to promote the progress of the Useful Arts within this Province."[84] In 1826, this was followed by similarly entitled legislation in Upper Canada which explained the rationale of patent legislation in terms of it being expedient "for the encouragement of Genius and of the Arts" so as to "secure an exclusive right to the Inventor of any New and Useful Art, Machine, Manufacture or Composition of Matter."[85] This formula continued into the *Patent Act*

1985 where section 2 now defines invention as meaning "any new and useful art, process, machine, manufacture or composition of matter, or any new and useful improvement in any art, process, machine, manufacture or composition of matter." Given this, it was perhaps a little surprising that the Canadian Supreme Court, by a bare majority, adopted a relatively conservative interpretation of the scope of patentable subject-matter so as to exclude protection for higher life forms. The majority did not agree with the majority decision in the United States *Chakarbarty* case that anything under the sun made by the hands of man was patentable.[86] The majority were of the view that since invention had been defined by reference to specific categories such as "manufacture" and "composition of matter," that Parliament had thereby signalled a clear intention to include certain subject-matter as patentable whilst excluding others as being outside of the confines of the Act. This interpretation allowed the majority to explore whether Parliament had intended to include higher life forms (even if made by the hands of man) as patentable subject-matter—a conclusion which the majority flatly rejected even though they accepted that lower life forms (whatever was encompassed by that expression) were patentable.[87]

The conclusion of the *Oncomouse* saga before the Canadian courts is not of course the end of the Canadian debate over patentability of higher life forms. The decision goes against the fact that the *Oncomouse* has been patented in many other countries including the United States, Japan and the European Patent Office.[88] The arena for debate may well now shift to the Canadian Parliament—not just because of the Supreme Court's decision but also because of the significant and important recommendations set out in Report of the Canadian Biotechnology Advisory Committee that was published shortly before the *Oncomouse* decision.[89] The position that is adopted by Canada on the interface between its patent law, biotechnology, biodiversity and the rights of inventors, the public and indigenous communities will be keenly awaited by both developed and developing countries alike. Canada as a developed country is already a key player in the biotechnology industry.[90] Canada also has a significant agricultural industry and is likely to possess considerable biodiversity of her own as well as indigenous communities to cater for and protect.[91] Canada's intellectual property law framework is similar to those in many other developed countries: nevertheless, whether there is agreement or not with the Canadian Supreme Court's decision against patentability of higher life forms, that decision has marked

Canada out as the first major industrialised nation where its highest court has rejected patent protection for higher life forms. Developing countries are likely to watch with keen interest the response of the Canadian Government. The majority of the Supreme Court whilst rejecting patentability of higher life forms under existing provisions were not saying that amendments should not be made so as to extend protection to such life forms. The majority recognised that this was an issue of policy for Parliament to consider and implicitly endorsed the need for a balanced approach. On this it is noted that the Canadian Biotechnology Advisory Report attempts just such an approach. [92] On the one hand, the report recommends protection for higher life forms with the exception of human bodies at any stage of development. At the same time the report recommends that special provisions be enacted to safeguard the interests of farmers[93], innocent bystanders[94] and research and experimental use. Of even greater interest to biodiversity rich developing countries is the clear recommendation that the Federal Government develop policies to harmonise its patent and intellectual property laws with the principles set out in the Convention on Biological Diversity 1992.[95] These are important issues that need to be examined and the response of the Canadian Government is likely to be eagerly awaited both within and outside of Canada.

2.2.2.8 The position in India

At the time when the TRIPS Agreement was signed, India's patent law was primarily to be found in the Patents Act 1970. Section 3 of that Act set out a list of things that were deemed not to be inventions within the Act. These were:

(a) an invention which is frivolous or which claims anything contrary to well established natural laws;
(b) an invention the primary or intended use of which would be contrary to law or morality or injurious to public health;
(c) the mere discovery of a scientific principle or the formulation of an abstract theory;
(d) the mere discovery of any new property of new use for a known substance or of the mere use of a known process, machine or apparatus unless such known process results in a new product or employs at least one new reactant;

(e) a substance obtained by a mere admixture resulting only in the aggregation of the properties of the components thereof or a process for producing such substance;
(f) the mere arrangement or re-arrangement or duplication of known devices each functioning independently of one another in a known way;
(g) a method or process of testing applicable during the process of manufacture for rendering the machine, apparatus or other equipment more efficient or for the improvement or restoration of the existing machine, apparatus or other equipment or for the improvement or control of manufacture;
(h) a method of agriculture or horticulture;
(i) any process for the medicinal, surgical, curative, prophylactic or other treatment of human beings or any process for a similar treatment of animals or plants to render them free of disease or to increase their economic value or that of their products

Whilst some of these exclusions, such as those touching on discoveries, are consistent with those found in patent laws of industrialised countries and the TRIPS Agreement, there are some which clearly test the TRIPS obligation to protect all inventions (whether products or processes) and in all fields of technology. What then is the position in India of biological inventions such as those that featured in the *Oncomouse* litigation and the *Howard Florey/Relaxin* case? Notwithstanding that the *Patents Act* 1970 sets out no express bar against patenting of inventions involving living organisms, these types of "inventions" were bound to raise tricky issues as is well demonstrated by the Canadian *Oncomouse* litigation. Questions may also arise under the Indian Act as to whether the mere purification or isolation of a compound from a natural substance amounts to invention. Even if it did amount to invention in a way that satisfied the novelty and inventive step requirements, there remains the fact that section 5 of the Indian Act excludes patentability for products (substances) intended for use, or capable of being used, as food or as medicine or as a drug. Medicine in this context is defined very broadly by section 2(1) and includes:

> all medicines for internal or external use of human beings or animals; all substances intended to be used for or in the

> diagnosis, treatment, mitigation or prevention of diseases in human beings or animals; all substances intended to be used or in the maintenance of public health, or the prevention or control of any epidemic disease among human beings or animals; insecticides, germicides, fungicides, weedicides and all other substances intended to be used for the protection or preservation of plants and all chemical substances which are ordinarily used as intermediates in the preparation or manufacture of any of the medicines or substances above referred to.

Such a definition could well exclude claims directed to the isolated relaxin hormone and the cDNA molecules in the *Howard/Florey Relaxin* case simply on the basis that as substances, they would fall within the definition of medicine and hence be excluded by section 5.[96]

A number of important amendments to the list of excluded items were made to the *Indian Patents Act* by the *Patents (Amendment) Act* 2002.[97] Of particular importance to the position of biological inventions are the following new exclusions from the definition of invention:

(a) The mere "discovery of any living thing or non-living substance occurring in nature."
(b) "Plants and animals, in whole or any part thereof, other than micro-organisms but including seeds, varieties and species and essentially biological processes for production or propagation of plants and animals."
(c) "An invention which, in effect, is traditional knowledge or which is an aggregation or duplication of known properties of traditionally known component or components."

The new exclusion of the "mere" discovery of living things or non-living substances is unlikely in itself to be controversial. The provision does not provide that living things can never form the basis of an invention and the question remains as to what is needed to convert the discovery into invention. This question is by no means confined to Indian patent law although the continuing bar under the Indian Patent Act against product patents in the area of medicine and drugs is likely to mean that the invention debate will be less intense than it might otherwise have been. In any case India has also made use of the flexibility conferred on Member States by Article 27(3)(b) of TRIPS to exclude plants, animals and essentially biological processes for the production of animals or plants. These are now excluded from the definition of invention although micro-organisms remain covered. Thus, it appears that the *Oncomouse* is likely to receive short shrift under the *Indian Patent Act*. Even though it is not a naturally occurring organism, it is still an animal and excluded from the definition of invention. It may also be excluded from the definition of invention under the amended provision that now catches "inventions, the primary or intended use or commercial exploitation of which would be contrary to public order or morality or which causes serious prejudice to human, animal or plant life or health or to the environment." In any case, to cap it all off, the *Oncomouse* is likely to be also caught in India as a type of medicinal product and hence not patentable under section 5. Essentially biological processes are also excluded from the definition of invention although new genetic engineering processes may escape on the basis that they involve substantial technical intervention by man.[98]

The Indian approach to the question of invention has been to set out an extensive list of things which are to be excluded. Some of these, such as the *ordre public* type bar and the exclusion of plants, animals and essentially biological processes find support in the TRIPS Agreement where strictly speaking the approach is to treat these items as potentially unpatentable rather than as not capable of amounting to an invention. Others find support in the Convention for Biological Diversity such as the exclusion of traditional knowledge from the definition of invention.[99] It is much too early to predict how this particular exclusion will work in practice. How will traditional knowledge be defined and how will it affect innovations that whilst based on traditional knowledge—advances the technology in some new specific manner?[100] Doubtless, other developing countries with rich biodiversity and traditional knowledge systems will follow and observe the Indian experience with keen interest. Ultimately, however, whatever is the position taken in India, what is needed is some broad international agreement on the position of traditional knowledge under "conventional" patent laws and copyright laws and on whether some new *sui generis* intellectual property right should be developed to cater for the interests of the rightful holders of traditional knowledge.[101]

2.2.2.9 The position in Singapore

The Patents Act of Singapore, as originally enacted, followed closely the *Patents Act* 1977 (United Kingdom) which is itself based on the European Patent Convention 1973.[102] Thus, whilst there is no express definition of what is an invention, there was a list of exclusions that followed closely the list set out in section 1(2) of the English Act and Article 52(2) of European Patent Convention 1973.[103] There were, however, also some differences. In the first place, the Patents Act of Singapore never incorporated an express bar against patenting animals, plants and essentially biological processes.[104] Second, in 1995, the *Patents Act* was amended and the list of exclusions in section 13(2) was deleted.[105] It has been argued elsewhere[106] that the deletion of section 13(2) cannot mean that the items formerly enumerated (including discoveries as such) are now *ipso facto* to be treated as inventions. Instead, what is more likely, is that the burden now falls more so than ever on the courts to determine whether the things that are claimed properly fall within the scope of invention on a case by case basis. In some respects, the statutory approach in Singapore on the question of invention has now moved closer to the Australian position. The general policy objective behind the grant of patent may well inform the debate on whether the thing for which protection is claimed is a proper subject-matter for the grant of a patent.[107] Thus, in *Merck & Co Inc v Pharmaforte Singapore Pte Ltd*, a case that involved patent claims over purer forms of chemical compounds (statins) useful for treating certain diseases, Chao Hick Tin JA stated that:

> In this regard, we must also point out that the fact that a discovery is made does not mean there is an invention. The latter does not follow from the former. This distinction was brought out by Lindley LJ in *Lane Fox* at page 49 where he said: "An invention is not the same thing as a discovery. When Volta discovered the effect of an electric current from his battery on a frog's leg, he made a great discovery, but no patentable invention. Again, a man who discovers that a known machine can produce effects which no one before him knew could be produced by it, may make a great and useful discovery; but, if he does no more, his discovery is not a patentable invention: ... He has added nothing but knowledge to what previously existed. A patentee must do something more; he must make some addition, not only to knowledge, but to previously known inventions, and must so use his knowledge and ingenuity as to produce either a new and useful thing or result, or a new and useful method of producing an old thing or result."[108]

Whilst the concept of invention implies some useful practical application of a discovery or fresh insight, this is not likely to be too problematic in many cases involving biological "inventions." Thus, in the case of inventions like the *Oncomouse*, the practical application and utility of the genetically engineered oncorodent is its use in carcinogenicity studies. Further, with due respect to the decision of the Canadian Supreme Court, it is unlikely that the courts in Singapore will hold that higher life forms such as oncorodents were not intended by Parliament to be capable of forming the basis of invention. Indeed, the Select Committee on the Singapore Patent Bill 1994 in deciding against a specific bar against animal and plant varieties noted that the general justification for patenting new life forms is that it provides an incentive for people to invest and innovate and that since the biotechnology industry relies on the patent system as an incentive mechanism, patenting was essential to maintaining the creation of benefits flowing from biotechnology research.[109] Similarly, the Singapore patent law is not likely to have problems (from the perspective of what is an invention) in extending recognition to genetically engineered bacterium or viruses such as those which featured in the *Chakarbarty* case. Neither is it likely to have any difficulties with claims directed towards genes and proteins as featured in the *Howard/Florey Relaxin* case—at least not where these are limited to proteins, genes and DNA molecules in cDNA or isolated (purified forms).[110]

2.2.3 Permitted exclusions from patentability

Aside from exclusions from patentability that arise within the context of the discussion of what is an invention, another highly important issue concerns the range of exclusions from patentability (whether internalised within or dealt with externally to the question of invention) permitted by international agreements. Some of these have been touched on already and what follows is a drawing together of the permitted exclusions by reference to the provisions in the TRIPS Agreement.

2.2.3.1 The *ordre public*/morality exclusion

Article 27(2) of the TRIPS Agreement provides that: "Members may exclude from patentability inventions, the prevention within their territory of the commercial exploitation of which is necessary to protect *ordre public* or morality, including to protect human, animal or plant life or health or to avoid serious prejudice to the environment, provided that such exclusion is not made merely because the exploitation is prohibited by their law." The inclusion of an *ordre public* type bar is not mandatory and it is to be noted that several major jurisdictions have not enacted any express bar to patentability based on Article 27(2).[111] Indeed, it should be pointed out that there are two broad views as to the appropriateness (and practicality) of assessing *ordre public* type considerations in assessing patentability of inventions. *Ordre public* considerations have nothing to do with the novelty of the invention or lack of intellectual merit in the making of the invention (inventive step or non-obviousness). Instead, the objection is based on some broad overriding concern that the exploitation of the invention is contrary to public safety or morality. If the patent system is seen as fulfilling the limited role of encouraging intellectual creativity and industrial innovation, it may be suggested that broader concerns of public safety and morality are best taken outside of the patent system. After all, the grant of a patent is not a certificate to use and certainly carries no presumption of general societal approval. On the other hand, there are those who argue that it is time that the patent system takes on a broader role of "managing technological change" as opposed to simply "promoting" technological change.[112] Whether the patent system has the expertise and the capabilities to manage and direct technological change is, however, bound to be a highly contentious issue.

Of those jurisdictions to have such a bar, the European Patent Office has certainly accumulated some experience with the operation of the bar. Indeed, it appears that the inspiration for Article 27(2) is likely to be found in Article 53(a) of the European Patent Convention 1973.[113] In recent times, application of the bar in opposition proceedings in Europe has been most hotly contested in the area of patents for genetically modified plants and animals. In all of these recent cases, the opposition failed. In the *Harvard Oncomouse* case, the Technical Board suggested that the bar required a careful weighing up of the arguments which in that case concerned suffering of animals and possible risks to the environment against the invention's usefulness to mankind.[114] When the matter was returned to the Examination Division for consideration, a broad range of principles and factors were taken account of in the balancing exercise. The statement of principles is particularly illuminating and bears repeating. These are first, the principle that patent law did not confer a positive right of use. Second, the principle that exceptions to patentability were to be narrowly construed. Third, the principle that all new technologies are normally afflicted with new risks. Fourth, that biotechnological inventions were not generally excluded from patent protection. These principles when taken in combination set up what might be described as a "light touch" approach to the operation of the bar. On the facts, given the possible benefits to mankind and reduction of animal suffering (less animals being needed to conduct carcinogenicity studies if oncomice were used), the Examination division found against the application of the bar.[115]

If *ordre public* objections failed in the case of genetically modified animals, they have had just as little success in Europe against genetically modified plants. In *Plant Genetic Systems/Glutamine synthetase inhibitors*, the EPO had to consider claims involving plants and seeds that had been genetically modified so as possess a gene encoding a protein that offered protection against herbicides. Opposition in this case was based on possible dangers to the environment through escape of the transgene. The attempt failed even though the Technical Board of Appeal defined *ordre public* as covering public safety and the physical integrity of individuals as part of society, including the environment. Morality was defined as the belief that some behaviour is right and acceptable whereas other behaviour is wrong such belief being founded on the totality of norms which are deeply rooted in a particular culture. *Ordre public* was not called into play since the evidence was insufficient to establish the degree of actual risk of environmental harm. The Technical Board of Appeal, in short, did not approach the need to protect the environment on the basis of some "precautionary principle." Instead, it chose to emphasise the point that whilst the patent office was at the cross road of science and technology—it was not there alone. There were other regulatory authorities that were charged with the specific task of regulating the use of technologies whether these were patented or not.[116] On the issue of morality, the Technical Board found that on the evidence (and given that traditional selective breeding was common place) none of the claims offended against conventionally accepted standards of conduct of European culture.

In the area of human genes and proteins, *ordre public*/ morality type objections were raised in the *Howard Florey/Relaxin* case. That case involved claims over the gene encoding for a protein that was produced in the body of pregnant women and which caused the pelvic ligaments to relax. Aside from opposition on the basis that there was no invention, a number of morality based objections were also raised. Thus, it was said that the invention was offensive as it involved the isolation of a gene through the use of tissue obtained from a pregnant woman. This was said to be against "human dignity" as it made use of a human condition for a technical process that was orientated towards profit. The patent claims were also said to amount to a modern form of slavery and dismemberment of women and to infringe the human right of self determination.[117] The Opposition Division of the EPO rejected all of these arguments. In doing so, the approach taken was that Article 53(a) was limited to those cases where the invention would be universally regarded as outrageous.[118] Further, the fact that the invention was based on tissue material that was taken from a pregnant woman did not mean that invention was immoral. Two significant points arose here. First, the tissue was taken with informed consent[119] and second, human tissues had for a long time been used as a source of useful products.[120] The arguments based on "dismemberment" and "slavery" were also rejected as the patent on the gene and protein did not confer any rights on any individual human being.[121] It followed that no individual rights of self determination were affected and it was not correct to categorise the patent as one over "life." Finally, the Opposition Division rejected the argument that there was a societal consensus that human genes should not be patented. The Opposition Division felt that the opinion of society on the patenting of genes was complicated and not yet definitely formed. In any case, the Opposition Division once again by implication eschewed the application of any precautionary approach to Article 53(a) as it was not the law that patents were to be granted only for inventions that were actively approved of by the public. In short, whilst Article 53(a) opened the door to fundamental ethical objections, the EPO was not the right institution to decide upon those questions. These questions had to be decided by society in general and it was only when there was overwhelming consensus of immorality that the invention could be excluded.

The European cases well illustrate the point that even in those jurisdictions which choose to enact exclusionary provisions in accordance with Article 27(2) TRIPS, that severe difficulties can arise in the application of the provisions. Much depends on the attitude or approach that is taken to *ordre public* and morality objections. One view, might be to take the European approach and draw a sharp distinction between the grant of a patent and the regulation of the use of technology. Save in the most extreme cases (where *ordre public* or immorality on the basis of universal abhorrence is established), patenting is an ethically neutral act as it does not demand that a patented invention should actually be capable of being exploited within the society conferring the patent. This is not a question of patent offices avoiding responsibility or ignoring the issue—rather it is a question of allocation of responsibilities in a way that best serves the interests of society at large. A good case could be made out that society as a whole should adopt a precautionary approach to environmental risks from GM foods, health dangers associated with new drugs and so forth. But, the question is whether that precautionary approach is best taken within or outside of the patent system. A precautionary approach would require active and continuous monitoring of the impact of new technologies in a way that the current patent system is ill-suited to meet. Indeed, is there a danger that over-reliance on the intellectual property system to police innovation and technology will give rise to a false sense of security? An invention that is unpatentable and unregulated is in many respects even more dangerous than one which is patented. At least the patentee can during the term of the patent prevent the unauthorised and uncontrolled exploitation of the invention! Of course what this really means is that there must be effective regulation of biotechnology irrespective of and independent of the patent decision. On this basis, there is force in the view that Article 27(2) is rightly confined to those exceptional cases where the *ordre public* or morality objection is clearly established. Thus, Professor Dworkin has argued that:

> Few would deny that there are major ethical issues relating to developments in biotechnology and genetic engineering; that there is a need to ensure that such ethical issues are properly addressed; that there should be adequate controls and monitoring of undesirable or questionable developments. The real question, though, is whether such control should be exercised in any significant way through the patent system. A rational answer must be "no".[122]

A different view, that has also been suggested, is that it is time for intellectual property law in general and patent law in particular to take on a wider role of promoting and managing or shaping technological change. After all, it might be said that the patent system by setting up an incentive system for promoting technological development cannot then be heard to say that the system is free of all responsibility when dangerous or morally questionable technologies surface before the patent office.

Patenting, it might be said, is not an entirely ethically neutral act.[123] Thus, Professor Drahos has more recently argued that:

> The controversy over biopiracy ... shows that many people now expect intellectual property to serve distributive values ... the failure to engage meaningfully with the role of intellectual property in the regulation of food, agriculture, biodiversity, the environment and health will lead intellectual property into a crisis of legitimacy much deeper than the one it is currently experiencing.[124]

Member countries of the WTO therefore have to decide whether they wish to implement Article 27(2) of TRIPS and if so whether they will apply the light touch approach of the European Patent Office.[125] If not, and if the view is taken that a more pro-active role is to be played by the patent system in managing technology, the resources to be allocated to patent offices will, at the very least, have to be carefully re-assessed—for otherwise the patent offices may have acquired responsibilities that they are unable to discharge. At present, it is very unlikely that the European Patent Office will alter its position.[126] There may, however, be some room within Article 27(2) of TRIPS for other Member States to apply the *ordre public*/morality provisions on a more open and aggressive basis if this is thought to be appropriate.[127] For example, it has been suggested by some commentators, that it may be open to Member States to find a biotechnology invention "immoral" where it is the product of an act of biopiracy involving deception and/or a breach of the source country's laws regulating access—at least where these laws are in conformity with the Convention on Biological Diversity.

Since the coming into operation of the TRIPS Agreement, the European Union has issued its Directive on the legal protection of biotechnological inventions in 1998.[128] The framing of this Directive gave the European Union the opportunity to clarify its own position in respect of the *ordre public*/morality exclusion in the area of biotechnology. Thus, whilst Article 6(1) sets out the general exclusion, Article 6(2) goes on to list out things which in particular are to be caught.[129] These are: processes for cloning human beings; processes for modifying the germ line genetic identity of human beings[130]; uses of human embryos for industrial or commercial purposes[131] and processes for modifying the genetic identity of animals which are likely to cause them suffering without any substantial medical benefit to man or animal, and also animals resulting from such a process.[132] These Articles have now been implemented by the European Patent Office through amendments to its Guidelines for Examination in European Patent Office issued in February 2001.[133] Whilst the spirit behind these specific examples of the operation of *ordre public*/morality bar is clear, the devil remains in the details and it is only right that the Recital of the Directive should explain that the examples are illustrative only. Might not other countries wishing to implement Article 27(2) of TRIPS follow suit and carve out through legislative provisions or patent office guidelines, examples of things which will offend against *ordre public* and morality within their own culture and society? If so, there seems to be no reason why such a list be confined to the matters set out in the European Union Directive: the list might also cover other matters touched on already such as the patenting of inventions which were made from use of biological material obtained by deception, fraud or in breach of the national law of the source country regulating access to genetic resources. After all, the European Directive itself is clearly cognizant of these wider issues. For example, Recital 26 provides that:

> Whereas if an invention is based on biological material of human origin or if it uses such material, where a patent application is filed, the person from whose body the material is taken must have had the opportunity of expressing free and informed consent according to national law.

A provision based on Recital 26 would clearly cover the sort of facts that arose in *Moore v Regents of the University of California*.[134] Might there not be sufficient flexibility with the *ordre public*/morality bar for countries, wishing to do so, to extend the bar to cover cases where informed consent of relevant indigenous communities had not been obtained as is required by the Convention on Biological Diversity (CBD)?[135] If the latter is fundamentally a Convention founded on ethical uses of the world's biodiversity—might not Article 26(2) of TRIPS provide the CBD with a point of entry into the patent system? The framers of the European Directive in fact tried to deal with these issues in Recital 27 which states that:

> Whereas if an invention is based on biological material of plant or animal origin or if it uses such material, the patent

> application should, where appropriate, include information on geographical origin of such material, if known whereas this is without prejudice to the processing of patent applications or the validity of rights arising from granted patents.

Recital 27, whilst in the ball park area of the issues dealt with by the CBD, is a rather tame provision as there does not seem to be any intention to attach consequences to a non-compliance. This can be contrasted with the language of Recital 26 which seems to support some consequences (undefined) attaching to a failure to obtain personal informed consent for biological material of a human origin. The drafting of Recital 27 reveals the considerable controversy behind the issue of the interface between TRIPS and CBD goals of prior informed consent, access and benefit sharing agreements, rights of indigenous communities and sustainable use of biodiversity. Some countries, such as the United States have taken the view that a requirement of certificate or proof of geographical origin is impractical especially in the case of agricultural products and is inconsistent with TRIPS. Others, are more amenable to a requirement that there should be disclosure of origin—but only in a manner such that the requirement does not become yet another substantive requirement for patentability.[136] Still other countries would argue in favour of clear provisions making such disclosures essential to the grant of and or enforcement of patent rights.[137]

2.2.3.2 The medical treatment exclusion.

Article 27(3)(a) of TRIPS also permits Members to exclude from patentability, diagnostic, therapeutic and surgical methods for the treatment of humans or animals. As in the case of the general *ordre public*/ morality bar, it is up to Member States to decide whether they wish to avail themselves of this exclusion. Countries which have implemented Article 27(2) are also likely to implement Article 27(3)(a).[138] Indeed some countries or groupings such as those in the European Patent Convention have had a medical treatment bar as part of their patent laws long before TRIPS was signed. Thus, Article 52(4) of the EPC 1973 provides that methods for the treatment of the human or animal body by surgery therapy or diagnostic methods practised on the human or animal body is not to be considered as inventions capable of industrial application.[139] This bar, like its TRIPS counterpart, does not apply to products used in the method of treatment. Countries like the United States on the other hand, which are generally more reluctant to bring in morality issues into the patent system, have had less problems with method of treatment patents. Thus, Grubb states that claims to medical treatment of humans have "been allowed for a long time" in the United States and that even "claims to surgical procedures are also patentable" although the latter type of patent has, understandably, given rise to controversy even within the United States.[140] The experience of the Members States of the EPC 1973 and the EPO with the bar tends to suggest that the bar will be interpreted narrowly.[141] Further, it should be stressed that products such as drugs and tools used in a method of treatment are not caught in any case by the bar. To be patentable, a drug must of course satisfy the novelty requirement: a requirement that might be thought to raise significant difficulties where the compound is already taught by the prior art base and especially so if that teaching included medical use. And yet, the story of bioprospecting is often the story of the search for biological compounds, known to indigenous communities, and which are already known to have some useful purpose. Can a scientist who manages to isolate and purify the active compound which reduces fever in a plant extract, claim that the active compound is new and patentable in its own right when the plant extract itself was already known? And what if the scientist discovers that the active compound has a new hitherto unrecognised use to treat hypertension—could he legitimately claim a fresh patent on the compound but this time limited to its new use? Or would such a claim offend the bar against patents for methods of treatment and/or the novelty requirement? In Europe, whilst these questions have given rise to considerable litigation and discussion, by and large, these have been resolved in favour of patentabilty.[142]

2.2.3.3 The animal, plant and essentially biological processes exclusion

Article 27(3)(b) of TRIPS allows Members to exclude from patentability, "plants and animals other than micro-organisms, and essentially biological processes for the production of plants or animals other than non-biological and microbiological processes … ." This provision is similar to one found in the European Patent Convention 1973[143] where it has, not surprisingly, been the subject-matter of considerable litigation in the context of the patentability of transgenic plants and animals. The approach of the European Patent Office has been one of cautious restraint.

In the *Harvard Oncomouse* case, the Technical Board of Appeal held that the right approach was to interpret exceptions to patentability narrowly and that the task was to find an interpretation that balanced the interest of inventors and society in general.[144] On this basis, the Examination Division found that the term "animal variety" was a sub-unit of a species. Since the claims in question were directed towards oncomammals, the bar against animal varieties did not apply on the particular facts.[145]

Countries choosing to exercise their right under Article 27(3)(b) of TRIPS to exclude animal and plant *varieties* should note that the European provisions, whilst similar, are not identical.[146] Much of the European debate over Article 53(b) of the EPC 1973 has concentrated on whether the bar can be applied where the claims are not limited to particular plant or animal *varieties*. The inventor can take himself outside of the exclusion by widening the scope of his claim to encompass more than one variety of plants and animals. On the other hand, Article 27(3)(b) of TRIPS refers to the patenting of animals or plants without any express limitation to "varieties." Can a Member State interpret this to mean that any claim covering plants or animals can be excluded under TRIPS even if the technical feasibility is not confined to particular varieties?[147] Further, what about "parts" of animals and plants. Can Article 27(3)(b) of TRIPS be applied in a way so as to exclude inventions involving use of body parts (human or otherwise) including cells and other substances found inside the animal or plant body?[148] What might be encompassed by the expression "essentially biological process for the production of animals and plants"? Is this to be confined to conventional reproductive techniques such as selective breeding and cross fertilisation or can it be stretched to cover genetic engineering processes used to produce transgenic living organisms?[149] Further, whilst Article 27(3)(b) allows Members to exclude animals, plants and essentially biological processes from patentability, it also requires that microorganisms, non-biological and microbiological processes to be treated as patentable.[150] Many types of biological inventions are likely to involve the use of microbiological processes and microorganisms. These cannot be excluded under Article 27(3)(b) as presently framed. Even though Article 27(3)(b) allows Members to exclude patent protection for plants, TRIPS does of course require Members to provide protection for plant varieties either by patents or by an effective *sui generis* system or a combination of the two. The shape of the *sui generis* system, however, is left to the individual Member States to determine although the protection that it offers must be "effective."[151]

2.2.4 The Review of Article 27(3)(b)

That Article 27(3)(b) was the subject of intense scrutiny and debate prior to its adoption in TRIPS is self evident from the fact the Article itself requires that it should be reviewed after the expiry of four years after the entry into force of the WTO Agreement. That date came in 1999 and to date the review has yet to be concluded.[152] Developing countries which are rich in biodiversity naturally see the review as an opportunity to start the process of harmonising TRIPS with the Convention on Biological Diversity. Could the bar on patents for animals, plants and essentially biological processes be made compulsory and extended to microorganisms and traditional knowledge? Industrialised countries at the cutting edge of biotechnology naturally take the other view that what is needed is a strengthening of protection rather than a watering down of the protection.[153] Notwithstanding the difficulties inherent in any re-examination of the substantive content of Article 27(3)(b), the Doha Ministerial Declaration of the WTO (2001) nevertheless expressly instructed the TRIPS Council to examine in its review, the relationship between TRIPS and the Convention on Biological Diversity and the protection of traditional knowledge and folklore. In this context a number of submissions have already been received. Three of these are summarised below to illustrate the range of issues and diverse views that have surfaced in the review of the Article.

2.2.4.1 The Swiss Submission on Article 27(3)(b)

The Swiss Submission asserts that Article 27(3)(b) as it stands represents a well balanced solution—one that takes account of the interests and needs of all Members of the WTO. As such, it does not propose any change in the Article although it does propose that Members be specifically authorised to require declaration of the source of genetic resources and traditional knowledge in patent applications.[154] The Swiss proposal whilst it does not go so far as to cover other information such as prior informed consent and access benefit sharing arrangements, indeed these were rejected, accepts that national law under its proposal "may foresee that the validity of granted patents is affected by a lacking or incorrect declaration of source if this was due to a fraudulent intention."[155] Beyond this, the Swiss proposal was that there was no need to amend Article 27(3)(b) so as to introduce a farmers' privilege defence as this was already covered by Article 30.[156] Lastly, there were the Swiss views on issue of protection of traditional knowledge. The Convention on Biodiversity[157] expressly recognises the importance of traditional knowledge of indigenous communities in promoting the sustainable use of biodiversity. Indeed Article 8(j) requires CBD Members to respect, maintain and preserve the knowledge, innovations and practices of indigenous and local communities. The problem, of course, is that the established intellectual property rights, especially patents are ill-suited to protect most types of traditional knowledge, innovations and practices. Patent law requirements of inventorship, novelty, inventive step and industrial application just do not fit the reality of how traditional knowledge is created communally and built up incrementally over long periods of time on a shared basis. The Convention on Biological Diversity recognises that it is important that modern day exploiters of biodiversity should share the benefits of any resulting inventions on a mutually agreed basis. But, how were indigenous communities (indeed source countries) to achieve this equitable sharing on mutually agreed terms if there was no real control over the genetic resources or traditional knowledge in the first place? One approach might be to enact national legislation designed to control access by linking bioprospecting to entry into agreements on a prior informed consent basis with terms as to benefit sharing.[158]Another approach might be to craft an intellectual property right for the holders of traditional knowledge. The provision in Article 27(3)(b) of TRIPS for a *sui generis* system to protect varieties of plants might provide a possible door for such a right to be created and recognised by both the CBD and WTO. On this issue, however, Switzerland took the view that the main forum for discussing intellectual property rights and traditional knowledge was the World Intellectual Property Organization. [159]

2.2.4.2 The African Submission on Article 27(3)(b)

The African Group took a dramatically different view on Article 27(3)(b) and its fit with the provisions of the CBD. In its submission, the Group drew a distinction between areas where a common understanding had yet to be reached amongst the delegations and those areas where agreement was possible.[160]

The first area identified as being one without a common understanding concerned the patenting of life forms. The Group asserted that these types of patents were regarded as unethical and contrary to the moral and cultural norms of many Members of the WTO. TRIPS and that Article 27(3)(b) should be amended so as to prohibit life patents by extending the exclusion to micro-organisms as well as non-biological and microbiological processes for their production.[161] The Group also maintained its position that the requirement to protect plant varieties should not undermine but should support the right of Members to protect important public policy goals relating to food security, nutrition, the elimination of rural poverty and the integrity of local communities. Another area without a common understanding concerned the issue of misappropriation of genetic resources and traditional knowledge. On this, the Group noted that the use of access contracts to regulate activities of researchers and the development of databases of traditional knowledge to assist patent offices assess novelty, inventive step and utility requirements whilst helpful did not provide an international mechanism to prohibit and prevent the misappropriation of resources. The Group also felt that the fact that work was on-going in the WIPO on protection of traditional knowledge was not a reason for delaying work within the WTO. Any conclusions reached by the WIPO would not be automatically applicable within or translated into the WTO and in any case the Group's view was that "work in the WIPO on genetic resources and traditional knowledge has been very slow and that it would ... not be appropriate to defer action under the mandate on Article 27(3)(b), which has a time frame, until the WIPO has completed its work." The Group also made the point that the WTO agreement had the advantage of being a single undertaking that provided for compulsory obligations on its members backed up with a dispute settlement mechanism. The Group felt that any solution to the concerns that patenting constitutes a misappropriation of genetic resources and traditional knowledge should similarly take the form of obligations that are enforceable within the WTO framework. Thus, unlike the Swiss proposal which sees no need to amend Article 27(3)(b) and which also advocates the rooting of the discussions on protection of traditional knowledge in the WIPO, the African Group finds both a need to revise TRIPS and to search for international solutions to the problem of biopiracy and traditional knowledge in all relevant international organisations especially the WTO. Yet another area that the African Group identified as being without common understanding concerned the relationship between TRIPS and the CBD in the context of the review of Article 27(3)(b).[162] The Group felt that what was needed were rights to protect genetic resources and traditional knowledge and that this could be achieved through requirements for "disclosure of the source of the genetic resources and traditional knowledge involved in the claimed invention, and for demonstration of compliance with the applicable procedures in the Member where the genetic resources and traditional knowledge originate."[163]

2.2.4.3 The Brazil, Bolivia, Cuba, Dominican Republic, Ecuador, India, Thailand, Peru and Venezuela Submission on Article 27(3)(b)[164]

The Brazilian submission, like the African Group, identified equity and protection against misappropriation of genetic resources as a key issue that had to be resolved so as to enable Members to meet their obligations under both TRIPS and the CBD. The Brazilian submission re-iterated earlier submissions that TRIPS should be amended so as to require applicants for a patent relating to biological materials or traditional knowledge, to provide as a condition to acquiring patent rights:

(a) disclosure of the source and country of origin of the biological resource and of the traditional knowledge used in the invention;
(b) evidence of prior informed consent through approval of authorities under the relevant national regime;
(c) evidence of fair and equitable sharing under the relevant national regime.[165]

In taking this position the Brazilian submission disagreed with views expressed by the United States that compulsory disclosure requirements for biological inventions amounted to discrimination between technologies.[166] This was on the back of the argument that different norms of disclosure for inventions based on biological resources and traditional knowledge would not amount to discrimination between fields of technology.[167]Further, the submission argued that the imposition of compulsory disclosure would not cause a legal and administrative nightmare for patent offices since the burden was on the applicant to provide the information.[168]

2.2.4.4 A Singapore perspective on the Review of Article 27(3)(b)[169]

A Singapore view on patentability of life forms and Article 27(3)(b) as set out in a December 2000 discussion "non-paper" is generally in favour of strong patent protection.[170] The non-paper accepts that considerable effort and expense is incurred in biotechnological research and that it is "only fair that the intellectual property created by research and development in biotechnology be recognised and protected through patents." The non-paper argues that except for reasons of *ordre public* and morality, patents are to be available for biological inventions in the same way as in other areas of science and industry. On this basis, the review of Article 27(3)(b) should not lead to a lowering of intellectual property protection for biotechnological inventions. Indeed, Singapore favoured discussion as to whether patent protection should be extended to all new inventions of plants and animals. The Singapore non-paper did recognise that there were possible shortcomings in the existing patent system in respect of claims for mere discoveries, over naturally occurring substances, over prior art which is not widely known such as traditional knowledge. These concerns could be addressed in a technical manner by improving the patent examination process (such as opposition proceedings) and more rigorous application of patent criteria of novelty, inventive step and industrial applicability.[171] On the much vexed issue of traditional knowledge, Singapore noted that there was no clear consensus as to the specific scope of traditional knowledge and that this was an impediment to discussion of specific commitments in the area. That aside, whilst Singapore supported moves to protect innovations by non-industrial communities, it felt that careful consideration was needed of the implications of having "differentiated systems of intellectual property for public domain knowledge developed by industrial and non-industrial communities."[172]

2.2.4.5 Reviewing Article 27(3)(b): The road ahead

The current and on-going review of Article 27(3)(b) has thrown up a range of issues from a possible extension of the provision to cover micro-organisms and all processes to produce animals and plants to the need to make disclosure of information about source, prior informed consent and compliance with national access/benefit laws a pre-condition to the grant of the patent. Developing countries with rich biodiversity and traditional knowledge stores are naturally keen on making disclosure compulsory. Some are prepared to go even further and suggest a banning of all patents on life and life processes.[173] Industrialised countries tend to support leaving Article 27(3)(b) alone and the taking of the debate over CBD and protection of traditional knowledge outside of TRIPS and into the WIPO. Other industrialised countries, whilst accepting that a disclosure system can be set up (perhaps by amendment of the Patent Co-operation Treaty) feel that compliance should be voluntary and not made a compulsory pre-requisite. Industrialised countries, such as the United States, also tend to the view that access contracts coupled with more extensive use of databases on biodiversity and traditional knowledge, would be sufficient to meet the CBD goals of equitable sharing of benefits on a prior informed consent and mutually agreed terms basis. They may also prefer to deal with the problem of fraud and deceit in gaining access and or non-compliance with national laws on the basis that the burden should be on the opposer/attacker to establish the facts and breaches rather than to place that burden on the applicant as a pre-condition (substantive or procedural) to the grant of the patent.[174] Whether the difference between these positions can be resolved in the near future remains to be seen.

2.2.5 State of the art and novelty issues in patent law

Aside from patent questions arising in connection with the meaning of invention and allowable exclusions from patentability, the biotechnology revolution has also put the spot light on the substantive requirements of novelty, inventive step and industrial applicability. Inevitably, some of the points overlap with the earlier discussion on invention and allowable exceptions. In the case of the novelty requirement, there is unlikely to be much disagreement over the rationale for the requirement: the avoidance of patent monopolies over something which is already in the public domain so as to protect the right of the public to practise that which is already known. The difficulty which biotechnology and bioprospecting has highlighted in recent years, however, is that the state of the art for the purposes of novelty enquiries differs from country to country. The point has already been made that early English patent law used a very limited concept of novelty that permitted patents to be granted for inventions which were new to the United Kingdom although known and used already outside of the United Kingdom. Notwithstanding that English courts tried to temper the narrow geographical reach of the state of the art under the *Patents Act* 1949 by recognising a notional domestic novelty test[175], the limitation of novelty to what was known by the public in the United Kingdom meant that inventions that were part of the public domain in some foreign country might still be patentable in the United Kingdom. This changed when the Patents Act 1977 was enacted. That Act, in line with the EPC 1973 provides in section 2(2) that the state of the art now comprises:

> all matter (whether a product, a process, information about either, or anything else) which has at any time before the priority date of that invention been made available to the public (whether in the United Kingdom or elsewhere) by written or oral description, by use or in any other way.

The new definition was significant in making expressly clear that the prior art base includes both written as well as oral information and uses that had the effect of making the claimed invention available to the public anywhere in the world. Following earlier case law, information would be regarded as available to the public where it was made known to one member of the public free from any bars of confidentiality.[176] Applying this world-wide notional novelty approach would mean that many traditional knowledge innovations would already fall into the prior art base and accordingly not be patentable. From the perspective of the holders of the traditional knowledge, the failure of patent law to protect such knowledge might be addressed through the introduction of a new *sui generis* right to protect traditional knowledge innovations. From the perspective of controlling biopiracy, a worldwide novelty approach to the state of art would at least mean that "bad patents" if granted could be challenged and revoked when found out.[177] Further, the prospect of such bad patents being granted could be reduced by the development of databases of traditional knowledge, use of access contracts as well as (although more controversially) introduction of compulsory disclosure of origin requirements discussed earlier.

The fact that a country employs a worldwide notional novelty approach does not however mean that disputes cannot arise at the margin of what is known and what is claimed to have been invented. The broad scope of the prior art base is counterbalanced by relatively tough tests for anticipation. Whether the test as to whether the prior art base anticipates the claimed invention is based on the concept of "an enabling disclosure" or "clear and unmistakable directions to make or do something which will now infringe" or "photographic novelty," claims directed towards active ingredients in an isolated/purified form may well escape the prior art base unless that isolated/purified form is already taught by that prior art base.[178] Thus, as Lord Hoffmann once pointed out, whilst Amazonian Indians knew of the beneficial anti-fever effects of extracts from the bark of the Cinchona tree, they did not know of quinine as $C_{20}H_{24}N_2O_2$. Neither would they have known of pills made from quinine sulphate.[179] From this perspective of patent law, whilst the traditional knowledge of the Amazonian Indians taught that the bark could be used to treat fevers, it did not make available the active compound in an isolated form. But, as Lord Hoffmann accepted, this raises an epistemological question: what does it mean to *know* something so that it can be part of the state of the art? In Lord Hoffmann's view the answer was that the invention claimed would be part of the art (known) if the information which has been disclosed enables the public to know the invention under a description to work the invention. On this basis, claims directed towards the bark of the Cinchona tree or even the use of the bark to treat fever would lack novelty: but claims directed towards and limited to the isolated active ingredient outside of its natural environment would be new (but not necessarily inventive).[180]

Leaving aside disputes over what traditional knowledge systems actually teach especially in respect of subsequently isolated and purified extracts or compounds, there is an even more fundamental problem that many countries do not in fact apply a world wide novelty standard.[181] For example, under the United States *Patents Act*, a mixed novelty system is employed. Under this system, the state of art available essentially covers: knowledge or use of the invention in the United States and patents or printed publications in the United States and elsewhere.[182] Knowledge or use of the invention in a foreign country will not count unless that knowledge or use exists in the form of a printed publication. Similarly, under the *Patent Act* 1990 (Australia), a mixed novelty system is used whereby publicly available documents published anywhere are taken into account as well as information made publicly available through the doing of an act in the patent area (essentially Australia).[183] As in the case of the United States, the Australian patent system has what might uncharitably be termed "a blinkered view" of the state of the art since prior traditional knowledge known overseas is ignored unless it happens to have been published as a document. The question that inevitably arises is whether there should be greater harmonisation in this era of global trade and intellectual property rights of the state of the art that is to be available in novelty and inventive step inquiries. If that state of the art is to continue to exclude prior oral traditional knowledge, the misgivings of countries with rich traditional knowledge stores will be readily understandable. If world wide novelty is good enough for the Member States of the European Union and other countries—why not for all? On the other hand if the state of art of some major industrial countries continues to exclude prior oral traditional knowledge, source countries will have little alternative but to build up databases of such knowledge in an attempt to inject the information into the prior art base. That may be no bad thing, but as a matter of principle, what is wrong with world wide novelty *and* databases to assist patent offices in assessing that prior art base?[184]

2.2.6 Inventive step issues in patent law

In the case of the requirement of inventive step (or non-obviousness), similar problems arise in respect of the state of the art as were discussed above in connection with novelty. If the state of art does not include oral traditional knowledge of foreign countries, bioprospectors obviously stand a much higher chance of proving novelty and inventive step. Thus, if traditional knowledge teaches that the oil extracted from crushed seeds of a plant can be used to repel insects, will a researcher who first identifies and isolates the active ingredient be able to claim a patent limited to that isolated ingredient? The isolated ingredient may well be novel even if the traditional knowledge is taken into account since that knowledge did not unequivocally teach the claimed invention: namely the isolated and purified active ingredient. But is it inventive? If the traditional knowledge is excluded on the basis that it is oral information, the skilled reader, who is now deemed in law not to know of that use, might well think it inventive to search and find an insect repelling ingredient in the extract of the crushed seeds. After all, if the prior art is interpreted as having no (legally) relevant teaching—the making of the invention almost necessarily establishes its own inventiveness. But, if the prior art includes the prior oral traditional knowledge, inventive step becomes a more significant hurdle. The question would be whether, without the benefit of hindsight knowledge of the invention, but with the knowledge that the extract of the crushed seeds repelled insects, it was obvious to look for the presence of some active ingredient in the extract. If it was obvious to the skilled reader to look, were there any difficulties that needed inventiveness to overcome in identifying the active ingredient? If the inventor was merely using known scientific, industrial techniques and processes to reach known or obvious goals, a serious issue as to whether there is any inventive step, in the absence of unexpected problems or difficulties, must arise. Merely being the first to succeed, whilst sometimes an indicator of inventive step, is not conclusive where there has been no long felt need or if the inventor was the first to try[185] What the cases on biopiracy reveal is that there is an urgent need to open the question of the prior art base that is relevant for an attack on lack of inventive step as well as the need for greater care in deciding whether inventions closely related to that prior art base are properly to be regarded as sufficiently inventive or "value added" as to deserve patent protection.[186]

2.2.7 Infringement and exclusive rights

One area where the reach of exclusive rights and biotechnology patents has seen movement in recent years in favour of the patentee concerns the new European provisions dealing with the propensity of living things to reproduce (with or without human intervention). This propensity when coupled with a patented invention, such as in the case of the oncomouse, raises the question as to whether patent rights are infringed by acts of what might be termed "natural reproduction."[187] In the case of product *per se* patents, the exclusive rights conferred will already under the patent laws of most countries include a right of making and a right of sale, disposal and use. It follows that if a defendant uses or disposes the offspring of oncomice parents, when that offspring possesses the activated oncogene that lies at the heart of the invention, an act of infringement will arise. Indeed, the fact that defendant was unaware that the second generation mice that he dealt with contained the oncogene is irrelevant as product patent infringement is usually a strict liability tort.[188] In the case of a patented process that is used to produce modified living organisms, the unauthorised use of that process can of course result in infringement—but what if the defendant has merely disposed of the offspring of parents produced by the process? If the offspring is properly regarded as being the direct product of the patented process—infringement can still arise in those jurisdictions which impose liability against the use, disposal or importation of products derived directly from a patented process.[189] But, what if a view was taken that the second generation living organisms were by definition not the direct products of the process? In Europe, the problem of self reproduction is now dealt with by Article 8 of the Directive on Biotechnology Inventions. Article 8(1) provides that:

> The protection conferred by a patent on a biological material possessing specific characteristics as a result of the invention shall extend to any biological material derived from that biological material through propagation or multiplication in an identical or divergent form and possessing those same characteristics.

In a similar vein, Article 8(2) deals with process patents and provides that:

> The protection conferred by a patent on a process that enables biological material to be produced possessing specific characteristics as a result of the invention, shall extend to biological material directly obtained through that process and to any other biological material derived from the directly obtained biological material through propagation or multiplication in an identical or divergent form and possessing those same characteristics.

These two Articles effectively ensure that liability will arise where the defendant disposes, uses, etc., second generation living organisms which derive from the first generation patented organism or where the first generation organism is the direct product of the patented process. The fact that the second generation organism is divergent does not make any difference so long as it possesses the same characteristics as the first generation organism.[190] Europe has thus acted to clarify the reach of patent rights against second generation living subject-matter connected with the patent—should other countries now follow suit and, if so, is there a need to re-examine the defences to infringement?

It is clear from the above discussion that part of the difficulty of fitting biological inventions within the patent law framework concerns the scope of the rights conferred on the patented invention. Aside from problems arising from the natural propensity of all living things to reproduce—there are also problems of applying the exclusive rights given the broad range of patents that may be granted. Patents, for convenience, fall into a number of categories. These are: product *per se* claims, product by process claims, use bound product claims and process claims. Process claims primarily protect the patented process although Article 28 of TRIPS extends the protection to products obtained directly by means of the patented process. In such cases, a reversal of the burden of proof arises in the circumstances set out in Article 34 of TRIPS. Use bound product claims differ from product *per se* claims in that the rights are limited to the claimed new use for the product. Product *per se* claims, on the other hand, protect the product irrespective of the use to which the product is put. In this way, product *per se* claims are naturally the strongest of the different types of patent. Product *per se* claims are usually disclosed by characterisation of the product—for example by description of its composition. Bosytn notes, however, that in cases where a *new* product is claimed whose structure cannot be described—that the disclosure may be based on a description of the process by which the product can be obtained.[191] These distinctions can give rise to tricky problems in the context of biological inventions and the scope of the claimed invention. A good example of this occurred in *Kirin Amgen Inc v Transkaryotic Therapies Inc*. This case concerned a protein, erythropoietin (EPO), that regulates the production of red blood cells. The existence of EPO was known and whilst it could be detected in the blood, it was never isolated from that source. The patentee was not the discoverer of EPO but was able to determine the amino acid sequence of the protein as well as to identify the gene that encoded the EPO protein. Subsequently, they were able to use known genetic engineering techniques to produce the EPO protein outside of the human body. The defendant in that case developed a method of increasing EPO production *in situ* within the human cells—a different process that involved gene activation. The technique was based on inserting a promotor near the endogenous EPO gene. It did not make use of an isolated EPO encoding sequence. In these circumstances, an issue arose as to construction of the claims and infringement. On construction, the Court of Appeal found that the claims were directed towards EPO produced by the disclosed process of expression. Interpreted on this basis, the claims were said to distinguish EPO produced by the claimed method from what was acknowledged to be part of the prior art namely uEPO.[192] Moving to the question of infringement, the Court of Appeal found that the defendant's variant had a material effect on the way in which the claimed invention worked.[193] This was because the claimed invention was based on an exogenous DNA sequence which had been made suitable for use in a host cell to produce EPO. There was no claim to the gene sequence *per se* as the latter would not be patentable. The defendant's variant was different as it used an endogenous DNA sequence. This made a functional difference given the level of generality at which the claimed invention was set out in the patent specifications.

The *Kirin Amgen* litigation in the United Kingdom well demonstrates the policy currents underlying so much of patent law. The inventor/patentee was the first to sequence the DNA for the EPO gene and to use genetic engineering techniques to clone the protein outside of the human body. Doubtless, considerable time, effort and expense were incurred in the process. The disclosure of the gene sequence provided others with important information that led to the development of other methods such as those used by the defendant to "obtain" EPO. Given that the inventor/patentee had no claim over uEPO as a product *per se*, the protection conferred by the patent was inevitably relatively "thin" and open to invention around. The mere fact that the information disclosed about the DNA sequence enabled the defendant to develop an alternative method to obtain EPO did not amount to infringement since that alternative method was functionally different from the claimed method. In short, the defendant was able to use the information disclosed in the patent specifications to develop an alternative non-infringing method. Whilst the inventor/patentee might complain that being the first to sequence the EPO gene did not confer the protection that they deserved—others will point to the fact that use of information in patent specifications to advance the art is part of the bargain leading to the grant of patent protection. The defendant by standing on the shoulders of a giant was able in this sense to see that much further. Indeed, some have even argued that the practice of granting product *per se* claims needs to be reassessed at least in the area of gene patents. A product *per se* patent requires proof that the product is new (not part of the prior art in the sense of it being available to the public), inventive and capable of industrial application. When granted, product *per se* patents usually result in strong protection since infringement is not dependent on any particular use. Thus a patentee who obtains a product *per se* patent on a gene will be able to exert control over all uses of the claimed gene (aside from the disclosed use) including downstream uses of the gene to make medicaments. Does this provide overprotection or too much reward for an inventor who can now "sit back" and licence others to develop new uses? Some commentators have argued that product *per se* gene patents should be limited to the disclosed use thereby effectively equating such gene patents with "use bound" product claims.[194] Other commentators strongly defend the existing patent regime and its application to biotechnology and gene patents.[195] At present, there is no doubting that the status quo in patent law supports the grant of product *per se* claims even over biological based inventions which may be hard for second comers to invent around. If there is a generally perceived abuse over the earning of "excessive royalties" or "inappropriate royalties" from downstream or other uses of gene based inventions, one approach may be to deal with this through more stringent and rigorous application of novelty requirements. Product *per se* claims should only be allowed where the product is truly new in the sense that it was not already taught by the prior art. As Lord Hoffmann points out, knowing a chemical (or indeed biological product) does not necessarily demand that its chemical formula be known—a product may be known under other descriptions, a point that is especially pertinent in the context of use of traditional knowledge.[196] Second, there is the more radical question as to whether the scope of the claims for gene product patents should be limited to disclosed uses. Still yet another approach may be to re-assess the allowable defences to infringement such as the introduction of an experimentation defence and to re-examine the conditions under which compulsory licences may be obtained.[197] Whichever side one takes on this debate, there is no getting away from the importance of the issue, an issue which will need a broad international consensus within the framework of TRIPS and the WIPO treaties if there is to be movement away from the current status quo. After all, inventors will argue that the possibility of broad *per se* claims in area of biological inventions encourages ground breaking innovation which can then lead to further useful research and development. If product *per se* claims were not available, might not some researchers take the view that it is better to be a second comer and to work in the area after the initial ground breaking work (for example sequencing and the working out of the first industrial application for the gene) is made known?

2.2.8 Defences in patent law

Article 30 of TRIPS sets the standard against which defences are to be measured in national patent laws of Member States. It provides that:

> Members may provide limited exceptions to the exclusive rights conferred by a patent, provided that such exceptions do not unreasonably conflict with a normal exploitation of the patent and do not unreasonably prejudice the legitimate interests of

> the patent owner, taking account of the legitimate interests of third parties.

Patent legislation usually sets out a range of defences and exceptions that might now be supported by this Article. This section will examine three areas where defences may be especially important in connection with biological inventions.

2.2.8.1 Exhaustion of rights

The first area, concerns exhaustion of rights. If patent rights are to be extended so as to impose liability where living organisms associated with patented inventions reproduce naturally, the question of innocent infringement arises. Should there be a general defence protecting "innocent bystanders from claims of patent infringement with respect to adventitious spreading of patented seed or patented genetic material or the insemination of an animal by a patented animal"? The Canadian Biotechnology Advisory Committee, from whose 2002 Report the quotation was taken, certainly thought so.[198] At the very least, where liability arises in connection with "natural reproduction," some limited defence based on exhaustion of rights may be needed. Thus, Article 10 of the European Directive states that:

> The protection [of Articles 8 and 9] shall not extend to biological material obtained from the propagation or multiplication of biological material placed on the market in the territory of a Member State by the holder of the patent or with his consent, where the multiplication or propagation necessarily results from the application for which the biological material was marketed, provided that the material obtained is not subsequently used for other propagation or multiplication.

In the United Kingdom, Article 10 has been implemented by Schedule A2 paragraph 10 of the *Patents Act* 1977.[199] The defence provides a limited area of exhaustion that applies where the multiplication or propagation necessarily results from the application for which the biological material was marketed by the patentee. Thus, Bently and Sherman explain "the defence will allow a farmer to sow a patented seed, to harvest and sell the resulting crop (for example to sell wheat for flour)."[200] It follows that in the United Kingdom, even though patent rights have been extended to include second generation living organisms associated with the patent, individuals who do no more than use biological material (wheat) that necessarily results from the purpose for which the seeds were marketed—have a defence to that form of infringement.[201]

2.2.8.2 Farmers' rights

The second area where biological inventions call out for special defences concerns the much discussed area of farmers' rights. This is large area that generally concerns the rights of those individuals who have done so much to conserve and develop biodiversity over the generations. These individuals, usually farmers, are in many ways the first stakeholders in the world's biodiversity whose contributions have been recognised by the Convention on Biological Diversity (1992). Farmers' rights and privileges are not just a matter of checks and balances within the patent system—they are also about recognising and protecting their contributions to traditional knowledge and ensuring that they are able to participate equitably in the age of modern biotechnology. Internationally, Professor Blakeney explains that farmers' rights as a concept was developed as a counterbalance to the recognition within the International Undertaking on Plant Genetic Resources (IUPGR) in 1989 that intellectual property protection in the form of plant breeders' rights were not incompatible with the goals of IUPGR. [202]At present, the International Treaty on Plant Genetic Resources for Food and Agriculture (ITPGR) defines farmers' rights as including: protection of traditional knowledge relevant to plant genetic resources for food and agriculture; the right to participate equitably in sharing the benefits arising from the use of plant genetic resources for food and agriculture; and the right to participate in making decisions at the national level on matters arising from the use of plant genetic resources for food and agriculture. The ITPGR also expressly states that the identified rights do not "limit any rights that farmers have to save, use, exchange and sell farm saved seed or propagating material."[203] The practice, custom and right of farmers in many communities to save seed from previous harvests for use in successive seasons is thus recognised by the international community.[204] Whilst the debate in the past over farmers' rights (especially the right to save and sow) has taken place in the context of plant varieties protection, the increasing use of patents to protect living organisms (plants and animals) demands that the issue of farmers' rights be addressed directly by the patent system. This is especially so as patent rights are generally stronger than plant varieties protection rights. For example, even Europe, with its relatively strong protection for biotechnology and patents, recognises in Article 11 of the European Directive the need to protect farmers' rights.[205] In the United Kingdom, this has resulted in amendments to the *Patents Act* 1977. Section 60(5)(g) sets out a new farmers' rights defence that applies to the:

> ... use by a farmer of the product of his harvest for propagation or multiplication by him on his own holding, where there has been a sale of plant propagating material to the farmer by the proprietor of the patent or with his consent for agricultural use. [206]

In the case of animals, section 60(5)(h) sets out a defence that covers:

> ... use of an animal or animal reproductive material by a farmer for an agricultural purpose following a sale to the farmer, by the proprietor of the patent or with his consent, of breeding stock or other animal reproductive material which constitutes or contains the patented invention.[207]

Important though these new English and European provisions are in recognising the validity of claims to farmers' rights within the patent law context, some may feel that the provisions do not go far enough. The English provisions whilst allowing for saving and using seed and the breeding of patented animals excludes sale or exchanges between farmers. Thus in the case of section 60(5)(g), Schedule A1 sets conditions restricting the movement of protected material from the holding and in any case the defence only applies to use by the farmer concerned for propagation or multiplication. Similarly, in the case of section 60(5)(h) and patented animals, use of the progeny for commercial sale is not permitted. Developing countries dependent on agriculture may of course challenge the patentability of plants and animals in the first place—those which do decide to confer patent protection are likely to look very closely at the shape and form of allowable farmers' rights as identified by ITPGR.[208] Even if countries adopt farmers' rights defences, this is unlikely to see the end of the dispute. Instead, it is likely to see the sharpening of the already acrimonious debate over use of technology to render plants and animals obtained from patented biological material, sterile and incapable of further multiplication or propagation. This in turn opens the door to an even wider debate: should such technology be allowed to be used by the industry as a sort of biological equivalent of copy lock protection and spoiler devices that are so common place now in the rush to protect copyright from the onslaught of digital copying? If so, will the world see a push for anti-circumvention legislation designed to penalise and catch technology which is intended to get around biological genetic copy-lock protection? And, if so, will there be a counter that any such legislation must at the least allow for such reproduction as is permitted by defences such as farmers' rights? On the other hand, if terminator technology is to be banned, how is this to be achieved? Is the use of terminator technology in a patented invention a ground for invoking *ordre public*/morality type provisions? Is this in any case enough or should legislation governing use of GM products prohibit the licensing of such products for use when they contain terminator technology? And finally, are there any useful environmentally sound purposes to which the technology could be put such as protecting the environment from the danger of escaping transgenes? Or is there a danger that the terminator gene itself might escape and render other plants and animals sterile? These are questions that are easy to ask but which may prove to be far more difficult to reach a general consensus on.[209]

2.2.8.3 Experimentation defence

The third area where discussion of defences in patent law and biological inventions has been particularly sharp concerns the right to conduct research and experiments on patented inventions. The Canadian Biotechnology Advisory Committee in 2002 explained that:

> ... patent holders gain the exclusive right to make, use, import and sell their inventions ... Subsequent inventions can usually be made only after further research or experimentation using the patented invention. However, without authorisation, these activities infringe on the patent holders' rights ... Access to basic or platform technology such as cell lines, plants and animals at a reasonable cost is crucial to research. The lack of clarity that currently exists in Canadian patent law can only cast a pall on university and independent researchers afraid of even the possibility of facing a patent infringement law suit. This chilling effect could lead to under-investment in basic

> research and the withholding of experimental results for fear that the disclosure of those results will draw the negative attention of the patent holder[210]

To this end the Committee recommended that the Canadian Government introduce a new defence stating that it is not patent infringement to use a patented product or process for private non-commercial purposes or to study the subject-matter of the invention to investigate its properties, improve upon it, or create a new product or process. Some countries already have defences in this area. For example, section 60(5)(a) of the *Patents Act* 1977 (UK) sets out a defence covering private non-commercial uses and section 60(5)(b) provides a defence for acts done for experimental purposes on the subject-matter of the invention.[211] The English experience is that these defensive provisions are usually interpreted conservatively. What will amount to experimental purposes? Certainly, whilst investigation to discover some new principle or test a new idea will be experimentation might it be better to follow the Canadian proposal and specifically cover investigation of properties and acts intended to improve the product or develop new products or processes?[212] In the United States, an experimentation defence whilst existing at common law appears to be even narrower in scope in that it may exclude experimentation for commercial purposes. Professor Drahos writes that:

> in the US the experimental defence ... is a creation of the courts. It has been frequently raised but rarely sustained. The reason why courts around the world rein in the experimental exemption relates to a simple economic argument. A liberal interpretation of the experimental exemption would allow the patentees' competitors free access to the invention, compromising the capability of the patentee to exploit the patent.[213]

If industrialised countries such as Canada and the United Kingdom recognise the importance of private non-commercial use defence as well as a defence to cover experimental use on the subject-matter of a patented invention in commercial settings, the same will be even more so in developing countries hurrying to gear up their industry to meet the new opportunities that biotechnology is said to offer. It is likely that many developing countries if they have not done so already will move quickly to introduce such defences in the near future.[214] What is important is to clarify that the experimentation defence goes beyond academic research and covers experimentation on the patented invention in a commercial context.[215]

2.3 BIOTECHNOLOGY AND OTHER INTELLECTUAL PROPERTY RIGHTS

Thus far the discussion on fitting biotechnology products within the intellectual property framework has concentrated on the law of patents. There are, however, other intellectual property rights which to a greater or lesser extent have some ability to protect aspects of biotechnology. These are summarised below.

2.3.1 Law of copyright

Copyright whilst playing a significant role in protecting literary and artistic works (and other copyright subject matter) in the area of biotechnology such as notes, articles, reports, research papers, charts, diagrams, photographs, drawings and so forth is unlikely to have any real impact on protecting the technology itself. In the first place, copyright does not create a true monopoly (unlike patents) since the protection is limited to acts of copying. An independent researcher who does not copy (directly or indirectly) a copyright work can research and compete all he wants without fear of copyright law. Second, copyright is said to protect the expressive elements of authorship rather than the facts, ideas or knowledge that is being expressed. Thus, the general view is that the copyright in written instructions on how to make a product is not infringed by following the instructions and making the product. So, if a paper describes a new genetic engineering process for gene splicing, a scientist who splices a gene using that process will not have committed copyright infringement (although he may be liable under patent law if the process is patented). Finally, in the area of databases such as collections of single nucleotide polymorphisms, expressed sequence tags, traditional knowledge, biodiversity and so forth, any copyright protection is likely to be limited to the elements of selection and arrangement that make the database original in the copyright sense of an intellectual creation.[216] Inevitably, this means that the copyright protection for such databases is likely to be thin since the mere use of information relating to individual entries is unlikely on its own to amount to infringement.[217]

2.3.2 Confidential information and trade secrets

Moving away from copyright, the law of confidential information and trade secrets also has a role to play in safeguarding biotechnology information and data that has not been released into the public domain. Even where the biological invention such as the oncomouse has been patented, there may well be significant pieces of information that have not been set out in the patent specifications. After all, even where the applicant for a patent is under a duty to disclose the best method of working, he will not usually have to disclose all that he knows in relation to that method. It will generally be enough if he has disclosed such as to enable a person skilled in the art perform that method. Furthermore, the mere fact that a product incorporating confidential information has been made and sold to the public does not mean that the information is thereby in the public domain. The mere fact that the information may eventually be discovered by a determined reverse engineer does not mean that the information is *ipso facto* publicly available upon the marketing of the product. A good example of how the law of confidence can protect confidential information in the form of genetic information contained in a product is the Australian case of *Franklin v Giddins*.[218] The case concerned a variety of nectarine in the form of bud wood that the defendant had stolen from the plaintiff's orchard. In an action for delivery up of the bud wood and trees, Dunn J. found that stolen bud wood contained a trade secret namely the genetic structure of the bud wood. This information was of value and could be treated as a trade secret in respect of which an obligation of confidentiality could be imposed on the defendant.

2.3.3 Plant varieties rights

The International Union for the Protection of New Varieties of Plants (UPOV) as its name suggests has as its main goal the granting of rights over new plant varieties.[219] The basic elements of UPOV 1991 are summarised in the paragraphs that follow.

UPOV 1991 permits breeder's rights to be granted where the variety is new, distinct, uniform and stable. Novelty has a much more restricted meaning than the absolute novelty requirement adopted by patent law.[220] A variety is deemed to be new, if at the filing date, propagating or harvested material of the variety has not been sold or disposed of by or with the consent of the breeder for purposes of exploitation in the territory of the Contracting Party in which the application has been filed earlier than one year before that date. In the case of territories other than the Contracting Party in which the application is filed, the period is extended to four years and in the case of trees or vines, six years. Thus, for example, if a breeder produces a variety of orchid and applies for protection in a Contracting State, that variety will be treated as new so long as he has not exploited it in that Contracting State more than one year before the application is made. Similarly, the variety will also be treated as new, even if he has exploited it elsewhere, so long as that was not more than four years before the application in the Contracting State.

Distinctiveness is defined as meaning a variety that is "clearly distinguishable from any other variety whose existence is a matter of common knowledge at the time of filing the application."[221] The requirement of uniformity is met by establishing that "subject to the variation that may be expected from the particular features of its propagation, it is sufficiently uniform in its relevant characteristics."[222] Finally, stability is established by showing that "its relevant characteristics remain unchanged after repeated propagation or in the case of a particular cycle of propagation, at the end of each such cycle."[223]

Where a variety has been registered, the rights conferred include the right to produce or reproduce (multiply) the variety, to condition for the purpose of propagation, to offer for sale, export, import and to stock the variety for the purposes of multiplication, conditioning and sale.[224] UPOV 1991 also extends the zone of liability to essentially derived varieties of the protected variety. Also caught are varieties which are not clearly distinguishable from the protected variety and varieties whose production requires the repeated use of the protected variety.[225]

Turning to the allowable exceptions, UPOV 1991 exempts acts done privately and for non-commercial purposes, for experimental purposes and for breeding other varieties.[226] Limited farmers' rights exceptions are also permitted under Article 15(2). This states that:

> each Contracting Party may, within reasonable limits and subject to the safeguarding of the legitimate interests of the breeder, restrict breeder's right in relation to any variety in

> order to permit farmers to use for propagating purposes, on their own holdings, the product of the harvest which they have obtained by planting, on their own holdings, the protected variety or a variety covered by Article 14(5)(a)(i) or (ii).

Further, a limited exhaustion principle is set out in Article 16 which applies to material which has been sold or otherwise marketed by the breeder or with his consent in the territory of the Contracting Party concerned including any material derived therefrom.[227]

The several revisions of UPOV since its signing in 1961 has been said to have led to a progressive strengthening of plant breeders' rights. [228] Aside from the fact that UPOV 1991 permits patent protection alongside plant varieties rights, two other significant points (amongst others) are worth stressing. First, UPOV 1991 sees a broadening of the zone of liability to include varieties which might be described as "near to" the protected variety. Thus, under Article 15(5) the rights as noted now reach out to any essentially derived variety, any variety not clearly distinguishable from the protected variety and even a variety (which whilst not essentially derived) whose production required the repeated use of the protected variety. Thus breeders who develop a new variety in a way that makes repeated use of the protected variety will find that the new variety is under the shadow of the first protected variety.

Second, UPOV 1991 also narrows the scope of the available defences. UPOV 1978 did not have any specific provision on defences and to that extent, Members of UPOV 1978 had some room to manoeuvre in carving out defences under national laws. UPOV 1991, on the other hand, as noted above, restricts the compulsory defences to the right of private and non-commercial use as well as a right to experiment. But, whilst the second breeder has a right of experimentation that appears to extend to experimentation with commercial objectives in mind, he might find that the holder of the rights in the protected variety is able to exercise control over a derived variety if, for example, it is an essentially derived variety. Further, the farmers' right exception to save and sow seeds that is permitted under UPOV 1991 is subject to the requirement of reasonableness and the legitimate interests of the breeder. Some countries may query as to what the interests of the breeder are doing in a provision that concerns farmers' rights when these are intended as a counterbalance to the exclusive privileges already conferred on breeders. As seems likely, these requirements may well be interpreted as meaning that exercise of farmers' rights are to be made subject to adequate compensation.[229]

2.4 CONCLUSION: *SUI GENERIS* PROTECTION AND THE CONVENTION ON BIOLOGICAL DIVERSITY 1992

The central objective of the Convention on Biological Diversity has been to promote sustainable use of the Earth's biodiversity in a manner that recognises the sovereign right of nation States to control and determine access[230] whilst at the same time respecting, preserving and maintaining the knowledge, innovations and practices of indigenous and local communities.[231] Much has already been written on the question as to whether these goals are consistent with the objectives of TRIPS and the extent to which the latter may be an impediment to a meaningful attainment of the CBD goals.[232] Doubtless, the debate will continue for some time in Asia, Indian Sub-Continent, Africa, South America, Europe, North America and the world at large. Indeed the very question as to whether sustainable development can be achieved in a manner that protects local and traditional communities and practices is by no means something on which there is uniform agreement.[233] Whatever is the view taken on that question, attempts must of course be made to reduce the areas where conflicts between TRIPS and the CBD may arise. One view, that might be taken, is that there is no conflict at all for CBD goals can, by and large, be achieved through the use of suitable mutually agreed terms that provide for access on a prior informed basis and with benefit sharing. The phenomenon of agreement smoothes the water and makes CBD consistent with TRIPS in the sense that CBD does not clash with the intellectual property rights mandated by TRIPS. After all, any of the intellectual property rights can be licensed and made subject to contractual agreements. But, is the phenomenon of agreement enough to make TRIPS consistent with the CBD? If compliance with the CBD merely requires the parties to make their own agreements for prior informed access with equitable benefit sharing—then, from a certain perspective, it does not seem to add up to very much or indeed to anything new.

Looking at TRIPS and "modern" intellectual property rights from the perspective of local and traditional communities, a question that must arise concerns whether these intellectual property rights are capable of protecting traditional knowledge and innovation. After all, if the source country (for the biodiversity and traditional knowledge) and local stakeholders enjoy legally enforceable controls over the biodiversity and traditional knowledge such that these are protected nationally and recognised internationally, then the source country and the local stakeholders will have a real bargaining chip to bring to the negotiation table.[234] Two separate but connected issues arise. First, there is the question as to who is to have the authority to grant permission to researchers to access and remove biological specimens. Much here will depend on the national law of the source country: often—for convenience, if for no other reason, it may be a Government body or a State body or some special organisation set up for the purpose of administering access rules.[235] Whilst members of the local or indigenous communities may not be involved in the administration of the process, Article 8(j) of the CBD certainly requires that their approval be obtained. Second, there is the question of ensuring an equitable and fair sharing of the benefits from the technology with the source country (Article 15(7)) and the relevant local or indigenous community (Article 8(j)). Both of these issues are dealt with at length by the recent Bonn Guidelines on Access to Genetic Resources and Fair and Equitable Sharing of the Benefits Arising out of their Utilisation.[236]

But aside from legislation or rules controlling the access to the genetic resources as suggested by the Bonn Guidelines, there is also the question as to the interface between intellectual property rights and traditional knowledge. Are there sufficient safeguards built into the patent and plant varieties protection systems that prevent or reduce the risk of "bad rights" being granted over material that was already part of traditional knowledge? This is a matter that has been touched on already. Some countries take the position that the risk of bad patents or plant breeders' rights can be reduced by simply setting up of databases and by use of terms in access agreements and by monitoring of patent applications overseas. After all, if a source country finds a traditional knowledge item has been patented overseas, then as in the *Turmeric* case, revocation proceedings can be brought. But, there is also the other view that this puts too heavy a burden on developing countries who may not have the resources to police patent applications around the world. Perhaps, some supra-national body should be set up to carry out this role?[237] Even better, some argue that national patent offices should play a more active role by at least requiring statements of origin and evidence of prior informed consent as part of the patent process.[238] Aside from the possibility of bad patents, there is also the question as to whether traditional communities can assert their own intellectual property rights over the genetic resources that they have developed and conserved and other aspects of their traditional knowledge base. In many cases, this will be very difficult as "modern" intellectual property rights are often ill-suited to meet the nature of traditional knowledge innovation given their open and communal nature with incremental development over many years.[239] What is really wanted, from the perspective of some biodiversity rich developing nations, is a *sui generis* system that can be tailored so as to recognise communally held and administered rights that are long lasting and which are supported internationally. TRIPS itself recognises in Article 27(3)(b) that *sui generis* rights may be one method of protecting plant varieties. TRIPS also sets out minimum standards and does not prevent Members from increasing the rights and by implication introducing new intellectual property rights so long as these are consistent with the general TRIPS provisions.[240] On this basis, Member states may be able to introduce new intellectual property rights protecting traditional knowledge of their local and traditional communities.[241] Of course, to work, these rights will need to be recognised by the international community and WIPO and may ultimately need to be backed up an international convention of its own (possibly under the auspices of WIPO). But, in the meantime, it has been suggested by some commentators that one way forward will be for a group of like-minded countries to develop *sui generis* traditional knowledge rights that are protected on the basis of reciprocity and not national treatment. After all, it has been pointed out that the United States took a reciprocity approach in 1989 when it introduced its new *sui generis* legislation to protect semi-conductors and the European Union similarly applied reciprocity and not national treatment in its Database Directive. Thus, Professor Drahos explains:

> The key idea would be to devise an all embracing model of protection for the physical, cultural and social resources of indigenous peoples ... It would then be possible to link the national statutory regimes of developing countries that were participating in the process ... Ideally, developing countries would have developed a common set of standards for the

> protection of indigenous knowledge ... Once a significant number of developing countries agreed to participate in such an arrangement and had demonstrated its feasibility, some Western countries would be likely to join. In this way, a regulatory model for the protection of indigenous knowledge could be networked and globalised.[242]

Thus, there is no doubting that biological inventions and biotechnology present many challenges to intellectual property law, its administrators, adjudicators, users and policy makers in this new millennium. Some of these are closely connected with hard black letter intellectual property law issues such as the meaning of invention in patent law, the range of available exclusions from patentability, the application of *ordre public* and morality bar, the state of the art in novelty and inventive step inquiries, the range of defences and exceptions (particularly exhaustion of rights, farmers rights and experimentation rights) in patent law. Whilst these are black letter law issues, there is also no getting away from the sharp question of policy that lies behind them including questions as to the role of the patent system beyond the horizon of an incentive to invent. They also include issues as to the rights of Members to develop *sui generis* systems to protect new plant varieties and to base these not on UPOV 1991 but UPOV 1978 or indeed on home grown systems that may have broader defences for farmers' rights.[243] They also include the question of validating the CBD through disclosure of origin and evidence of prior informed consent and benefit sharing as part of the process of acquiring intellectual property rights as well as the issue of new *sui generis* rights to protect traditional knowledge (and folklore) nationally and internationally.[244] The one thing that is clear is that the time has come to apply the principle of "*carpe diem*" and try to bring some of these issues and questions to a satisfactory conclusion.

ENDNOTES

1 Editor's note: This chapter is a shortened version of a paper submitted by the author which originally included a discussion on the following patent law issues: "Industrial Application," "Scope of Claims," and "Compulsory Licences."

2 *Nature*, April 2, 1953.

3 By Norman Borlaug.

4 Cohen and Boyer developed a technique using restriction enzymes and ligases to "cut and paste" genes into a bacterium. This technique lies at

the heart of the process of producing transgenic organisms and helped to throw open the door to modern genetic engineering. The technique was patented in the United States (US Patent 4,237,224). The patent proved to be a winner for the patent owners (Universities of Stanford and California) generating "hundreds of millions of dollars in royalty payments" by the time that the patent expired in 1977. See Grubb, *Patents for Chemicals, Pharmaceuticals and Biotechnologym*, Oxford University Press, 1999, at page 233 and also at page 374. Grubb notes that when the patent expired, Stanford's annual royalty income dropped from $50 million to $15 million. See also "Licences worth a billion" at (http://www.biomedcentral.com/news/20030527/01).

5 By Luc Montagnier's team at Pasteur Institute, France, Robert Gallo's team at National Cancer Institute, USA and Jay Levy's team at University of California, San Francisco, United States.

6 Awarded to Kary Mullis. The polymerase chain reaction technique uses a type of DNA polymerase that is heat resistant to greatly amplify small amounts of DNA. The PCR technique is one of the essential tools of modern biotechnology and was the subject-matter of a patent dispute.

7 This was the FLAVRSAVR tomato produced by Calgene. Genetically modified foods are of course very much in the news at present. Not only do these products of biotechnology raise questions of patentability, they have also engendered considerable debate on a wide range of issues ranging from possible environmental harm, labelling and evaluation procedures, moratoriums and trade relationships within the World Trade Organization.

8 The team included Craig Venter, Claire Fraser, Hamilton Smith, and United States researchers. The living organism was the bacterium *Hemophilus influenzae*. Craig Venter went on to play an important role in the eventual unravelling of the human genome. Available online: (http://www.bio.org/er/timeline.asp).

9 This was Dolly, a lamb that was cloned from a cell taken from the udder of an adult sheep. The pioneering work by Dr Ian Wilmut and Dr Keith Campbell of the Roslin Institute in Scotland in collaboration with PPL Therapeutics, involved somatic cell nuclear transfer techniques. This technique lies at the heart of modern cloning. The technique is the subject-matter of patent applications with patents having already been granted in the United Kingdom to Genron Bio-Med—the United States company that has been licensed to exploit the invention. See generally, Wilmut, Campbell and Tudge, *The Second Creation. The Age of Biological Control by the Scientists who cloned Dolly*, Headline Book Publishing, 2000. Dolly died in February 2003.

10 US Patent No. 5,695,967 granted to in respect of a technique behind the creation of the world's first artificial chromosome by Athersys Inc. See http://www.athersys.com/. The significance of artificial chromosomes is that the technology will facilitate transfers of genes between organisms in manner that avoids the problems associated with cut and paste techniques using vectors such as bacteriophages.

11 This was the first time that the genome of a multi-cellular organism had been sequenced. Work on *C. elegans*, organ development and cell death

led to the award of the 2002 Nobel Prize for Physiology or Medicine to Sir John Sulston, Dr Sydney Brenner and Robert Horvitz. The successful decoding of the genome of *C.elegans* also increased expectations that the attempt to decode the human genome would be successful. The Human Genome Project itself can be traced back to 1988 when the National Institutes of Health (USA) set up an Office for Genome Research. The objective of the Human Genome Project was to sequence the entire human genome in the expectation that the information would, amongst other things, lead the way to a better understanding of disease and open the doors to new therapies and treatments. Two "rival" groups were eventually involved in the "race" to decode the human genome. First, there was the Human Genome Project led by the National Institutes of Health and the Wellcome Trust (with participation of researchers from many centres around the world). The second was the initiative of Celera Genomics led by Craig Venter. The two teams used different techniques and strategies to sequence the genome. The decoding of the human genome raised issues concerning the patentability of gene fragments and the question of public accessibility to the gene sequences. See generally, *The Human Genome Project*, Edited by Dennis and Gallagher, Nature, 2001 and also Davies, *Cracking the Genome. Inside the Race to Unlock Human DNA*, The Free Press, 2001.

12 This was Chromosome 22 which is the second smallest human chromosome. The euchromatic portion of chromosome comprises some 33.5 million base pairs. At the time, it also included the largest continuous sequence of base pair sequences from any organism (22 million). Available online: (http://www.sanger.ac.uk/HGP/Chr22).

13 The official announcement was made at the White House, USA, by President Clinton, Prime Minister Tony Blair and members of the Human Genome Project Team and Celera Genomics on June 26, 2000. The Human Genome Project draft was published in *Nature* on February 15, 2001 and the Celera Genomics draft was published in *Science* on February 16, 2001. The final completed version of the human genome was released by the International Human Genome Sequencing Consortium on April 14, 2003.

14 The decision was announced on August 10, 2001. Federal funds could be used for research on adult and umbilical stem cells as well as stem cells taken from established stem cell lines for which the "life and death" issue had already been made. No federal funds were to be used for research on other human embryonic stem cells.

15 The decoding of the *M. grisea* genome followed fast on the heels of the decoding of the rice genome. The Whitehead Institute/MIT Centre for Genome Research explained that by studying the genes, scientists will gain a better understanding of host/pathogen interaction. It is said that this may in turn lead to development of more durable and resistant rice strains. Other measures such as use of fungicides have not been satisfactory on account of cost, environmental harm and the fact the fungus has the ability to evolve into forms resistant to fungicide. Available online: (http://www-genome.wi.mit.edu/media/2002/pr_02_riceblast.html).

16 See Bains, *Biotechnology From A to Z*, Oxford University Press, Second Edition. See also the *Shorter English Oxford Dictionary*, CD-ROM version 2.0 which defines biotechnology simply as "the industrial application of biological processes." Biological is in turn defined as something pertaining to "the nature of biology or the phenomena of living organisms." See also Article 2 of the Convention on Biological Diversity 1992 which defines biotechnology as meaning "any technological application that uses biological systems, living organisms, or derivatives thereof, to make or modify products or processes for specific use."

17 See generally Wei, *An Introduction to Genetic Engineering, Life Sciences and the Law*, SNP, 2002 at Chapter 1.

18 See the FLAVRSAVR tomato, note 7 above. This tomato has a modified gene that delays the ripening process. The idea being that the tomato can stay on the vine longer and develop a fuller taste. The technology (anti-sense technology) involves neutralising the gene that produces the protein that leads to ripening and softening of flesh in the fruit. See Reiss and Straughan, *Improving Nature? The Science and Ethics of Genetic Engineering*, Cambridge University Press, Canto edition 2001 at pages 132–139.

19 See for example *Plant Genetic Systems/Glutamine Synthetase Inhibitors* [1905] EPOR 357 which concerned insertion into the plant genome, a gene that produced a protein that conferred protection against a class of herbicides. The idea being that the genetically modified plant would be less likely to be damaged by herbicides. See Reiss and Straughan, *Improving Nature? The Science and Ethics of Genetic Engineering*, Cambridge University Press, Canto edition 2001 at pages 139 *et seq*.

20 See for example the patent granted to Monsanto by the European Patent Office (EPO). Euro Patent No. 301,749. The patent is concerned with a process for genetically engineering plants such as soybean plants. In May 2003, the patent was upheld but in a limited form. Originally, the patent claims were not limited to soybean plants. The Opposition Division of the EPO ruled that the claims should be limited to the soybean plant (and not any plant) so as to ensure compliance with the disclosure requirements set out in Article 83 of the European Patent Convention 1973. Available online: (http://www.european-patent-office.org/news/pressrel/2003_05_06_e.htm).

21 See for example the transgenic "oncomouse" which involved the incorporation of an activated oncogene into the genome of a laboratory mouse. The idea being that the "oncomouse" could be used to test for carcinogenic substances and to assess the effectiveness of therapies. See Reiss and Straughan, *Improving Nature? The Science and Ethics of Genetic Engineering*, Cambridge University Press, Canto edition 2001 at pages 169–171. The patentability of the "oncomouse" (oncorodents and indeed oncomammals) has been the subject-matter of considerable controversy in Europe, Canada and elsewhere. See *Harvard Oncomouse Patent* [1990] EPOR 501; [1991] EPOR 525. The saga of the "oncomouse" in Europe may still not yet be over. In November 2001, the EPO Opposition Division held that the "oncomouse" patent whilst valid should be limited to transgenic rodents containing the additional oncogene (as opposed to oncomammals). This latest decision may be taken to the EPO Technical

Board of Appeals. In Canada, the saga of the oncomouse before the courts is finally over with the matter reaching the Supreme Court in 2003. See *Commissioner of Patents v President and Fellows of Harvard College* [2002] SCC 76 which by a bare majority rejected the product claims on the basis that the "oncomouse" was not an invention within the language of the Canadian Patents Act. See Wei, *Mus Musculus and Homo Sapiens: Murine Metaphysics and the Canadian Supreme Court*, [2003] SJLS 38.

22 See note 10 above.

23 The first cloned mammal was Dolly the Sheep. See note 8 above. Dolly, was followed shortly by Polly. Polly was a cloned sheep with a human gene inserted so as to express the human protein in the milk. For another example of a cloned but transgenic sheep, see Tracy, a cloned female sheep with the human gene that produces a protein called *alpha 1 antitrypsin* (AAT). Patients suffering from emphysema have reduced amounts of AAT, the latter being a protein that protects the lungs. The gene for AAT was inserted into the genome of a cloned female sheep in such a way that the gene expressed the protein in the milk produced by the clone after birth. The human protein could then be extracted for use. See Reiss and Straughan, *Improving Nature? The Science and Ethics of Genetic Engineering*, Cambridge University Press, Canto edition 2001 at pages 166–168.

24 Often times the drugs are isolated/purified versions of active ingredients naturally occurring in living organisms or which involve (to a greater or lesser extent) natural living processes. In other cases, the drug may be a synthetic version of a natural compound. In other cases, the drug may be a modified version of a natural substance. See for example Tracy and the production and "harvesting" of AAT referred to in n.22 above. See also *Howard Florey/Relaxin Patent Application* [1995] EPOR 541 which concerned patents over the human gene encoding for the hormone "Relaxin." The patent claims included the gene (probably in cDNA form) as well as to the hormone. The hormone causes pelvic ligaments to relax during child birth.

25 Aside from new drugs, genetic engineering also holds out the promise of gene therapy for a range of diseases from cystic fibrosis to immune problems, Alzheimer's disease and so on. At present, it seems that successful gene therapy still lies some way in the future although the increased pace of embryonic stem cell research and therapeutic cloning may push the science and technology forward. Reiss and Straughan, *Improving Nature? The Science and Ethics of Genetic Engineering*, Cambridge University Press, Canto edition 2001 at pages 202 *et seq*. See however, *Straits Times*. June 14, 2003 carrying a *New York Times* report that there is building evidence that gene therapy (using current techniques) can result in increased risk of cancer.

26 There have been several well-known but thus far unsubstantiated reports that the first cloned human baby has been born in recent years.

27 But, see Dr. Vandana Shiva, *Protecting Our Biological and Intellectual Heritage in the Age of Biopiracy*, 1996, Research Foundation for Science and Technology and Natural Resource Policy, India. Dr Shiva argues that this does not mean that the indigenous peoples are unaware of the existence of the active ingredient. They know of it in their own terms and within their own knowledge system. Dr Shiva argues that "the difference in

epistemological foundations does not make indigenous knowledge systems inferior, it just makes them different."

28 These will include the structure of access and benefit arrangements as well as the need to protect traditional knowledge, innovations and practices of indigenous communities—if not within intellectual property systems then possibly under some new *sui generis* system. See generally Sherman, *Regulating Access and Use of Genetic Resources: Intellectual Property Law and Biodiscovery*, [2003] EIPR 301. Sherman points out that first generation biotechnology issues (many of which are not completely resolved) concern questions of patentability. Second generation issues concerned the scope of protection—in particular the impact of patents on downstream research and development in the context of patents over diagnostic and research tools, reach through claims and infringement. Third generation issues concern the impact of patent law on upstream products: biodiversity and protection of traditional knowledge.

29 The paper will focus on the position in Singapore, United Kingdom and Europe and will also touch briefly on the position of other countries for comparative purposes. In doing so the author is aware that there remains considerable debate and uncertainty even within Europe on many patent law and intellectual property issues and that the international position is fluid and dynamic. That being so, the author apologises in advance for any errors or omissions in the discussions that follow.

30 In UK, the BPO has taken the view that the controversy over use of landmines and the enactment of the *Landmines Act* 1998 means that these are caught by the morality bar. See *CIPA Guide to the Patents Act*, 5th ed., Sweet & Maxwell, at para.1.19.

31 Indeed, see Article 4quater Paris Convention (1979) states that "The grant of a patent shall not be refused and a patent shall not be invalidated on the ground that the sale of the patented product or of a product obtained by means of a patented process is subject to restrictions or limitations resulting from the domestic law."

32 (1602) 1 WPC 1.

33 Grubb, *Patents for Chemicals, Pharmaceuticals and Biotechnology*, Oxford University Press, 1999 at page 9.

34 Note also that early Venetian patent law (The Decree of Venice 1474) also set out a patent system that was rooted in domestic novelty. See Grubb, note 33 above at pages 10–11.

35 See also *Edgeberry v Stephens* (1691) 1 WPC 35 holding that inventor included the person who imported an invention into the UK: "whether learned by travel or by study it is the same thing." See also the discussion on the point in Blanco White, *Patents for Inventions*, Stevens, 4th ed. at page 222.

36 The new law came into force on June 1, 1978.

37 The European Patent Convention 1973 is not a document of the European Communities, nevertheless it is worth noting that there is a high degree of correlation between the membership of the two.

38 See PA 1977, ss. 2 and 7.

39 It is also often said that part of the consideration for the grant of the patent is the disclosure by the patentee of his invention in his patent specifications—the point being that after expiry of the patent term, third parties will be free to use that disclosure to work the invention.

40 See *Perspectives on Intellectual Property: IP in Biodiversity and Agriculture*, edited by Peter Drahos and Michael Blakeney, Sweet & Maxwell, 2001 at pages v–vi. Compare also the views of the Commission on Intellectual Property Rights (CIPR): *Integrating Intellectual Property Rights and Development Policy*, 2002 at page 6 that intellectual property rights are best seen as a means by which nations and societies can promote the fulfilment of human economic and social rights.

41 Similarly, the *Patent Law Treaty* 2000 is also silent on the question of what amounts to an invention or patentable subject-matter.

42 See Li Westerlund, *Biotech Patents. Equivalency and Exclusions under European and US Patent Law*, Kluwer International, 2002 at page 24.

43 Carlos M Correa, *Access to Plant Genetic Material and Intellectual Property Rights* at pages 117–18 published as a paper in *Perspectives on Intellectual Property: IP in Biodiversity and Agriculture*. 2001. Sweet & Maxwell.

44 See Graham Dutfield, *Protecting Traditional Knowledge and Folklore: A Review of Progress in Diplomacy and Policy Formulation*, October 2002 at page 20. The latter is a draft paper prepared for the UNCTAD/ICTSD Capacity Building Project on Intellectual Property Rights and Sustainable Development. Available online: (http://www.ictsd.org/iprsonline/unctadictsd/docs/Dutfield2002.pdf). Dutfield's reference to genetic and biochemical resources is likely to include genes (genetic) and proteins (biochemical).

45 See Correa, note 43 above at page 118. The Shorter Oxford English Dictionary, CD-ROM version 2.0 defines micro-organism as an organism that is to small to be seen except with the aid of a microscope such as bacteria and viruses. The Oxford Dictionary of Biology, 1996, defines it as including bacteria, viruses, protozoans and some algae and fungi.

46 See Correa note 43 above at page 118.

47 Query also the relationship between Article 27(1) and Article 27(3)(b). Article 27(1) demands patent protection for any invention in any field of technology. Article 27(3)(b) gives Member countries a limited right to exclude from patentability certain things (but not including micro-organisms, non-biological and micro-biological processes). Can a Member country take the view that even though micro-organisms are expressly left out of the exclusion, that a Member country can achieve the same result by falling back on Article 27(1) and holding that micro-organisms are not in any case inventions? This would, with respect, place a strained construction on Article 27.

48 See generally Dutfield, note 44 above at page 29, notes that NGOs as well as certain groups of countries, including the African group, have argued for a review of Article 27 to provide that plants, animals and all other living organisms and their parts are not patentable. Dutfield comments that whilst there may be some strategic advantages for developing countries

to adopt such a position, that there is at present no prospect for such a position being adopted by the WTO.

49 Directive 98/44/EC.

50 Biological material is defined in Article 2 as meaning "any material containing genetic information and capable of reproducing itself or being reproduced in a biological system."

51 See also Kamstra, Doring, Scott-Ram, Sheard and Wixon, *Special Report on Biotechnological Inventions: The EC Directive*, Sweet & Maxwell, 2002. The authors point out at para. 3.33 that the language of the directive "isolated from the environment" is a clear echo of a similar provision in EPO Guidelines (pre February 2001) that a "substance found in nature that has first to be isolated from its surroundings" may result in a patentable invention. Thus the authors continue "In this way, the need for isolation is seen as the hallmark of an invention as opposed to a discovery in this context: a crude exudate appearing on the stem of a plant is a discovery; a compound isolated from it is an invention (and if it is novel, involves an inventive step and is susceptible of industrial application, it is a patentable one)." See also Bostyn, *The Prodigal Son: The Relationship Between Patent Law and Health Care*, [2003] Medical Law Review 11, 67 at page 73 that the process of isolation and purification of a substance from nature is not always straight forward and may require the expenditure of considerable time effort and research.

52 Note also that whilst Article 4.1 of the Directive states that plant and animal varieties are not patentable, the width of the exclusion is narrowed considerably by Article 4.2. This provides that inventions which concern plants or animals shall be patentable if the technical feasibility of the invention is not confined to a particular animal or plant variety.

53 The EPC 1973 was amended in 2000.

54 See *Guidelines for Examination in the EPO*, October 2001 Revision at Chapter IV, para. 2.3 where it is explained that "If a new property of a known material or article is found out, that is mere discovery and unpatentable because discovery as such has no technical effect and is therefore not an invention ... If however that discovery is put to practical use then this constitutes an invention which may be patentable ... To find a previously unrecognised substance occurring in nature is also mere discovery and therefore unpatentable. However, if a substance found in nature can be shown to have technical effect, it may be patentable. An example of such a case is that of a substance occurring in nature which is found to have an antibiotic effect. In addition, if a micro-organism is found to have existed in nature and to produce an anti-biotic, the micro-organism itself may also be patentable as one aspect of the invention. Similarly, a gene which is discovered to exist in nature may be patentable if a technical effect is revealed, e.g., its use in making a certain polypeptide or in gene therapy."

55 *Ibid.* at Chapter IV, para. 2.3 which explains that for computer programs, whilst these are in the list of excluded items "as such," claim to computer programs will not be excluded if there is a technical effect over and above the technical effects of running any computer program

56 Note also that Article 53(b) excludes from industrial applicability, methods of treatment of the human or animal body by surgery, therapy or diagnostic methods (but not products used in the method). Lord Hoffmann has pointed out that the cumulative effect of these provisions is to render the question of what is an invention under the EPC 1973 (and the United Kingdom Patents Act 1977) largely academic. See generally *Biogen Inc v Medeva plc* [1997] RPC 1. But note that there may a residue of cases where the question of what is an invention is not a waste of time. See *Genentech Inc's Patent* [1989] RPC 147. In that case, Mustill LJ took the view that where the alleged invention concerned something already existing in nature and which was far removed from mechanical and chemical inventions to which so much of patent law related to, the issue of invention could not be lightly treated. See also the *Guidelines for Examination in the European Patent Office* which provides that in Chapter IV para. 2.2 that the question as to whether there has been any invention is separate from the question of novelty, inventive step and industrial applicability.

57 [1995] EPOR 541. The decision has been confirmed by the Technical Board of Appeal. See Bostyn, *The Prodigal Son: The Relationship Between Patent Law and Health Care*, [2003] Medical Law Review 11, 67 at page 76.

58 Complementary DNA (cDNA) is made by copying the mRNA of the relaxin gene back into DNA. The difference between cDNA and genomic DNA (the gene as it exists in nature) is that genomic DNA possesses non-coding segments called introns that are removed as part of the process of transcription of the gene into mRNA template. A cDNA version of the gene thus does not include the introns. See also Li Westerlund, note 42 above at para. 2.2.9 where the author argues that cDNA are not natural products.

59 These were the guidelines prior to the amendment in October 2001.

60 Note that the guidelines on "discovery" have since been amended in October 2001. The amended guidelines are set out in note 54 above.

61 The new guidelines also follow the Directive in stating at C-IV 2a.2 that an element isolated from the human body or otherwise produced by means of a technical process, which is susceptible of industrial application, including the sequence or partial sequence of a gene, may constitute a patentable invention, even if the structure of that element is identical to that of a natural element. The guideline explains that such an element "is not *a priori* excluded from patentability since it is for example the result of technical processes used to identify, purify and classify it and produce it outside the human body, techniques which human beings alone are capable of putting into practice and which nature is incapable of accomplishing itself." The new guidelines also state in C-IV 2a1 that in the case of European patent applications concerning biotechnological inventions, the provisions of the EPC are to be applied and interpreted in accordance with the European Union Directive. See also Bostyn, note 57 above at page 71 that "an invention must have a technical character, must achieve a technical effect, or imply a technical contribution."

62 Section 6 of the Statute of Monopolies 1624 stated that patents could be granted "... over the sole working or making of any manner of new manufactures within this realm ..."

63 [1960] ALR 114.

64 (1994) 122 ALR 417.

65 Note that there are some extra bars for innovation patents. See note 73 below.

66 See also *NV Philips Gloeilampenfabriken v Mirabella International Pty Ltd* (1993) 44 FCR 239.

67 See also APO Manual of Practice and Procedure, September 2002 at para. 8.2.2A for a summary of the leading Australian cases on "manner of manufacture." The manual is available online: (http://www.ipaustralia.gov.au/pdfs/patents/manual/Part208.pdf).

68 Ricketson, *The Law of Intellectual Property*, Law Book Co, 1984 at para. 48.42. See also generally, Ludlow, *Genetically Modified Organisms and Their Products as Patentable Subject-matter in Australia*, [1999] EIPR 298.

69 APO Manual of Practice and Procedure, September 2002 at para. 8.2.2A.

70 *Ibid.* at para. 8.2.5.3. See also para. 8.2.14.3 where it said that the Patent Office Practice is that the isolation and cultivation of naturally occurring micro-organisms which has some new use, satisfies the requirement of technical intervention. A claim for a biologically pure culture of naturally occurring micro-organism without any specified ingredients is also acceptable provided the micro-organism has a new use.

71 *Ibid.* at para. 8.2.14.1. See also para. 8.2.15.2 where it is said that a new plant or animal (providing it is not naturally occurring) can be regarded as a manner of manufacture if it involves technical intervention by man and is useful in economic affairs.

72 Ricketson, *The Law of Intellectual Property*, Law Book Co, 1984 at para. 48.42 and the Practice Note of the Australian Patent Office (1980) 50 AOJP and also Practice Note No 6 1991. See also the APO Manual of Practice and Procedure, September 2002 at para. 6.1.2 that the *Rank Hovis* decision applies to all life forms.

73 Note APO Manual of Practice and Procedure, September 2002 at para. 8.5.1 that human genes, tissues and cells lines are outside the scope of the bar. It should also be noted that the *Patent Act* 1990 of Australia as amended also sets out provisions relating to "innovation patents." The standard of inventiveness for innovation patent is different than for a normal or standard patent in that a substantial contribution to the working of the invention may be enough. In the case of innovation patents, there is a further specific bar in section 18(3) against the patenting of plants and animals and the biological processes for the generation of plants and animals. This bar does not apply to standard patents.

74 Title 35, enacted 1952.

75 *Ibid.* section 100(a).

76 See Durham, *Patent Law Essentials. A Concise Guide*, Quorum Books, 1999 at para. 4.2 that truths of nature cannot be patented under the US Patent Act even by those who discover the truth. See also *Diamond v Chakrbarty* (1980) 65 L Ed 2d at page 150 that not every discovery is patentable viz the laws of nature, physical phenomena and abstract ideas.

77 (1980) 65 L Ed 2d. The first case upholding patentability over modified living organisms was the decision of the US Court of Customs and Patent Appeals in *Re Bergy* 596 F 2d 952 (1979).

78 Art.1, Para 8 Clause 8.

79 (1980) 65 L Ed 2d at page 150.

80 *Ibid*, at page 150.

81 These include the "oncomouse" (US Patent 4,736,866), maize plants in *Exparte Hibberd* 227 USPQ 443, seeds and seed grown plants in *Pioneer Hi Bred Intl Inc v JEM Ag Supply Inc* 200 F.3d 1374 as well as a genetically engineered oyster. See *Exparte Allen* 2 USPQ 2d 1425. See also the US Patent and Trademark Office Notice—1077 Official Gazette 24 (1987) that the US PTO is now examining claims directed to multicellular living organisms including animals.

82 See Li Westerlund, note 42 above at para. 2.2.7 that "extensively interpreted ... the invention concept [in US law] would also encompass the kinds of subject-matter that require human intervention to make them available in a useful form by way of isolating or purifying naturally occurring products." Westerlund notes at para.2.2.8 that a large number of patents have been granted in USA over cDNA molecules and purified proteins. Westerlund gives the example of *Re Bergstrom*, 427 F 2d 1394. This case involved patent claims for purified prostaglandin found to be patentable since it was by definition new and useful since the purified substance could be used for medicinal purposes. Westerlund explains that in naturally occurring secretions, the concentration is too low for medical use. Suppose then that there is a compound that even when mixed in its natural secretions, could be and is used for some purpose such as repelling insects. If the only advantage of isolation and purification is to make it more convenient or effective for the old use—is that enough? It is submitted that this will not be so much a question of novelty or invention as much as possible obviousness and lack of inventive step. But note that there are older US cases holding where the applicant is claiming a patent in respect of the discovery of some natural phenomenon—that must come from the application of the law of nature to some new useful end. See for example *Funk Bros. Seed Co. v Kalo Inoculant Co.* 333 US 127 (1948) which concerned a mixture of naturally occurring nitrogen fixing bacterium. Westerlund explains at para. 2.2.4 that all the inventors had done was to recognise the natural properties and take advantage of them. The US Supreme Court in *Chakrabarty* distinguished *Funk*—pointing out that "by contrast, the patentee has produced a new bacterium with markedly different characteristics from any found in nature and one having the potential for significant utility. His discovery is not nature's handiwork but his own. ..." See (1980) 65 L Ed 2d at page 151. See also Correa, note 43 above at page 112.

83 2002 SCC 76.

84 *Ibid.* at para. 40. Geo 4, c.25.

85 Preamble of 7 Geo. 4, c5.

86 See Bastarache J. for the majority at 2002 SCC 76 at para. 158.

87 Numerous arguments based on a close reading of the *Patents Act* and its relationship to the *Plant Breeders Rights Act* were given. They also included arguments that the detailed provisions of the Act as a whole were not well suited to protecting higher life forms. For example, it was said that broad patent protection for higher life forms would raise problems over farmers' rights, innocent infringement and the need for experimentation and research defences. Other problems concerned with slippery slope and patents over human life also featured strongly. The majority felt that given these problems, it was preferable to hold that genetically engineered higher life forms were not patentable subject-matter rather than to hold that they were and to leave it to the courts or Parliament to develop the necessary refinements, qualifications and exceptions. See generally, Wei, *Mus Musculus and Homo Sapiens: Murine Metaphysics and the Canadian Supreme Court*, [2003] SJLS 38.

88 In Europe, see *Harvard Oncomouse Patent* [1990] EPOR 501 and [1991] EPOR 525. Note also that the EPO announced on 7 November 2001 that the Oncomouse patent had been confirmed by the Opposition Division albeit in a form restricted to transgenic oncorodents as opposed to transgenic oncomammals in general.

89 June 2002. This is a report to the Government of Canada, Biotechnology Ministerial Coordinating Committee. Copies of the report are available online: (http://www.cbac-cccb.ca).

90 See *Straits Times*, June 24, 2003 for an article by Audrey Tan quoting an *Ernst and Young* Report. "Beyond Borders: The Global Biotechnology Report 2003" that the top ten biotechnology countries are: United States, Canada, Germany, Britain, France, Australia, Sweden, Israel, Switzerland and Netherlands.

91 According to the Economist, *Pocket World in Figures*, 2003, about 2.5 per cent of Canada's GDP originates from agriculture.

92 See note 86 above. The Report noted that the purpose of patent rights was to achieve public good and endorsed the views of Justice Jackson of the United Supreme Court that "The primary purpose of our patent system is not the reward of the individual but the advancement of the arts and sciences. Its inducement is directed to disclosures of advances of knowledge which will be beneficial to society; it is not a certificate of merit, but an incentive to disclose." See *Sinclair & Carroll Co Inc v Interchemical Corporation* 325 US 327 (1945) at pages 330–31. It followed from this that patent rights ought to be judged not in and of themselves but in terms of their effects on society as a whole. This, the CBAC pointed out at page 8, necessarily involved a balancing approach.

93 Farmers' rights in this context means the right to save and sow seeds or to breed patented animals so long as the progeny are not sold as commercial propagating material or in a manner that undermines the commercial value of the invention to the creator.

94 This concerns innocent infringement arising from adventitious spreading of patented seed or patented genetic material or the insemination of an animal by a patented animal. The Report also recommended that Canada

examine the position of liability and redress for adventitious spreading of genetic material.

95 The Report recommended policies to encourage the sharing of benefits of research involving genetic material, to participate in the discussions over implementation of the CBD and the Bonn Guidelines; to comply with the Bonn Guidelines within Canada as well as internationally, to sign and ratify the International Treaty on Plant Genetic Resources for Food and Agriculture and to generally encourage and facilitate benefit sharing arrangements between users of genetic resources and traditional and local communities within Canada. The Report is also sensitive to the needs to protect traditional knowledge and in this respect supports the efforts be undertaken in this regard by the World Intellectual Property Organization in examining the possibility of developing a new form of intellectual property right. The Report also shows sensitivity to concerns over biopiracy driven by state of art novelty searches that exclude oral knowledge. Thus the Report also makes the important recommendation that prior art should include both written as well as oral traditional knowledge that has been made available to the public.

96 Process claims are however allowed under section 5. India's patent laws have been severely criticised for having eroded the scope of patent protection. See generally, Grubb, note 33 above at page 35. Note that under Article 65(2)&(4) of TRIPS, India effectively has until 2005 to provide for patent protection for pharmaceutical products. Article 70(8) however requires that India accept patent applications, *inter alia*, for pharmaceutical products from the date of entry into force of the WTO Agreement. Further, Article 70(9) requires India to grant exclusive marketing rights where applications have been made under Article70(8). Disputes over India's compliance with these provisions resulted in a successful complaint by the United States to the WTO. See Grubb, note 33 above at page 43.

97 The Patents (Amendment) Act also sets out a new general provision that "invention means a new product or process involving an inventive step and capable of industrial application." For a discussion, see Bhattacharya, TRIPS, *Indian Patents (Amendment) Act and India's Agendas in the Next Ministerial Meeting at Mexico*. The paper is available online: (http://www.sisshyd.net/siss/docs/swapan_bhattacharya.doc).

98 Note also that the exclusion of plants and animals includes "parts thereof." Does this go beyond what is permitted by Article 27(3)(b) of TRIPS. Will this include, for example, proteins and genes on the basis that the living body essentially comprises proteins, genes, etc?

99 Another approach to dealing with traditional knowledge might have been to exclude patentability on the basis that much of traditional knowledge will already be in the state of the art. This is especially so if the state of art is defined as including both oral as well as written information available to the public. The problem, however, is that some traditional innovative practices may be secret and hence not available to the public in any event. In such a case, a person who manages to learn of the secret and who tries to patent it—should, if the facts come to light, fail, simply because he is not in fact the inventor.

100 Will the courts take the view that the exclusion only bites where the patent claims effectively duplicate the traditional knowledge innovation without adding anything new?

101 Note that whilst India has excluded traditional knowledge from the definition of invention under the *Patents Act* 1970, she has also taken steps to provide for the "conservation of biological diversity, sustainable use of its components and the equitable sharing of the benefits arising out of the use of biological resources." See the Biological Diversity Act 2002 (passed in 2002) and the draft Community Intellectual Property Rights Bill 1994. These are posted online:(http://www.grain.org/brl/tk-brl-en.cfm).

102 The Singapore provisions on "invention" have been discussed extensively elsewhere and so this section will only set out a brief summary of the interface between invention, biotechnology and the Singapore Act. See, Wei, *Inventions, Genes and Napoleonic Victories*, (1997) 9 SacLJ 1 and also Wei, *An Introduction to Genetic Engineering, Life Sciences and the Law*, SUP, 2002 at para. 4.3 *et seq*.

103 See section 13(2) of the Patents Act Cap.221. The text of Article 52(2) of the EPC 1973 excluding discoveries etc "as such" from the definition of invention is set out above.

104 Query, however, whether the Singapore Patent Office (The Intellectual Property Office of Singapore) and the courts might not simply examine whether these fall within the general meaning of invention.

105 See Singapore Hansard, November 1, 1995 which explains that section 13(2) was deleted as part of the measures needed to ensure that the Singapore Act complied with the TRIPS Accord. It seems that fears that the list of exclusions might mean breach of Article 27 (patents to be available for all inventions in all fields of technology) was the motivation behind the deletion. Note, however, the point made earlier that TRIPS does not in fact set out any definition of invention and that Member countries must have enjoyed some latitude within the "ball park" to carve out their own definition of invention.

106 See Wei, *Inventions, Genes and Napoleonic Victories*, (1997) 9 SacLJ 1.

107 See also the decision of Hoffmann LJ in *Societe Technique de Pulverisation Step* v *Emson Europe Ltd* [1993] 513 where it was said in the context of whether there was an "inventive step" that this might be answered by reference to the general policy of the Patents Act to reward and encourage inventors without inhibiting improvements of existing technology by others. Did the invention deserve protection of a patent monopoly? But, see also *Molnlycke AB v Proctor & Gamble* [1994] RPC 49 and the Singapore case of *Ng Kok Cheng v Chua Say Tiong* [2001] 3 SLR 487 that the question of whether the invention deserved protection was not helpful. Whilst the "Hoffmann question" is certainly one that is difficult to apply, there is no doubting the qualitative and judgmental nature of the inventive step inquiry. This approach to inventive step may also serve to give some support for the Australian policy based approach on the related question of what is an invention in the first place.

108 [2000] 3 SLR 717 at page 733. The English case quoted is *Lane Fox* v *Kensington and Knightsbridge Electric Lighting Co* [1892] 3 Ch 424. On this basis, the essence of invention appears to revolve around the practical or useful application of the results of some discovery or new insight. See also *Househill Coal and Iron v Neilson* (1843) 1 WPC 673 where it was said that an abstract philosophical principle could not be patented until it was applied to reach a practical result and benefit not previously attained. This may be a tighter definition than the current Australian approach of asking whether there is a mode or manner of achieving an end result which is a artificially created state of affairs of utility in the field of economic endeavour.

109 See Report of the Select Committee on the Patents Bill, Parl.5 of 1994 at page vi. The Singapore position with respect to patentability of genetically modified organisms is discussed in Wei, *Mus Musculus and Homo Sapiens: Murine Metaphysics and the Canadian Supreme Court*, SJLS [2003] 38. In the case of claims in respect of human beings, these may be rejected on the basis of the bar in section 13(3) against patents the publication or exploitation of which would be generally expected to encourage offensive, immoral or anti-social behaviour. See also Article 10(1) of the Constitution of the Republic of Singapore which prohibits slavery.

110 Note that in the *Merck & Co Inc v Pharmaforte Singapore Pte Ltd* [2000] 3 SLR 717, an issue did arise over whether the mere act of purifying a known compound could result in a patentable invention. The Singapore Court of Appeal, dealt with this issue not in relation to the question of invention but in the context of novelty and inventive step. On novelty, the Court of Appeal following English cases held at [2000] 3 SLR 717 at page 723 that a purer form of a known compound or a dimensional limitation of a known product could be novel and patentable. On the facts, however, the purification was found to have been obvious and lacking in inventive step. The English cases referred to included *Badische Anilin Und Soda Fabrik v Societe Chimique des Usines Du Rhone & Wilson* (1898) 14 RPC 875. See also *Genelabs Diagnostics Pte Ltd v Institut Pasteur & Anor* [2001] 1 SLR 121 where the Singapore Court of Appeal upheld patent claims directed towards the human immunodeficiency virus (HIV2) and its antigens of a stated amino acid sequence. The practical utility of the virus and antigens was its use in test kits and the like. The case did not raise any issues as to the meaning of invention and in respect of patentability chiefly concerned novelty, inventive step and sufficiency. Whilst some of the claims were directed towards the HIV-2 virus, it is probable that these claims when interpreted in the light of the specifications will not include the virus as discovered in its natural environment. As in the United Kingdom and Europe, it is likely that claims to gene fragments when the function or purpose of the gene fragment remains unknown is likely to be rejected. See C.IV para.2.3 of the Guidelines for Examination in the European Patent Office which states that "a gene which is discovered to exist in nature may be patentable if a technical effect is revealed e.g. its use in making a certain polypeptide or in gene therapy." See also C.IV para. 4.6 discussed below on industrial application.

111 See for example the *Patent Acts* of Canada, the United States and Australia. Note however that section 18(2) of the Australian *Patents Act* 1990 contains

an express bar against patenting human beings and biological processes for their generation. Note also that Australia retains the link between invention and the term "manner of manufacture" as used in section 6 of the Statute of Monopolies. Section 6 allowed grant of patent rights over manner of manufacture provided, *inter alia*, that the grant is "not contrary to law nor mischievous to the State ... or generally inconvenient." Ludlow argues that the whole of section 6 has been imported into Australia. See Ludlow, *Genetically Modified Organisms and Their Products as Patentable Subject-matter in Australia*, [1999] EIPR 298 at page 310.

112 See *Perspectives on Intellectual Property: IP in Biodiversity and Agriculture*, note 40 above at pages v–vi.

113 This provides that "European patents shall not be granted in respect of inventions the publication or exploitation of which would be contrary to *ordre public* or morality, provided that the exploitation shall not be deemed to be so contrary merely because it is prohibited by law or regulation in some or all of the Contracting States."

114 [1990] EPOR 501 at page 513.

115 [1991] EPOR 525. But note that in November 2001, the EPO Opposition Division, whilst confirming the patent, limited it to oncorodents as opposed to all oncomammals. It is probable that this was done as the *ordre public* arguments would have been more cogent if the claims applied to any non-human oncomammal. See also *Leland Stanford/Modified Animal* [2002] EPOR 16 which concerned an immuno-compromised mouse that had been implanted with human hematopoietic tissue. The claims extended to include any "chimeric non-human mammalian host." On the issue of morality, the Opposition Division carried out the balancing test and found in favour of the invention. The medical benefits included use in testing AIDS therapies. The dangers said to arise from xenotransplantation were found to be hypothetical and that in order for them to be taken into account, the dangers had to be conclusively documented hazards. The Opposition Division also noted that xenotransplantation was in any case already subject to regulatory control.

116 Indeed, in Europe the regulation and control of genetically modified foods has been made the subject of a United States complaint to the WTO. A EU/US Summit attempt to break the deadlock in June 2003 failed. In July, the EU Parliament passed new laws on the labelling of all GM foods with more than 0.9 per cent of GM material. Available online: (http://www.ictsd.org/weekly/03-07-03/story3.htm). The new regulations will also require the food industry to segregate GM plants from conventional plants and to place strict controls to stop the accidental mixing of GM food into traditional food imports. It also appears that a new European Food Safety Authority is to be set up and that members of the EU are free to legislate their own rules to prevent or reduce the danger of environmental damage arising from the escape of transgenes. The intensity of the dispute over the risks associated with GM foods well illustrate the difficulties that patent offices will face if they are compelled to examine the environmental safety of GM foods on a precautionary basis. If such a principle was adopted it is likely that most GM foods and organisms would be caught. See also the

Cartegena Protocol on Biosafety to the CBD. The Protocol is set to come into force on 11 September 2003 and deals with the need to ensure an adequate level of protection in the field of the safe transfer, handling and use of living modified organisms resulting from modern biotechnology that may have diverse effects on conservation and sustainable use of biodiversity. The precautionary principle states that: "In order to protect the environment, the precautionary approach shall be widely applied by States according to their capabilities. Where there are threats of serious or irreversible damage, lack of full scientific certainty shall not be used as a reason for postponing cost-effective measures to prevent environmental degradation." Contrast this with the "sufficiently substantiated" test adopted in the *Plant Genetics* case. That case and the subsequent regulation of GM foods in Europe shows that a society that is pro-patent is not necessarily anti environmental safety. Singapore has signed and ratified the CBD 1992 but has not done so for the Cartagena Protocol. Singapore has set up a Genetic Modification Advisory Committee (as long ago as 1999). The GMAC has issued guidelines on the release of agriculture-related genetically modified organisms and is working towards bio-safety guidelines and GM foods. It has been reported that the GMAC supports caution and that she may move towards compulsory pre-market approval system (to be timed with labelling guidelines to be issued by Codex Alimentarius). See *Straits Times*, May 28, 2003.

117 See *Perspectives on Intellectual Property: IP in Biodiversity and Agriculture*, note 40 above at pages vi that "intellectual property rights by allowing for the commodification of the most basic biological information, have the potential to turn traditional groups into trespassers in their own cultures. The design of future intellectual property rights will have to pay much more attention, one suspects, to the international human rights framework." See also Beyleveld and Brownsword, *Mice, Morality and Patents*, Common Law Institute of Intellectual Property (1993) and Ford, *The Morality of Biotech Patents: Differing Legal Obligations in Europe*, [1997] 6 EIPR 315 that the European Convention on Human Rights may yet provide another means of activating the morality debate in patent law.

118 The Opposition division cited the EPO Guideline C-IV 3.1 that the test is whether the public in general would find the invention so abhorrent that patent rights were inconceivable.

119 Query what would have been the position of the EPO if there was deception or a failure to obtain a proper consent such that the medical researchers were in breach of some ethical obligation? See for example the well known case of *Moore v Regents of the University of California* 793 P.2d 479)(Cal. 1990). For discussion, see Wei, *An Introduction to Genetic Engineering, Life Sciences and the Law*, SUP, 2002 at para. 4.39 *et seq*. In the context of biopiracy and the need to protect the rights of indigenous communities under Article 8(j) of the CBD, might it be possible that a researcher who takes genetic material by deception or in breach of national laws and rules governing access, will find that the invention is sufficiently tainted as to operate the morality bar? This is certainly a question that needs to be explored urgently—especially as it may provide a means (although this is controversial) for requiring proof of prior informed consent and origin of

the raw sources in a manner that might not require any modification of TRIPS.

120 Of course, there is a world of difference between the taking of tissue samples for research with and without informed consent. In Singapore see the Ethical Guidelines for Gene Technology published by the National Medical Ethics Committee in February 2001 on the need for informed consent. See also the extensive review of human tissue banking practices and the recommendations of the Singapore Bioethics Advisory Committee on Human Tissue Research, November 2002. The work of the Bioethics Advisory Committee has since resulted in a draft Bill to regulate biomedical research in Singapore. It is probable that after consultation that the Bill will be presented to Parliament sometime in 2004.

121 The point being that the claims as interpreted in the light of the specifications would not extend to the gene or protein as it occurs in nature.

122 Evidence to UK House of Lords Committee on the Biotech Directive 1994, HL Paper 28 HMSO March1 1994 and cited by Curley and Sharples, *Patenting Biotechnology in Europe: The Ethical Debate Moves On*, [2002] EIPR 565. See also *Leland Stanford/Modified Animal* [2002] EPOR 16 that "so long as the invention has a legitimate use, it cannot be the role of the EPO to act as a moral censor."

123 See Drahos, *Biotechnology Patents, Markets and Morality*, [1999] EIPR 441 that "since the whole point of patenting is to exclude others from access to informational resources of the patent, it is hard to see how patenting can be described as ethically neutral. The act of exclusion will always affect someone's interest." Contrast, Crespi, *Patenting and Ethics: A Dubious Connection*, [2001/2002] 3 BSLR 71 at 78 that "most professional patent practitioners are somewhat dubious as to the wisdom or appropriateness of introducing ethical and moral questions into a law which is primarily based on the assessment of originality, innovativeness and practical advances in science and technology." See also Bostyn, note 57 above at pages 84 and 85 for similar views that questions relating to the desirability of exploitation cannot be taken within the patent system.

124 See *Perspectives on Intellectual Property: IP in Biodiversity and Agriculture*, note 40 above at page vi. Professor Drahos however notes that whilst the TRIPS provisions (Article 27(2)) are disappointing from the perspective of "an amoral conception" of patent law, it would be a mistake to hold that the European Community is a supporter of the moral conception of patent. For similar views, see Sherman, *Regulating Access and Use of Genetic Resources: Intellectual Property Law and Biodiscovery*, [2003] EIPR 301 at page 305. Sherman argues that "while there is no denying the important role that patents play in macro-economic policy, there is no reason why the patent system, as a regulatory tool, should only be used in a pursuit of economic ends, nor any reason why "external" factors such as the impact of technology on the environment or health should not fall within the core remit of the patent system." See also Geertrui van Overwalle, *Belgium Goes its Own Way on Biodiversity and Patents*, [2002] EIPR 233 at page 235 where it is argued that "the bioindustry might find itself one day being confronted with public opinion taking the view that ethical concerns are more

important than mere financial gain, greater competitiveness, maximalisation of monopolies, economic growth and biotechnological development."

125 The Patents Act (Singapore) provides in section 13(2) that "an invention the publication or exploitation of which would be generally expected to encourage offensive, immoral or anti-social behaviour is not a patentable invention." This provision, whilst enacted before TRIPS, is supported by Article 27(2) of TRIPS. The question remains how widely or restrictively the provision will be interpreted in Singapore. Note that the United States/ Singapore Free Trade Agreement signed in 2003 specifically permits exclusions based on Article 27(2) of TRIPS.

126 Note however the changes made to the Guidelines for Examination in the European Patent Office as a result of the EU Directive of Biotechnological Inventions, 98/44/EC. These are set out below.

127 See C.IV 3.3a of the Guidelines for Examination in the European Patent Office, February 2001 ed. which states that "the EPO has not been vested with the task of taking into account the economic effects of the grant of patents in specific areas of technology and of restricting the field of patentable subject-matter accordingly. The standard to apply for an exclusion under Article 53(a) is whether the exploitation of the invention is contrary to *ordre public* and morality in this technical field."

128 See generally Kamstra et al, note 51 above.

129 The list is explained by para. 38 of the Recital in terms that the operative part of the Directive should also include an illustrative list of inventions excluded so as to "provide national courts and patent offices with a general guide to interpreting the reference to *ordre public* and morality" but that the list "obviously cannot presume to be exhaustive and whereas processes, the use of which offend against human dignity, such as processes to produce chimeras from germ cells or totipotent cells of humans and animals are obviously also excluded from patentability."

130 Para. 40 of the Recital to the Directive states that "there is consensus within the Community that interventions in the human germ line and the cloning of human beings offends against *ordre public* and morality" and that it is important therefore to exclude unequivocally from patentability processes for modifying the germ line genetic identity of human beings and processes for cloning human beings.

131 Query whether this bar will include stem line cell cultures obtained from human embryos and which are used in stem cell research aimed at finding cures for diseases and ailments? On this note that para. 17 of the Recital notes the significant progress made in treating disease thanks to medicinal products derived from elements isolated from the human body and the role that the patent system plays in encouraging these developments. Further, para. 42 states that whilst uses of human embryos for industrial or commercial purposes are excluded, such an exclusion does not affect inventions for therapeutic or diagnostic purposes which are applied to the human embryo and useful to it. The latter qualification deal with inventions applied for treatment/diagnostic purposes to the human embryo. It does not cover the development of stem cell lines from a human embryo.

132 This essentially endorses the balancing approach taken by the *Harvard Oncomouse* case before the EPO.

133 See C.IV para. 3.3b of the 2001 Guidelines.

134 793 P.2d 479.

135 Indeed, it seems that Belgium considered taking such an approach in its 2000 proposal to amend its *ordre public* provision to cover inventions developed in breach of the key CBD provisions. See Dutfield, note 44 above at page 24. For a critical analysis of the Belgium proposals, see Geertrui van Overwalle, *Belgium Goes its Own Way on Biodiversity and Patents*, [2002] EIPR 233. The author argues that the narrow interpretation of *ordre public* means that the latter concept does not "offer a gate of entry for the equitable sharing and the origin indication condition." The author does however support the conclusion that CBD equitable sharing objectives should be integrated into Belgium patent law.

136 If disclosure is required, further decisions will be needed as to whether the disclosure should go beyond geographical origin and include prior informed consent and access benefit arrangements.

137 See International Centre for Trade and Sustainable Development, Doha Round Briefing Series, Intellectual Property Rights, vol. 1, No. 5 of 13, February 2002. The report is available online: (http://www.ictsd.org/pubs/dohabriefings/doha5-ipr-rev.pdf). One way around the reluctance to carve out new patentability requirements might be to try and extend *ordre public*/morality bar to cover those cases where fraud etc has been proven. But, even this might not satisfy the demands of biodiversity rich countries as they may prefer a provision that requires the applicant to affirmatively state and prove geographical origin and evidence of prior informed consent and access benefit sharing arrangements. Could this be implemented in a manner consistent with TRIPS by making disclosure a procedural requirement? Could it be argued that disclosure of origin and source is needed to establish that the applicant is in fact the inventor and not merely a naked bio-pirate? These are hard issues that need careful appraisal by the international community. See also See Dutfield, note 44 above at page 25. Note that in the insurance contracts, there is a well developed principle of *uberrimae fidei* or utmost good faith that requires an applicant to disclose all facts material to the risk to be insured. If insurance law can make such a demand (based on the nature of the contract and the applicant's special knowledge), is it so unacceptable for a similar principle to be applied to applications for patent protection especially in the light of the CBD 1992?

138 In the case of Singapore, see section 16(2)&(3) PA Cap 221. Grubb explains the exclusion as based on the idea that a doctor must be able to treat his patient as he sees fit without fear of being sued for infringement. See Grubb, note 33 above at page 219.

139 The bar is really based on public policy rather than lack of industrial applicability. Thus, Art. 53(c) EPC as amended in 2000 has reformulated the bar as an exception to patentability rather than as claims that lack industrial application. Proposals are afoot to amend the UK Patents Act to reflect this. See Consultations on the Proposed Patents Amendment Bill, (http://www.gov.uk/about/consultations/patact/effect.htm).

140 See Grubb, above at note 33. Grubb also notes that the US response was to enact the Physician Immunity Statute which exempts from infringement, performance of a medical activity by a medical practitioner and related health care entities.

141 See for example the extensive guidelines on what amounts to surgery, therapy and diagnosis in C.IV 4.3 of the Guidelines for Examination in the European Patent Office, February 2001. See also the discussion in Bently and Sherman, *Intellectual Property*, Oxford, 2001 at page 365. Note also the controversy as to whether genetic screening techniques are covered by the exclusion of diagnostic methods practised on the human or animal body? Early cases in the EPO suggesting that screening methods fall outside the exclusion. Later cases suggest a broader approach to diagnosis that may cover screening methods (at least those which are applied in situ). See *Non-Invasive Measurement/Bruker* (1998) OJEPO at 308 and compare *Device and Method for Sampling Substances Using Alternative Polarity/Cignus* (2002) OJEPO 4. Both of these cases are discussed in the context of BRAC 1 Gene patents by Bostyn, note 57 above at page 101.

142 Patents for second and subsequent medical uses of known substances are allowed in Europe using the Swiss Claim formula: "use of a substance or composition X for the manufacture of a medicament for therapeutic application Z" so long as the application is new and inventive. See C.IV para. 4.2 of the Guidelines for Examination in the European Patent Office, February 2001. In UK, Swiss Claims were accepted as valid in *Schering's Applications* [1985] IPD 8032 (Pat. Ct.). But note also the use of Swiss Claim formula and the changes (when in effect) made by the Revision to the EPC by the Diplomatic Conference in Munich in 2000. The Diplomatic Conference amended Article 54 of the EPC so as to permit claims directed to the product for the new specified use. See Article 54(4) which as amended reads "[Article 54] shall not exclude the patentability of any substance or composition, comprised in the state of the art, for use in a method [of treatment], provided that its use for any such method is not comprised in the state of art." Article 54(5) reads "[Article 54] shall also not exclude the patentability of any substance or composition referred to in paragraph 4 for any specific use in any method [of treatment] provided that such use is not comprised in the state of the art." Singapore's statutory provisions on methods of treatment and novelty are the same as those in the current *Patents Act* 1977 (UK) and whilst there has yet to be any decision in the area, it is probable that claims for second and subsequent medical uses will be accepted at least when presented in the Swiss formulation. Note that the United States/Singapore Free Trade Agreement (2003) permits the use of Article 27.3(a) of TRIPS.

143 See Article 53(b) EPC which states that "plant or animal varieties or essentially biological processes for the production of animals or plants" are not patentable under the EPC 1973. Microbiological processes or the products thereof are not covered.

144 [1990] EPOR 501 at page 510.

145 See also *Plant Genetics Systems/Glutamine Synthetase Inhibitors* [1995] EPOR 357 and *Novartis/Transgenic Plant Patent* decision [1999] EPOR 123 and

on appeal at [2000] EIPR N-49. In the latter case, the Enlarged Board of Appeal held that Article 53(b) of the EPC did not apply where a specific plant variety was not claimed. See now also CIV. Para. 2a.2 and Para. 3.4.1 of the Guidelines for Examination in the EPO, February 2001, that inventions which concern plants or animals are patentable provided the application of the invention is not confined to a single plant or animal variety. These guidelines are consistent with Article 4(2) of the European Directive on biotechnological inventions which sets out a similar provision. In the United Kingdom, see now also para. 4, Schedule A2 of the PA 1977. For discussion of the European position on animal and plant varieties, see Kamstra *et al*, note 51 above at pages 27–28 and also at pages 34–35.

146 Singapore has not implemented provisions based on Article 27(3)(b). In any case the United States/Singapore Free Trade Agreement (2003) now prevents any exclusions based on Article 27(3)(b). In the case of Australia, it is to be noted that there is no express exclusion of animal, plants and biological processes for standard patents but there is such an exclusion for innovation patents. See PA 1990, section 18 as amended.

147 But even if this approach is taken, it does not follow that inventions like the oncomouse can be excluded. If the view is taken that the oncomouse is a product of genetic engineering, the genetic engineering process will be patentable. Might it be argued that Article 27(3)(b) of TRIPS implicitly requires that animals or plants that are the product of such a process be treated as patentable? Compare Article 53(b) of EPC 1973 which expressly makes clear that products of microbiological processes are not to be caught by the exclusion.

148 See for example the *Patents Amendment Act* 2002 (India) which excludes "plants and animals in whole or any part thereof other than micro-organisms but including seeds, varieties and species and essentially biological processes for the production or propagation of plants and animals." But see note 146 below that micro-organisms includes human, plant and animal cells.

149 See CIV para 3.4.2 of the Guidelines for Examination in the European Patent Office, February 2001 which explains the European thinking that a process for the production of plants or animals is essentially biological if it consists entirely of natural phenomenon such as crossing and selection. Para. 3.5 goes on to explain that microbiological process includes genetic engineering and that the product of a microbiological process may also be patentable *per se*.

150 See CIV para 3.5 of the Guidelines for Examination in the European Patent Office, February 2001 which explains that micro-organism includes "bacteria and other generally unicellular organisms with dimensions beneath the limits of vision ... including plasmids and viruses and unicellular fungi (including yeasts), algae, protozoa and, moreover, human, animal and plant cells." Thus a proposal for a draft ASEAN Framework Agreement on Access to Biological and Genetic Resources, February 2000 that would exclude plants, animals, micro-organisms or any parts thereof will find itself clashing with Article 27(3)(b) of TRIPS.

151 In the case of Singapore, the United States/Singapore Free Trade Agreement (2003) requires Singapore to adhere to the International Convention for the Protection of New Varieties of Plants (UPOV) 1991. This means that Singapore will have to enact Plants Breeders Rights legislation in the near future as well as to allow for patent protection for new plant varieties where conditions of patentability are met. In the case of India, the Patents Amendment Act 2002 excludes protection for plants. Consistent with her obligations under Article 27(3)(b), India enacted the Protection of Plant Varieties and Farmers Rights Act in 2001. India is not at date of writing a member of UPOV. Article 27(3)(b) of TRIPS does not compel adherence to UPOV—what it does demand is some *sui generis* form of effective protection for plant varieties.

152 Professor Drahos notes that right from the start, there were disputes even over what was meant by "review." For developing countries such as India, the African group, Thailand etc, review meant "substantive review" and opened up Article 27(3)(b) to re-negotiation. For the United States, Professor Drahos points out that review meant fact finding. See Drahos, *The TRIPS Reviews and the CBD: A Dress Rehearsal?* published as a chapter in *Perspectives on Intellectual Property: IP in Biodiversity and Agriculture*, Sweet & Maxwell, 2001 at page 62.

153 See Drahos, supra note 152 at page 64 that "the US will continue to push for a version of Article 27(3)(b) that fits its own maximalist model. This model is close to its own domestic position. Irrespective of what is being said by the EC concerning Article 27(3)(b), domestically its law is evolving in a way that is seeing the restrictions on patentability being narrowed. Like the US, Europe wants investment flows to be directed into its biotechnology and pharmaceutical sectors."

154 This is to be done by an amendment to the Patent Cooperation Treaty 1977.

155 WTO Doc: IP/C/W400/Rev. 1, June 18, 2003 at page 2.

156 Article 30 of TRIPS allows limited exceptions to the exclusive rights conferred by a patent provided that such exceptions do not unreasonably conflict with a normal exploitation of the patent and do not unreasonably prejudice the legitimate interests of the patent owner, taking account of the legitimate interests of third parties. Switzerland has indicated that it intends to introduce a farmers' right defence based on this Article in its patent law. Note that in UK, a farmers' right defence has already exists. See section 60(1)(g) and (h) PA 1977. For discussion, see Bently and Sherman, *Intellectual Property Law*, 2001 at para. 5.4.2.

157 Switzerland has signed and ratified the CBD.

158 The Swiss see the proposal to require evidence of country of origin of the biological resources and traditional knowledge as sufficient to enable source countries to police compliance with national access legislation.

159 The Swiss view is that it is critical to develop a clear definition of what traditional knowledge encompasses and what are the objectives of protection. Until this is resolved, movement ahead, whether at WIPO or other fora, is bound to be slow. Switzerland also noted that biodiversity

rich countries could reduce the spectre of bad patents being applied for and granted in respect of traditional knowledge innovations by documenting the information in a written form that is more readily accessible to patent offices. Issues concerning protection of traditional knowledge are closely related to folklore. Professor Blakeney explains that folklore is typically discussed in copyright or copyright plus terms whilst traditional knowledge would be broad enough to embrace traditional knowledge of plants and animals in medical treatment and as food. Thus discussion of protection for traditional knowledge would shift the debate from copyright to patent law and biodiversity rights. See Blakeney, *Protection of Traditional Knowledge under IP Law*, [2000] EIPR 251. The question remains as to what is encompassed by traditional knowledge. Some consensus on this is needed if there is to be international movement forward. See generally Heath and Sabine, *Intellectual Property: Suitable for Protecting Traditional Medicine*? [2003] IPQ 69.

160 Areas of possible agreement were identified as follows. (a) Members have the right under TRIPS to adopt appropriate protection for plant varieties by *sui generis* systems drawing on the International Treaty of Plant Genetic Resources, the Convention on Biological Diversity, the 1978 Act of UPOV and the African Model Law on Protection of Rights of Local Communities, Farmers, Breeders and Regulation of Access to Biological Resources. (b) Irrespective of the type of *sui generis* system adopted, Members to have the right to exclude non commercial use of plant varieties and the system of seed saving and exchange amongst farmers. (c) Members have the right to require within their domestic laws, the disclosure of sources of any biological material that constitutes some input in the inventions claimed and proof of benefit sharing. (d) Traditional knowledge and inventions of local communities should be protected under appropriate regimes and on the understanding that TRIPS only sets out minimum standards and does not prevent Members from adopting other areas of protection. (e) It is important to identify and document genetic resources and traditional knowledge as a way of assisting searches and examinations for novelty and inventive step. Note that in the case of Singapore, the US/Singapore Free Trade Agreement (2003) requires adherence to UPOV 1991 for plant protection.

161 WTO Paper. IP/C/W/404 at page 2. The African Group also asserted that patents on life forms also made the exception in Article 27(2) concerning *ordre public* and morality. Query whether the Group wishes to go beyond a discretionary exclusion principle to a mandatory exclusion for all life patents.

162 This area is really part of the general problem of protecting traditional knowledge of local and indigenous communities.

163 Note that the African Group felt that disclosure was best achieved by an amendment to Article 29 TRIPS. Compare this with the Swiss proposal above. The African Group also goes further than the Swiss proposals in that the disclosure requirements apply to information on compliance with access regulations of the country of origin.

164 For convenience, the Brazilian submission. See WTO docs: IP/C/W/403.

165 The Brazilian submission, like the African Group, accepted that databases and access contracts whilst helpful suffered from limitations in that they did not amount to an international solution. See also Heath and Sabine, note 159 above at page 82 that "a system whereby lack of consent regarding the use or access of biological material renders the patent prone to cancellation would appear to be nothing out of the ordinary from a doctrinal point of view." See also the on going discussions within WIPO in connection with the draft substantive Patent Law Treaty (SCP/10/2). One proposal (on which substantive discussion has not yet taken place) is to include a provision allowing Contracting Parties to require compliance with applicable laws on public health, nutrition, ethics in scientific research, environment, access to genetic resources, protection of traditional knowledge and other areas of public interest in sectors of vital importance for their social, economic and technological development.

166 See for example the US position taken in IP/C/W/ 257.

167 Specifically, it was argued at page 3 of the Brazilian submission that "Before a patent is granted, it would ... be important to verify the extent of the prior existing knowledge that it utilises and the 'inventiveness' involved in the invention. Procedures adopted for the granting patents often have to be different depending on the field of technology. For instance, in the case of micro-organisms, the nature of the invention demands that the micro-organisms that are used are deposited prior to grant of the patent...." Query also whether compulsory disclosure requirements can be supported on the basis that the information provided is essential to assessing whether there is an *ordre public*/morality objection that can be raised.

168 Contrast this with the US views in IP/C/W/257. Note also whether any distinction can be drawn here between agricultural inventions and drugs and pharmaceuticals on the basis that it is often more difficult even for the applicant to be sure of the source country identity in the case of plants and seeds in the field of agriculture. Note also that whilst it may be for the applicant to provide the evidence, the patent office will still have to evaluate that evidence and in the course of so doing resolve factual as well as legal issues such as meaning of source country and the content and scope of national access laws. These are bound to be time consuming and lengthy exercises.

169 Reference should also be made to an ASEAN Workshop on the TRIPS Agreement (February 15, 2001), available online: (http://www.grain.org/docs/asean-tmk-en.pdf). That workshop organised by the UN Development Programme (UNDP) appears to have taken the position that the review of Article 27(3)(b) should seek to exclude patentability for plants and animals. Cf. the Singapore position described below. See also one early proposal for a Draft ASEAN Framework Agreement on Access to Biological and Genetic Resources (2000), available online: (http://www.grain.org/docs/asean-access-2000-en.pdf). That proposal stated that ASEAN shall not allow the patenting of plants, animals, micro-organisms or any parts thereof and traditional indigenous knowledge. It also proposed that ASEAN shall not allow the prospecting or application of intellectual property rights on genetic material of human origin. Note, however, that the status of this proposal is not entirely clear. It appears that the February

24, 2000 proposal was possibly prepared by (or connected with) representatives from Philippines, (Elipdio V. Peria of the South East Asia Regional Institute for Community Education—SEARICE) for consideration by an ASEAN Working Group for Nature Conservation and Biodiversity in June 2000 (the SEARICE proposal for convenience). Since 2001, the 12th Meeting of the ASEAN Working Group on Nature Conservation and Biodiversity (June 2002) agreed to set up a Technical Board to consider a Draft Agreement and the Bonn Guidelines. The Technical Experts Panel met in July 2003 and a further meeting to finalise a Draft prior to circulation to ASEAN bodies for approval is planned for later this year. At time of writing it does not appear that a Draft Agreement has been finalised and it is likely that the details of any concluded Framework Agreement will be substantively different from the SEARICE proposal made in 2000. Readers should refer to the Framework Agreement when finalised, adopted and made available, for the provisions that are actually agreed upon. The comments on the proposal for a Draft Agreement in this paper is based solely on the SEARICE proposal dated February 24, 2000.

170 The Singapore "Non-paper" on TRIPS JOB (00)/7853 can be found online: (http://www.cptech.org/ip/wto/tc/singapore.html). Note that the position set out in the 2000 Non-paper does not necessarily reflect the current Singapore position.

171 Query whether this means that there will be support for universal standard of the state of art based on world wide novelty (without discrimination between written and oral knowledge). Query also whether there will be support for making disclosure of geographical origin and traditional knowledge sources compulsory and if so whether this will extend to access/benefit arrangements. On this the non-paper notes that Singapore is a party to the CBD and that the CBD recognises the sovereign right of States over their genetic resources. It followed that there was no objection to the principle of benefit-sharing on a commercially viable fair and transparent basis. The non-paper stressed, however, that the CBD left it to individual States to decide the terms for access and that this flexibility should be kept. The non-paper did not support using TRIPs to enforce benefit sharing arrangements and it thus appears to follow that she will not be in favour of making disclosure of access benefit arrangements compulsory as a precondition to the grant of a patent. See also the early SEARICE proposal for a draft ASEAN Framework Agreement on Access to Biological and Genetic Resources (2000) above at note 164a. That proposal, *inter alia*, supported the setting up of a database on biological and genetic resources as well as procedures making prior informed consent a pre-condition to access to ASEAN biological and genetic resources. The proposal also contained provisions on fair and equitable sharing of benefits. Whilst the proposal did not expressly state a view on whether disclosure of origin and evidence of prior informed consent and entry into access benefit arrangements should be compulsory in the patent application process, the tenor of the 2000 proposal certainly leant in that direction. Note however that readers should refer to the actual Framework Agreement when finalised, adopted and made available for provisions that are actually agreed upon.

172 Compare and contrast the views of CIPR, *Integrating Intellectual Property Rights and Development Policy*, 2002. CIPR agrees at page 78 that without a deeper understanding of what traditional knowledge involves it will be difficult to move forward towards international norms. But, on the other hand, CIPR also encourages developing countries to adopt a minimalist approach to patent law that would exclude from patentability diagnostic, therapeutic and surgical methods for the treatment of humans and animals, animals and plants as well as new uses of known substances. CIPR also advocates for developing countries a restrictive interpretation of micro-organisms as well as provisions linking disclosure of source and access benefit arrangements to the grant and/or enforceability of biological patents. See CIPR 2002 Report at pages 84–87,116–122.

173 See Martin Khor, *TRIPS Council Debates Patents on Life, Traditional Knowledge and Article 27.3(b)* available online: (http://www.sacredearth.com/ethnobotany/news/trips1.htm). Khor notes that many developing countries have come out in support of either or both the African and Brazilian submissions. Khor also notes that the EC has shown willingness to discuss mandatory disclosure requirements but leaves open whether this should be done at the WTO or WIPO. See also Khor, *Intellectual Property, Biodiversity and Sustainable Development: Resolving the Difficult Issues*, 2002. See also *Bridges Trade BioRes*, September 26, 2002. See also the views of the NGO, Genetics Resources Action International (GRAIN). GRAIN takes the view that biodiverse rich developing countries rather than arguing for a new intellectual property right to protect traditional knowledge should seek the banning of all patents on living things. See GRAIN, The TRIPS Review at a Turning Point, available online: (http://www.grain.org/publications/trips-july-2003-en.cfm).

174 The point being that if an opposer/attacker of the patent can show that fraud or deceit or breach of relevant national access laws, that the patent might be revoked or rendered unenforceable. See generally the discussion in Heath and Sabine, note 159 above at page 80 *et seq*. Note that the US/Singapore Free Trade Agreement (2003) provides that a patent may only be revoked on grounds that would have justified a refusal to grant the patent or that pertain to insufficiency of or unauthorised amendments to the patent specification, non-disclosure or misrepresentation of prescribed material particulars, fraud and misrepresentation. But, whilst fraud *on* the patent office might lead to a court holding the patent to be unenforceable, what if deceit relates to the source provider of the genetic material? See for example, albeit in a different context, *Moore* v *Regents of the University of California* 793 P2d 479. See also *Regents of the University of California* v *Eli Lilly* 119 F.3d 1559 which concerned a breach of NIH protocols against use of uncertified plasmids. The patent application stated that certified plasmids had been used. The Appeals Court refused to hold that the patent was unenforceable as they concluded that the Patent Office would have granted the patent even if they had known of the correct position. But see here the amendments made in India by the Patents Amendment Act 2002. That Act introduced two new grounds for opposition: (a) that the specifications do not disclose or wrongly mentions the source or geographical origin of biological material used for the invention and (b)

that the invention is anticipated having regard to the knowledge, oral or otherwise, available within any local or indigenous community in India or elsewhere. Further, if the attacker/opposer can show that claimed invention is nothing more than traditional knowledge—the patent can be revoked for want of novelty. The problem here of course is that not all countries recognise foreign oral knowledge as forming part of the prior art base—a problem discussed below.

175 *Fomento* v *Mentmore* [1956] RPC 87 (CA).

176 See note 175 above, and also the Guidelines for Examination in the European Patent Office D-V at para 3.1.3.1.

177 By "bad patent" what is meant is a patent granted in ignorance of the fact that the invention is already in the prior art base in some foreign country. See the examples given by Professor Blakeney, *Intellectual Property Aspects of Traditional Agricultural Knowledge*, published as a Chapter in *Perspectives on Intellectual Property: IP in Biodiversity and Agriculture*, Sweet & Maxwell, 2001. Perhaps one of the best known is the US patent granted over the use of turmeric for wound healing. That use was part of traditional knowledge in India and the US PTO revoked the patent when the Indian Government was able to provide documentary evidence that the use was part of the prior art. Supporters of the patent system will point to this case as vindication of the existing system for the patent was revoked. Supporters of indigenous knowledge and patent law reform might disagree and argue that given the costs of revocation proceedings, etc., the patent should never have been granted. See Dutfield, note 44 above at page 22. For discussion of meaning of biopiracy and wrong patents, see CIPR, *Integrating Intellectual Property Rights and Development Policy*, 2002 at page 74.

178 In Singapore, see *Genelabs Diagnostics Pte Ltd v Institut Pasteur* [2001] 1 SLR 121 that for a prior publication to anticipate, it must be established that following the teachings in the prior publication would inevitably lead to the invention covered by the patent. "The prior disclosure must not only identify the subject-matter of the claim in the later patent it must do so in a way that enables the skilled man to make or obtain it, a kind of enabling disclosure." Other hard patent law issues on novelty that have arisen concerns whether knowledge of the amino acid sequence of a protein means that the knowledge also discloses the gene. This is unlikely since the redundancy built into the genetic coding system means that there may be numerous different possible gene sequences that could encode for the protein. See in USA, *Re Bell* 26 USPQ 2d 1529 and Grubb, note 33 above at page 235. See also Schertenleib, *The Patentability of DNA based Inventions in the EPO and the European Union*, [2003] EIPR 125 for a summary of novelty issues in connection with disclosures in gene libraries and the views expressed in the Trilateral Projects between the EPO, USPTO and JPO. The latter refers to a useful comparative study of the way these patent offices apply patent law criteria in the area of biotechnology. Project B3b concerned the status of nucleic acid molecule based inventions whose inventions are inferred based on a homology search. Project B3b also sets out a discussion of reach through claims and patentability of DNA fragments and is available online: (http://www.european-patent-office.org/tws/sr-3-b3b_bio_search.htm). Trilateral project 24.1 concerned claims,

patentability and unity of invention and is available online: (http://www.european-patent-office.org/tws/sr-3-bio.htm).

179 *Merrell Dow Pharmaceuticals Inc* v *HN Norton & Co Ltd* [1996] RPC 76 at page 88.

180 But see generally, Vandana Shiva, *Protecting our Biological and Intellectual Heritage in the Age of Biopiracy*, 1996. Dr Shiva argues that if bad patents are to be avoided, such as those over Neem extracts, more recognition must be given to non-western knowledge systems

181 Singapore applies a standard of world wide novelty. See section 14(2) PA Cap 221. In the case of India, see note 169 above and the extended area for anticipation by reference to traditional knowledge.

182 See section 102 US Patents Act Title 35. Note also that unlike the United Kingdom, EPC, Singapore, Australia and many other countries, the priority date at which the novelty of an invention is assessed under US law is the date of invention (as opposed to the date of filing).

183 See Schedule 1 of the *Patents Act* 1990 (as amended).

184 See Correa, note 43 above at page 129. Professor Correa argues that the novelty requirement should be defined so as to exclude patentability for "any subject-matter which was made available to the public, by means of a written description, by use or in any other way, in any country before the date of filing, including use by local and indigenous communities and deposit of a material in a germplasm bank or other deposit institution where such material is publicly available." See also Dutfield, *Indigenous Peoples, Bioprospecting and the TRIPS Agreement: Threats and Opportunities* also published as a Chapter in *Perspectives on Intellectual Property: IP in Biodiversity and Agriculture*, Sweet & Maxwell 2001 at page 143 where the US mixed novelty system is described as one which could legalise the misappropriation of traditional knowledge. Dutfield, like so many commentators, feels that the EPC system which makes no distinction as to geographical source of prior knowledge is much fairer. See also G. Bodeker, *Indigenous Medical Knowledge: The Law and Politics of Protection* where it said that the World Conservation Union (IUCN) recommends more "exacting standards of novelty and inventive step so that the failure of IPR law to adequately protect traditional knowledge is not compounded by the ability of others to hold patents for inventions closely derived from such knowledge" and that prior art should "include public domain knowledge in any part of the world whether published or not." The latter paper was presented to the Oxford Intellectual Property Research Centre in 2000. A copy of the overheads is available online: (http://www.oiprc.ox.ac.uk/EJWP0300.pdf). See also above at note 95 for the position of the Canadian Biotechnology Advisory Commission. Note also that CIPR in its 2002 Report, *Integrating Intellectual Property Rights and Development Policy*, also supports an absolute novelty standard covering all public uses of information anywhere in the world. See also generally *Intellectual Property Rights: Implications for Development (August 2003)*, UNCTAD-ICTSD, at and note that the draft substantive Patent Law Treaty (WIPO) SCP/10/2 and accompanying regulations proposes a definition of prior art that includes oral knowledge and uses on a worldwide

basis. A copy of the paper is available online: (http://www.wipo.int/scp/en/documents/session_10/pdf/scp10_2.pdf).

185 See Wei, *An Introduction to Genetic Engineering, Life Sciences and the Law*, SUP, 2002 at page 195. In the United Kingdom and Singapore, see especially *Windsurfing International v Tabur Marine Great Britain* [1985] RPC 59, *Biogen Inc* v *Medeva plc* [1997] RPC 1 and *Genetech Inc's Patent.* [1989] RPC 147. See also C.IV para. 9.3 of the Guidelines for Examination before the EPO, July 1999 which states, *inter alia*, "the question to consider ... is whether at the priority date of that claim, having regard to the art known at that time, it would have been obvious to the person skilled in that art to arrive at something falling within the terms of that claim. If so the claim is bad for lack of inventive step." For the US position, see Grubb, note 33 above at page 64 that the general approach is the same as in UK save that the US courts more readily permit mosaicing and hindsight analysis. If so, inventive step is an even more formidable requirement in US law. See also generally, Durham, *Patent Law Essentials. A Concise Guide*, Quroum Books 1999 at page 96 and also Jaenichen, McDonell and Haley Jr., *From Clones to Claims*. Heymanns, 2002 at page 321 for a summary of the US position on inventive step.

186 The author is not suggesting that all patents for inventions arising out of uses of traditional knowledge lack novelty or inventive step—merely that the cases highlighted in the literature give some cause for concern. See for example the *Quinoa* patent, the various *Neem* patents, the *Enola Bean* patent, the *Nuna bean* patents, the *P. niruri* patent and the *Maca* patent and the other examples discussed variously by Professor Blakeney, *Intellectual Property Aspects of Traditional Agricultural Knowledge*, published as a Chapter in *Perspectives on Intellectual Property: IP in Biodiversity and Agriculture*, Sweet & Maxwell, 2001, Dutfield, note 44 above, K Puri, *Is Traditional or Cultural Knowledge a form of Intellectual Property*, 2000 available online: (http://www.oiprc.ox.ac.uk/EJWP0100.pdf), Vandana Shiva, *Protecting our Biological and Intellectual Heritage in the Age of Biopiracy*, 1996 and Gari, *Conservation, Use and Control of Biodiversity: Local Regimes of Biodiversity Versus the Global Expansion of Intellectual Property Rights*, published as a Chapter in *Perspectives on Intellectual Property: IP in Biodiversity and Agriculture*, Sweet & Maxwell, 2001.

187 Recital 46 of the European Directive on Biotechnological Inventions explains that: "Whereas, in view of the fact that the function of a patent is to reward the inventor for his creative efforts ... and thereby encourage inventive activities, the holder of the patent should be entitled to prohibit the use of patented self-reproducing material in situations analogous to those where it would be permitted to prohibit the use of patented, non-self reproducing products, that is to say the production of the patented product itself."

188 See for example, section 60(1)(a) PA 1977 (UK) and section 66(1)(a) PA Cap 221 (Singapore). Query whether this needs re-thinking in the light of the possibility of patented living organisms reproducing without any intervention by man. Should a farmer be liable for making a patented invention when the act of making occurred on his property without his knowledge and without his involvement? See for example the current patent

litigation in Canada between Monsanto and a Canadian farmer over Canola plants carrying a gene that confers protection to a herbicide. Monsanto asserts that the farmer planted and harvested the GM Canola whereas the farmer asserts that if this occurred—it was accidental and a result of GM seeds blowing onto his land from nearby fields. Even assuming that the latter is proven the fact that the defendant did not knowingly infringe is not per se a defence to product patent infringement. Should there be a defence to cover innocent accidental use of a patented invention in such circumstances? See generally the Canadian Biotechnology Advisory Commission Report 2002. Note that it has been reported that Monsanto will not sue in those cases where GM seeds have accidentally crossed over.

189 See section 60(1)(c) of the UK *Patents Act* 1977 and Article 64(2) of the EPC. In Singapore, a similar provision is found in section 66(1)(c) of the *Patents Act* (Cap. 221).

190 Liability for divergent but same characteristics is similar to the doctrine of equivalents and purposeful interpretation of patent claims in infringement actions. In the United Kingdom, these Articles have been implemented by Schedule A2 paras. 7&8 of the *Patents Act* 1977. See also Article 9 of the Directive which provides that the protection conferred by a patent on a product containing or consisting of genetic information "shall extend to all material ... in which the product is incorporated and in which the genetic information is contained and performs its function." In UK this is implemented by Sch A2, para. 9 of the *Patents Act* 1977.

191 See Bostyn, note 57 above at page 74. Bostyn also notes that in *Kirin Amgen Inc v Transkaryotic Therapies Inc* [2002] EWCA 1096 and [2003] RPC 3 at para. 29 that the UK CA stressed that the Guidelines for Examination in the EPO (CIII 4.7b) allowed claims for products defined in terms of a process for manufacture only if the products themselves fulfilled the requirements of patentability. For case comments, see Gilbert and Wilson, *Broad Biotech Patents in the United Kingdom after Amgen*, [2000/2001] 3 BSLR 108, Thomson and Kempton, *Construction Issues in Pharmaceutical and Biotech Cases*, [2002] EIPR 591 and also Sheraton and Sharples, *The Court of Appeal Puts Biogen Insufficiency Back where it Belongs*, [2002] EIPR 596.

192 The CA noted at para. 31 that the claims interpreted thus would be consistent with Article 64(2) EPC which allows patents to extend to products directly obtained by the patented process. If the patent could extend to such products there was no reason why the claim could not be drafted to do just that.

193 Applying the Protocol to Art. 69 EPC, *Wheatley v Drillsafe* [2001] RPC 133 and *Improver Corporation v Remington Consumer Products Ltd* [1990] FSR 181.

194 See generally, White, *Gene Compound Per Se Claims: An Appropriate Reward?* [2000/2001] 6 BSLR 239. White gives as an example of the problems that might arise, the case of *Chiron v Organon Teknika* [1994] FSR 202, [1994] FSR 258 and [1995] FSR 589. In that case a patent (product per se claim) was obtained over the gene sequence for the Hepatitis C virus. Claims to a vaccine acting on the virus were rejected (downstream claims) since the

specifications did not enable the making of the vaccine. White points out that even though the downstream claims to the vaccine were deleted, Chiron has taken the position that any subsequent inventor who uses the patented gene to make such a vaccine will necessarily infringe unless a licence is obtained. See also the suggestion of Bostyn that under the EU Biotechnology Directive, the requirement that the industrial application of a gene must be disclosed, might be taken to mean that the patent is to be limited to use of the gene for the disclosed industrial purpose (a type of use bound product claim). See Bostyn, note 57 above at page 81. See also generally the views of CIPR, *Integrating Intellectual Property Rights*, 2002. CIPR also warns against the danger of overly broad product per se patents over genes and proteins on grounds that these blur the distinction between invention and discovery and dilute the novelty and inventive step requirement. See especially at pages 14, 117, 126–30.

195 Crespi, *Gene Compound Claims: Another View*, [2001/2002] 1 BSLR 3. Crespi notes that product per se gene patents have been attacked on the basis that whilst it is always possible to invent around traditional product patents—genes when patented cannot be easily invented around. To this, at page 4 he replies, *inter alia*, that there is no principle of patent law "that limits patents to objects that can be designed around."

196 *Merrell Dow Pharmaceuticals Inc v HN Norton & Co* [1996] 76.

197 Consider for example the recent waivers (August 30, 3003) granted by the WTO to the domestic supply requirement in Article 31 of TRIPS (compulsory licences) in the context of the public interest in health and crises such as those caused by HIV.

198 Patenting of Higher Life Forms and Related Issues. Report to the Government of Canada Biotechnology Ministerial Coordinating Committee, June 2002.

199 The UK provision is not limited to biological materials marketed in Member States of the EU.

200 Bently and Sherman, *Intellectual Property Law*, Oxford, 2002, at page 510.

201 *Ibid.* note at page 510 that other uses such as selling the seed to other farmers for propagating new crops will not be permitted.

202 Blakeney, *Intellectual Property Aspects of Traditional Agricultural Knowledge*, published as a chapter in *Perspectives of Intellectual Property: IP in Biodiversity and Agriculture*, Sweet & Maxwell, 2001, at page 44.

203 See Adcock, *Farmers' Right or Privilege*, [2001/2] 3 BSLR 90.

204 Note that whilst ITPGR defines farmers rights in connection with plant genetic resources, similar points are likely to arise with animals.

205 Not so surprising given the strength of the farming community in the European Union. The Canadian Biotechnology Advisory Committee in its report, Patenting of Higher Life Forms and Related Issues, (2002) has also recommended a farmers' privilege defence in its patent law to save and sow seeds from patented plants or to breed patented animals so long as the progeny are not sold as commercial propagating material or in a manner that undermines its commercial value to its creator.

206 Note that the width of this defence is cut down by provisions in Schedule A1 of the *Patents Act* 1977. These include the following two important qualifications. First, the defence only applies to plant groups set out in Schedule A1 (various fodder plants, cereals, potatoes, oil and fibre plants). Second, if the defence applies, this is subject to payment of equitable remuneration (which must be sensibly lower than the amount charged for the production of protected material of the same variety in the same area with the holder's authority). The duty to pay equitable remuneration does not apply to small farmers as defined in the Council regulation on Community Plant Varieties Rights.

207 This defence is not subject to any duty to pay equitable remuneration. Use for an agricultural purpose includes making an animal or animal reproductive material available for the purposes of pursuing the farmers' agricultural activity. It does not include sale within the framework or for the purposes of commercial reproduction activity. See section 60(6B).

208 In the case of India, the *Patents Amendment Act* 2002 excludes from patentability plants, animals, seeds, varieties and species and biological processes for the production of animals and plants. India also enacted the *Plant Varieties and Farmers' Rights Act* 2001. That Act whilst setting up a system to protect plant varieties allows farmers to "save, use, sow, resow, exchange, share or sell his farm produce including a seed of a variety protected under this Act in the same manner as he was entitled before the coming into force of this Act." See section 39 of the Act. Adcock notes that if India decides to apply for membership of UPOV, the main area of contention is likely to be the issue of farmer's rights. Adcock explains that "the scope of the farmers' privilege varies in different national laws, but generally farmers were allowed to continue their tradition of using a part of one year's harvest as seeds for the next and to exchange seeds with their farm neighbours. These activities were not considered part as a part of "commercial marketing" under Article 5(1) of the 1978 Convention. However, this form of farmers' privilege falls well short of what is allowed under the farmers' rights provisions in [the Indian Act]." See Adcock, *Farmers' Right or Privilege*, [2001/2] 3 BSLR 90 at page 92. Adcock also notes that UPOV 1991 provides that farmers' rights must recognise the legitimate interests of the breeder and that this usually means payment of compensation (equitable remuneration) for use of farm saved seed. See Article 15(2) UPOV 1991. See also the extensive farmers' rights provisions in the Organization of African Unity's (OAU) Model Law for the Protection of the Rights of Local Communities, Farmers, Breeders and for the Regulation of Access to Biological Resources. Part V sets out farmers' rights that include the right to save, use and exchange and sell farm saved seed/propagating material of farmers' varieties and to use a new breeders variety to develop farmers' varieties, including material obtained from gene banks or plant genetic resource centres. This right does not permit the sale of farm saved seed/propagating material on a commercial scale. Adcock also notes at page 93 that UPOV has been critical of these provisions and wants to see them narrowed down. If so much dispute can arise over the scope of farmers' rights within UPOV and plant varieties legislation, it is likely that similar problems will arise in patent law. The OAU Model Law

is available online: (http://www.grain.org/docs/oua-modellaw-2000-en.doc).

209 For discussion of the technology, see Swanson, *Genetic Use Restriction Technologies (GURTS): Impact on Developing Countries*, Int. J. Biotechnology, Vol. 2 Nos. 1/2/3, 2000, *Potential Impact of Genetic Use Restriction Technologies on Agricultural Biodiversity and Agricultural Production Systems*, FAO, CGRFA/WG-PGR-1/01/7, Choi, *The Terminator's Back: Controversial Scheme Might Prevent Transgenic Spread*, Scientific American, 30 and Coghlan, *No Escape for Alien Genes*, New Scientist, May 10, 2003.

210 Patenting of Higher Life Forms and Related Issues. Report to the Government of Canada Biotechnology Ministerial Coordinating Committee, June 2002, at page 14.

211 In Singapore, similar defences are set out in section 66(2)(a) and (b) PA Cap 221.

212 See *Monsanto v Stauffer Chemical* [1985] RPC 515, *Auchinloss v Agricultural and Veterinary Supplies* [1997] RPC 649, *Klinsche Versuche (Clinical Trials) II* [1998] RPC 423 and *SKF Laboratories v Evans Medical* [1989] FSR 513. See also the discussion in Bently and Sherman, *Intellectual Property Law*, 2001 at page 506 and also Grubb, note 33 above, at pages 162–63.

213 Drahos, *The TRIPS Reviews and the CBD: A Dress Rehearsal*? Published as a chapter in *Perspectives on Intellectual Property Rights: IP in Biodiversity and Agriculture*, Sweet and Maxwell, 2002, at page 65. See also Durham, *Patent Law Essentials. A Concise Guide*, Quorum Books, 1999 at page 149 citing *Douglas v United States* 181 USPQ 170 states that whilst "a kitchen experimenter amusing himself on a rainy afternoon might practise a patent without infringing, but experiments conducted for commercial purposes are likely to violate the patent, if they involve making or using the claimed invention." In the US special statutory provisions exist dealing with testing of drugs in the context of applications for licence approvals. See *Roche Products Inc. v Bolar Pharmaceutical Inc* 221 USPQ 937 (denying such a defence at common law) and its reversal by the Drug Competition and Patent Term Restoration Act 1984. Grubb is of the view that the Bolar Exception contravenes TRIPS as it applies only to pharmaceutical inventions and amounts to technological discrimination. On the other hand, CIPR advocates an express Bolar type exception for all developing countries. See *Integrating Intellectual Property Rights and Development Policy*, 2002 at page 122. See also Correa, note 43 above at page 122, states that the US defence is narrow and covers experimentation for philosophical (scientific) purposes to create products outside of the scope of the patent.

214 In the related context of UPOV 1991, Article 15 provides that plant breeders' right do not extend to acts done for private non-commercial purposes and for the purposes of experimentation.

215 See *CIPA Guide to the Patents Acts*, Fifth Ed. Sweet & Maxwell, at para. 60.14 that the UK experimentation defence can cover acts which have in view an ultimate commercial purpose.

216 See Article 10 of TRIPS that "Compilations of data or other material ... which by reason of the selection or arrangement of their contents constitute

intellectual creations shall be protected as such. Such protection, which shall not extend to the data or material itself, shall be without prejudice to any copyright subsisting in the data or material itself."

217 For fuller discussion, see Wei, *An Introduction to Genetic Engineering, Life Sciences and the Law*, SUP, 2002 at Chapter 3. See also Laddie, Prescott & Vitoria, *The Modern Law of Copyright and Designs*, Butterworths, 3rd ed. at Chapter 38 and Karnell, *Protection of Results of Genetic Research by Copyright or Design Rights*, [1995] 8 EIPR 355. In Europe, note the European Database Directive that has led to a new *sui generis* European database right. Compilations of data (including genetic data) may be protected under the database rights against unauthorised use and extraction. See Bovenberg, *Should Genomics Companies set up Database in Europe? The EU Database Protection Directive Revisted*, [2001] EIPR 361. See also Ng-Loy Wee Loon, *Patenting Genes—A Closer Look at the Concepts of Utility and Industrial Applicability*, IIC Vol.33, No.4/2002 393.

218 [1978] Qd R 72. See also Wei, *Surreptitious Takings of Confidential Information*, Vol. 12 No.3 Legal Studies. See also Correa, note 43 above at page 126. Correa cites a US case (*Pioneer Hi-Bred v Holden*) recognising protection of inbred lines as a trade secret.

219 UPOV was signed in 1961 and revised in 1972, 1978, and 1991. The 1991 Act came into force on April 24, 1998. UPOV 1978 is now closed for membership. New applicants must join UPOV 1991. Note also that in the case of Singapore, the US/Singapore Free Trade Agreement (2003) requires Singapore to ratify or accede to UPOV 1991.

220 See Article 6 UPOV 1991.

221 See Article 7 UPOV 1991. Query what amounts to common knowledge. Contrast UPOV 1978 where Article 6 expressly provided that common knowledge can be established by factors such as cultivation or marketing already in progress. Is the fact that a variety is being cultivated by indigenous farmers overseas something relevant to proving common knowledge under UPOV 1991?

222 See Article 8 UPOV 1991.

223 See Article 9 UPOV 1991.

224 See Article 14 UPOV 1991. Note that subject to allowable defences, the rights extend in the case of harvested material, to entire plants and parts obtained through the unauthorised use of propagating material of the protected variety unless the breeder has had reasonable opportunity to exercise his rights against the propagating material. A similar provision applies to products made directly from harvested material through the unauthorised use of the harvested material unless the breeder has had a reasonable opportunity to exercise his rights against the harvested material. See Article 14(2)(3) UPOV 1991. The term of protection is to be not less than 20 years and for trees and vines—not less than 25 years. See Article 19 UPOV 1991.

225 See UPOV 1991 Article 14(5).

226 See UPOV 1991 Article 15. The last defence also applies to the other variety unless caught by Article 14(5).

227 But exhaustion does not apply if the acts involve further propagation or an export of material of the variety which enables propagation to a country which does not protect the variety except where the exported material is for consumption purposes.

228 See the views of the International Environmental Law Research Centre available online: (http://www.ielrc.org/Content/BP03031T.html).

229 See Adcock, *Farmers' Right or Privilege*, [2001/2] 3 BSLR 90 at page 92. Adcock explains that UPOV 1991 provides that farmers' rights must recognise the legitimate interests of the breeder and that this usually means payment of compensation (equitable remuneration) for use of farm saved seed. Adcock also points out at page 93 that the UPOV is likely to take issue with India on its farmers' right defences in its Plant Varieties and Farmers' Rights Act 2001 in the same way that it objects to the farmers' right defences proposed by the OAU's Model Law for protecting the rights of local communities, farmers and breeders and for the regulation of access to biological resources. It is also interesting to note that it has been reported that India intends to join UPOV 1978 rather than UPOV 1991. This may not be possible given that membership of UPOV 1978 is closed. Still, under Article 27(3)(b) of TRIPS, India could try and justify her new Plant Varieties and Farmers' Rights Act 2001 on the basis that it is *sui generis* legislation that provides effective protection (UPOV 1978 standard) for plant varieties. See also a proposal for a draft Malaysian Protection of Plant Varieties Bill 1999. This proposed farmers' rights covering: propagation by small farmers on their own holdings using the product of the harvest from the protected variety planted on their own holdings, exchange of propagating material by small farmers within reasonable limits and the sale of farm saved seeds where the small farmer cannot make use of his own farm saved seeds on his own holding due to natural disasters or emergencies or any other factors beyond the small farmer's control, provided the amount sold is not more than what is required by his own holding. Available at the Genetic Resources Action International (GRAIN) website: (http://www.grain.org/brl/pvp-brl-en.cfm). For a discussion of Plant Breeders Rights in Canada, see Derzko, *Plant Breeders' Rights in Canada and Abroad: What are These Rights and How Much Must Society Pay for Them*, McGill Law Journal 39 [1994] 144. For Asia, see Egelyng and Blakeney, *Plant Variety Protection in Asia: Some Issues of Implementation and Implications for Germplasm Exchange Networks*, published as a Chapter in *Perspectives on Intellectual Property: Issues in Biodiversity and Agriculture*, Sweet & Maxwell, 2002.

230 Article 3 CBD 1992.

231 Article 8j CBD 1992.

232 See the collection of articles published in *Perspectives on Intellectual Property: IP in Biodiversity and Agriculture*, above at note 40.

233 See Gari who argues that "development as the empowerment of the local ecological and cultural contexts around biodiversity questions many of the assumptions of the global green developmentalism" in Gari, *Conservation, Use and Control of Biodiversity: Local Regimes of Biodiversity Versus the Global Expansion of Intellectual Property Rights*, published as a

Chapter in *Perspectives on Intellectual Property: IP in Biodiversity and Agriculture*, Sweet & Maxwell, 2002 at page 6.

234 See for example Blakeney, *Protection of Traditional Knowledge under IP Law*, [2000]EIPR 251 at page 255 who notes that in Australia "under current intellectual property law there is no obligation for companies which utilise the traditional medical knowledge of Aboriginal peoples to provide any compensation to recognise their equity in the commercial exploitation of this knowledge."

235 This in itself can be a complex issue for some nation States. See Nnadozie, Access to Genetic Resources and Intellectual Property Rights: Regulatory Framework in Nigeria, published as a Chapter in *Perspectives on Intellectual Property: IP in Biodiversity and Agriculture*, Sweet & Maxwell, 2002

236 These are not prescriptive rules and were adopted by COP VI/24. A copy of the guidelines is available online: (http://www.biodiv.org/decisions/default.asp?dec=VI/24&print=1). For detailed discussion, see Jeffrey, *Bioprospecting: Access to Genetic Resources and Benefit Sharing under the Convention on Biodiversity and the Bonn Guidelines*, (2002) 6 Sing JICL 747. The guidelines touch on competent national authorities, participation of stakeholders, prior informed consent, mutually agreed terms, benefit-sharing and other matters.

237 See for example something along the lines of a global biotechnology collecting society suggested by Professor Drahos. The society could police patent applications as well as administer intellectual property rights granted over traditional knowledge. Drahos, *Indigenous Knowledge, Intellectual Property and Biopiracy: Is a Global Bio-Collecting Society the Answer*? [2000] 6 EIPR 245. See Dutfield, note 44 above at page 35 where the views of Professor Drahos are discussed. See also Heath and Sabine, note 159 above at page 77 that whilst the Neem patent was revoked before the EPO, revocation procedures are expensive and costly. The authors, however, also comment that the fears of expropriation through third party patenting seem overblown as in many cases the patent claims are directed towards purer or more stable forms of the active ingredients of the product and not to the product as known and used by the traditional community. Heath and Sabine also make the point at page 88 that there is no general acceptance of the position, that where traditional knowledge is used as a basis for further research and development of new products, that compensation is to be paid. After all "all inventors stand on the shoulders of giants." See also Gupta, *Compensating Local Communities for Conserving Biodiversity: How Much, Who will, How and When*, available online: (http://www.sristi.org/papers/compensating).

238 Note that UPOV is apparently not against disclosure of origin of genetic resources since this will facilitate an examination of whether a variety qualifies for protection. Available online: (http://www.upov.int/en/about/pdf/international%20harmonization.pdf).

239 See Puri, *Is Traditional or Cultural Knowledge a form of Intellectual Property*? Paper presented to Oxford University Intellectual Property Research Centre on January 18, 2000. Available online: (http://www.oiprc.ox.ac.uk/EJWP0100.pdf). See also Dutfield, *Indigenous Peoples, Bioprospecting and*

the TRIPS Agreement: Threats and Opportunities, published as a Chapter in *Perspectives on Intellectual Property: IP in Biodiversity and Agriculture*, Sweet & Maxwell, 2002, at page 144.

240 Article 1(1) TRIPS.

241 See Heath and Sabine, note 159 above, at page 74 where it is noted that just as some countries have opted for additional protection for utility models, so too additional protection for traditional medicine can also be devised.

242 See Dutfield, note 44 above, where the views of Professor Drahos are quoted at page 41. Some countries have already started formulating national laws protecting traditional knowledge. These include Philippines (*Indigenous Peoples Rights Act* 1997, *The Traditional and Alternative Medicines Act* 1997, Community Intellectual Property Rights Bill 2001—still in draft form), India (The Biological Diversity Act 2002, The Karnataka Community Intellectual Property Right Bill 1994—not enacted, the Community Intellectual Property Rights Bill 1994—not enacted). A list of countries that have legislation or proposals to protect traditional knowledge—together with the legislation—can be found at the website of Genetic Resources Action International (GRAIN): (http://www.grain.org/brl/tk-brl-en.cfm). Note also the Part IV of the OAU Model Law on The Protection of Rights of Local Communities, Farmers and Breeders and for Regulation of Access to Biological Resources. Dutfield notes at page 41 that in April 2002 an International Seminar on Traditional Knowledge was organised by India with participation of Brazil, Cambodia, Chile, China Colombia, Cuba, Egypt, Kenya, Peru, Philippines, Sri Lanka, Thailand and Venezuela. The conclusion reached which may well herald more action to come was that "the ability of patent offices in a national jurisdiction to prevent bio-piracy as well as to install informed consent mechanisms to ensure reward to TK holders, does not *ipso facto* lead to similar action on the patent application in other countries. A need was therefore expressed for an international framework for protecting TK."

243 But not in the case of Singapore as the US/Singapore Free Trade Agreement (2003) requires Singapore to adhere to UPOV 1991. Singapore will have to apply the higher standards agreed upon to all Member States of the WTO under the TRIPS most favoured nation principle. Some of the areas where Singapore has agreed to implement "higher" patent standards are: accession to UPOV 1991, exclusion of patentability only as defined in Article 27(2) (*ordre public*/morality) and 27(3)(a) (methods of treatment of humans and animals) of TRIPS, provision of a cause of action against pharmaceutical products made or distributed in breach of contract between the patentee and a licensee whether the breach occurs in or outside of Singapore and compulsory licences. Professor Drahos, commenting on the use of free trade agreements to negotiate intellectual property accords on a bi-lateral basis, has commented that "if both the US and the EC continue to negotiate bilateral agreements which impose higher standards than TRIPS with other Members of TRIPS, the MFN principle will operate to globalise rapidly the new standards ... By the time the US and the EC come to the MTN table on intellectual property many of the issues currently being raised in TRIPS reviews may have been settled bilaterally.

The only question will be whether to 'fold' those bilateral negotiated standards into TRIPS." See Drahos, *The TRIPS Reviews and the CBD: A Dress Rehearsal?* Published as a chapter in *Perspectives on Intellectual Property: IP in Biodiversity and Agriculture*, Sweet & Maxwell, 2002 at page 67.

244 See the helpful survey in Sherman, *Regulating Access and Use of Genetic Resources: Intellectual Property Law and Biodiscovery*, [2003] EIPR 301. Sherman supports at least considering the possibility of making it a condition of patentability, that applicants obtain prior informed consent from access providers and also to disclose in their patent application geographical origin of relevant biological material.

CHAPTER 3

Plant Genetic Resources, Biological Inventions and Intellectual Property Rights: The Case of India

S. K. VERMA*

3.1 INTRODUCTION

Since the adoption of the Convention on Biological Diversity (CBD), 1992, and the Agreement on Trade-related Aspects of Intellectual Property Rights (TRIPS), 1994, as a part of the WTO Agreement, the ownership over biotechnological inventions has become a debatable issue at the national and international levels. The increasing surge in patents and other intellectual property rights (IPRs) related to genetic resources, and their effect on the development and sustainability of agriculture has further made it an area of great concern, particularly for developing countries. In addition, the issue of biopiracy has also become quite significant.[1]

A close look at these two treaties clearly establishes many inter-linkages between the two. The main overlapping and conflicting areas in these treaties are the ownership/protection and access to biological and genetic resources on the one hand and access to technology in biological inventions on the other. The TRIPS Agreement obliges the states-parties to grant patents "in all fields of technology" [including biotechnology] and protect plant varieties through patents or a *sui generis* system or combination of both. The CBD, on its parts, requires members to

* Director, Indian Law Institute; Professor of Law, University of Delhi.

conserve and preserve the bio-diversity and the eco-system and has mandated them to protect and allow access to biological and genetic resources in accordance with the provisions of the Convention. Another treaty of relevance in this area is the recently concluded International Treaty on Plant Genetic Resources for Food and Agriculture (PGRFA Treaty), adopted on November 3, 2001, which incorporates, to a large extent, the philosophy of the CBD.

India is a party to all the three treaties. Recent controversy in India over the controversial patents granted by the US Patent Office and the EPO on *turmeric*, *basmati* and *neem* (all were based on the knowledge widely shared in India)[2] has brought the issue of biopiracy to the centre-stage in all the legislative efforts undertaken by the Government of India to comply with its international obligations under these treaties. Though the of *turmeric* and *neem* patents have been revoked in the US and the EU respectively, these cases have highlighted certain gaps in the whole procedure of granting and revoking patents on bio-products, and the very issue of IPRs has become very controversial in India. On *turmeric* the patent was granted to the University of Mississippi Medical Centre in December 1993 on its use in normal healing, particularly in chronic and acute wounds, which was successfully challenged by the Indian Council of Scientific and Industrial Research (CSIR), on the ground that the alleged invention was part of public domain knowledge in India. On the basis of documented evidence, the patent was cancelled. Similarly, *neem* patent, granted to W. R. Grace of the U.S., was revoked by the European Patent Office (EPO) after representations made by certain NGOs.[3] In the case of the *basmati* rice patent, the USPTO granted US-based Rice Tech. Inc. a patent on September 2, 1997. In response to a petition from the Government of India to the USPTO, Rice Tech. Inc. surrendered four claims (out of its 20 far-reaching claims) in September 2000 and 11 more claims in August 2001. Rice Tech. Inc. presently holds patents on five claims and is selling *basmati* after developing its novel lines named BAS-867, RT-117, and RT-112. Because of these developments, the new high yielding, photoperiod-insensitive aromatic super fine rice strains developed by the Indian Agricultural Research Institute will not be marketed internationally as "basmati" rice using the geographical indication specific to the region, but is marketed simply as aromatic rice at a huge economic loss to the country.

There are numerous other cases where the patents have been granted on genetic resources obtained from developing countries without their knowledge and consent. Patents have been granted without any further improvement of the genetic resources,[4] such as in the cases of *kava*, *barbasco*, and *endod*, among others. There can also be cases where the possessors of those resources may not know about the actual grant of the IPRs on those plant materials and genetic resources. Such cases, occurring on regular basis in different parts of the world, have created an unsavoury controversy. In response to the industrialised countries' demand that the developing countries should make all out efforts to combat IP "piracy," the developing countries have expressed their own widespread concern over "gene-piracy," and have demanded their fair share and right over their genetic resources, which is the basis of all growth in biotechnology in the developed world. Central to the bio-privatisation of knowledge and biodiversity is the devaluation of local and traditional knowledge and the creation of monopoly rights on plant genetic resources by claiming novelty over that which is already in the public domain in the developing world. The result? People in these countries lose access to the knowledge and resources vital to their survival, creativity and to the conservation of cultural and biological diversity. These developments have highlighted the close linkages between biodiversity and IPRs on biotechnology, particularly when it involves the protection of traditional knowledge, innovations and creativity.

This paper examines the issues of ownership and access to genetic resources, on the one hand, and the IPRs over biotechnological inventions, on the other, which are at the centre of this whole controversy. For this, the paper first looks into the reasons underlying the controversy, followed by the international framework on the ownership and protection of biological inventions. The CBD will be examined closely for this purpose. This paper will then take a stock of Indian legislative efforts to address these issues.

3.2 GENETIC RESOURCES AND BIOTECHNOLOGY

The conservation and sustainable utilisation of plant genetic resources (PGRs) is broadly recognised as important for the developments in biotechnology. PGRs are the "raw material" for the biotechnology industry. Genes, folk varieties, and land races are used to develop new varieties by biotechnology. It is estimated that about 6.5 per cent of all genetic research undertaken in agriculture is focused upon germplasm derived from wild species and land races.[5] Until the advent of molecular biology and genetic engineering, plant breeding depended on access to genetic variability within a species for its success. Genetic engineering has, however, rendered the transfer of genes across sexual barriers possible, and has thus enhanced the economic value of biodiversity.[6]

Through biotechnology, the desirable characteristics of a plant's genetic resources (PGRs) are synthesised through rDNA technology, and a new variety is created. Techniques which use rDNA technology have made it possible to break through natural species barriers systematically by moving genes from one species to another that do not combine in nature. Genetically modified (GM) crops, developed by using input traits (e.g., resistance to insect pests and plant diseases), output traits (e.g., delayed fruit ripening, better taste, elimination of saturated fats in cooking oils, elimination of allergens, better delivery of necessary nutrients), and agronomic traits (e.g., resistance to drought, salinity, acidity, flood, etc. and increase in crop yield) have also been made possible by this technology.

PGRs have thus considerable potential value for plant and animal breeding, food, chemical, pharmaceutical, medicine and environmental industries.[7] It is estimated that 80 per cent of world population depends upon botanical medicines. Through modern technologies, such as chemical prospecting, screening as well as molecular mapping, valuable information about their genetic formation can be gathered and put to use for different purposes. It is also important to note that genetic resources are a store of knowledge. As "genotypes" which embody information about the genetic constitution of micro-organisms, plants and animals, they become the subject matter of patents and plant breeders' rights (PBRs), even though their patentability is questionable *per se* on the grounds of novelty and disclosure. PGRs have thus become a prolific source of IPRs.

Research and development in the field of biotechnology is principally confined to developed countries, particularly in private hands (mainly with MNCs). The PGRs for research and development which were available to them free of charge until recently originated from developing countries and were collected and stored by developed countries in their *ex-situ* conservation centres. The products or plant varieties, particularly created or developed from these genetic resources, are protected through patents and plant breeders' rights (PBRs) in developed countries and are not freely accessible to developing countries. These protected products are exported to developing countries at high prices, after "value-adding" without acknowledging the source or making due payment for the cultivation and protection of these "raw materials." The traditional communities and indigenous people in developing countries, who have conserved, preserved and developed these PGRs, which rightfully belong to them, and have transmitted knowledge thereto to seed companies and research institutions in developed countries over the years have not received any reward or benefits in return. They are instead made to pay high prices for improved varieties which have been developed out of these resources. Since their genetic resources have contributed to the overall wealth and the development of the global economy and of the economies of the developed countries, it is important that these communities and developing countries are compensated for using these PGRs.[8]

The areas of medicine and agriculture, which are profoundly affected by biotechnology, particularly through rDNA technology are both very critical to developing countries. The seeds, produced through rDNA technology, with desired characteristics, have the potential to revolutionise agricultural productivity, keeping in mind the carrying capacity of the land which is limited not only in India but in other developing countries as well. The new seed products with new traits introduced provide agronomic benefits such as disease resistance, pest resistance, herbicide tolerance, and also extend the shelf-life of harvested produce. For countries whose economies are based on agriculture, the application of techniques of modern biotechnology is the only answer to improve biomass productivity of food, fuel, fodder and a variety of raw materials for industrial purposes. In the area of medical biotechnology, the production of more effective vaccines has become possible. Molecular probes and monoclonal antibodies have proved to be very powerful tools for the diagnosis, prognosis and treatment of human tumours. Hybridoma technology and genetic engineering have helped in the development of immunodiagnostics that are sensitive, specific, cost-effective and easy to use. The DNA finger-printing technique in medico-legal cases, especially disputed parentage linkage analysis in disease conditions, is gradually finding increased usage all over the world.

3.3 INTERNATIONAL FRAMEWORK ON PLANT GENETIC RESOURCES AND IPRS

Biodiversity is basic to achieving progress in improving the productivity of plants, animals, marine life and all living organisms. Food, medicine, industrial products are derived both from the domesticated and wild components of biodiversity. Biodiversity provides the feedstock to the biotechnology industry. Biological diversity is primarily concentrated in the tropics, where the developing countries are primarily located. It is a well-documented fact that developing countries are rich in world's flora and fauna and 80 per cent of the earth's terrestrial biodiversity is confined to these countries. Mega biodiversity countries also have the largest concentration of resource-poor indigenous communities. India is one of the 12 mega biodiversity countries of the World. With only 2.5 per cent of the land area, India accounts for 7–8 per cent of the recorded species of the World. India is equally rich in traditional and indigenous knowledge, both coded and informal. The Indian Gene Centre represents one of the eight important Vavilovian Centres of origin and crop plant diversity of cultivated plants and their wild relatives. It is immensely rich in medicinal and aromatic plant species that occur in diverse ecosystems. It is estimated that of the 20,000 species of angiosperms in India alone, there are 9,500 species of ethnobotanical importance.[9]

In order to protect biodiversity and its sustainable use, the Convention on Biological Diversity (CBD) is aimed at the: (i) conservation of biological diversity; (ii) sustainable use of components of biological diversity; and (iii) fair and equitable sharing of benefits arising out of utilisation of genetic resources and appropriate transfer of relevant technology. Different provisions of the Convention give effect to these objectives which are found in Article 1 of the CBD.

Article 15 of the Convention establishes the ownership of a State over its genetic resources and the "prior and informed consent"[10] of the State as a pre-requisite for access to these genetic resources.[11] Genetic resources are no more the "common heritage of mankind" as was declared in Article 1 of the International Understanding on Plant Genetic Resources (IU) adopted under the auspices of the FAO in 1983 which allowed free access over them.[12] As a consequence of this mandate under the IU, there had been the free-of-charge use of genetic resources by all, with the result that there was free access to the seed banks and agricultural research centres of the Consultative Group on International Agricultural Research Work (CGIAR).[13] This policy, nevertheless, led to the growth of the Green Revolution.

But whereas the CBD has declared genetic resources as the property of each sovereign State, the TRIPS Agreement has mandated countries to introduce IPRs in the field of biotechnology. Article 27(1) of the TRIPS Agreement provides:

> ...patents shall be available for any inventions whether products or processes, in all fields of technology, provided that they are new, involve an inventive step and are capable of industrial application[14]

Article 27(2) of the TRIPS Agreement provides an important exception in favour of protecting the environment (which must also include biodiversity), where Member States may exclude from patentability those inventions which are necessary "to avoid serious prejudice to the environment." But, whereas plants and animals other than micro-organisms, and essentially biologically processes for the production of plants may be excluded from patentability, plant varieties are to be protected "either by patents or by an effective *sui generis* system or by any combination thereof."[15]

The mandate to introduce IPRs for biological inventions is thus a significant step in the development of policies which would restrict the flow of information and the complete abandonment of the principle of common heritage. The germplasms stored in the international agricultural research centres (IARCs) around the world would now be regulated under terms of the PGRFA Treaty. [16]

The principle of national sovereignty over PGRs is balanced by paragraph (2) of Article 15 of the CBD which obliges Contracting Parties to create conditions to facilitate access to genetic resources for environmentally sound uses by other Contracting Parties, and not to impose restrictions that run counter to the Convention objectives. It further provides that access to genetic resources of a Contracting Party "shall be on mutually agreed terms," based on the "prior informed consent" of the Contracting Party providing such resources.[17] The country accessing the genetic resources shall develop and carry out scientific research on those genetic resources with the full participation of the Contracting Party providing the genetic resources,[18] which shall also be entitled to share the research results and the benefit arising from the commercial use of its genetic resources. Such sharing shall be based upon "mutually agreed terms."[19]

These provisions thus create two-way obligations for owners of genetic resources: to protect them and to allow access to them on mutually agreed terms. Hence, the owners cannot refuse to share these resources *per se*. However, the most troublesome terms in the Article are the references to "mutually agreed terms" and "prior informed consent," which need a well-structured mechanism before access is allowed. The CBD emphasises the use of bilateral agreements between providers and use of resources.

The CBD also recognises that access to genetic resources and benefit-sharing arising out of the use of genetic resources cannot be separated from the traditional knowledge of indigenous and local communities. Traditional knowledge can be highly valuable in identifying sources of new products derived from genetic resources, including pharmaceuticals and crop varieties,[20] hence, the prior informed consent of the holders of knowledge would be significant. Therefore, any system created under Article 15 to enable the access to genetic resources must give due place to the rights of the relevant indigenous people and communities.

The Convention specifically obliges the Contracting Parties to protect and promote the rights of communities, farmers and indigenous peoples *vis-à-vis* their biological resources and knowledge system.[21] This is in recognition of the fact that informal innovations by farmers are the main reason for the stability and sustainability of the agricultural system in most developing countries, and their knowledge in the creation, conservation and protection of new plant and animal varieties is necessary to the preservation of the eco-system.

Traditional knowledge[22] arises as an issue in association with genetic resources under Article 8(j) of the CBD. It recognises the contributions of local and indigenous communities to the conservation and sustainable utilisation of biological diversity through traditional knowledge, practices and innovations, and provides for the equitable sharing of benefits with such people arising from the utilisation of their knowledge, practices and innovations. It requires the Contracting Parties to take legislative and administrative action in three vital aspects:

1. To respect, preserve, maintain the knowledge, innovations and practices of indigenous and local communities embodying traditional lifestyles relevant to the conservation and sustainable use of biological diversity;
2. To promote the wider application of such knowledge, innovations and practices with the approval and involvement of the holders of such knowledge, innovations and practices; and

3. To encourage the equitable sharing of the benefits arising from the utilisation of such knowledge, innovations and practices.

The first category of issues is most complex and difficult to define. Respecting the traditional knowledge of indigenous and local communities can be understood as requiring such traditional knowledge to be accorded a status comparable to that given to other types of knowledge, innovations and practices, particularly to scientific knowledge. Hence, a proper mechanism needs to be devised at the national level, which should properly reflect this mandate by defining the availability, scope and use of this knowledge and practices. It could be in the form of a *sui generis* system or any other form of IPRs, such as patents, geographical indications and trade secrets. It is, however, not only the mechanism of protecting those rights, either through IPRs or a *sui generis* system, that is important, but also what constitutes those rights. In this context, the role of "farmers' rights" also becomes an important issue.

The implementation and action on the second and third categories of issues depend very much on the outcome of the debate on the first category of issues. If they are well defined and identified by way of legislation, the transfer of traditional technology and the conservation of that knowledge could be facilitated, as well as the sharing of benefits arising from their utilisation. The value of traditional knowledge in PGRs, however, may be examined in the context of its commercial validity, the cultural identity of the traditional communities and biological diversity of the area. A wider application of traditional knowledge for the *in-situ* conservation of biodiversity would facilitate traditional technology transfer by the holders of such knowledge to potential users.[23]

The Convention further mandates that information concerning indigenous and traditional knowledge and technologies should be included among the information to be exchanged and, where feasible, repatriated between the Parties.[24] Technological cooperation between the Contracting Parties should also include cooperation regarding indigenous and traditional technologies.[25] The Convention, however, does not provide any mechanism for the fair and equitable sharing of benefits as has been stated in Article 8(j) and other provisions.

The International Treaty on Plant Genetic Resources for Food and Agriculture (PGRFA Treaty) provides such a mechanism, involving the exchange of information, access to and transfer of technology, capacity-building and sharing of benefits arising from commercialisation (Art. 13) which is to be regulated through a standard material transfer agreement (MTA). It aims at the conservation and sustainable use of plant genetic resources for food and agriculture, and the fair and equitable sharing of benefits derived from their use, for sustainable agriculture and food security.[26] The Treaty defines PGRs as "any genetic material of plant origin of actual or potential value for food and agriculture."[27] The Treaty affirms each State's sovereign rights over their PGRs for food and agriculture, and proscribes the acquisition of IPRs over these PGRs. Article 12.3(d) of the Treaty which states that "recipients shall not claim any intellectual property or other rights that limit the facilitated access to plant genetic resources for food and agriculture, or their genetic parts and components in the form received from the Multilateral System" became very controversial, leading to abstentions by Japan and the United States from voting on the adoption of the Treaty. It recognises the rights of local and indigenous communities and farmers of all regions of the world, particularly those in the centres of crop origin and diversity, and mandates the Contracting Parties to protect and promote their rights, which will not be limited to the traditional rights of farmers to save, use, exchange and sell farm-saved seed and propagating material.[28] It further provides broad guidelines for states concerning the scope of the rights to be protected under this heading, but the responsibility for realising farmers' rights[29] has been given to member states. This includes the protection of traditional knowledge, farmers' entitlement to a part of benefit-sharing arrangements and the right to participate in decision-making regarding the management of plant genetic resources. However, the Treaty is silent with regard to farmers' rights over their landraces (folk varieties).

While none of these is necessarily IPR-related, Article 3 provides that "Nothing in this Article shall be interpreted to limit any rights that the farmers have to save, use, exchange and sell farm-saved seeds/ propagating material, subject to national law and as appropriate." The overall significance of the PGRFA Treaty lies in the fact that it is the first Treaty providing a legal framework which not only recognises the need for agro-biodiversity conservation and sustainable use of plant genetic resources for food and agriculture but also delineates a regime for access and benefit sharing, and in this process creates direct and indirect links to intellectual property instruments.[30]

3.3.1 Technology transfer related to biotechnology

Closely related to the issue of ownership over PGRs is the issue of IPRs over biotechnology and the transfer of technology. Under the CBD, the obligation "to facilitate access to genetic resources" under Article 15(2) is inter-twined with Article 16, the principal provision in the whole Convention relating to technology transfer related to biotechnology. In fact, the Convention does not impose a duty on States to allow access to their genetic resources or to part with their technological know-how unless there exists a *quid pro quo* arrangement *inter se* between the parties. Article 16 provides that:

> Each Contracting Party, recognizing that *technology includes biotechnology* and the both access to/and transfer of technology among Contracting Parties are essential elements for the attainment of the objectives of this Convention, undertakes subject to the provisions of this Article to provide and/or facilitate access for and transfer to other Contracting Parties of technologies that are relevant to the conservation and sustainable use of biological diversity or *make use of genetic resources and do not cause significant damage to the environment....*[31]

However, the "technology subject to patents and other intellectual property rights, such access and transfer shall be provided on terms which recognise and are consistent with the adequate and effective protection of intellectual property rights."[32] Thus, it enjoins members to recognise proprietary rights in genetic-based technology and protect them through patents or other measures in order to provide effective protection. However, a developing country which provides genetic resources should be given "access to and transfer of technology, [by a Contracting Party] which makes use of those resources, on *mutually agreed terms*, including technology protected by patents and other intellectual property rights" by taking legislative, administrative or policy measures.[33] It thus imposes a duty on the holders of technology and IPRs, who make use of genetic resources collected from developing countries to establish a *quid pro quo* arrangement which connects the access to genetic resources to the transfer of technology.

There is also the obligation of the Contracting Parties to cooperate in this regard, "subject to national legislation and international law in order to ensure that such rights are supportive of and do not run counter to its objectives."[34] Further, Article 22 provides that the CBD "shall not affect the rights and obligations of any Contracting Party deriving from any existing international agreement except where the exercise of those rights and obligations would cause a serious damage or threat to biological diversity." Both provisions together provide a strong case for CBD to prevail over the obligations under any other agreement, including TRIPS. What is not clear, however, is that in case of a conflict between the two, which will get precedence: the obligations under the TRIPS Agreement or the CBD? Can non-compliance with IPR obligations be justified if they are not supportive of the objectives of the CBD, including the one contained in Article 8(j)? However, a reasonable question may also be raised as to whether the members of one Convention are dictated by the provisions of another Convention (i.e., are the parties to the TRIPS Agreement subjected to the provisions of the CBD?). Since there is a close connection between the biotechnology and genetic resources, can it not be argued that life-forms should be kept out of the purview of the TRIPS,[35] particularly when they have the environmental impact for which TRIPS provides an exception in Art. 27(2)? Will the developed countries, the principal holders of IPRs in biotechnology, be agreeable to subordinate the TRIPS Agreement to the CBD and part with the technology to developing countries which require biotechnology to solve their food and health problems, but lacking the capacity to pay for it? But the weakness of these provisions is nevertheless evident in view of the fact that the Contracting Parties are only obliged to "cooperate"; there is no affirmative assertion about the substantive obligation in this regard.[36]

The sharing of profits and access to technology on "mutually agreed terms" are the troubling spots in the whole scheme of the CBD. Those who develop the new plant or animal varieties, pharmaceuticals or chemicals, based on genetic resources, are to share their profits with the owner of those resources on *mutually agreed terms*, provide effective participation in biotechnological research activities by those Contracting parties, especially developing countries, which provide the genetic resources for such research.[37]

The linking together of genetic resource sharing with technology transfer is perceived by the developed world as an interference with their contractual relationships and an encroachment into their proprietary know-how and technologies. Such views put in jeopardy the transfer of technology to developing countries without first providing for an effective protection of technology through IPRs.

The United States has not ratified the CBD so far, which it perceives as weakening the IPR regime. Its biotechnology industry has raised objections to the Convention alleging that it: (1) provides a basis for the parties, particularly developing countries, to reduce IP protection, and (2) opens the door to compulsory licensing arrangements by them. There are fears that because of the immense potential of biotechnology to solve the developing countries' food and health problems, they may introduce compulsory licenses for biotechnology related patents.[38] Developed countries perceive the CBD as a threat to further research and development in biotechnology.

Article 16 of the CBD, on the other hand, stems from the acknowledgement that conservation of biological diversity generates opportunity costs for biodiversity-rich countries that are not in control of the technologies which are necessary to achieve the Convention's objectives. It establishes a legal framework that seeks to reduce those costs, yet without undermining the international intellectual property system. Firstly, access to and transfer of technology should take place "under fair and most favourable terms." The common meaning of that term indicates that technology transfer contracts should adopt conditions prevailing on the international technology market (unless parties mutually agree to concessional and preferential terms), without price discrimination or market segmentation. It is apparent that the term "mutually agreed" does not allow for compulsory licenses since a compulsory license, by definition, is not "mutually agreed." Where, however, compulsory licenses are granted, the remuneration paid by the country acceding to the protected technology should be adequate in the circumstances of each case, taking into account the economic value of the authorisation. Other conditions, as established by Article 31 of the TRIPS Agreement and Article 5A of the Paris Convention for the Protection of Industrial Property, are also applicable to compulsory licenses of patented, environmentally sound inventions. Nevertheless, the factors determining transfer of biotechnology are essentially the same as those determining transfer of technology in general which will also encompass the returns and quantum of royalty.

It is significant to note that Article 8(1) of the TRIPS authorises its members, in formulating or amending their national laws and regulations to "adopt measures necessary to protect public health and nutrition, and to promote the public interest in sectors of vital importance to their socio-economic and technological developments," provided such measures are consistent with other TRIPS provisions. A member is also authorised to issue compulsory licenses in cases of public non-commercial use[39] or to remedy anti-competitive practices.[40] The TRIPS Agreement further provides that the protection and enforcement of IPRs should contribute to the promotion of technological innovation and transfer and dissemination of technology, "to the mutual advantage of producers and users of technological knowledge and in a manner conducive to social and economic welfare and to a balance of rights and obligations."[41] Article 66(2) of the TRIPS Agreement provides that developed countries shall establish incentives to enterprises and institutions in their territories for the purposes of promoting and encouraging technology transfer to least developed countries. Thus, these TRIPS provisions are consistent with Articles 16(4), 17 and 19 of the CBD, which refer to transfer of technology, that is largely under the control of the private sector in developed countries, to developing countries,

Given the strong views of the developed countries towards IPRs, protecting the rights of indigenous people and rewarding them for their contribution in preservation, conservation and further development of genetic resources, in accordance with the CBD mandate, becomes a difficult task.

3.3.2 IPRs on biological inventions and benefit-sharing

In order to check biopiracy and to give access to genetic resources, some mechanism needs to be devised to the mutual benefit of the owners of genetic resources and the users who need access to them for biotechnology related research and development. The CBD merely lays down the framework for the access to genetic resources and sharing of benefits arising out of the use of these resources, but to effect these mutual obligations requires further implementation at the national and international level.

The interface between access to genetic resources and benefit-sharing, on the one hand, and intellectual property rights, on the other, has two different aspects. First, genetic resources which are conserved either *in-situ* or *ex-situ*, may have been modified by means of human intervention and acquire characteristics that are not found in nature. Where those modifications are new, involve an inventive step and are capable of industrial application, they may be protected by patents (depending on specific provisions found in national laws regarding patentable subject-matter). PGRs that consist in plant varieties that are new, distinct, sufficiently uniform and stable may qualify for protection under national laws, through patents or a *sui generis* system or a combination thereof. Other modified resources that do not qualify for protection under existing intellectual property mechanisms, such as landraces and traditional varieties, which nonetheless are of great relevance to the subsistence of local communities and possibly for the conservation and development of plant genetic resources, may be considered by national laws to constitute subject-matter protectable under national laws relating to traditional knowledge. Access to genetic resources, which are privately controlled through trade secrets or other means, will depend on authorisation by right holders and on licensing agreements.

The second context in which intellectual property rights are relevant to the framework regulating the access to genetic resources and benefit-sharing is the recording of interests in inventions that arise from access to or use of genetic resources and traditional knowledge. A number of regional and national laws have provided for such records or documentation by requiring patent documents to disclose the origin of the genetic resources used in the development of inventions, and to show that prior informed consent has been obtained from the competent authorities and traditional knowledge holders. The purpose of such disclosure is to provide a mechanism to verify compliance with national laws and contracts concerning access to genetic resources and benefit sharing. India has set-up a Traditional Knowledge Digital Library on its traditional biological wealth and medicinal plants in a digital form in accordance with an international format to facilitate the diffusion of information and to ward off the incidence of biopiracy since March 2003. The Library has profiled the medicinal plants used in Indian systems of *Ayurvedic*, *Unani*, and *Siddha* medicine.

The CBD provides for positive benefits to be granted to the holders of biological knowledge for their contributions to the earlier, non-patented foundations on which patented innovations rest. This foundation may be in the form of information, such as the knowledge in India of the use of *neem* leaves as pesticides in stored grain, or *turmeric* as an antiseptic.

This foundation may be significant to development of a new variety or a compound, by working on that knowledge and adding an element of novelty of trivial nature, without any credit or benefit returned to the people or a public funded agency, like the Indian Council of Agricultural Research, who have helped in its conservation and development. Plant breeders' rights, under the UPOV Convention for example, negate the contribution of farmers as breeders and hence undermine farmers' rights. Similarly, patents allow the usurpation of indigenous knowledge by multinational biotechnology enterprises which engage in minor tinkering or trivial translation.

At the international level, the administrative implementation of the concept of indigenous and local communities' rights, however, is beset with many problems because of the complex quantitative and qualitative dimensions of recognising the inventive and value addition components of their contribution. At present, there is no international legal instrument (except for the PGRFA Treaty, to an extent, which provides for material transfer agreements) which adequately recognises indigenous and local communities' rights over their knowledge, innovations or practices. It is nevertheless difficult to classify traditional knowledge, innovations and practices within the traditional mould of intellectual property, as practiced in developed countries, which is individualistic and monopolistic in nature. However, some sort of intellectual property protection for indigenous and local communities may be valuable in this regard at the national level or bioprospecting agreements at the international level. It is, however, doubtful, whether these communities will be able to enforce their rights because of lack of financial, technical and legal means to claim such rights and to ensure their effective implementation. A *sui generic* system may, however, accommodate these challenges.[42]

In this context, the very term "access" needs clarification. What kind of activity would constitute access? Physical takings, collections, exchanges or something else? Access is often defined by geographical scope, and the scope of genetic resources covered, rather than by the nature of the physical activity that constitutes it. The innovations and knowledge of the local and indigenous communities are often inherent in the genetic resource as intangible components, and only the information given by the community makes the resource useful and interesting to users outside that community.[43]

A further problem related to giving effect to the obligation of facilitating access to genetic resources is to define the precise ambit of the term "prior informed consent." Any measures adopted in this regard need to strike a balance between the need to control access to ensure benefit-sharing and "mutually agreed terms," and the need to ensure that access procedures, as well as requirements for prior informed consent and benefit-sharing, are flexible and simple. As "prior informed consent" requires the full disclosure of the reasons of the activity, the specific procedure, potential risks and full implications of the activity, capacity-building among indigenous and local communities would be necessary.

When a Contracting Party enters into a material transfer agreement on genetic resources, it may include clauses for capacity building, which may also be considered as one of the modes of benefit sharing. Capacity-building may include the inculcation of negotiation skills, increased understanding of environmental management issues and legal support. While these terms are *mutually agreed* upon, the legislative framework should also lay down minimum conditions on access and benefit-sharing. In this regard, the Andean Pact Common Regime on the Common System on Access to Genetic Resources[44] is an example, requiring the bio-prospecting applicant to provide legally correct, complete and trustworthy information.[45] In the Philippines, Executive Order No. 247 was issued in May 1995. The Executive Order, "Prescribing Guidelines and Establishing a Regulatory Framework for the Prospecting of Biological and Genetic Resources, their By-Products and Derivatives, for Scientific and Commercial Purposes," established a framework to regulate bio-prospecting and a benefit-sharing mechanism at the national level. It established a Competent National Authority to give effect to the Order.[46]

In recent years, there has been a surge in international bio-prospecting activities in general and entities from developed countries have concluded such agreements with developing countries from different regions of the world.[47] These ventures have laid down frameworks for access and benefit-sharing, which may be useful towards framing any mechanism at the international level, and they also reflect exercises which have been conducted on "mutually agreed terms." Nevertheless, to benefit more from such joint prospecting ventures and to conserve their rich endowment of biological diversity, the developing countries should undertake a greater percentage of the risk-sharing by performing more of the "value adding" functions at the local level. This will enable them to dictate what amounts to an equitable compensation to the indigenous people or rural communities involved.[48] National level measures, besides addressing the issues raised above, can also outline the nature of the monetary and non-monetary benefits—depending on its needs and priorities in each given case—that will accrue to the country through bio-prospecting relationships. These measures will also require the sharing of the benefits with indigenous and local communities involved in research programmes.

While framing a legislative and administrative set-up at the national level, it must be noted that biotechnology research is generally location-specific, particularly in agriculture because of the need to adapt to local soil and climatic conditions. An agreement with a foreign party should have a *quid pro quo* arrangement which allows access to genetic resources in exchange for indigenous research and production facilities, as well as the training of local manpower. This will help in the diffusion of technology locally and would be in line with the CBD, which mandates the *in situ* conservation of biological resources. To facilitate the realisation of the objectives of the CBD, which require Member States to "respect, preserve and maintain" the traditional knowledge of indigenous and local people, the law should require IPR applications to include mandatory disclosure of the country of origin and the local community which provided the knowledge about the resources pertaining to the patentable subject matter, as well as the proof of their consent.

3.4 LEGISLATIVE EFFORTS IN INDIA

In India, research and development activities in the area of biotechnology is carried out mainly by the public funded agencies. These include government agencies, universities and research institutions. In the agriculture sector, it is principally centred on crop improvement and creating new varieties.[49] As a result, numerous varieties of fruits, vegetables, pulses, crops and cereals have been created. However, strong views have been expressed against genetically modified plants as creating risks to biodiversity and also affecting human and animal health, though these doubts have been termed as ill-founded. In recent years, the introduction of genetically modified *Bt Cotton* has generated fair amount of controversy in the country despite a conditional sanction from the Genetic Engineering Approval Committee (GEAC) of the Department of Biotechnology (DBT) on March 26, 2002 being granted to Monsanto-Mahyco Biotech Ltd., an American company, for commercial cultivation. A case pending before the Supreme Court of India was filed by the

Research Foundation for Science, Technology and Ecology challenging the legitimacy of the 1998 field trials of *Bt Cotton*. The Research Foundation points to irregularities, violations of biosafety laws and guidelines in previous years, and the susceptibility of the crop to pests and diseases. Similarly, The Indian Council for Agricultural Research (ICAR) has claimed that *Bt Cotton* developed by it is superior to Monsanto cotton because it contains multiple pest resistant genes. The high price of GM seeds is another issue.

Any legislative action in the areas of intellectual property rights over biological inventions and plant variety protection needs to take into account the special circumstances of India. Up to 70 per cent of the population of the country is dependent on agriculture and 10–15 per cent on agriculture-related industry for jobs and income with small land-holdings, based on traditional means of agriculture, using simple tools for agricultural purposes. Like other developing countries, seed saving from their harvests for further propagation, and the selling and exchanging of seeds is a common practice among Indian farmers. It should be noted that the right to sell seeds is totally excluded under the UPOV Convention, except by the plant breeder. Looking into the Indian seed sector, only 20 per cent of seed demand is met by the formal sector (which include government agencies, private seed companies, cooperative societies and other registered participants) and 80 per cent by the informal sector which is not under the control of official monitoring bodies. Farmers are therefore big players in the seed market. Hence, to sustain Indian agriculture, farmers' rights are to be treated as ownership rights over PGRs.

It is also important to note that MNCs are big players in the seed sector of the world economy and also in India.[50] There is no mechanism to protect the innovations of farming communities and to compensate them if any new variety fails to germinate, or if it is not eco-friendly or if it is hazardous to health. As seeds are the first link in the food chain, through control over the seed sector, MNCs can control the food system and may thus affect the food security of the country. It has been argued that if all farmers in India, who are the original breeders of the plant varieties (or propagating material) are forced out of the market, the seed industry will have a 7.5-billion-dollar market every year.[51] It is against this background that the plant variety protection and IPRs over biological inventions have become a debatable issue in India. Farmers are fearful of high seed prices and less control over their harvest. It will also lead to more reliance on cash crops than food crops, affecting food security in the country.[52] There is also the fear of a reduction in biodiversity (through practices such as monocultures), resulting in increased crop vulnerability to natural forces and plant diseases.

In order to give effect to its international obligations, India has adopted three inter-related legislative instruments on intellectual property rights, plant genetic resources and biodiversity: the Patents (Amendment) Act 2002 which has become effective on 30 May 2003; the Plant Variety Protection and Farmers' Rights Act, 2001, and the Biological Diversity Act, 2002. In practice, since patents fall within purview of the Ministry of Industry and Commerce, and matters related to plant varieties are the concern of the Ministry of Agriculture, while biodiversity issues are dealt with by the Ministry of Environment and Forests, there seems to be a lack of effective cooperation in the drafting of these three pieces of legislation, resulting in the overlapping of the functions carried out by these governmental bodies. There are strong linkages between these three pieces of legislation. The *Patents Act* sets out the patent framework applicable biotechnological innovations, the *Plant Variety Protection* law provides a *sui generis* system for plant breeders' rights (PBRs) in accordance with Article 27.3(b) of the TRIPS Agreement, while the *Biological Diversity Act* provides a mechanism to protect and share plant genetic resources (PGRs), as mandated under the CBD.

3.4.1 Patents (Amendment) Act, 2002

The Patents (Amendment) Act provides for the patentability of biotechnological processes. The *Explanation* to section 5 of the Act provides that "for the purposes of this section, 'chemical processes' includes biochemicals, biotechnological and microbiological process."[53] Where a patent is sought for an invention based on biological material, it is necessary to deposit the biological material along with the specifications with a depository institution, disclosing the source and geographical origin of the biological material used in the invention.[54]

It also incorporates provisions for the protection of biodiversity and traditional knowledge by refusing to grant patents or revoking patents if the application mentions the wrong source or geographical origin of the biological material.[55] This measure is taken to protect the folklore or knowledge belonging to the local or indigenous communities of any country.[56]

In compliance with the TRIPS Agreement, "an invention the primary or intended use or commercial exploitation of which could be contrary to law or morality or which causes serious prejudice to human, animal or plant life or health or to the environment" has been made non-patentable under section 3. Similarly, "Plants and animals other than micro-organisms in whole or any part thereof including seeds, varieties and species and essentially biological processes for production or propagation of plants and animals" are not patentable. Patents will not be granted for plant varieties or essentially biological processes, though it leaves open the patentability of plants and animals generated through micro-organisms, non-biological and microbiological processes. The "discovery of any living or non-living substance occurring in nature" is also not patentable. Further, "an invention, which in effect, is traditional knowledge or which is an aggregation or duplication of known properties of traditionally known component or components" is similarly non-patentable. However, it is often difficult to check unscrupulous patenting on traditional knowledge because of the lack of documentation and validation.

3.4.2 Plant Variety Protection and Farmers' Rights Act, 2001

The plant varieties, which are not patentable under the Patents (Amendment) Act, are specifically dealt under the Plant Variety Protection and Farmers' Rights Act. The main focus of the Act is to establish a system of plant breeders' rights (PBRs). The Act is extended to all categories of plants, excluding micro-organisms (which are patentable).

It is primarily based on the UPOV Convention,[57] providing a *sui generis* system for PBRs, but it includes a number of provisions not present in the UPOV Convention. For instance, it recognises the role of farmers as cultivators and conservers, and the contribution of traditional, rural and tribal communities to the country's agro-biodiversity by making provision for benefit-sharing and compensation, and also protecting the traditional rights of the farmers,[58] and has thus acknowledged that farmers' rights can be conceived as intellectual property rights. The Act, in fact, has taken into account the specific socio-economic interests of the various stake-holders in the seed sector—from private seed companies to public corporations and research institutions, and resource-poor farmers.

Section 3 of the Act envisages a "Plant Varieties and Farmers' Rights Protection Authority" (the "Authority"), which, among others, is empowered to regulate benefit-sharing arrangements. These arrangements are meant to provide individuals or groups with the possibility of receiving financial compensation when a protected variety is developed using their genetic resources. The Authority, in determining the appropriate amount of compensation under section 26 of the Act, will take into account the extent and nature of the use of the claimant's genetic resources in the development of the variety, and the commercial utility and demand in the market of the variety so developed. The Act also establishes the National Gene Fund, in which the amount accruing from benefit-sharing arrangements is credited. Under section 45 of the Act, the amount collected in the Fund is to be utilised towards making benefit-sharing payments due to claimants, compensating the village community involved in the exploitation of the plant variety in question, and towards the conservation and sustainable use of genetic resources. To give effect to the rights of village or local communities, and to carry out benefit-sharing arrangements, the central government may devise one or more schemes as provided for under section 46 of the Act.

Chapter VI of the Act is devoted to farmers' rights, which protects the traditional rights of farmers to save, use, exchange, share or sell their farm produce of a protected variety, which is in line with Article 15(2) of the 1991 Act of the UPOV Convention. However, the farmer is not entitled to sell "branded" seed.[59] It also acknowledges the rights of farmers to register new varieties which they have bred or developed, such that they are entitled to receive protection just like any other breeder under the Act.[60] A farmer engaged in the conservation of genetic resources (landraces and wild relatives of economic plants) and their improvements, through selection and preservation, is entitled to receive recognition and reward from the Gene Fund. The Act also recognises the rights of the communities (once their contribution is quantified) who are entitled to compensation from the Gene Fund. The Act only provides for compensation to the community if their contribution to the evolution of a variety is verified and accepted. It falls short of granting them any proprietary rights. It allows communities to file claims for their contribution to the development of a protected variety.[61] This position is also reflected under the Biodiversity Act, 2002. The grant of specific intellectual property rights to a community, where such rights are monopolistic in nature, will be fraught with certain administrative and legal problems, particularly in relation to its precise ambit and enforceability.

Under section 29 of the Act, the registration of a variety is not allowed in cases where prevention of commercial exploitation of such variety is necessary to protect public order or public morality, or human, animal or plant life and health, or to avoid serious prejudice to the environment.[62] The central government can exclude any genera or species from the purview of protection on grounds of public interest. Chapter VII of the Act makes provisions for the compulsory licensing of protected varieties in the public interest if the right-holder does not arrange for the production and sale of seeds to ensure that the protected seeds are available to farmers. In line with the patent statute, the proposed legislation provides that the Authority will determine the duration of the license (which may vary from case to case), terms and conditions of the license (royalty and other remuneration to the breeder of the variety) and will ensure that the compulsory licensee of the variety possesses the adequate means to provide, the seeds or its propagating material to farmers at reasonable market prices.[63]

The provisions on benefit-sharing and compensation will be subject to the rules, guidelines and schemes to be framed by the central government and the authority.

3.4.3 The Biological Diversity Act, 2002

The Act gives effect to the mandate of the CBD and, to some extent, the PGRFA Treaty. It addresses some issues which are relevant to biodiversity management in general and specific PGR management issues. The main focus of the Act is to regulate access to genetic resources and associated knowledge by foreign individuals, institutions or companies with the goal of securing the equitable sharing of benefits arising out of the use of these resources with the local people, who are the conservers of biological resources and holders of knowledge and information relating to the use of these resources, and to protect the bio-diversity related knowledge of local communities. For this purpose, the Act envisages the *National Biodiversity Authority*, *State Biodiversity Boards* and *Biodiversity Management Committees*. Under Section 18 of the Act, the *National Biodiversity Authority* (NBA) is the nodal body which oversees the implementation of the Act and is responsible for issuing guidelines for granting access to, and the equitable sharing of benefits derived from the use of, genetic resources.

The Act proposes to set up Biodiversity Funds at central, state and local levels. Section 27 of the Act provides for the proceeds from the Fund to be used for the conservation and development of those areas from which genetic resources have been accessed.

Section 36(5) of the Act requires traditional knowledge related to biodiversity to be respected and protected by the Central Government through such measures as recommended by the NBA. These measures may include the registration of such knowledge at the local, state or national levels, and other measures of protection, including a *sui generis* system of intellectual property protection. Under section 37 of the Act, state governments are to notify National Heritage Sites (which are important from a biodiversity standpoint), in consultation with local self-government institutions in order to identify and monitor areas rich in biological resources for the purposes of *in-situ* and *ex-situ* conservation.

To address the problem of biopiracy, the Act has elaborate provisions related to granting foreign individuals access to biological resources. Under section 3 of the Act, companies or associations cannot obtain any biological resources found in India or knowledge associated thereto for the research, commercial utilisation, or for bio-survey and bio-utilisation purposes without the prior approval of the NBA. Similarly the research results relating to biological resources occurring or obtained from India cannot be transferred to any of them for monetary consideration without the approval of the NBA. However, under section 4 of the Act, the publication of research papers or dissemination of knowledge through seminars or workshops is exempted provided such publications comply with the policy guidelines of the central government. Similarly, collaborative research projects involving the transfer or exchange of biological resources or information relating thereto between institutions, including government-sponsored institutions, are exempted from the application of sections 3 and 4, if they conform to these guidelines.

A foreign party, as defined under the Act, who intends to obtain any biological resources occurring in India or knowledge associated thereto for research, or other purposes specified in section 19 of the Act, will have to get the prior approval of the NBA. These purposes include commercial utilisation, or bio-survey and bio-utilisation, or transfer the results of any research relating to biological resources occurring in, or obtained from, India. Under section 20 of the Act, no transfer of any biological resources or knowledge associated thereto can take place without the permission of the NBA. The NBA, when granting approval under section 21 of the Act, will ensure the equitable sharing of benefits on terms and conditions *mutually agreed* upon between the person applying for such approval, the local bodies concerned and the relevant benefit-claimers.

The Act also seeks to address the question of the rights of holders of traditional knowledge by setting-up a system of benefit-sharing. In this regard, the NBA is empowered under section 18 of the Act to frame guidelines for access and the equitable sharing of benefits, to advise the central government on matters relating to conservation and sustainable use of biological diversity and advise the state governments in the selection of areas to be notified as heritage sites. The NBA will consult with local bodies to ensure the equitable sharing of benefits. Section 21 of the Act envisages a benefit-sharing scheme involving the joint ownership of IPRs with the NBA or with identified claimers.

In matters relating to IPRs, the Act is very stringent. It requires an inventor seeking any kind of IPR in or outside India, for any invention based on any biological research or information on a biological resource obtained from India, to obtain the *prior permission* of the NBA. If a person applies for a patent, the prior permission of the NBA is required after the patent is accepted, but before the sealing of the patent by the concerned patent authority. Further, the NBA, when giving its approval, may impose a benefit-sharing fee or royalty or both, or impose conditions which include the sharing of financial benefits arising out of the commercial utilisation of such rights. Under section 6 of the Act, this provision will not be applicable to a person making an application for any rights under the plant variety protection legislation.[64] The NBA is also empowered under section 18(4) of the Act to take the necessary measures to oppose the grant of IPRs in any country outside India on any biological resource or associated knowledge derived or obtained from India. But this scheme has an interface with the Patents Act if the patent is filed in India. It is doubtful whether the Act will have extra-territorial jurisdiction in this regard.

State Biodiversity Boards will deal with matters relating to access to genetic resources by Indians for commercial purposes and will restrict any activities that are contrary to the objectives of conservation, sustainable use and the equitable sharing of benefits. Under section 7 of the Act, local populations and communities in a particular area, who have been practicing indigenous medicine, will not be subjected to the rigours of the Act. Any contravention of these provisions is punishable under the Act.

The functions of the *Biodiversity Management Committees* under section 41 of the Act are related to the conservation, sustainable use and the *documentation of biodiversity* at the local level. Though the *State Biodiversity Boards* (at the state level) and the *Biodiversity Management Committees* (at the local level) will monitor and protect the bio-resources at their respective levels, and will be consulted in facilitating access to those resources, the final decision will lie with the NBA.

Section 27 of the Act provides for the money in the *National Biodiversity Fund* is to be used to channel benefits to benefit-claimers, to conserve biological resources, to develop those areas in which such biological resources or knowledge associated thereto have been accessed, and to promote the socio-economic development of such areas.

On the issue of benefit-sharing, separate bodies (with similar functions) have been constituted under the Plant Variety and Farmers' Rights Act *and* under the Biological Diversity Act which are engaged in regulating access to genetic resources and traditional knowledge. A composite piece of legislation could have avoided this overlapping. The Biodiversity Act focuses mainly on biopiracy and benefit-sharing, and does not provide any mechanism to check the impact of monoculture on biodiversity that is generated by the introduction of IPRs to agro-biotechnology. In the area of benefit-sharing, further fine-tuning will need to be done when the law is finally put in place. A clear understanding is needed of issues such as the royalty amount, the transfer of technology tools (with or without patent or *sui generis* system protection), the training of the local scientific community, and the other monetary benefits transferred.

It is doubtful, however, whether the proposed provision on the joint ownership of IPRs, under section 21 of the Act, will be acceptable to private multinational companies in the business of biotechnology unless there are clearly perceptible advantages to the technology-holder, or the IPR pertains to an orphan and neglected crop which does not hold much value for the technology holder.

The idea of a Fund under the Act enshrines the principle that creators and holders of knowledge do not have rights in that knowledge. Their only reward is a potential financial contribution from this Fund to be decided by higher authorities. Furthermore, it is not clear whether the reward will be in the form of only monetary benefits or whether it will also be in kind. Will it involve a one-time payment or a continuous process of periodic payments for ongoing contributions towards the conservation and cultivation of genetic resources. Since most of the holders of traditional knowledge are resource-poor and are many a time landless farm labourers, a reward in the form of land will help improve their condition, as well as help in the protection of the environment, and the conservation and cultivation of genetic resources. The Act also does not recognise biodiversity-related community IPRs. The provision for such a right could have been made under a *sui generis* system like Plant Variety and Farmers' Rights Act because the patent system is inherently incapable of doing so. But the idea of granting patents to local communities, proposed by few in India, is fraught with a few drawbacks and it is doubtful whether the local communities will be able to withstand challenges from formal plant breeders, who are well-equipped to defend their rights.[65]

Section 41 of the Act provides for the documentation of biodiversity in order to check potential biopiracy and also to help the local *Biodiversity Management Committees* to effectively challenge the IPRs granted in foreign jurisdictions. On the subject of traditional knowledge of medicinal plants, the *Traditional Knowledge Digital Library* has already been set-up by the Government of India. There are also various experiments on documentation that have been undertaken by the village communities, particularly in Kerala, which is one of the states in India with the richest levels of biological diversity. But not all of them are success stories. In an experiment in the *Pattuvam* village in Kerala, the village undertook to register all its natural resources and knowledge pertaining to these resources. The Register was accompanied by the People's Biodiversity Declaration asserting that no monopoly claims on life forms will be accepted by people living in that area. Other provisions detailed, for instance, the conditions under which experiments on life forms collected in the territory of *Pattuvam* could be carried out. The Register was kept as a secret, and information sharing was allowed only in exceptional cases. The Register was thus not aimed at containing the commercial exploitation of local resources by others, but mainly to stop them from asserting rights over prior local knowledge. But there have been problems with this form of documentation.

First, while registers can be very effective to countering patent claims by others over knowledge held locally, they cannot stop the utilisation of genes from plants produced in a given village by outsiders who will then be able to patent novel products and processes after prospecting those genes. Second, a register does not help anyone claiming rights over knowledge. On the contrary, the register is meant to show that such knowledge is in the public domain and is, therefore, not patentable. Third, while open registers can accessed by anyone for a fee, closed registers, as in *Puttuvam* experiment, would be confined to local communities.

They also have very narrow utility because merely acknowledging the knowledge of local people has no bearing on the fact that those who conserve biological resources, or who create and hold knowledge and information relating to the use of those biological resources, are also the "owners" of these resources and should thus have the right to determine the conditions of their sale. The ultimate decision-making body under the Act is the NBA, which may over-ride the interests of these knowledge holders. Benefit-sharing is meant merely as an attempt to make the bargain offered to current owners of knowledge and genetic resources slightly less bitter. To avoid biopiracy, it thus sacrifices farmers and local communities' rights and denies them any rights over their knowledge and inventions.

Furthermore, the issues related to the mode of benefit-sharing and the probable stakeholders thereto are fraught with many problems. This was evident in the case of the *Aarogyappacha* (*trichopus Zeylanicus travancoricus*) experiment, which resulted in an immune-enhancing, anti-stress and anti-fatigue drug *Jeevani* based on the knowledge provided by the *kani* tribe from Kerala.[66] The scientists working with the Government of Kerala's Tropical Botanical Garden and Research Institute (TBGRI) helped to develop the drug out of the active ingredients of the plant. The rights to manufacture *Jeevani* were transferred to a private manufacturer, the Arya Vaidya Pharmacy (Coimbatore) Ltd. for a licence fee of Rupees ten *lakhs* (US$24,000) for seven years with a 2 per cent royalty payable on all sales. The TBGRI decided to give 50 per cent of the fee and royalty to the *Kanis*.[67]

The benefit-sharing arrangement became very controversial as between the numerous stake-holders, including the Kerala Forest Department, as the plant was grown only in a protected area. Once it became commercially viable, the problem of over-extraction of the plant also came to light, raising concerns about its sustainable extraction from its natural habitat. It was also realised by the scientists that, without IP protection, the drug would not generate enough revenue from mere licensing activities alone.

This case, however, has highlighted the potential of genetic resources and the role of indigenous and local communities in their beneficial use, which has also helped the development of the indigenous communities involved. The effective use of intellectual property to protect the rights of the parties involved is a necessary condition for generating the funds which are subjected to the benefit-sharing exercise. But other measures are also required to supplement these IPRs in the benefit-sharing exercise. These include identifying the stakeholders and defining their roles, the sustainable extraction of the bio-resources, acknowledging local informants in patent applications, and other modes of benefit-sharing.[68] The Biological Diversity Act outlines the benefit-sharing framework mainly when a foreign party who seeks access to genetic resources is involved. The Act does not deal adequately with a case similar to the *Aarogyappacha* situation, where the stakeholders were entirely locals and Indian nationals.

3.5 CONCLUSION

The recent developments in biotechnology have highlighted its potential in every field of human activity, particularly in food, medicine, chemicals, animal and plant breeding and environmental problem-solving. Access to PGRs, the raw material for biotechnology, is an essential pre-requisite for the further growth of biotechnology. The holders of PGRs, mainly developing countries, have been deprived of the benefits from their use so far. On the other hand, the technology-holders, mainly from developed countries, through IPRs over these resources after genetically improving them, have restricted the further use of these resources. The two international treaties, the CBD and the TRIPS Agreement, have a common agenda: to put in place a system that ensures the unhindered access to genetic resources and the technology developed therefrom to the respective parties. Any new system needs to take into account the concerns of both the developed and developing biodiversity-rich countries.

Biodiversity-rich countries should thus put in place a system which provides a harmonious construction to their obligations under the TRIPS Agreement and the CBD, ensuring access to their biological resources, while developed countries must transfer the technology used in prospecting these resources. A benefit-sharing mechanism *must be* properly devised: it should reward those who conserve genetic resources and while allaying the fears of technology-holders who are interested in obtaining proper returns from their research and development efforts. The TRIPS Agreement mandates for patents on any "invention," including biotechnology inventions. But the TRIPS Agreement does not provide any definition of "invention," and thus individual countries may decide what they perceive as an invention, giving them a handle to exclude DNA sequences and life forms from patentability. The country may also lay down the requirements regarding novelty and require disclosure of the source from which the material was accessed in any IPR application relating to PGRs.

To give practical shape to the concept of access and benefit-sharing at the international level, it should have a CBD-centric approach, which may include the following lines of action:

(a) The term "invention" must be defined under the TRIPS Agreement, in the absence of which the governments should have the option to exclude all life forms and related knowledge from IPR systems, and for this purpose, necessary changes must be made to Article 27(3)(a) of the TRIPS.[69] A less restrictive form of effective protection can be devised through a *sui generis* system for life forms.
(b) To facilitate the realisation of the objectives of the CBD regarding the equitable sharing of benefits, the TRIPS Agreement should mandatorily specify that norms of disclosure pertaining to an IPR application should reveal the country of origin, and the community which provided the knowledge about the resources pertaining to the subject matter, as well as the proof of consent of such country. This will require the re-casting of Article 29 of the TRIPS Agreement. In other words, the applicant must satisfy the requirement that the provisions of the CBD have been fulfilled.[70]
(c) In order to avoid any unwarranted exploitation of biological and genetic resources, efforts should be made to document the knowledge related to them and clear modalities should be adopted to regulate access to that knowledge at national and international levels.
(d) There should be clear rules establishing commitments by governments not to grant, or to cancel, patents on PGRs, accessed from international germplasm banks,[71] or where the knowledge,

though not properly documented, was in the public domain as in the case of *turmeric* or *neem*. The harmonisation of national patent laws in this area is therefore necessary.

ENDNOTES

1 The CBD entered into force on December 29, 1993 and presently has 187 parties; TRIPS, on the other hand, currently has 148 members.

2 Another important case of biopiracy is the patent sought on *phyllanthus niruri* (commonly known as Bhadharti in Sanskrit and Jaramla in Hindi) for the cure of jaundice or viral hepatitis. Use of *Phyllanthus niruri* for treatment of jaundice has been an ancient and well-recorded innovation in the Indian system of medicine. The Fox Chase Cancer Centre of Philadelphia has applied to the EPO for its use in curing viral hepatitis B.

3 See generally, Shayana Kadidal, "Subject-Matter Imperialism? Biodiversity, Foreign Prior Art and the *Neem* Patent Controversy," 37 IDEA at pages 371 and 375 (1997).

4 See, for example, US patent no. 5,304,718 on quinoa granted to researchers of the Colorado State University. See Pat Roy, Mooney, "The Parts of Life: Agriculture Biodiversity, Indigenous Knowledge, and the Role of the Third System," *Development Dialogue*, Special Issue, at pages 152–54 (Uppsala, 1998).

5 McNeely, "Biodiversity and Agricultural Development: The Crucial Institutional Issues," in D. R. Lee and C. B. Barett (eds.) *Tradeoffs or Synergies? Agricultural Intensification, Economic Development and the Environment*, 399 at page 404 (Wallingford, CABI 2001).

6 See J. P. Mishra, "Biodiversity, Biotechnology and Intellectual Property Rights: Implications for Indian Agriculture," 3 *J. W. Intel. Property* 211 at page 212 (2:2000).

7 J. Straus, "Biodiversity and Intellectual Property" (unpublished paper presented to AIPPI, Japan in Feb. 2001). McManis, quoting World Resource Institute, observes that about one-quarter of all prescription drugs in the United States contain as their active ingredient a compound extracted or derived from plants worth 60 billion dollars in the developed world. Around the world, almost 121 prescription drugs are made from higher plants, almost half of which come from the tropics, and 74 per cent of which were discovered by following up on native folklore claims. See Charles R. McManis, "The Interface Between International Intellectual Property and Environment Protection: Biodiversity and Biotechnology," 76 *Washington U.L.Q.* 255 at page 273 (1:1998).

8 M. S. Swaminathan, "Implementing the Global Biodiversity Convention: IPR for Public Good," 20 *Vikalpa* 3 (4:1995).

9 Manju Sharma. 1999. The Potential of Biotechnology. In *Bioresources and Biotechnology : Policy concerns for the Asian region* 6. Edited by Suman Sahai. Gene Campaign, at page 10.

10 "Prior informed consent" is broadly understood to mean consent to an activity that is given after receiving full disclosure regarding the reasons

for the activity, the specific procedures the activity would entail, the potential risks involved, and the full implications that can realistically be foreseen. See, UNEP Doc. UNEP/CBD/TKBD/1/2, Oct 18, 1997, at page 26.

11 CBD, Article 15(1) and (5).

12 See Article 5 of the IU.

13 The CGIAR, established in 1971, is an informal association of 58 public and private sector members that supports a network of 16 international agricultural centres. It holds one of the world's largest *ex-situ* collections of plant genetic resources in trust for the world community. It contains over 500,000 accessions of more than 3,000 crop, forage, and agro-forestry species in the "genoplasm" banks of these centres. The collection includes farmers' varieties and improved varieties and, in substantial measure, the wild species from which those varieties were created.

14 Emphasis added.

15 TRIPS Agreement, Article 27(3).

16 The CGIAR has placed its collections under the auspices of the FAO which will be made available under a standard Material Transfer Agreement (MTA). It is the CGIAR's stated policy that such germplasm is held in trust for the world community and should not be subject to IPRs by the Centres or the recipients of the material. Under the PGRFA Treaty access to these genetic resources shall be provided only for research, breeding and training in food and agriculture; for multiple-use crops (food and non-food), their importance in food security will be the determinant factor for their accessibility; the recipient shall not claim any IPR or other right over these genetic resources (or their genetic parts). See Article 12 of the Treaty.

17 CBD, Paragraphs 4 and 5 and Article 15.

18 CBD Article 15(6).

19 CBD Article 15(7).

20 See UNEP/CBD/IC/2/14.

21 CBD, Articles 8 and 10.

22 In the context of CBD, the traditional knowledge has been defined to mean "knowledge, innovations and practices of indigenous and local communities embodying traditional lifestyles relevant for the conservation and sustainable use of biological diversity." Available online: (http://www.biodiv.org/socio-eco/traditional/what-is.asp).

23 CBD, Article 10 further reinforces the mandate of Article 8.

24 CBD, Article 17(2).

25 CBD, Article 18(4).

26 PGRFA Treaty, Article 1.

27 PGRFA Treaty, Article 2.

28 PGRFA Treaty, Article 9.

29 "Farmers' Rights" have been defined by FAO in International Understanding on Plant Genetic Resources in 1983, as "rights arising from

the past, present and future contributions of farmers in conserving, improving, and making available plant genetic resources, particularly those in centres of origin or diversity." See FAO Conf. Res. 8/83, 5/89 and 3/91.

30 Philippe Cullet and Radhika Kolluru, "Plant Variety Protection and Farmers' Rights: Towards a Broader Understanding," XXIV *Delhi Law Review* 41 at 48 (2002).

31 CBD, Article 16(1) (Emphasis added by author).

32 CBD, Article 16(2).

33 CBD, Article 16(3).

34 CBD, Article 16(5).

35 Some developing countries have already excluded the patentability of existing biological materials. For example, the Mexican law excludes the patentability of all genetic materials; the Argentine patent law, and the ANDEAN countries' (Bolivia, Colombia, Ecuador, Peru and Venezuela) Decision 344 do not allow the patentability of materials existing in nature. The Brazilian patent law (1996) stipulates that no patents shall be granted with respect to living beings or "biological materials found in nature," even if isolated, including the "genome or germplasm" of any living being. See CGRFA (FAO) Background Study Paper No. 8 on "Access to Plant Genetic Resources and Intellectual Property Rights" by Carlos M. Correa, page 9 (April 1999).

36 Cooperation has been emphasised under Article 18 (CBD) also for the "development and use of technologies, including indigenous and traditional technologies" relevant to the objectives of the Convention.

37 CBD, Article 19(1). Emphasis is placed on *in-situ* research, where feasible.

38 The CBD was signed by the US on June 4, 1993, only after a number of US pharmaceutical and biotechnology firms and organisations that were previously opposed to the CBD changed their position, who feared that their continued opposition to the Convention might simply exclude them from exploring PGRs in developing countries, Because of its strong stand on IPRs, it is doubtful that the US will ratify the Convention in its present format.

39 TRIPS, Article 31(b).

40 TRIPS, Article 31(k).

41 TRIPS, Article 7. See also Article 19, CBD.

42 It is reported that every region of the world is dependent on genetic material, which originated in other regions for 50 per cent of its basic food production, and, for several regions of the world, this dependency is close to 100 per cent. See Carlos M. Correa, above at note 35, at page 2.

43 See the case of medicinal plant *arogyapaacha* (referred later in this paper) in India, about which the tribal people passed on the knowledge about the useful properties of the plant.

44 Decision 391, July 1996.

45 *Ibid*. Article 22.

46 For more details, see Doc. UNEP/CBD/COP/3/20, October 5, 1996.

47 See World Resources Institute, *Biodiversity Prospecting: Using Genetic Resources for Sustainable Development* 2 (1993).

48 For some examples on bio-diversity prospecting, see S. K. Verma, "Biodiversity and Intellectual Property Rights" 39 *JILI* 203, at pages 212–13 (1997).

49 Charak K. S. and Manju Sharma, "Biotechnology in Agriculture, Challenges and Opportunities," 51 *Indian Farming* 10–18 (8:2001); R.T.Gahukar, "Biotechnology in Plant Protection," 24 *Pesticides Information* 13–18 (1:1998).

50 R. T. Gahukar. 2003. Issues Relating to the Patentability of Biotechnological Subject Matter in Indian Agriculture. 78 *JIPRs* 9–22: 17.

51 Vandana Shiva, "Biodiversity Totalitarianison : IPRs as Seed Monopolies," 32 *Eco & Pol. Weekly* 2582 (Oct–Dec 1997).

52 See M. S. Swaminathan, "Ethics and Equality in the Use and Collection of Plant Genetic Resources: Some Issues and Approaches," in International Plant Genetic Resource Institute, *Ethics and Equity in Conservation and Use of Genetic Resources for Sustainable Food Security*, 7 (1997).

53 Section 5 of the 1970 Patents Act relates to inventions where only methods or processes of manufacture are patentable. Products of such processes are presently not protected under the Act. Under the TRIPS Agreement Article 65 (4), India is obliged to provide product patents by January 1, 2005.

54 See section 10(d).

55 Under the new provision (p) of section 64, a patent can be revoked when "the complete specification does not disclose or wrongly mention the source or geographical origin of biological material used for the invention."

56 Section 64(q). This provision is in line with the Bonn Guidelines on Access to Genetic Resources and Fair and Equitable sharing of the Benefits Arising out of their Utilisation (adopted at Hague in 2002), paragraph 16(d)(ii), suggesting Parties to adopt "measures to encourage the disclosure of the country of origin of the genetic resources and of the origin of traditional knowledge, innovations and practices of indigenous and local communities in applications for intellectual property rights."

57 Union Internationale Pour La Protection Des Obtentions Vegétalé (International Union for the Protection of New Varieties of Plants), 1961 has been amended in 1972, 1978 and 1991. The 1991 Act is in force since April 1999.

58 *Ibid.* See sections 39 and 41.

59 Any seed put in package or any other container and labelled to indicate as protected variety is a branded seed.

60 Section 39. The extent to which this provision will be meaningful in practice is, however, open to debate. To obtain protection, farmers' varieties must conform to the UPOV criteria of distinctness, uniformity and stability. Given that breeding efforts of farmers typically occur *in-situ*, and that farmers (unlike breeders in formal breeding programmes) cannot entirely control the agro-ecological conditions in which varieties are bred, it is

questionable to what extent varieties claimed by farmers will meet these qualifying criteria.

61 See section 41 of the Act.

62 Compare with Article 27(2), TRIPS Agreement, and the Patents (Amendment) Act, sec. 3(b).

63 See sections 48 to 51 of the Act.

64 In these circumstances, the Plant Variety Protection Act will be applicable.

65 Philippe Cullet, "Revision of the TRIPS Agreement concerning the Protection of Plant Varieties," 2 *J. W. Intel. Property* 617, at page 649 (4:1999).

66 See for details of this case, UNEP and WIPO joint submission, on "The Role of Intellectual Property Rights in the Sharing of Benefits from the use of Biological Resources and associated Traditional Knowledge: Selected Case Studies," 32–50 (April 2000).

67 This was done as per the guidelines of the Council of Scientific and Industrial Research (CSIR).

68 Benefits-sharing should include other inputs such as non-monetary contributions through capacity-building, awareness creation, education, removal of informational asymmetries, sharing of research findings, acknowledgement of knowledge providers on product packages and on patent applications. See note 65 above, at page 44.

69 On IPRs, the PGRFA Treaty provides, "Recipients shall not claim any intellectual property or other rights that limit the facilitated access to the plant genetic resources for food and agriculture, or their genetic parts or components, in the form received from the Multilateral System." Article 12 (3). The Treaty, however, is limited to food and agriculture, and the use of PGRs for other biotechnological inventions is outside its purview.

70 The Patents (Amendment) Act (India) provides such a provision. But there is no such provision in Plant Variety and Farmers' Rights Act.

71 It is, however, doubtful whether such a rule can have a retrospective operation, made applicable to those IPRs/patents granted before the coming into force of the CBD.

CHAPTER 4

Patenting of Higher Life Forms: A Canadian Perspective

CATHERINE GECI[1] AND BARTHA MARIA KNOPPERS[2]

4.1 INTRODUCTION

Intellectual property protection is indispensable. Patents, trade secrets and copyrights provide systems for intellectual property protection. Yet, while a patent guarantees the open publication and the exclusive use of an invention for commercialisation, a trade secret hides the results of an experiment, the process used to create a product, or the product itself (until it is commercialised and sold). Copyright protects original works of authorship fixed in a tangible medium of expression. Although protecting an invention by secrecy is a common feature of certain forms of industrial research[1], patenting is the method of choice in the field of biotechnology and pharmaceuticals. Patents on DNA sequences, protein molecules, and drugs derived from these substances have been filed worldwide[2]. Some of these patents have sparked technical, ethical and social concerns because of their implications[3].

Among the issues that currently fuel debate in the field of intellectual property, the patentability of higher life forms raises concern, especially in Canada. Indeed, since the Canadian Supreme Court's decision in *Harvard College v. Canada (Commissioner of Patents)*[4], discrepancies between the Canadian, American and European patent regimes have been

1 M.Sc., Student (Third Year), Faculty of Law, Université de Montréal.
2 Professor of Law, Canada Research Chair in Law and Medicine, Université de Montréal.

highlighted. Moreover, the Supreme Court of Canada's majority decision in *Harvard College* does not parallel the recommendations concerning the patentability of higher life forms put forth by the Canadian Biotechnology Advisory Committee (CBAC)[5]. Thus, we will first review the CBAC's recommendations on the patentability of higher life forms, followed by the Supreme Court's decision pertaining to the patentability of the "oncomouse". Finally, we will address the ethical considerations for the patenting of higher life forms, both at the regional and international levels.

4.2 CIPO'S POSITION AND THE CBAC'S RECOMMENDATIONS ON THE PATENTABILITY OF HIGHER LIFE FORMS

The report issued in June 2002 by CBAC entitled *Patenting of Higher Life Forms and Related Issues* was intended to provide advice and suggest directions to the government. After careful consideration of the principles and values guiding the CBAC[6], 13 recommendations were put forward, nine of which will be discussed below.

First, no country allows patents on the human body, Canada included. The CBAC supports this position. It recommends that the *Patent Act*[7] be amended to explicitly state in general terms that "no patent shall be granted in human bodies at any stage of development."[8] However, this restriction does not prevent the patenting of genes, partial DNA sequences, proteins, cell lines, or stem cells of human, animal or plant origin. In fact, the Manual of Patent Office Practice (MOPOP), published by the Canadian Intellectual Property Office (CIPO)[9], includes specifications relating to biological material, nucleotide and amino-acid sequence listings, as well as hybrid and gapped sequences. Although the CIPO maintains that human, animal and plant proteins, genes and cells are patentable, it has always sustained the position that the *Patent Act* does not allow for the patenting of higher life forms such as plants and animals.

Second, concerning the patenting of higher life forms such as plants, seeds and non-human animals, the CBAC's recommendation propose that if they meet the criteria of novelty, non-obviousness and utility, they should be to be recognised as patentable subject matter. It is interesting to note that this recommendation fueled much debate amongst members of the Committee. Indeed, some members held the view that the extension of patents should be granted to higher life forms while others suggested the opposite. The arguments in favor of patenting higher life forms included:

1) that patents provide the necessary financial incentive to industry to invent, disclose and make available new technology to the Canadian public by helping industry attract investment and recoup its costs of research and development (within the scope of three limitations: the farmer's privilege, the innocent bystander privilege and the experimental use exception; see text below);
2) that the availability of patent protection fosters openness and innovation in the scientific community by providing an alternative to trade secrecy protection;
3) that Canada may suffer economically if it does not follow its major trading partners such as the United States, the European Union and Japan who allow patents on higher life forms;
4) that patents on DNA sequences which are currently permitted can be used to claim control over a whole plant or animal. If patents on whole plants and animals are explicitly allowed, differentiation between specific patent rights that pertain to whole plants and animals and those that pertain to molecular sequences only could create an opportunity to balance corporate interests and to ensure the respect of reasonable boundaries for patent rights[10].

At the other side of the spectrum, arguments against the patenting of higher life forms were considered. These included:

1) Patenting plants and animals raises serious moral and ethical questions relating to biodiversity, animal rights, economics and environmental sustainability, and the commodification of life;
2) Patents on higher life forms are unnecessary since patents on DNA sequences, genes, or the process necessary to invent a plant or animal, as well as trade secrets or plant breeders' rights sufficiently protect the inventor's interests;
3) Patents on higher non-human life forms threaten to undermine the economic viability of industries that rely on plants and animals[11].

The recommendations formulated by the CBAC were not meant to be absolutist. Rather, they had the overall public good in mind. The formulation of patent policy with respect of higher life forms necessitates a commitment to justice in order to balance the interests of the various stakeholders and the effects of patents on society as a whole. That was why it was maintained that the rights of patent holders must not extend too far. The scope of patent rights with respect to higher life forms should, according to the CBAC, be subject to certain limits in order to ensure that the scope of the patent rights granted is no greater than the patent rights granted over other non-biological inventions and to make certain that patent rights do not unreasonably prejudice other industries and institutions. The limitations to patent rights in the field of biotechnology would include the farmer's privilege, the protection for innocent bystanders, and the research and experimental use exception.

The CBAC's recommendation for the farmer's privilege is that it should be explicitly included in the *Patent Act*[12]. It specifies that farmers should be permitted to save and sow seeds from patented plants or to breed patented animals, as long as the progeny are not sold as commercial propagating material or in a manner that undermines the commercial value to its creator of a genetically engineered animal. Relationships between the different legislative texts that provide some type of protection to farmers such as the *Patent Act*[13], the *Plant Breeder's Rights Act*[14], and the *Animal Pedigree Act*[15] would need to be harmonised. At the international level, plant breeders' rights were recognised under the International Convention for the Protection of New Varieties of Plants (UPOV) of 1961. A revision of the UPOV Convention in 1991 allowed countries to provide both patent and plant variety protection to plants. Thus, a breeder has rights to prevent others from breeding the same plant and from breeding plants that are significant derivatives of the original plant[16]. But Canada has not yet ratified the 1991 version of UPOV. If Canada decides to permit patents on plants, it would either have to carve out a patent exclusion so that a genus or species subject to plant breeders' rights cannot be patented, or it must ratify the 1991 UPOV Convention.[17] Incidentally, the farmer's privilege is part of the European Community's patent law: the farmer may reproduce non-human animals and certain plants (the latter for a relatively small fee) for his or her own use, without the consent of the patent holder.

The need for protection of innocent bystanders stems from the fact that the reproduction of patented seeds, genetic material and animals cannot always be controlled or known by those who grow the plants or raise the animals. The reproduction of patented inventions without the permission of the patent holder constitutes infringement. The CBAC therefore recommends that the *Patent Act* include provisions that protect innocent bystanders from claims of patent infringement with respect to the adventitious spreading of genetic seed or patented genetic material or the insemination of an animal by a patented animal.

The final exception, the experimental use exception, attempts to balance the interests of the patent holders in commercialising their inventions with those of society in fostering further research. Indeed, patent legislation in many countries states that research using, and experimentation on, a patented invention is not an infringement of the patent holder's rights[18]. However, the extent of the experimental use exemption varies widely. In the United States for example, the exemption only applies to research having the purpose of "philosophical enquiry," which means that the research has no reasonable possibility of being commercially applied. In the European Union, the experimental use exemption allows industrial research on the invention itself, rather than the mere use of the invention[19].

In Canada, the full scope of the experimental use exemption has not yet been fully outlined by the courts, especially with regard to biotechnological inventions. The consensus is that the exemption permits persons other than the patent holder to use a patented invention for a non-commercial purpose, usually research, or to determine if the invention works as described in the patent[20].

A lack of clarity on the scope of the research exemption can easily become a pitfall for independent and university researchers. Furthermore, since both genetically engineered crops and animal breeding often become the platform for new research, the scope of the exemption as it applies to the patenting of whole plants and animals can become the focal point for scientists who need to know what research they can or cannot conduct without infringing a patent. In order to fill the void created by the uncertainty of the breadth of the research exemption, the CBAC recommended that there should not be a patent infringement when a patented process or product is used either privately and for non-commercial purposes, or to study the subject matter of the patented invention to investigate its properties, improve upon it, or create a new product or process. But, if a research tool is consumed in an experiment, the researcher would be required to purchase the right to use that tool in the experiment through a license fee. With the incorporation of the CBAC's recommendations into current patent law, Canada's policies would be aligned with those of the European countries abiding by the *European Community Patent Convention*[21], and would not prevent it from complying with its international trade obligations. In addition, this view would be consistent with the Nuffield Council on Bioethics' recommendation that companies should work together to extend the concept of the 'research exemption' throughout the industry for DNA sequences which appear in patents and which have a use in research[22].

The CBAC's position does not reflect that of the CIPO. To reiterate, CIPO has always sustained that the *Patent Act* does not allow for the patenting of higher life forms such as plants and animals. Canadian case law has also addressed the patentability of certain biological material and lower life forms. For example, cell lines derived from higher life forms are patentable as was established in *Re Application for Patent of Connaught Laboratories*[23]. Also, other types of lower life forms have been deemed patentable subject matter: micro-organisms, for example, are patentable if they are reproducible *en masse* and in a uniform fashion[24]. Plant cell lines containing transgenic genes are equally patentable[25]. However, the CBAC maintains the view that there is no bright line between the patent claims that can be made with respect to DNA sequences and cell lines, which are patentable, and those relating to whole plants, seeds and non-human animals which are not[26].

4.3 THE "ONCOMOUSE DECISION"

The Supreme Court of Canada was asked to determine whether the "oncomouse" (a transgenic mouse used for cancer testing) was an "invention" under the *Patent Act*. By a five to four majority, the Court held that higher life forms were not patentable because they were neither a "manufacture" nor a "composition of matter" within the meaning of "invention" under the act. The majority held that a reading of the words of the *Patent Act* supports such a conclusion. It also decided that the wording of section 2 of the Canadian *Patent Act* should be strictly construed and that higher life forms were not implicitly incorporated within the definition of an invention. However, it should be noted that this was a 5-4 decision.

According to the four dissenting judges, the "oncomouse" results from a scientific achievement that alters every cell in the body of an animal. This altered form does not exist in nature but is an inventive "composition of matter" resulting from human modification of the mouse's genetic material and should therefore be patentable. Nevertheless, the entire Court pointed out that, regardless of whether the "oncomouse" was deserving of patent protection, it was up to Parliament to draw the line between lower life forms which were patentable and higher life forms which were not. Nothing prevented Parliament from deciding that the patenting of higher life forms should be allowed, either generally or subject to certain exclusions or limitations on patent rights[27].

This decision overturned the conclusion reached by the Federal Court of Appeal[28]. The Federal Court of Appeal had issued a 2-1 split decision by which the majority held that the "oncomouse", as a genetically-modified mouse used in cancer research, was a "composition of matter" within the scope of the meaning of "invention" under the *Patent Act*. Therefore, before the ruling of the Supreme Court, the definition of "invention" included genetically modified, non-human mammals for a short time.

The only other Canadian court case involving the patentability of higher life forms decided at the level of the Supreme Court of Canada is *Pioneer Hi-Bred Ltd. v. Canada (Commissioner of Patents)*[29]. In this case, a new soybean variety was obtained by hybridisation. This soybean variety was held not to be an invention according to the *Patent Act* because it did not meet with the traditional conditions and requirements of a patent. However, effective patent protection can still be obtained in Canada for biotechnological inventions involving the genetic manipulation of higher life forms provided that the claims are correctly worded. For example, in the case of *Monsanto v. Schmeiser*[30] the patent enforced by Monsanto related to a genetically engineered plant. The claims in the Monsanto patent did not specifically claim such a plant. The patent actually claimed a chimeric gene and plant cells that contained this chimeric gene. In this case, the Supreme Court of Canada upheld the validity of the patent, and more importantly held that Schmeiser's reproduction and growth of a transformed plant equated to the reproduction of the claimed gene and plant cells containing the gene. Patent infringement was held to have occurred. In other words, the holder of a patent over an artificially constructed gene, as well as cells containing that gene can prevent others from growing plants that contain that gene or cells, even though the patent does not cover the entire plant.[31]

It is interesting to note that in no country with a patent system comparable to Canada has a patent on the "oncomouse" been refused. Indeed, the patent on the "oncomouse" in the United States was issued on April 12, 1988[32], and its European equivalent was issued on May 31, 1992[33]. However, both in the United States and Europe, the patenting of the "oncomouse" did meet with some opposition.

The patentability of life forms is a question that has already been addressed by the American courts. In fact, in 1980 the Supreme Court ruled in *Diamond v. Chakrabarty* that a human-made micro-organism is patentable[34] as a "manufacture" or a "composition of matter" within the meaning of the patent statute. In that case, the Court opined that the patentee had produced a bacterium with markedly different characteristics from any found in nature which had the potential for significant utility. The bacterium was not nature's handiwork, but the patentee's own. Although a microbacterium is a "lower life form" and a mammal is a "higher life form," the same principle applied in *Chakrabarty* was considered for the patenting of the "oncomouse". The United States Patent and Trademark Office (USPTO) was the first to grant a patent to the "oncomouse". This ruling by the USPTO was challenged by a consortium of animal rights groups. However, after several appeals, the Court of Appeal for the Federal Circuit eventually ruled that the Animal Legal Defense Fund lacked the necessary standing to challenge the USPTO's authority to grant animal patents[35]. The challenge was thus dismissed without the validity of the patent having been determined. Furthermore, as to the scope of the "oncomouse patent", it is interesting to note that the patent on the "oncomouse" that was granted in its initial form covered any non-human transgenic mammal, unlike the EPO decision where the patent covers only transgenic rodents with the cancerous gene.

Similarly in Europe, the patenting of living organisms such as the "oncomouse" raised a plethora of issues. Indeed, the European Patent Office (EPO) initially rejected the "oncomouse" patent application stating that the mouse was an "animal variety" and therefore was excluded from patentability. However, in 1992, the EPO Appeal Board eventually ruled that the claims were allowable and the "oncomouse" patent was accepted. Opposition notices were immediately filed by 16 different parties claiming that the patent violated European morality provisions. The opposition notices filed were mainly from animal rights and anti-vivisectionist groups from the UK, Germany and Austria. In deciding whether the "oncomouse" should be rejected on morality grounds, the EPO balanced the potential risks to the environment, any suffering of the animal, and concerns about the cloning of human genes against the potential benefits that the mouse offered to mankind. Eventually, the EPO Appeal Board decided that the benefits offered by the "oncomouse" outweighed the potential risks and the patent was granted. It is also interesting to note that the Opposition Division of the European Patent Office (EPO) responsible for the "oncomouse" case decided to limit this patent to transgenic rodents with the cancerous gene, and not to extend the scope of the patent to all mammals as the US decision allowed.[36] Therefore, inventions relating to animals are patentable if the technical feasibility of the invention is not confined to a specific plant or animal variety. If an animal can be obtained only through genetic engineering, to the exclusion of any natural breeding, the invention relating to such an animal may be protected by a patent.

The same risk/benefit analysis used in the case of the "oncomouse" has also been performed on a subsequent European patent application—Upjohn's Hairless Mouse—which was genetically engineered to be completely hairless or bald. Its purpose was to provide an animal model for testing hair restorative products and wool production techniques. The EPO Appeal Board, in applying the risk/benefit analysis, decided that the benefits to humans offered by the Upjohn's Hairless Mouse did not outweigh either the risks posed or any suffering of the animal, and so this patent application was refused[37]. Therefore, in Europe, a patent is not simply granted for a non-human organism that presents different characteristics from any other known organism. Other considerations, such as risk-benefit evaluations, or animal welfare considerations are relevant to determinations of an invention's patentability.

Since the granting of the patent on the "oncomouse", the patentability of living organisms has been reiterated in Directive 98/44/EC of the European Parliament and of the Council of July 6, 1998 on the legal protection of biotechnological inventions. The Directive 98/44/EC allows for the patenting of living organisms as well as for human genes. More specifically, an element isolated from the human body, including a sequence or partial sequence of a gene, by techniques of identification, purification, characterisation and multiplication, may constitute a patentable invention, even if the structure of that element is identical to that of the natural element[38]. The inventions relating to living organisms and genes that are eligible for patent protection in the European Union must fulfill the conditions of patentability: novelty, inventive step and industrial application[39]. Furthermore, the Directive allows for the patenting of plants and animals provided that the application of the invention is not technically confined to a single plant or animal variety.

Therefore, a patent for a novel gene sequence that confers a benefit to a plant will extend to any plant in which the gene has been artificially inserted. Finally, it bears noting that the preamble of the Directive states that:

> Whereas if an invention is based on biological material of human origin or if it uses such material, where a patent application is filed, the person from whose body the material is taken must have had an opportunity of expressing free and informed consent thereto, in accordance with national laws.[40]

It remains to be seen if this "preambular" statement will be translated, at the national level, into an explicit consent requirement or simply notification of the possibility of eventual commercialisation and patenting.

4.4 ETHICAL FRAMEWORK FOR THE PATENTING OF HIGHER LIFE FORMS

4.4.1 CBAC principles

The relationship between patent law and ethics is not foreign; yet harmonising both fields is difficult. With respect to biotechnology, many ethical and social considerations must be taken into account when designing a comprehensive framework for the patentability of higher life forms. In Europe, the "oncomouse" decision[41] and the Greenpeace decision[42] both highlight the difficulties that confront patent law when ethical concerns are raised. In an attempt to address these social and ethical considerations, the CBAC has proposed recommendations relating to biotechnology within the scope of the principles and values it chose to guide it, namely: justice, accountability, autonomy, beneficence, respect for diversity, knowledge and caution[43]. It concentrated on the application of these principles through: benefit-sharing, the protection of traditional knowledge and the issue of the commodification of life.

In its report entitled, *Patenting of Higher Life Forms*, CBAC discusses the key social and ethical issues involved in deciding whether higher life forms should be patentable in Canada. Its recommendations reflect the desire to improve the patent system, to share the benefits of biotechnological inventions, and to respect traditional knowledge in relation to intellectual property. The ethical framework proposed by the CABC may orient the eventual direction of Canada in the field of biotechnology. Developing and refining these proposed principles is undoubtedly one of the CBAC's highest priorities[44].

4.4.1.1 Benefit-sharing

In relation to benefit-sharing, CBAC's recommendation is based partly on the Human Genome Organization (HUGO) Ethics Committee's *Statement* on the subject. HUGO's recommendations included: (1) that all humanity share in, and have access to, the benefits of genetic research; (2) that benefits not be limited to those individuals who participated in the research; (3) that there be prior discussion with groups or communities on the issue of benefit-sharing; (4) that even in the absence of profits, immediate health benefits as determined by community needs could be provided; (5) that at a minimum, all research participants should receive information about general research outcomes and an indication of appreciation; (6) that profit-making entities dedicate a percentage of their annual net profit to healthcare infrastructure and/or to humanitarian efforts[45]. That general benefits of new research and novel medicines should be available to all does not parallel the traditional view that benefit-sharing is limited to the sharing of royalties from patent fees or profits from sales of compounds. According to the HUGO *Statement*, benefit-sharing could imply giving free medicine to the patients who gave blood samples to mediate drug discovery for instance. Therefore, pharmaceutical companies also have a moral responsibility towards the community in the context of gene and protein patenting[46].

Another document which inspired the CBAC's recommendations was the Convention on Biological Diversity (CBD)[47] to which Canada has been a party since 1992. The CBD reiterates that states have sovereign rights over their biological resources. As a party to the Convention, Canada has agreed to "facilitate access to the genetic resources in their territory to other parties, obtain prior informed consent when accessing those resources, and take measures to achieve a fair and equitable sharing of the results of research and development and the benefits arising from the commercial and other utilisation of genetic resources within the member country that provided the resources."[48] Also, the Bonn *Guidelines on Access to Genetic Resources and Fair and Equitable Sharing of the Benefits Arising out of their Utilization*[49] provide guidance for the development of access and benefit-sharing regimes and inform the practices of stakeholders in access and benefit-sharing arrangements regimes. Through legal, administrative and policy measures, the disclosure of the country of origin of the genetic resources and the origin of traditional knowledge, innovations and practices of indigenous and local communities in applications for patent or other intellectual property protection is envisioned[50].

The aforementioned documents support CBAC's recommendation on benefit-sharing. The role of government and stakeholders involved in funding research, and establishing guidelines or codes of conduct for the ethical conduct of research, involves developing policies and practices for the sharing of benefits derived from research involving genetic material. Within the context of research based on human genetic material specifically, the CBAC recommends that the benefits be shared with the groups or communities who provided the material. With respect to research based on plant and animal genetic material, the CBAC recommends that Canada continue to participate in the implementation and compliance of international agreements, ratify the *International Treaty on Plant and Genetic Resources for Food and Agriculture*[51], and generally, encourage and facilitate benefit sharing arrangements between the users of genetic resources and traditional and local communities within Canada. One of the benefit-sharing mechanisms that could be developed might include possible formulas for the sharing of benefits based on different benefit-indicators[52].

It is interesting to note that CBAC's draft recommendation is much more succinct than the recommendations adopted in the final report. Indeed, in contrast with the draft recommendation suggesting that "the federal research granting councils, the National Committee on Ethics in Human Research and other relevant bodies explore options for sharing the benefits of research (including its commercial exploitation) with the communities or populations involved in the research,"[53] the final report elaborates explicitly on the benefit-sharing of human, animal and plant genetic material research.

4.4.1.2 Traditional knowledge

Traditional knowledge may be defined as the knowledge, innovations and practices of indigenous and other local populations, embodying traditional lifestyles and practices adapted to the local environment[54]. The use of traditional knowledge for researchers may narrow their search for sources of new medicinal compounds or other patentable material. Indeed, the commercialisation of products derived from genetic resources of the holders of traditional knowledge has proved that traditional knowledge may actually be an asset of significant economic value to the community of which the knowledge holders are part. Benefit-sharing arrangements may thus become increasingly important for the community. One example of such an arrangement is the bioprospecting agreement between Costa Rica and Merck and Co., which enabled Merck to look for medicinal compounds in the rainforests of Costa Rica in exchange for financial assistance to protect the rainforest, as well as a share of any patent that results from the bioprospecting activity[55].

Addressing the issue of protecting traditional knowledge within the patent system is equally of value. The World Intellectual Property Organization (WIPO) has in fact established an Intergovernmental Committee on Intellectual Property and Genetic Resources, Traditional Knowledge and Folklore, which is considering a new intellectual property scheme that specifically addresses community-based knowledge and its protection. Similarly, the *Cartagena Agreement*[56] recognises plant breeders' rights and controls access to genetic resources thereby reaffirming that traditional knowledge may not be restricted to modern national boundaries and that cooperation may prove useful.

In addition, the possibility of considering traditional knowledge as prior art in the view of patent authorities has been suggested[57]. Indeed, prior art has generally been defined as written or published descriptions of the invention undergoing examination by the patent authorities. Therefore, knowledge that has been transmitted orally would not be taken into account when determining whether an invention is sufficiently novel so as to be granted a patent. However, many databases or registries of traditional knowledge have been created to put such knowledge into the public domain. From the Canadian perspective, the CBAC recommends that the CIPO provide guidance to patent examiners on assessing whether traditional knowledge that has been made public through oral as well as written or published means may be considered prior art.

4.4.1.3 Commodification of life

Applying patent law to higher life forms undoubtedly raises issues concerning the commodification of life as well as genetic material since an invention that is patented may be commercialised. An example of this type of commodification is exemplified in *Moore v. Regents of the University of California*[58] where the removal and patenting of Moore's cells by his physician resulted in the development of an anti-cancer drug without his informed consent.

It is interesting to note that the Canadian Parliament does not have jurisdiction within the *Patent Act* to regulate matters pertaining to human life and genetic material, or to animal ownership and animal welfare outside of the patent scheme; rather, "legislation governing property and contract rights between individuals, including the ownership of non-human animals and plants, falls under provincial jurisdiction."[59]

The CBAC suggested that other principles for the ethical framework should be further considered in the underlying moral and philosophical debate on biotechnology and intellectual property. They would include whether or not humanity should have the right to own life and manipulate life, further discussion on the principles of biodiversity, environmental protection, responsible stewardship of life, non-malfeasance, freedom to explore, and finally, respect for human rights and dignity[60].

4.4.2 The international ethical framework

One of the international agreements that has had an enormous impact on intellectual property rights is the Agreement on Trade-Related Aspects of Intellectual Property Rights (TRIPS). Essentially, TRIPS provides that all member states of the World Trade Organization (WTO) must develop a patent regime, or something similar to a patent regime at the very least, for the protection of biological resources. More specifically, article 27.3(b) relates to genetic resources and biological diversity. Although TRIPS is designed to ensure that all technologies and their products may be patented, including those formerly considered unpatentable (pharmaceutical and medical processes and their products, biological material, plants and microorganisms), certain exceptions are permitted. According to article 27.3(b), member countries are allowed to exclude plants and animals from patentability as well as certain biological material[61]. Higher life forms could therefore be excluded from patentability. Article 27.3(b) thus provided a source of heated debate since most developing nations wish to expand the scope of the article whilst other countries (the United States for one) propose to narrow this exception. Canada has not yet adopted a formal position on this matter[62].

The Convention on Biological Diversity is especially important in the contexts of traditional knowledge and benefit-sharing as discussed in the paragraphs above. It also specifies for the first time in a legally binding document that biological diversity of each and every country is the possession of that country (Articles 3 and 10). However, it is important to highlight the differences between the CBD and TRIPS[63]: (1) The CBD confers sovereign rights to national states over their biological resources while TRIPS proposes that the rights of individual states to the patenting of biological resources are largely restricted; (2) TRIPS does not provide for any benefit-sharing between the provider of the materials and the holder of the patent while the CBD does; (3) TRIPS does not recognise granting prior informed consent before receiving access to the biological resources of a given state while the CBD does; and (4) TRIPS gives greater weight to private property and private interests while the CBD attributes priority to public interest and community possessions (once state sovereignty is recognised). Ultimately, these inconsistencies could in fact impede international discussion on the issue of patenting of higher life forms, especially from an ethical and societal viewpoint.

Not only have international agreements influenced the debate on the patenting of higher life forms, but certain documents have significantly contributed to the discussion by addressing the question of the patentability of genetic material. The international consensus is that biotechnological inventions are subject to the same criteria as other inventions in the field of technology. Furthermore, although a DNA sequence may not be patentable in its original form since it constitutes a part of the common heritage of humanity[64] and does not meet patentability criteria, DNA that has been isolated with a proven function of industrial application may be patented. We have already seen that the 1998 European *Directive on Biotechnological Inventions* maintains this position.

A similar phenomenon is observed at the national level. For example, the UK Nuffield Council on Bioethics has proposed an ethical framework for gene patenting[65]. Specifically, it provides two main recommendations: first, that patents on DNA sequences be the exception rather than the rule; and second, that the tests of inventiveness and usefulness be more rigorously applied to applications for genetic patents. In relation to the patenting of higher life forms, it is possible to speculate that the same requirements that are considered for DNA patenting could apply to the patenting of higher life forms.

Finally, advocacy organisations are diametrically opposed to the patentability of genetic material for fear that it may be exploited commercially for nothing more than profit[66]. Yet, the concerns related to the patenting of genetic material do not always address the patenting of higher life forms *per se*. In fact, the American Medical Association makes the distinction quite clear: "... DNA sequences, however, are not tantamount to human life, and it is unclear where or whether qualities uniquely human are found in genetic material."[67] Therefore, even though the link between the patenting of DNA and life forms is tangible, there may not be any synchronisation between the patentability requirements for genetic material and those for the patenting of higher life forms.

Moreover, UNESCO's 1997 *Universal Declaration on the Human Genome and Human Rights* stipulates in Article 4 that: "The human genome in its natural state shall not give rise to financial gain." Yet, where there is eventual patenting, UNESCO in its *International Declaration on Human Genetic Data* (2003) incorporated HUGO's (2000) concept of benefit-sharing in Article 6 which states that: "a) There should be reciprocity and exchange of information with fair return; b) There are various mechanisms available for fair returns, for example, non-exclusive licenses, copyright, monetary, non-monetary (e.g., publication or credits, database pools, and central repositories; etc.) Any fees should not restrict the free flow of scientific information and equitable access."

Indeed, UNESCO's 2003 *Declaration* elaborates further in Article 19 on the Sharing of Benefits:

(a) In accordance with domestic law or policy and international agreements, benefits resulting from the use of human genetic data, human proteomic data or biological samples collected for medical and scientific research should be shared with the society as a whole and the international community. In giving effect to this principle, benefits may take any of the following forms:
   (i) special assistance to the persons and groups that have taken part in the research;
   (ii) access to medical care;
   (iii) provision of new diagnostics, facilities for new treatments or drugs stemming from the research;

(iv) support for health services;
(v) capacity-building facilities for research purposes;
(vi) development and strengthening of the capacity of developing countries to collect and process human genetic data, taking into consideration their specific problems;
(vii) any other form consistent with the principles set out in this Declaration.

(b) Limitations in this respect could be provided by domestic law and international agreements.

4.5 CONCLUSION

While this Canadian contribution to the debate on intellectual property rights has concentrated on the patenting of higher life forms and in particular on the divergent positions taken on the "oncomouse," the ethical issues spill over from the plant or animal "kingdoms" to encompass humans. This is only natural under an "ecosystems approach" to ethical issues.

Even while strengthening the criteria of patentability, there is no doubt that we need to move beyond the "patentability" debate. This is all the more evident considering that "the international intellectual property regime for the development of genetic resources has been so carved up by patents and licenses that it is becoming, in the view of many, an "anti-commons"."[68] This, together with commercial interests and the approach of State sovereignty over genetic resources, has hampered an international approach because it limits the possibility of benefit-sharing as well as the construction of international, publicly accessible, genetic material and data.

It is our opinion that we need further experience in developing the benefit-sharing approach in practice. Most importantly, we should encourage cross-licensing, and where public health is at stake, compulsory, non-exclusive licensing. Another idea is the creation of patent pools that aggregate licenses using a joint venture for administration. Finally, an independent and non-profit patent clearinghouse is perhaps the most novel reform to be suggested:

> A 'clearinghouse' is any agency that brings together seekers and providers of goods, services or information, thus matching demand and supply. A patent clearinghouse would function in much the same way as a copyright collective—it would

> administer the rights of several patent owners; authority would be granted by the patent owner to the collective to set license terms to others who would be permitted to work the patent. The patent clearinghouse would be made available to all users of the technology and users would pay only for those patents they require. The fee would be standard and, given the lack of negotiation, the transaction cost would be low.[69]

Similar to the notion of global public goods from the HUGO *Statement on Genomic Databases*[70], this approach would ensure fair access and fair economic return. It is our opinion that as much effort should be put into the debate on licensing, on public repositories and on benefit-sharing as we have done for patents. Seeing as Canada is not in conformity with its international counterparts on patenting, it is in these three domains that common ground can be found. It is there that the benefits of biotechnology will be realised and made accessible to all.

ENDNOTES

1 Darryl R. J. Macer, "Inventions, patents and morality," in UNESCO, *Encyclopedia of Life Support Systems*, 2001, available online: (http://www.biol.tsukuba.ac.jp/~macer/Papers/ipmoral.htm).

2 Organisation for Economic Co-operation and Development (OECD), *Compendium of Patent Statistics*, Paris, 2003, pp. 25–26; Sandy M. Thomas, M. M. Hopkins and M. Brady, "Shares in the human genome: The future of patenting DNA," (2002) 20 *Nature Biotechnology* 1185; Mike Scott and Jill Valentine, "Impact of gene patenting on R&D and commerce" (2003) 21(7) *Nature Biotechnology* 729; Richard J. Warburg, Arthur Wellman, Todd Buck and Ligler Schoenhard, "Patentability and maximum protection of intellectual property in proteomics and genomics," (2003) 4(1) *Pharmacogenomics* 87.

3 Richard E. Gold and Timothy A. Caulfield, "The Moral Tollbooth: A Method that Makes Use of the Patents System to Address Ethical Concerns in Biotechnology," (2002) 359:9325 Lancet 2268; Sandy Thomas, Michael Hopkins, and Max Brady, "Shares in the human genome: Future of patenting DNA," (2002) 20 *Nature Biotechnology* 1185; Timothy A. Caufield, "From human genes to stem cells: new challenges for patent law?", (2003) 21(3), Trends in Biotechnology, pp. 101–102; Editorial, "Patenting pieces of people," 21(4) *Nature Biotechnology* 341.

4 *Harvard College v. Canada (Commissioner of Patents)*, 2002 SCC 76.

5 Canadian Biotechnology Advisory Committee (CBAC), *Patenting of Higher Life Forms*, Ottawa, 2002.

6 *Ibid.* at page 42. See also, *infra* (Section 4.4).

7 R. S., c. P-4, §1.

8 The term "human bodies" used in CBACs first recommendation results from a change in the Interim report by which the term "human beings" was replaced with "human bodies" since the word "being" denoted the metaphysical concept of a human, rather than the biological aspect. Furthermore, the "stages of development" range from the zygote to the adult human body.

9 Chapter 17.

10 Canadian Biotechnology Advisory Committee (CBAC), see note 5 above, at pages 10–11.

11 *Ibid.*, at page 11.

12 R. S. 1985, c. P-4

13 *Ibid.*

14 1990, c. 20.

15 R.S., c. 8 (4th Suppl.).

16 Canadian Biotechnology Advisory Committee (CBAC), *Biotechnology and Intellectual Property: Patenting of Higher Life Forms and Related Issues—Interim Report to the Government of Canada Biotechnology Ministerial Coordinating Committee- Executive Summary*, Ottawa, 2001, at page 17.

17 *Ibid.*

18 *Ibid.* at page 19.

19 *Ibid.* Recently, in the United States, a decision by the Court of Appeals for the Federal Circuit in *Madey v. Duke* (CAFC No. 01-1567, October 3, 2002), adopted a narrow scope of interpretation as concerns the unlicensed use of academic researchers using other researchers' patented materials and techniques. Duke invoked the experimental use exception in its defense against John M. J. Madey for allegedly infringing his patent on free electron laser (FEL) technology. Arguing that the school's role was to teach and expand knowledge, rather than to profit from patented discoveries, Duke claimed that it owed Madey nothing. However, Duke was not entitled to shelter under the experimental use exception, which exempts infringing uses that are "solely for amusement, to satisfy idle curiosity, or for strictly philosophical inquiry." Another ruling by the CAFC involves the narrow interpretation of exemptions. It was stated in *Integra v. Merck KgaA*, CAFC No. 02-1052, June 6, 2003, that researchers may conduct studies on drugs as well as medical devices only if it serves the purpose of providing data to the Food and Drug Administration when applying for the approval of generic drugs.

20 See above note 16, at page 17

21 76/76/EEC.

22 Nuffield Council on Bioethics, *The Ethics of Patenting DNA*, London, 2002, at page 61.

23 (1982) 82 C.P.R. (2d) 32 (C.B.A.)

24 *Re Application of Abitibi Co.*, (1982) 62 C.P.R. (2d) 81 (C.B.A.)

25 *Monsanto v. Schmeiser et al.*, (2004) CSC. 34.

26 Canadian Biotechnology Advisory Committee (CBAC), see above note 16, at page 17.

27 This view, that it is Parliament's responsibility to establish policy in the patenting of higher life forms, is supported by CBAC.

28 *President and Fellows of Harvard College* v. *Commissioner of Patents*, (2000) 7 C.P.R. (4th) 1 (F.C.A.)

29 (1989) 25 C.P.R. (3d) 257 (S.C.C.).

30 2004 C.S.C. 34.

31 Canadian Biotechnology Advisory Committee (CBAC), see above note 16, at page 17.

32 US Patent No. 4,736,866.

33 European Patent No. EP0169672.

34 *Diamond v. Chakrabarty*, (1980) 447 U.S. 303.

35 Shelly Rowland and Jared Scarlett, "The World's Most Litigated Mouse," (2003) 13 NZ Bio Science, available online: (http://www.bsw.co.nz/articles/xfactor13.html).

36 Munich, November 7, 2001 (Official Information): "The EPO opposition division dealing with Harvard University's 'oncomouse' patent has decided to maintain it in amended form ...", available online: (http://www.european-patent-office.org/news/presser1/2001_11_07_e.htm).

37 See Rowland and Scarlett, above at note 35.

38 European Commission, *Report from the Commission to the European Parliament and the Council—Development and Implications of Patent Law in the Field of Biotechnology and Genetic Engineering*, Brussels, 2002, at page 16.

39 *Ibid.*

40 European Parliament and the Council of the European Union, Directive 98/44/EC of the European Parliament and of the Council of July 6, 1998 on the legal protection of biotechnological inventions, France, July 1998, available online: (http://europa.eu.int/eur-lex/pri/en/oj/dat/1998/l_213/l_21319980730en00130021.pdf) (last accessed: May 27, 2004).

41 Oncomouse [1989], Official Journal of the European Patent Office (Exam) 476; [1990] Official Journal of the European Patent Office, 476, 490 (IBA); [1991] E.I.P.R. 250.

42 *Greenpeace U.K. v. Plant Genetic System NV*, Case No. T 0356/93_3.34 dated. February 21, 1995. In this decision, the EPO Opposition Division held that it was only necessary to consider ethical questions once a certain ethical threshold had been passed. In other words, an exception to patentability based on morality grounds should only be considered when the invention would universally be regarded as outrageous and when an overwhelming consensus would exist to the effect that no patent should be granted. Thus, the Opposition Division in this case did not revoke the patent for a genetically engineered plant on the grounds that it was inherently immoral and that it created environmental risks.

43 Although the CBAC has proposed guidelines for the development of biotechnology, it has acknowledged that it is the Parliament's responsibility to establish policy in respect to the patenting of higher life forms.

44 Canadian Biotechnology Advisory Committee (CBAC), see above note 5, at page 37.

45 Hugo Ethics Committee, *Statement on Benefit Sharing*, London, 2000.

46 D. R. J. Macer, "Inventions, patents and morality," in UNESCO, *Encyclopedia of Life Support Systems*, 2001, available online: (http://www.biol.tsukuba.ac.jp/~macer/Papers/ipmoral.htm); see also Lorraine Sheremeta and Bartha Maria Knoppers, "Beyond the Rhetoric: Population Genetics & Benefit-Sharing," (2004) *Health Law J*, at 6 (to be published).

47 United Nations Environment Programme (UNEP), *United Nations Conference on Environment and Development: Convention on Biological Diversity*, (1992) 31 I.L.M. 818.

48 Canadian Biotechnology Advisory Committee (CBAC), see above note 5, at page 19.

49 United Nations Environment Programme (UNEP), *Guidelines on Access to Genetic Resources and Fair and Equitable Sharing of the Benefits Arising out of their Utilization*, UNEP/CBD/COP/6/20, 2002.

50 Lorraine Sheremeta and B.M. Knoppers, see note 46 above, at page 5.

51 This treaty is a revision of the 1983 International Undertaking on Plant Genetic Resources in an attempt to harmonise it with the requirements of the CBD, and addresses farmers' rights as well as access to privately-held plant genetic collections.

52 Darryl R. J. Macer, "Inventions, patents and morality," in UNESCO, *Encyclopedia of Life Support Systems*, 2001, available online: (http://www.biol.tsukuba.ac.jp/~macer/Papers/iprmoral.htm).

53 Canadian Biotechnology Advisory Committee (CBAC), see above note 16, at page 21.

54 Canadian Biotechnology Advisory Committee (CBAC), see above note 5, at page 19.

55 Bartha Maria Knoppers, "Biotechnology—Sovereignty and Sharing," in T. A. Caulfield and B. Williams-Jones, eds., *The Commercialization of Genetic Research: Ethical, Legal, and Policy Issues*, (New York: Kluwer Academic/Plenum Publishers, 1999) at page 7.

56 The parties to the Cartagena agreement include members of the Andean community such as Bolivia, Columbia, Peru, Ecuador and Venezuela. The text to the Agreement is available online: (http://www.comunidadandina.org/ingles/treaties/trea/ande_trie1.htm).

57 Canadian Biotechnology Advisory Committee (CBAC), see above note 5, at page 20.

58 249 Cal. Rptr., 494, 504, 508 (Cal. Ct. App. 1988).

59 Canadian Biotechnology Advisory Committee (CBAC), see above note 5, at page 35.

60 *Ibid.*

61 Biological material including plants and animals other than micro-organisms and essentially biological processes for the production of plants and animals, other than non-biological and microbiological processes. The exception also provides the option of excluding patents on certain processes related to medical diagnostics and treatment of humans or animals.

62 Canadian Biotechnology Advisory Committee (CBAC), see above at note 5.

63 The differences between the CBD and TRIPS were outlined in a paper by Beatrix Tappeser and Alexandra Baier, *Who Owns Biological Diversity? A Brief Description of the Debate over the Rights to Biological Diversity in the North-South Context*, (Berlin: Heinrich Boell Foundation, 2000).

64 International Council of Scientific Unions, "Statement on Gene Patenting (June 1992)," (1993) 44:2 Int. Dig. Hlth. Leg. 363; UNESCO-International Bioethics Committee (IBC), *Report of the IBC on Ethics, Intellectual Property and Genomics*, (Paris, 2002), art. 4, UNESCO—General Conference, *Universal Declaration on the Human Genome and Human Rights*, (*Paris*, 1997), art. 4; International Society of Bioethics (SIBI), *Bioethics Declaration of Gijón*, (Gijón, 2000), rec. 8.

65 Nuffield Council on Bioethics, see above at note 22.

66 Indigenous People's Council on Biocolonialism, *Declaration of Indigenous Peoples of the Western Hemisphere Regarding the Human Genome Diversity Project*, (Phoenix, 1995), at pages 13 and 21.

67 American Medical Association, "E-2.105 Patenting Human Genes," (1998), available online: (http://www.ama-assn.org/ama/pub/category/8431.html).

68 Kennedy, D. "Agriculture and the Developing World," (2003) 302 *Science*, at page 357.

69 Sheremeta, Lorraine, and Richard Gold, "Creating a Patent Clearinghouse in Canada" A Solution to Problems of Equity and Access," (2003) 11(3) *Health Law Review*, 18, at page 19.

70 Hugo, *Statement on Genomic Databases*, December 2002.

CHAPTER 5

Intellectual Property Rights and Biodiversity Conservation: Reconciling the Incompatibilities of the TRIPS Agreement and the Convention on Biological Diversity

MICHAEL I. JEFFERY* Q.C.

5.1 INTRODUCTION

The interrelationship between intellectual property rights (IPRs) and biodiversity conservation is necessarily tied to an understanding of the current global economic climate as well as the geographical location of genetic resources. Such an understanding should take into account not only inter-governmental relations, but also the role of the private sector in resolving conflict between the two. The Convention on Biological

* BA, LL.B, University of Toronto, LL.M, Osgoode Hall, York University, Canada. The author is currently Professor of Law and Director, Centre for Environmental Law, Macquarie University, Sydney, Australia and former Chair of the Environmental Assessment Board of Ontario, Canada. Professor Jeffery is currently Deputy Chair of the World Conservation Union's (IUCN) Commission on Environmental Law. The author gratefully acknowledges the exceptional contributions of his research assistants Elaine Johnson and Su Ts'en Lin of Macquarie University Centre for Environmental Law in the preparation of this paper.

Diversity (CBD)[1] is important to business in that it promotes conservation of the very resources that business seeks to exploit, however, a number of companies and organisations while having heard of the CBD, have very little understanding of its scope and how it affects them.[2] This lack of understanding may stem from the fact that the CBD will affect business in an indirect and subtle way. In recent years, however, there is much more information on the CBD that is relatively easy to access and in many cases business friendly.

In the mid-1990s there was evidence that some industries avoided working in countries where access and benefit-sharing laws have been introduced after having been developed without the input of industry and this serves to highlight the important role that industry has in developing workable legislation.[3]

The role of industry is fundamental in the context of use of genetic resources, as it has the capacity to generate huge profits from the commercial use of such resources, and therefore also benefits. It is hoped that if these benefits are shared equitably with the providers of such resources, including holders of traditional knowledge, the promotion of conservation and sustainable use of biodiversity will be enhanced and available for use by future generations. Industry players therefore need to be aware of their obligations under the CBD, even where such obligations extend above and beyond the requirements of national IPR regimes.

Incompatibilities between the Agreement on Trade-Related Aspects of Intellectual Property Rights (the TRIPS Agreement)[4] and the CBD arise primarily because many biological resources are located in the "South" (or "developing") countries, where natural resources have not been available or exploited to the same extent as those of the "North" countries. For this reason, the economic burden of conservation lies heavily with the South countries, whilst the use of those resources is often associated with countries of the North that possess the technological and economic capacity to develop them into marketable commodities. IPRs are relevant to all States involved in biodiversity conservation and the use of biological resources, as those States using genetic resources require protection for the technological advances arising from the use of biological resources, whilst provider States require the protection of traditional knowledge, including indigenous and local knowledge used in the development of such products, as well as the equitable sharing of benefits arising from the use of their resources.

The first international agreement on the conservation of biodiversity to acknowledge the existence of IPR regimes within its text is the 1992 Convention on Biological Diversity (the CBD).[5] One of the obstacles during negotiations leading up to adoption of the CBD was the doctrine of genetic resources being considered the "common heritage of humankind."[6] Countries of both the North and South were opposed to the application of this concept to the convention-developing countries because it implies free access to their resources, and developed countries because it raises the possibility of benefit-sharing and the open transfer of technologies.[7]

The TRIPS Agreement is the most comprehensive, setting the minimum level of intellectual property rights, which must be provided by all State parties to the General Agreement on Tariffs and Trade (GATT)[8] and subsequently by all member States of the World Trade Organisation (WTO). Members may implement more extensive protection provided that such protection does not contravene the provisions of the TRIPS Agreement. Also relevant to IPR protection and biodiversity is the *International Convention for the Protection of New Varieties of Plants* (the UPOV Convention)[9], which provides a framework for IPR protection of plant varieties, referred to as plant breeders' rights (PBRs) or plant variety rights.[10] IPRs (in particular patents) grant monopoly rights as incentives for technological innovation, or "development." By definition, they are proprietary interests over subject matter outside the public domain. This limited recognition and protection of intellectual property is problematic as it fails to acknowledge systems of knowledge that have evolved over time, as scientific knowledge does, but whose evolution has not taken place in a laboratory.[11]

Under IPR regimes, public or community-based knowledge is considered "common heritage" that should be made freely available.[12] This poses a problem for indigenous communities whose local knowledge, passed down through generations, is used by bioprospecting companies to locate and understand the properties of biological organisms to be used in creating a patentable product. If IPRs were available to such communities, this could create monetary incentive for local communities to conserve valuable genetic resources. Some commentators, however, are sceptical of the effectiveness of IPRs as a solution to conservation because for thousands of years many indigenous communities have preserved knowledge and resources without any legal incentives.[13] However, as communities begin to disintegrate, traditional ecological knowledge is often lost, creating a need for a means of preservation of such knowledge and resources.[14] It must also be considered that the beneficiaries of benefit-sharing may not see monetary reward as the most appropriate or welcome form of compensation for use of their knowledge. This point complicates the concept of benefit-sharing with the issue of ethics and effectiveness of regimes.[15] The extension of IPRs, where possible, to cover traditional knowledge may, however, be counter-productive in promoting the development of new products beneficial to the wider community because of the additional financial expenditures and delay on the part of companies negotiating acceptable arrangements.[16]

The purpose of this paper is to provide an overview of the problems faced in reconciling the incompatibilities of IPR regimes and biodiversity conservation, in particular between the TRIPS Agreement and the CBD. These instruments will be examined with a focus on the environmental legal aspects of the interaction between intellectual property rights and biodiversity conservation, and some possible solutions to such conflicts will be put forward. The paper suggests that the interface between the TRIPS Agreement, UPOV and the CBD needs to be better co-ordinated to avoid conflict and to ensure that they are developed in a cohesive and integrated manner.

5.2 KEY PROVISIONS OF INTERNATIONAL CONVENTIONS AND AGREEMENTS RELATING TO IPR ISSUES

5.2.1 The Convention on Biological Diversity

The CBD is a convention that covers virtually all aspects of biodiversity, including issues of sustainable use of biodiversity and biotechnology[17], as well as contentious issues affecting North/South relations such as access and benefit-sharing and the transfer of technology.[18] Within this convention there is explicit recognition that there is a significant role for existing intellectual property rights in the regulation of biodiversity conservation and use.[19]

There was pressure during UNCED negotiations to reach an agreement before Rio in the hope that the Convention could be opened for signature there in June 1992. This pressure resulted in parties being forced into making concessions and forcing an agreement sooner than otherwise would have been the case. It has also been argued that this rush has made the convention at times contradictory and often unclear.[20] The final text of the convention was completed and adopted on May 22, 1992 opened for signature on June 5, 1992 in Rio de Janeiro and entered into force on December 29, 1993.

During the negotiations of the Convention, some parties wanted biodiversity to be considered the "common heritage of humankind," with precedent for this principle existing in the 1983 FAO *International Undertaking on Plant Genetic Resources* where it is stated that "plant genetic resources are a heritage of humankind to be preserved, and to be freely available for use, for the benefit of present and future generations."[21] As genetic resources are located primarily in the South, countries of the North generally supported this principle, as it guaranteed them free and open access to the gene banks and other biological resources found in the South.[22] With the majority of biological resources found in the South, the "common heritage of humankind" doctrine effectively amounted to an obligation of the countries of the South to protect biodiversity and genetic resources for the exploitation of the richer, industrialised countries of the North. IPR regimes created further tension in this context, as they provided protection primarily for the biotechnology industry.[23] In this way, benefits accrued to the North without being shared with countries of the South, who had to forego the economic benefits that could be gained through the use of their resources (e.g., logging and agriculture) in order to preserve them under the common heritage doctrine. During negotiations, the South rejected the doctrine, seeking to maintain sovereignty over their resources and to have the North provide benefits in return for the use of the resources. Given that neither the North or the South was entirely happy with the concept of "common heritage of humankind," the concept of biological conservation being a "common *concern* of humankind" was developed.[24] Through this new concept, a balance between the North's concern for protecting biological resources in the South, and the South's interest in benefiting from resources found within their borders was achieved.[25]

5.2.1.1 Article 15: Access to Genetic Resources

In Article 15(1), by recognising a State's sovereign rights over its natural resources, the authority over access to these resources lies with the national government and is subject to national legislation. With each State having control of access, there is much discretion for it to decide how to regulate access to their natural resources.[26] This access has to satisfy the requirement that there is "prior informed consent"[27] of the party providing the resources, and where this access is granted it will be on "mutually agreed terms[28]." The control that nation States have over access to resources is qualified by an obligation imposed by the CBD to "endeavour to create conditions to facilitate access to genetic resources for environmentally sound uses by other Contracting Parties and not to impose restrictions that run counter to the objectives of this Convention."[29]

Article 15(7) requires that:

> Each Contracting Party shall take legislative, administrative or policy measures, as appropriate, and in accordance with Articles 16 and 19 and, where necessary, through the financial mechanism established by Articles 20 and 21 with the aim of sharing in a fair and equitable way the results of research and development and the benefits arising from the commercial and other utilisation of genetic resources with the Contracting Party providing such resources. Such sharing shall be upon 'mutually agreed terms'.

There is no specific reference in Article 15(7) to intellectual property rights, however the obligations imposed on the Parties to facilitate the fair and equitable sharing of benefits in accordance with Article 16 requires the Contracting Parties to take the measures in a manner that is "on terms which recognise and are consistent with the adequate and effective protection of intellectual property rights."[30]

5.2.1.2 Article 16: Access to and Transfer of Technology

Article 16 specifically relates to the access to and transfer of technology, which is considered to be essential if the objectives of the CBD are to be achieved. There is an obligation placed on the Parties to establish a framework in which to provide and facilitate access to and transfer of technology to the Contracting Parties. While minimum requirements are set out, the way in which these requirements are given effect are left to the Contracting Parties.[31]

Article 16(1) of the CBD includes in its definition of technology, biotechnology, and specifically "technologies that are relevant to the conservation and sustainable use of biological diversity or make use of genetic resources and do not cause significant damage to the environment."[32] By defining "technology" in this way it ensures that traditional and indigenous applied knowledge also falls within this provision.[33]

Under Article 16(2) access to and transfer of technology "shall be provided and/or facilitated under fair and most favourable terms, including on concessional and preferential terms where mutually agreed"[34]. The terms "fair and most favourable" and "concessional and preferential" are not defined within the Convention, however the language is consistent with the United Nations Framework Convention on Climate Change (UNFCCC), the Protocol on Substances that Deplete the Ozone Layer (Montreal Protocol) and Agenda 21.[35] It is recognised in this paragraph that *"in the case of technology subject to patents and other intellectual property rights, such access and transfer shall be provided on terms which recognise and are consistent with the adequate and effective protection of intellectual property rights."*[36] It has been suggested that the adoption of the phrase "adequate and effective protection," was meant to establish a link specifically to the TRIPs Agreement, which utilises this language.[37]

Article 16(3) deals with the transfer of technology that specifically makes use of genetic resources, however, it does not create an obligation for the transfer of the technology that makes use of the resources to the Contracting Party that is providing the genetic resources. The Article purely provides for the establishment of legislative, administrative or policy measures that would facilitate the access and transfer of the technology, but the manner in which this obligation is to be met is left to the parties to decide.[38] Significant in this Article is the fact that there is a specific reference to technology that is protected by patents and other intellectual property rights as well as the fact that obligations under this Article are to be "in accordance with international law." This international law that the obligations must be accordance with would include any international law that applies to intellectual property rights, such as the TRIPS Agreement, World Intellectual Property Organization (WIPO) administered multilateral treaties, and bilateral agreements and other regional treaties such as the European Community Directive on the Legal Protection of Biotechnological Inventions.[39]

Article 16(4) is an extension of the obligations placed on Contracting Parties in Article 16(3) to encourage the provision of access to and transfer of technology by the respective party's private sector, "for the benefit of both governmental institutions and the private sector of developing countries[40]." As in Article 16(3), there is no obligation created which forces the private sector to jointly develop or transfer technology to developing countries. It is unlikely that developed countries would have participated in the negotiations of the CBD had such an obligation been created with the force of a binding commitment.[41]

During the negotiations leading up to the CBD, many developed countries were concerned that the CBD had the potential to undermine intellectual property rights regimes worldwide, and this Article found its way into the CBD as a means of emphasising these concerns of the developed nations.[42] There is disagreement as to whether or not intellectual property rights in fact support the objectives of the CBD. While there may be conflicts between the two[43], the requirement that Contracting Parties "shall cooperate in this regard subject to national legislation and international law in order to ensure that such rights are supportive of and do not run counter to its objectives"[44] should erase any conflict.

5.2.1.3 Article 8(j): *In-situ* Conservation

Unlike Article 15 that refers only to genetic resources, Article 8(j) has a much wider scope as to the resources it includes. The qualification that the article's implementation is subject to national legislation was introduced in order to maintain relationships that had been established between some States and indigenous groups prior to the Convention being complete.[45] Article 10(c) is considered to be a natural consequence of Article 8(j) as it requires that Parties "protect and encourage customary use of biological resources in accordance with traditional cultural practices that are compatible with conservation or sustainable use requirements." As a result, it is necessary to consider the customary use of these resources in the development of policy and legislation with regard to access to genetic resources.[46]

As Dutfield[47] notes, it is significant that the use of the word "holder" suggests that there is some type of ownership or legal entitlement at the least, and so have some rights over their "knowledge, innovations and practices"[48] regardless of whether or not they can attract intellectual property right protection.[49] This Article of the CBD is an acknowledgement by the international community that they understand the importance and value of traditional "knowledge, innovation and practices" to modern society.[50]

5.2.2 The TRIPS Agreement

Unlike biodiversity conservation, which is a relatively new area of international law, the international regulation of intellectual property regimes dates back as far back as the late 19th Century with the 1886 *Berne Convention*[51] and the 1883 *Paris Convention.*[52] Whilst intellectual property developed and expanded over the next 100 years, the Uruguay Round of trade negotiations under the *General Agreement on Tariffs and Trade* (GATT)[53] saw efforts to harmonise national and regional intellectual property laws through the TRIPS Agreement, which was finalised in 1993, and entered into force on January 1, 1995.[54] The Uruguay Round also resulted in the creation of the World Trade Organisation (the WTO) and the TRIPS Agreement is now binding on all members of the organisation. The TRIPS Agreement is the most comprehensive treaty in its field, setting forth minimum standards for protection of IPRs, requiring effective and appropriate enforcement measures and effective procedures for multilateral prevention and settlements of inter-governmental disputes.[55] Members may implement more extensive protection over and above the minimum standards provided such protection does not contravene the provisions of the TRIPS Agreement.[56] This is one area where protection of traditional ecological knowledge may be possible. For example, in 1989, Kenya passed its *Industrial Property Bill*[57] which allows for patents to be granted relating to traditional medicinal knowledge. Such a piece of legislation is not in conflict with the TRIPS Agreement, and attempts to bridge the gap between the TRIPS Agreement and the CBD on this matter.

The TRIPS Agreement was meant to be implemented by Members within one year of its entry into force.[58] However, developing countries and the least-developed countries are generally afforded a further four years and 10 years respectively[59] in which to implement the requirements of the Agreement. During this time, however, they are expected to take significant interim measures in protecting IPRs. Despite differential treatment in implementation dates, the Agreement upholds what have been key features of intellectual property conventions: the *national treatment* and *most favoured nation* (MFN) principles.[60] The national treatment principle promotes non-discrimination between a Member's nationals (i.e., its citizens and corporations) and the nationals of another Member, whilst the MFN principle prohibits discrimination between the nationals of other Members.[61] In addition, Members are required to make available fair and equitable judicial procedures and remedies for the effective enforcement of IPRs.[62]

The TRIPS Agreement does not define intellectual property in its own right, but simply states that intellectual property refers to seven categories of IPRs, namely, copyright and related rights, trademarks, geographical indications, industrial designs, patents, layout designs of integrated circuits and protection of undisclosed information (including trade secrets or test data).[63] Of these categories, patents are potentially the most useful in terms of use of genetic resources, but trade secrets may also be relevant, as well as geographical indications, and possibly trademarks.[64]

5.2.2.1 Patents

Through Article 27, the TRIPS Agreement places an obligation on Member states to enact legislation that will make patents available for both products and processes in *all* fields of technology provided that they are "new, involve an inventive step and are capable of industrial application."[65] The rationale behind this article is to ensure that no material is excluded from patent law, including drugs and medicines, farm chemicals and products produced outside of the country.[66]

Despite the broad nature of the framework patent provisions within the TRIPS Agreement, there are some allowable exclusions within Article 27. One such exception is the "*ordre public* or morality" provision in Article 27(2). Whilst neither of these terms are defined within the Agreement, the article states that they include the protection of "human, animal or plant life or health or to avoid serious prejudice to the environment."

The exclusion provided for in Article 27(2) is broad in its application, and has the potential to be far-reaching for at least two reasons. First, for some societies or cultures, the patenting of life-forms and their components in general would be considered inherently immoral. Second, many traditional societies have put forward the proposition that the monopoly protection of products derived from traditional ecological knowledge and community-based resources is exploitative and morally wrong.[67] These considerations raise the question—could such patents be outlawed in countries where this view is prevalent? Dutfield explores this point by explaining that legal experts appear to assume that such broad legislation would not be compatible with the TRIPS Agreement, as the Agreement requires exclusions to be applied narrowly on a case-by-case basis.[68]

Further possible exclusions relate to diagnostic, therapeutic and surgical methods as well as plants and animals (other than micro-organisms) and biological process (other than microbiological processes).

On this point, the Agreement states that Members have the obligation to provide protection of plant varieties either through patents, an "effective" *sui generis* system, or a combination of the two.[69] It is important to bear in mind that these exclusions are subject to the national treatment principle which prohibits legislators from discriminating between foreign nationals and those of the Member's country.

It has been noted that while there exist these discretionary provisions for providing exclusions within national patent laws, the pressure of attracting trade may force countries to provide protection for certain materials and processes which they would ordinarily be inclined, and entitled, to exclude.[70] Even without this pressure, many developing countries are finding that they must revise their patent laws in order to become TRIPS-compliant. This involves removing exceptions so that technologies such as pharmaceuticals are afforded protection under patent laws.[71]

5.2.2.2 Trade secrets

Trade secret law is relevant to the use of biodiversity, particularly in terms of the seed industry, where it is commonly employed to protect inbred parent lines of hybrids, which could otherwise be used by competitors to develop rival products.[72] Article 39 of the Agreement deals with the protection of undisclosed information, or trade secrets. This article provides for the protection of information that cannot be protected by patent law, or information that the holder does not want to be made publicly available. Trade secrets are distinct from patent laws in that they do not provide monopoly protection, but instead deny public access to the information. This does not prevent others from developing and using the same information, but simply allows holders of the information to be protected from publicly disclosing such information.

The requirements of Article 39(2) are such that Members must ensure that natural and legal persons are able to prevent "information lawfully within their control from being disclosed to, acquired by, or used by others without their consent in a manner contrary to honest commercial practices."[73] In order for information to be protected it must be secret, have commercial value because it is secret, and have been subject to reasonable steps by the person in control of it to be kept secret. However, since the range of information that may be protected by trade secrets is broader than in the case of patents, it is suggested that they may be used to encompass scientific information as well as traditional knowledge.[74] This would be a useful component in bringing together the provisions of the TRIPS Agreement and the CBD, as the CBD (in Article 8j) implies protection of the "knowledge, innovations and practices" of indigenous or local communities embodying traditional lifestyles.

5.2.2.3 Geographical indications

Section 3 of Part II of the TRIPS Agreement deals with regulation of geographical indications, which are "indications which identify a good as originating in the territory of a Member, or a region or locality in that territory, where a given quality, reputation or other characteristic of the good is essentially attributable to its geographical origin."[75] They are similar to trademarks, but distinct in that they identify a product according to a particular territory, whereas trademarks identify a product according to its brand or a particular company.[76] It is suggested that geographical indications, although focused on regulation of beverages and foodstuffs to date,[77] could be applicable to protecting traditional ecological knowledge.[78] This aspect of geographical indications will be discussed further in section 5.4.

5.2.3 Plant breeder's rights

Plant breeder's rights (PBRs) are a relatively new concept, arising because IPR regimes did not originally allow patents to be held over living organisms.[79] Without IPR protection, developers of new plant varieties would be likely to receive little reward for their innovations, thus providing less incentive for development of the industry. Lack of recognition for innovation in this area is compounded by the fact that the products of such innovation—new plant varieties—are living organisms that are easily replicable.

5.2.3.1 The UPOV Convention

PBRs have developed as a *sui generis* form of IPRs, distinct from ordinary patent rights, and are extended to the international community through the *International Convention for the Protection of New Varieties of Plants* (the UPOV Convention), as amended.[80] The UPOV Convention has been considered by some developed countries to be capable of satisfying the *sui generis* requirement of Article 27(3)(b) of the TRIPS Agreement,[81] which states that "members shall provide for the protection of plant varieties either by patents or by an effective *sui generis* system or by any combination thereof."

The UPOV Convention was signed in Paris in 1961, entering into force in 1968, and derives its abbreviated name from the Union for the Protection of New Varieties of Plants which was established under the Convention. The convention has since been revised twice (the current version being the 1991 Act) and is a framework convention, placing an obligation on member states to create national legislation to grant and protect PBRs.[82] Such rights are to be protected where the plant variety is:

(i) *new* (i.e., has not yet been offered for sale with the consent of the breeder),
(ii) *distinct* (i.e., clearly distinguishable from any other plant variety),
(iii) *uniform* in its relevant characteristics (subject to variation from particular features of its propagation), and
(iv) *stable* (i.e., remains unchanged after repeated propagation).[83]

In its original form, the convention effectively created two exceptions to the protection of PBRs: the "farmer's privilege" and the "research and development" exception.[84] In practice, primary producers often save seeds from past crops for replanting in the next season. To allow producers to replant crops from saved seeds without having to pay additional royalties is what has been referred to as "farmer's privilege." "Farmer's privilege" was allowed in effect (although not specifically) under the 1978 version of the Convention as it provided for breeders to be given the right to exclude others only from *commercially* marketing or selling the product, thereby leaving open the possibility of creating national legislation that allowed for replanting by farmers without the payment of additional royalties.[85] The 1991 Act of the UPOV Convention extends PBRs to all forms of production, effectively abolishing the potential for the "farmer's privilege." It does, however, permit member states to limit the scope of PBRs in their national legislation "within reasonable limits and subject to safeguarding of the legitimate interests of the breeder,"[86] for the purposes of establishing a "farmer's privilege," thereby allowing such privilege to exist on a case-by-case basis.[87] The 1991 Act limitations on "farmer's privilege" rights are likely to impact smaller primary producers to the greatest extent, particularly those in developing countries, where most of the seed used in production is saved from the previous harvest.[88]

The research and development exception to PBRs is found in Article 15 which provides for the use of protected plant varieties for research and development purposes by other breeders without authorisation from the rights holder.[89] The article distinguishes PBRs from the patenting of other genetic material as it allows open access to genetically modified resources.[90] Such relatively unrestricted access has been limited to some extent by the 1991 Act, which provides that where a plant variety is "essentially derived" from a protected variety, the right holder of the protected variety enjoys rights over both types of plant. "Essential derivation" exists where a plant variety is derived from the use of a protected variety, and the derived variety is not clearly distinguishable from the protected variety, containing virtually all of the protected variety's genes.[91] This concept extends PBRs considerably, giving seed companies substantial increases in their rights, which may pose a threat to the farmer's rights of control over their own food production.[92]

PBRs are distinct from patent rights in that they contain exceptions such as those outlined above, and whilst the UPOV Convention is silent on whether plant varieties may be subject to both PBRs and patent legislation, some countries expressly forbid the patenting of plant varieties. This is the case in most European countries.[93] Despite a clear distinction between the two forms of protection, it appears that the 1991 revision of the Convention, by expanding breeder's control over propagation and limiting the "farmer's privilege," has resulted in PBRs becoming more closely related to patent rights in terms of their criteria for protection.[94] Some authors have expressed concern that that this transformation is likely to have a negative impact on biodiversity conservation and rural farming communities.[95] In particular, the lack of recognition and IPR protection in favour of indigenous communities and countries of origin that is often associated with traditional IPR regimes and biodiversity conservation may now apply to PBRs as well. This means that the contributions made by such communities to the development of new varieties of plants, through the identification and conservation of the relevant biological resources, as well as genetically improving plant varieties over many years, remains unrewarded and open to exploitation.[96]

5.2.3.2 International Undertaking on Plant Genetic Resources

During the 1970s, with increased efforts in the collection and conservation of plant genetic resources and the 1978 revision of the UPOV Convention expanding its scope to non-European nations, the international community turned its attention toward a means of effectively managing *ex-situ* biodiversity conservation, particularly in the form of seed collection.[97] In 1983, in response to this concern, the Food and Agriculture Organisation of the United Nations (FAO) adopted the *International Undertaking on Plant Genetic Resources* (IU).[98] The IU is a non-binding agreement administered by the Commission on Genetic Resources for Food and Agriculture[99] and is set apart from the CBD and the UPOV Convention in that it has a more tightly defined scope than the CBD and was created with the intent of having a more universal application than the UPOV Convention, which was established primarily to meet the needs of a group of developed nations.[100] Tension between the North and South countries during negotiations was sparked by a 1979 publication by Pat Mooney entitled *Seeds of the Earth* and revolved around accusations that countries of the North were using seeds from the South in the development of plant genetic resources, making huge profits with little acknowledgement of the contribution of the South. As a result, the FAO became the battleground for what has been termed the "seed wars," which complicated the 1983 negotiations considerably.[101]

The IU is relevant to a discussion of the incompatibilities between IPRs and the CBD in that it was built on the principle of plant genetic resources being the "common heritage of mankind," a concept specifically rejected during the negotiations leading up to the CBD. Pressure from plant breeders, particularly those of the North, lead to a revision of the IU regarding the "common heritage" principle resulting in a 1989 Resolution which accepted that plant breeder's rights under the IU were not in conflict with the definition of such rights under the UPOV Convention.[102] In further breaking down the application of the "common heritage" principle, the 1989 Resolution introduced "Farmer's Rights" which are designed to recognise the contributions of farmers in "conserving, improving and making available plant genetic resources,"[103] whilst a further resolution in 1991 confirmed the sovereign rights of nation states over their plant genetic resources.[104]

Negotiations regarding the revision of the IU to facilitate its harmonisation with the CBD were concluded in November 2001 with the presentation of the revised IU which was converted to a legally-binding text: the *International Treaty on Plant Genetic Resources for Food and Agriculture (ITPGR)*.[105] The new treaty is now set to come into force on June 29, 2004 having been ratified by the 40th State 90 days earlier on March 31. It establishes a multilateral system of access and benefit-sharing, under which States are allowed free access to certain genetic resources, and contains a funding strategy involving the creation of a Multilateral System to facilitate access to over 64 major crops.[106] Where the Multilateral System using these genetic resources results in the development of a commercial product, the funding strategy provides for an equitable share of monies derived therefrom to be used for programmes to assist small farmers in developing countries. The ITPGR also provides for the recognition of the contributions of farmers to the conservation and development of plant genetic resources. [107]

5.3 INCOMPATIBILITIES BETWEEN THE TRIPS AGREEMENT AND THE CBD

The relationship between IPR regimes and the CBD is complex and disputed. As a result, there exist several conflicting views on how well the two are able to be harmonised. Dutfield identifies three current realms of thought on the topic:[108]

> *Pro-patent.* This view puts forward the proposition that patents and IPRs support the CBD and its objectives in that when corporations are protected under IPR regimes, they will be more willing to invest in "natural product research" and more likely to participate in benefit-sharing and technology transfer agreements. It is thought that this, in turn, will help protect biodiversity conservation by providing incentives for careful preservation of these valuable resources.
>
> *Anti-patent.* Opponents to the pro-patent view assert that by creating patents over living organisms we are encouraging the destruction of biodiversity and creating monopolies that are unfair and immoral. This view says that such patents also support "biopiracy," which is the unauthorised use of biological resources or the knowledge held by indigenous communities or developing countries.
>
> *Pragmatic.* The pragmatic view states that whilst there are difficulties in reconciling the incompatibilities between TRIPS and the CBD, the best way to achieve reconciliation is through

amendments and additions to our existing systems of IPR protection.

It is important to bear in mind these differing views on IPRs and the CBD when discussing the possible incompatibilities and how they might be resolved.

Central to a discussion on the incompatibilities between IPRs and biodiversity conservation is the issue of "biopiracy." This term is used to describe the removal of genetic resources without consent or compensation, and is often alleged by developing countries, but also occurs in developed countries. [109] Biopiracy involves the exploitation of either citizens of a State or the State itself. In terms of the exploitation of citizens, holders of traditional ecological knowledge have been identified as the primary victims. In terms of the exploitation of the State itself, developing countries are considered to be the most common victims, as they frequently lack the resources and capability to protect their natural resources from exploitation. In addition, as has been noted earlier, such resources are typically concentrated in the South, therefore making them more susceptible to the practice of biopiracy.[110]

The issue of biopiracy is one which must be considered seriously by stakeholders in the biotechnology industry, as demonstrated by the recent action taken by the *San* people of the Kalahari—the aboriginal people of Southern Africa—against the South African government. In this case, the *San* people took action against the South African Council for Scientific and Industrial Research (CSIR) over a patented active molecule (P57) from the Hoodia plant, which was patented by the CSIR who then sold rights for further development sold to the UK herbal medicine company, Phytopharm. The issue here was the misappropriation of the traditional medicinal knowledge of the *San* people in that the molecule was extracted from the Hoodia plant, which the *San* people had been using for years as an appetite suppressant. Phytopharm developed the product further and sold the rights to the US drug company Pfizer, which aims to market a new obesity treatment based on the Hoodia plant within the next three years. It is expected that the product will generate around $6 billion in market value.[111]

A legal settlement was reached between the South African *San* Council and the CSIR, and on March 24, 2003 a Memorandum of Understanding was signed between the two recognising the contribution of both the San and the CSIR in developing the product, and included the requirement for a benefit-sharing agreement to be put in place. The agreement, signed two days later, stipulates that the *San* people will receive 8 per cent of all "milestone payments" the CSIR receives from Phytopharm and 6 per cent of all royalties CSIR receives once the drug is commercially available.[112] It has been noted that difficulties may arise in the sharing of benefits given the confidentiality of the CSIR's agreement with the foreign drug companies, and the likelihood of difficulties in calculating and monitoring a fair distribution of royalties for the *San* people.[113] The case does, however, highlight the importance in recognising traditional ecological knowledge through benefit-sharing agreements, and obtaining informed consent before traditional medicinal knowledge is used in the creation of marketable products.

It has been found that since the introduction of the CBD, pharmaceutical companies are collecting genetic resources from far fewer countries than they previously had, and are relying much more on *ex-situ* sources and other organisations such as botanic gardens to collect such resources for them. Because these companies have become more dependent on these collaborations with other organisations, the availability of IPRs is no longer the prime concern of pharmaceutical companies in determining who to collaborate with in the collection of genetic resources.[114]

Many pharmaceutical products are discovered through the study of their traditional uses,[115] however many pharmaceutical companies as their primary source, rely on literature and databases, rather than ethnobotanical knowledge[116]. In this way, companies gain access to the relevant knowledge without triggering benefit-sharing obligations.[117]

5.3.1 Maintaining and preserving traditional ecological knowledge systems

A major aspect of the incompatibilities between the TRIPS Agreement and the CBD is the recognition of traditional ecological knowledge (TEK), and the associated provisions of access and benefit-sharing, and technology transfer. Protection of local and traditional knowledge is necessary, not only for the sake of the upholding the principles of economic and social equity, which are reasons in themselves to protect and benefit such societies, but also in serving the interests of global trade and the bioprospecting industry. As the "pro-patent" view outlined above suggests, this may in turn lead to the promotion of sustainable use and conservation of biological resources. This is because it is thought that as genetic resources are often developed and conserved by local and traditional communities, respecting, maintaining and preserving such knowledge may assist in it remaining useful in this capacity.

There exists inequity between the lack of IPR protection concerning traditional knowledge of genetic resources in the South, and the availability of such protection for the technology in countries of the North which have been developed using such genetic resources. The knowledge of traditional peoples and communities (i.e., those "embodying traditional lifestyles")[118] has been recognised only relatively recently by western knowledge systems as important and valuable in both the development of new products derived from genetic resources and, therefore, also in the conservation of biological diversity. Given the fact that use of traditional ecological knowledge to locate plants for the development of marketable drugs (termed "ethno-pharmacology")[119] can dramatically increase the success of bio-prospectors in locating pharmacologically active compounds showing positive effects, from one successful sample in 10,000 to one in two,[120] it is likely that many of these plant-based medicines are derived using traditional ecological knowledge systems. The contribution made by traditional ecological knowledge toward the global economy proves difficult to calculate, however, some studies have attempted research on the question. For example, in 1985 it was estimated that of the 120 plant-derived pharmaceutical products available, 75 per cent were discovered through the study of traditional medicinal use.[121] More recently, a 1996 study revealed that the base compound in the majority of 150 plant-derived prescription drugs correlated with those used in traditional medicines.[122]

Traditional knowledge, by its very nature, is not capable of being protected under conventional IPR regimes, such as those to be provided for by Member states of the TRIPS Agreement. Of all the regimes available for protection of intellectual property, patents probably have the most potential to be useful in the protection of traditional ecological knowledge. However, conventional patentability standards are not capable of adequately protecting traditional ecological knowledge for several reasons.[123] First, in order for an invention to be patented, it must be new. Traditional knowledge is often passed down through generations. Therefore, under conventional patent laws, it loses its novelty and becomes part of the public domain. Second, the financial disadvantage often associated with members of traditional communities, particularly those in developing countries, means that such communities are likely to face difficulties in the development and enforcement of patent legislation.[124]

The TRIPS Agreement fails to address the issues arising from protection of traditional knowledge, and provides only for provision of IPR regimes that work to protect owners of conventional knowledge, such as biotechnology companies. Article 27(3)(b) of the agreement provides for the inclusion of PBRs into national legislation, either through patents or an "effective *sui generis*" IPR regime. However, this article is probably not comprehensive enough to include traditional ecological knowledge beyond the PBRs provided for by the UPOV Convention. In addition, the exact meaning of the article is unclear, providing no definition of what is to be taken to be an "effective" *sui generis* regime. A further concern is that *sui generis* systems require development and enforcement of complex legislation on an individual State basis. As traditional ecological knowledge is often appropriated from developing countries with limited resources, or communities unaccustomed to the operation of the Western commercial world, communities may never see the benefits of a *sui generis* IPR regime.[125]

5.3.2 Access and benefit-sharing

At present, few benefits are afforded to owners of traditional knowledge that is used in the development of commercial products derived from genetic resources. In fact, Posey estimates that less than 0.001 per cent of profits from drugs developed using such knowledge systems have been passed on to the owners of such knowledge.[126] In contrast to, and perhaps in conflict with, the TRIPS Agreement, the CBD attempts to address the issues surrounding exploitation of traditional knowledge through its access and benefit-sharing provisions, which will be discussed below.

In implementing the CBD, countries are faced with the need to strike a balance between controlling and facilitating access to genetic resources, in a world where biodiversity resources exist largely in the South and the technology to develop it exists largely in the North. The dilemma arises because bioprospecting companies investing significant amounts of capital (both intellectual and financial) into development of the genetic resources are likely to be looking for access to genetic resources that also protects their IPRs from exploitation by unauthorised users. Provider countries, on the other hand, may wish to enact national legislation restricting access to their resources where proper compensation or payment of royalties is not forthcoming. If the legislation of provider countries becomes too restrictive, however, it is likely to drive users of those resources away, resulting in the loss of opportunity by provider countries to derive any benefits at all.[127]

The access and benefit-sharing provisions of the CBD[128] are introduced in its Objectives, which include the "fair and equitable sharing of the benefits arising out of the utilisation of genetic resources, including by appropriate access to genetic resources and by appropriate transfer of relevant technologies."[129] This clause encapsulates the need for a balance between facilitating access to genetic resources and sharing the benefits arising from such access, the negotiation of which has been referred to as the "grand bargain."[130] Article 15 of the CBD qualifies this clause further, by requiring that access is allowed only with "prior informed consent"[131] and on "mutually agreed terms."[132] Thus, provider States may condition access upon informed consent, and on any other terms deemed appropriate, within an enforceable contract, bearing in mind their obligation to facilitate access to genetic resources in accordance with the objectives of the CBD.[133]

Under Article 27 of the TRIPS Agreement, countries are required to make available IPR protection in the form of patents for products and processes in all fields of technology, regardless of whether the invention is a product or process, with few exceptions.[134] This far-reaching application of patent law into national legislation has meant that developing countries (the majority of provider countries) have had to create IPR regimes to protect the innovation of companies making use of their biological resources, such as pharmaceutical companies, regardless of whether or not they are able to share in the benefits.[135] Even where exceptions to IPR protection exist, provider countries are finding themselves under increasing pressure to develop patent legislation in order to avoid deterring biotechnology industries from investing within their territories.[136]

The access and benefit-sharing provisions of the CBD are directly incompatible with current IPR regimes, such as those that may be derived from the national implementation of the TRIPS Agreement. This is due to the fact that protection of IPRs may hinder the benefit-sharing and technology transfer objectives of the CBD whilst failing to afford provider countries recognition and reward for the contributions made by their people through the provision of traditional knowledge and stewardship of resources.[137]

5.3.3 Ownership and prior informed consent

As the CBD requires the "prior informed consent" (PIC) of Member states for access to genetic resources within their control, users of such resources, particularly those within the private sector, are faced with difficulties of identifying exactly from whom such consent should be obtained from. This difficulty arises because although the CBD recognises the sovereign right of states to *control* access to their biological resources, *ownership* of these resources will determine whose consent is required to gain access. Such ownership is created on a case-by-case basis through individual country tenure systems.

As treatment of ownership varies widely between States, from traditional common tenure to state-enforced private property rights,[138] such a task may prove cumbersome for those who are seeking to comply with the provisions of the CBD within that particular country or those seeking to adhere to best practice measures.[139]

Trade-related IPRs have become a new and powerful way of establishing ownership over natural products and genetic resources. This new kind of ownership over genetic resources creates difficulties for bioprospecting companies in determining from whom they must obtain PIC. The issue becomes particularly complicated when it involves local and indigenous communities, whose IPRs in the case of genetic resources are poorly defined, and whose concept of ownership may differ considerably from conventional views. Although the CBD requires consent from Member states, this does not prevent such states from applying PIC provisions to individuals or communities, including traditional communities, further increasing the onus on bioprospecting companies to ensure proper consent has been obtained.[140]

5.3.4 Transfer of technological capability

Assuming that access and benefit-sharing agreements for the use of genetic resources is a desired outcome of a resolution of the incompatibilities between IPR regimes and the CBD, it is important to take into account the fact that in order for access and benefit-sharing agreements to work effectively, there must be sufficient capacity in provider countries to legislate, monitor and effectively enforce regulations which govern bioprospecting companies. Given that these countries are frequently countries of the "South," with limited resources, capacity building in relation to regulation of genetic resources is a major issue. This is a need which is recognised and addressed within the CBD, and more specifically through the Bonn Guidelines[141], which were adopted at the sixth meeting of the Conference of the Parties in 2002 (COP VI).

As access and benefit-sharing are not provided for through the TRIPS Agreement, the Guidelines are another area in which the two agreements are not compatible, and need to be considered in attempts to reconcile the two.

The Bonn Guidelines act as a guide to developing access and benefit-sharing agreements between parties, are indicative in their nature, rather than prescriptive and are therefore country-specific in their implementation.[142] They deal with capacity building in access and benefit-sharing agreements, and are likely to be particularly useful in assisting bioprospectors when negotiating such agreements on a case-by-case basis under the CBD. The Guidelines make it clear that overall strategies on this topic should be available at a national or regional level to further assist implementation of the objectives of the CBD in private agreements.[143] This is to ensure that the conservation and sustainable use of biodiversity, as well as the equitable sharing of benefits, are promoted within the agreements. The Guidelines expand on some of the key concepts of access and benefit-sharing included in the CBD. These are prior informed consent (PIC), mutually-agreed terms, and benefit-sharing.

The basic principles of PIC as set out in the Guidelines include legal certainty and clarity, access at a minimum cost, transparency of restrictions on access, and obtaining consent of the national authority as well as the relevant stakeholders—indigenous or local communities—where appropriate.[144] In particular, the first three of these principles are available to ensure that the system developed facilitates, rather than restricts, access.[145] The Guidelines attempt to address the difficulties in establishing ownership of genetic resources discussed above, as it calls for the establishment of a competent authority for providing evidence of PIC. This should help to reduce transaction costs by providing a focal point for negotiations and in determining from whom consent should be obtained, an aspect of PIC which has caused much frustration in the past.[146]

Probably the most contentious aspect of PIC in terms of IPR regimes and the TRIPS Agreement is the requirement to provide details of specific uses of the genetic resource to which access is being requested. Such a requirement may be seen to be incompatible with the nature of the research being undertaken, as it potentially could involve disclosure of information that would ordinarily remain confidential until such time as a patent was granted over the final product. Any regulations relating to access and benefit-sharing agreements must therefore take into account the need for disclosure of such information in fulfilling the PIC requirements of the CBD, as well as the need to protect confidentiality so that bioprospecting companies are not placed at a competitive disadvantage by disclosing such information. This issue becomes more complicated given that bioprospecting often takes place on public lands, where the information may be available to many stakeholders.[147]

When negotiating access and benefit-sharing agreements, the Guidelines include a suggestion that such agreements should provide that the use of genetic resources should include joint research and possibly joint ownership of IPRs "according to the degree of contribution."[148] This suggestion has the potential to create tension between the TRIPS Agreement and the CBD, as it implies a certain level of erosion of IPRs and the monopoly status of patents.

Finally the Guidelines place an emphasis on non-monetary capacity-building, which includes joint ownership of relevant IPRs and access to scientific information. Providing for capacity building within access and benefit-sharing agreements is considered important in ensuring fair and equitable benefit-sharing, which will hopefully lead to increasing developing countries' (and the world's) ability to conserve and maintain biological resources so that they may be available for many years to come.

5.3.5 Derivative products

In some sectors of the biotechnology industry, such as pharmaceuticals, the majority of commercial products contain products derived from, or patterned on, genes found in nature.[149] Derivative products are not defined by the CBD and it is therefore up to member States to provide such a definition. The sale and use of derivatives of genetic resources are often included in access and benefit-sharing agreements made between providers and users of the resources.[150] This generally involves an agreement to pay royalties not only for use of the genetic resources itself, but also for the use of any derivatives of that resource.[151]

In dealing with regulation of derivative products and benefit-sharing relating to such products, many jurisdictions have provided definitions for terms such as "derivative," "by-product" and "synthesised product."[152] However they fail to set out where these terms are to be applied, for example, whether or not they are to be applied to access and benefit-sharing agreements and prior informed consent provisions of national legislation.[153]

Regulating access and benefit-sharing in relation to derivatives presents regulators with difficulties in that without agreements relating to use of derivatives, there is concern that companies may produce derivatives within the source country, and will thus be able to export without the constraints of benefit-sharing. As most products in some sectors of the industry are made from derivative products, this possibility seriously inhibits the effectiveness of the agreements that have been made. The alternative is to attempt to control derivatives through agreements. However, this would require a broad definition of the products subject to access and benefit-sharing agreements, which may prove to be unworkable as derivatives of genetic resources can be found everywhere in every day life. A possible solution to this problem may be for countries to regulate access over only the genetic resources themselves, but to provide that the use of derivatives must be subject to benefit-sharing agreements.[154]

5.3.6 *Ex-situ* conservation

Ex-situ conservation and collections of components of biological diversity exist in a diverse body of facilities, which include gene banks, in-vitro plant tissue and microbial culture collections, captive breeding of animals, artificial propagation of plants, and the collection of living organisms within zoos, aquaria and botanic gardens.[155] Such collections are used for the purposes of research, public education and awareness and conservation, and are playing an increasing role in the development of genetic diversity for the purposes of agriculture and medicine through genetic engineering.

The CBD deals with *ex-situ* conservation through Article 9, but makes it clear that such conservation measures should predominantly be for the purposes of complementing *in-situ* conservation. Importantly, plants and animals removed from their country of origin, and kept in *ex-situ* collections prior to entry into force of the CBD (December 29, 1993) are exempt from the CBD,[156] which means that repatriation of these resources, and therefore also access and benefit-sharing agreements, will be an ongoing problem. This provision benefits countries of the North as many genetic resources collected before this date are situated in the North. The Andean Pact provides us with an example of a regional agreement attempting to solve this problem, as it encourages *ex-situ* conservation centres to sign contracts with the Competent National Authority, thereby including genetic resources collected prior to 1993 to be subject to access and benefit-sharing arrangements.[157]

5.3.7 Are IPRs slowing the rate of innovation in biotechnology?

One of the benefits of protecting biodiversity, other than for its own intrinsic value, is that it will be available for future use in many capacities including for ecological, genetic, social, economic, scientific, educational, cultural, recreational and aesthetic purposes.[158] Conserving biodiversity for scientific purposes is necessary for promotion of innovation and technological growth. Nowhere is this more important to the survival of humankind than in the development of research for medicinal purposes.[159] The granting of patents over new inventions in this field is viewed by some as acting to inhibit innovation, a situation that has been described as the "tragedy of the anticommons."[160]

The "tragedy of the anticommons" arises when many gene fragments are patented in isolation. During the research and development (R&D) stage of biotechnological advances, costs may rise significantly when R&D involves the use of many gene fragments subject to patents.[161] The danger here is that the potentially huge transaction costs involved in paying for license to access each gene fragment may be so high in some cases that R&D is no longer financially justifiable. Where innovation in development of health products using biotechnology is financially prohibitive as a result of excessive patenting, the purpose for which biodiversity is being preserved through the CBD—so that it may be available for future scientific research—becomes redundant. It will therefore be important that those countries implementing the TRIPS Agreement ensure that their own IPR regimes are able to meet the social and economic welfare needs of society as well as the protection needs of the holders of intellectual property rights.[162]

5.3.8 IPRs and the erosion of biodiversity

Dutfield identifies two aspects of IPR regimes (in particular, patents) that have the potential to threaten biodiversity: monocultures and crop-agrochemical linkages.[163] The first aspect refers to the proposition that by applying IPR regimes to the development new agricultural products, incentives to develop seeds with a maximum demand in the marketplace, and that can be widely cultivated, are increased. The result is that agriculture is encouraged to move toward a more centralised breeding regime, where diversity of agro-cultures is discouraged, leading to the advent of the monoculture.[164] This is likely to affect biodiversity conservation in that such agricultural systems may replace more biodiversity-rich ecosystems. However, it must be noted that such systems may also have the potential to reduce the loss of biodiversity if they are able to produce at a higher rate than more diverse agricultural systems (thereby reducing the need to clear biodiversity-rich land for the sake of cultivation).[165]

Crop-agrochemical linkages to IPRs refer to genetically modified crops being created as part of an agricultural "package" where crops are developed as resistant to a certain herbicide marketed by the same company who created that particular crop. This practice is to promote use of the company's herbicide product over and above its competitors. Environmentalists, however, assert that these "packages" may encourage excessive use of herbicides, accelerate resistance amongst pests, or the resistant properties could cross over to other plants or weeds, which would be so powerful as to dominate ecosystems and become what has been termed a "superweed."[166] IPRs are relevant to this discussion as both the crop seeds and the herbicide are likely to be protected by patents. However it has been noted that they probably cannot be held solely to blame, and that perhaps the patent office is not the most appropriate place in which to address issues of genetically engineered pest-resistant crops.[167]

5.3.9 The UPOV Convention

The provisions of the UPOV Convention on plant variety rights have been criticised as having the potential to erode the protection of biodiversity, therefore undermining the objectives of the CBD. These criticisms focus on the Convention's requirements for granting plant breeders' rights (PBRs), which are uniformity, stability, distinctness and novelty.[168]

The uniformity and stability requirements of the Convention may prove to give an unfair disadvantage to traditional and local communities who are more likely to breed varieties of plants that are genetically diverse, and therefore more likely to be more robust varieties in changing, unstable conditions. The Convention not only makes it more difficult for such societies to gain access to its provisions, but also tends to encourage varieties that are not genetically diverse, which may be seen as running counter to the conservation and equity provisions of the CBD.[169] In addition, the requirement that plant varieties be distinct and new may also have an inequitable effect in that those breeders with the resources to acquire PBRs could misappropriate genetic resources from local communities who do not have the financial, legal and technical support to acquire such PBRs.

It must be noted that whilst links may exist between IPR regimes and the erosion of biodiversity in the above contexts, IPRs may not be the sole cause of such erosion. There is therefore a need for further research in this area, and the application of the precautionary principle in the meantime may be appropriate to avoid any of the potential environmental and social impacts.[170]

5.4 RECONCILING THE DIFFERENCES

If the differences between the two agreements are to be reconciled, it will be necessary to take the *pragmatic* approach outlined by Dutfield and included in section 5.3 of this paper. This approach recognises that whilst there maybe serious difficulties in reconciling the two, building on our existing IPR and biodiversity conservation regimes will be the most practical and achievable approach to bridging the gap.[171]

The pragmatic approach is examined in the discussion below, and was highlighted by the WTO declaration of the Fourth Ministerial Conference in Doha, Qatar (the Doha Declaration).[172] The Declaration specifically instructs the Council for the TRIPS Agreement to examine the relationship between the TRIPS Agreement and the CBD, as well as the protection of traditional knowledge and folklore and "other relevant new developments" that are raised by Member states during the review of the TRIPS Agreement.[173] A review has since been undertaken of both Article 27(3)(b) of the Agreement, as well as the entire Agreement itself, and it has been agreed that the Council shall work with both the World Intellectual Property Organisation (WIPO) and the CBD in addressing the issues raised in this respect.[174]

The findings of the review include India's suggestion that patents inconsistent with Article 15 of the CBD not be granted, that Article 27(3)(b) of the TRIPS Agreement be implemented only after five years from the end of the current review, that technology transfer should be on fair and mutually advantageous terms, as well as suggesting that Article 27(3)(b) be amended to make it consistent with the CBD.[175] Some of these concerns, as well as a discussion on providing non-Member states with "observer status" in negotiations of agreements, are addressed in the brief description below on how the two agreements may be reconciled.

5.4.1 Using the TRIPS Agreement as a framework for reconciling the differences

Although the TRIPS Agreement allows for the creation of effective *sui generis* systems which may eventually evolve into a system embodying protection of traditional knowledge, an alternative method of protection of this type of knowledge may be through disclosure requirements at the time of patent registration to include the country of origin of the biological materials and the traditional knowledge related thereto. The application should further require evidence that prior informed consent has been obtained and the nature of the compensation paid (if any).[176]

Adding access and benefit-sharing provisions to the TRIPS Agreement, for example through amendment of Article 27,[177] is another suggestion of how to reconcile the differences between the two international treaties. This approach, however, has been criticised as creating unmanageable complications in the use of genetic resources.[178] Other suggestions include the expanded use of patent law, trade secrets and geographical indications in protecting indigenous knowledge.

5.4.1.1 Patents

Some of the problems identified with patent law and its impact on biodiversity conservation within the CBD may be addressed through adjustments to patent law regimes. Dutfield suggests some possible alterations, which include applying the precautionary principle to take into account the potential environmental and social impacts of patenting life forms; expanding the interpretation of the *ordre public* and morality exclusion within Article 27(2); reforming the standards of *novelty* so that traditional knowledge cannot be as easily misappropriated by those with greater financial resources and access to patentability laws; including requirements for certification or country of origin in the process of applying for IPRs.[179] Of course, these types of amendments would all be subject to implementation by national governments. It should also be noted that in any case, if patents were to be used as a method for recognising traditional knowledge, some significant barriers do exist to the implementation of such a provision, such as the fact that the information required for a patent specification is expressed in a technical way, which may not be within the expertise of indigenous and local communities, as well as taking into account the significant amount of financial resources needed to acquire patent protection.[180]

5.4.1.2 Trade secrets

It has been suggested that the trade secret may prove useful in the protection of traditional ecological knowledge.[181] This is based on the fact that not all knowledge within traditional communities is shared, and that some individuals may have access to information due to their status in the group, which may be converted into a trade secret to be owned by either that individual or the group as a whole.[182] This practice is under way in Ecuador, where a database of TEK trade secrets is being developed and intended for use by the private sector. It must be noted, however, that whilst this is a possibility for the future, and on an individual-nation basis, the TRIPS Agreement does not go far enough in providing for protection of indigenous IPRs under trade secrets.[183]

5.4.1.3 Geographical indications

The geographic indication provisions of the TRIPS Agreement could be used to develop laws protecting traditional ecological knowledge and help to maintain locally grown goods, such as *Basmati* rice, which has been the subject of much controversy in recent years.[184] Where products are distinct due to the origin of their production, the *appellation of origin* provision comes into play. This aims to protect the original producers from having their good reputation destroyed by the development of a similar product at another location or nation, or by those without the traditional "know-how" to produce a superior product.

In the case of *Basmati* rice, which is cultivated in Northern India and Pakistan, two foreign companies (from the US and France) have been accused of appropriating the good reputation of the product to sell a similar product themselves. It has been suggested that India and Pakistan could challenge this action using the geographical indication provisions of the TRIPS Agreement on the basis that the US and French companies, in marketing their product as "Basmati" rice, are misleading consumers as to the origin of the product, thereby harming the reputation of true *Basmati* rice.[185] This suggestion, however, will be subject to the two countries protecting geographical indications themselves, as the TRIPS Agreement does not require Members to protect geographical indications unless the country of origin does so as well.[186]

5.4.2 Integrating the relevant conventions: Observer status

In order to avoid potential future conflicts and to promote greater interaction between the key IPR and biodiversity agreements, all parties to the debate will need to be given the opportunity to identify such conflicts and to contribute to finding effective and workable solutions. Such solutions should minimise the possible adverse impacts of IPRs on biodiversity conservation and therefore on its future availability for use by industry.[187] This may require members of different agreements having observer status within other key agreements, a concept which has in fact been suggested by Members of the WTO through the Doha Declaration which states that the WTO Members agree to negotiations on "procedures for regular information exchange between multilateral environmental agreement (MEA) Secretariats and the relevant WTO committees, and the criteria for the granting of observer status."[188]

Granting of observer status would include, for example, signatories of the TRIPS Agreement being invited to Conferences of the Parties (COPs) held by Contracting Members under the CBD in which changes to the Convention are negotiated. Guests to the COP meetings would not be given voting power, but may still have some input into how the agreement is developed and any amendments that are made, so that both the agreements are developed in coordination with each other.

5.4.3 Concluding comments

It is becoming increasingly important to ensure that the incompatibilities between the necessity of protecting intellectual property rights and the conservation and protection of biological diversity are effectively minimised. It is only recently that these issues are gaining national and international attention and the recent Doha Declaration evidences a new commitment on the part of the international community to take some practical steps in this regard.

One cannot approach a discussion of these issues without seriously considering how to bridge the apparent gulf between affording effective IPR protection with respect to traditional and local knowledge and existing IPR regimes that protect conventional forms of knowledge and integrating the two. The CBD explicitly recognises the obligation on Contracting Parties to respect, preserve and maintain knowledge of indigenous and local communities and the access and benefit provisions incorporating the concept of prior informed consent are integral to the achievement of the CBD's objectives and goals.

IPR regimes and the protection of intellectual property rights, on the other hand, are also given explicit recognition in the CBD and are of course the main focus of the TRIPS Agreement. What has been lacking to this point in time is the development of a comprehensive mechanism to properly ensure that the two principal international instruments in the context of biological diversity are not operating at cross-purposes. In this writer's respectful view, it is in this direction that the debate should now proceed.

ENDNOTES

1 *United Nations Conference on Environment and Development: Convention on Biological Diversity*, 5 June 1992 UNEP/Bioprospecting.Div./N7BINC5/4, reprinted in 31 I.L.M. 818 (1992) (entered into force on December 29, 1993) [hereinafter the CBD]. 187 parties (168 signatures) as at August 1, 2003.

2 Kerry ten Kate and Sarah A Laird, *The Commercial Use of Biodiversity: Access to genetic resources and benefit-sharing*, (UK: Earthscan Publications Ltd, 1999) at pages 292–312.

3 *Ibid*, at page 294.

4 *Agreement on Trade-Related Aspects of Intellectual Property Rights*, April 15, 1994, Marrakesh Agreement Establishing the World Trade Organisation, Annex 1C, GATT Doc. MTN/FAII- A1C, 33 I.L.M. 1197 [hereinafter the TRIPS Agreement].

5 See above at note 1.

6 David Hunter, James Salzman, and Durwood Zaelke, *International Environmental Law and Policy*, 2nd ed., (New York: Foundation Press, 2002) at pages 933–934. This concept arose from the 1983 Food and Agriculture Organisation of the United Nations (FAO) International Undertaking on Plant Genetic Resources.

7 *Ibid*, at page 934.

8 *General Agreement on Tariffs and Trade*, October 30, 1947, 61 Stat. A3, 55 U.N.T.S. 187 [hereinafter GATT].

9 *International Convention for the Protection of New Varieties of Plants*, reprinted at www.upov.org (53 member States as at 31 July 2003) [hereinafter UPOV Convention]. The convention was adopted in Paris in 1961 and established the International Union for the Protection of New Varieties of Plants. It was revised in 1972, 1978 and 1991.

10 Graham Dutfield, Intellectual Property Rights, Trade and Biodiversity: Seeds and Plant Varieties, (UK: Earthscan Publications/IUCN, 2000) at page 27.

11 Biswajit Dhar, Sachin Chaturvedi, and R. V. Anuradha, Regime of Intellectual Property Protection for Biodiversity: A Developing Country Perspective (India: RIS and IUCN, 2001) at page 69.

12 *Ibid*, at page 74.

13 See for example Paul J. Heald, The Rhetoric of Biopiracy (2003) 11 *Cardozo J. Int'l & Comp. L.* 519, (Symposium: Traditional Knowledge, Intellectual Property, and Indigenous Culture).

14 Paul J Heald, see above note 13 at page 525.

15 Biswajit Dhar, Sachin Chaturvedi, and R. V. Anuradha, see above note 11 at page 71.

16 Paul J. Heald, see above note 13 at pages 531–532.

17 David Hunter, James Salzman and Durwood Zaelke, see above note 6 at page 932.

18 Michael I. Jeffery, "The Impact of Trade and Intellectual Property Rights on Biodiversity Conservation: Setting the Boundaries," presented at the World Jurist Association 21st Biennial Conference on the Law of the World, 22 August 2003, Adelaide, at page 6.

19 *Ibid*, at page 6.

20 David Hunter, James Salzman, and Durwood Zaelke, see above note 6 at page 933.

21 Report on the Conference of the FAO, U.N. Food and Agriculture Organization, 22nd Sess., U.N. Doc. No. C 83/Rep. (1983) (Rome, Nov. 5–23, 1983) extracted in Hunter *et al.*, (2002) at page 934.

22 David Hunter, James Salzman, and Durwood Zaelke, see above note 6 at page 934.

23 Protection of IPRs was a requirement of many countries of the North in the negotiations leading up to the CBD.

24 David Hunter, James Salzman and Durwood Zaelke, see above note 6 at page 934.

25 *Ibid*, at page 934.

26 Kerry ten Kate and Sarah A Laird, see above note 2 at page 16.

27 CBD Article 15(5).

28 CBD Article 15(4).

29 CBD Article 15(2).

30 CBD Article 16(2).

31 CBD Article 16.

32 CBD Article 16(1).

33 Michael I. Jeffery Q. C., "Bioprospecting: Access to Genetic Resources and Benefit-Sharing under the Convention on Biodiversity and the Bonn Guidelines" (2002) 6 *Singapore J. Int'l & Comp. L.* 747 at page 766.

34 CBD Article 16(2).

35 Michael I. Jeffery Q. C., see above note 33 at page 766.

36 CBD Article 16(2).

37 Graham Dutfield, see above note 10 at page 34.

38 Michael I. Jeffery Q. C., see above note 18 at page 12.

39 Michael I. Jeffery Q. C., see above note 33 at page 767.

40 CBD Article 16(4).

41 Michael I. Jeffery Q. C., see above note 33 at page 768.

42 Michael I. Jeffery Q. C., see above note 18 at page 8.

43 Graham Dutfield, see above note 10 at page 34.

44 CBD Article 16(5).

45 Lyle Glowka, "A Guide to Designing Legal Frameworks to Determine Access to Genetic Resources" (Gland, Switzerland, Cambridge, and Bonn; IUCN 1998) at page 15.

46 *Ibid*, at page 16.

47 Graham Dutfield, see above note 10 at page 35.

48 CBD Article 8(j).

49 Graham Dutfield, see above note 10 at page 35.

50 Lyle Glowka, see above note 45 at page 15.

51 Berne Convention for the Protection of Literary and Artistic Works (1886).

52 Paris Convention for the Protection of Industrial Property (1883).

53 GATT see above at note 8.

54 The TRIPS Agreement. See above at note 4.

55 Anne Fitzgerald, *Intellectual Property*, 2nd ed., (Sydney, Australia: Lawbook Co., 2002) page 45. See the TRIPS Agreement, preamble.

56 The TRIPS Agreement, see above note 4 at Article 1.

57 *Industrial Property Bill* (1989), Kenya Gazette Supplement 92 (bills No 18), 1399–1459, cited in Graham Dutfield, see above note 10 at page 19.

58 The TRIPS Agreement, see above note 4 at Article 65(1).

59 *Ibid*, Articles 65(2) and 66(1).

60 MFN principle: The TRIPS Agreement, Article 4. See also Article 5. National Treatment principle: The TRIPS Agreement, Article 3. An illustration of this principle would be that a copyright work produced in another *Berne Convention* or *Paris Convention* country outside of Australia would qualify for the same copyright protection under Australian law as if it were originating in Australia. Fitzgerald, *supra* note 55 at page 40.

61 This means that any concession granted to one Member's nationals within any Member country must also be granted to all other Member's nationals. Graham Dutfield, see above note 10 at page 19.

62 The TRIPS Agreement, see above note 4 at Part III, Section 2, Articles 42–49.

63 Article 1.2 of the TRIPS Agreement states that "for the purposes of this Agreement, the term 'intellectual property' refers to all categories of intellectual property that are the subject of Sections 1 through 7 of Part II."

64 David Downes, Integrating Implementation of the Convention on Biological Diversity and the Rules of the World Trade Organisation. IUCN, Gland and Cambridge; Downes notes that geographical indications may also be relevant.

65 The TRIPS Agreement, Article 27 (1).

66 Maria Kruger, "Harmonising TRIPS and the CBD: A Proposal from India," (2001) 10 *Minn. J. Global Trade* 169, at pages 184–185.

67 Graham Dutfield, see above note 10 at page 20.

68 *Ibid*, at page 20.

69 The TRIPS Agreement, see above note 4 at Article 27(3).

70 See Klaus Bosselmann, "Plants and Politics: The International Legal Regime Concerning Biotechnology and Biodiversity" (1996) 7 *Colo. J. Int'l Envt'l L. & Policy* 111.

71 David Downes, see above at note 64.

72 Graham Dutfield, see above note 10 at page 25.

73 The TRIPS Agreement, see above note 4 at Section 7, Part II, Article 39.

74 See Michael I. Jeffery Q. C., see above note 18 at page 17

75 The TRIPS Agreement, see above note 4 at Article 22(1).

76 Moran W, "Rural Space as Intellectual Property," *Political Geography*, 12, pages 263–277. Cited in Graham Dutfield, see above note 4 at page 24.

77 Protection for geographical indications for wines and spirits is provided for specifically within Article 23. This is an indication of the influence of heavy wine and spirit exporters, such as France, in the negotiations of the TRIPS Agreement. Graham Dutfield, see above note 10 at page 24.

78 Graham Dutfield, see above note 10 at page 85.

79 Sam Johnston and Faharna Yamin, "Intellectual Property Rights and Access to Genetic Resources," in John Mugabe, Charles V. Barber, Gudiun Henne, Lyle Glowka and Antonio La Vina (eds), *Access to Genetic Resources: Strategies*

for Sharing Benefits, (Kenya: African Centre for Technology Studies, 1997) at page 249.

80 UPOV Convention see above at note 9.

81 Michael I. Jeffery Q. C., see above note 18 at page 19.

82 UPOV Convention, see above note 9 at Article 2.

83 *Ibid*, at Article 5. Articles 6–9 set out the definitions of these criteria.

84 Sam Johnston and Faharna Yamin, see above note 79 at page 249.

85 Lyle Glowka, Françoise Burhenne-Guilmin, and Hugh Synge in collaboration with Jeffrey A. McNeely and Lothar Gündling, *A Guide to the Convention on Biological Diversity*, (Gland and Cambridge; IUCN, 1994), at page 88.

86 UPOV Convention, see above note 9 at Article 15(2).

87 Lyle Glowka, Françoise Burhenne-Guilmin and Hugh Synge, see above note 85 at page 88.

88 Graham Dutfield, see above note 10 at 29. See also Graham Dutfield, Background Paper, (written for the IUCN Project on the Convention on Biological Diversity and the International Trade Regime), "Intellectual Property Rights, Trade and Biodiversity: The Case of Seeds and Plant Varieties," IUCN, Gland, Switzerland, June 1999, at page 33 for a relevant case study on this aspect of "farmer's privilege."

89 Article 15(iii) of the UPOV Convention, which states that "breeder's rights shall not extend to ... acts done for the purpose of breeding other varieties."

90 Lyle Glowka, Françoise Burhenne-Guilmin, and Hugh Synge, see above note 85 at page 88.

91 *Ibid*, at page 88.

92 Michael I. Jeffery Q. C., see above note 18 at page 20. See also: Lyle Glowka, Françoise Burhenne-Guilmin, and Hugh Synge, see above note 85 at page 88; WWB/CIEL Joint Discussion Paper, "Biodiversity & Intellectual Property Rights: Reviewing Intellectual Property Rights in Light of the Objectives of the Convention on Biological Diversity," Gland and Geneva, Switzerland, 2001, at page 16.

93 Graham Dutfield, see above note 10 at page 28.

94 Although it is important to note that the move toward patent-like protection of plant variety rights is denied by supporters of the 1991 revision: see *Ibid*, at page 29.

95 Sam Johnston and Faharna Yamin, see above note 79 at page 250.

96 *Ibid*, at pages 250–251.

97 D. S. Tilford, "Saving the Blueprints: The International Legal Regime for Plant Resources," (1998) 30 *Case Western Reserve Journal of International Law*, 373, at page 409.

98 *International Undertaking on Plant Genetic Resources*, Resolution 8/83, FAO Conference, 22nd Session, Rome, November 1983.

99 Originally called the Commission on Plant Genetic Resources.

100 D. S. Tilford, see above note 97 at page 410.

101 Graham Dutfield, "TRIPS-related Aspects of Traditional Knowledge" (2001) 33 *Case Western Reserve Journal of International Law* 233 at page 264.

102 Agreed Interpretation of the International Undertaking, Resolution 4/89. Extract of the 25th Session of the FAO Conference, Rome, November 11–29, 1989, Para 1, available online: (http://www.fao.org/ag/cgrfa/IU.htm#documents) (last accessed September 11, 2003).

103 Farmers' Rights, Resolution 5/89. Extract of the 25th Session of the FAO Conference, Rome, November 11–29, 1989, available online: (http://www.fao.org/ag/cgrfa/IU.htm#documents) (last accessed September 11, 2003).

104 Resolution 3/91. Extract of the 26th Session of the FAO Conference, Rome, November 9–27, 1991, available online: (http://www.fao.org/ag/cgrfa/IU.htm#documents) (last accessed September 11, 2003).

105 *International Treaty on Plant Genetic Resources for Food and Agriculture*, November 2001, available online: (http://www.fao.org/ag/cgrfa/itpgr.htm#text) (last accessed September 11, 2003). Under Article 28, the Treaty shall enter into force the 90th day after deposit of the 40th instrument of ratification, acceptance, approval or accession.

106 Access is allowed to those genetic resources listed in Annex I of the International Treaty on Plant Genetic Resources for Food and Agriculture.

107 Commission on Genetic Resources for Food and Environment, available online: (http://www.fao.org/ag/cgrfa/itpgr.htm).

108 Graham Dutfield, see above note 10 at page 41. These views are set out in Box 5.1.

109 Christopher Hunter, "Sustainable Bioprospecting: Using Private Contracts and International Legal Principles and Policies to Conserve Raw Medicinal Materials," (1997) 25 *B. C. Envtl. Aff. L. Rev.* 129, at pages 138–141.

110 *Ibid*, at pages 138–141.

111 Dr Gerard Bodeker, "Traditional Medical Knowledge, Intellectual Property Rights and Benefit Sharing," (2003) 11 *Cardozo J. Internationa'l & Comp. L.* 785, at page 796. (Symposium: Traditional Knowledge, Intellectual Property, and Indigenous Culture).

112 Council for Scientific and Industrial Research, *Media Release: The San and the CSIR announce a benefit-sharing agreement for potential anti-obesity drug*, March 24, 2003. Available online: (http://www.csir.co.za/plsql/ptl0002/PTL0002_PGE013_MEDIA_REL?MEDIA_RELEASE_NO=7083643) (accessed September 26, 2003). Milestone payments are paid subject to agreed technical performance targets of the molecule during clinical development, whilst royalties are paid based on sales which are not to commence before 2008. The income will be deposited into a San Hoodia Benefit Sharing Trust.

113 Gerard Bodeker, see above note 111 at page 796.

114 Kerry ten Kate and Sarah A Laird, see above note 2 at pages 58–59.

115 75 per cent of the 120 pharmaceutical products derived from plants in 1985. *Ibid*, at page 61.

116 Defined as "the use of people's knowledge and experiences of the medicinal properties of plants and other genetic resources to guide drug discovery." *Ibid*, at page 61.

117 *Ibid*, at page 62.

118 The CBD refers to indigenous people as "indigenous and local communities embodying traditional lifestyles." See, for example, the Preamble of the CBD see above note 1.

119 Other uses of traditional ecological knowledge include for cosmetic or agricultural purposes.

120 United Nations Development Program, *Conserving Indigenous Knowledge: Integrating two systems of innovation*, An independent study by the Rural Advancement Foundation International, 1994, New York. Cited in Biswajit Dhar, Sachin Chaturvedi, and R. V. Anuradha, see above note 11 at page 70.

121 Farnsworth N. R., Akerele O., Bingel A. S., Soejarto D. D., and Guo Z., "Medicinal Plants in Therapy," *Bulletin of the World Health Organisation*, 1985, vol. 63, pages 965–981. Cited in Kerry ten Kate and Sarah A Laird, see above note 2 at page 61.

122 Grifo F., Newman D., Fairfield A. S., Bhattacharya B., and Grupenhoff J. T., "The Origins of Prescription Drugs," in Grifo F., and Rosenthal (eds.) *Biodiversity and Human Health*, 1996, Island Press, Washington DC. Cited in Kerry ten Kate and Sarah A Laird, see above note 2 at page 61.

123 See Graham Dutfield, see above note 101 at pages 253–258 for a more detailed critical analysis of the patent system in protecting TEK.

124 Willem Pretorius, "TRIPS and the Developing Countries: How level is the playing field?" in Peter Drahos and Mayne R. (eds.), *Global Intellectual Property Rights: Knowledge, Access and Development*, (New York: Palgrave MacMillan, 2002), at page 187.

125 *Ibid*, at page 187.

126 Posey D., "Intellectual Property Rights for Native Peoples: Challenges in Science, Business and International Law," paper presented for the International Symposium on Property Rights, Biotechnology and Genetic Resources, Nairobi, Kenya, 1991. Cited in Willem Pretorius, see above note 124 at page 186.

127 Lyle Glowka, "Bioprospecting, Alien Invasive Species, and Hydrothermal Vents: Three Emerging Legal Issues in the Conservation and Sustainable Use of Biodiversity" (2000) 13 *Tulane Environmental Law Journal* 330 at pages 331–332.

128 Provisions regarding access are Articles 3 and 15 of the CBD. Article 3, which recognises State sovereignty over genetic resources, and Article 15, which specifically refers to State control of access to genetic resources through national legislation. Provisions relating to benefit-sharing are Articles 8(j), 15(6), 15(7), 16 and 19(1)(2) of the CBD.

129 CBD, see above note 1 at Article 1.

130 Gollin, M., "An Intellectual Property Rights Framework for Biodiversity Prospecting," in Read *et al.*, *Biodiversity Prospecting*, WRI, Washington DC, 1993. Cited in Kerry ten Kate and Sarah A Laird, see above note 2 at page 4.

131 CBD, see above note 1 at Article 15(5).

132 *Ibid*, at Article 15(4).

133 Obligation to facilitate access in Article 15(2) of the CBD. Objectives in Article 1 of the CBD.

134 Exception are listed in Article 27(2)–(3), and include Members being able to choose to exclude from patent protection inventions to protect *ordre public* or morality, or methods of treatment for humans or animals, or biological processes.

135 Downes D., see above at note 64.

136 Bosselmann K., "Focus: Plants and Politics: The International Legal Regime Concerning Biotechnology and Biodiversity" (1996) 7 *Colorado Journal of International Environmental Law and Policy* 111 at pages 126–128.

137 John Mugabe *et al.*, "Managing Access to Genetic Resources: Towards Strategies for Benefit Sharing," in Mugabe J *et al.*, eds., *Biopolicy International Series No. 17*, (Kenya: ACTS/Initiatives Publishers/WRI, 1996) at page 10.

138 Columbia University School of International and Public Affairs, *Access to Genetic Resources: An Evaluation of the Development and Implementation of Recent Regulation and Access Agreements*, Environmental Policy Studies Working Paper 4, Biodiversity Action Network, Columbia, 1999, at page 9.

139 See Kerry ten Kate and Sarah A Laird, see above note 2 at pages 32–33 for more detailed analysis on how to comply legally and in terms of best practice.

140 Henrietta Fourmile, "Using PIC procedures under the Convention on Biological Diversity to protect Indigenous Traditional Ecological Knowledge and Natural Resources Rights" (1998), 16 *Indigenous Law Bulletin* 27.

141 Conference of the Parties to the Convention on Biological Diversity, Access and Benefit-Sharing as Related to Genetic Resources, Bonn Guidelines on Access to Genetic Resources and Fair and Equitable Sharing of the Benefits Arising out of their Utilisation, U.N. Environment Programme, 6th meeting, U.N. Doc. UNEP/CBD/COP/6/24 (2002) [hereinafter the Bonn Guidelines].

142 See subsection A (Key Features) of Section I (General Provisions) of the Bonn Guidelines, *Ibid.* See also Michael I. Jeffery Q. C., see above note 33 at page 795.

143 The Bonn Guidelines, see above note 141 at Clause 22.

144 *Ibid*, at Clause 26(a)–(d).

145 Michael I. Jeffery Q. C., see above note 33 at page 797.

146 Kerry ten Kate and Sarah A Laird, see above note 2 at page 326.

147 Columbia Study, see above note 138 at page iii.

148 The Bonn Guidelines, see above note 141 at Clause 43.

149 Kerry ten Kate and Sarah A Laird, see above note 2 at page 70.

150 Lyle Glowka, see above note 45 at page 35.

151 Kerry ten Kate and Sarah A Laird, see above note 2 at page 17.

152 See *Ibid*, at page 19 for some examples of such definitions from the Philippines Executive Order and Implementing Regulations, the Andean Community Decision 391 and the Costa Rica Law 7788.

153 *Ibid*, at page 18.

154 *Ibid*, at page 20.

155 Lyle Glowka, Francoise Burhenne-Guilmin and Hugh Synge, see above note 85 at page 52.

156 CBD, see above note 1 at Article 15(3).

157 Andean Pact, Decision 391: *Common Systems on Access to Genetic Resources*, available online: (http://users.ox.ac.uk/~wgtrr/andpact.htm) (last accessed September 19, 2003).

158 CBD, see above note 1 at Preamble, paragraph 1.

159 This concept is also important in the field of agro-biotechnology. See Graham Dutfield, see above note 10 at page 16 for examples of how patent law can obstruct innovation in this field.

160 Heller M. A., and Eisenberg R. S., "Can Patents Deter Innovation? The Anticommons in Biomedical Research," *Science*, 280, pages 698–701. Cited in *Ibid*, at page 15.

161 *Ibid*, at page 16.

162 See *Ibid*, at pages 15–17.

163 *Ibid*, at pages 44–50.

164 This proposition is put forward by Walter Reid, *Genetic Resources and Sustainable Agriculture: Creating Incentives for Local Innovation and Adaptation*, Biopolicy Series no. 2, African Centre for Technology Studies, Nairobi. Cited in *Ibid*, at pages 44–45.

165 *Ibid*, at page 46.

166 *Ibid*, at page 47.

167 *Ibid*, at pages 46–49.

168 TRIPS Agreement, see above note 4 at Article 5. Articles 6–9 set out the definitions of these criteria.

169 See Graham Dutfield, see above note 10 at page 50.

170 *Ibid*, at page 55.

171 *Ibid*, at page 41.

172 World Trade Organisation, *Fourth Session of the Ministerial Conference, Ministerial Declaration*, 20 November 2001, Doha, November 9–14, 2001. Adopted November 14, 2001. WT/MIN(01)/DEC/1. [hereinafter Doha Declaration].

173 *Ibid*, at para. 19. This article adds further that in undertaking this work, the Council should be guided by the objectives and principles of the TRIPS Agreement, taking into account the "development dimension."

174 Dr. Gerard Bodeker, see above note 111 at pages 790–791.

175 *Ibid*, at pages 791–792.

176 Willem Pretorius, see above note 124 at pages 187–188.

177 This was suggested by Brazil. See David Hunter, James Salzman and Durwood Zaelke, see above note 6 at pages 966–968.

178 *Ibid*, at page 967.

179 Graham Dutfield, see above note 10 at pages 77–78.

180 Graham Dutfield, see above note 101 at pages 255–257. Dutfield notes that, for example, that it would cost around US$20,000 to prepare and prosecute a patent in the United States. This cost is likely to make patents prohibitive for indigenous and local communities.

181 *Ibid*, at pages 258–260.

182 Josephine R. Axt I *et al.*, *Biotechnology, Indigenous Peoples and Intellectual Property Rights*, 93-478 CONG. RES. SERVICE REP. FOR CONGRESS 63 (1993). Cited in *Ibid*, at page 259.

183 *Ibid*, at pages 259–260.

184 Graham Dutfield, see above note 10 at page 85.

185 *Ibid*, at page 87.

186 TRIPS Agreement, see above note 4 at Article 24(9).

187 Michael I. Jeffery Q. C., see above note 18 at pages 23–24.

188 Doha Declaration, see above note 172 at paragraph 31(ii).

CHAPTER 6

A Brief Review of Legislation on Access to Genetic Resources and the Protection of Traditional Knowledge in Selected Megadiverse Countries[1]

JORGE CAILLAUX* AND SUSANNA E. CLARK†

6.1 INTRODUCTION

The Convention on Biological Diversity (CBD) of 1993, has triggered and paved the way for some of the most interesting discussions in the realm of international bio-policy. The discussion revolves around the context for access to genetic resources and benefit-sharing and the search for legal mechanisms that protect indigenous peoples' traditional knowledge, which is often related to the genetic resources in question.

* Legal Director, Corporación Drokasa (a Peruvian group of corporations working in agriculture and pharmaceuticals); Regional Vice Chairperson for South America, IUCN Commission on Environmental Law; President, Peruvian Society for Environmental Law; Visiting Professor of Environmental Law, Pontificia Universidad Católica de Lima.

† B.A. 1998, Cornell University; J.D. 2004, Washington University School of Law.

Over 50 countries around the world have high levels of biological diversity and those with the highest levels of biodiversity are recognised as Megadiverse countries, many of which have initiated policy and regulatory initiatives directed towards regulating access to genetic resources and protecting traditional knowledge, and some have adopted specific legislation[2]. Likewise, many academic institutions and private companies have made efforts to adapt their policies on access to biological material, to respond to the new paradigm that recognises that access is no longer free but regulated by conditions outlined in accordance with CBD. These include "prior informed consent," "mutually agreed upon terms," "partnerships," and "benefit-sharing." New policies and legal guidance is also provided by the Bonn Guidelines on Access to Genetic Resources and the Fair and Equitable Sharing of Benefits (2002) and on the recently adopted International Treaty on Plant Genetic Resources for Food and Agriculture (2003). International negotiations on the subject traditional knowledge, especially within the World Intellectual Property Organization's (WIPO) Intergovernmental Committee on Genetic Resources and Intellectual Property, Traditional Knowledge and Folklore, have also been instrumental in informing and orienting policy developments in various countries and regions.

In any case, countries which are either developing or implementing specific access and traditional knowledge policies and laws face considerable challenges that include the following:

- limited capacity to negotiate mutually beneficial terms in bio-prospecting projects;
- unlimited sources of national genetic resources available outside of the national jurisdiction (e.g. botanical gardens or ex situ collections);
- practical difficulties in controlling access to and use of genetic resources and related traditional knowledge;
- problems related to compliance with access and traditional knowledge rules;
- a limited research and technological culture which leads to insufficient policy and legal incentives that might serve to add value to national resources;

- external pressure deal with traditional knowledge issues in a particular way, stemming from other more "powerful" fora, such as the World Trade Organisation (WTO); and
- the difficulty of effectively incorporating and streamlining the legitimate interests of indigenous communities with regard to the protection of their traditional knowledge.

This chapter seeks to contribute to the identification of common legal and practical problems that Megadiverse countries face in developing and implementing policies and laws on access to genetic resources and the protection of traditional knowledge.[3] This chapter also contains some suggestions which address several of these problems, how to facilitate increased participation in international fora, and how to promote cooperation among countries with similar interests at stake[4].

The chapter is divided into five parts. The first part provides an overview of policy and legal progress made in some noteworthy countries. The second party includes several examples of institutional policy positions held by several important companies, associations and institutions (*ex-situ* centres). The third part identifies several critical issues that must be taken into account when creating access and traditional knowledge processes (policy and regulation). The fourth part provides the readers with an overview of a concrete example of legislation which has been introduced to protect traditional knowledge in Peru, along with a highlight of some of its key features. Finally, the fifth part offers recommendations regarding some of the main issues addressed throughout the paper and the future outlook.

6.2 PROGRESS IN POLICIES AND LAWS REGARDING ACCESS TO GENETIC RESOURCES AND TRADITIONAL KNOWLEDGE

Several countries have taken important steps towards the establishment of policies and norms on access and the protection of traditional knowledge.

In Brazil, legislation on access to genetic resources and benefit-sharing was passed following a process initiated in 1995 with a Senate Bill (Proposed Law 306, 1995) and supplemented with a proposal by the Federal Government's Inter-ministerial Group on Access to Genetic

Resources. The Executive Branch approved the Provisional Measure 2,126-8 on 26 January 2001[5]. It is also important to mention policies and norms created at the state level. These include, for example, Acre State's Law 1,235 that governs control instruments on access to genetic resources (1997), and Amapa State Law 0388/97 on Genetic Resource Access (1997).

China has yet to create a specific standard for access to genetic resources. However, legal instruments such as the Wildlife Protection Law (1989), the Charter for Protection of Wild Flora (1997), the Charter for Seed Management (1991), and the Livestock Reproduction Charter (1994), include clauses that govern the title and access to rights on genetic material and species. Chapter 5 of China's National Biodiversity Report to the CBD suggests the need for a standard on access and benefit-sharing, given the fact that current standards do not address the issue in its entirety.

Costa Rica approved a Biodiversity Law (Law 7788, 1998) that includes procedural guidelines, basic requirements and an institutional framework for access to genetic resources. This law also contains a very detailed section on intellectual property and traditional knowledge. In compliance with this legislation, the National Commission for Biodiversity Management (CONAGEBIO) will need to formally approve a specific charter on access to genetic resources, and has prepared a draft proposal to this effect.

India does not currently have a standard that specifically regulates access to genetic resources. Nevertheless, important steps have been taken towards the adoption of a special framework, such as the establishment by the Ministry of Environment and Forests in 1995 of an Expert Committee charged with the drafting of a general law on biodiversity, including access to genetic resources. A draft Biodiversity Act was later prepared that includes general declarations on the institutional framework, and several specific resolutions regarding the conservation and sustainable use of biodiversity, as well as aspects related to access to genetic resources and benefit-sharing. This Act proposes the establishment of national, state and local authorities, together with special committees. These authorities would be responsible for fine-tuning access procedures through special decrees.[6]

In the case of Indonesia, Law 12 (Law on Cultural Practices, 1992) contains several declarations that refer to the use of and access to genetic resources. Nevertheless, they are quite general and therefore further regulation of the institutional framework (authorising agencies), administrative procedures, and conditions of access (including monitoring) are needed.

Mexico does not have specific legislation concerning access to genetic resources and benefit-sharing. In 1997, the National Commission for the Knowledge and Use of Biodiversity (CONABIO) and the Senate prepared a bill for a proposed law on access to genetic resources. This initiative sought to further develop Articles 87bis and 87bis 1 (regarding prior informed consent and benefit-sharing) of the General Law on Ecological Balance and Environmental Protection. This represents an integral approach to access to genetic resources that would promote participation from the private sector (and smallholders) in the use of Mexico's biological resources. In synthesis, Mexico's legal framework (together with CBD) would likely lead to the use of specific regulations on the issue of access.

In South Africa's case, the Senate's Environment Committee and the Department of Environmental Issues and Tourism initiated a process in 1995 to develop a general national policy on conservation of biological diversity. In 1997, a White Paper on Conservation and Sustainable Use of South Africa's Biological Diversity was published in the Official Gazette. The normative framework for the implementation of this document is currently under development. Provincial governments will be responsible for implementing the legislation and controlling access to genetic resources.

The Andean countries (Bolivia, Colombia, Ecuador, Peru and Venezuela) have developed shared legislation within the framework of the Andean Community of Nations (otherwise known as CAN, an acronym based on its Spanish title). CAN approved Decision 391 regarding the Common Framework on Access to Genetic Resources in 1996, which has been converted into the cornerstone for a series of national policies and norms related to the access of genetic resources and benefit-sharing. Bolivia published its Supreme Decree 24676 in 1997 that provides a very specific framework for the implementation of Decision 391. Colombia and Venezuela are directly implementing Decision 391 without any corresponding national regulations. Ecuador is currently approving a Charter on Access to Genetic Resources, and Peru is following a similar process. It is also important to mention CAN's Regional Biodiversity Strategy that advocates the design of joint guidelines and actions for access to genetic resources.

Finally, the United States of America does not have any special regime for access to genetic resources given that its legal framework favours the principle of common law. In practice, depending on the type of land tenure (federal, state or private) owners have the right to condition access to genetic resources and natural resources in general, in a way that serves them best, or in accordance with the relevant laws, as the case may be. Property rights generally include ownership of the associated natural resources on a tract of land, including above-ground and subterranean resources. While in the case of *ex-situ* genetic resources, it is generally accepted that anyone can have access to material maintained in seed banks, botanical gardens and other modalities (intellectual property rights prevailing when applicable). However, there might be exceptions and special conditions for access. This is especially true in the case of resources belonging to the National Program of Genetic Resources, which is considered to be national property.

6.2.1 Common Elements of Proposed Frameworks Regulating Access to Genetic Resources

The majority of proposed frameworks follow a sequence involving a request for access, setting conditions for access, signing agreements, and final approval by the relevant authorities. There are parallels in the structures and procedural flows, although these vary depending on the instrument in question. In Costa Rica and the CAN countries, the similarities are noteworthy.

Traditional and indigenous knowledge on biological diversity and genetic resources is clearly a priority for the majority of the Megadiverse countries. In fact, the incidence of megadiversity is closely related to cultural diversity. In this respect, several of the legislative initiatives include references with varying degrees of specificity on how to approach the issue of resource access on indigenous lands. Nevertheless, none of the initiatives deal in any detail with the issue of reaching prior informed consent with communities or indigenous groups that share similar resources and knowledge. Along these lines, each of the countries includes a reference to the necessity of establishing mechanisms to protect traditional knowledge associated with genetic resources in their proposed legal instruments (CAN's Decision 391, Costa Rica's Law 7788, Brazil's Provisional Measure). This opens an interesting panorama for the development of an *ad hoc* or *sui generis* special legal regime or framework designed to protect this knowledge.[7]

None of the proposals or standards reviewed here distinguish between the type of bio-prospecting (access to agricultural resources, medicinal plants or micro-organisms), and the final objective of bio-prospecting (to carry out taxonomic activities or for commercial goals), nor is special consideration given to centres of *ex-situ* conservation. In general, the same rules apply irrespective of the activity.[8] It is also interesting to note that, with the exception of the United States, all of the countries in question have either chosen or are working on specific norms on access to genetic resources. Another important issue is that none of these countries has opted for revising and adapting sector-specific norms that existed prior to the CBD and that generally govern aspects related to the collection of biological material. Table 6.1 allows for a comparison between the countries on core issues.

Furthermore, with the exception of Bolivia[10], none of the Megadiverse countries have yet to develop true strategic planning processes for access and benefit sharing. Following the legal mandate of the CBD, countries have evidently initiated policy and legislative processes as a matter of course. Concrete examples are lacking in the following areas:

- integrated and comprehensive market and demand analyses for genetic resources at the national level;
- evaluations of market structure and characteristics;
- needs analyses of the principle actors and stakeholders;
- cost-benefit analyses of a specific access norm or framework;
- institutional priorities at the national level;
- existing institutional scientific and administrative capacities; and
- non-juridical considerations that surround the issue of access to genetic resources.

It is not surprising then that a complex issue such as the access to genetic resources would produce very detailed norms and frameworks with an emphasis on procedural aspects. At the very least, one could conclude at first glance that the procedures designed for CAN, Costa Rica and Brazil are not especially easy or expeditious, although this is not necessarily bad. It is the State's privilege to regulate access in the way that best reflects its interests. Nevertheless, it is very important to take

TABLE 6.1 Treatment of critical issues in genetic resource access by country*

Countries	Ownership or rights over genetic resources	Specific legislation (special norm)	Protection of indigenous knowledge	Prior informed consent	Responsible authority bio-prospecting	Catalogued types of conservation	Centers of *ex-situ*
Brazil	Not defined	Yes	Yes (general reference to be defined)	With the State	Federal level (Inter-agency council)	No	Access subject to contracts for transfer of material (under legal conditions).
China	State	No		With the State			
Costa Rica	State	Yes	Yes (general referendum)	With the State	Technical office of CONAGEBIO	Yes	Agreements on the transfer of material (currently being formalized)
India	State	No	Mandate of the Biodiversity Act (special legislation)				
Indonesia		No					

TABLE 6.1 Treatment of critical issues in genetic resource access by country* (cont'd)

Mexico	State	No	General treatment under the Law of Ecological Balance		Secretary of the Environment and Natural Resources (SEMARNAT)		
South Africa	State	No					
CAN countries	State or the Nation	Yes	Yes	With the State or communities	Varies from country to country (Ministry of Environment, sector institutions, etc.)	Relative (depends on who carries out bio-prospecting)	Special treatment (model access contracts)
Peru			Peru Law 27811 on the Protection of Collective Knowledge of Indigenous Peoples Related to Biodiversity (2002).				
US	Private (as a general rule)	No			Federal, State or private representatives, depending on the specific case)	No	Special procedures (principle of free access)

* This table includes very general information. In several cases, sector-based legislation responds to some of the criteria of differentiation (China and Indonesia). Blank spaces indicate a lack of available information.

into account the possible consequences and implications that excessively rigid or complex procedures would have on interested parties. Research centres and companies are nearly unanimous in their response to the question of how legal frameworks for access should be characterised: these frameworks should be simple, clear and unambiguous.[11]

The concept of "transaction costs" is useful in this regard. The core issue is how to value the costs of a system which regulates access to genetic resources—the cost of supporting a specialised administration, operational and administrative costs, costs for the stakeholders—when compared to the potential benefits over the short, medium and longer terms. The response to this issue should be used to adjust the structure of the access regime or system. Finally, it is also relevant to analyse if any of the access systems have had a positive impact in biodiversity conservation policies and actions "in the field," considering that this objective is important to the CBD.

6.3 INSTRUMENTS AND PRACTICES OF INSTITUTIONS AND CORPORATIONS CONNECTED WITH ACCESS TO GENETIC RESOURCES AND THE USE OF RELATED TRADITIONAL KNOWLEDGE

The number of instruments and practices used by different institutions to adapt to the principles of the CBD has gradually increased. Countries of origin and suppliers of genetic resources are not the only parties to try to regulate access to their resources, as companies, universities, professional associations, *ex-situ* conservation centres in general (botanical gardens, seed banks, centres for conservation and storage of micro-organisms) and the different agents engaged in bio-prospecting, have also begun to deliberate on how to best comply with the mandates of the CBD.

The establishment and use of codes of conduct, institutional policies, model contracts (binding once signed), and best practice manuals are just some of the tools that reflect institutional points of view on the scientific and economic issues related to access to genetic resources.

Policy and regulatory efforts must take these instruments into account. As non-binding tools, their use provides an important reference point for negotiations involving bio-prospecting arrangements. A wealth of instruments exist today, whereas just seven or eight years ago no useful legal or "soft law" experiences existed, allowing for the design of proposals that are better adapted to the needs of different stakeholders. There is a tendency to trivialise the importance of these instruments. However, experience shows that they can be extremely useful in understanding the needs and priorities of different stakeholders and sectors, as well as an example of how they function, including their contribution to the generation of confidence between the relevant parties, mainly corporations, research centres and other private and public institutions.

Several of these institutional initiatives and instruments are detailed below. It should be noted that these instruments vary substantially in

TABLE 6.2 Documented policies, model contracts, codes of conduct, and experiences in legal access to genetic resources following the ratification of the Convention on Biological Diversity

a)	Kew Botanical Garden's Policy on Access to Genetic Resources and Benefit Sharing (adopted in 1998).
b)	Model contracts elaborated by the US National Cancer Institute [Letter of Intention (1990), Letter of Collection (1992) and Memorandum of Understanding (1995)].
c)	Model contracts of the Strathclyde Institute for Drug Research.
d)	Proposal for an International Code of Conduct on the Sustainable Use and Access to Micro-organisms, sustained by the principle storage facilities and institutions that have *ex-situ* collections of micro-organisms (1999).
e)	Glaxo Wellcome's Policy for Acquiring Sources of Natural Products (1992).
f)	Novo Nordisk Document: Acquisition of Natural Resources for the Development of New Pharmaceuticals (1995).
g)	Institutional Polices of Shaman Pharmaceuticals (1994).
h)	Principles of Access to Genetic Resources and Benefit Sharing for Botanical Gardens (2000).
i)	FAO Code of Conduct for Collection of Germplasm.
j)	Position Document of the European Council of the Chemical Industry on the Protection of Indigenous Knowledge and Access to Genetic Resources (2000).
k)	Document on the Institutional Position of CGIAR on Genetic Resources, Biotechnology and Intellectual Property Rights (1998).
l)	Document on the Institutional Position of the Association of Systematic Collection on access to specimens and genetic resources.

content and form. Each initiative includes core commitments to share monetary and non-monetary benefits in exchange for access to genetic resources and, in some cases, to traditional knowledge as well.

These initiatives are important inasmuch as they portray institutional responses to the CBD and to the issue of access to genetic resources in particular. It should be noted that US institutions subscribe to the principles of the CBD even in the absence of US government ratification. In this respect, it is important to understand the needs and interests of the commercial and scientific sectors of the biotechnology industry, in order to propose more effective policy and regulatory alternatives that more evenly respond to the interests of the Megadiverse countries without abandoning the needs of these sectors.

6.4 ELEMENTS TO CONSIDER TOWARDS ACHIEVING COMPLIANCE WITH AND ENFORCEMENT OF POLICIES ON ACCESS TO GENETIC RESOURCES

It is very difficult to identify each and every problem faced by the Megadiverse countries when developing and effectively implementing genetic resource access policies and norms. However, several elements that should be considered when developing these policies are readily identifiable. These include shared concerns and common issues that can be acknowledged and highlighted as factors that may influence the way access policies and norms are applied. A concise evaluation of the most pertinent of these issues follows.

6.4.1 Legal status of genetic resources

It is important to clearly define the legal status of genetic resources in order to establish who holds title to related rights and what these rights might include. In the case of the CAN countries, for example, Decision 391 determines that genetic resources are either denominated as national heritage or state property depending on the specific country. In Brazil, the term genetic wealth is used, and access and use of this wealth in any form is subject to approval by national authorities. While China does not have specific legislation, its Rules for Wildlife Protection stipulates that wildlife resources belong to the State, thereby providing a clear definition of ownership rights. In Costa Rica, both genetic and biochemical resources are considered State property.[12] This type of official status is delineated in most legal systems which regulate access, and together with the distinct sovereign right to regulate natural resource use found in each of the different countries, it allows the State to intervene as the responsible authority. As mentioned above, the exception to the rule is the US, where private property rights extend to natural resources and by extension, to private rights over genetic resources as well, subject of course to existing titles (Federal, State or individual) to the property on which these resources are found.

One of the crucial issues regarding ownership arises when negotiating a projected royalty or compensation to be paid when the company or research institution authorised to use a genetic material develops a commercial product. Who has the right over this income? Normally the access contract signed by those participating in the joint venture settles this issue with a specific clause or section providing a rule. Normally, projects do not reveal royalty levels. However, anecdotal evidence suggests that, for example, in the case of royalties for the use of traditional knowledge, these range between 1 per cent and 5 per cent of the commercial benefits generated by products. Monetary benefits are not—at least in the short term—of relevance.

6.4.2 Prior informed consent and mutually agreed terms

The existence of a license to access genetic resources implies the need for each country to establish certain conditions that promote reliable information, transparency, and specific contractual commitments that embody the concept of prior informed consent (PIC), while ensuring that contracts for the transfer of genetic material are made on mutually agreed terms (MAT). Both PIC and MAT can be considered, however, at different levels and with different stakeholders involved in the access process. Obviously, specific mechanisms are needed to establish the best possible conditions for PIC and MAT when dealing with access to community or indigenous-owned biological resources or traditional knowledge. In this respect, it makes sense to recognise that shared knowledge and resources exist between communities and indigenous groups, both within countries and between indigenous groups in different countries. One should also approach this situation realistically and recognise that bringing *all* communities together in agreement and establishing the same conditions for their approval would be quite unlikely. In these cases, special mechanisms should be developed (co-managed funds, for example) to mitigate and resolve opposing decisions between communities and other potential conflicts.[13]

6.4.3 Role of stakeholders and participatory processes

Although it may seem obvious to state that each actor fulfils a specific function in the negotiation of a bio-prospecting project, it is important that the policies and norms clearly reflect each and every one of these possible functions so as to promote cooperation and collaborative efforts. Policies and norms that successfully promote close rapport are the best guarantee that these projects will result in diverse benefits for the countries of origin. Thus, a detailed analysis of the interests of each actor and the promotion of participative processes (both in the design of policies and norms and in the negotiations themselves) help guarantee the acceptance of basic consensus on project objectives and goals. It is clear that the negotiation process calls for the development of negotiating skills and capacity, that could be provided by the respective State or country or independent institutions, in order to help parties find the best possible agreement and prevent potential conflicts and excessive negotiating costs.

6.4.4 Cooperation and collaboration

The evaluation of existing pilot experiences and norms for access in Megadiverse countries seems to clearly indicate that the basic premise consists of *controlling* the flow of genetic resources. Access procedures are oriented towards this control. Incentives designed to promote cooperation and collaboration between stakeholders in industry, government, research institutions, and indigenous communities are few or non-existent. It is therefore important to define an unambiguous State policy to control the flow of resources, not through restrictions on access, rather through incentives that promote effective opportunities for cooperation and the establishment of joint ventures for bio-prospecting. This could constitute the best way to regulate the flow of resources and control access. As considered on a number of occasions during the discussions leading up to CAN's Decision 391, another legitimate option is, of course, the use of control regulations based on restricted access. Such measures would need to be evaluated, however, to see if they perpetuate illegal flows or even destructive competition between Megadiverse countries. This underscores the importance of fully evaluating the costs and benefits of an ultra-protectionist access regime. In sum, it is important to address the rules of a very old market of genetic materials characterised by its free flow over national borders normally carried on by the individual scientist participating in specific research projects. These resource flows are probably reduced by increased customs control over the importation of plants and all kinds of biological organisms, which originated mostly in pest and disease control measures. This is why, any policy regarding access to genetic materials should provide for mechanisms that change this state of affairs.

6.4.5 Negotiation capacity

This section does not refer to the negotiation capacity of policy-makers before the different international fora (which should be strengthened in all countries), but rather to the parties' technical capacity to negotiate different types of bio-prospecting arrangements. Starting with the responsible authority for the access procedures (whichever it may be) and including national scientists or institutions that prepare or participate in the design of bioprospecting projects, limitations exist in their capacity to negotiate contracts and other agreements, given the multiple, potential avenues allowed under the principles of the CBD (and those that may be required by legislation). This could be an opportunity for independent institutions to offer its services to facilitate dialogue and negotiation between all parties, such as was the case of the Peruvian Society for Environmental Law in the ICBG Project signed between Washington University, Searle Pharmaceuticals, Universidad Cayetano Heredia, Museo de Historia Natural and CONAP.[14]

6.5 THE LEGAL PROTECTION OF TRADITIONAL KNOWLEDGE: SOME OPTIONS AND ALTERNATIVES FROM THE ANDEAN REGION

Decision 486 of the Andean Community of Nations on a Common Regime on Industrial Property (enacted in 2001) requires that if traditional knowledge (source country) or genetic resources (country of origin) from one of the five Member States of the Andean Community of Nations (Peru, Bolivia, Ecuador, Colombia, and Venezuela) is used, then a patent applicant may be required (at the discretion of the examiner) to provide evidence that the traditional knowledge or resources used in the invention were legally obtained.[15] This is what has been described as "*defensive protection of traditional knowledge.*"

6.5.1 Defensive protection of traditional knowledge: The Andean Regime (Decision 486) and disclosure requirements.

The patent system is a two-way mechanism: on one hand it impacts and affects traditional knowledge rights when promoting property rights protection without promoting the CBD's objectives and, on the other hand, it can become an effective resource for defensively protecting traditional knowledge.[16] The primary change needed, to expand the use of the current patent system in order to utilise it as a defensive measure against misappropriation of traditional knowledge[17], is the development of rules ensuring that prior art searches take existing traditional knowledge into account as part of the state of art.[18] For example, the US Patent Office (USPTO) follows a procedure that calls for defensive measures. The USPTO prefers granting a patent that might be based in part on prior art that is unaccounted for, instead of conducting a more exhaustive search that could prove to be too costly. An issue that needs to be addressed in this context is the need to facilitate access to traditional knowledge resources that are in the public domain and which should be taken into account in prior art searches. The USPTO's practice of allowing challenges to a patent *after* it has been granted is arguably not the most efficient or just system. The US patent's approval serves as notice to interested parties who then have a certain time period to present their case against the patent's inclusion of traditional knowledge that has not been accounted for. However, this is an inequitable process because it shifts the burden to the parties harmed by an unlawful patent, rather than having the party granted the patent, and directly benefiting from it, absorb the costs of fulfilling a complete disclosure requirement in a patent application.

It should be the responsibility of the patent applicant to describe all material traditional knowledge used in an invention. Further measures could include requiring the patent applicant to conduct a prior art search for traditional knowledge and to disclose the source country or community of the traditional knowledge that was used in the invention process. Shifting the burden onto indigenous peoples makes the process, in practice, extremely biased and unfair given the limited resources and capacity that indigenous communities, and their organisations, have.

The Peruvian regulation on plant breeders' rights first put into practice the requirement that an applicant provide evidence that materials were legally accessed, the origin of the genetic material contained in the plant variety, and the origin of knowledge (including traditional knowledge) that was used in connection with the variety.[19] Decision 391 of the Andean Community on a Common Regime on Access to Genetic Resources and Decision 486 on a Common Regime on Industrial Property (2001) also includes this requirement.

Traditional knowledge could also be protected through *positive measures* and this is an area that should be addressed more concretely as an option in addition to current defensive measures.[20] Positive protection refers to the conveyance of rights to indigenous peoples for their traditional knowledge.

The current patent system fails to take traditional knowledge into account as prior art when examining the novelty and inventive step requirements, despite the fact that much traditional knowledge has been widely documented and made public. The systematisation of traditional knowledge in databases could function as a defensive measure to protect traditional knowledge. One part of the solution could involve an effort to expand the codification of traditional knowledge, such as in registers or databases.[21] These in turn could be administered on a national level and be tied to an international system that is accessible by patent reviewers for prior art searches on a worldwide scale. Progress in this area would also be achieved if the Patent Cooperation Treaty system and national patent offices required a review of traditional knowledge resources in patent searches. Another part of the solution could be to require patent applicants to disclose the source of traditional knowledge used as any part of the claimed invention, and to provide evidence of prior informed consent, and of equitable benefit-sharing with the source communities and countries.[22] However, organising and disseminating traditional knowledge through registers and databases may have adverse impacts on the interests and cultures of indigenous communities.[23]

The Andean Community Decision 486 on a Common Regime on Industrial Property, has made great headway by requiring patent applicants to disclose if any traditional knowledge forms part of the claimed invention. Patent applicants have the burden of providing evidence of prior informed consent and equitable benefit-sharing with source communities and countries when they incorporate traditional knowledge into a claimed invention. It is essential to require that a patent applicant disclose traditional knowledge used in an invention, forming part of the state of the art or prior art, in order to promote the progress of science on both a small and on a larger scale. Requiring disclosure of traditional knowledge in a patent application would create an incentive for the maintenance of traditional knowledge systems on a small scale by protecting the development and ownership rights of traditional practices. On a larger scale, traditional knowledge systems would be supported by the continued maintenance of biodiversity *in-situ* by indigenous communities, and by the elevation and promotion of the status of traditional knowledge itself.[24] Such a requirement also promotes the goal of Article 8(j) of the CBD—to promote the wider use of traditional knowledge. Furthermore, prior art or the state of the art usually refers to the complete body of knowledge publicly available before filing a patent application, or before a priority date (if one is claimed). It is therefore not only incomplete, but professionally unethical to exclude publicly available traditional knowledge from patent applications and patent searches.

Acknowledging the widespread role of traditional knowledge in the development of pharmaceutical products, and its essential role in protecting biodiversity, we must take a step further in the direction of upholding traditional knowledge systems with an international effort founded on global interests.[25] The usefulness of traditional knowledge is indisputable, and one way the patent system is benefiting mankind is by disseminating this knowledge and using it for new developments. This is a worthwhile effort for both indigenous communities and the researchers or entrepreneurs involved. Therefore, both parties must be protected and provided with incentives. The incentives for those engaged in research and development group are already integrated into the temporary monopoly rights granted by the patent system, leaving the present need to provide indigenous groups with the benefits they deserve.

Defects in the current patent systems, with regard to an under-protection of traditional knowledge, should be corrected to solve an imbalance between the inherent flaws of the patent system and the public benefits derived from access to and use of indigenous knowledge.[26]

6.5.2 Positive protection of traditional knowledge: An overview of Law 27811 of Peru

Indigenous peoples' rights over their resources, intellectual efforts and developments should also be safeguarded with positive protection measures. The responsibility to conserve resources in order to safeguard future opportunities for research and development is a global one.

Peruvian Law No. 27811 (Law 27811) protects the biodiversity-related traditional knowledge possessed by indigenous communities. Law 27811 was enacted on August 10, 2002. Peru became the second country, after Panama to establish this type of legal measure for protecting traditional knowledge. Panama focused on expressions of folklore. Under Law 27811, indigenous communities can assert rights over collectively-held knowledge that is related to biological diversity[27], and prevent the unauthorised use of indigenous traditional knowledge. Law 27811 was Peru's first effort to implement Article 8(j) of the CBD and article 63 of the national Industrial Property Law of 1996. The law seeks to protect collective knowledge in order to benefit the communities that are its holders.[28] It encourages indigenous communities to freely exchange knowledge between their communities.[29] Along these lines, it establishes that communities will benefit by sharing their knowledge with other communities, and taking part in negotiations to allow its use. Representative community organisations and leaders must obtain the prior informed consent of the communities in order to authorise the use of traditional knowledge on their behalf.[30]

Law 27811's coverage is limited to the protection of traditional knowledge related to the uses and properties of biodiversity, thereby excluding (or leaving undecided) the protection of their practices and innovations. Its coverage is further limited to the protection of collective knowledge—knowledge that is developed and held by the community as a whole—and therefore does not belong to any one individual within the community.[31]

There is an ongoing debate about whether the existing legal instruments can adequately protect traditional knowledge or if the characteristics of traditional knowledge call for novel legal solutions. The protection of collective knowledge and sharing of benefits can possibly be achieved through a variety of intellectual property and other legal instruments, such as with contracts, trade secrets, registers, measures to prevent unfair competition, and bio-prospecting agreements, although this might require an adjustment of their traditional uses to include these new areas of protection.

Under Law 27811, if an interested party intends to use the knowledge for a commercial or industrial purpose, then a license must be signed. The underlying rationale is that requiring signatures will promote a discussion to establish mutually agreed terms. Law 27811 also provides unfair competition procedures to defend against the misappropriation or unauthorised use of traditional knowledge.[32] In addition, a claim can be presented to the national authority against someone who reveals, acquires, or uses collective knowledge in bad faith, while under an obligation to maintain its confidentiality, or without obtaining prior informed consent. The competent authority can also initiate a claim itself, either in response to an action or as a precautionary measure.

As mentioned above, under the discussion on defensive measures, Law 27811 also recommends the establishment of registers, which document collective knowledge and which vary in degrees of confidentiality. These registers may be publicly accessible or accessible only to the indigenous communities. The goals of the register system are to preserve and protect traditional knowledge, and to provide the competent national authority, INDECOPI, with the information necessary to defend the rights of indigenous communities related to their traditional knowledge.[33] Law 27811 establishes three types of registers, each with a distinct level of confidentiality. These include the National Public Register, which provides a defence against patents based on knowledge that is clearly in the public domain, a National Confidential Register, and Local Registers.

Law 27811 also creates a National Fund for the Development of Indigenous Peoples which has yet to be implemented.[34] This fund serves as a depository for the monetary benefits from license agreements and all indigenous communities have the right to access the Fund's financial resources to support conservation projects on their lands. The fund will eventually be administered by communities themselves. Law 27811 further establishes a Council specialising in the protection of indigenous knowledge[35], and a Council of national experts and representatives of indigenous and local communities charged with monitoring the system, providing technical and legal assistance to indigenous peoples' representatives, and supervising the national fund, among other duties.

As under Decision 486, Law 27811 also integrates the protection of traditional knowledge into existing intellectual property regimes by requiring an interested party to present a license at the same time as when he applies for a patent. Use of collective knowledge for industrial or commercial purposes requires a license that is signed by the communities' representative and the third party. The law regulates the minimum requirements of these licenses by requiring:

1) compensation to the indigenous communities of at least five per cent of gross sales of commercial products that are derived from the acquisition of collective knowledge;
2) the provision of research results; and
3) assistance in strengthening the indigenous communities' representative organisations. This will involve capacity building in enhancing their negotiating skills and their awareness of Law 27811.[36]

Law 27811 requires evidence of prior informed consent from the communities providing the knowledge. The element of prior informed consent seeks to ensure that communities have a choice over whether to disclose certain knowledge that might be culturally sensitive, for example, if that knowledge is used for industrial, commercial, or scientific purposes by third parties. The law requires a third party to negotiate with an organisation representing the communities that hold the relevant knowledge. These organisations must, in turn, inform the largest number of communities that might overlap in sharing the knowledge in question so that they can take part in the negotiation process or present their concerns.[37]

Law 27811 further specifies that licenses must be:

1) written (both in Spanish and the appropriate indigenous language);
2) in force for a maximum of three years; and
3) registered with INDECOPI.

The license is confidential, but still allows for other non-exclusive licenses for the same knowledge to be granted by different communities.

Furthermore, the knowledge can continue to be developed by present and future generations without restrictions arising from the license.[38]

6.6 OPTIONS AND RECOMMENDATIONS: PROMOTING COMPLIANCE WITH GUIDELINES ON ACCESS TO GENETIC RESOURCES AND THE FAIR AND EQUITABLE DISTRIBUTION OF BENEFITS

This section proposes several suggestions and recommendations, based on two critical assumptions. First, that genetic resources are shared and are found dispersed throughout the world (in *ex-situ* conservation sites, for example). Secondly, that these resources are relatively easy to access, and controlling of the flow of these resources is quite difficult.

It is important to keep in mind that the nearly indiscernible nature of genetic resources, together with the ease of transporting them from one site to another, creates a veritable challenge to finding effective control measures against illegal access. The recommendations made below can be used by the Megadiverse countries when designing rules for access.

a) *South–South Cooperation*

South–South cooperation, especially between the Megadiverse countries, is clearly a vital measure needed to strengthen institutional and human resources capacities. Understanding and sharing national experiences from negotiating bio-prospecting projects and the problems and challenges faced during their implementation can be extremely useful. In South America, the existing ties between the eight countries that are parties to the Amazon Cooperation Treaty (also known by its Spanish acronym as the TCA) should be fully exploited, especially in light of the agreements to locate its Permanent Secretariat in Brazil and the personal support of former President Cardoso to raise the importance of Amazon issues. Likewise, the technical capacity in the field of biotechnology in countries such as India and Brazil, and the enormous taxonomic skill capacity of Costa Rican and Brazilian institutions, should be used to formalise a technical cooperation program between the Megadiverse countries.

b) *Clarity and simplicity*

Clarity and simplicity are essential conditions for the effective and efficient implementation of access rules in each of the countries. If the Megadiverse countries view bio-prospecting as an opportunity to create national benefits, the policy and regulatory framework must be absolutely unambiguous in order to guarantee legal security to all stakeholders. Clarity and simplicity should also not be confused with leniency. The access regime or framework can be very strict and precise but clear rules are needed to make it readily understood with little room for differing interpretations.

c) *Flexibility*

The Megadiverse countries might consider flexibility as a quality of their access regimes, such that their regimes will be able to accommodate different modalities or types of bio-prospecting arrangements, as well as its numerous objectives, and the various types of contractual agreements. However, flexibility does not imply leniency here either. In this sense, the regulatory and policy processes should begin by recognising that each bio-prospecting project presents distinct challenges and issues that cannot easily be anticipated *ex-ante*. For example, bio-prospecting for marine micro-organisms differs considerably from the collection and evaluation of medicinal plants. In fact, the context of each bioprospecting project also varies notably in terms of its objectives, potential markets, and the providing country's national scientific capacities. This is why the capacities of national agencies to conduct negotiations should be strengthened, together with the establishment of a flexible legal framework. A second, and possibly more complex, option would consist of designing specific procedures for each type of bio-prospecting project.

d) *Intellectual property*

All countries—whether developed or developing—should adopt coherent positions on intellectual property rights in order to ensure that the objectives of the CBD are effectively met. Naturally, there may not be consensus on every aspect, as can be seen in the debate surrounding Article 27(3)(b) of the TRIPS agreement regarding whether intellectual property rights should be extended to cover life forms. However, disclosure requirements in patents—concerning the legal origin of genetic resources and traditional knowledge—as proposed in Andean legislation (Decision 391 and Decision 486 and in Brazil and Costa Rica), could be a common negotiating tool, especially for countries with megadiversity and important indigenous populations. Furthermore, the acceptance of this requirement by industrialised countries could further the implementation of the CBD and ensure legal certainty with regard to the nature and origin of potentially patentable inventions, especially when they incorporate biological or biologically derived materials.

These countries could also adopt a common position calling for stricter and more comprehensive evaluations by patent offices when determining the level of innovation or the scope of the state-of-the-art during patent assessments of biotechnological inventions. It might also be useful to make similar recommendations to the TRIPS Council and the CBD Conference of Parties, or to request that WIPO carry out further technical research on the viability of this option. Initiatives proposed to these institutions should be aimed at establishing some type of mechanism to increase the technical rigor of patent evaluations and other types of intellectual property rights related to biological and genetic resources. Such a mechanism would also require that basic information on medicinal plants and their uses, and traditional innovations, is provided by the requesting party and that the evaluators show more diligence when evaluating this information. In the case of the TRIPS review, emphasis could be placed on the formal procedures outlined in Article 29, rather than on the substantial review of Article 27(3)(b).

e) *Basic conditions*

While it is unlikely that a uniform legal framework for access would be adopted given the individual characteristics of each country, with the exception of some regional blocs such as the Andean Community, the Megadiverse countries could agree on essential conditions for negotiating bio-prospecting projects and access contracts. This would not require an agreement on detailed and comprehensive baselines. Each national and regional context and each negotiation has its own specific considerations, and therefore requires a certain degree of flexibility. However, the Megadiverse countries may need to agree upon certain basic conditions that have to be present in any bio-prospecting agreement entered into with third parties. These might include the training of national professionals, applying a portion of the benefits to strengthen national institutional or scientific capacities, or investing in activities that provide value to *in-situ* resources.

Another possibility is the use of a collectively established minimum percentage for royalties or dividends earned from the commercial or industrial products manufactured. This would be used to establish a lower limit below which these countries will not accept. This limit could vary between two and five per cent, such that a country would not accept any bio-prospecting proposal if the royalty rate went below this. The advantage to this lies in that the basic negotiating conditions would be clearly established, thus strengthening the entire block of countries.

f) *Biodiversity fund*

While the suggestion of sharing benefits in a just and equitable fashion between countries that share similar levels of biodiversity is interesting, each country will, in practice, look out for its own interests and needs. A way to ensure that at least a portion of the benefits derived from the negotiation process leading to access and use of genetic resources is utilised in a mutually beneficial way, would be to establish a trust fund (or other financial mechanism) for the Megadiverse countries. This shared fund could be used to channel resources to small *in-situ* projects in participating countries, selected through a screening process which has been agreed upon. It might also be used to exclusively finance basic or taxonomic research or other activities related to the conservation and valuation of the countries' biological wealth.

g) *Information systems*

It is very important that the Megadiverse countries have an information system that would disseminate data on their experiences and progress made in designing policies and rules for access. It could also be used to inform intellectual property agencies of the details of bio-prospecting projects, their research and development focus, the stakeholders involved, the permits issued, and so forth. Shared information would be especially useful for evaluating patent requests and for issuing Certificates of

Acquisition. Contact and communication between patent offices and access authorities is a fundamental consideration in monitoring efforts.

h) *Non-monetary benefits*

Countries should include provisions for non-monetary benefits in the legal framework and negotiation regime for bio-prospecting projects. Obviously, provisions should also be included for the use of royalties or other instruments for sharing larger-scale economic benefits at the commercialisation or industrialisation stage. Human resource and institutional capacity development could be strengthened by including stipulations for technology transfer, training, and the provision of minimum infrastructure that would be required for research efforts. The most effective approach might be to promote bio-prospecting projects as collaborative efforts that place a premium on these capacity development issues, rather than establishing royalties based on possible future benefits in the commercial phase.

i) *Jurisdiction*

Although it is a politically controversial and debatable issue, it would also be important to consider some type of ultra-national jurisdiction to review cases of possible compliance breaches or illegality. When dealing with sanctions, the most effective approach might be to file a complaint under the jurisdiction of one of the European countries or even the US, depending on the specific participants in a given bio-prospecting project. In cases of possible restitution or indemnification, the political and legal implications will have to be evaluated by each country, along with the basic terms and conditions of the access contracts.

j) *Directives*

With respect to post-CBD declarations for access and benefit sharing, it is important not to get caught up with negotiating Directives which are not binding on the parties to the convention, where the content of these Directives is not particularly innovative or new to the Megadiverse countries. These Directives have been influenced by the legal and policy frameworks which many countries have already created, and not vice versa. It would be better to establish directives that are relevant to resource *users* and not for those that supply resources as countries of origin.

k) *Congruent national legislation*

One should not lose sight of the importance of the codes used in many countries to regulate access to and use of biological samples for research purposes. These codes (which include rules for permits issued under CITES) must have a clear relationship with the more specific codes or principles related to genetic resources.

l) *Medicinal plants*

Medicinal plants, their by-products and their use have an enormous commercial value potential for Megadiverse countries. Many cases exist, such as in Peru, where industry exploits this type of resource without adhering to an access system for the associated genetic resources. Clarity must be sought regarding the type of legal regime that applies to this type of activity, as there is a tendency to assume that it should not be subject to legal regulation. Explicit resolutions are therefore required.

m) *Definitions and system limits*

Finally, and perhaps most importantly, policy and legal frameworks must be thoroughly unambiguous with regard to definitions, especially with respect to what is really meant by "access." The legal regime that controls access must also be very clearly defined in terms of its scope and boundaries, addressing questions such as: Does it apply to medicinal plants? Does it apply to taxonomic research? Do the same rules apply to nationals and foreigners? The success of an access regime will largely depend on these variables.

6.7 FINAL COMMENTS

The development of policies and rules for access in the Megadiverse countries should be based on a very simple and obvious premise. Even though this group of countries retains and "controls" most of the planet's biological wealth, their ability to effectively control the use of this wealth *outside* of their national jurisdictions is limited.

Also, if one takes into account that biological wealth can be found and obtained with fewer restrictions from other sources, such as *ex-situ* conservation sites—botanical gardens and seed banks—or marine sites outside of national jurisdiction, the issue of effective control becomes extremely relevant when designing related policies and norms.

That said, it is clear that if the Megadiverse countries adopt a shared position, the course and tendencies of international law regarding access to genetic resources can be changed. Cooperative efforts and actions should push the Megadiverse countries towards the establishment of certain basic rules that protect their common interests. The harmonisation of policy and regulatory frameworks would be an important step in that direction. As mentioned above, these do not need to be complicated: a clear and unambiguous system that can be adapted to the different modalities of bio-prospecting and that offers legal guarantees to all parties involved, would constitute a clear and resolute message. The basic foundation is situated in our national scientific and biotechnology capacities. Collaborative and cooperative agreements with external institutions are of fundamental importance, and the local private sector and national research institutes must be engaged in the process of designing and implementing policies and laws regarding access to genetic resources.

Finally, it is noteworthy to insist on a global partnership towards the design and implementation of a legal system that can bring some equity to a common concern of humanity—the conservation of cultural diversity as a prerequisite of biodiversity conservation—in order to assure the concrete objectives of the Biodiversity Convention are met. This requires legal recognition of traditional knowledge over the use of plants, biological and genetic resources existing in the lands and ecosystems where they have developed over the centuries. To accomplish such a challenging task the international institutions concerned with trade, the protection of IPRs, the conservation of biodiversity and the goals of sustainable development will need to accelerate their work and efforts to send a clear message to the global community to halt all bilateral and other multilateral negotiations that could hamper the effectiveness and significance of the rule of International Law in the field of what we could start recognising as Biodiversity Law.

ENDNOTES

1 This chapter is based on a paper prepared by Jorge Caillaux and Manuel Ruiz entitled: Legislative Experiences on Access to Genetic Resources and Options for Megadiverse Countries (2002). This work has been updated with additional information and content, especially regarding access to genetic resources and the protection of traditional knowledge in the Andean region.

2 The term "Megadiverse" refers to some 12 countries. There is no unanimous point of view on exactly which countries are Megadiverse, but it is generally agreed that the following are included: Australia, Brazil, Bolivia, China, Colombia, Ecuador, India, Indonesia, Madagascar, Mexico, Peru, United States, Venezuela and Zaire (Democratic Republic of Congo). Nevertheless, many other countries (while not megadiverse) possess large and extremely important reserves of biological wealth, including: Costa Rica, Cuba, Fiji, the Gambia, Malaysia, Nigeria, the Philippines, South Africa, Thailand, and several others. It is important to keep in mind that the majority of these countries are characterised as developing countries.

3 We offer a brief review of advances made in the regulatory framework and public policy in the following countries: Brazil, China, Costa Rica, India, Indonesia, Kenya, Madagascar, Mexico, South Africa and the Andean Community of Nations.

4 This paper does not address debates and discussions arising from the increasing bilateral trade negotiations in course which include IPR issues normally imposed by developed countries. Bilateralism will become an uphill battle for developing countries and may result in treaties with much higher IPR standards. This situation and trend may risk the pragmatism of legal discussions and the inclusion of traditional knowledge protection issues.

5 The formal name of this standard is "Provisional Measure 2,126-8 that regulates Chapter II, para. 1 and 4 of Constitutional Article 225, articles 1, 8(j), 10 (c), 15 and 16 (3)(4) of the Convention on Biological Diversity related to access to genetic heritage, protection and access of associated traditional knowledge, distribution of its related benefits, access and technology transfer for its use, among other articles."

6 Editor's note: A more up-to-date account of the position in India can be found in Professor Verma's discussion in Chapter 3.

7 In Peru, a "Proposal for a Regime of Protection of Collective Knowledge of the Indigenous Peoples" was prepared in the context of a participatory process lead by the National Institute for the Protection of Competitiveness and Intellectual Property (INDECOPI). The CAN countries are also committed to developing a *sui generis* framework under the conditions established by Decision 391 and in the context of the Regional Biodiversity Strategy.

8 Decision 391 distinguishes between access contracts signed with research centres (Art. 36) and *ex-situ* conservation centres (Art. 37). Proposals for regulatory frameworks in Ecuador, Bolivia and Peru also take this issue into account but have not yet arrived at a clear solution.

9 This table includes very general information. In several cases, sector-based legislation responds to some of the criteria of differentiation (China and Indonesia). Blank spaces indicate a lack of available information.

10 In the case of Bolivia, the planning process took place following approval of Decision 391 and its operational charter. The planning process was designed to more effectively apply the norms.

11 For more information, see Ten Kate, Kerry and Laird Sarah. 1999. The Commercial Use of Biodiversity: Access to Genetic Resources and Benefit Sharing. Earthscan Publications Ltd., London. See, in particular, Chapter 10.

12 Every one of these countries has made a distinction between genetic resources (over which the State exercises rights) and biological resources, over which multiple forms of rights are exercised (property, possession, use). Naturally, the panorama becomes more complicated when property rights are exercised (for example over a crop or animal) and when the State has an interest or rights over the genetic components of these same resources.

13 While beyond the scope of this paper, special attention should be placed on the effects and impacts of bioprospecting in general on the life and organisation of indigenous communities. Problems between communities with differing perceptions on the advantages or possibilities offered by bioprospection projects will no doubt arise. The concept of a communal split could be used to evaluate the seriousness of this problem. It is also important to note that indigenous communities, in the approval process of projects, do not always weigh incentives aimed at providing economic benefit for the community, as many communal perspectives often prioritise solid religious and cultural doctrines. Simply put, the right to participate in a shared fund can serve to reduce tension between communities that approve projects without being able to *directly* participate in them.

14 For further details of the ICBG project see: Rosenthal, J. P. 1999. "Drug Discovery, Economic Development and Conservation: The International Cooperative Biodiversity Groups." Pharmaceutical Biology, vol. 37, Supp. 1999. Swets & Zeitlinger Publishers.

15 "Negative or preventive protection of traditional knowledge refers to the use of mechanisms to impede traditional knowledge from being misappropriated. For example, the prior art search (for traditional knowledge) during patent procedures and ensuring [the] non-obviousness of an invention are two ways through which negative protection can be ensured. It is a preventive measure and a reaction to an action (filing of a patent)." Manuel Ruiz, "The International Debate on Traditional Knowledge as Prior Art in the Patent System: Issues and Options for Developing Countries," Trade-Related Agenda, Development and Equity (T.R.A.D.E.), Occasional Paper 9 (South Centre, October 2002) 19.

16 *Ibid.* at page 13.

17 There are various definitions of "traditional knowledge," and it is important to clarify what we are referring to under this term. A good working definition is WIPO's description of "traditional knowledge" as including: "... tradition-based literary, artistic or scientific works; performances;

inventions; scientific discoveries; designs; marks, names and symbols; undisclosed information; and all other tradition-based innovations and creations resulting from intellectual activity in the industrial, scientific, literary or artistic fields." WIPO, "Intellectual Property Needs and Expectations of Traditional Knowledge Holders," WIPO Report on Fact Finding Missions on Intellectual Property and Traditional Knowledge (1998–1999) Geneva, April 2001.

18 See note 15 above.

19 Supreme Decree 008-96-INDECOPI, 1996.

20 See section 6.5.2 below on the positive protection of traditional knowledge under Peruvian national law.

21 There are many issues surrounding the creation of registers and databases. For one, the incorporation and codification of indigenous knowledge in a database raises concerns about how this will impact indigenous peoples' cultures and the granting of positive protection for their traditional knowledge. One solution is to maintain several register systems, each with a different level of confidentiality. The indigenous groups would take part in deciding what traditional knowledge should be included in the public domain and what traditional knowledge should only be accessible to patent reviewers.

22 Requiring the disclosure of origin of genetic resources in patent applications was one of the possible user measures discussed—a measure that has attracted increasing support at the WTO and WIPO from a range of developing countries and, more cautiously, from the EC and Switzerland (see BRIDGES Trade BioRes, June 13, 2003, available online: http://www.ictsd.org/biores/03-06-13/story1.htm).

23 Laird, S. *Biodiversity and Traditional Knowledge. Equitable Partnerships in Practice*. (London, Earthscan Publications, 2002).

24 CIEL, "Comments on Improving Identification of Prior Art. Recommendations on Traditional Knowledge Relating to Biological Diversity Submitted to the United States Patents and Trademark Office" (August 1999).

25 For example, in the EU, Directive 98/44/EC on the legal protection of biological inventions encourages member states to require patent applicants to include information on the *geographical origin* of biological material (Recital 27). However, only Denmark has so far implemented this requirement, with Germany, Sweden, Belgium, Portugal, Switzerland and Norway in the process of setting up their regulations. The Norwegian proposal goes one step further by also requiring the provider country to be specified (if it is different from the country of origin) and evidence of prior informed consent. The country is also in the process of developing rules to govern the access to genetic resources in Norway. See BRIDGES Trade BioRes, vol. 3 no. 20; 14 November 2003.

26 Dutfield, G. *Intellectual Property Rights: Trade and Biodiversity*. (London, Earthscan Publications, 2000).

27 Law 27811 defines "collective" and "biological."

28 Law 27811, articles 5 and 12.

29 Law 27811, article 6.

30 *Ibid.*

31 Law 27881, article 10. "One important and widely acknowledged aspect about traditional knowledge is that it does not imply static [or] necessarily old knowledge. Rather, traditional knowledge is often dynamic and adaptive to changing cultural patterns and a wide range of external influences, including occupation of indigenous people's lands, market pressures over certain resources, resettlement, etc. Traditional knowledge often flows in oral forms and is not codified in writing or in systematised forms (i.e., books or databases). For some a key feature is its *collective nature*: knowledge is generated collectively in complex communal manners where no one individual can be recognised as a creator."

32 Law 27881, article 67.

33 INDECOPI is the competent national authority in charge of registering licenses, managing the national public and confidential registers, and overseeing administrative procedures. Law 27811, article 64.

34 Law 27811, article 37.

35 Law 27811, article 63.

36 Ruiz, Manuel & Isabel Lapeña, "New Peruvian Law Protects Indigenous Peoples' Collective Knowledge," Bridges: Between Trade and Sustainable Development, Year 6 No. 6, (September 2002) 15, available at http://www.ictsd.org/.

37 Law 27811, article 6.

38 See Ruiz & Lapeña, above at note 36.

CHAPTER 7

Intellectual Property Engineering: The Role of the Chemical, Pharmaceutical and Biotechnology Industries

PETER DRAHOS*

7.1 INTRODUCTION

Intellectual property rights were important to chemical firms in 19th-century Europe and to US and European pharmaceutical companies in the 20th century. The relationship was one of mutual importance. Because these companies wanted intellectual property rights, especially patents, they took an interest in lobbying governments on their design. A cycle of regulatory growth was thus created. As the chemical and pharmaceutical industries took more interest in the design of intellectual property rights, the strategies of the larger companies came to be more and more based on the use of intellectual property rights and this in turn meant that the companies had a greater and greater incentive to influence their design.[1] The business model paradigm of these industries took it as axiomatic that there had to be strong intellectual property rights—the stronger the better.

In the 1980s this cycle of regulatory growth underwent something of a quantum jump. US, European and Japanese companies, including pharmaceutical and chemical companies set aside their

* Regulatory Institutions Network, Research School of Social Sciences, Australian National University.

differences and campaigned for the inclusion of an agreement on intellectual property rights in the Uruguay Round of Multilateral Trade Negotiations. Those negotiations produced an agreement known as the Agreement on the Trade-Related Aspects of Intellectual Property Rights (TRIPS). TRIPS, in the eyes of the chemical and pharmaceutical companies that had been amongst its prime movers, was a major step in the globalisation of standards of patent, trade secret and trade mark protection, the three areas of most importance to these companies. Of major significance was the obligation on states to make available patents for products and processes without discrimination as to field of technology.[2] TRIPS was, however, far from perfect. Ultimately the handful of multinationals that had steered TRIPS through the Uruguay Round wanted an even higher set of standards. A letter from Pfizer Inc. in 1994 to the United States Trade Representative (USTR) captures this thinking quite nicely:

> Finally, GATT does not do it. Many Indians mistakenly (often very honestly) believe that if they endorse GATT they will have solved their IP and pharmaceutical patent issue. Not so, particularly if they truly want to create an environment that attracts investment and provides better medicine—legalistically agreeing to something (GATT) that brings this into play in ten years or more achieves neither of these two objectives.[3]

TRIPS did not turn out to be, as many developing countries had hoped, the end of multinational companies' plans for the globalisation of intellectual property rights. In fact, as the discussion below will show, in many ways it was only the beginning.

The remainder of this chapter is divided into four sections. The first section draws on the considerable scholarship surrounding the genesis of TRIPS and tells the story of TRIPS concentrating in particular on the role that was played by Pfizer. The second part explains how the trade regime has been used to create a global regulatory ratchet for intellectual property rights. The third section shows how US industry uses the ratchet. As a result of this ratchet, "TRIPS-plus" standards are proliferating in the national laws of many developing countries. The fourth part discusses the effects of this proliferation from the point of view of development. A conclusion then follows.

7.2 THE STORY OF TRIPS

TRIPS is one of 28 agreements that make up the Final Act of the Uruguay Round of Multilateral Trade Negotiations, the negotiations that had begun in Punta del Este in 1986 and culminated in 1994 with the signing of the Final Act and the creation of the WTO. The TRIPS Agreement requires all WTO members to adhere to minimum standards of intellectual property protection.[4] All developing countries and many developed countries had to reform their domestic intellectual property law in order to conform to the obligations in TRIPS.

On the face of it, TRIPS represents a puzzle. Why did other countries agree to TRIPS? At the time of the negotiations the US as the world's principal exporter of intellectual property, had much to gain from the globalisation of intellectual property rights via the trade regime, while the economic and social consequences for developing countries were (and are) serious. For example, TRIPS requires countries to recognise patents on pharmaceutical products and this has implications for both the cost of patented medicines, as well as the long-term fate of the generic industries in those countries.[5]

Susan Sell in her study of TRIPS points out that some 12 US corporations were primarily responsible for the lobbying that brought TRIPS into being.[6] Other studies of TRIPS have come to a similar conclusion.[7] TRIPS was not a case of simple lobbying because it required the drafting of a detailed international agreement containing US standards of intellectual property protection and then ultimately steering it through a multilateral trade negotiation involving more than one hundred states and that lasted from 1986 to 1993. The key to explaining how this was achieved lies in a small number of corporations creating ever widening circles of influence that brought more actors and networks into the cause of global intellectual property rights. The activities of Pfizer Corporation during this time illustrate how TRIPS came to be an output of private nodal governance.

Pfizer, more than most pharmaceutical corporations, had invested in developing countries and so saw the threat to international markets that generic manufacturers in countries like India posed for the R&D pharmaceutical industry. It also saw that developing countries were increasingly using their superior numbers in the World Intellectual Property Organization (WIPO) to put forward initiatives that favoured their own position as net importers of foreign technology. During the early 1980s a small group of Washington-based policy entrepreneurs had conceived of the idea of linking the intellectual property regime to the trade regime. Pfizer executives, including the CEO Edmund Pratt, were amongst the leading proponents of this idea. Essentially their policy idea was to get an agreement on intellectual property into the General Agreement on Tariffs and Trade (GATT). Amongst other things, such an agreement would be enforceable under GATT dispute resolution procedures. It was a radical idea. States had moved cautiously in ceding sovereignty over intellectual property rights within the context of WIPO.

Pfizer executives began to use their networks in two important ways. The first way consisted of network activation. Pfizer executives used their established business networks to disseminate the idea of a trade-based approach to intellectual property. Pratt began delivering speeches at business fora like the National Foreign Trade Council and the Business Round Table outlining the links between trade, intellectual property and investment. As a CEO of a major US company, he could work the trade association scene at the highest levels. Other Pfizer senior executives also began to push the intellectual property issue within national and international trade associations.[8] Gerald Laubach, President of Pfizer Inc., was on the board of the Pharmaceutical Manufacturers Association and on the Council on Competitiveness set up by President Ronald Reagan; Lou Clemente, Pfizer's General Counsel, headed up the Intellectual Property Committee of the US Council for International Business; Bob Neimeth, Pfizer International's President was the Chair of the US side of the Business and Industry Advisory Committee to the OECD. The message about intellectual property went out along the business networks to chambers of commerce, business councils, business committees, trade associations, and peak business bodies. Progressively Pfizer executives who occupied key positions in strategic business organisations were able to enrol the support of these organisations for a trade-based approach to intellectual property. With every such enrolment, the business power behind the case for such an approach became harder and harder for governments to resist.

The second way in which Pfizer operated was through the interlinking of networks. One of the nodes that played a pivotal role in the negotiations over intellectual property was the Advisory Committee on Trade Negotiations (ACTN). ACTN had been created in 1974 by Congress under US trade law as part of a private sector advisory committee system.[9] The purpose of this system was to ensure a concordance between official US trade objectives and US commerce. ACTN existed at the apex of this system. Pratt, with the assistance of other senior executives within Pfizer, began to put himself forward within business circles as someone who could develop US business thinking about trade and economic policy. In 1979 Pratt became a member of ACTN and in 1981 its Chairman. During the 1980s representatives from the most senior levels of big business within the US were appointed by the President to serve on the committee (Pratt was appointed by President Carter). The Committee was a purely advisory one, but with direct access to the USTR and the duty of advising him/her on US trade policy and negotiating objectives in the light of national interest. Out of this business crucible came the crucial strategic thinking on the trade-based approach to intellectual property.

With Pratt at the helm, and the CEOs of IBM and Du Pont Corporation serving, the ACTN began to develop a sweeping trade and investment agenda. John Opel, the then Chairman of IBM, headed this Task Force. During Pratt's six years of chairmanship ACTN worked closely with William E. Brock III, the USTR from 1981–1985 and Clayton K. Yeutter, the USTR from 1985–1989 helping to shape the services, investment and intellectual property trade agenda of the US.

ACTN's basic message to the US government was that it should pull every lever at its disposal in order to obtain the right result for the US on intellectual property. There were a lot of possible levers. US Executive Directors to the IMF and World Bank could ask about intellectual property when casting their votes on loans and access to bank facilities; US aid and development agencies could use their funds to help spread the IP gospel. Over time the message was heard and acted upon. Provisions protecting intellectual property as an investment activity were automatically included in the Bilateral Investment Treaty program which the US was engaged in with developing countries in the 1980s. Means of influence of a personal and powerful kind also began to operate. Shultz, the Secretary of State discussed the IP issue with then Prime Minister Lee Kuan Yew, stated Jacques Gorlin in his 1985 analysis of the trade-based approach to IP.[10] President Reagan in his message to Congress of 6 February 1986 entitled "America's Agenda for the Future" proposed that a key item was much greater protection for US intellectual property abroad.[11] This was consistent with ACTN's recommendation that the development of a US strategy for intellectual property be endorsed by the President and Cabinet. The ground was being prepared for intellectual property to become the stuff of big picture political dealing and not just technical trade negotiation.

So far as ACTN was concerned, folding intellectual property standards into the GATT was the single best way in which to spread those standards. Realistically ACTN realised that the negotiation of a broad intellectual property agreement would be a long process. But this process would not start unless intellectual property was put on the agenda of the next trade round. For this to happen a Ministerial Conference of Contracting Parties of the GATT would have to issue a declaration containing, amongst other things, a form of words opening the way for the negotiation of an IP code. Here ACTN ran into a fundamental problem. Both Opel and Pratt had been pushing the IP agenda with the USTR, at first with William Brock and then his successor Clayton Yeutter. In 1981 Brock had formed the Quadrilateral Group (Quad) of countries, for the purpose of trying to develop a consensus for a new round of multilateral trade negotiations. In the early 1980s there were differences of view between Europe and the US on the desirability and content of a future trade round. Without the agreement of the US and Europe the prospects of a multilateral trade round getting off the ground were slim. The Quad consisted of the US, the EC, Japan and Canada. Once these countries had achieved a consensus on an agenda for a multilateral trade round, the round would most likely begin. Yeutter saw the centrality of intellectual property to the round, but the problem was, as he explained to Pratt and Opel, that when he went to meetings of the Quad there was no real support from the other Quad members to merge IP and trade.

The problem facing Pratt and Opel was clear enough. They had to convince business organisations in Quad countries to pressure their governments to include intellectual property in the next round of trade negotiations. That meant first convincing European and Japanese business that it was in their interests for intellectual property to become a priority issue in the next trade round. With a strong Quad consensus, there was a real likelihood of intellectual property making it onto the agenda for the next trade round. Without such a consensus developing countries would be able to block an initiative on intellectual property. The time frame for the consensus-building exercise was roughly six months. The Ministerial Conference to launch a new trade round was scheduled to take place at Punta del Este in Uruguay in September of 1986. The USTR had been working hard to convince the remainder of the Quad of the IP issue, but it had to become much more than just a talking point at the Ministerial Conference.

Pratt and Opel's response was swift. In March of 1986 they created the Intellectual Property Committee (IPC).[12] The IPC was an ad hoc coalition of 13 major US corporations; Bristol-Myers, DuPont, FMC Corporation, General Electric, General Motors, Hewlett-Packard, IBM, Johnson & Johnson, Merck, Monsanto, Pfizer, Rockwell International and Warner Communications. It described itself as "dedicated to the negotiation of a comprehensive agreement on intellectual property in the current GATT round of multilateral trade negotiations."[13]

Europe was the key target for the IPC. Once Europe was on board Japan was likely to follow, or at least not to raise significant opposition. Canada, despite its Quad membership, was not really a player. It was the support of European and Japanese corporations that was crucial. What followed was a consensus-building exercise carried out at the highest levels of senior corporate management. CEOs of US companies belonging to the IPC would contact their counterparts in Europe and Japan and urge them to put pressure on their governments to support the inclusion of intellectual property at Punta del Este. Small but very senior and powerful business networks were activated. The IPC also sent delegations to Europe in June 1986 and Japan in August of 1986 to persuade businesses in those countries that they also had an interest in seeing the GATT become a vehicle of globally enforceable intellectual property rights. The IPC's efforts in the lead-up to Punte del Este brought it success, for both European and Japanese industry responded by putting pressure on their governments to put intellectual property on the trade agenda. Ultimately the linkages that were created between US, European and Japanese companies led to the joint release in 1988 of a suggested draft text of an agreement on intellectual property.[14]

The Ministerial Declaration on the Uruguay Round of 20 September 1986 contained a negotiating mandate on intellectual property rights.[15] In the seven years that followed, US trade negotiators with the assistance of the many networks that had been enrolled and activated in the cause of global intellectual property rights, were able to deliver a strong agreement on intellectual property in the form of TRIPS.

7.3 THE GLOBAL INTELLECTUAL PROPERTY RATCHET

During the period that TRIPS was being negotiated (1986–1993) there were suggestions that if developing countries agreed to TRIPS the US would ease off negotiating intellectual property standards bilaterally.[16] During the 1980s the US had set the scene for TRIPS through a series of strategic bilateral negotiations on intellectual property with countries like South Korea and Brazil. Provisions on intellectual property also became part of its bilateral investment treaty program during this time. One of the incentives that was held out to developing countries for the successful negotiation of TRIPS was that the US would desist from using its trade enforcement tools to obtain the standards that it wanted.

The reality turned out to be somewhat different. During the 1990s the US actually intensified the level of its bilateral activity.[17] It used its trade enforcement tools under its Trade Act to review the intellectual property standards of larger and larger number of countries and it concluded many more bilateral agreements related to intellectual property than it had in the 1980s. In effect, it had created without anybody really noticing a global regulatory ratchet for intellectual property. Moreover the ratchet only travelled in one direction—up. Thus while many areas of business regulations were experiencing deregulation during the 1980s and 1990s, intellectual property was experiencing regulation.

The US was the principal architect of the global regulatory ratchet for intellectual property, with the EU to a lesser extent also making use of it.

In short form this ratcheting process is dependent upon:

(a) a process of forum shifting[18]: a strategy in which the US and EU shift the standard-setting agenda from fora in which they are encountering difficulties to those fora where they are likely to succeed (e.g., from WIPO to the WTO to BIPs);
(b) co-ordinated bilateral and multilateral IP strategies; and
(c) the entrenchment in international agreements of a principle of minimum standards.

The principle of minimum standards plays a vital role in this strategy. Each bilateral or multilateral agreement dealing with intellectual property contains a provision to the effect that a party to such an agreement may implement more extensive protection than is required under the agreement or that the agreement does not derogate from other agreements providing even more favourable treatment.[19] This means that each subsequent bilateral or multilateral agreement can establish a higher standard.

Bilateral agreements are also being drafted in ways to ensure that developing countries are integrated into multilateral IP regimes with maximum speed. Developing countries are being obliged to comply with multilateral standards in conventions to which they are not a party, to ratify multilateral treaties or both. So, for example, the US-Jordan FTA requires Jordan to give effect to Articles 1–14 of the WIPO Copyright Treaty (1996) and to ratify Articles 1–22 of the International Convention for the Protection of New Varieties of Plants (1991) (UPOV Convention).[20]

The global ratchet for IP consists of waves of bilaterals (beginning in the 1980s) followed by occasional multilateral standard-setting (See Figure 7.1 below). Each wave of bilaterals or multilateral treaty never derogates from existing standards and very often sets new ones. A detailed comparison of the provisions of all of the multilateral and bilateral treaties on intellectual property is beyond the scope of this chapter. An example of the global ratchet in action can be seen by comparing the intellectual property provisions of NAFTA with TRIPS and the subsequent bilateral treaties.

Where the US or the EU are at any given moment in the cycle of ratcheting is determined essentially by how much effective resistance they are meeting in terms of their negotiating objectives. The bilateralism

FIGURE 7.1 The Global Intellectual Property Ratchet

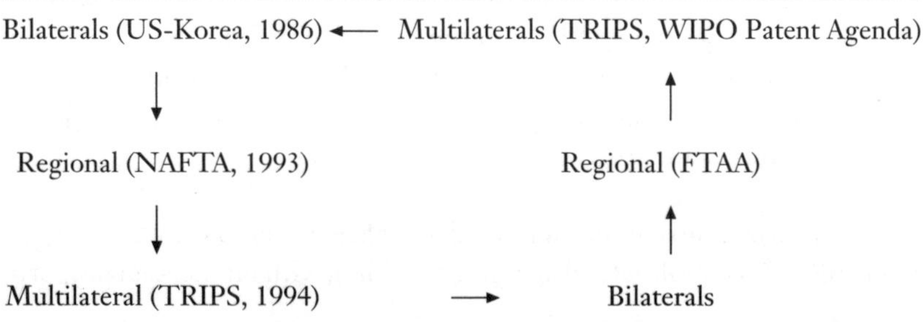

that preceded TRIPS and that laid the foundation for TRIPS was triggered by the resistance that the US encountered on its intellectual property agenda at the GATT. Presently, it is clear that the US in particular is in a bilateral phase. The Ministerial Declaration that launched the Doha round of multilateral trade negotiations in 2001 contained only a modest work programme in relation to TRIPS with geographical indications being the principal item listed for negotiation. Bilaterally, however, the US has been busily negotiating free trade agreements (FTAs) with countries that it sees as being important regional models. The list below summarises the state of play:

1. US-Jordan (2001)
2. US-Chile (2003)
3. US-Singapore (2003)
4. US-Southern African Customs Union
5. US-Central American FTA
6. US-Morocco
7. US-Australia

The focus on FTAs at this time can also be explained in terms of the effective resistance that the US has been encountering at the TRIPS Council over the last several years. The TRIPS Council was the venue in which African states in June of 2001 launched an initiative aimed at examining the role of intellectual property rights in access to medicines. The end of 2001 saw WTO members agree to the Declaration on the TRIPS Agreement and Public Health, a Declaration that the US pharmaceutical industry counted as a blow against its interests and which it did its best to downplay.[21] Similarly, the review of Article 27(3)(b) that was started in 1999 has not run the way that the US would have liked. In essence the US wants to bring TRIPS into line with what is its own domestic position—"virtually anything is patentable".[22] Instead what eventuated during the course of the review was a very wide-ranging dialogue in the TRIPS Council that raised many issues about patents, including the need to better integrate the provisions of TRIPS with a regulatory approach towards biodiversity that states had agreed to in the context of the Convention on Biological Diversity.[23] Developing countries were able to resist US proposals in the context of the TRIPS Council because outside of the Council they were being given assistance by civil society actors.[24] These actors were helping to provide technical expertise and through global campaigning they were instrumental in creating around TRIPS a moral atmosphere in which it was judged unfair to developing countries. This in turn expanded the art of the possible when it came to TRIPS. Moreover, it was to the advantage of both civil society and developing countries that the TRIPS Council was one highly visible forum on which they could concentrate their attentions.

This effective resistance in the TRIPS Council has led to forum shifting by the US. In the FTAs that it has recently concluded it has sought and in many cases obtained standards of intellectual property from the other state that bring that state closer to the US domestic position.[25] A good illustration of this can be found in the provisions of the US-Singapore FTA that deal with patents. Under the US-Singapore FTA the parties may only exclude those inventions from patentability that are specified in Article 27.2 and 27.3(a) of TRIPS.[26] Article 27.3(b) of TRIPS has been bypassed in other words.

TRIPS also bars its members from using its provisions to address the issue of the exhaustion of intellectual property rights. The US-Singapore FTA, however, deals with the exhaustion issue by requiring each party to give the patent owner a remedy against a third party who disturbs a contractual arrangement between a patent owner and licensee.[27] TRIPS does not specifically address the rights of generic manufacturers to make use of a patented drug prior to the patent expiring for the purposes of obtaining marketing approval of their generic product from their relevant regulatory authority. However, as Canada pointed out in the Canada–European Community pharmaceutical products case, the understanding of key players such as the US in the TRIPS negotiations was that this exception was preserved by Article 30 of TRIPS.[28] Moreover, the state practice after TRIPS came into force was also consistent with the understanding that a regulatory review exception was permitted by Article 30.[29] The scope of this Article 30 exception is, in the case of the US-Singapore FTA, limited to obtaining marketing approval including in cases where the export of the generic version is permitted. It would seem, therefore, that even if a Singaporean generic manufacturer could take advantage of an export market that was not patent-barred, it would not be able to export in commercial quantities to that market until the patent in Singapore had expired. The compulsory licensing provision of the US-Singapore FTA is, unlike TRIPS, drawn in the negative. This means that compulsory licensing is prohibited except in specified circumstances (to remedy anticompetitive acts, for public non-commercial use, national emergency or other circumstances of extreme urgency).[30] It also contains an express restriction on the transfer of "know how", something not to be found in TRIPS. A country like Singapore that agrees to this kind of provision on compulsory licensing is clearly circumscribing the rights it would otherwise have under TRIPS to enact a wider provision. The restriction on "know how" is also important since "know how" licensing agreements frequently accompany a patent licensing arrangement and enable the licensee to make efficient use of the patent. Without access to "know how", the commercial value of access to a patent is often worth much less to a licensee.

It is also worth noting that countries by adopting this kind of provision for compulsory licensing in their patent law may be going even further than the US does. Compulsory licensing is not part of US patent law, but provisions on compulsory licensing are to be found in other parts of US law such as the Clean Air Act and the Atomic Energy Act.[31] In addition, compulsory licences are a key remedy in the context of antitrust litigation. Countries that adopt a restrictive approach to compulsory licensing as part of their patent law and do not compensate by having licensing access provisions in other parts of their law are clearly offering patent owners stronger rights than exist in US domestic law.

Another example of the way in which the US is using FTAs to bring other countries into line with its own domestic provisions is to be found in Article 16.8 of the US-Singapore FTA. This provision deals with the treatment of information by a regulatory authority that relates to the safety or efficacy of a pharmaceutical or agricultural product and is required to be submitted by that authority for the purposes of obtaining marketing approval. TRIPS deals with this situation somewhat succinctly in Article 39.3. Members are required to protect such data against "unfair commercial use" provided that it required "considerable effort" to generate, that it is undisclosed and that it is a new chemical entity. The US-Singapore FTA takes this open and flexible standard and converts it into something much more specific. Under it, Singaporean authorities cannot, in effect, rely on the information that has been submitted for the purposes of giving approval to a third party (a generic manufacturer) unless, of course, the original party submitting the information consents to such use. The period of non-reliance is five years for pharmaceutical products and 10 years for agricultural chemical products. This obligation to maintain the exclusivity of the data applies even if it has not been submitted in Singapore, but in another country and Singaporean authorities are relying on marketing approval by a regulatory authority in that country. Further the obligation to maintain this exclusivity of data is independent of the period of patent protection in the product. These provisions essentially bring Singapore into line with US law.[32]

7.4 THE DRIVER IN THE DRIVER'S SEAT

The previous section provided examples of how FTAs are being used by the US to bring countries into line with US domestic standards of intellectual property protection. The section on TRIPS showed how TRIPS itself was the product of a highly sophisticated and co-ordinated international campaign by a group of multinationals with US multinationals in a leadership role. Lobbying understates the actual process of what occurred. It was in reality a form of private governance that might best be described as nodal governance. This process of nodal governance, which has evolved over the last 20 years within the US, has resulted in a centrally co-ordinated process of standard-setting for sectors of key importance to multinational companies—intellectual property rights, services and investment. Developing countries have had no answer to this centrally co-ordinated strategy. Whenever they are successful in mounting resistance in one forum such as the TRIPS Council, they encounter a forum-shifting response in which the US shifts the negotiating agenda from that forum to another. The global intellectual property ratchet is precisely the product of this centrally co-ordinated strategy of forum shifting.

Driving the global intellectual property ratchet is a networked private nodal governance that is formally woven into US policy and law-making at the highest levels. The Advisory Committee for Trade Policy and Negotiations, the committee that was so important in the context of TRIPS remains at the apex of a private sector advisory system that advises and influences US trade policy. This system is made up of 33 advisory committees that have provision for approximately 1,000 members.[33] It is a three-tiered system with ACTPN at the top, six policy advisory committees in the second tier and 26 sectoral, functional and technical advisory committees in the third tier. ACTPN's members include individuals drawn from the highest levels of US business. It is, as we saw in the section on TRIPS, a strategic agenda-setting committee that looks at the broad goals that the US should pursue in trade negotiations.

In the case of agreements that relate to intellectual property the technical detail of these agreements is monitored by a third tier committee, the Industry Functional Advisory Committee on Intellectual Property Rights for Trade Policy Matters (IFAC). The membership of IFAC is made up of 20 members drawn from Industry Sector Advisory Committees and another 20 drawn from the private sector areas who provide the committee with technical expertise in intellectual property.[34] This technical expertise is vital to the committee's work and complements the strategic work of ACTPN. Under its charter IFAC is to provide detailed technical advice on trade agreements negotiated by the USTR.[35] In the case of the US-Singapore FTA, IFAC, in the words of its report, "advised US negotiators on, and reviewed draft texts, of the US–Singapore FTA intellectual property chapter".[36] Importantly, IFAC reviewed the US-Singapore FTA in the context of other multilateral and bilateral agreements and initiatives that the US had achieved. In other words, IFAC is a committee that gets its hands dirty by reviewing and drafting specific agreements. It does this technical work across all US trade initiatives in intellectual property, whether bilateral, regional and multilateral. It is thus able to co-ordinate at a technical level the work it does across these different fora, thereby ensuring that US trade negotiating initiatives push intellectual property standards in the direction that US industry would like. The technical expertise on IFAC, as well as the expertise available to it from the corporate legal divisions of its members means that, for example, it can evaluate a country's intellectual property standards in detail when that country seeks WTO accession and it can provide detailed assessments of the standards that USTR negotiators must bring home in a negotiation.

Formally IFAC must report to the President, the USTR and Congress when the President notifies Congress of an intention to enter into a trade agreement. This formal role, however, represents only a small part of a more complex system of private sector nodal governance. Members of IFAC work outside of the committee to ensure that the US remains committed to an agenda of globalising US standards of intellectual property. So, for example, the Biotechnology Industry Organization, which represents more than 1,100 organisations and is a member of IFAC has over the years independently lobbied the USTR on the question of intellectual property rights. Its agenda is a matter of public record and is neatly summarised in a letter of January 29, 2003 to the USTR, Robert Zoellick: "[t]he United States' intellectual property system is the best in the world, and BIO advocates the establishment of global standards protecting intellectual property comparable to those in the United States."[37]

Naturally when BIO sits on IFAC it brings its advocacy position with it. A seat on IFAC means that BIO is able, in co-operation with the other members, to provide technical and drafting advice to the USTR as to the kind of standards that meet the desires of the organisations that BIO represents. There are a number of incentives for the USTR to be attentive to the suggestions of IFAC, including the superior technical expertise of the committee, the fact that the negotiating mandate in the Trade Act of 2002 requires the USTR to seek standards of protection comparable to US domestic law and that IFAC must ultimately write a report, as it did in the case of US-Singapore FTA, that endorses the agreement as being in the economic interests of the US. The upshot is that the standards that members of IFAC seek are very often the ones they achieve, especially in bilateral negotiations where the US almost always has superior bargaining power. So, for example, BIO has urged that where there are delays by trading partners in the granting of patents there be compensatory extensions of the patent term and it has also advocated that trading partners adopt US standards of data protection for pharmaceutical products. Articles 16.7 and 16.8 of the US-Singapore FTA implement these US domestic standards in Singapore. BIO also works in other ways outside of IFAC. It, for example, responds to the USTR's request for public comment on which countries should be the subject of "Special 301" listing and as a recognised international NGO in WIPO it can be active in pushing its position on patents in the WIPO Patent Agenda process.

To sum up: the members of IFAC become intimately involved in trade negotiations on intellectual property, not just advising but reviewing drafts and helping to decide objectives. Most importantly, they track US negotiating objectives across negotiations in different fora, thereby ensuring that these objectives are consistently pursued and pursued in a way that is most likely to bring long term success. Shifting from bilaterals to multilaterals has been at the centrepiece of US strategy for the last 20 years and has proven to be highly effective.

7.5 INTELLECTUAL PROPERTY RIGHTS AND DEVELOPMENT: FUZZY VALUES, HARD RULES

The Doha Round of trade negotiations that was launched in Doha, Qatar in November 2001 has been referred to as a "development round," the idea being that this round, in apparent contrast to previous rounds, will pay some attention to the needs of developing countries. Some reference to a fairer development agenda is an almost obligatory part of speech-making for Western leaders. The policy elites that operate in the global corridors of power of institutions such as the World Bank, the IMF and WTO spend their time writing reports that symbolically utilise warm and fuzzy development values. Thus a recent World Bank report says that development is about "improving the quality of people's lives, expanding their ability to shape their own futures."[38] It is now clear that major development problems such as lack of market access for developing countries' exports, ill health and lack of education in developing countries "can be solved only with cooperation from high-income countries".[39] And in addition "[p]oor people and poor countries should have greater voice in international forums".[40] Here we have a group of fuzzy values that include co-operating with the poor, recognising their autonomy and helping to empower them. How do these values square with the detailed technical rule-making that goes on with respect to intellectual property rights in trade fora?

7.5.1 Autonomy

The value of autonomy implies at the level of rule-making for developing countries that one should set rules that do not limit the opportunities of poor countries and that leave them with some sovereign discretion over informational resources. The very concept of development, it might be argued, implies rule diversity. Yet the practice of rule-making in trade fora is about the globalisation and harmonisation of one set of intellectual property standards. The standards of intellectual property that the US is globalising are its domestic standards, standards that meet its own economic needs and fit with its cultural and philosophical traditions. Strong patent standards may make sense in the US because, amongst other things, it has 3,676 scientists and engineers in R&D per million people, but surely they make no sense in a country like Rwanda that has only 35 per million. Around the world many people have deeply-held reservations about the patentability of plants, animals and human genetic resources, reservations that are based on a variety of ethical perspectives and traditions, including religious, indigenous and environmental ones. Yet the US has relentlessly pushed in TRIPS and subsequent bilateral agreements what the US Supreme Court has declared to be its domestic position, namely that anything under the sun is patentable.[41] It is equally relentless in seeking to impose upon the world a system of agriculture that is really a system of technology in which the farmer becomes the lessee of patented seeds, plants, fertilisers and pesticides. Fears that this technology does not meet the needs of subsistence farmers around the world, that it carries with it environmental risks that have not been properly assessed, that it cuts across farmer traditions such as the saving and exchange of seed or that it requires economies of scale that few countries can really exploit tends to be brushed aside by the US as disguised protectionism. It responds by threatening litigation in the WTO, knowing that its weight of lawyers will more than likely tilt the playing field in its favour.

Ignoring moral diversity in the definition of intellectual property rules while seeking through those rules to universalise its own cultural perceptions is a US practice to be found in other parts of intellectual property. The US was successful in excluding from TRIPS the recognition of authors' rights, those rights that are based on European philosophical traditions that recognise an indissoluble link between creators and their works (the key ones being the right to paternity and the right to integrity). Hollywood in the form of the Motion Picture Association Of America (MPA) has been opposed to these rights because they are potential interferences in its world-wide systems of production, marketing, distribution and exhibition. The right of integrity, for example, gives authors, potentially at least, some rights over how their works might be used in a film. Directors may also use the right to exercise some control over the commercial fate of their films—preventing, for example, the colourisation of a film shot in black and white.

Yet at the same time actors like the MPA invoke free speech values to argue that there should be no restrictions on the circulation of US film, television and other copyright works. Of course, there is a trade agenda because, as has been known for a long time, trade follows the film. The practical upshot of these free speech/free trade arguments is a constant pressure to remove quotas. No quota is too low to be ignored.

When Indonesia imposed a screen quota requiring its First Run theatres to show at least two Indonesian films each month for a minimum of two days, both the MPA and the International Intellectual Property Alliance raised the matter with the USTR as part of their recommendation in 1993 to list Indonesia under the 301 process. The endgame for Hollywood is no restriction on its capacity to dominate any type of screen in the world at any time and place.

7.5.2 Empowerment

Empowerment is another fuzzy value that routinely makes it into the "development-speak" of western policy elites. Whatever empowerment means, it surely does not mean transferring wealth from the poor to wealthy. Yet by imposing its own standards of intellectual property on developing country economies the US has changed the *terms of trade* of those economies. Developing states, which are net importers of intellectual property, will have to make greater payments to the US for the use of intellectual property rights than otherwise would have been the case. A study by the World Bank, for example, pointed out that the net rent transfers to the US from the patent provisions of TRIPS would be about $19 billion per year.[42] This figure only represents a beginning since it does not cover many other valuable areas of intellectual property like copyright that relates to the software, music and film industries.

7.5.3 Co-operation

Finally, we arrive at the value of co-operation, perhaps the primary value in development rights talk these days. How does this value square with the reality of technical rule-making in the international intellectual property regime? With more than 20 million dead and more than 40 million people infected by HIV, cooperation in fighting AIDS would seem to be beyond argument. Consider, however, the history of the WTO when it comes to the critical issue of defining intellectual property rights in ways that would encourage generic manufacturers to provide cheap anti-retroviral therapies for poor people in developing countries. In the WTO, negotiations follow a basic pattern in which inner circles of key players (for example, the Quad) forge a consensus that is then progressively expanded to include those in the outer circles. During the TRIPS negotiations and when the rules on patenting were being decided, no African negotiator, the continent worst affected by AIDS, ever made it into the key inner circles of decision-making. During the negotiations, the "Green Room" process was used to discipline developing countries so that consensus decision-making could be projected to the outside world. (The Green Room refers to high-level negotiations between key players over unsettled parts of the negotiating text.) Because of the pressure of these Green Room processes, developing country negotiators began to refer to them as the "Black Room" consultations.[43]

After the signing of the TRIPS Agreement, co-operation has continued to remain elusive. In 1997 the South African government introduced a bill that gave the health minister some discretion in setting conditions to ensure the supply of affordable medicines. South Africa has the biggest HIV-infected population in Africa. The bill was signed by President Mandela on December 12, 1997. It specifically allowed the importation into South Africa of patented medicines which had been put onto another market with the consent of the patent owner. The idea was to encourage the importation of patented medicines from the cheapest market (parallel importation), a form of importation that was allowed within the European Union, amongst other places. The response of the US officials was to turn the passage of the South African bill into a trade matter. Agencies of the US government such as the USTR, the Department of Commerce and the State Department, with the assistance of officials from the European Commission, began to pressure South Africa to change the bill. One of their arguments was that the South African government, in passing the Medicines bill, would be in breach of its obligations under TRIPS. In 1998 the pressure on South Africa intensified. The USTR listed South Africa under its trade law for possible trade sanctions if it did not comply with the demands of the US pharmaceutical industry and, in February 1998, 41 pharmaceutical companies began proceedings in South African courts against the South African government, naming Nelson Mandela as first defendant. The trade dispute continued to climb up the totem pole of political importance. Senior officials from the US and the EU continued to draw attention to South Africa's obligations under TRIPS. Sir Leon Brittan, the then Vice-President of the European Commission, wrote to Thabo Mbeki, at that time the Deputy President of South Africa, drawing his attention to South Africa's obligations under TRIPS.[44] At the August 1998 US-South Africa Binational Commission meetings in Washington, Vice President Gore made the protection of US pharmaceutical patents the central issue.[45]

In March 2001, 39 pharmaceutical companies came to the Pretoria High Court armed with most of South Africa's intellectual property barristers and a barrage of arguments against the Medicines Act. TRIPS surfaced again, the line of argument being that TRIPS required that patents be "enjoyable without discrimination" as to the field of technology.[46] The South African Medicines Act was said to discriminate against pharmaceutical patents. In April of 2001 the pharmaceutical companies withdrew from the litigation because of a highly effective global public campaign by civil society.[47] It put TRIPS, patents and the price of pharmaceuticals firmly in the spotlight. With the debate threatening to spill over into the cost of drugs generally, and hard questions being asked about the patent system, it was time for the large pharmaceutical industry to withdraw to the corridors of Washington and the WTO.

At a special meeting of the TRIPS Council in June 2001, developing states pushed for the recognition of a reading of TRIPS that permitted them to deal with health crises. Ultimately this produced the Declaration on TRIPS and Public Health at a Doha WTO Ministerial in November of 2001, a Declaration that affirms the right of developing countries to protect the health of their populations. The Doha Declaration was of enormous symbolic importance to developing countries, but it did leave unsettled a practical detail. The Declaration affirmed the right of developing countries to issue compulsory licences over pharmaceutical patents, but it did not change the restrictions on the export of patented products under TRIPS. As a UNIDO study showed in 1992, most developing countries do not have a sophisticated pharmaceutical industry and so the capacity to issue domestic compulsory licences is of little practical value.[48] Today only a handful of developing countries have significant innovative capabilities in the pharmaceutical sector (Argentina, Brazil, China, India, Korea, Mexico and Thailand) and of these only India has been a major exporter. Under the TRIPS Agreement these countries face export restrictions on patented products.

During the course of 2002 and 2003 the members of the TRIPS Council worked to find a solution to the problem of export. A consensus solution was announced in August of 2003.[49] Symbolically a solution was needed to allay the concerns of western publics and more importantly to preserve the WTO as a forum in which technical rule-making on intellectual property could continue. Instead of a simple statement of principle that would permit developing country generic manufacturers to export medicines to the countries that needed them, the solution comes in the form of six pages of provisions that set up a complex system of licensing and monitoring by states and the TRIPS Council.[50] For example, the system set up by the draft means that a generic manufacturer in an exporting country is dependent upon *both* the exporting and importing country each complying with the mandatory system of notification and conditions. The consequences of failure to comply are not spelt out. Generic manufacturers would in practical terms have to monitor the bureaucracies of two countries in relation to every act of export in relation to a single product (potentially many bureaucracies).

The detail of the provisions reveals a familiar pattern in rule-making when developed and developing countries meet at the negotiating table. Developing countries are drawn into complex juridical webs that they do not have the resources to disentangle and that ultimately do not serve them. The main pharmaceutical exporting nations (USA, UK, Japan, Germany, France and Switzerland) have indicated that they will not use the system *as importers*. This suggests that the pharmaceutical companies (including the generic affiliates of multinationals) in these countries may use the system *as exporters*. Generic manufacturers in developing countries may well face strong price competition in the export markets left to them under the system from these companies. This price competition is likely to be subsidised by the lucrative domestic markets of these companies, markets that would remain protected under the proposed system. In the long run this will simply increase the dependency of least-developed countries upon individual acts of charity or politicised development aid programmes.

The debates over AIDS, patents, TRIPS and the right to health are complex, but lying at the heart of the problem is a simple structural reality. Developing countries that are members of the WTO have to recognise patents on pharmaceutical products. The only reason that the price of patented anti-retroviral therapies have come down from US$15,000 per year to less than US$300 per year is because a few generic manufacturers like the Indian company Cipla were able to make the drugs at a price closer to marginal cost. They were able to manufacture because of their domestic patent position. However, all those developing countries with serious generic manufacturing capabilities either do or will soon have to recognise pharmaceutical patents as part of their TRIPS obligations. This will have two basic effects, one short term and the other longer term. In the short term, the capacity of these countries to export to other developing countries will slowly dry up. In the longer term, the generic industries of the main developing country exporters will become integrated into the manufacturing and distribution strategies of US and European pharmaceutical multinationals. The effect will be to drive prices up, not down.

7.6 CONCLUSION

For some time now the US has had an historically unprecedented opportunity to use its stock of knowledge to further the development of the many poor states in the world. As measured by indicators such as number of scientific publications, number of students in higher education and number of scientists, the US has a greater volume of knowledge located within it than any other country.[51] No hegemonic power has had such a world of knowledge available for utilisation and creative use. Since knowledge has the quality of being non-rivalrous in consumption, it follows that the US would not itself lose the knowledge it utilised for development purposes (and in fact would probably add to it since the application of knowledge generally leads to more knowledge). Moreover, treating knowledge as part of a global intellectual commons would not be inconsistent with the US pursuing its own economic growth. The principle of the intellectual commons is not, as the free software movement has shown, inconsistent with the development of business models.

However, for the time being the US state and US multinationals remain committed partners in the institutional project of information feudalism, that is the project of acquiring and maintaining global power based on the ownership of knowledge assets. Patent attorneys in US corporations are able to draft patent claims that travel the institutional pathways of international treaty law arriving as domestic obligations in other states that stipulate what potential competitors may or may not do with US informational assets. This is private networked governance that draws upon public nodes of authority such as the USTR to legitimise and enforce its privately drafted property law. It is global in its reach.

At a deeper level the global intellectual property paradigm is a negative vision. The basis of competition lies in the development of skills. The acquisition of skills by newcomers disturbs roles and hierarchies. After India built a national drug industry it began exporting bulk drugs and formulations to places such as Canada. A developing country that had acquired skills threatened those at the top of an international hierarchy of pharmaceutical production—the US, Japan, Germany, and the UK. Underneath the individualist ideology of intellectual property there lies an agenda of under-development, of maintaining an economic hierarchy in the world. Today's global intellectual property paradigm is all about protecting the knowledge and skills of the leaders of the pack.

ENDNOTES

1 For the history see Graham Dutfield, *Intellectual Property Rights and the Life Science Industries: A Twentieth Century History*, Ashgate, England, 2003. See also Peter Drahos with John Braithwaite, *Information Feudalism: Who Owns the Knowledge Economy?*, (London: Earthscan, 2002), chap. 3.

2 See Article 27.1 of TRIPS.

3 Letter from C. L. Clemente, Senior Vice President—Corporate Affairs, Pfizer Inc. to Joseph Papovich, Deputy Assistant US Trade Representative for Intellectual Property, June 7, 1994.

4 For an analysis of its provisions see D. Gervais, *The TRIPS Agreement: Drafting History And Analysis* (London, Sweet and Maxwell, 1998).

5 See Commission on Intellectual Property Rights, Integrating Intellectual Property Rights and Development Policy, London, 2002, chap .2.

6 S. Sell, *Private Power, Public Law: The Globalization of Intellectual Property Rights*, (Cambridge: Cambridge University Press, 2003).

7 M. Ryan, *Knowledge Diplomacy: Global Competition and the Politics of Intellectual Property* (Washington DC: Brookings Institution Press, 1998); Peter Drahos with John Braithwaite, *Information Feudalism: Who Owns the Knowledge Economy?* (London: Earthscan, 2002); D. Matthews, *Globalising Intellectual Property Rights* (London and New York: Routledge, 2002).

8 See "Pfizer: Protecting Intellectual Property in a Global Marketplace," *Harvard Business School*, 1992, at page 8.

9 See Private Sector Advisory Committee System, USTR, 1994 Annual Report, available online: (http://www.ustr.gov/reports).

10 Jacques Gorlin, "A Trade-Based Approach for the International Copyright Protection for Computer Software", September 1, 1985, 47, fn 47.

11 See *BNA's Patent, Trademark & Copyright Journal*, 31, February 13, 1986, at page 285.

12 See Edmund Pratt, "Intellectual Property Rights and International Trade," speech to US Council for International Business, available online: (http:/ /www.pfizer.com/pfizerinc/policy/forum).

13 IPC, "Accomplishments and Current Activities of the Intellectual Property Committee," June 14, 1988.

14 Basic Framework of GATT Provisions on Intellectual Property, Statement of Views of the European, Japanese and United States Business Communities, The Intellectual Property Committee, Keidanren (Japan), UNICE (Europe), June 1998.

15 Document MIN.DEC of 20 September 1986, reprinted in Terence P. Stewart (ed.), *The GATT Uruguay Round: A Negotiating History (1986-1992)*, vol. 3, (Deventer, Boston: Kluwer Law and Taxation Publishers, 1986), at pages 1–10.

16 See, for example, the statement by a member of the office of the USTR Emory Simon in "Remarks of Mr Emory Simon," Symposium: Trade-Related Aspects Of Intellectual Property, 22 (1989), *Vanderbilt Journal of Transnational Law*, at page 370.

17 See P. Drahos, "BITs and BIPs—Bilateralism in Intellectual Property", 4 (2001), *Journal of World Intellectual Property*, at page 791.

18 For a detailed explanation of this strategy and some examples see John Braithwaite and Peter Drahos, *Global Business Regulation* (UK: Cambridge University Press, 2000), chap. 24.

19 See, for example, Article 1702 of NAFTA, Article 1.1 of TRIPS, Article 4.1 of the US-Jordan FTA and Article X1 of the US-Nicaraguan BIT.

20 *Ibid*. See Article 4.1.

21 See Susan K. Sell, "TRIPS and the Access to Medicines Campaign" 20 (2002), *Wisconsin International Law Journal*, 481, at pages 518–519.

22 See *Hughes Aircraft Co. v. United States*, 148 F.3d 1384, 1385 (Fed. Cir. 1998).

23 For an overview and summary see Boniface Guwa Chidyausiku, "Article 27.3(b) of the TRIPS Agreement: The review process and developments at national and regional levels," in Christophe Bellmann, Graham Dutfield and Ricardo Meléndez-Ortiz (eds.) *Trading in Knowledge* (London and Sterling: Earthscan, 2003), at page 101.

24 See Susan K. Sell, "TRIPS and the Access to Medicines Campaign" 20 (2002), Wisconsin *International Law Journal*, 481; Ruth Mayne, "The Global Campaign on Patents and Access to Medicines: An Oxfam Perspective" in Peter Drahos and Ruth Mayne (eds), *Global Intellectual Property Rights: Knowledge Access and Development*, Palgrave, Macmillan, 2002, at page 244.

25 Under the Bipartisan Trade Promotion Authority Act of 2002 the Congress has stated that one overall negotiating objective for the US is to obtain in bilateral and multilateral agreements provisions that "reflect a standard of protection similar to that found in United States law". See Section 2102(b)(4)(A)(i)(II), codified as 19 USC 3802.

26 See Article 16.7.1 of the US-Singapore FTA.

27 See Article 16.7.2 of the US-Singapore FTA.

28 See WT/DS114/R 4.15.

29 Canada pointed out that Germany, Italy, Japan, Portugal, Argentina, Australia and Israel had allowed an exception to patent rights for the purposes of generic producers obtaining marketing approval.

30 The US pushed for such a compulsory licensing provision in the context of the TRIPS negotiations but was unsuccessful. See Jayashree Watal, *Intellectual Property Rights in the WTO and Developing Countries* (New Delhi: Oxford University Press, 2001), at page 320.

31 See Donna M. Gitter, "International Conflicts Over Patenting Human DNA Sequences in the United States and the European Union: An Argument for Compulsory Licensing and a Fair-Use Exemption" 76 (2001), *New York University Law Review*, at pages 1623, 1681–1682.

32 See Jayashree Watal, *Intellectual Property Rights in the WTO and Developing Countries* (New Delhi: Oxford University Press, 2001), at pages 200–201.

33 A description is to be found in The President's 2002 Annual Report on the Trade Agreement Program, available online: (http://www.ustr.gov/reports/2003.html).

34 The members are, International Intellectual Property Alliance, The Gorlin Group, Law Offices of Hope H. Camp, representing Eli Lilly and Company, Cowan, Leibowitz & Latman, P.C., Anheuser-Busch Companies, Sidley, Austin, Brown & Wood, LLP, representing Biotechnology Industry Organization, Covington and Burling representing Microsoft Corporation, Merck & Company, International Anticounterfeiting Coalition, Intellectual Property Owners Association, Pfizer, Pharmaceutical Research and Manufacturers of America, The Engineered Wood Association, Georgia-Pacific Corporation, Business Software Alliance, Lark-Holton Global Consulting, Levi Strauss & Company, Tuttle International Group, Procter & Gamble, Distilled Spirits Council of the United States, Rubber and Plastics Manufacturers Association.

35 The Charter is available online: (http://www.ita.doc.gov/td/icp/Charter-23.html).

36 See The US-Singapore Free Trade Agreement (FTA) The Intellectual Property Provisions: Report of the Industrial Functional Advisory Committee on Intellectual Property Rights for Trade Policy Matters (IFAC-3), February 28, 2003, at page 3.

37 The letter is available on BIO's website: (http://www.bio.org).

38 World Bank, *The Quality of Growth* (NY: Oxford University Press, 2000), at page xxiii.

39 *World Development Report 2000/2001: Attacking Poverty* (NY: Oxford University Press, 2001), at page 188.

40 *World Development Report 2000/2001: Attacking Poverty* (NY: Oxford University Press, 2001), 12. See also, Deepa Narayan *et al.*, *Voices of the Poor: Can Anyone Hear Us?*, World Bank, (NY: Oxford University Press, 2000), chap. 7.

41 *Diamond v. Chakrabarty* 206 USPQ 193, 200 (1980).

42 See Global Economic Prospects and the Developing Countries, World Bank, Washington DC, 2002, at page 137.

43 Peter Drahos with John Braithwaite, *Information Feudalism: Who Owns the Knowledge Economy*? (London: Earthscan, 2002), at page 135.

44 See Oxfam Background Briefing, "South Africa vs. the Drug Giants: A Challenge to Affordable Medicines," available online: (http://www.oxfam.org.uk/cutthecost).

45 The details of this international effort are described in "US Government Efforts To Negotiate the Repeal, Termination or Withdrawal of Article 15(c) of the South African Medicines and Related Substances Act Of 1965," United States Department of State, Washington D.C. 20520, February 5, 1999.

46 See Article 27.1.

47 See Ruth Mayne, "The Global NGO Campaign on Patents and Access to Medicines: an Oxfam Perspective" in Peter Drahos and Ruth Mayne (eds.) *Global Intellectual Property Rights: Knowledge Access and Development* (Hampshire, UK: Palgrave, Macmillan, 2002), chap. 15.

48 Robert Ballance, Janos Progany, and Helmet Forstener, *The Worlds' Pharmaceutical Industries: An International Perspective on Innovation, Competition & Policy*, UNIDO, 1992.

49 See WTO News: 2003, Press Releases, Press/350, August 30, 2003.

50 See Implementation of Paragraph 6 of the Doha Declaration on the TRIPS Agreement and Public Health, IP/C/W405, August 28, 2003.

51 Thomas Schott, "Global Webs of Knowledge," *American Behavioural Scientist*, 44 (2001), at pages 1740–1751.

CHAPTER 8

Traditional Knowledge, Biological Resources and Drug Development: Building Equitable Partnerships to Conserve, Develop and Respect Biocultural Diversity[1]

STEVEN R. KING*, JULIE ANNE CHINNOCK†, MICHAEL J. BALICK‡, SILVIANO CAMBEROS SANCHEZ§, KATY MORAN**, AND CHARLES LIMBACH††

8.1 INTRODUCTION

The protection, utilisation and conservation of Traditional Knowledge (TK) have become an important global issue for many countries, cultures, organisations and peoples. The current international debates and

* Ethnobotany and Conservation, Napo Pharmaceuticals Inc, 213 E. Grand Ave. South San Francisco, CA 94080.

† The National College of Naturopathic Medicine, Portland, OR, JAChinnock@aol.com.

‡ Institute of Economic Botany, The New York Botanical Garden, Bronx, New York, 10458.

§ Calle Aurelio L. Gallardo, Col. Ladron de Guevara, Jalisco, Mexico.

** HFC , 24 Chauncy Court, Cambridge, Mass. 02138.

†† 18950 Pesante Rd, Prundale, California 93907.

negotiations taking place within many international fora such as the Convention On Biological Diversity, (CBD), the World Intellectual Property organisation (WIPO) and the World Trade Organization (WTO) are focusing on reconciling many fundamental ethical, legal and moral issues. One of the most frequently discussed issues is the potential conflict between the mandates of the CBD and the Trade Related Aspects of Intellectual Property Rights (TRIPS).

WIPO is actively working to understand, define and moderate the complex evolution of the global community's attempts to respect both the IPR system and the holders of TK and biological resources.[2] (WIPO, 2001, 2002a, b, c, d, e, f). Two recent papers by the Head of the Genetic Resources, Biotechnology and Associated Traditional Knowledge section of WIPO have summarised the ethical, moral and legal issues with great depth, clarity and compassion.[3] There are many extremely capable legal experts, diplomats, scholars, social scientists and fortunately increasing numbers of Traditional Knowledge holders (earthcall.org) guiding this debate. The United States Patent and Trademark Office (USPTO) is also trying address the issues associated with patents and the protection of Traditional Knowledge.[4]

In the meantime, local communities and cultures continue to live and seek protection from inappropriate exploitation as well as opportunities to improve, enhance and advance their lives, communities, cultures and ecosystems. This chapter presents two examples of the process of actual direct collaboration with the holders of Traditional Knowledge and the countries in which they live. This discussion provides one other critical dimension to the discussion and debate. In Article 1 of the CBD, there are three well known objectives: the conservation of biological diversity; the sustainable use of biological diversity's components; and the fair and equitable sharing of benefits arising out of the utilisation of genetic resources. There are, however, very few specific discussions of how individuals, organisations, or corporations have worked to address and accomplish these three mandates and objectives. We hope that this chapter contribution will be of use to any groups or organisations seeking to collaborate directly with the holders of traditional knowledge.

After introducing the key issues and themes of this chapter, we will present details of two specific partnerships with the cultures and countries of Belize and Tanzania. Shaman Pharmaceuticals Inc. worked to address the complex issues mentioned above in the course of multiple years of collaboration with local cultures, national scientists and government agencies. With this account of two distinct collaborations, we hope to stimulate analysis, dialogue, and discussion on Traditional Knowledge, biological resources, intellectual property rights, and the equitable sharing of benefits. In following sections of this chapter, we present several examples of organisations conducting ethnobotanical research and development activities around the world.

8.2 BIOCULTURAL DIVERSITY AND INDIGENOUS PEOPLES

It is well known that tropical ecosystems are being destroyed at a rapid pace.[5] In addition to the diminishing flora and fauna, human cultures living in the forest are dwindling in numbers as well. As the ecosystems are destroyed, the cultures that depend on it are destroyed as well. The conservation of both biological and cultural diversity, or "biocultural diversity", is essential in conserving both the ecological systems and the human cultures nurturing these systems.[6] Tropical ecosystems have long been a location for both industrial and scientific research. Great discoveries and achievements, as well as financial benefits, have often been accompanied by the exploitation and destruction of genetic resources.

There is no longer any doubt, however, that indigenous peoples must share in the benefits derived from products developed based on their knowledge, technology, and forest management. One of the key question is how these benefits can be distributed in the most fair and effective manner.[7] Obviously, each country and relationship will be different, and ensuring equitable sharing usually involves a complex series of steps. Fair and equitable benefit-sharing is often complex, but not impossible, and efforts should continue to be made.[8] Intellectual property rights (IPRs) are a Western concept originally established to protect commercial inventions.[9] Many feel that *sui generis* legislation may be needed to protect the rights of indigenous peoples.[10] Posey and Dutfield proposed the concept of Traditional Resource Rights (TRR), which are "equitable integrated Rights, including IPR".[11] The concept of TRR may more appropriately reflect the concerns of indigenous people than IPR.[12] These are based on fundamental human rights and include both tangible and intangible resources. They are actually not one set, but a bundle of rights, combining various international agreements "in an effort to build a solid foundation for more equitable systems of protection and benefit sharing".[13]

8.3 INDIGENOUS PEOPLES' ORGANISATIONS AND MANDATES

Indigenous Peoples are directly challenging the global IPR system. Indigenous Peoples are now leading many of the efforts in IPR, Biological Diversity, and cultural conservation.[14] They have set up organisations such as the Indigenous Peoples' Biodiversity Network (IPBN), the World Council of Indigenous Peoples (WCIP), and the Coordinating Body of Indigenous Organizations of the Amazon Basin (COICA).[15] These are people who constitute less than 4 per cent of the world's population, but make up 95 per cent of the world's cultural diversity[16], and are using the issued mandates and alliances to initiate steps towards positive interpretation and implementation.

The International Alliance of Indigenous-Tribal Peoples of the Tropical Rainforest (IAIP) has released a document, titled "The Biodiversity Convention—the concerns of Indigenous Peoples", which address the objectives of the Convention on Biological Diversity (CBD) and Article 8(j) in particular, calling for support to "help indigenous peoples carry out our own process of mutual consultation on our rights, our knowledge, our biodiversity".[17]

Therefore, in addition to, and possibly more important than, the many international agreements and declarations, there are existing indigenous mandates and charters, often directly stating demands on these issues. These include the aforementioned IAIP's mandate, which explicitly condemns "those who use our biological diversity for commercial and other purposes without our full knowledge and consent".[18]

Quite obviously, there are many methods of collaboration and each case is very different and holds a unique set of circumstances. In addition, each community has its own set of individual needs. Relationships and transactions will always be dynamic and case-specific.[19] As Clay argues in *Generating Income and Conserving Resources: 20 Lessons From the Field*[20], "There is no single blueprint for success." It is up to the individual, company, or institution to initiate these reciprocal partnerships and to follow cultural and national laws. Positive and negative examples should be documented and published so that monitoring, dialoguing, digesting, and assessing these methods are feasible exercises.

TABLE 8.1

Indigenous Mandates and Charters in 1990s
UN Declaration on the Rights of Indigenous Peoples, 1993
Mataatua Declaration on Cultural and Intellectual Property Rights of Indigenous Peoples, 1993
The COICA/UNDP Statement, 1994
Charter of Indigenous Tribal Peoples of the Tropical Forests, 1992
Recommendations from the Voices of the Earth Congress, 1993
Kari-oca Declaration and Indigenous Peoples' Earth Charter, 1992
Consultation on Indigenous Peoples' Knowledge and Intellectual Property Rights, 1995
UNDP Consultation on Indigenous Peoples' Knowledge and Intellectual Property Rights, 1995
World Council of Indigenous Peoples: Declaration of Principles, 1984
UNDP Consultation on the Protection and Conservation of Indigenous Knowledge, 1995

One of the most important aspects in these collaborations at all levels is the role of the indigenous groups, who must become full partners in the negotiations, and be supplied with complete information about the intended research. Highest priority should be given to their ability to accept or reject offers of research collaboration or to negotiate agreements with legal counsel on their teams. Communities will often partake in an equitable collaboration, if the researchers are open and honest about their goals and methods, as well as their commitments to the community, and can guarantee them fairly negotiated contracts and agreements. They may also rely on the reputation of other projects that groups have been involved with and what has been said about them, true or not. Because of both past and ongoing wrongs in research methods, some communities are, for good reason, hesitant to collaborate. There exists, for many, a positive view of the renewed interests in traditional knowledge and natural resources combined with fair compensation. Many tribal and indigenous communities however, choose not to "share" their healing systems, made up of plant medicines, local ecology, spiritual care, and more.[21] But if equitable sharing and positive biocultural benefits can be attained, partnerships can be amicably made. As one member of Costa Rica's *KéköLdi* indigenous group has stated: "We are happy to assist scientists who want to analyse the medicinal properties of the plants in our forests. We only ask them to assist us too, in our efforts to protect our forests."[22]

8.4 SHAMAN PHARMACEUTICALS INC.

Shaman Pharmaceuticals was a mid-stage pharmaceutical company in the process of developing traditional pharmaceuticals identified through a multi-disciplinary process of ethnomedicine and ethnobotany, biology, and natural products chemistry. In the Senate Foreign Relations Committee Hearing on the US ratification of the Convention of Biological Diversity, Shaman's CEO and founder, Lisa Conte, testified as to the significance of the Convention for the recognition of both biological diversity and cultural rights. She stressed the Convention's importance, "... because it defines not only biodiversity conservation, but also the sustainable use of biodiversity and of the equitable sharing of benefits that arise out of that use".[23] She also explained Shaman's philosophy and procedures "to equitably compensate indigenous societies for their intellectual contributions to the identification of useful products in the drug discovery process".[24] This was the foundation for Shaman's commitment to several layers of reciprocity, directly related to ethnomedical collaborations with communities, which are discussed below.

8.4.1 Shaman's focused benefit sharing and reciprocity

From the start of the company, and before the Convention on Biological Diversity (CBD) was opened for signature in 1992, Shaman Pharmaceuticals has focused on reciprocity issues through balanced collaborations between the company and the communities with which it works.[25] It has addressed biodiversity and conservation, as well communal compensation and reciprocity at all stages of the relationship. Because traditional knowledge is an irreplaceable cultural resource and direct acknowledgment is inherent, Shaman has set up three time frames for reciprocity: the short, medium, and long terms. These were developed to provide benefits to communities throughout the drug discovery process. Because of the nature of the pharmaceutical industry, there is a long lead time before a drug is actually on the market, and the company thought it inappropriate to delay reciprocity until this happened. Short and medium term methods address this time issue. Short term reciprocity, which we will focus on in this chapter, devotes 10–15 per cent of the field research funds to immediate community needs, as defined directly by the community. Reciprocity can be in the form of services, or of supplies which are lacking in the community, but this is decided on by the community itself and not by Shaman.

Medium term reciprocity involves projects that transpire in several months or years, and include major parts of the CBD, technology transfer and sustainable development goals. This involves working with local universities, governments, Traditional Healers Associations, Federations, and other groups to benefit the community. These intentions are stated in Article 10(e) of the CBD, which calls for the encouragement of cooperation between government authorities and the private sector in developing methods for sustainable use of biological resources.

Long term benefits are those that are distributed after a product reaches the market. Compensation is carried out by The Healing Forest Conservancy (HFC), a non-profit organisation founded by Shaman Pharmaceuticals, to develop and implement methods to deliver long-term compensation back to the communities with which the company has worked.[26] The overall philosophy is that a portion of company profits will be returned to *all* communities and countries in which Shaman has worked, regardless of where the plant or information that led to its discovery was encountered.[27] This method was designed to provide benefits to a large number of groups, reducing the risk that exists in drug discovery for each individual group. Only a small, unpredictable percentage of products will ever reach the market, so the benefit as well as the risk is spread out among all groups to increase opportunities for compensation and speed up the return time. All of these stages have been discussed in much more detail in previous publications.[28]

Shaman has worked to comply with the CBD and extended the methods of reciprocity and collaboration to include opportunities that were not included in the Convention. Case studies of how Shaman worked to implement CBD policies, principles, and guidelines into applicable research practices are included in publications which provide the details of collaborations in Nigeria[29], Cameroon[30], Guinea[31], and Uganda.[32] We now add to these case studies a description in the next two sections of how partnerships were created in Belize and Tanzania.

8.4.2 Belize: Ethnobotanical research collaboration

Belize is a small country about the size of the state of Massachusetts. It was previously known as British Honduras until 1973 and gained independence from Britain in 1981. It lies on the East coast of Central America in the heart of the Caribbean Basin, with Mexico bordering to the North, Guatemala to the West and South, and flanked by the Caribbean Sea on the East. On the Caribbean side lies the longest barrier reef (185 miles) in the Western Hemisphere, and the second longest in the world. Approximately 30–50 per cent of the forest is still intact—depending on whose estimates you use—and another 20 per cent is being selectively logged. Although, in some areas, like the South, contracts are being given to foreign logging companies, who control up to 200,000 acres of forest in that region.[33]

The *Maya* were the first known inhabitants of Belize, beginning as early as 1500 B.C. There still exists a significant proportion of *Maya* (*Yucatec*, *Mopan*, and *Kekchi*), making up 7–10 per cent of the population throughout the entire country. In the 17th century, the British arrived to cut mahogany for export. They eventually brought African slaves who now represent the 8 per cent Garifuna (Carib) population. There are actually six distinct cultural groups in Belize in addition to *Maya* (7–10 per cent), including Creole (mixed European and African) (40 per cent), Mestizo (mixed *Maya* and Spanish) (33 per cent), Garifuna (8 per cent), East Indian (3 per cent), and Mennonite (3 per cent) populations.[34]

Like traditional cultural practices everywhere, traditional medicine in Belize is in danger of extinction. Many of the codices (books) that were the written teachings of *Maya* medicine and its practice were burned by the Spanish Conquistadors. The practice or teaching of traditional medicine, along with other traditional practices of the *Maya*, were banned and then declined. Changing from written to oral, this continued for generations until the last few decades, when traditional teachings were felt to be irrelevant to life in the modern world. Healers, ethnobotanists, and interested younger Belizeans have made it their work to chronicle the remnants of Belizean traditional medicine before it is all lost.[35] Many of the healers who still retain this knowledge are old and work is being done to capture their vast "oral libraries" of healing knowledge. One of the greatest and most well-known *Maya* doctor-priests of Belize, Don Eligio Panti, died in February of 1996. Much of his experience and knowledge died with him.[36] Fortunately, he had worked for years with Dr. Rosita Arvigo and Michael Balick, who recorded many of his uses of Belizean plants. Dr. Arvigo, who was his apprentice, continues to see many of Don Eligio's patients. Don Eligio will not be forgotten, and now, neither will much of his valuable healing pharmacopoeia.

Dr. Arvigo, with Gregory Shropshire and Michael Balick set up the Ix Chel Tropical Research Foundation (IXTRF) in the Cayo District of Belize. IXTRF is a Belizean NGO dedicated to traditional medicine, ethnobotany, Belizean culture, and rainforest conservation. It is home to *The Belize Ethnobotany Project*, a joint project with the New York Botanical Garden to record traditional uses of plants and carry out cooperative studies, such as with the National Cancer Institute, to test rainforest plants for AIDS and cancer fighting substances.[37] It also assisted in the formation of the Belize Association of Traditional Healers (BATH) and the acquisition of Terra Nova, an extractive reserve for medicinal plants.[38] Through the project, a reference collection of plants has been built at the Belize College of Agriculture and the Belize Forestry Department. Creative approaches to reciprocity in exchange for information have been developed. A significant portion of the profits made from *Rainforest Remedies*, a medicinal plant book which Arvigo and Balick compiled and wrote on the healing plants of Belize, have gone to individual collaborating healers to help construct clinics, support apprentices, and to achieve other personal goals further enhancing traditional healing.[39] Conferences, classes, and lectures on ethnobotany and healing have taken place and have helped rekindle the interest of the younger generations, as well as respect for the traditional healer's knowledge. An employee profit-sharing herbal extract industry has also been started, and is run as a cooperative venture with local farmers.

The Healing Forest Conservancy (HFC) has successfully completed several pilot projects to contribute to the discussion of long term compensation. One of these occurred in Belize in conjunction with IXTRF and BATH. Results of all pilot projects are shared with other cultural groups and countries to give them concrete examples for analysis. Because land demarcation is an important aspect and the first step towards sustainable management, it is often one of the highest priorities for indigenous groups. When BATH sought a way to protect Terra Nova from approaching poachers and loggers, they decided that demarcating the 6,000-acre tract would help and requested assistance. The HFC and the Rex Foundation funded the surveying and demarcation of this area. This successful cooperation between a government, a traditional healers association, and outside groups is a useful example for other groups who desire to demarcate their land. This was the first major collaboration between Shaman, through the HFC, and indigenous groups and other organisations in Belize.[40]

8.4.2.1 Prior informed consent and relationship building

Shaman Pharmaceuticals initiated interest in Belize due to its existing indigenous populations, rainforest and the continued use of traditional medicine by its people. It is one of the over 25 countries, in Latin America, Africa, and Asia that have collaborated with Shaman scientific teams. Michael Balick, an ethnobotanist with extensive field research in Belize was involved in the planning process, as was Julie Anne Chinnock, a natural products ethnobotanist at Shaman, who had lived and worked in Belize previously.[41] A cultural background report on Belize was prepared by Shaman's in-house medical anthropologist as part of the pre-fieldwork preparation, a practice which has been suggested by several authors.[42] The Southwest part of the country was chosen due to the existing *Mopan* and *Kekchi Maya* communities there. An NGO, the Toledo Eco-Tourism Association (TEA), who had expressed interest in working with Shaman, was contacted to seek a possible collaboration with people in the community. This was a NGO set up by, and a representative of, the people in several communities of the Toledo District. It was decided after reviewing their objectives as an organisation and receiving their permission, that they would be an appropriate liaison in order to conduct an ethnomedical field research collaboration. It is important to highlight that other NGO's and groups do exist in the region, but this one appeared to have commendable objectives, was proactive in inviting us to collaborate, had one of the largest representations of the people in the communities, and was accepted by many people in the 14 village areas. Sometimes individuals, groups, or communities can represent themselves in collaborations, but sometimes they do not "have the legal, technical, social, or political expertise or power to effectively structure an exchange in their own interests and may require the assistance of other organisations such as activist NGOs."[43] This is partially the case in Southern Belize, although many self-representative groups do exist and are currently forming and reinforcing their presence and objectives in the country.

The self-defined purposes of the TEA were to provide alternatives to ecological destruction, to set up manageable and controlled income-generating activities (including eco-tourism) as the name suggests, to improve public health and education in the district, to protect the environment, and to preserve the culture and the values of the indigenous communities. They are also actively involved in current projects to prevent illegal and destructive logging in the Toledo District.[44]

The Toledo *Maya* still maintain slash and burn farming (milpa) methods. In recent times, their environment is being sacrificed for short term economic gain. Timber concessions are being granted and misguided development schemes are utilising non-sustainable harvest methods.[45] Tourism had become an economic alternative, but was developing into another means of forest and cultural demise. There was, and remains, the immediate need for protection of the indigenous groups residing in this natural area. There are still many traditional uses of the forest in this area, with much knowledge held by the local people. This adds greater strength to the demand that these natural areas be protected from over-development.[46] The TEA was formed to help keep this area from biological and cultural destruction, while producing income for the communities as well. As Jason Clay has argued, "success [in resource use] will only be achieved if very specific local conditions are taken into account in the design and implementation of conservation and development strategies for each community".[47] This is exactly what the TEA attempted to do by concentrating its efforts on a small number of communities and using non-timber forest products and ecotourism in an ecological and productive manner. They received commendations and recommendations from the RainForest Action Network and other groups for their efforts in conservation and sustainable development.[48]

8.4.2.2 The prior informed consent process

Contact regarding this research project was established with the TEA in June 1994, in the form of a introductory letter of interest, a proposal to visit and do research, articles describing past collaborations, commitments and research methods, as well as an open invitation for questions and concerns. Prior Informed Consent (PIC) was requested from the healers and the communities. Although Spanish, Creole, Garifuna, and several forms of *Maya* are all spoken in Belize, English is the central language and is spoken by most people, and therefore the most appropriate language to be used for all written correspondence. PIC is one of the most important aspects of the CBD, and in the context of TRRs and IPRs. It is an authorisation from the communities within the research jurisdiction, based on the description (in the local language) of the intended work, the possible implications, the intended benefits, and among other things, how and by whom the genetic resources will be used. This information gives the communities the ability to negotiate, comply or deny access.[49] The Convention on Biological Diversity addresses PIC in Article 15(5), stating that:

> Access to genetic resources shall be subject to prior informed consent of the Contracting Party providing such resources, unless otherwise determined by the Party.

In accordance with the CBD and the important need for PIC, all parties and communities involved in the collaboration with Shaman were fully informed of the company's objectives and goals and the potential for commercialisation prior to the collaborative research being conducted. This is a vital aspect in any research program and needs to be initiated at the beginning of any program and openly maintained throughout the relationship, in order to have enough time to discuss problems, goals, and aspirations before the research begins. There will always be changes and questions and the discussions should be ongoing.[50]

A meeting was held to discuss Shaman's request and to come to a decision on their proposal to begin collaborating. The company's objectives and methods were described to the group and the potential advantages and disadvantages discussed and debated between them. The TEA then decided that they would approve and help facilitate the research, including interviews and plant collections, and that a committee be formed to observe and monitor Shaman's work. Two interested villages extended an invitation. Permission was then granted, in writing, by the TEA Executive Committee.

Planning activities began, such as setting and verifying dates, confirming existing government permits, and picking a convenient date for a follow-up public meeting to discuss details of reciprocity. Discussions of objectives continued via phone and fax, and additional materials were sent upon request. Joint goals were expressed by both parties to be considered and discussed further at the follow-up meeting. Discussions took place on the appropriate amount of daily salaries each healer and other workers would receive for their work on the project. Specific suggestions on salaries were given by the members of TEA and other Belizean organisations and individuals. Medium and long term benefit information was also relayed both in writing and verbally.

8.4.2.3 Discussions and ethnobotanical research

The field expedition began several weeks later, with the team consisting of Balick and Chinnock, a Belizean herbal healer from the western part of the country, Polo Romero, and a Mexican medical doctor, Silviano Camberos Sanchez, trained in both medicine and ecology. Mr. Romero learned his healing methods while working in rubber, mahogany, and chicle camps. He is now a well-known healer who specialises in treating snake bites. Dr. Sanchez had extensive training in ethnobotany and had worked for 10 years with the Huichol Indians in Western Mexico.

Shaman's ethnomedical/botanical approach to drug discovery was largely based on, and begins with, the work of the field research teams. The representatives from Shaman always included an ethnobotanist and a physician. Both of these team members play key roles in the interviewing and plant collecting process. Most of the healers are experts in various disciplines, including the flora of the region that comprises their botanical pharmacopoeia and the diseases that are present in the geographic area. Having both an ethnobotanist and a physician on the research team enhanced its ability to understand the healers' botanical medicine knowledge.[51]

Upon Shaman's arrival in Belize and before the actual research work began, immediate informal discussions about the collaboration occurred. Individuals spoke with the ethnobiomedical team about the objectives of the research and Shaman's work with indigenous people from other countries. Healers were previously identified by members of the two communities and had accepted the invitation to collaborate. Over a 10-day period, ethnomedical interviews and research activities were carried out, while botanical voucher and bulk collections were made. The team interviewed, in total, four *Maya* healers and one village health care worker/herbalist who provided descriptions of Type II diabetes patients and the local plants used to treat them. Translators were hired in some cases to translate both *Kekchi* and *Mopan Maya*. Collectors were also hired to accompany the team when plant collections were made.

Through direct interviews, conversations, and case presentations of Type II diabetes, the team worked with the healers and discussed signs and symptoms, age groups, and disease identification. They talked about the names given to both the disease and the medicines used. In several field walks of the surrounding forest, the team located and collected botanical voucher specimens for taxonomical identification and plant collections for analysis.

8.4.2.4 Focused benefit-sharing and reciprocity

The community meeting took place on a set date and at least one representative from each village attended. The meeting was composed of mostly TEA members, although several other individuals came. The meeting began with a declaration by the TEA president, that reciprocity should be distributed at the community level and that related decisions should be directed through local cultural councils: Alcalde's Association and the Toledo *Maya* Cultural Council (TMCC) representing all the indigenous people of the local communities. During our time in the field, there was one suggested healer who requested a large personal monetary payment (US$20,000) in exchange for meeting with him. The Shaman team politely declined to accept his offer as Shaman was able to comply financially or according to our previous discussions and guidelines of compensation. These guidelines were based on Shaman's codes of reciprocity and were approved earlier and by this declaration of the Southern group in Belize. The "community benefit" approach to reciprocity is used by other groups as well. This declaration coincides with a vote taken in 1993 by BATH. They decided that reciprocity and profits in ventures with pharmaceutical companies for access to their plants should be returned to the community and not to individuals.[52]

The group then presented a statement of thanks for Shaman's acknowledgment of *Maya* culture and the healers' knowledge. This *acknowledgment* was and is *extremely important* to all the culture groups that we have collaborated with. It is an issue of *fundamental dignity* and *respect* which is outside the realm of money and contracts. They also expressed concerns about the false promises they were given by researchers in the past, citing specific examples of graduate students and anthropologists who had lived in their communities for lengths of time and had failed to send "even a photo or a copy of their theses or books."

The Shaman team then thoroughly explained the company's purpose and objectives, and reciprocity was discussed in great detail. Everyone in attendance introduced themselves and each individual stated their thoughts and opinions and asked questions. Ideas of short-term reciprocity were offered by the community members and one idea was formally presented to build several village nurseries to promote reforestation and the growth of non-timber crops. This project was to be part of a larger project that was then being proposed to the Belizean government. Three nurseries were to be built to initiate re-forestation, research, and employment for the members of the community. The intention was to eventually grow medicinal plants, fruit trees, and other economically viable crops to help support these communities. It also included training and workshops on sustainable crops and development. This was an opportunity which could, eventually, be open to all villagers, for education and income generating purposes.

There was another extensive long-term project suggested which was deemed unfeasible and beyond the available budget. After some discussion, a vote was taken and a majority decision was reached to proceed with the nursery project. Informational packets about the company, papers detailing past projects and collaborations, and 60 copies of *Rainforest Remedies*[53], a book on Belizean Medicinal Plants, were distributed to all the attendees and for reference at the community health centres in each village.

In accordance with our standard procedures, during the course of our research we adhered to things that all responsible field research teams do. We provided emergency medical care and transport. We held a supplemental one day health clinic at the community's request, treating over 60 people with minor ailments. The clinic was held with Dr. Camberos Sanchez and the village health worker/herbalist working together. The traditional healer and Dr. Camberos Sanchez made joint evaluations of most of the patients. Some of the patients were prescribed or treated with botanical medicines from the herbalist. The Western medicines were provided by the medical physician, when needed, and were regarded as a complement to their own therapeutics.

Compensation for daily wages was given for translators, healers, collectors, and other local participants. Payment was given for food and lodging, through the TEA's existing Homestay program. As part of medium term reciprocity, a commitment was given to return and to hire people in the same communities for potential recollections. This was done nine months later, when a plant that a local healer suggested was collected in a greater quantity for testing. The Shaman team also sent photographs and written material from their trip back to the villages. Voucher specimens of each plant collected, with collection data, were identified and mounted on archival paper and sent to the Belize College of Agriculture and the Belize Forestry Department. Test data from all analyses carried out on Belizean plants was sent to several organisations in Belize, including Ix Chel and the TEA.

8.4.2.5 Observations from Belize

Here are some observations highlighting both the advancements and limitations that the team experienced. The biggest challenge that may be encountered in any work with communities is finding a group that is representative of the whole community. Although the TEA is a progressive, productive group, not all of the members of the community were fully represented by them or by any organisation that we found in the country. There were some other more encompassing groups, such as the Toledo *Maya* Cultural Council, suggested by members of the community while we were there, and these groups will most likely be facilitators for extended medium and long term reciprocity arrangements. Along these same lines is deciding on a project for reciprocity that would affect the community as a whole. The project that was chosen does have a direct impact on many people and an indirect one on even more, yet it is not something that all community members chose to participate in. There are existing factions in these communities which can make these and other decisions even more difficult.

This research did stimulate much discussion in the community, and created links where they did not exist before. People met to discuss the threat of losing their important traditional knowledge and culture. The research, as well as the discussions, reinforced the interest in traditional knowledge. The Belizean herbal medicine book, *Rainforest Remedies*[54], was widely valued and more copies were requested by and sent to schools and community organisations. Many children participated, watched the research and collection activity and expressed a new interest in the healers. This project also helped to generate discussions for future research and benefit sharing projects with Shaman and others. It also eased some of their doubts about working with researchers and helped prepare them for negotiations regarding the sharing of future equitable benefits.

During the course of our work, a US researcher, Jeffrey Augello, a student at the School for International Training, requested to accompany us in the field. He had previously studied Shaman's objectives and observed and documented our work. He had discussions with numerous people in the communities before, during, and after the team was there. He then compiled a report entitled *Bridging the Gap: An Analysis of the Pharmaceutical Industry and Their Emerging Role in the Conservation Movement* which was distributed later in the US and Belize. Mr. Augello's unbiased observations were very much an asset to our research. As part of his assessment, he came to four main conclusions about the community's opinion of our methods and research:

1. The majority of villagers showed support and participated in the project;
2. Those who knew Shaman's purpose, but chose not to participate, still supported the research;
3. Those who knew little about the company or project, showed little reaction or interest;
4. Those who knew even less or were unaware of the company or project, were interested in participating in the future and learning more about the project.

For the purposes of self-assessment, there were additional lessons which we collectively learned overall through our own observations and all channels of feedback:

1. It is important to continue to attempt to *identify* an organisation that *represents all or the majority of the communities' interests*, or to personally contact all representative parties and groups in the communities in which we work.
2. It is essential to keep *prior informed consent* as an integral part of the conception and planning of a project. This should be done well *in advance of the research* taking place to accommodate communication limitations, and so that the largest number of people have the opportunity to participate in the collaboration and decision making discussions.
3. *Feedback*, in the form of relevant publications and results, should be provided to the communities, especially schools, clinics, and health care centres to further their knowledge and interest in traditional healing and medicine.

4. *Reciprocity* should be initiated from the community and be focused on strengthening the majority of the community directly or indirectly. Reciprocity should be an issue discussed before, during, and after the entire research process, so as to allow time and thought for a realistic assessment of the risks and options, and the value of intellectual and natural resources.

8.4.2.6 Follow-up and conclusion

For several years after the field research occurred, there was frequent multi-lateral communication between Shaman, the TEA, the individuals who assisted in the research, the Belizean government, and others. A Biodiversity Task Force Working Group was formed by the Belizean Department of Forestry in order to discuss the key issues unfolding related to research and natural resource collections. The TEA has proceeded with the nursery project using the funds supplied by Shaman. They have built three nurseries in separate villages and are planning to expand the projects to more villages and incorporate them with their Community Conservation Areas for further research, education, and income-generating projects. They have held several workshops on botany, nursery and agroforestry practices in these communities and are currently growing a variety of species in the nurseries. The test results of the plants collected in Belize that Shaman sent back are being shared with the local traditional healers and health workers. The TEA was awarded the world prize for socially responsible tourism in Berlin in 1996.

By utilising a combination of the various laws, declarations, and mandates that now exist, and striving to comply with the CBD, stressing factors such as PIC and focused benefit sharing at various stages, effective research combined with fair and equitable benefit-sharing and reciprocity can be a foundation for equitable partnerships.

8.4.3 Tanzania: Ethnobotanical research collaboration

Tanzania has a population of 30 million and over 100 cultural groups. Traditional medicine is thriving in Tanzania as it is throughout the rest of Africa.[55] Many African nations, such as Nigeria, have officially incorporated traditional medicine practitioners into their national public health care programs.

In 1991 Shaman was contacted by Mr. David Scheinman of the Tanga AIDS Working Group (TAWG) and Rural Development Associates (RDA). The TAWG is an interdisciplinary group that links physicians, health workers, traditional healers, people living with AIDS (PLWAs) and social scientists. TAWG focuses on increasing research on medicinal plants that show promising results in the treatment of HIV/AIDS patients in Pangani, Tanzania.[56] The core focus of TAWG is to treat people living with AIDS (TAWG has treated 4,000 people as of 2004) with traditional medicines, provide compassionate care and conducts applied ethnomedical research. The efforts of TAWG was sought to bridge the gap between traditional and hospital medicine, and to provide much needed integrated health care to PLWAs.

The initial collaboration involved Shaman providing literature searches on the biology, chemistry and efficacy of many of the plants utilised to treat people living with AIDS. The literature data provided by Shaman indicated that there was data which supported the use of several of the treatments used by the traditional healers, including a treatment for oral thrush, a major opportunistic infection caused by AIDS. This type of data was important and well received by the TAWG.

In 1992 one of the authors, Steven King, visited the Tanga region, met with healers, patients, and nurses from the hospital and other biomedical staff. As part of this initial process, Shaman provided a US$2,000 contribution to support the collection, preparation and delivery of traditional plant medicines to patients in the Tanga area.

Through discussions and correspondence, Shaman and TAWG agreed to proceed with an exploratory visit by a Shaman-trained physician who was also a skilled ethnobotanist. In 1993, Dr. Charles Limbach worked for one month in the Tanga region and trained local healers, physicians and technicians in Shaman's ethnobotanical field research methods. The skills learned in this exploratory collaboration were utilised by the TAWG group to further their own primary objectives and to collaborate with Shaman and with other international and national organisations.

8.4.3.1 Relationship and capacity building

In 1994 scientists from the Institute of Traditional Medicine (ITM) at the Muhimbili University College of Health Sciences in Dar es Salaam contacted Shaman about a potential collaboration. One of the ITM's mandates is to research and provide recommendations on the safety and efficacy of traditional plant medicines of importance to public health in Tanzania. The ITM had been collaborating with the United States National Cancer Institute (NCI) as well. In this relationship, medium term focused benefit sharing was initiated first, followed by a workshop exchange as a form of capacity building and technology transfer.

In September 1994, Shaman sponsored the Director of the ITM, Dr. Rogasian Mahunnah, to attend a meeting on intellectual property rights held in Costa Rica by the American Society of Pharmacognosy. Dr. Mahunnah then visited Shaman's facilities in California to review our facility and operations. Shaman then began financially supporting the research programs of the ITM, including US$11,274 for an ITM diabetes research project. The ITM also requested literature searches and equipment for their laboratory facility.

8.4.3.2 National level prior informed consent and agreements

Shaman submitted an Agreement of Principles to the ITM and Muhimbili. This contractual agreement had been utilised by Shaman in multiple countries. In each previous case, collaborating countries, NGOs and culture groups modified and negotiated a variety of aspects of the agreement. In Tanzania, the Board of the Muhimbili University reviewed the draft agreement and began a process of negotiation. While the agreement was being negotiated Shaman was invited to Tanzania to conduct a capacity-building workshop and to initiate collaborative field research. Shaman sent an ethnobotanist and physician team, comprising of Ms. Rowena Richter and Dr. Kariem Ali, to conduct the workshop and field research.

The ITM had expressed interest in evaluating Shaman's ethnomedical field interview methodology. The ITM scientist planned to combine our methods with their own expertise to enhance their capacity to engage in plant medicine research for public health issues in Tanzania. Once the Shaman team had obtained the required research permits they conducted a four-day workshop. The workshop was held in Tanga, Tanzania in collaboration with the previously described TAWG. With their previous success in integrating traditional medicine, healers, health care workers and the local hospital, TAWG provided expertise for the workshop. The workshop involved 14 participants, representing five Tanzanian community health and conservation organisations. The four days involved lectures, interview techniques, and all technical aspects of documenting the preparation of phyto-medicines.

8.4.3.3 Prior informed consent and focused benefit-sharing in Mwanga and Moshi districts

Two weeks before the workshop and the field research, a scientist from the ITM visited the villages that the Shaman team hoped to work with. Those communities that wished to potentially collaborate gave their prior informed consent to meet with the field teams.

Before the research teams visited any villages in Mwanga, traditional healers and traditional birth attendants representing each village met with the research teams in a central location. A total of 44 men and women attended the meeting, including the chairman and secretary of the Mwanga Association of Healers, and district medical officer. Speaking in Swahili, Tanzania's national language, Shaman's research and development focus was described and explained to them. The meeting lasted for several hours and the representatives of the villages related their past negative experiences with researchers who had not provided compensation or reciprocity and who never returned to share their results. The Shaman team described its multiple levels of focused benefit-sharing, and informed them that each healer would be paid for their time, knowledge and expertise. After a dialogue between the parties, the representatives gave their prior informed consent for the teams to conduct the interviews. It was also requested that the same group meet again a second time after the interviews in the villages had been conducted. The research team conducted the research over the next five days. The second meeting began with the Shaman research team inviting comments on their work. The healers mentioned that it would have been better if more time had been allowed to discuss the plant medicines during the interviews.

The discussion then moved on to the immediate focused benefit-sharing arrangements. In every Shaman research collaboration, 10–15 per cent of the overall budget is designated for immediate focused benefit-sharing with the communities. The funds in this case, a sum of US$6,750, was divided equally between the Mwanga and Moshi districts. The people of each district determined how they wished to allocate the funds for the benefit of their respective communities. The Shaman team learned that the timing of the benefit-sharing discussion was important. The team had followed the advice of the chairman of the Mwanga Association of Healers, Mr. Milkiel Msemo, and had not brought up the topic of focused community benefit-sharing at the first meeting. Several healers at the meeting informed the Shaman team that they had demonstrated proper respect by discussing focused community benefits at the second meeting after the work was done. The Shaman team was told that if they had brought this topic up at the initial meeting, it would have easily been misinterpreted as insulting behaviour.

At the time of this research project, the Mwanga Association of Healers had been experiencing internal strife, and the meeting and the research team's visit helped re-invigorate the organisation. One of their revised goals was to work more closely with the physicians in the government hospitals for the benefit of their patients. The group agreed that the establishment of a central office would help their organisation gain strength, as well as credibility, and help them towards their goal of increased integrated collaboration. The association was not ready to build this facility at that time and they asked us to hold the funds that we had committed until they were ready to begin construction. The Shaman team agreed and the director of the ITM later facilitated the transaction. The association built what they had visualised, which comprised offices, wards and a laboratory. The Government of Tanzania gave them 15 acres of land on which these structures were built. A medicinal plant garden was planned for another plot of land.

In the Moshi district, prior informed consent was discussed and granted in each of the five villages. After the discussions, one individual healer chose to not participate. When the interviews were completed, each village determined how they wished to utilise the resources made available to them under the focused benefit-sharing arrangements. They requested that the Shaman team purchase and deliver building materials to them rather then giving them the actual funds. This request was honoured by the Shaman team. The Village of *Uchira* decided to purchase the materials necessary to install electricity and lights in the local health clinic so that women delivering babies at night would be able to do so with adequate light. The *Mayuyuni* village had a partially constructed health clinic made from local bricks and they elected to purchase 45 bags of cement to complete its construction. Women in the village of *Mayuyuni* had been travelling to the nearest clinic to deliver babies, often having to pay as much as a year's wages for transportation. The community was therefore eager to complete their clinic. Two other villages elected to buy mattresses, sheets and blanket for their clinics. The women participated actively in the decisions made on the type of focused benefits that each village chose to receive. It appeared that they influenced the choices made in the five communities and steered the discussions towards issues that affected women, children and childbirth in the community.

8.4.3.4 Follow-up, data return and conclusions

After the field research described above, the Shaman/ITM team returned to Dar es Salaam and presented a summary of its work to the physicians and officials at Muhimbili. Copies of the data forms and duplicates of the plant herbarium specimens were deposited at the ITM, Tanzania Forestry Research Institute and the National Herbarium. There was also continued focused benefit-sharing in the medium term. After this the Shaman team returned to the United States, and a taxonomist at the Missouri Botanical Garden identified the plants. These determinations, along with newly published scientific names and supporting literature, were sent to the botanists at the ITM for them to review. Shaman also provided an additional US$11,274 for a second phase of research support for ITM's research programs. Shaman also continued to return data from the biological assays on Tanzanian plants, as part of its agreement with Tanzania.[57] This data return has proved beneficial to the treatment of patients in Tanzania.

One specific plant, called *Zingiri*, demonstrated activity in an in-vitro cell-based assay of herpes simplex, a viral infection that is often pronounced in people with weak immune systems. Prior to learning of the Shaman anti-viral data, Mr. Kassomo, a regional traditional healer had been utilising *Zingiri* to treat mouth sores. After learning of this lab data, Kassomo began treating patients suffering from herpes zoster and other herpes viral infections. The results were promising. As a result, this well-known local plant medicine has become widely utilised in the Tanga Aids Working Group treatment programs. Mr. Kassomo began to deliver the plant medicine to the Bombo Hospital and it is also being utilised to treat fungal infections.[58] Mr. Kassomo has become well-known for his herpes treatments and patients come to him from Kenya and Tanzania to receive treatment. Shaman did not pursue any research or development on this plant or any compounds from it. This is an example of an important local public health benefit.

In September 1996 an ethnobotanist, a physician from the ITM and four *Masaai* were sponsored by Shaman to attend a meeting of the International Society of Ethnobiology in Nairobi and a public health workshop was conducted by Dr. Thomas Carlson, the head of Shaman ethnomedical field research.

The relationship between Shaman and Tanzania was initiated as a long term partnership. Between the years of 1992–1997 a total of US$226,577 was invested in a combination of research support, focused benefits, purchases of research materials and reciprocity. The numerous partners in Tanzania continue to collaborate with a diverse set of national and international partners to research, develop, utilise and conserve the rich biocultural diversity of this country.

8.5 ORGANISATIONS UTILISING TRADITIONAL ETHNOBOTANICAL KNOWLEDGE IN RESEARCH AND DEVELOPMENT PROGRAMS

8.5.1 International Cooperative Biodiversity Group (ICBG) projects in Nigeria, Cameroon, Suriname, Peru, Vietnam, Laos and Mexico

The objectives of the International Cooperative Biodiversity Groups (ICBG) are to focus on natural products drug discovery, economic development and biodiversity conservation. The accomplishments of this program over the past 10 years are impressive and the specific programs have been described in detail elsewhere.[59] In addition to the bioactive compounds isolated, scientists trained and research conducted, the program has been the most transparent government-sponsored international experiment conducted to date, testing the various processes and methods of implementing the guiding principles of the Convention On Biological Diversity. The ICBG program requires and has a strong focus on prior informed consent. The ICBG participants must demonstrate agreements that provide for the protection of traditional knowledge and IPR contracts that are linked to benefit sharing.

The ICBG program provided 11 major grants between 1993 to 2002. Ethnobotanical and ethnomedical research has been utilised in varying degrees in nine of these 11 major grants. All of these nine major grant programs also utilised a variety of other research and collection activities. The research programs that put the largest emphasis on ethnobotanical and ethnomedical knowledge in the drug discovery process were the programs implemented in Cameroon and Nigeria[60], Peru[61], Vietnam and Laos[62], Surinam and Madagascar[63], and Mexico; a program that was ultimately cancelled.[64]

The ICBG programs are highly dynamic and complex in their goals, methods and accomplishments. No single, simple objective can be identified, measured or highlighted. Several of these programs placed a high priority on anti-malarial and anti-parasitic diseases such as the *Drug Development and Conservation of Biodiversity in West Africa*[65] program and *Peruvian Medicinal Plant Sources of New Pharmaceuticals*.[66] In the West African program, ethnomedical field research methodology yielded a 69 per cent activity rate out of 500 anti-malarial extracts tested. Activity rates of 40–48 per cent were reported for other parasitic diseases such as *leishmania* (40 per cent) and *trypanosomiasis* (48 per cent). In addition, a total of 47 isolated and characterised molecular leads for drug development activities were isolated in this program as of 1999.[67]

The ICBG program in Peru has also demonstrated the importance of collaborating with traditional healers who treat malaria. This research team demonstrated that anti-malarial-targeted ethnomedicinal plants utilised by the *Aguaruna* communities yielded a statistically significant number of anti-malarial extract leads when compared to plants collected on a random.[68]

The demonstrated utility of ethnobotanical research to identify anti-parasitic extracts and compounds around the world should lead to increased collaboration with traditional healers in many cultures. It is likely that a number of infectious diseases can be effectively managed with local botanical and phytomedicines. These treatments are being evaluated and, when shown to be safe and effective, should be made available as standardised extracts in regional public health programs. There are efforts underway to do this in Africa, Southeast Asia and Latin America.

8.5.2 South Africa, the *San* Bushmen, Phytopharm plc and P57

The South African Council for Scientific Research and Industrial Research (CSIR) received a patent on an extract of the *Hoodia* cactus in 1996. This *Hoodia* cactus has been part of the traditional knowledge of the *San* Bushman of Southern Africa for centuries. The *San* use this species to suppress appetite and thirst when they search for food in the desert or during times of famine. In 1997 CSIR licensed this extract, now called P57, to a small British pharmaceutical company Phytopharm plc. This development stage product P57, derived from the traditional knowledge of the *San* Bushman, is being investigated for its ability to treat obesity and has a very large sales potential. In the United States, is it estimated that there are 35–65 million obese people. In 1998, Phytopharm plc subsequently licensed P57 to Pfizer Pharmaceuticals, one of the largest pharmaceutical companies in the world. In 2001, the *San* Bushman threatened to take legal action against CSIR because no access or benefit-sharing agreement had been made with the *San* to allow CSIR to patent and license this extract based on the indigenous knowledge of the *San*.[69] In March 2002, the *San* and CSIR created a memorandum of understanding which recognised the *San* as the custodians of traditional knowledge associated with the uses of a large variety of plant materials, including the *Hoodia* cactus.[70] The *San* in turn acknowledged that it was necessary for the CSIR to protect the work that had been done in isolating the active ingredient in the plant by patenting it in the CSIR's name. Finally, in March of 2003, the CSIR issued a press release stating that the *San* and CSIR had created a benefit-sharing agreement for the potential anti-obesity drug P57. This was the reverse of how the process *should* have taken place: the CSIR should have initiated the PIC, access and benefit sharing process *before* beginning work on the *San* Bushman pharmacopeia.

In July 2003, Phytopharm plc announced that Pfizer had decided to halt its clinical development of P57 for the treatment of obesity and to return all rights to Phytopharm. Phytopharm has indicated that a great deal of pre-clinical and clinical data had been generated with Pfizer and that they would now seek another partner to complete the product development.[71]

The problems with the timing of the access and benefit-sharing process and agreement highlight the importance of following proper procedures when working with the holders of traditional knowledge. The ethnobotanical knowledge of the *San* Bushman and the discovery of P57 is, however, another example of the effectiveness of collaborating with the holders of traditional knowledge.

8.5.3 Ethnobotanical research in Samoa: The antiviral compound *Prostratin*

Prostratin was identified during field studies in Western Samoa, by Dr. Paul Cox, an ethnobotanist from Brigham Young University and currently the Director of the US National Tropical Botanical Garden. His primary sources for information about this plant were two Samoan healers, Mariana Lilo and Epenesa Mauigoa, both of whom died in 1993. The healers were using the bark from the stem of the mamala tree to treat a disease they called *fiva samasama*—"yellowing fever," or hepatitis. The bark was used to treat viral infections; the leaves were used to treat back pain; and the root to alleviate diarrhoea. These elderly women also taught Dr. Cox details of 121 different herbal remedies from 90 species of flowering plants.[72]

Selected samples of these native remedies were sent to scientists at the US National Cancer Institute (NCI), where plant-derived substances are routinely screened for activity against different diseases. In 1992, Dr. Michael Boyd and his colleagues at NCI isolated the active chemical from the samples, *Prostratin*, and discovered its powerful effects against HIV, which suggested that *Prostratin* could be used to activate viral reservoirs.[73] HIV reservoirs are a barrier to curing the HIV infection. They may persist for up to 60 years in some patients and are where latently infected cells continue to be present after acute HIV infection. These latently infected cells are invisible to the immune system and are not susceptible to available anti-viral drugs. Many international leaders pursuing HIV and AIDS research and therapy now see latent virus activation as a possible strategic requirement for future advances in the therapeutics of HIV infection and AIDS.[74]

The Medical Director of the AIDS Research Alliance (ARA), Stephen J. Brown, M. D., took notice of NCI's work with *Prostratin* in 1999 and began to direct research on the compound. Most recently, a study in the November 15, 2001 issue of the journal *Blood* confirmed the earlier work of researchers at several institutions—including NCI, ARA and UCLA—where it was learned that *Prostratin* exhibited dual action, inhibiting HIV replication while activating dormant, or "latent," HIV.[75]

In one study, researchers at the NCI and Jefferson Medical College in Philadelphia demonstrated that *Prostratin* could activate dormant HIV in cells taken from HIV-positive patients. The authors suggest that future studies should examine combination therapies involving *Prostratin* and other anti-HIV drugs to activate pockets of dormant HIV in the hope of eradicating the virus.

Data from Dr. Jerome Zack at UCLA indicates that *Prostratin* can induce replication of the latent pool of virus without initiating T-cell replication.[76] Highly active antiretroviral therapy (HAART) often reduces viral load to undetectable levels and can significantly delay progression to symptomatic AIDS. But HIV remains hidden or dormant in various "reservoirs" of the body, and the viral "rebound" that almost always occurs when antiretroviral therapy is discontinued is largely due to continued replication of HIV within these reservoirs despite HAART.

Dr. Zack has described his next research steps[77]:

> Further in-vitro studies will be performed to fully define the effects of *Prostratin* on cells in the immune system. Collaborative studies are planned to assess the effects of *Prostratin* in SIV models, with the eventual intent of bringing this type of approach to clinical trial in infected patients.

Ultimately, the likelihood is that *Prostratin* will be tested as an adjunct to HAART—possibly in combination with additional therapies to boost immune response or target cells that are actively producing the virus. Recently published data has amplified the importance of trying to solve the problem of the latency of the HIV virus.[78] Clearly this compound, derived from a partnership with indigenous healers, has already provided significant medical and scientific advances in field of basic AIDS therapy research.

In August 2001, the AIDS Research Alliance signed an agreement with the Prime Minister of Samoa that was facilitated by Dr. Cox, guaranteeing that a total of 20 per cent of all ARA profits from the development of the antiviral drug *Prostratin* would be returned to Samoa according to the following formula: 12.5 per cent to the government, 6.7 per cent to the village, and 0.4 per cent to each of the families of the two healers who participated in the research. Prior to this national-level agreement, the village council of Falealupo, Samoa negotiated a convenant called "The Falealupo Covenant." This agreement focused on the equitable transfer of benefits as part of the process of collaborative field research. As of 2001, more then US$480,000 in benefits—including schools, medical clinics, water supplies, an aerial rainforest canopy walkway and an endowment for the rainforests—have been transmitted as a result of this covenant.[79]

8.5.4 MerLion Pharmaceuticals Pte. Ltd., Singapore

MerLion Pharmaceuticals was founded in 2002 as one of Singapore's first drug research and development companies. MerLion was created through the privatisation of the former Centre for Natural Products Research (CNPR). The CNPR was established in 1993 to screen natural products samples for new pharmaceutical leads. MerLion acquired all the assets of CNPR, including the natural product library of GlaxoSmithKline (GSK), which is one of the world's largest and most diverse natural product samples. The natural product library of GSK includes natural products derived and isolated from soil samples, marine organisms and terrestial plants. This GSK natural product library, like most large natural product collections, is likely to contain a relatively small number of plants collected based on their use by indigenous peoples of Southeast Asia and other regions of the world. The approach of MerLion is based on high throughput screening, natural product chemistry and medicinal chemistry. Their focus is on the discovery of novel bioactive compounds. MerLion has already established screening partnerships with large pharmaceutical companies such as Fujisawa Pharmaceuticals Co. Ltd., Merck & Co. Inc. and Abbot Laboratories. The company does not conduct ethnobotanical field research. MerLion does, however, explicitly state its company policy: "A significant portion of any royalty payment is expected to be shared with the indigenous local communities in which the samples were collected to support science training and education."[80]

8.5.5 Napo Pharmaceuticals Inc.

One example of a late stage product that is based on collaboration with indigenous people and traditional knowledge is the anti-diarrhoea compound SP-303. This compound was originally developed by Shaman Pharmaceuticals Inc. It was purchased by Napo Pharmaceuticals Inc. in December 2001.

SP-303 was isolated from a plant that is utilised by indigenous people in the Northwestern Amazon basin of South America to treat diarrhoea and other gastro-intestinal problems.[81] SP-303 works via a novel mechanism of action that inhibits the secretion of chloride ions without causing constipation or other side effects associated with opiate-derived anti-motility drugs.[82] SP-303 is well suited to treating cholera and 900,000 doses have been provided for free, as a dietary supplement, to 26 countries in Latin America, Africa and Southeast Asia. There are two pathways through which this compound is being developed for international utilisation. One pathway is the traditional pharmaceutical development of the compound for Irritable Bowel Syndrome (IBS-D diarrhoea predominant), and HIV-associated diarrhoea in both developed and lesser developed nations. The other path is being pursued by a non-profit pharmaceutical company to develop and distribute this compound as a very low cost treatment for paediatric diarrhoea in the biodiversity-rich countries. Paediatric diarrhoea kills more then two million people each year and access to safe, low-cost anti-diarrhoea therapies are urgently needed.

Napo Pharmaceuticals Inc. has adopted the long-term benefits-sharing obligations of Shaman Pharmaceuticals Inc. Napo Pharmaceuticals will utilise the Healing Forest Conservancy (HFC) as the mechanism to implement the long-term benefit-sharing process described in the earlier sections on Shaman Pharmaceutical's benefit-sharing processes.

8.6 RESPECT, DIGNITY AND INTELLECTUAL CREDIT

Some of the most important concerns of indigenous peoples that have collaborated with Shaman Pharmaceuticals Inc. were the issues of respect, dignity, intellectual credit and acknowledgement. In fact the Western IPR system has not yet been able to appreciate or reconcile this fundamental issue. Indigenous peoples wish to be recognised and accorded proper respect for their intellectual contributions to the world's pharmacopia. The US patent system does not allow for a healer, who may have guided scientists to a plant that has yielded important pharmaceuticals, to be recognised as a true "inventor." The list of pharmaceuticals that have been developed based on traditional knowledge is well-known.[83] The authorship of a scientific paper and contracts that provide for benefit-sharing does not address this problem. Textbooks in high schools and medical schools should confer the appropriate intellectual credit to the relevant indigenous communities as a matter of dignity, ethics and respect for the past, present and future innovations that indigenous peoples have provided to the global health care system.

8.7 CONCLUSION

The complex legal and policy issue associated with the use of traditional knowledge and biological resources will require medium and long term international analysis, negotiation and some changes in the international regimes of access and benefit-sharing. This process of change will require time, patience and active listening to traditional and indigenous communities. During this process of change, some traditional communities will continue to seek equitable opportunities to develop and conserve their traditional knowledge and biological resources. The authors hope that the experiences described in this chapter may provide some useful examples so that local partnerships can be created in the midst of the international negotiations on access, benefit-sharing and legal regimes. There is no doubt that cultural diversity and biological diversity is disappearing at a dramatic rate. Any and all approaches that can support the long term vitality of communities and their ecosystems should be pursued in a respectful and collaborative manner.

ENDNOTES

1 The authors would like to acknowledge the contributions of the following groups and individuals: In Belize the country, the people, and the traditional healers and communities, specifically the Mopan and Kekchi *Maya* and Creole communities of the Toledo and Cayo Districts; the government of Belize, specifically Rafael Manzanero and the Department of Forestry; the Belize College of Agriculture, including Hugh O'Brien and Carol August; all the people at Ix Chel Tropical Research Centre, especially Drs. Rosita Arvigo and Gregory Shropshire; and all the members of the Toledo Ecotourism Association. We also want to acknowledge the following individuals: Leopoldo Romero, Isidoro Peck, Sebastian Pop, Victor Cho, Alfredo Sho, Estefenia Bolon, Emeterio Pop, Felipe Teck, Roberto, and Petronia Teul, Jose Tot, Julian Pau, Laura Benitez, Pablo Cocom, Rolando Cocom, Candido Coh, William Schmidt, Braulio Ah, Faustino Cucul, Romualda Chun, Ken DuPlooy, Ben Piper, Santiago Ash, Alfredo Villoria, Victor Tzub, Incensia Sho, Reyes Chu, Kanah Petru, Marcos Sho, Benito Canti, and many others in the Punta Gorda area.

In the Tanzania collaboration. Ms Rowena K. Richter, and Karriem Ali who conducted the workshop, a portion of the field research and whose reports and writing formed much of the Tanzania section. Special recognition for his work and thanks are due to Mr. David Schienman of the Tanga Aids Working Group, who first contacted Shaman in 1991. The Muhimbili University College of Health Sciences, The Institute of Traditional Medicine, especially Dr. Rogasian Mahunnah, Mainen Moshi, Febronia Uisso, Boniface Mhoro. The Tanga Aids Working Group, including Dr. Ana Chaze, Abdullah Mohamed, Drs. Tubeti and Mbersero, the Tanzania Forestry Research Institute. The traditional healers and traditional birth attendents of the Wapare, Wagweno, Wasambaa, and Wachagga people of Mwanga and Moshi districts, the Mwanga Association of Traditional healers, the Ministry of Cultural Affairs, Moshi; and The Maternal Child Health Program of Mwanga District.

2 See, for example, the following reports from the World Intellectual Property Organization (WIPO): WIPO, "Annex B Extracts from the Peruvian ICBG Agreements" in "Report of Peruvian fact finding mission" in *WIPO Global Intellectual Property Division: Intellectual Property Needs and Expectations of Tradtional Knowledge*, volume 3, July, draft report, (2000) WIPO, Geneva; WIPO, *Report on the Review of Existing Intellecual Property Protection of Traditional Knowledge. Protection of Traditional Knowledge.* WIPO/GRTK/IC/4/7 of November 5, 2002; WIPO, *Traditional Knowledge and Intellectual Property Rights-Document submitted by the European Community and its Member States.* WIPO/GRTK/IC/3/16 of June 14, 2002, Annex at page 4; WIPO, *Elements of* Sui Generis *System for the Protection of Traditional Knowledge.* WIPO/GRTKF/IC/3/8 of 29 March 2002; WIPO, *Progress Report on the Status of Traditional Knowledge as Prior Art*, document WIPO/GRTK/IC/2/6 (2002); WIPO, *Technical Proposals on Databases and Registries of Traditional Knowledge and Biological/Genetic Resources.* WIPO/GRTK/IC/4/14 of 6 December 2002; WIPO. *Initial Report on the Technical Study on Disclosure Requirements Related to Genetic Resources and Traditional Knowledge, InterGovermental Committee On Intellectual Property and Genetic Resources, Traditional Knowledge and Folklore.* WIPO/GRTK/IC/4/11 (2002).

3 See Carvalo, N. P., *From Shaman's Hut to the Patent Office: How Long and Winding is the Road.* 41 Rev. ABPI 3 (Brazilian Association of Intellectual Property), 1999. Also, see Carvalo, N.P. 2003. From Shaman's Hut to the Patent Office: In Search of Effective Protection for Traditional Knowledge. Paper presented at Conference On Biodiversity, Biotechnology and the Legal Protection of Traditional Knowledge, 4–6 April, in Washington University School of Law.

4 See Radding, R. J. 2003. Interfaces Between Intellectual Property and Traditional Knowledge and Folklore: A US Perspective. *NYSBA Bright Ideas.* Spring/Summer Vol. 12, No.1: 11–17.

5 See, for example, Farnsworth, N. R., O. Akerle, A. S. Bingel, D. D. Soejarto, and Z. G. Guo. 1985. Medicinal Plants in Therapy. *Bulletin of the World Health Organization* 63: 965–981; Farnsworth, N. R. 1988. Screening Plants for New Medicines. In *Biodiversity*. Edited by E.O. Wilson and Francis M. Peters. Washington DC: National Academy Press, pages 83–97 ; Iwu, M. 1996. Implementing the Biodiversity Treaty; How to Make International Co-operative Agreements Work. *TIBTECH* 14 March: 78–82; McNeely, J., K. Miller, W. Reid, R. Mittermeier, and T. Werner. 1990. *Conserving the World's Biological Diversity, International Union for Conservation of Nature and Natural Resources*. World Resources Institute, Conservation International, World Wildlife Fund-US, and the World Bank, Gland Switzerland; Wilson, E. O. 1993. The Current State of Biological Diversity. In *Biodiversity*. Washington DC: National Academy Press, pages 3–18; World Resources Institute (WRI), The World Conservation Union

(IUCN), and United Nations Environment Programme (UNEP), (1992) Kathleen Courier, ed. *Global Biodiversity Strategy*. WRI, IUCN, & UNEP.

6 See, for example, Balick, M. J., and P. A. Cox. 1996. *Plants, People, and Culture: The Science of Ethnobotany*. W. H. Freeman/Scientific American Library; Moran, K. 1992. Ethnobiology and US Policy. In *Sustainable Harvest and Marketing of Non-Timber Forest Products*. Edited by Mark Plotkin and Lisa Famolare. Washington DC: Island Press, at pages 289–301; Moran, K., S. R. King, and T. J. Carlson. 2001. Biodiversity Prospecting: Lessons and Prospects. *Ann. Rev of Anthropol.* 30: 505–526.

7 See Moran, K., S. R. King, and T. J. Carlson, above at note 6; Moran K. 1998. Mechanisms for benefit-sharing: Nigerian case study. *Case Studies on Benefit-Sharing Arrangements*, Secretariat, Convention on Biological Diversity, Fourth Conference of the Parties (COP 4), Bratislava, Slovakia; King, S. 1994. Establishing Reciprocity: Biodiversity, Conservation and New Models for Cooperation Between Forest-Dwelling Peoples and the Pharmaceutical Industry. In *Intellectual Property Rights for Indigenous Peoples: A Source Book*. Edited by Tom Greaves. Oklahoma City: Society For Applied Anthropology, at pages 69–82.

8 See Greaves, T. 1994. IPR, A Current Survey. In *Intellectual Property Rights for Indigenous Peoples: A Source Book*. Edited by Tom Greaves. Oklahoma City: Society For Applied Anthropology, at pages 3–16; Posey, D., and G. Dutfield. 1996. *Beyond Intellectual Property: Toward Traditional Resource Rights For Indigenous Peoples and Local Communities*. Ottawa, Canada: International Development Resource Center.

9 See Posey, D. "International Agreements and Intellectual Property Right Protection for Indigenous Peoples" in Tom Greaves, ed., *Intellectual Property Rights for Indigenous Peoples: A Source Book*. (1994) Society For Applied Anthropology, Oklahoma City, at pages 223–252.

10 See Tobin B. 1994. "Putting the commercial cart before the cultural horse: a study of the ICBG Agreements". Paper Presented at the Symposium of Indigenous Peoples of Latin America: Indigenous Peoples, Biodiversity and Intellectual Property, 27–30 September in Santa Cruz, Bolivia (on file with the Peruvian Society for Environmental Law: SPDA); Tobin, B. 2001. Redefining Perspectives in the Search for Protection of Traditional Knowledge: A Case Study from Peru. In *Review of European Community and International Environmental Law* (RECIEL) 10 (1): 47–64. Blackwell Publishers.

11 Posey, D., and G. Dutfield. 1996. *Beyond Intellectual Property: Toward Traditional Resource Rights For Indigenous Peoples and Local Communities*. Ottawa, Canada: International Development Resource Center.

12 See Chapter 10 by Donna Craig in this publication.

13 See Posey, D. 1995. *Indigenous Peoples and Traditional Resource Rights; A Basis For Equitable Relationships*. Oxford: Green College Center for Environmental Policy and Understanding; and see above note 11.

14 See, for example, the efforts of The South and Meso American Indian Rights Center (SAIIC) and the Call of the Earth Circle (http://earthcall.org/)—an Indigenous Peoples Initiative on Intellectual Property Policy.

15 See Posey, D. above at note 13.

16 Burger, J. 1987. *Report From the Frontier: the State of the World's Indigenous Peoples.* London: Cultural Survival Inc.

17 Available online: (http://iaip.gn.apc.org/IFB/cbd-ip~1.htm).

18 *Ibid.*

19 See Laird, S. A. 1994. Natural Products and the Commercialization of Traditional Knowledge. In *Intellectual Property Rights for Indigenous Peoples: A Source Book*. Edited by Tom Greaves. Oklahoma City: Society For Applied Anthropology, at pages 145–162; Laird, S. A. 2002. *Biodiversity and Traditional Knowledge Equitable Partnerships in Practice.* London, Earthscan Publications Ltd., 503 pages; Kate ten K., and Laird S. A., eds., 1999. *The Commercial Use of Biodiversity: Access to Genetic Resources and Benefit-Sharing.* London, Earthscan.

20 Clay, Jason. 1996. *Generating Income and Conserving Resources: 20 Lessons from the Field.* Baltimore, Maryland, WWF.

21 See McGowan, J., and I. Udeinya. 1994. "Collecting Traditional Medicines in Nigeria; A Proposal for IPR Compensation". In *Intellectual Property Rights for Indigenous Peoples: A Source Book*. Edited by Tom Greaves. Oklahoma City: Society For Applied Anthropology, at pages 57–68.

22 Palmer, P., J. Sanchex, and G. Mayorga. 1993. *Taking Care of Sibo's Gifts: An Environmental Treatise from Costa Rica's KékoLdi Indigenous Reserve*. San Jose, Costa Rica: Editorama.

23 Conte, Lisa. 1994. Testimony of Lisa Conte, President and CEO of Shaman Pharmaceuticals, Inc. before the Senate Foreign Relations Committee, Hearing on the Convention on Biological Diversity, 12 April 1994.

24 *Ibid.*

25 See King, S. 1994. Establishing Reciprocity: Biodiversity, Conservation and New Models for Cooperation Between Forest-Dwelling Peoples and the Pharmaceutical Industry. In *Intellectual Property Rights for Indigenous Peoples: A Source Book*. Edited by Tom Greaves. Oklahoma City: Society For Applied Anthropology, at pages 69–82.

26 See Moran, K. 1999. "Health: indigenous knowledge, equitable benefits". IK Notes, Africa Region, World Bank, available online: (http://www.worldbank.org/aftdr/ik/default.htm); and Moran, K. 2000. Bioprospecting: Lessons from benefit-sharing experiences, *Int. J. Biotechnology*, vol. 2, nos. 1/2/3: 132–144.

27 See King, S., & T. Carlson. 1995. Biocultural Diversity, Biomedicine and Ethnobotany: The Experience of Shaman Pharmaceuticals. *Interciencia—Journal of Science and Technology of the Americas*, vol. 20, no. 3: 134–139; Moran, Katy. 1997. Returning Benefits From Ethnobotanical Drug Discovery to Native Communities. In *Biodiversity and Human Health*. Edited by Francesca Grifo and Joshua Rosenthal. Washington DC: Island Press, at pages 243–264; Moran K. 1998. Mechanisms for benefit-sharing: Nigerian case study. *Case Studies on Benefit-Sharing Arrangements*. Secretariat, Convention on Biological Diversity, Fourth Conference of the Parties (COP 4), Bratislava, Slovakia.

28 See Bierer, D. E., T. J. Carlson, and S. R. King. 1996. Integrating Indigenous Knowledge, Tropical Medicinal Plants, Medicine, Modern Science and Reciprocity into a Novel Drug Discovery Approach. *NetScience* 2 (no. 5). (http://www.awod.com/netsci/Issues/May96/feature2.html). Tempesta, M. & S. King. 1994. Chapter 33 Ethnobotany as a Source For New Drugs. *Annual Reports in Medicinal Chemistry* 29. Academic Press, Inc., San Diego, at pages 325–330. See also King, S. at note 25 above, King and Carlson; Moran, K. at note 27 above.

29 Carlson, T., M. Iwu, S. R. King, C. Obialor, and A. Ozioko. 1997. Medicinal Plan Research in Nigeria: An Approach for Compliance with the Convention on Biological Diversity. *Diversity*, vol. 13, no. 1: 29–33.

30 Sunderland, T., B. Jaff , N. Ndam, and J. Jato. 1997. "Conservation Through Utilisation—A Case Study: Capacity Building and the Institutional Context For Biodiversity Conservation in Cameroon". Presented to the UK Tropical Forest Forum Workshop: The African Rainforests and the Conservation of Biodiversity, 17–24 January, in Limbe Botanic Garden, Cameroon.

31 Carlson, T., B. Foula, J. Chinnock, and S. R. King, G. Abdourahmaue, M. Bah, A. Bah, S. Cisse, M. Camara, R. Richter. 2001. Case Study on Medicinal Plant Research in Guinea: Prior Informed Consent, Focused Benefit Sharing, and Compliance with the Convention on Biological Diversity. *Economic Botany*. 55(4): 478–491.

32 Nelson-Harrison, S. T., S. R. King, C. Limbach, C. Jackson, A. Galiwango, S. K. Kato, B. R. Kanyerezi. 2002. Ethnobotanical research into the 21st Century. In *Ethnomedicine and Drug Discovery*. Edited by Iwu and Wootton. Elsevier Science B. V. at pages 283–307.

33 Ito, T. M. and M. Loftus. 1997. Cutting and Dealing: Asian Loggers Target the World's Remaining Rain Forests. *US News and World Report*, 10 March, 39–41.

34 Hartshorn, G., L. Nicolait, L. Hartshorn, G. Bevier, R. Brightman, J. Cal, A. Cawich, W. Davidson, R. DuBois, C. Dyer, J. Gibson, W. Hawley, J. Leonard, R. Nicolait, D., Weyer, H. White, and C. Wright. 1984. *Belize Country Environmental Profile, A Field Study*. Robert Nicolait and Associates, Belize City.

35 Arvigo, R., and M. Balick, 1993. *Rainforest Remedies: One Hundred Healing Herbs of Belize*. Twin Lakes, WI: Lotus Press.

36 See Thomas, R. "Eligio Panti, 103, Maya Healer With Modern Ties." Obituary page in *New York Times*, Saturday, February 10, 1996.

37 See Arvigo and Balick, above at note 35. See also, Balick, M. J., R. Arvigo, G. Shropshire, and R. Mendelson. 1996. Ethnopharmacological Studies and Biological Conservation in Belize. In *Medicinal Resources of the Tropical Forest: Biodiversity and Its Importance to Human Health*. Edited by Michael J. Balick, Elaine Elisabetsky, and Sarah Laird. New York: Columbia University Press, at pages 326–333.

38 See Balick, M. J., R. Arvigo, and L. Romero. 1994. The Development of an ethnobiomedical forest reserve in Belize: it's role in the preservation of biological and cultural diversity. *Conservation Biology* 8(1): 316–317.

39 See Arvigo and Balick, above at note 35.

40 See King, S., T. Carlson and K. Moran. 1996. Biological Diversity, Indigenous Knowledge, Drug Discovery and Intellectual Property Rights. In *Valuing Local Knowledge; Indigenous People and Intellectual Property Rights*. Edited by Stephan Brush, and Doreen Stabinsky. Washington DC: Island Press, at pages 186–208; Moran, Katy. 1997. Returning Benefits From Ethnobotanical Drug Discovery to Native Communities. In *Biodiversity and Human Health*. Edited by Francesca Grifo and Joshua Rosenthal. Washington DC: Island Press, at pages 243–264.

41 See Balick, M. J., R. Arvigo, G. Shropshire, J. Walker, D. Campbell, and L. Romero. 2002. Belize ethnobotany project: Safeguarding medicinal plants and traditional knowledge in Belize. In *Ethnomedicine and Drug Discovery*. Edited by Iwu and Wootton. Elsevier Science B. V. at pages 283–307.

42 See Daly, D. C., and C. F. Limbach. "The Contribution of the Physician to Medicinal Plant Research" in Michael J. Balick, Elaine Elisabetsky, and Sarah Laird, eds. *Medicinal Resources of the Tropical Forest: Biodiversity and Its Importance to Human Health*. (1996) Columbia University Press, New York, at pages 48–62; Elisabetsky, E. & R. Setzer. "Cabocla Concepts of Disease, Diagnosis, and Therapy: Implications for Ethnopharmacology and Health Systems in Amazonia." in E. P. Parker, ed. *The Amazon Caboclo: Historical and Contemporary Perspectives*, Studies in Third World Societies Series, no. 32. (1985) Williamsburg, VA: College of William and Mary Department of Anthropology, at pages 243–278,

43 Balick *et al*. (1996), above at note 37. See also Kloppenberg J., and T. Gonzales. "Between State and Capital: NGO's as Allies of Indigenous Peoples" in Tom Greaves, ed. *Intellectual Property Rights for Indigenous Peoples: A Source Book*. (1994) Society For Applied Anthropology, Oklahoma City, at pages 163–178.

44 Toledo Eco-Tourism Association Brochure. (1992) Belize, Central America.

45 Augello, Jeffrey. 1994. *Bridging the Gap: An Analysis of the Pharmaceutical Industry and Their Emerging Role in the Conservation Movement*. School for International Training, Belize.

46 *Ibid.*

47 See above note 20.

48 Hayes, R. Letter of recommendation from Randall L. Hayes, Executive Director of Rainforest Action Network. San Francisco, April 14, 1995.

49 See Posey, above at note 13.

50 See King, above at note 25.

51 See King and Carlson, above at note 27.

52 See Balick, *et. al.* above at note 35.

53 See Arvigo and Balick, above at note 35.

54 *Ibid.*

55 See Iwu, M. M, *Handbook of African medicinal plants* (1993) CRC Press, Boca Raton, Florida; Kokwaro J. O, *Medicinal plants of East Africa*, 2nd edition. (1993) Kenya Literature Bureau, Nairobi; Johns, Timothy E., E.

B. Mhoro, Pius Sanaya, and Ebi K. Kimanani. 1994. Herbal remedies of the Batemi of Ngorongoro District, Tanzania: A quantitative appraisal. *Economic Botany* 48: 90–95.

56 Scheinman, D. 2000. An integrated Program for Developing Medicinal Plants: A case study from Tanga, Tanzania. Paper presented to Medicinal Plants Forum for Commonwealth Africa, 5 December, in Cape Town, South Africa.

57 Richter, R. K. and T. J. S. Carlson. 1998. Reporting biological assay results on tropical plants to host country collaborators. *J. Ethnopharmacology* 62: 85–88.

58 See Scheinman, above at note 56.

59 Rosenthal, J., ed. 2000. Drug discovery, economic development and conservation: the International Cooperative Biodiversity Groups. *Pharmaceutical Biology*, vol. 37.

60 Schuster B. G., J. E. Jackson, C. N. Obijiofor, C. O. Okunji, W. Milhous, E. Losos, J. F. Ayafor, and M. M. Iwu. 1999. Drug development and conservation of biodiversity in West and Central Africa: A new standard of collaboration with indigenous people. *Pharm Biol* 37 (Suppl): 84–99.

61 Lewis, W. H., G. Lamas, A. Vaisberg, D. G. Corely, and C. Sarasara. 2000. Peruvian Medicinal Plant Sources of New Pharmaceuticals. *Pharm Biol* 37 (Suppl): 69–84.

62 Soejarto, D. D., C. Gyllenhaal, J. C. Regalado, J. M. Pezzuto, H. H. S. Fong, G. T. Tan, N. T. Hiep, L. T. Xuan, D. Q. Binh, N. V. Hung, T. Q. Bich, N. N. Thin, P. K. Loc, B. M. Vu, B. H. Southavong, K. Sydara, S. Bouamanivong, M. J. Oneill, J. Lewis, X. Xie, G. Dietman. 1999. Studies on Biodiversity of Vietnam and Laos: The UIC-Based ICBG Program, *Pharm Biol* 37 (Suppl): 100–113.

63 Kingston D. G. I, M. Abdel-Kader, B-N Zhou, S-W Yang, J. M. Berger, H. van der Werff, J. S. Miller, R. Evans, R. Mitter meier, L. Famolare, M. Guerin-McManus, S. Malone, R. Nelson, E. Moniz, J. H. Wisse, D. M. Vyas, J. J. K. Wright, and G. S. Aboikonie. 1999. The Suriname International Cooperative Biodiversity Group Program: Lessons from the first five years. *Pharm Biol* 37 (Suppl): 22–34.

64 Berlin, B., E. A. Berlin, J. C. F. Ugalde, L. G. Barrios, D. Puett, R. Nash & M. Gonzalez-Espinoza. 2000. The Maya ICBG: Drug Discovery, Medical Ethnobotany, and Alternative Forms of Economic Development in the Highland Maya Region of Chiapas, Mexico. *Pharm Biol* 37 (Suppl): 127–144.

65 Schuster *et al.* 1999, see above at note 60.

66 See Lewis *et al.* 2000, see above at note 61.

67 Schuster *et al.* 1999, see above at note 60.

68 Lewis, W. H. 2003. Pharmaceutical Discoveries Based on Ethnomedicinal Plants: 1985 to 2000 and Beyond. *Economic Botany* 57(1): 126–134.

69 Hirshler, B. "African Tribe May Get Rich From Anti-obesity Drug". Reuters, Health, 9 November 2001. Available online: (http://dailynews.yahoo.com./h/nm/20011109/hi/obesity_12.html).

70 Kahn, T. 2002. Prickly Dispute Finally Laid to Rest: *San* Reach Agreement with CSIR Over Use of Appetite-suppressing Cactus. *Johannesburg Business Day*. Available online: (http://allafrica.com/stories/200203220129.html).

71 Phytopharm. (2003) "Pfizer returns rights of P57," available online: (http://www.phytopharm.com/press/Rel%2080finalfinal.htm).

72 Cox, P. A. 1994. The ethnobotanical approach to drug discovery: strengths and limitations. In *Ethnobotany and the Search For New drugs*. Edited by Prance, G. and J. Marsh. Ciba Foundation Symposium 185: 25–41. London: Academic Press.

73 See Gustafson, K. R., J. H. Cardellina, J. B. McMahon, R. J. Gulakowski, J. Ishitoya, Z. Szallasi, N. E. Lewin, P. M. Blumberg, O. S. Weislow, J. A. Beutler, R. W. Buckheit, G. M. Cragg, P. A. Cox, J. P. Bader, and M. R. Boyd. 1992. A non-promoting phorbol from the Samoan medicinal plant Homalanthus nutans inhibits cell killing by HIV-1. *Journal of Medicinal Chemistry* 35: 1978–1986; and Gulakowski, R. J., J. B. McMahon, R. W. Buckheit, Jr., K. R. Gustafson, M. R. Boyd. 1997. Antireplicative and anticytopathic activities or *prostratin*, a non-tumor producing phorbol ester, against human immunodeficiency virus (HIV). *Antiviral Res* 33 (2): 87–97.

74 Gulakowski *et al.* 1997. *ibid.* See also Kulkowsky, J, D. M. Culnan, J. Roman, D. Geethanjali, M. Scnell, M. R. Boyd, R. J. Pomerantz. 2001. *Prostratin*: Inhibition of HIV-1 infection and induction of latent viral expression suggest a potential adjuvant therapy for HAART. *Blood* 98: 3006–3015.

75 See Kulkowsky *et al.* (2001), *ibid.*

76 Korin, Y., D. G. Brooks, S. Brown, A. Korotzer, Z. A. Zack. 2002. Effects of Prostratin on T-Cell Activation and Human Immunodeficiency Virus Latency. *Virology*. vol. 76, no. 6: 8118–8123.

77 *Ibid.*

78 Persaud, D., Zhou, Y., Siliciano, J. M., Siliciano, R. F. "Latency in Human Immunodeficiency Virus Type 1 Infection: No Easy Answers". (2003) *J. Virol.* 77 at pages 1659–1665.

79 Cox, P. A. "Ensuring equitable benefits: the Falealupo Covenant and the isolation of the anti-viral drug prostratin from a Samoan medicinal plant". (2001) *Pharmaceutical Biology* 39 at pages 33–40.

80 Available online: (http://www.MerLionpharma.com/main_policy.html).

81 Carlson, T. J. S., S. R. King, 2000. Sangre de Drago (Croton lechleri Müell.-Arg.)—a phytomedicine for the treatment of diarrhoea. *Health Notes: Review of Complementary and Integrative Medicine*. 7(4): 315–320.

82 See Gabriel S. E., S. E. Davenport, R. J. Steagall, V. Vimal , T. Carlson, and E. J. Rozhon. 1999. A Novel Plant-Derived Inhibitor of cAMP-Mediated Fluid and Chloride Secretion. *American Journal of Physiology*. 279 (39): G58–G63; and Holodniy, M., J. Koch, M. Mistal, J. Maimares Schmidt, A. Khandwala, J. E. Pennington and S. B. Porter. 1999. A Double Blind, Randomized, Placebo-Controlled Phase II Study to Asses the Safety and Efficacy of Orally Administered SP-303 for Symptomatic Treatment of Diarrhea in Patients With AIDS. *The American Journal of Gastroenterology*. Vol. 94, no. 11: 3267–3273.

83 See, for example, Farnsworth *et al.* (1985), above at note 5.

CHAPTER 9

The Legal Framework in China Protecting Intellectual Property Rights in Traditional Chinese Medicines[1]

WANG XI*, YANG HUAGUO† AND ZHOU YANFANG‡

9.1 INTRODUCTION

Chinese medicine is one of the treasures of Chinese traditional culture, the result of several thousand years of fighting against diseases, and the most intact national medical system in the world till now. Over the past few years, with the recognition of the side-effects of Western medicine and an enhanced awareness of environmental protection, there has emerged a trend of "back to nature" and "green consumption." Due to its natural properties and minimal side-effects, Chinese medicine has gained wider and wider acceptance. The World Health Organization has commented that "Chinese medicine is a good example of the world's traditional medicine,"[2] and recommends it to countries all over the world.

The 21st century is a century in which intellectual property rights have gained substantial attention. China has successfully joined WTO.

* Professor, Associate Dean of School of Law, Director, Environmental and Resources Law Institute (ERLI), Shanghai Jiao Tong University.

† PhD (Environmental Law) Candidate, School of Law, Shanghai Jiao Tong University.

‡ LLM (Environmental Law) Candidate, School of Law, Wuhan University.

To operate under the WTO rules, it is very important to enhance the protection of Chinese medicine with intellectual property rights. A long time ago, when the production of Chinese medicine was still on a small scale, a prescription of Chinese medicine was protected by way of a secret recipe, and the protective measures are the well-known traditional rules of "handing down in the family from ancestors" and "passing to sons not daughters." Therefore, intellectual property right protection of Chinese medicine has had a considerably long history. Now, this traditional method of protection has fallen behind the times. China has thus issued a series of laws and regulations to protect intellectual property rights in Chinese medicine.

This chapter describes and analyses the legislative framework and the major regulatory systems relating to intellectual property protection for Chinese medicine. International treaties and practices are also compared and analysed. Recommendations for improving the intellectual property system protecting Chinese medicine are proposed at the end of the chapter.

9.2 THE LEGISLATIVE FRAMEWORK OF INTELLECTUAL PROPERTY RIGHTS PROTECTING CHINESE MEDICINE

The framework of intellectual property rights protecting Chinese medicine is composed of laws and regulations in different sections, and the following is a summary of the major laws and regulations which have been enacted.

1. *Patent Law* of the People's Republic of China
   The law was promulgated on March 12, 1984, amended on September 4, 1992, and amended again on August 25, 2000. It mainly provides for the conditions for granting patent, the term of patent protection, patent application procedures and compulsory licenses for patented inventions. There are 8 Chapters in total with 69 Articles. The Rules for Implementing the Patent Law took effect on July 1, 2001.

2. *Trademark Law* of the People's Republic of China.
   The law was promulgated on August 23, 1982, amended on February 22, 1993, and amended again on October 27, 2001. There are 8

Chapters in total with 43 Articles. It mainly provides for application procedures for trademark registration, the extension of registered trademarks, transfers and licences, the protection of registered trademarks, trademark use regulations and disputes settlement procedures. The Rules for Implementing the Trademark Law took effect on September 15, 2002.

3. *Anti-Unfair Competition Law* of the People's Republic of China
The law was promulgated on September 2, 1993. There are 5 Chapters in total with 33 Articles. It mainly provides for rules for preventing unfair competition practices and related legal responsibilities.

4. *Pharmaceutical Administration Law* of the People's Republic of China
The law was promulgated on September 20, 1984, and amended on February 28, 2001. There are 10 Chapters in total with 106 Articles. It mainly provides for rules relating to the management of, and legal responsibility for, medicine production and distribution. Detailed rules of its implementation took effect on September 15, 2002.

5. *Regulations on Protection of Varieties of Chinese Medicine*
The regulations were promulgated by the State Council on October 14, 1992. There are 5 Chapters in total with 27 Articles. They mainly provide for the classification, examination and approval, and protection of protected medicine varieties.

6. *Regulations* on *Protection of New Varieties of Plants*
The regulations were promulgated by the State Council on March 20, 1997. There are 8 Chapters in total with 46 Articles. They mainly provide for the content and categorisation of plant variety rights, the conditions for plant variety applications, and the terms of protection for plant variety rights.

7. *Provisions on Patent Administration of Chinese Medicine*
The provisions were promulgated on September 5, 1995 by the State Administration of Traditional Chinese Medicine[3]. They mainly provide for application procedures for Chinese medicine patents, patent management, and patent protection.

9.3 THE PROTECTION OF INTELLECTUAL PROPERTY RIGHTS RELATING TO CHINESE MEDICINE

9.3.1 Patent protection for Chinese medicines

Patent protection is the most effective way to protect the pharmaceutical invention, and has been used by countries around the world as the main method of protecting pharmaceutical inventions. Patent protection for Chinese medicine in China is reflected in *Patent Law* of the People's Republic of China, and its Implementing Rules, as well as *Provisions on Patent Administration of Chinese Medicine*. The *Patent Law* of 1985, in view of maintaining social benefits and safeguarding public health, did not provide patent protection for medicine and substances acquired through chemical methods. It only protected the methods of producing medicine. The amended *Patent Law* of 1993 added the protection of medicines and extended the effect of method patents to the products produced directly by these methods. Thereafter, great progress has taken place in the number of patent applications for Chinese medicines. In 1993 alone, the patent applications for Chinese medicine reached 2,196, surpassing the total number from 1985–1992 (see Table 9.1). The amended *Patent Law* of 2000

TABLE 9.1 Patent application of Chinese medicine in China 1985–1995 (unit: case)[4]

Year	Inventions	Utility models	Designs
1985	76	33	0
1986	59	81	1
1987	128	173	11
1988	162	196	8
1989	193	217	19
1990	323	196	11
1991	378	363	30
1992	863	513	46
1993	2196	483	28
1994	1813	763	50
1995	1021	210	26
Total	7212	2828	230

followed the regulation of medicine under the 1993 *Patent Law*, and all inventions in medical fields receive patent protection in China.

9.3.1 The subject matter protected by Chinese medicine patents

They are mainly the inventions and creations in Chinese medicine field. According to Article 3 of the Provisional Provisions on *Patent Administration of Chinese Medicine*, they include preparations (including effective chemical monomers, effective elements and effective parts extracted from plants, animals and minerals) of Chinese medicine and methods and processes for their production; machines and equipment for Chinese medical treatment and their production processes; health care medicines, cosmetics, foods, soft drinks and seasonings containing Chinese medicine; testing preparations and hygienic materials; designs and patterns for packaging and containers of Chinese medicines; and other inventions and creations related to Chinese medicines.

9.3.2 The acquisition and utilisation of Chinese medicine patents

The most important conditions for granting Chinese medicine patents over Chinese medicines are novelty, inventiveness and practical applicability. Novelty means that, before the date of filing, no identical invention or utility model has been publicly disclosed in publications in the country or abroad or has been publicly used or made known to the public by any other means in the country; nor has any other person filed previously with the Patent Administration Department under the State Council an application which describes the identical invention or utility model and was published after the said date of filing.[5] Inventiveness means that, as compared with the technology existing before the date of filing, the invention has prominent substantive features and represents a notable progress, or that the utility model has substantive features and represents progress.[6] Practical applicability means that the invention or utility model can be made or used and can produce effective results.[7] Generally speaking, the wider the scope of patent rights protection, the greater the effectiveness of the protection obtained. The scope of patent protection is based on the proposed claims in the application document, and the claims are described through the technical disclosures. Therefore, in order to achieve better patent protection, it is important to analyse clearly the existing techniques before the application and, on this basis, demarcate the widest scope of patent protection possible. Besides, because of the territorial limits of patent rights, territorial issues should also be considered when applying for a patent.

The purpose of patent protection is to generate economic benefits in the market which are brought about by the protected technological innovation. It is not necessary to apply for a patent over an innovation without a potential market value; otherwise, the applicant has to bear the cost of maintaining that patent right. Therefore, once patent protection is applied for, the patent holder should actively seek to exploit the patented technology and carry out the permitted trading activities within the limited protection period in order to achieve the full economic potential of the patented technology. As for innovations with substantial market potential, the patent holder should apply for further patent protection in respect of further research in order to extend the term of protection. Thus, the patent system pushes scientific research closer to the market, and greatly promotes the application of technological innovation to production.

9.3.3 The term of protection for Chinese medicine patents

The term of protection for patented inventions is 20 years, while that of utility models and designs is 10 years, from the date of application.

At present, the situation in China concerning Chinese medicine patents is as follows:

1) The quantity of Chinese medicine patents is small. Many entities and individuals do not pay enough attention to the use of patents to protect their inventions and creations through the patent system.
2) Most of the patent applicants are individuals. Table 9.2 shows that the quantity of application from medical companies, universities and research institutions are declining. In 1995, their applications only amounted to 12 per cent of the total applications. The patent authorisation rate for applications by individuals is about 30 per cent, while the rate for pharmaceutical companies, universities and research institutions is about 70 per cent. The applications submitted by individual applicants usually consist of prescriptions only, without

reports of animal tests and clinical observation. As those applications are considered as disclosing incomplete inventions, they are therefore usually rejected. However, while the applicants did not get the patent authorisation they had sought, the release of their technological information in their patent application usually puts them in a disadvantaged position. But not only are those applicants disadvantaged, it is also not good for the Chinese medicine industry as a whole because the technological information released can be retrieved by others worldwide. It is actually a loss of Chinese medicinal information resources.[8]

3) The inventiveness of Chinese medicine is on the low side; from the point of patent application categories, compound preparations occupy a considerable proportion (See Table 9.2). The applications that relate to extraction and purification of effective elements are even less. Compound preparations of Chinese medicine mainly protect Chinese medicine prescriptions, and most inventions of this type adopt routine technologies. However, the applications that relate to extracted and purified effective elements are more important than the other kinds of applications. Those applications are more important after China joined the WTO and has had to face challenges from, and the technological monopolies of, foreign pharmaceutical industries. In addition, developing the technology for extracting effective elements is helpful for Chinese medicines to go to world market, because the purified compounds have no problems of heavy metals and quality control. So, China should have more applications related to the extraction and purification of the effective elements of Chinese medicine.

TABLE 9.2 Technical categories of patent applications for novelty of Chinese medicine 1987–1995

Technical categories	1987	1989	1991	1993	1995
Compound	39 (30.5)	85 (44)	126 (33.3)	1109 (50.5)	545 (53.3)
Effective part	4 (3.1)	12 (6.6)	3 (0.79)	80 (3.6)	3 (0.3)
Effective monomer	0 (0)	4 (2.1)	1 (0.26)	8 (3.6)	0(0)
Total	43 (33.60)	101 (52.3)	130 (34.4)	1197 (54.5)	548 (53.6)

NOTE: The figures in brackets are the percentages amount to the total applications that year.

4) The proportion of professional invention applications is low (see Table 9.3) and the quantity is decreasing (See Figure 9.1), which reflects the fact that enterprises and scientific research units in China are not making full use of this powerful weapon of patents to protect their intellectual property rights.

TABLE 9.3 Amount of professional inventions and non-professional inventions in patent application 1987–1995

	1987	1989	1991	1993	1995
Non-professional inventions	74 (57.8)	118 (61.1)	276 (70.6)	1593 (72.5)	854 (83.6)
Professional inventions	54 (42.2)	75 (38.9)	111 (29.4)	603 (27.5)	167 (16.4)
Research organisations	20 (15.6)	29 (15)	29 (7.7)	130 (5.9)	38 (3.8)
Colleges & universities	9 (7)	12 (6.2)	12 (3.2)	67 (3.1)	16 (1.6)
Hospitals	7(5.5)	13 (6.7)	18 (4.8)	88 (4.0)	17 (1.7)
Enterprises	16 (12.5)	19 (9.8)	47 (12.4)	316 (14.4)	89 (8.7)
Social groups	2 (1.6)	2 (1)	5 (1.3)	2 (0.09)	7 (0.7)

NOTE: The figures in brackets are the percentages of the total applications that year.

FIGURE 9.1 Quantity of Chinese medicine patent applications for professional inventions in China[11]

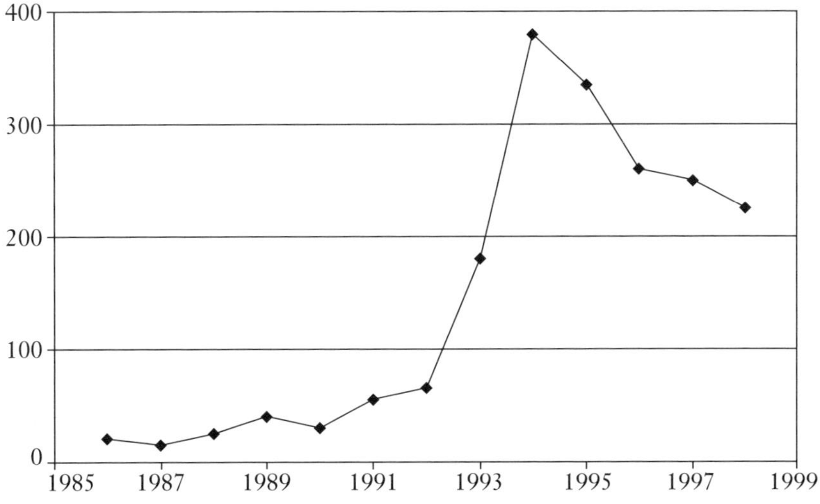

5) There are few international applications. International patent applications under the Patent Cooperation Treaty (PCT) are a shortcut commonly adopted to obtain patent protection in foreign countries. Statistics show that, at present, there are only 1,728 Chinese herbal medicines and plant medicines which have used the PCT system, accounting for 7 per cent of the published Chinese herbal medicine and plant medicine-related patent applications in the world. Among the 7 per cent, the US ranks first, accounting for 35.7 per cent of these patents, followed by the following countries (in order) France, Japan, Germany, the UK, Korea and China (2.1 per cent).[9] China became a PCT member state in 1994 and the Chinese Patent Administration became a PCT accepting and searching agency. Figure 9.2 shows that, from 1994–2001, PCT applications of Chinese medicine totalled only several dozens. 99.7

FIGURE 9.2 Number of PCT patent applications in China for Chinese medicine 1994–2001[12]

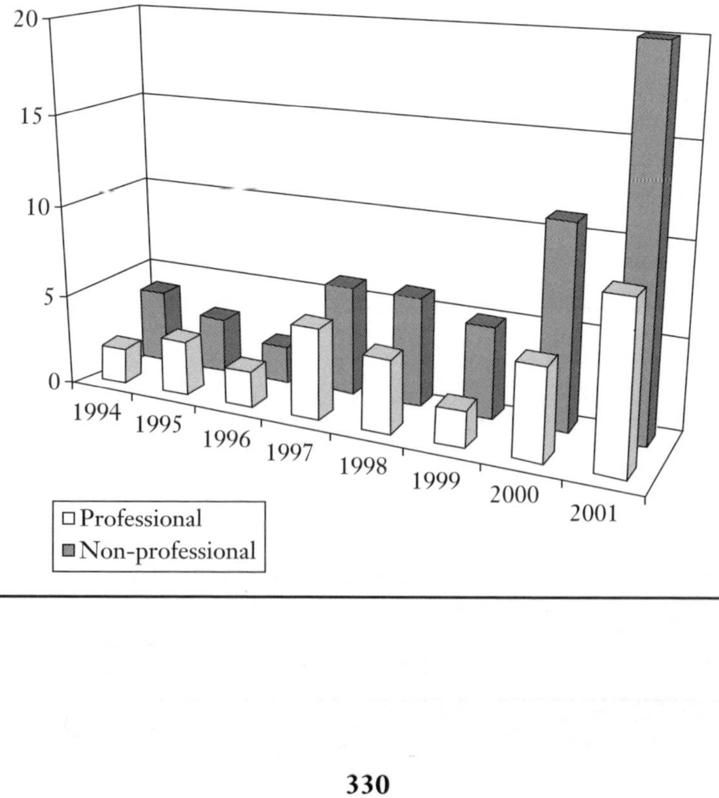

per cent of the Chinese herbal medicines and plant medicines which applied for patent protection in China have given up the opportunity to apply for patent protection overseas, which makes it possible for foreign countries to freely use Chinese herbal medicine and plant medicine patent technology. Chinese herbal medicine will thus lose its competitive advantage in the international market. In the meantime, patent applications made by foreign pharmaceutical enterprises in China are increasing. (See Figure 9.3)[10]

Moreover, there are some problems that need to be addressed urgently by the patent system. Firstly, the time period for a patent application relating to Chinese medicines to be reviewed and approved is too long. It lasts an average of three years, from the filing date of the patent application for a Chinese medicine patent, before the patent is granted or refused. From the applicant's viewpoint, this application process is time-consuming compared with the application process for plant variety protection. Moreover, after the publication of the patent, there is no time limit set by the law for substantive reviews of the patent

FIGURE 9.3 Number of Chinese medicine patent applications by foreign pharmaceutical enterprises 1994–1997[13]

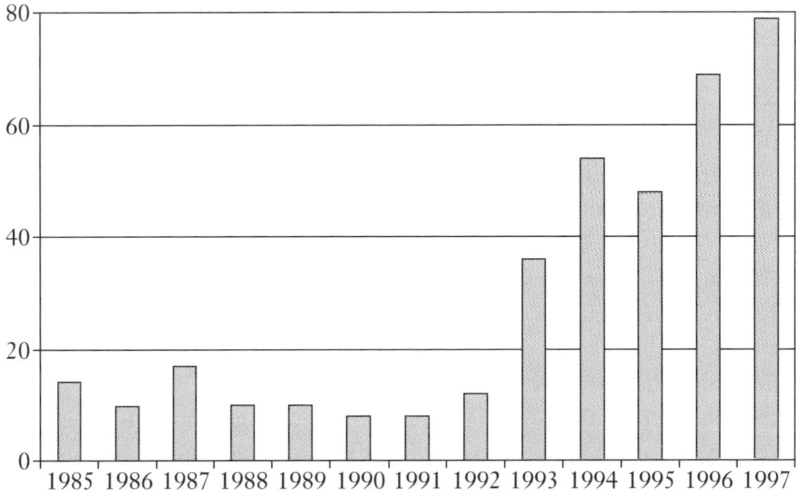

application. This results in an unlimited and prolonged period of substantive review.[14]

Secondly, inventors have a wrong understanding of the nature of patent protection for Chinese medicines. Many scientific researchers think that simply adding to or subtracting several components from a patented Chinese medicine compound would not be considered an infringement of the patent, and that, therefore, the patent over the Chinese medicine is not capable of protecting core technologies. Due to these misperceptions, as well as their reluctance to disclose the invention, most inventors are not willing to apply for a patent.

The third problem lies in the judicial redress available when Chinese medicine patents are infringed. What concerns people widely is how, and using what standards, to assess whether an infringement of a Chinese medicine patent has occurred. The fourth problem is that there is no time limit for the patent nullity review process, which leads to the potential for limitless extensions to an infringement suit.[15]

After China's entry into WTO, the Chinese have been paying more attention to the protection of intellectual property rights. From 2003, the patent protection system has been adopted by the whole pharmaceutical field, which has greatly encouraged patent applications for Chinese medicines. Statistics show that, in 2001, patent applications for Chinese herbal medicines totalled 2,772, and for the first time, the annual applications exceeded 2,500. From January 1, 2002 to September 27, 2002, patent applications for Chinese medicine totalled 1,447 with the following characteristics: firstly, there is a trend of increased applications from enterprises and research institutes. Individual applications have long been a major part of all patent applications. However, with professional inventions increasing rapidly, the ratio of professional inventions to non-professional inventions has changed, from 1:11 in 2002, to 1:5 in 2003, especially in the field of medicine. Professional inventions, especially from the applications made by enterprises, increased by 35 per cent compared to 2002. Secondly, there is a trend of decreasing applications from individuals. Years of practical experience with patent-related matters indicates that it is extremely hard to exploit the patent after it has been granted. Larger amounts of capital investment for pharmacological and clinical experiments are usually needed before one is granted a license for producing a new medicine. Therefore, although some individuals acquire patent rights, they have no way to produce the patented medicine, and thus no way to benefit from the market. At the same time, they have to pay an increasing patent fee to the patent agency. As time passes, many patents are given up by their owners, thereby striking at the enthusiasm of individual patent applicants. Statistics show that non-professional inventions have decreased by 55 per cent this year from 2002. This means that patent applications from individuals have become more rational and mature, reversing the previous situation of blindly submitted patent applications.[16]

In conclusion, as domestic patent applications for Chinese medicines increase, the distribution of applicants will tend to become more reasonable, and patents will play a more significant role in protecting and promoting the development of the Chinese medicine industry.[17]

9.4 THE ADMINISTRATIVE PROTECTION SYSTEM FOR CHINESE MEDICINES

Before the *Patent Law* was amended in 1993 and patent protection was available for medicines, China relied mainly on administrative regulations to protect intellectual property rights in medicines. After 1993, both systems operate concurrently. Administrative Protection refers to the protection of intellectual property rights in medicines under administrative regulations promulgated by State administrative agencies apart from patent and trademark protection. These administrative regulations include: systems for protecting new Chinese medicines, varieties of Chinese medicines and plant varieties. The legislation protecting new medicines is the *Pharmaceutical Administration Law*, with detailed rules for its implementation found in the *Provisions on New Medicine Protection and Technical Transfer*. The legislation protecting varieties of Chinese medicine is the *Regulations on Variety Protection of Chinese Medicine*. The legislation protecting plant varieties is the *Regulations on Protection of New Varieties of Plant*.[18]

9.4.1 The legal protection of new Chinese medicines

The Ministry of Public Health issued the *Provisions on New Medicine Protection and Technical Transfer* in 1987, a piece of legislation which provides for someone who develops a new medicine to be awarded a "Certificate of New Medicine" after that medicine is reviewed and approved by the State Health Department. Without permission of the original developer, other entities shall not reproduce the new medicine which has been approved by the Ministry within the following time frames starting from the date of the issuance of the "Certificate of New Medicine.": eight years for medicine in category I, six years for medicine in category II; four years for medicine in category III; three years for medicine in category IV. This protection is accorded to all medicines, and not just for Chinese medicines. After China's entry into the WTO, the State Council promulgated the *Regulations for Implementing the Pharmaceutical Administration Law* of the People's Republic of China on August 4, 2002, which entered into force on September 15, 2002. The State Pharmaceutical Supervision and Management Administration adopted *Provisions on Pharmaceutical Registration Management* (on a trial basis) on October 15, 2002, which entered into force on December 1, 2002. According to these two important regulations, administrative protection of new medicines has been abolished and replaced by a safety monitoring period of less than five years which is in accordance with the TRIPS Agreement. Article 34 of the Regulations provides that, based upon the need to protect public health, the State Pharmaceutical Supervision and Management Administration may establish a monitoring period no longer than five years for a new medicine produced by a pharmaceutical enterprise. During this period, no permit shall be given to any other enterprise to produce or import the monitored medicine. The monitored medicine can only be produced by the protected enterprise. This is a new system for monitoring and administration of new medicines with characteristics of intellectual property protection.

9.4.2 The protection of varieties of Chinese medicines

Regulations on Protection of Varieties of Chinese Medicine, which entered into force in 1993, provide special intellectual property protection for Chinese medicines. Article 2 of the Regulations provides that the regulations are applicable to all Chinese medicines produced in China, including final products of Chinese medicines, extracted substances of natural medicines and their preparations, and artificial products of Chinese medicines. It is obvious that the regulations have a broad scope of application: all the Chinese medicine varieties that have not been patented qualify for variety protection.

The conditions for variety protection of Chinese medicines are very general. Novelty or creativity is not required. Medicines which have been publicised or publicly used can also be protected by this system. The protected Chinese medicine varieties can be divided into two categories: those that have special effects for specific diseases and those manufactured goods that have characteristics similar to wild medicinal materials, as well as those that are used to prevent and cure special diseases qualify for first-level protection. Those that qualify as first-level protected varieties, and those that have been deleted from first-level protection but have remarkable effects towards specific diseases, and those effective substances and special preparations that are extracted from natural medicines can apply for second-level protection. Once an application is approved by Ministry of Public Health, the Ministry will issue a "Certificate of Protected Variety of Chinese Medicine" to the applicant. The certificate will be published in the State Communiqué of Protected Varieties of Chinese Medicine. The terms of protection for first level protected varieties are respectively 30 years, 20 years, and 10 years. These terms can be extended under special circumstances. The term of protection can be extended with the Ministry's approval but each extension period shall not exceed the original period of protection. The protection term of second-level protected varieties of Chinese medicines is seven years. Upon the expiry of this term of protection, an extension of another seven years can be obtained.[19]

Within the term of protection, the protected Chinese medicine variety can only be produced by the enterprise holding the "Certificate of Protected Variety of Chinese Medicine." If the protected Chinese medicine is produced by other enterprises before approval is given, those that have not applied for the Certificate can, within six months after the issuance of the Communiqué, apply to the Ministry of Public Health for the certificate. Those that do not apply for the certificate within the time limit must cease production within a specified deadline.

After eight years of development, the protected varieties of Chinese medicine under the *Regulations on Variety Protection of Chinese Medicine* are not confined to prepared medicines that are already produced with governmental approval. Chinese medicines that have been issued with "Certificate of New Medicine" can also qualify for variety protection.

Variety protection of Chinese medicines is complementary to patent protection, and its function is similar to the additional protection certificates issued by some developed countries. It is an extension and enhancement of the intellectual property rights in medicine inventions. It can be treated as a balance to the administrative protection which only foreigners enjoyed in the past. Although it is rational in some ways, it has the following shortcomings. Firstly, because variety protection does not require novelty, medicines which are not original formulations can obtain protection. Existing technologies that have entered into the public domain should not be protected. The fact that specific enterprises are permitted to monopolise existing technologies will definitely harm the public interest. Secondly, the fact that varieties which are being produced by more than one enterprise can be protected could possibly force the other enterprises producing the same variety to pay a fee to apply for similar protection, and thus add to the burdens of these enterprises. Thirdly, the fact that the other enterprises are permitted to enjoy the same variety protection may also harm the interests of the originator of the protected variety, conflict with the pre-existing patent rights and thus weaken the protection given by the patent system, because variety protection exists side by side with patent protection for medicines. Fourthly, the long term of protection for medicine varieties may lead to high prices for medicines over a long time, which is adverse to the interests of patients. Lastly, variety protection applies only to the varieties produced domestically, and not to the varieties imported into China by foreigners, which can be criticised as discriminatory and in conformity with the National Treatment Principle in the TRIPS Agreement. Therefore, the relevant governmental departments have been consulting widely to prepare amendments to the Regulations since China joined the WTO.[20]

9.4.3 Plant variety protection

In 1997, China implemented the *Regulations on New Plant Variety Protection*. New plant varieties include plant varieties that are cultivated or developed from wild plants with characteristics of novelty, distinctiveness, consistency and stability, and that are properly named. Plant varieties that are protected by the new plant variety right should belong to a genus or family listed in the National Plant Variety List. The term of protection for creepers, forest trees, fruit trees and ornamental trees is 20 years. For other plant varieties, the term of protection is 15 years.

9.4.4 Trademark protection for Chinese medicines

China implemented the *Trademark Law* in 1982. The law provides that medicines for human consumption must use registered trademarks, and those that are not registered are not to be sold in the open market. Article 41 of the *Pharmaceutical Administration Law* of People's Republic of China provides that "except Chinese medicinal materials and prepared herbal medicine ready for decoction, medicines must use registered trademarks; those that do not use registered trademarks shall not be distributed in the market. The registered trademarks must be marked on the package or label of the medicine." This makes trademark registration compulsory for medicines, and makes the management of trademarks an integral part of intellectual property rights in Chinese medicines.

The duration of a registered trademark is 10 years. Upon expiry of the term of protection, an application for an extension of the registration is possible, and each extension is for 10 years. After the registration of medicine trademarks, a monopoly is obtained in the country where the registration takes place.

Because patents and trademarks are both important components of intellectual property and their protection completely conforms to the provisions of the TRIPS Agreement, they will be continually improved and enhanced since China has entered into the WTO. The subject matter protected by trademarks and patents is not the same, with trademarks protecting brands and patents protecting the technical content of medicines. The two will not be in conflict and will complement each other.

The old names of Chinese medicine have a long history in China, and enjoy a good reputation both in and outside the country, such as "Tong Ren Tang" of Beijing, "Da Ren Tang" of Tianjing. They are household names in China.

The following problems exist in trademark applications in respect of Chinese medicinal products:

1) The quantity and distinctiveness of Chinese medicine trademarks is low. Many Chinese medicine enterprises do not sufficiently understand trademark registration and in many enterprises, one trademark is used by more than one, or even a hundred products, while a Japanese enterprise Wu Tian owns more than 7,000 registered trademarks at home and abroad.

2) The relationship between the names of medicines and their trademarks is not properly handled. Many trademarks of medicine do not conform to the requirement in the *Trademark Law* that "trademarks shall not use the common names of products."
3) The awareness of trademarks is very weak and famous brands have been lost to registrations made overseas. For example, "Su Xiao Jiu Xin Wan" and "Niu Huang Qing Huo Wan" have been registered in Japan and Korea. The US has more than 200,000 international trademarks and 25,000 are registered in China, while China has a mere 11,000 internationally registered trademarks.
4) The clarity and distinctiveness of trademarks are inadequate. The public in China are still used to distinguishing Chinese medicine through their common names, not their trademarks. And some enterprises put trademarks in unobtrusive places, which results in the situation mentioned above.
5) Lack of trademark registration for native Chinese medicinal materials.
6) Designs of Chinese medicine trademarks lack competitiveness.[21]

9.4.5 Commercial secrets protecting Chinese medicines[22]

The *Anti-Unfair Competition Law* entered into force on September 2, 1993. Under this legislation, commercial secrecy is defined as technical or business information that is not known by the public, that can bring economic benefits to the holder of the commercial secret, has practical use and is kept secret by the rights holder. The subject matter of intellectual property rights protection concerning Chinese medicine is mainly its prescription and production technology. The production technology of Chinese medicine is complicated and highly technical, while the prescription is also complex and diverse, making it very difficult to reverse engineer the prescription and production technology. Therefore, from the point of the technology features in the field of Chinese medicine, commercial secrecy protection is an effective way to protect intellectual property rights in Chinese medicine.

Article 10 of the *Anti-Unfair Competition Law* clearly defines the actions that infringe commercial secrecy. The Article provides that traders shall not infringe commercial secrecy by: 1) theft, bribery, threats of force or other unfair acts to obtain commercial secrets; 2) disclosing, using or allowing other people to use the commercial secrets obtained through the acts above mentioned; 3) violating an agreement or the requirements of the holders of the secret by disclosing, using or allowing other people to use the commercial secret. When a third party obtains, uses or discloses the commercial secret, where he knows or ought to know of the illegal acts mentioned above, this is treated as an infringement of commercial secrecy.

The protection of commercial secrets does not have definite duration. Due to the different methods of protecting commercial secrets and patented inventions, the effects and scope of protection are also different with their own advantages and disadvantages. Although the legal effects of patent protection are strong, it can be acquired only at the cost of disclosing its technical content. The contents of a commercial secret need not be publicised, which seems to be better than the former. However, in order to safeguard public interest, industrialised medicinal products must conform to the medicinal standards of the State in order to be granted medicine production approval, which makes it difficult to keep the prescription and production technology a secret. Moreover, if a third party independently develops a medicine that has been kept secret by an enterprise, that third party may apply for patent protection. Although the enterprise still has priority of use, it is subject to the limitations of the third party's patent rights over the medicine, and cannot expand its production scale.

Many famous Chinese medicines in China are using commercial secrets to protect their intellectual property rights, e.g., Yunnan Bai Yao. Experience shows that as long as the enterprise properly uses protective measures, it can very effectively use commercial secrecy to protect its intellectual property rights in Chinese medicines.

For the present, problems exist in the following areas: 1) improper understanding and use of commercial secrets; 2) violation of agreements with the holder of the commercial secrets: by illegal disclosures during the implementation of technical development, service, consulting and transfer contracts; violation of the provisions on qualified uses; exceeding time limits, territorial limits or amount limits, or allowing others to use the commercial secrets belonging to one's unit or company; 3) illegal acquisition through theft, inducement, coercion or violations of commercial ethics.

9.5 COMPARING THE METHODS OF PROTECTION

9.5.1 Content of protection

Patent rights, variety protection and the protection of new medicines monitoring period are exclusive rights, all of which allow for control to be exercised over medicinal products, but the content of control differs to some degree. Variety protection confers full rights over production, use and distribution of the medicine, but no rights to control importation, while the patent rights and new medicine monitoring period protection include the right to control importation. The *Patent Law* provides that, without the permission of the patentee, it is illegal to import the patented products for the purpose of production and distribution. In other words, without the permission of the patent holder, the import of patented products is illegal. The *Provisions for Implementing Pharmaceutical Administration Law* also provide that, during the new medicine variety monitoring period, permitting other enterprises to import the variety is not allowed.

In addition, variety protection rights for Chinese medicines and the new medicine monitoring period protection rights are not controlling rights in a complete sense. The *Regulations on Variety Protection of Chinese Medicine* provide that the protected variety of Chinese medicine may only be produced within the protection term by the enterprises that have acquired the "Certificate of Protected Variety of Chinese Medicine." As for the protected varieties that are in short supply for clinical uses, the State Pharmaceutical Supervision and Management Administration may permit other enterprises to produce them as well. The *Provisions on Pharmaceutical Registration and Administration* provide that technology relating to new medicines, generally speaking, can only be transferred once, and the enterprise that accepts the transfer shall not transfer the technology again. Therefore, the Pharmaceutical Supervisory Administration limits the holder of variety protection rights and new medicine monitoring period protection from transferring or permitting others to produce the medicines, and the latter cannot freely dispose of their rights.

Patent law in China adopts the "first to file" principle: when two or more applicants apply for the same invention, patent rights are granted to the one who first applies for it. Patent rights are exclusive and the same invention can be granted only one patent. *Provisions on*

Pharmaceutical Registration and Administration provides that when a new medicine enters into a monitoring period, if the State Pharmaceutical Supervision and Management Administration has permitted other applicants to carry out clinical studies of the medicine, the application can continue to be processed; as for those medicines conforming to the provision, the State Pharmaceutical Supervision and Management Administration may approve production or importation, and monitor the new medicine produced by domestic enterprises at the same time. According to the *Regulations on Variety Protection of Chinese Medicine*, more than one pharmaceutical enterprise can obtain protection for the same variety. It is obvious that the exclusiveness of new medicine monitoring period protection and variety protection of Chinese medicine are less than strong.

9.5.2 Acquisition of rights

Only medicine inventions which satisfy the novelty, creativity and practicability requirements of the *Patent Law* can qualify for patent protection; only new medicines conforming to the *Provisions on Pharmaceutical Registration and Administration* and passing the approval process can obtain the "Certificate of New Medicine." As for those Chinese medicine varieties that have met the pharmaceutical standards of the State, province, autonomous region or municipality, and the medicine marketed has the "Certificate of New Medicine," if approved by the Chinese Medicine Variety Protection Assessment Committee in the respects of medical, pharmaceutical distributional and management content, the "Certificate of Protected Chinese Medicine Variety" can be awarded. That is to say, the acquisition of the rights is different. Comparatively speaking, patents focus on the protection of the technology developed in the research process; new medicine monitoring period protection emphasises novelty and the efficacy, safety and the quality of the medicine; and variety protection starts with the protection of existing Chinese medicine, setting standards for producers, thus regulating production and distribution. With newly developed Chinese medicine qualifying for variety protection, the sense of intellectual property rights protection in variety protection grows. From the different ways by which these rights are acquired, new medicine monitoring period and variety protection incorporate intellectual property rights into the supervision and administration of pharmaceuticals. These are intellectual property rights in pharmaceuticals with Chinese characteristics.

9.5.3 Terms of protection, territorial limits and remedies

The term of protection for medicine patent is 20 years from the date of application; the longest new medicine monitoring period is five years, from the date recorded on the medicine production approval document; the terms of protection for variety protection can be divided into two levels, the longest is 30 years which can be extended. The scopes of new medicine monitoring period protection and the variety protection are confined to China. As for the medicine patent, applications for patent protection in other countries around the world are permitted. Therefore, considering the term of protection, scope of protection, content and territorial limits, new medicine monitoring protection and variety protection of Chinese medicine are not the best choices of intellectual property to protect pharmaceutical products.

In China, when patent rights are infringed, the patent holder can request the department in charge of the patent administration to settle the problem according to the law, or he can bring the case to the People's Court. What the department in charge can do is just to order the infringing party to stop. For medicines that have acquired new medicine monitoring period protection or variety protection, the protection of rights is closely related to hospital management. Without the permission of the rights holder, the Pharmaceutical Supervision and Management Administration shall not permit others to produce or distribute the medicine, and thus put an end to the infringement. The Pharmaceutical Supervision and Management Administration can protect the rights holder through administrative enforcement. It can even directly revoke the production and distribution permits of the infringing enterprise. The Pharmaceutical Supervision and Management Administration will punish those who imitate new medicines or protected varieties of Chinese medicine without authorisation. The transaction costs involved here are low while efficiency levels are high, when compared to patent protection. Therefore, in China, protecting intellectual property rights in medicines through the administrative measure of the Pharmaceutical Supervision and Management Administration is better than that of patent protection.

Many Chinese enterprises are actively applying for variety protection of their Chinese medicines, which provides clear evidence of their negative attitude towards patent protection.

9.6 CONFLICTS BETWEEN LAWS RELATED TO THE PROTECTION OF INTELLECTUAL PROPERTY RIGHTS IN CHINESE MEDICINES

9.6.1 Conflicts between domestic law and international law

9.6.1.1 International laws related to intellectual property rights in Chinese medicines

A. Paris Convention for the Protection of Industrial Property ("Paris Convention")

The *Paris Convention for the Protection of Industrial Property* ("*Paris Convention*") is the world's earliest international convention related to the protection of industrial property rights, such as trademarks and patents. It was signed on March 24, 1883 and entered into force in 1884, under the promotion of the French government. From its conclusion, it has been amended six times, and the present executive text is the amended version from the Stockholm Conference in 1967. On March 15, 1985, China became a member state under the Convention. The scope of protection of the *Paris Convention* is extensive, encompassing patents, utility models, designs of industrial products, trademarks, service trademarks, producer names, geographical indicators or origin marks, anti-unfair competition and so forth. "Industrial property rights" refer not only to "industry" in its narrow sense, but also includes business, agriculture and excavation, as well as manufactured and natural products. The provisions of the *Paris Convention* can be divided into three categories: National Treatment Principle, Priority Rights Principle, and the basic standards required for the protection of trademarks and patent (Common Rules Principle).

B. TRIPS Agreement

The *TRIPS* Agreement: was one of the series agreements finally concluded during the Uruguay Round negotiations, and was signed on April 15, 1994. The *TRIPS* Agreement has seven parts and 73 Articles: general provisions and basic principles; standards concerning the availability, scope and use of intellectual property rights; enforcement of intellectual property rights, acquisition and maintenance of intellectual property rights and related *inter-parties* procedure; dispute prevention and settlement; transitional arrangements; institutional arrangements. Its goal is to reduce distortions and impediments to international trade, taking into account the need to promote effective and adequate protection for intellectual property rights, and to ensure that measures and procedures to enforce intellectual property rights do not themselves become barriers to legitimate trade.

Compared with the other existing international conventions on intellectual property rights, it extensively provides standards of protection for intellectual property rights, sets requirements for intellectual property rights enforcement and remedies, provides ways for settling international disputes concerning intellectual property rights, expands the scope of patent protection, mainly to include the protection of medicine and industrial products, and unifies the term of protection for patented inventions to 20 years.[23]

It reflects the following principles of intellectual property protection: 1) National Treatment Principle (similar to the *Paris Convention*); 2) Principle of Protecting Public Order, Social Ethics and Public Health; 3) Independence of Locality of Patent (from *Paris Convention*); 4) Priority Right Principle (from *Paris Convention*); 5) Principle of Reasonable Restriction on Rights (preventing abuses of rights); 6) Principle on Dispute Resolution (Related to Trade Retaliation); 7)Transparency Principle; and 8) Judicial Review Principle.

C. Convention on Biological Diversity

The *Convention on Biological Diversity* is an important convention in the area of international environmental protection. It was concluded in Rio de Janeiro on June 5, 1992, and took effect on December 29, 1993. It took effect on China on the same day. The *Convention on Biological Diversity* sets up a legal framework for the preservation and sustainable use of biological resources and biodiversity. It clarifies the key areas of preservation and sustainable use of biological resources and biodiversity, provides for basic measures of preservation and sustainable use and sets down general principles concerning the acquisition of genetic resources, technology transfer and biological technology benefits-sharing. The goals of the Convention are: first, the protection of biodiversity; second, the sustainable use of components of biodiversity; third, the fair sharing of benefits generated by genetic resources. These three goals are the outline of the whole Convention and form the framework of the Convention.[24]

The objectives of the *Convention on Biological Diversity* point out that, the human use of biological resources should conform to principles like "the conservation of biological diversity, the sustainable use of its components and the fair and equitable sharing of the benefits arising out of the utilisation of genetic resources." According to Article 2, the "Country of origin of genetic resources" means the country which possesses those genetic resources under *in-situ* conditions. According to Article 15, the State has sovereignty over its natural resources, and "Access to genetic resources shall be subject to prior informed consent of the Contracting Party providing such resources," and the party which provides genetic resources has the right to "(share) in a fair and equitable way the results of research and development and the benefits arising from the commercial and other utilisation of genetic resources with the Contracting Party providing such resources."

Article 15 of the *Convention on Biological Diversity* puts forward a number of principles for genetic resources acquisition and benefit-sharing. Determining and sharing intellectual property rights is an important factor in acquiring genetic resources within a certain limit and sharing the benefits fairly and rationally. Article 17 requires the promotion of information exchange between the parties, including technical and scientific information, as well as indigenous and traditional knowledge. This knowledge includes the technology transfers referred to in Article 16. This Article in fact recognises the value of indigenous and traditional knowledge and experiences, including the Chinese medicine system, in implementing the Convention. The value of such knowledge is equal to the value of the technologies referred to in Article 16. Article 18 requires the parties to promote international scientific cooperation. The information exchanged and produced as a result of such cooperation is also related to intellectual property rights. According to the fourth subsection of this Article, the parties should, in accordance with the goals of the Convention, encourage methods for the development and use of related technologies, including indigenous and traditional technology. Article 19 requires parties to adopt measures to provide opportunities for other parties, especially developing countries who provide genetic resources for the researches, to participate in bio-technology research. This Article also requires the parties to adopt practical measures to ensure that parties, especially the developing countries, have the priority to obtain the fruit and benefits generated by the bio-technology which is developed from the of genetic resources provided by those countries. Intellectual property rights form the basis for meeting this requirement.[25]

9.6.1.2 The conflict between the Regulations on Variety Protection of Chinese Medicine and the Paris Convention and the TRIPS Agreement

Article 2 of the *Paris Convention* (1967 version) provides for the National Treatment Principle and specifically provides that it's not necessary for citizens of member states to have residence or a place of business in the countries where he applies for intellectual property protection to enjoy industrial property rights. Article 3 of the *TRIPS* Agreement provides that parties to this agreement, in the area of intellectual property rights protection, shall accord nationals of the other Member states treatment that is no less favourable than that it accords to their own nationals.

As mentioned above, the recipients of variety protection of Chinese medicine do not include foreign enterprises. They are confined to domestic enterprises that produce Chinese medicine varieties. This is obviously in conflict with the *Paris Convention* and the National Treatment Principle espoused in the *TRIPS* Agreement. It's noteworthy that the *Provisions on Pharmaceutical Registration and Administration* grant foreign pharmaceutical enterprises national treatment. It provides that the foreign enterprises which have to comply with the formalities of importing medicines registration should be represented by its Chinese branches or a Chinese agent. We suggest that, when amending the *Regulations on Variety Protection of Chinese Medicine* in the future, particularly the nationality provisions concerning the applicant seeking registration, more attention should be paid to the relevant provisions in the *Provisions on Pharmaceutical Registration and Administration*. This will improve the consistency between the domestic laws.

9.6.2 Conflicts among domestic laws[26]

The existing *Patent Law*, *Pharmaceutical Administration Law*, *Regulations on Variety Protection of Chinese Medicine* and *Provisions on Pharmaceutical Registration and Administration* were promulgated at different times and by different governmental departments. They were introduced in the early 1990s reflecting the policies of a planned economy. Unlike the patent protection system, the other systems of protection incorporate intellectual property rights into pharmaceutical administration, through administrative methods of protection, by the pharmaceutical supervision and administration departments. Conflicts between the two categories of protection are therefore inevitable.

The conflict between the *Regulations on Variety Protection of Chinese Medicine* and the *Patent Law* is worth special attention. The *Regulations on Variety Protection of Chinese Medicine* do not apply to the case of Chinese medicine varieties that apply for patent rights. If two enterprises applied for variety protection and patent protection over the same product, and obtained variety protection and patent protection respectively, what would be the legal effects of those two rights? Before the amendment of the *Pharmaceutical Administration Law*, the *Regulations on Variety Protection of Chinese Medicine* was merely an administrative regulation, its power falling short of *Patent Law*. Therefore, under to the *Patent Law*, without the permission of patent holder, even if a "Certificate of Variety Protection of Chinese Medicine" has been obtained, a third party is not allowed to produce, use or distribute this medicine. Article 36 of the amended *Pharmaceutical Administration Law* provides that the State enforces variety protection system of Chinese medicines.

As a matter of legal theory, as a special law, the effect of the *Pharmaceutical Administration Law* should be better than that of the *Patent Law*, which is the general law. Therefore, the conflict between the *Regulations on Variety Protection of Chinese Medicine* and the *Patent Law* will probably become the focus of future controversies in this area. The *Provisions on Pharmaceutical Registration and Administration* strengthens the coordination with *Patent Law*, and properly settles the problems of intellectual property rights in medicines. For example, the provision in Article 11 regarding the status of medicine patents, the rights that come with them and certificates of non-infringement, the provision in Article 12 about the disputes arising from the patent registration process, the provision in Article 13 about patented medicines. We suggest that provisions are needed to enhance the coordination between *Regulations on Variety Protection of Chinese Medicine* and *Patent Law*. In addition, it is necessary to add conflict provisions in future amendments so as to settle the problem of conflicts between variety protection rights and the patent rights.

Because medicine patents are protected by the *Patent Law*, while the monopoly acquired through administrative measures only receives protection from administrative regulations and rules, the protective effect of the *Patent Law* is higher than administrative protection. Therefore, the administrative protection system should not be in conflict with patent protection system. They should be compatible and in harmony with each other to bring them into full play.

9.7 RECOMMENDATIONS FOR IMPROVING INTELLECTUAL PROPERTY PROTECTION FOR CHINESE MEDICINES[27]

With China's entry into the WTO, it is necessary for the traditional Chinese medicine industry to adopt internationalised operational standards, and an intellectual property rights system which is in consistent with international rules is indispensable here. As such, we present the following proposals:

A. To establish a comprehensive and integrated legislative framework for intellectual property rights protection of traditional Chinese medicine.

The intellectual property rights system is composed of laws and regulations in different sectors of law. For example, the protection of Chinese medicines involves the *Patent Law*, *Trademark Law*, *Pharmaceutical Administration Law*, *Regulations on Variety Protection of Chinese Medicine*, and so forth. Every specialised law often has its own legislative goals and objectives, while the object of intellectual property rights takes different forms in different periods. Depending on the stage of development which the medicine is in, it may be protected by technical secrecy laws, under the *Patent Law*, under the protection of new medicine administration law, or under the protection of trademark law and the *Regulations on Variety Protection of Chinese Medicine*. Therefore, attention should be paid firstly to the integrity of the protection system, and the coordination between the different sectors of law. Different forms of intellectual property rights should be considered as an interrelated whole. When overlapping protection occurs, it is especially important to coordinate between the two or more overlapping laws and regulations. Secondly, coordination between intellectual property rights laws and other laws, regulations and policies should also be focused, such as technology innovation law, law on transfer of technological achievements, secret keeping law. From the State's point of view, both the diversity of laws and the coordination between different laws and regulations are needed. Only in this way can intellectual property rights protection be strengthened and an integrated intellectual property protection system constructed.

B. To strengthen the enforcement of laws against infringements of intellectual property rights over traditional Chinese medicines.
   (i) To strengthen the enforcement of laws against infringement and to improve laws related to intellectual property related dispute resolution. Corresponding measures are needed to ensure the enforcement process in order to strike severely at intellectual property rights infringement.
   (ii) To develop the necessary legal services related to intellectual property rights, and to encourage, induce and develop intermediary service agencies.

C. To establish a database of traditional Chinese medicine and to enhance intellectual property rights protection of Chinese medicine

China should establish a database of traditional Chinese medicine which can prevent patent applications for traditional Chinese medicines as well as increases the value of traditional Chinese medicine. We suggest that the World Health Organisation (WHO), through the world intellectual property rights organisations, intervene and support the establishment of a database of traditional Chinese medicines.

D. To enhancc the intellectual property rights protection of traditional Chinese medicine through the use of "subjective" articles in the TRIPS Agreement.

Today, when economic globalisation becomes the trend, WTO members should accept the TRIPS Agreement. As a member state of WTO, China may, under the TRIPS Agreement, improve its laws and regulations related to intellectual property rights over Chinese medicines and strengthen intellectual property rights protection over Chinese medicinal knowledge through the use of the "subjective" articles found in the TRIPS Agreement (e.g., the definitions of "invention," "availability," "exceptions," "parallel import," "compulsory licensing" and "transitional period").

E. To train more legal experts specialising in intellectual property rights, especially experts in intellectual property protection for traditional Chinese medicines.

(i) Colleges and universities, research institutes and enterprises which specialise in Chinese medicine should train, within the shortest time period, a team of experts familiar with the WTO's general principles and related rules, through lectures or training programs abroad.

(ii) To raise the awareness of Chinese medicine industry of intellectual property rights and help the industry to understand basic concepts and the significance of intellectual property protection, and to raise the sense of intellectual property rights law and help the industry to protect their intellectual property rights. In addition, more concrete and effective mechanisms should be established in order to protect inventors and to benefit of right holders.

(iii) To incorporate intellectual property rights into the whole process of science and technology management, to avoid repetition when applying for project establishment, to ensure the novelty and authoritativeness of projects, and to promote the generation of related intellectual property rights.

F. To make national law and regulations consistent with the relevant international laws.

ENDNOTES

1 Editor's note: The original text prepared by the authors is in Chinese. While reasonable efforts have been taken by the authors and the editor to faithfully translate the text into English, inevitable linguistic imperfections may have prevented a more accurate reflection of the more nuanced expressions of the authors in the original text. The Chinese text is available from Professor Wang Xi who may be contacted at wangxi@sjtu.edu.cn.

2 See http://www.cnm21.com/NEWS/yytx_32.htm (in Chinese).

3 Editor's note: The State Administration of Traditional Chinese Medicine (SATCM) is a state bureau under the Ministry of Public Health in China. Its primary role is to regulate Traditional Chinese Medicine and Pharmacology (TCMP), to develop the science of TCMP, and promote the development of TCMP.

4 Tables 9.1–9.3 are cited from Hong Jing, *et al.*, "Counter measures for intellectual property protection of Chinese medicines," *World Science and Technology: Modernization of Chinese Medicine*, vol. 3, no. 1, 2000, pp. 32–38.

5 Article 22, *Patent Law* of the People's Republic of China.

6 *Ibid.*

7 *Ibid.*

8 http://www.sipo.gov.cn/sipo/zscqb/fazhi/t20020802_7413.htm (in Chinese).

9 http://chanye.sina.net/zl/2003-06-23/171142.shtml (in Chinese).

10 Jiao Quan, *et al.*., "The present situation of intellectual property right protection of Chinese medicine and the countermeasures," *Journal of Nanjing Medical University* (Social Science Edition.), no. 1, March 2002, pp. 34–37.

11 http://www.yy2000.com/yiyaozhengce/zhishichanquanbaohu_4.htm (in Chinese).

12 *Ibid.*

13 Zhang Weibo, "The present situation of patent protection and related research," *World Science and Technology: Modernization of Chinese Medicine*, vol. 3, no. 1, 2001, pp. 40–46.

14 Zhang Tao, "Problems of the current intellectual property protection for Chinese medicine and the ways of solution," *World Science and technology: Modernization of Chinese Medicine*, vol. 4, no. 1, 2002, pp. 59–60.

15 *Ibid.*

16 http://www.gzyy.org/2003/0701/20030701020.htm (in Chinese).

17 See note 9 above.

18 Wang Beiying, "Intellectual property protection of Chinese medicine and medicine of minority nationalities," *Hunan Journal of Chinese Medicine*, vol. 5, no. 1, 1999, pp. 1–3.

19 Wang Bing, *et al.*, "Current situation of intellectual property protection for Chinese medicine," *World Science and Technology: Modernization of Chinese Medicine*, vol. 3, no. 5, 2001, pp. 71–75.

20 http://www.mhpie.com.cn/ (in Chinese).

21 http://www.bjzx.gov.cn/wcqh/dhfy/fyg/z10.htm (in Chinese).

22 Zhang Xuemei, "Ways for intellectual property of Chinese medicine," *Chinese Pharmaceutical Industry*, vol. 11, no. 10, 2002, pp. 38–39.

23 http://www.ec.com.cn/ec/publish/article/200212/200212_39_17919.xml?style=zhengZtArticle.xsl (in Chinese).

24 Wang Xi, *International Environmental Law*, Law Press China, 1998, p. 239.

25 http://www.people.com.cn/wsrmlt/jbzl/haoxf/A101.html (in Chinese).

26 Wang Xiaohu, "Issues of intellectual property rights of Chinese medicine," *Journal of Chinese New Medicine*, vol. 12, no. 2, 2003, available online: (http://www.bjinfobank.com/IrisBin/search.dll?SpSearch).

27 See note 21 above.

CHAPTER 10

Biological Resources, Intellectual Property Rights and International Human Rights: Impacts on Indigenous and Local Communities[1]

DONNA CRAIG*

10.1 INTRODUCTION

Some 200 million Indigenous people (4 per cent of the world's population) live in environments ranging from polar ice and snow to tropical deserts and rainforests. They are distinct cultural communities with land and other rights based on historical use and occupancy. Their cultures, economies and identities are inextricably tied to their traditional lands and resources. Hunting, fishing, trapping, gathering, herding or cultivation continue to be carried out for subsistence—food and materials—as well as for income.[2]

---

* Associate Professor, Centre for Environmental Law, Macquarie University, Australia; Director, Environmental and Indigenous Rights Program. The author acknowledges the research assistance by Abi Srikhanta, Law Student Volunteer, Macquarie University Centre for Environmental Law. The discussion in this chapter was substantially based on a working paper submitted to the Australian Human Rights Centre in 2003 entitled "Global Sustainable Development: Human Rights, Environmental Rights and Indigenous Peoples" (Working Paper 2003/3). It is available online at http://www.ahrcentre.org/Publications/craig_indi_rts.htm

Indigenous Peoples also provide valuable resources and knowledge related to plant and animal use, including methods of preparation, storage and management, which is of global economic significance. Their biogenetic resources already form the basis of sizeable seed, pharmaceutical and natural product industries. Natural resource management, soil fertility maintenance, stream and coastal conservation, and forest and agricultural system models provide viable, time-tested options for sustainable development adapted to microclimate variations and local socio-political ecosystems.

Yet Indigenous Peoples confront increasing external pressures on their lands, territories, resources, knowledge, innovations and practices. Even the recognition of their past endowments to world food and medicinal sources, as well as their significant contributions to agriculture, water and forest management, has done little to offset their political marginalisation.

10.1.1 The role of traditional ecological knowledge in conserving biodiversity

Traditional Ecological Knowledge, as defined by Johnson, covers "a body of knowledge built by a group of people through generations living in close contact with nature. It includes a system of classification, a set of empirical observations about the local environment, and a system of self management that governs resource use."[3]

Traditional Ecological Knowledge not only refers to Indigenous communities, but also incorporates the knowledge base of hundreds of millions of members of predominately rural societies who depend on the natural environment for their livelihood. Their knowledge has been passed on over many thousands of years, accumulating intricate, detailed and sacred understandings of the local land to form their cultures and knowledge systems.[4] The traditional relationship which indigenous communities have with nature is such that the concepts of biodiversity and conservation are foreign to them. Instead it is an "integral part of human existence, in which utilisation is part of the celebration of life"[5]. These include notions of stewardship and totems that are fundamental to biodiversity conservation.

It is vital to incorporate Traditional Ecological Knowledge into international law and policy, as it will assist in the preservation of local knowledge, encourage participation by these communities in environmental management and (with prior informed consent) provide a framework for access and equitable benefit-sharing. Age-old practices are not only beneficial to these communities but also provide examples of appropriate sustainable conservation, strategies displaying efficient management techniques for soil, water, fisheries and forestries, which have wider applications.

10.1.2 Ownership and protection of traditional ecological knowledge

Ownership and property are Western legal concepts that do not easily transpose into traditional and Indigenous systems. The notion of transferability is the least compatible element of property. This is because traditional and Indigenous Peoples identify themselves within communities who are tied to the land, often based on spiritual connections. There is often no single identifiable individual that could stand as the property owner of lands and biological resources.

Hansen and VanFleet argue that traditional knowledge is usually collective in nature and is often considered to be the property of the community as a whole:

> It is transmitted through specific cultural and traditional information exchange mechanisms, for example, maintained and transmitted orally through elders and specialists (breeders, healers, etc.), and often to only a select few people within a community.[6]

The rich and complex systems of traditional knowledge protected and transmitted through customary law regimes are often undermined by dominant legal systems. Attempts by Indigenous Peoples to assert and protect their own approaches to Traditional Ecological Knowledge, in an increasingly globalised world, has often taken the form of a debate about the appropriateness, use and abuse of intellectual and cultural property rights. These issues will be canvassed briefly as they will be dealt with by authors in the other chapters.

10.1.3 Who are Indigenous Peoples?

> There are approximately 15,000 culturally-distinct ethnic communities in the world today[7] and, while the diversity to be

> found among these cultures is both marvellous and extraordinary, most Indigenous Peoples share a sense of communal responsibility for their land and its living resources.[8]

The definitions of Indigenous Peoples are varied and problematic in some parts of the world. The Special Rapporteur of the United Nations Economic and Social Council Sub-Commission on the Prevention of Discrimination of Minorities has defined Indigenous Peoples in the following manner:

> Indigenous communities, Peoples and nations are those which, having a historical continuity with pre-invasion and pre-colonial societies that have developed on their territories, consider themselves distinct from other sectors of the societies now prevailing in those territories, or parts of them. They form at present non-dominant sectors of society and are determined to preserve, develop and transmit to future generations their ancestral territories, and their ethnic identity, as the basis of their continued existence as Peoples, in accordance with their own cultural patterns, social institutions and legal systems.[9]

The *International Labour Organisation (ILO) Convention 169* "Concerning Indigenous Peoples in Independent Countries" (1989), identifies Indigenous Peoples as:

a) tribal Peoples in countries whose social, cultural and economic conditions distinguish them from other sections of the national community, and whose status is regulated wholly or partially by their own customs or traditions or by special laws or regulations, and
b) Peoples in countries who are regarded by themselves or others as Indigenous on account of their descent from the populations that inhabited the country, or a geographical region to which the country belong, at the time of conquest or colonisation or the establishment of present state boundaries and who, irrespective of all their legal status, retain, or wish to retain, some or all of their own social, economic, spiritual, cultural and political characteristics and institutions.

The fundamental principle established by ILO 169 is that of self-identification, "as Indigenous or tribal shall be regarded as a fundamental criterion for determining the groups to which the provisions of this convention apply."[10]

10.1.4 What are indigenous intellectual and cultural property rights?

Intellectual and cultural property refers to Indigenous knowledge, whether it is in the form of biological knowledge, customary knowledge or created tangible materials, that is passed on from one generation to the next.

A Study on the Protection of Cultural and Intellectual Property of Indigenous Peoples by Daes argues that the separation of "intellectual" and "cultural" property is inappropriate. Instead, a holistic and integrated view of Indigenous heritage, encompassing all aspects of their lives, is essential. This is a more compatible view as it reflects Indigenous philosophies of oneness with their Peoples and lands:

> ... heritage includes all expressions of the relationship between the people, their land and the other living beings and spirits which share the land, and is the basis for maintaining social, economic and diplomatic relationships—through sharing—with other Peoples. All of the aspects of heritage are interrelated and cannot be separated from the traditional Territory of the people concerned. What tangible and intangible items constitute the heritage of a particular Indigenous Peoples' must be decided by the people themselves...[11]

In formulating the concept of property rights to protect Indigenous culture, it is important to recognise the needs and rights of Indigenous Peoples' under international and domestic law. In failing to do so, we will have a system of property rights that does not adequately address their needs and furthermore may work to disintegrate their community.

The following is a list of some key heritage rights that Indigenous Peoples in Australia call for in relation to intellectual and cultural property:

- The right to own and control Indigenous intellectual and cultural property,

- The right to define what constitutes Indigenous intellectual and cultural property and/or Indigenous heritage,
- The right to ensure that any means of protecting Indigenous intellectual and cultural property is premised on the principle of self-determination, which includes the right and duty of Indigenous Peoples to maintain and develop their own cultures and knowledge systems and forms of social organisation,
- The right to authorise, or to refuse to authorise, the commercial use of Indigenous intellectual and cultural property in accordance with customary law,
- The right to benefit commercially from the authorised use of Indigenous intellectual and cultural property, including the right to negotiate terms of such usage,
- The right to protect Indigenous sites, including sacred sites,
- The right to control the disclosure, dissemination, reproduction and recording of Indigenous knowledge, ideas and innovations concerning medicinal pants, biodiversity and environmental management,
- The right to own and control management of land and sea, conserved in whole or part because of their Indigenous cultural values.[12]

The international law for the protection of intellectual property has been developed with virtually no regard for the needs of Indigenous Peoples for the protection of their cultural and intellectual property (usually embodied in their communal lifestyles). They were developed to protect the marketable property of non-Indigenous corporations. This is a restricted form of property which is severed from the original components of the "invention" and the cultures which may have nurtured its initial stages. It is the "modification" or "discovery" through non-Indigenous technology which is usually rewarded and protected by intellectual property rights.

Indigenous Peoples, in contemporary society, require an economic base. This is even the case where many of their activities and lifestyle remain "traditional." In many situations their ecosystems have been altered, and political circumstances changed, so that they cannot (or do not wish) to live a totally subsistence lifestyle. The economic and sustainable use of resources may be consistent with the maintenance of

Indigenous lifestyle or cultural adaptation over time. Intellectual property rights are one type of legal strategy that is being considered by Indigenous Peoples, to protect their biological resources, cultural practices and to develop an economic base required by contemporary circumstances.

It is difficult to formulate a version of intellectual and cultural property rights appropriate for Indigenous Peoples at the present time. Some of the difficulties with existing laws are as follows:

- Indigenous Peoples are not given recognition, as legal "persons," to enforce international conventions on intellectual property.
- There is little experience with identifying the Indigenous knowledge or resource "component," when it is modified by industrial users and with placing an economic value on such a "component." Such knowledge is usually part of a culture that cannot be segmented by Indigenous Peoples or others.
- Intellectual property laws require an individual group, or other legal entity, to make the claim. Indigenous knowledge is often communally held.[13] This is not an impediment in itself, if groups who control knowledge and resources can be identified. The boundaries of groups and the "exclusivity" of knowledge and practice may be problematic.
- Intellectual property rights, in the form held by Indigenous Peoples, may not be readily marketable. Large scale marketing may also impact on the cultures and lifestyles which produced the knowledge and technologies.
- Indigenous Peoples would require greater resources and capacity building to avail themselves of intellectual property laws.[14]

The intellectual and cultural property rights of Indigenous Peoples require further consideration and development having regard to the specific provisions of the *Convention on Biological Diversity*[15] which are discussed in a later section of this chapter.

The emphasis in this chapter will be on important international legal standards relating to human and environment rights of Indigenous Peoples to their biological resources. The difficulties in developing the most appropriate forms of intellectual property rights for the recognition of Indigenous rights and aspirations does not mean that there is a legal void. There is a rich and diverse range of applicable international legal norms. The challenge is to find practical and enforceable means to implement them in the international and domestic context. Indigenous Peoples' have their own distinct views on how this should be done and their approaches require much greater research, support and consideration by the international community and nation States.

10.2 SUSTAINABLE DEVELOPMENT STRATEGIES

Indigenous Peoples are inevitably impacted by decisions and plans which go beyond their land and involve Peoples from the dominant culture. A key issue which must be addressed is how we recognise the requirements of Sustainable Development and the needs of Indigenous Peoples' for self-determination (including their own development strategies). It is fundamental that Indigenous Peoples must have legally recognised title to their land, seas and natural resources and the power to control their use and management in a way that they consider appropriate.

Following the United Nations Conference on the Human Environment,[16] several declarations have stated the basic right of Indigenous Peoples to exercise self-determination to achieve sustainable development:

> Development should respect, maintain and enhance the diversity of natural life and human culture to maintain and expand the availability of options for this and future generations ... This requires that homogenisation of land use and human lifestyles be avoided.[17]

The *Declaration of San Jose* defines the right to ethno-development as:

> the amplification and consolidation of ... a culturally distinct society's own culture, through the strengthening of its capacity to guide its own development and exercise self-determination ... and implying an equitable and proper organisation of power.[18]

This chapter explores evolving standards and legal approaches to human, environmental and Indigenous rights and the extent to which they potentially contribute to sustainable development. It will be argued that Indigenous intellectual and cultural property rights need to be understood, and recognised, in the context of these rights under international law.

10.3 STANDARDS AND APPROACHES TO HUMAN AND ENVIRONMENTAL RIGHTS OF INDIGENOUS PEOPLES

Traditionally, international law has focused on state sovereignty and nation states have predominated as legitimate parties. This has changed to a limited extent, in regimes such as the human rights conventions, which focus on the rights of the individuals. The role of Non-Government Organizations (NGO's) in the negotiation and implementation of some global and regional environmental conventions has also challenged the dominant concept that international law purely regulates the relationship between nation states. These new challenges, in modern international law, relate to the:

- concept and formulation of the rights (including substantive and procedural rights);
- need to address the collective rights of Peoples (particularly raised in *ILO 169* and the *Draft UN Declaration on the Rights of Peoples*);
- enforcement, monitoring and financing of the obligations of developing nations on an equitable basis (sometimes involving differential responsibilities for the "North" and "South");
- need to develop practical, affordable and innovative implementation strategies that empower, legitimise rights (in terms of the dominant political order), work effectively for local communities and Indigenous and tribal Peoples and address urgent needs such as poverty;
- promotion of the rapid dissemination and adaptation of comparative experiences relating to national implementation.

Often, Indigenous Peoples are seeking both collective and individual rights. The predominant Western legal traditions, based on social contract theory, tend to put individual rights against the State.[19] Indigenous strategies often involve this defensive role but they also assert their collective rights and (internal) collective obligations to maintain and continue to evolve their cultures and nations in the face of threats such as discrimination, dispossession, environmental change and the cultural and economic impacts of the dominant society.

Because Indigenous Peoples have integral and unique relationships with the earth, including land, seas, resources, wildlife, they do not fragment or compartmentalise their rights and obligations relating to their ecological, spiritual, cultural, economic and social dimensions.[20]

The accumulated knowledge acquired in this way, has become a matter of global interest and exploitation.[21] This can also be seen as a fundamental illustration of sustainable development as it draws "wisdom" from the idea of integrating these dimensions. Sustainable development has now become the central focus of modern environmental policy and rapidly evolving human rights, such as the right to development and the right to a healthy environment, as enshrined in the national constitutions of the Philippines, Pakistan, and India.

Human rights are often characterised as follows:

- Civil and political rights;
- Economic, social and cultural rights;
- The (evolving) right to development and the right to a healthy environment.

Article 1 of the *Declaration on the Right to Development*[22] reads:

> The right to development is an inalienable human right by virtue of which every human person and all Peoples are entitled to participate in, contribute to and enjoy economic, social, cultural and political development, in which all human rights and fundamental freedom can be fully realised.

International law and policy relating to sustainable development has been promoted by the *Rio Declaration*, *Agenda 21*, *Convention of Biodiversity* (CBD), *Framework Convention on Climate Change* (FCCC) and the *Forest Principles* which were the key outcomes of the *United Nations Conference on Environment and Development* (UNCED) in 1992.[23] The rights of Indigenous Peoples' are specifically mentioned in each of these global declarations and instruments except for the FCCC. The *Plan of Implementation*[24] developed at the *World Summit on Sustainable Development* (Johannesburg, 2002) contains some significant soft law provisions relating to Indigenous rights.

Arguably, basic provisions in international human rights instruments have become part of international customary law, known as *jus cogens*, and they are inextricably related to the rights to environment and development. Important *jus cogens* norms are as follows:

- the right to be free from genocide (including cultural genocide)

- the right to life (including the right of people not to be deprived of their own means of subsistence)
- the right of Peoples to self-determination[25]

Ward goes on to argue that these provisions in human rights instruments (now *jus cogens*) establish:

> [T]he right to be free from hunger, the right to an adequate standard of living, the right to health, free personal development, sustainable community development using environmental and social impact assessments, and the right to integrity of the community as a whole.[26]

10.3.1 The International Covenant on Economic, Social and Cultural Rights

After the adoption of the *Universal Declaration of Human Rights* (UDHR), the United Nations' Commission on Human Rights commenced drafting two human rights' conventions which are relevant to Indigenous Peoples' rights to ecologically sustainable development.

Article 1(2) of the ICESCR provides that:

> [A]ll Peoples may, for their own ends, freely dispose of their natural wealth and resources without prejudice to any obligations arising out of international economic co-operation, based upon the principle of mutual benefit and international law. In no case may a people be deprived of its own means of subsistence.

Indigenous Peoples assert their rights as "people" under this provision, but prefer the terminology of Peoples associated with the right to self-determination. Article 15(1c) provides that States recognise the right to "benefit from the protection of the moral and material interests resulting from any scientific, literary or artistic production of which he is the author."

10.3.2 International Covenant on Civil and Political Rights

Article 1(2) of the ICCPR is identical to Article 1(2) of the ICESCR. Article 18 of the ICCPR states that everyone shall have a right to freedom of thought, conscience and religion. Article 27 provides for the rights of minorities:

> In those States in which ethnic, religious or linguistic minorities exist, persons belonging to such minorities shall not be denied the right, in community with other members of their group, to enjoy their own culture, to profess and practise their own religion, or to use their own language.

10.3.3 Human Rights relating to intellectual property in biological resources

Hansen and VanFleet argue that:

> Since the adoption of the *Universal Declaration of Human Rights* (UDHR) in 1948, intellectual property (IP) has been considered a fundamental human right of all Peoples. Article 27 of the Declaration states that everyone has the '*right to protection of the moral and material interests resulting from any scientific, literary or artistic production of which he is the author.*' Since 1948, many international human rights instruments and documents have reinforced the importance of IP as a human right.[27]

Specific consideration needs to be given to Article 27 of UDHR, which also states, "Everyone has the right to freely participate in the cultural life of the community, to enjoy the arts and to share in scientific advancement and its benefits." Other international human rights instruments addressing intellectual property include Article 15 of the *International Covenant on Economic, Social and Cultural Rights* (ICESCR), Article 15 of the *International Labour Organization Convention No. 169* (ILO 169), Article 8(j) of the *Convention on Biological Diversity* (CBD) and Article 29 of the *Draft Declaration on Indigenous Rights*.[28]

10.3.4 Specific international legal instruments relating to the rights of Indigenous Peoples

The international legal status of Indigenous Peoples, as self-determining nations, remains an enduring and controversial issue in international law. This situation continues even though there is increasing domestic legal recognition of various forms of Indigenous self government within many nations. The fear of succession, and other political factors, has influenced the international position adopted by States. The right of self-determination remains a central concern in the negotiation of the UN *Draft Declaration of Indigenous Rights*. It is clear that this right is the focal point for asserting contemporary Indigenous claims for their integrated and comprehensive rights.

10.3.4.1 ILO Convention 169

In 1989 the International Labour Organisation adopted a new convention, *ILO 169, Concerning Indigenous and Tribal Peoples in Independent Countries*. Some Indigenous Peoples and other commentators consider that *ILO 169* undermines Indigenous aspirations by emphasising "participation" or "consultation" rather than self-determination. However, taken as a whole, *ILO 169* is the most significant international treaty, so far, that recognises the integrated and comprehensive rights of Indigenous and Tribal Peoples.

These Articles of the Convention are relevant to achieving systematic and co-ordinated action that is necessary to protect the integrated rights of Indigenous Peoples:

- 7.1 illustrates some elements of self-determination: "The Peoples concerned shall have the right to decide their own priorities ..." but then is qualified, "for the process of development."
- 7.2 and 7.3 refer to improved living conditions with "Indigenous participation and co-operation." The carrying out of studies, although only "where appropriate," should include assessment of "social, spiritual, cultural and environmental impact."
- 3.1 and 13.2 incorporate concepts of Indigenous rights, requiring governments to "respect the special importance for the cultures and spiritual values of the Peoples" and their territories (which covers the total environment of areas which the peoples concerned occupy or otherwise use).
- 14.1 is a recognition of Indigenous rights to "ownership and possession ... over the lands which they traditionally occupy." Furthermore, this provision extends to give rights to Peoples who do not have exclusive use of certain lands, but traditionally require access to it, such as "nomadic Peoples and shifting cultivators."

- 14.2 and 14.3 establishes the responsibility of governments to "guarantee effective protection of their rights of ownership and possession" and provide adequate legal mechanisms to resolve possible land claims.
- Article 15.1 states, "The rights of the Peoples concerned to the natural resources pertaining to their lands shall be especially safeguarded. These rights include the right of these Peoples to participate in the use, management and conservation of these resources."

ILO 169 tends to be regarded as a "floor" and not the "upper level" of Indigenous rights. It was negotiated at the same time as the *Draft UN Declaration of Indigenous Rights.* Many Indigenous Peoples prefer the stronger language in the *Draft Declaration.* ILO is expressed in a form to encourage ratification by the maximum number of nations, some of which give poor recognition to Indigenous rights at the present time. International standards will develop under this convention along with other human rights and environmental conventions as well as "soft law" instruments such as the Universal Declarations by the United Nations.

10.3.4.2 Draft Universal Declaration on the Rights of Indigenous Peoples

In 1982 the Economic and Social Council of the United Nations authorised the establishment of a Working Group on Indigenous Populations to meet annually as part of the Sub-Commission on the Prevention of Discrimination and Protection of Minorities. The Mandate of the Working Group was:

- to review developments pertaining to the promotion and protection of the human rights and fundamental freedoms of Indigenous Peoples; and
- to give special attention to the evolution of standards concerning the rights of Indigenous populations.

The two major matters for Working Group deliberations are a "Review of Developments" and "Standard Setting." Since 1985 the Working Group has decided to meet its "Standard Setting" mandate by formulating a *Draft Declaration on the Rights of Indigenous Peoples.* The process has involved hundreds of Indigenous Peoples in UN meetings and work for over 10 years. The *Draft Declaration* has been passed up to the Sub-Commission and it eventually will be considered by the UN General Assembly. Within the next few years it will be a UN Declaration with the same status as the *UN Declaration on Human Rights*. The Working Group Draft will be amended by Nation States in this process.

However, the Working Group version of the *Draft Declaration* (1993) is the most comprehensive, integrated and strongest articulation of Indigenous rights, by Indigenous Peoples, to date. This version expresses the international standard developed by Indigenous participants over a very long period of deliberation. This was one of the most participatory NGO processes, particularly including Indigenous Peoples, in UN history. The *Draft Declaration* needs to be read holistically as the clearest articulation of the integrated rights of Indigenous Peoples in evolving international law and policy.

The clear and unqualified right to Indigenous self determination is contained in Article 3. Other rights (including management rights) to lands, resources, waters, seas, biological resources, the recognition of intellectual and cultural property and the rights of Indigenous Peoples to determine their own development priorities are contained in Articles 25 to 30. These are more powerful reflections of the contemporary aspirations and needs of Indigenous Peoples than the provisions in ILO 169.

The *Draft Declaration* is slowly proceeding through the UN process. It will remain important to consider what parts of it are reflected in other treaties, discussed above, international customary law and *jus cogens*.

10.4 EVOLVING APPROACHES TO HUMAN RIGHTS AND THE ENVIRONMENT

The overlaps in the approaches to human rights have caused the United Nations to begin preparing a *Declaration of Principles on Human Rights and the Environment*.[29] This *Draft Declaration* commences:

1. Human rights, an ecologically sound environment, sustainable development and peace are interdependent and indivisible.
2. All persons have the right to a secure, healthy and ecologically sound environment. This right and other human rights, including civil, cultural, economic, political and social rights are universal.

The World Conservation Union (IUCN) has prepared a draft of an umbrella global treaty to provide a legal framework for sustainable development. It is known as the *Draft Covenant on Environment and Development.*[30] This is a very important indicator of future trends in international environmental law. It includes respect for all life forms. It recognises the right to development but has regard to the urgent need to maintain and restore the earth's ecological systems.

The United Nations *Meeting of Experts on Human Rights and the Environment* (2002) has reviewed the progress made since the United Nations Conference on Environment and Development (Rio de Janeiro, 1992).[31] They concluded that there was a growing and close connection between human rights and environmental protection in the context of sustainable development. Important developments have occurred at the national and international level. The experts particularly noted that the linkage is reflected in recent developments relating to procedural and substantive rights, in the activities of international organisations and in the drafting and application of national constitutions[32].

There is a wealth of case law, particularly in developing nations, upholding the constitutional right to environmental quality.[33] This often required innovative approaches to standing and public participation as seen in the famous Philippines case of *Oposa vs.Factoran*[34] and in the *Aarhus Convention on Access to Information, Public Participation and Access to Justice in Environmental Matters (1998).* The decisions of international treaty bodies (including courts and commissions) often recognise the violation of a fundamental human right as the cause, or result, of environmental degradation.[35]

Some human rights treaties, such as the *Convention on the Rights of the Child* and *ILO 169 Concerning Indigenous and Tribal Peoples in Independent Countries*, the *African Charter on Human and Peoples Rights* and the *Protocol of San Salvador to the American Convention on Human Rights* expressly recognise the right to live in a healthy or satisfactory environment.[36] Respect for human rights is broadly accepted as a pre-condition for sustainable development and that environmental protection is a pre-condition for the enjoyment of human rights—they are interdependent and interrelated.[37] This is now reflected in national and international practices and developments.[38] It is also understood that poverty is at the centre of a number of human rights violations and is at the same time a major obstacle to achieving sustainable development.[39]

It no longer makes any sense to talk about "categories of rights." None of the human rights instruments attempt any ranking—all rights and freedoms are placed on an equal footing. "All rights are, like humans themselves, inextricably singular and social."[40] Therefore, "first" and "second" generation should be approached as a unity rather than a duality.[41] Brownlie maintains that there has been an assumption lying behind the classical formulation of human rights standards that "group rights would be taken care of automatically as a result of the protection of the rights of individuals."[42] This approach has been inadequate to protect the rights of Indigenous Peoples and there is an urgent need to advance international law in the direction of a more unified conceptual framework.

International Labour Organisation Convention 169 (ILO 169) and the *Draft Declaration on the Rights of Indigenous Peoples* by the UN Commission on Human Rights, Sub-Commission on Prevention of Discrimination and Protection of Minorities provide examples of the integrated rights approach, with the *Draft Declaration* being a better example. ILO 169 and *Draft Declaration* should be understood within the wider framework of international environmental, Indigenous rights and human rights law. This is discussed by Posey who argued that there has been a gradual evolution of *sui generis* "Traditional Resource Rights."[43] Developing new forms of intellectual and cultural property rights should be a part of this process, and not an impediment to it.

Thus, Indigenous rights in international law and policy are not the "poor relation." They are a catalyst for developing more unified and effective approaches to human rights and sustainable development which should be recognised and implemented.[44]

10.5 AN EXAMPLE OF AN INTEGRATED RIGHTS APPROACH: TRADITIONAL RESOURCE RIGHTS AND *SUI GENERIS* SYSTEMS

Sui generis is the Latin word for "unique" or "of its own kind." In a legal context, the reference to a *sui generis* system involves an alterative or modified framework to the existing law, governed by fundamentally different principles and mechanisms.

Posey clarifies the definition and application of a *sui generis* approach in the discussion of Article 27.3(b) of the *Trade Related Aspects of Intellectual*

Property Rights Agreement (TRIPS)[45], which provides for the "... the protection of plant varieties either by patents or by an effective *sui generis* system or by any combination thereof." *Sui generis* systems in this context can mean a modification of existing intellectual property law, a new intellectual property right or an alternative to intellectual property rights.

The *sui generis* system referred to in TRIPS illustrates the acknowledgement that current intellectual property laws, specifically by way of patents, may be an inappropriate method of protection of Indigenous culture and heritage.

At a time when the difficulties in adapting existing Western legal structures to enhance conservation of biodiversity and empower Indigenous and local communities become manifest, the emergence of the concept of Traditional Resource Rights (TRR) appears to be timely. The "Traditional Resource Rights" concept was first elaborated in an article by Posey entitled: "Traditional Resource Rights: De Facto Self-determination for Indigenous Peoples,"[46] and it has been proposed as a specific example of a *sui generis* system of legal rights.

The term "Traditional Resource Rights" seeks to go beyond limited concepts of intellectual property rights and describes the many "bundles" of rights existing and being developed which can be utilised for the protection of and compensation for the use of traditional knowledge and resources. Traditional resources include plants, animals, and other material objects, like minerals and cultural artefacts, which may have intangible (e.g., sacred, ceremonial, heritage, or aesthetic) qualities. Traditional resources may also be totally intangible, metaphysical, or non-quantifiable with no physical manifestations, such as systems of knowledge. The term "property" is inappropriate, since property in traditional societies frequently has intangible, spiritual manifestations, and, although worthy of protection, can belong to no human being.

Traditional Resource Rights encompasses not only conventional intellectual property rights mechanisms but basic rights and customary law defined in, or accommodated by, national and international laws, agreements and declarations. The TRR concept can form the basis for *sui generis* systems for protection and benefit-sharing. Also, it could be implemented locally, nationally and internationally as a set of principles to guide the process for dialogue between Indigenous and local communities, and governmental and non-governmental institutions. Traditional Resource Rights could, for example, guide the development of innovative contracts providing benefits to local communities in exchange for the transfer of information and biogenetic material.

In short, TRR-guided negotiations can offer challenging opportunities for new partnerships based on increased respect for Indigenous Peoples and their knowledge, new codes of ethics and standards of conduct, socially and ecologically responsible practices, and holistic approaches to sustainability. At the very least TRR-oriented discussions are certain to be more fruitful than those based on intellectual property rights because Traditional Resource Rights bring the environmental concerns of local communities, and issues relating to sustainable development and global trade, into the human rights debate. The process of developing Traditional Resource Rights will involve further dialogue, debate and consciousness-raising.

Traditional Resource Rights consists of the following bundles of rights, which are supported by the legally and non-legally binding agreements stated in Table 10.1.

The transfer of plant and animal genetic materials takes on a new dimension since such materials should appropriately be seen as technological transfers as they are the application of traditional knowledge and lifeways systems. The establishment of global funds, such as the one for "Farmers' Rights" to compensate local farmers for their "contributions in conserving, improving and making available plant genetic resources"[48], will become essential to effect the equitable sharing of the benefits of biodiversity conservation. The provision of funding, loans and foreign aid (by nations, multilateral lending institutions and other agencies), affecting and involving Indigenous Peoples, should require the development of TRR *sui generis* provisions.

10.6 COMPLIANCE WITH INTERNATIONAL STANDARDS

The enforcement of international law and policy, relating to the human and environmental rights of Indigenous Peoples, is often inadequate with the possible exception of *Convention on the Rights of the Child, ILO 169* and the optional protocol under the *Convention on Civil and Political Rights*. Regional human rights conventions (Europe and the Americas) arguably have stronger enforcement and complaint mechanisms. Increasingly, remedies and settlements being sought by Indigenous Peoples involve co-management regimes. Many disputes, such as the *Awas Tingni* case discussed below, arise out of resource allocation and management decisions on Indigenous lands that are made without their involvement.

TABLE 10.1 Traditional Resource Rights[47]

RIGHT (bundle)	SUPPORTING AGREEMENTS: legally binding	SUPPORTING AGREEMENTS: non-legally binding
Human rights	ICESCR, ICCPR, CDW, CERD, CG, CRC, NLs	UDHR, DDRIP, VDPA
Right to self-determination	ILO169, ICESCR, ICCPR	DDRIP, VDPA
Collective rights	ILO169, ICESCR, ICCPR	DDRIP, VDPA
Land and territorial rights	ILO169, NLs	DDRIP
Right to religious freedom	ICCPR, NLs	UDHR
Right to development	ICESCR, ICCPR, ILO169	DDHRE, DDRIP, DHRD, VDPA
The right to privacy	ICCPR, NLs	UDHR
Prior informed consent	CBD, NLs	DDRIP
Environmental integrity	CBD	RD, DDHRE
Intellectual property rights	CBD, WIPO, GATT, UPOV, NLs	
Neighbouring rights	RC, NLs	
Right to enter into legal agreements, such as contracts and covenants	NLs	
Cultural property rights	UNESCO-CCP, NLs	

TABLE 10.1 Traditional Resource Rights[47] (cont'd)

Right to protection of folklore	NLs	UNESCO-WIPO, UNESCO-F
Right to protection of cultural heritage	UNESCO-WHC, NLs	UNESCO-PICC
Recognition of cultural landscape	UNESCO-WHC	
Recognition of customary law and practice	ILO169, NLs	DDRIP
Farmers' Rights		FAO-IUPGR

KEY:

Legally binding agreements in force (with number of State Parties)

CBD:	Convention on Biological Diversity (1992)
CDW:	Convention on the Elimination of all Forms of Discrimination Against Women
CERD:	Convention on the Elimination of all Forms of Racial Discrimination (1966)
CG:	Convention on the Prevention and Punishment of the Crime of Genocide (1948)
CRC:	Convention on the Rights of the Child
GATT:	Final Act Embodying the Results of the Uruguay Round of Multilateral Trade Negotiations (1994)
ICESCR:	UN International Covenant on Economic, Social and Cultural Rights (1966)
ICCPR:	UN International Covenant on Civil and Political Rights (1966)
ILO169:	International Labour Organisation Convention 169: Convention Concerning Indigenous and Tribal Peoples in Independent Countries (1989)
NLs:	National laws
RC:	Rome Convention for the Protection of Performers, Producers of Phonograms and Broadcasting Organisations (1961)
UNESCO:	UNESCO Convention Concerning the Protection of the World Cultural and Natural Heritage (1972) (WHC)
UNESCO:	UNESCO Convention on the Means of Prohibiting and Preventing the Illicit Import, Export and Transfer of Ownership of Cultural Property (1970) (CCP)

TABLE 10.1 Traditional Resource Rights[47](cont'd)

UPOV:	International Union for the Protection of New Varieties of Plants (1961, revised in 1972, 1978 and 1991)
WIPO:	The World Intellectual Property Organisation, which administers international IPR agreements, such as:
	The Convention of Paris for the Protection of Industrial Property (1883, revised most recently in 1967)
	The Berne Convention for the Protection of Literary and Artistic Works (1886)
	The Madrid Agreement Concerning the International Registration of Trademarks (1891)
	The Lisbon Agreement for the Protection of Appellations of Origin and their International Registration (1958)
	The Patent Cooperation Treaty (1970)
Non-legal agreements	
DDHRE:	UN Draft Declaration of Principles on Human Rights and the Environment (1994)
DDRIP:	UN Draft Declaration on the Rights of Indigenous Peoples (formally adopted by the UN Working Group on Indigenous Populations in July 1994)
DHRD:	UN Declaration on the Human Right to Development (1986)
FAO-IUPGR:	FAO International Undertaking on Plant Genetic Resources (1987 version)
RD:	Rio Declaration (1992)
UDHR:	Universal Declaration of Human Rights (1948)
UNESCO-F:	UNESCO Recommendations on the Safeguarding of Traditional Culture and Folklore (1989)
UNESCO-PICC:	UNESCO Declaration on the Principles of International Cultural Cooperation (1966)
UNESCO-WIPO:	UNESCO-WIPO Model Provisions for National Laws on Protection of Expressions of Folklore Against Illicit Exploitation and Other Prejudicial Actions (1985)
VDPA:	UN Vienna Declaration and Programme of Action (1993)

10.6.1 Inter-American human rights regime

The Organization of American States (OAS) is a regional agreement, founded on the principle that States, comprising North, Central and South Americas, must unify their efforts to ensure personal liberty and social justice based on essential human rights. The OAS system promotes the protections of human rights by establishing substantive norms, supervisory institutions, and accessible petition procedures. Member States of the OAS must accept the human rights standards indicated in the *Charter of the Organization of American States* and the *American Convention on Human Rights* which are enforced by the Inter-American Commission on Human Rights.

The characteristic that distinguishes it from the United Nations system is the accessibility of the "communication" of a petition which is not restricted to Non-Government Organizations or member states. The individual, his family relations or a third party may initiate proceedings. The Commission can appoint moderators to oversee "friendly settlement" proceedings whereby the parties agree, acting in good faith, to attempt to reach a resolution of the violations and have a six month deadline. A restriction on the OAS system for the protection of human rights is that similar proceedings cannot be ongoing in the United Nations system concurrently. The finding of a violation of a member State and subsequent ruling of the Inter-American Commission is not legally binding on the parties. However, should the member State or Commission wish to pursue the matter further, they may petition the Inter-American Court of Human Rights for a hearing. The State must first accept the jurisdiction of the Court in order to make any decision legally binding on the parties and any non-compliance will be then enforceable in the domestic court system.

A recent decision of the Inter-American Court of Human Rights, *The Mayagna (Sumo) Indigenous Community of Awas Tingni v. The Republic of Nicaragua* (Awas Tingni), was a landmark decision of the Court that recognised duties of the State to demarcate and preserve the integrity of ancestral lands of Indigenous Peoples within its boundaries. It further recognised the right of all persons to expeditious and fair access to competent tribunals as not only a pillar of the American Convention but a Rule of Law in democratic societies.

The Court stated that it is not enough for Nicaragua to acknowledge the rights of Indigenous Peoples to their ancestral territories. It must put this recognition into practice by not engaging in actions that would diminish or affect Indigenous rights or interests in ancestral lands. This decision indicates that compliance may require an effective system of national implementation to give practical meaning to the legal rights of Indigenous Peoples. As compensation for moral damage, by allowing the harvesting of natural resources on traditional

Awas Tingni land without notification, consultation or compensation, the Nicaraguan government was required to pay a monetary award of US$50,000,000.

10.6.2 United Nations Permanent Forum on Indigenous Peoples

The announcement of the United Nations Decade for the World's Indigenous Peoples was indicative that the recognition of the fundamental rights of Indigenous Peoples will continue to evolve internationally and nationally. The Permanent Forum on Indigenous Peoples, a new subordinate organ of the United Nations Economic and Social Council, has an innovative internal organisation. It comprises eight representatives of Indigenous Peoples and eight experts chosen by the member states of the United Nations, a combination not previously seen in other United Nations entities. The Forum is in response to the growing body of work on Indigenous issues at the international level and the resounding success and participation of Working Groups[49] under the Human Rights Commission.

10.7 RECOGNITION OF INDIGENOUS RIGHTS IN INTERNATIONAL ENVIRONMENTAL LAW

10.7.1 World Heritage Convention

The *World Cultural and Natural Heritage Convention* (1972) provides for the identification and protection of cultural and natural heritage which is of "outstanding universal value." A World Heritage List is compiled under the auspices of UNESCO. The State parties to the Convention also provide some (limited) funds for the protection of the places on the list.

Examples of criteria for "cultural" properties require that they should:

- be an outstanding example of a traditional human settlement or land use which is representative of a culture (or cultures), especially when it has become vulnerable under the impact of irreversible change; or,
- be directly or tangibly associated with events or living traditions, with ideas, or with beliefs, with artistic and literary works of

outstanding universal significance. (Note: The Committee considers that this criterion should justify inclusion in the List only in exceptional circumstances or in conjunction with other criteria).

The criteria for "natural" properties includes places which:

- be outstanding examples representing major stages of earth's history, including the record of life, significant on-going geological processes in the development of landforms, or significant geomorphic or physiographic features; or
- be outstanding examples representing significant on-going ecological and biological processes in the evolution and development of terrestrial, fresh water, coastal and marine ecosystems and communities of plants and animals; or
- contain superlative natural phenomena or areas of exceptional natural beauty and aesthetic importance; or
- contain the most important and significant natural habitats for *in-situ* conservation of biological diversity, including those containing threatened species of outstanding universal value from the point of view of science or conservation.

Of the 754 properties listed sites (as at July 3, 2003), 582 were selected for their cultural importance and 149 for their natural significance. The rest are joint cultural and natural heritage sites.

The World Heritage Site of Tongariro National Park in New Zealand was selected due to the area's importance in Maori mythology and the sacred nature of the mountains. The World Heritage Committee concluded after considering its inclusion under the criteria that it was:

> an outstanding example of an associative cultural landscape tied to the cultural identity of the Maori people[50].

It would appear from the above that the Convention may be useful in protecting the cultural heritage of some Indigenous Peoples although the recognition of their concerns and values, through criteria, has been slow. A factor will be the willingness of the World Heritage Committee and "expert" advisers such as the World Conservation Union to pay heed to the interests of Indigenous Peoples when considering the inclusion of new nominations and already listed properties under the new criteria. However, ultimately, the extent to which the religious and cultural importance of places and objects for ethnic minorities and Indigenous Peoples is taken into account in the World Heritage List depends upon: (a) whether governments are willing to consult Indigenous Peoples; (b) whether national legislation to implement the Convention allows for a flexible or broad interpretation of "cultural and national heritage"; and (c) whether the Committee is prepared to take the view that cultural and natural properties important to Indigenous People constitute part of the heritage of humankind of sufficient importance to justify the expense of their protection[51]. Precedents do exist and some places that are important to an Indigenous People are now on the World Heritage List, such as Tongariro and Uluru Kata Tjuta (Ayers Rock) in Australia, which are sacred to Indigenous Peoples.

10.7.2 Convention to Safeguard Intangible Cultural Heritage

The intangible nature of much of Indigenous knowledge and culture has been an overriding cause for the incompatibilities that these communities face with intellectual property. By the early 1980s the awareness of the concept of intangible expressions of spirituality emerged[52]. In October 2003, by overwhelming majority, the member States of UNESCO adopted the *International Convention to Safeguard Intangible Cultural Heritage*.

The primary aims are to assist in the preservation of intangible heritage and customs, raise awareness at all levels and to integrate international participation. Specific requirements such as the drawing up of national inventories of cultural property to be protected, funding provided by States parties to UNESCO and the establishment of an Intergovernmental Committee.

This Convention, possibly a few years away from international implementation, illustrates the progressive developments towards Indigenous heritage and cultural protection. Further, it highlights the inadequacies of current legal attempts at providing protection through international intellectual property law.

10.7.3 The Convention on Biological Diversity

The *Convention on Biological Diversity* (CBD), seeks to guide and govern the use and conservation of biogenetic resources and traditional knowledge, while protecting local communities and Indigenous Peoples. The primary role and sovereignty of States is not challenged by the CBD. For example, Article 1 of the Convention states:

> The objectives of this Convention ... are the conservation of biological diversity, the sustainable use of its components and the fair and equitable sharing of the benefits arising out of the utilisation of genetic resources, including by appropriate access to genetic resources and appropriate transfer of relevant technologies, taking into account all rights over those resources and to technologies, and by appropriate funding.

The CBD places Indigenous and traditional knowledge, as well as traditional technologies and biogenetic resources, under nation-state sovereignty. Thus, no matter how liberal or generous provisions might appear, Indigenous Peoples are faced with a difficult conundrum. On the one hand their contributions, central to sustainable development and conservation, and rights as decision-makers and beneficiaries are recognised far beyond any previous international binding legal convention. However, Indigenous Peoples are reluctant to accept that ultimate control over resources lies with nation-states. Few Indigenous groups are willing to allow this *a priori* usurpation of their fundamental rights of self-determination no matter what promises and favourable interpretations may arise.

There is no reason to expect that the CBD will significantly contribute to the resolution of basic issues raised in the *Draft UN Declaration on the Rights of Indigenous Peoples*, namely their call for self-determination. However, it may help pave the way for the development of useful instruments that work towards more equitable partnerships with Indigenous Peoples.

Intellectual and cultural property rights and Traditional Resource Rights are clearly mechanisms for renegotiating the terms of these partnerships, which would be built upon the recognition, application, and compensation for Indigenous technologies and knowledge. Unfortunately, the CBD does not provide any explicit legal means to recognise, protect or compensate Indigenous Peoples, nor do such mechanisms exist in any other global legal forum.

The CBD itself refers to Indigenous Peoples in several significant sections. Article 8(j) is the most important of these sections:

> Subject to its national legislation, respect, preserve and maintain knowledge, innovations, and practices of Indigenous and local communities embodying traditional lifestyles relevant for the conservation and sustainable use of biological diversity and promote their wider application with the approval and involvement of the holders of such knowledge, innovations and practices and encourage the equitable sharing of the benefits arising from the utilisation of such knowledge, innovations and practices.

The Explanatory Guide to the CBD[53] notes that the proviso of subjecting these obligations to national legislation is unusual. The objectives of the article could be defeated since the wording implies that existing national legislation will take precedence. It also could be taken to imply that these concerns of Indigenous Peoples can be respected and preserved without addressing outstanding issues of Indigenous Peoples' rights to land and biological resources. It is obvious that such communities cannot continue these traditional practices in isolation from the land and biological resources that they need[54], and this recognition would be consistent with a growing body of international obligations such as *ILO 169* and the *Draft Universal Declaration on the Rights of Indigenous Peoples.*

If Article 8(j) is to be given legal meaning, which respects the concerns of Indigenous Peoples, some fundamental issues must be addressed:

- Indigenous concepts of conservation and sustainable use need to be much better understood by the wider national and international community. This should be facilitated by providing the resources, and access, for Indigenous Peoples to express these concepts directly in their own words. It also involves the recognition of wide cultural diversity even within small groups of Indigenous Peoples.
- Indigenous knowledge, innovation and practices are also poorly understood. Ethnographic and ethnobiological studies are limited and have not necessarily been undertaken for the policy purpose of conservation and sustainable use of biological diversity. The knowledge and practice is deeply embedded in Indigenous culture and appropriate research and policy development will need to be undertaken through Indigenous control or partnership.

- The expression "Indigenous and local communities embodying traditional lifestyles" needs to be critically considered. Many Indigenous Peoples, with strong traditional links and involvement, may be excluded from Article 8(j) because of their employment or where they live. In particular, it fails to consider the realities of contemporary Indigenous culture. The Australian Government briefing for the first meeting of the Conference of Parties stated that Australia considers that the phrase "embodying traditional lifestyles" should not imply that such communities do not change and would include Indigenous Peoples who follow traditional customs but do so in a "non-traditional" way.
- Contracting parties are meant to promote wider application of Indigenous knowledge with the approach and involvement of relevant Indigenous people. The holder/s of the knowledge or technology may be an individual, group or community. This will make the participatory provisions difficult to implement without sound applied anthropological studies and co-operation from individuals and communities. It is unclear who can, or should, determine the issue of who are the "holders" of knowledge and technology.
- The provision for the "equitable sharing" of benefits, from the wider applications, raises the same issues discussed above. Will "equity" be determined from an Indigenous perspective and does it imply the recognition of cultural and intellectual property rights held by Indigenous Peoples? At the very least Indigenous Peoples will expect that the wider application of their knowledge, practices and technology would be preceded by recognition of Indigenous concerns in the first part of Article 8(j). The analogy is with the idea of a "trust." If national governments are to use Indigenous knowledge, innovations and practices, for the wider public "good," then there should be a clear obligation towards the Indigenous Peoples who have developed them. It would be against the intent (see Preamble) of the Convention to construe Article 8(j) purely as a means of appropriating Indigenous knowledge without reciprocity. The legal and practical forms of this reciprocity remain to be worked out under the Convention.

Article 10(c) requires contracting parties to "Protect and encourage customary use of biological resources in accordance with traditional cultural practices that are compatible with conservation and sustainable use requirements."

Most of the Articles in the Convention recognise that non-Indigenous laws, policies and practices will change as we learn more about biodiversity and strategies to protect it. Indigenous culture has always been subject to some change. Indeed, this is why some of their biodiversity strategies and protective systems have been so effective. If expressions such as "customary use" and "traditional cultural practices" are interpreted as protecting only past, or existing, uses and practices this would deny contemporary Indigenous self-determination and undermine many of the purposes of the Convention. The relevant focus is Indigenous sustainable use. Judgments about "traditionality" will impede Indigenous co-operation on these issues.

Some of these specific Indigenous Peoples' issues have been dealt with in a Work Programme of the CBD Conference of Parties (COP) from 1996 onwards. The COP (VI/10) requested that the CBD Working Group on Article 8(j) address the issue of *sui generis* systems for the protection of traditional knowledge and identified the following issues on which to focus:

a. Clarification of relevant terminology;
b. Compiling and assessing existing Indigenous, local, national and regional *sui generis* systems;
c. Making available this compilation and assessment through the clearing-house mechanism of the Convention;
d. Studying existing systems for handling and managing innovations at the local level and their relation to existing national and international systems of intellectual property rights, with a view to ensure their complementarity;
e. Assessing the need for further work on such systems at the local, national, regional and international levels;
f. Identifying the main elements to be taken into consideration in the development of *sui generis* systems;
g. The equitable sharing of benefits arising from the utilisation of traditional knowledge, innovations and practices of Indigenous and local communities, taking into account the work carried out by the Intergovernmental Committee Intellectual Property and Genetic Resources, Traditional Knowledge and Folklore with a view to promote mutual supportiveness, and existing regional, subregional, national and local initiatives.[55]

The latest COP and Ad-hoc meetings (2003) focused on improving both conceptual approaches and regulatory and implementation strategies for better State application of Article 8(j).[56] Recognition of the following illustrate the widening of international legal concepts: definitional problems of Article 8(j), inappropriateness of codifying traditional knowledge by Western scientific methods and also intellectual property law outside a *sui generis* approach, and the need for research ethics to formulate codes of conduct when studying traditional knowledge and customs.

Recommendations for practical improvements include: strengthening importance of participation by Indigenous communities, capacity building within States with the aid of indicators to measure retention and loss of traditional knowledge and cultures, requesting States to identify key threatening processes against the intentions of this Article, and adherence to structured report writing to comprehensively illustrate the nations position on the application of Article 8(j).

Article 6 requires Contracting Parties to develop national strategies, plans or programmes for the conservation and sustainable use of biodiversity. This is one of the most important obligations for implementation, under the Convention.

The identification and monitoring provisions in Article 7 involve national surveys or inventories of biological diversity. Article 14 deals with environmental impact assessment and minimising adverse impacts. Those activities must involve affected Indigenous Peoples in a significant way. These Articles will provide important bases for Indigenous participation in planning for biodiversity conservation at the national and local levels and complement the rights in Articles 8(j) and 10(c) of the CBD.

10.7.3.1 CBD intellectual and cultural property issues

A close analysis of the CBD reveals a serious risk that Indigenous Peoples will be seen as a "resource" for biological diversity rather than as Peoples who hold legal and cultural rights in relation to it. This poses serious ethical and practical issues in seeking to involve Indigenous Peoples. Indigenous knowledge is a considerable source of wealth in the pharmaceutical and other industries and a constant focus of research activity. At the present time, virtually none of the profits are returned to Indigenous Peoples. Several Articles in the CBD are primarily concerned with promoting commercial access to genetic resources and promoting the commercial access and transfer of technology. Articles 15 and 16 make no specific provisions for Indigenous Peoples and they have to be read in the context of the earlier articles such as 8(j).

The promotion of access to genetic resources and proposals to patent genes, could eventually deny Indigenous people the biological resources they have managed for thousands of years. These issues are of concern to Indigenous and non-Indigenous Peoples. The provisions for increased access to genetic resources need to be considered in the context of proposals to patent animal and life forms with the possible reduction in biodiversity because of monopolies in ownership and control.

The provisions for the access and transfer of knowledge and technology (Articles 16, 17 and 18) include Indigenous and traditional knowledge and technology. The term "technology" can encompass such knowledge and technology (in Article 16) and it is explicitly referred to in Articles 17 and 18. The only basis for Indigenous "control," "participation" and "benefit" is contained in Article 8(j). The scene is set for wide use of Indigenous knowledge and practices relating to biodiversity. However, few jurisdictions have developed legislation and Codes of Conduct which will ensure that some of the benefits are returned to Indigenous communities.

One strategy for Indigenous Peoples is to use existing intellectual property law for their own benefit where possible. At the same time, they are pushing for changes to intellectual property laws to encompass their cultural concerns and collective forms of "ownership." Proposals for national biodiversity laws will need to consider existing and alternative frameworks for addressing the intellectual and cultural property rights appropriate for Indigenous Peoples.

The language of the CBD, however, encourages rather than obliges States to protect the rights of Indigenous Peoples and to develop national legislation to respect, preserve and maintain the knowledge, innovations and practices of traditional Peoples. National laws are required to protect the intellectual property and traditional resource rights of communities embodying traditional lifestyles. The active approval by and involvement of Indigenous, traditional and local communities in conservation and development activities is fundamental for the successful implementation of the CBD. Furthermore, equitable sharing of benefits and development of effective forms for compensation are critical, as are mechanisms to protect local communities from the adverse effects of external technologies that weaken their effectiveness in conservation efforts.

Much research is needed to understand the effectiveness of traditional technologies. Research, monitoring, and inventory criteria, priorities, and methods need to be guided and controlled by Indigenous and local communities. Finally, to successfully implement the provisions of the CBD, financial mechanisms will have to be made available to Indigenous and local communities.

10.7.4 International Convention to Combat Desertification in Countries Experiencing Serious Drought and/or Desertification

The *International Convention to Combat Desertification in Countries Experiencing Serious Drought and/or Desertification* 1994, does not specifically mention Indigenous or traditional Peoples, but it does give significant emphasis to local Peoples, local communities, local populations, and local organisations. It also recognises local and traditional knowledge, know-how, practice, and skills. These are mentioned throughout the text, but given prominence in Article 17.

Article 9 calls for the preparation and implementation of National Action Programmes (NAPs), including regional and subregional programmes, to combat desertification. These programmes call for a participatory process based on lessons from field action, as well as the results of research. These NAPs are similar to the national plans called for in the CBD, and they should specify the respective roles of government, local communities and land users and the resources available and needed.

Article 10(3) allows that NAPs can include such things as local and regional early warning systems, strengthening of food security systems (including storage and marketing), and establishment of "alternative livelihood projects that could provide incomes in drought prone areas." Article 16 deals with information collection, analysis and exchange. Data banks and networks are called for that address the needs of local communities and ensure the adequate protection and return for local and traditional knowledge that is provided.

Article 17 deals with research and development and requires Signatories to:

> protect, integrate, enhance and validate traditional and local knowledge, know-how and practices, ensuring, subject to their respective national legislation and/or policies, that the *owners*

> *of that knowledge will directly benefit on an equitable basis and on mutually agreed terms from any commercial utilisation of it or from any technological development derived ...*

Article 18 treats the subjects of transfer, adaptation and development of technology. Article 19 calls for capacity building, educational, and public awareness measures, including training in alternative technologies, conservation, and research. The Article also calls for action:

> by fostering the use and dissemination of the knowledge, know-how and practices of local people in technical cooperation programmes, wherever possible;
> by adapting, where necessary, relevant environmentally sound technology and traditional methods of agriculture and pastoralism to modern socio-economic conditions ...

This raises serious issues about what, if any, mechanisms will be used to protect Indigenous rights to intellectual and cultural property.

Articles 20 and 21 deal with financial resources and mechanisms and call for assistance from the Global Environmental Facility (GEF) and international lending institutions. It also recognise debt swaps "and other creative mechanisms." Article 21(3) calls on States to utilise participatory processes involving non-governmental organisations, local groups and the private sector, in raising funds, in elaborating as well as implementing programmes and in assuring access to funding by groups at the local level.

A "Global Mechanism" is also established in Article 21(5) to guide, inform, advise and facilitate States in their attempts to finance relevant programs and projects. Such a mechanism should address the specific concerns of Indigenous, traditional, and local communities.

In general, the *Convention to Combat Desertification* (COD) offers significant promise to some local communities and, in as much as Indigenous communities are local communities, this should not go unnoticed. As with the CBD, the call for wider use and application of local and traditional know-how, knowledge, practice, and skills may be well-intentioned, but without adequate provisions for protection and just compensation for such use, such a call is dangerous.

The provisions of the *Convention to Combat Desertification* go further than the CBD in their protection of intellectual, cultural, and scientific property rights. However, no specific mechanisms are proposed, nor even any process to develop such provisions. This situation should signal to Indigenous and local communities an even greater and more urgent need to develop their own guidelines for technology access, transfer, and protection.

Although the COD has somewhat stronger wording in support of local communities and their traditional knowledge, know-how, and practices, it suffers the same problems as the CBD. These include extension of State sovereignty over traditional resources. It recognises and only tacit guarantees of Indigenous rights. Furthermore, the COD does not enjoy the general application and international grassroots support of the CBD. Consequently it is less likely that the COD will be moulded by public sentiment in favour of Indigenous Peoples. Nonetheless, there is no reason that such pressures could not be mobilised, since the *Convention to Combat Desertification* is yet another major international agreement that can and should serve as a pivotal point for the integration of human and environmental rights.

10.8 NATIONAL RECOGNITION OF CUSTOMARY LAW

Some nations have recognised the customary laws of Indigenous Peoples to use and manage their knowledge and biological resources through the common law or through statute. In the Canadian[57], New Zealand[58], and Australian experience the recognition of native title has encompassed related customary laws for the use of land and natural resources. In *Mabo v. Queensland*[59], the Australian High Court recognised the existence of native title which entitles Indigenous Peoples in Australia to the use and enjoyment of ancestral lands in accordance with their unique laws and customs. Four judges—Brennan, Dean, Gaudron, and Toohey, JJ—explicitly rejected a narrow view of "traditional law or custom." Justice Brennan stated:

> Of course in time the laws and customs of any people will change and the rights and interests of the members of the people among themselves will change too. But so long as the people remain as an identifiable community, the members of whom are identified by one another as members of that community living under its laws and customs, the communal native title survives to be enjoyed by the members according to the rights and interests to which they are respectively

> entitled under the traditionally based laws and customs, as currently acknowledged and observed. It is immaterial that the laws and customs have undergone some change since the Crown acquired sovereignty provided the general nature of the connection between the Indigenous people and the land remains.[60]

A Canadian Supreme Court Case has decided that the Canadian Federal Government owes a fiduciary obligation to Indigenous Peoples when they dispose of ancestral or reserve land[61]. This Court also held that native title includes practices that form an integral "part" of an Indigenous community's distinctive culture such as the Indigenous use of fisheries[62]. An argument can be made that native title necessarily includes Indigenous management of marine resources, wildlife, natural resources, land and waters the intellectual and cultural property associated with it.

In the context of Canada, the recognition of native title has led to the negotiation of some modern treaties which settle Indigenous land claims, allocate rights to natural resources (and royalties from their exploitation) and set up comprehensive regimes for Indigenous participation in environmental assessment, development decisions and the management of land, seas, natural resources and wildlife (Canadian Regional Agreements)[63]. Native title rights and Regional Agreements are granted constitutional protection[64].

The jurisprudence, whereby longstanding treaties between governments and Indigenous Peoples are being interpreted in the modern context, also gives greater emphasis and recognition to Indigenous customary laws relating to the sustainable use and management of biological resources and associated intellectual and cultural property.

10.9 CONCLUSION

The international law and policy relating to human rights, including the intellectual and cultural property rights, of Indigenous Peoples, is evolving rapidly. It currently falls short of the *sui generis* system for protecting the integrated rights of Indigenous people that Posey advocates. However, it is becoming increasingly clear that this type of system accords closely with a growing body of international law and policy specifically relating to Indigenous rights and the aspirations of Indigenous Peoples for self-determination.

In many contexts the global recognition of the integrated human and environmental rights of Indigenous Peoples would facilitate sustainable development and benefit the wider community. This reality should not obscure the many conflicts over priorities and strategies that can occur between the Indigenous Peoples and the environmental movement. Much work remains to be done in understanding human rights, environment and development rights and specific Indigenous rights. The sometimes strained relationship between the environmental and Indigenous rights movements raises fundamental ethical, legal and moral issues.

In some situations there is desperate urgency to meet basic needs and alleviate poverty in Indigenous communities. There are limited experiences with poverty reduction specifically directed at Indigenous Peoples.[65] The International Working Group for Indigenous Affairs has published a series of articles discussing needs-based approaches versus rights-based approaches[66] Maria Quispe concludes that this dichotomy can be a trap when planning economic and social policy involving Indigenous Peoples. A rights-based approach usually tries to:

1. Make People's needs become a right;
2. Promote Peoples knowledge about the existence of their rights; and
3. Develop political strategies to make people's rights become reality.[67]

The argument continues that we should never be afraid to re-think certain rights and how we try and make them mean something beneficial.[68] Traditional rights and development approaches have failed Indigenous Peoples and they are increasingly irrelevant to Indigenous self-determination and sustainable development:

> There is a need to further develop an integrated approach to working with Indigenous Peoples' rights and development simultaneously as it would contribute to the on-going work on designing effective poverty reduction strategies.[69]

ENDNOTES

1 The author wishes to dedicate this chapter to her good friend and colleague Dr Darrell Addison Posey from the Oxford Centre for Environment Ethics and Society. Darrell died on March 7, 2001 after many decades of incredibly courageous activism and academic work promoting the rights of Indigenous

Peoples particularly in relation to their intellectual and cultural property rights. This chapter draws on his fundamentally important life long work, as so many others have throughout the world. His rare generosity, intellect and leadership will be greatly missed.

2 The World Conservation Union, World Wide Fund for Nature and United Nations Environment Programme, *Caring for the Earth*, 1991.

3 Johnson, M. 1992. *Lore: Capturing Traditional Environmental Knowledge.* Dene Cultural Institute/IDRC, Hay River, page 4.

4 IUCN Inter-Commission Task Force on Indigenous Peoples, *Indigenous Peoples and Sustainability Cases and Actions*, IUCN, The Netherlands, 1997. The author was a member of the IUCN Inter-Commission Task Force on Indigenous Peoples.

5 Posey, D. A. 1999. Introduction: Culture and Nature—The Inextricable Link. *Cultures and Spiritual Values of Biodiversity*, UNEP, page 7.

6 Hansen, S. A., and VanFleet. 2003. Traditional Knowledge and Intellectual Property: A Handbook on Issues and Options for Traditional Knowledge Holders in Protecting their Intellectual Property and Maintaining Biological Diversity. *AAAS*, page 3.

7 UNEP. 1992. *Saving Our Planet: Challenges and Hopes*, Nairobi, Kenya.

8 Rural Advancement Foundational International. 1994. *Conserving Indigenous Knowledge: Integrating Two Systems of Innovation*, Commissioned by the United Nations Development Programme, New York, page 3.

9 UN ESOSOC (1986) *Study of the Problem of Discrimination Against Indigenous Populations*, United Nations Economic and Social Council, E/CN.4Sub.2/1986/7 and Add.1-4.

10 Posey Supra Note 4 at page 4.

11 UN Economic and Social Sub-Commission on Prevention of Discrimination of Minorities, *Study on the Protection of Cultural and Intellectual Property of Indigenous Peoples*, undertaken by Special Rapporteur, Erica-Irene Daes.

12 ATSIC Indigenous Reference Group, *Our Culture: Our Future*, written and researched by Janke T., and Frankel M., Michael Frankel & Company and Terri Janke, 1998, pages 47–48.

13 Yamin, F. and D. Posey. 1993. Indigenous Peoples, Biotechnology And Intellectual Property Rights. 2(2), *Review of European Community and International Environmental Law*, 143.

14 *Ibid.*

15 *United Nations Conference on Environment and Development: Convention on Biological Diversity*, June 5, 1992 UNEP/Bioprospecting.Div./N7BINC5/4, reprinted in 31 I.L.M. 818 (1992) (entered into force Dec 29, 1993).

16 United Nations Conference on the Human Environment Stockholm, 1972, at page 2.

17 *Cocoyoc Declaration*, 1974.

18 *Declaration of San Jose* UNESCO, 1981.

19 Clinton, R. N. 1990. The Rights of Indigenous Peoples as Collective Group Rights. 32 *Arizona Law Review*, 739 at page 740.

20 Posey, Supra Note 4 at pages 3–16.

21 *Ibid* at page 3.

22 GA. Resolution 128, UN GAOR (41st Meeting), UN Doc. A/Res/41/128 (1986).

23 Craig, D. & D. Ponce Nava, 1995. Indigenous Peoples' Rights and Environmental Law. In *UNEP's New Way Forward: Environemental Law & Sustainable Development*. Edited by Sun Lin & Y. Kurukulasuriya.

24 *Plan of Implementation* by World Summit on Sustainable Development (September 4, 2002)

25 See Ward, E., *Indigenous Peoples between Human Rights and Environmental Protection*, Copenhagen: Danish Human Rights Centre, 1993, at pages 121–122.

26 *Ibid.*

27 Hansen and VanFleet, see note 6 above.

28 *Ibid.*

29 Meeting of Experts on Human Rights and Environment—Geneva, May 16–18, 1994.

30 IUCN, *Draft Covenant on Environment and Development*, (2nd ed.) Commission on Environmental Law, 2000. The latest Draft can be accessed through the IUCN ELP website: (http://www.iucn.org/themes/law).

31 UN, Final Text (16 January 2002) *Meeting of Experts on Human Rights and the Environment* , OHCHR.

32 *Ibid.*

33 Craig, D., N. Robinson, and K.L. Koh, eds. 2002. *Capacity Building for Environmental Law in the Asian and Pacific Region ; Approaches and Resources* (Two Volumes), Asian Development Bank, Manila. See vol. 1, chapter 11: "Judicial Decisions and Alternative Dispute Resolution".

34 GR No 101083, July 30, 1993.

35 See note 16 above at page 2.

36 *Ibid* at page 2.

37 *Ibid* at page 3.

38 *Ibid* at page 3.

39 *Ibid* at page 3.

40 Shutkin, W. A. 1991. International Human Rights Law and the Earth: the Protection of Indigenous Peoples and the Environment. 31, 3, *Virginia Journal of International Law*, 479–511 at page 487.

41 *Ibid* at page 488.

42 Brownlie, I., in Crawford (ed.), *Rights of Peoples*, 1998, at page 16.

43 Posey, D., *Traditional Resource Rights: International Protection and Compensation for Indigenous Peoples and Local Communities*, IUCN, Gland, Switzerland, 1996.

44 For further discussion and Guidelines see IUCN Task Force on Indigenous Peoples, *Indigenous Peoples and Sustainability: Cases and Actions* (1997), Beltran, J., and Phillips,A., *Indigenous Peoples and Protected Areas: Principles, Guidelines and Case Studies*, IUCN, Gland, Switzerland (2000) and Craig, D "Recognising Indigenous Rights through Co-Management regimes: Canadian and Australian Experiences," (2002) vol. 6, *New Zealand Journal of Environmental Law* ; pages 199–255.

45 *Agreement on Trade Related Aspects of Intellectual Property Rights*, April 15, 1994, Marrakesh Agreement Establishing the World Trade Organisation, Annex 1C, GATT Doc. MTN/FAII- A1C, 33 I.L.M. 1197.

46 In Van der Vlist, L., ed., *Voices of the Earth*, Centre for Indigenous Peoples and International Books, Amsterdam, Netherlands, pages 217–239.

47 This table is based on a similar production in Posey, see note 43 above at page xiv.

48 Food and Agriculture Organisation of the United Nations, Resolution 4/89.

49 Under the Sub-Commission on the Protection and Promotion of Human Rights, the Working Group on Indigenous Populations comprised of a panel of experts created a Draft Declaration of Indigenous Rights and provided a platform for Indigenous issues. Under the direction of the Commission on Human Rights, the Working Group on the Draft Declaration on the Rights of Indigenous Peoples continues the shaping of the Draft Declaration for adoption of the Commission and is comprised of member states with the consultation and extensive participation of Indigenous groups.

50 See (http://www.unesco.org/whc/nwhc/pages/doc/main.htm) for more information about this and all other World Heritage sites.

51 Posey, see note 43 above at pages 54–55.

52 UNESCO, General Conference 32nd Session, Press Release, available online: (http://portal.unesco.org/en/ev.php@URL_ID=16783&URL_DO=DO_TOPIC&URL_SECTION=201.html) (accessed November 18, 2003).

53 IUCN Environmental Law Centre, *The Convention on Biological Diversity: An Explanatory Guide*, Bonn, IUCN Biodiversity Program, 1994, at page 48.

54 *Ibid* at page 93.

55 Working Group on Article 8(j) and Related Provisions of the Convention on Biological Diversity, "Conference of the Parties," UNEP/CBD/COP/6/20, Paragraph 34, available online: (http://www.biodiv.org/programmes/socio-eco/traditional/decisions.asp) (accessed November 18, 2003).

56 *Ibid*. See also Ad-Hoc Open Ended Inter-Sessional Working Group on 8(j) Provisions of the Convention on Biological Diversity, "Composite Report on the Status and Trends Regarding the Knowledge, Innovations and Practices of Indigenous and Local Communities Relevant to the Consideration and Sustainable User of Biodiversity" UNEP/CBD/WG8J/3/4, September 28, 2003, available online: (http://www.biodiv.org/doc/meeting.asp?wg=WG8J-03) (accessed November 18, 2003).

57 See *Calder v. Attorney General for British Columbia* 1973 34 DLR (3rd) 145.

58 *Te Weehi v. Regional Fisheries Officer* 1986 1 NZLR 680.

59 *Mabo v. State of Queensland* 1992 175 CLR 1.

60 *Ibid* at 61 and 70.

61 *Guerin v. the Queen* (1983) 144 DLR (3rd) 193 S. C.

62 *R v. Sparrow* (1990) 1 SCR 1, 75.

63 See Netheim, G., D. Craig, and G. Meyers. 2002. *Indigenous Governance Structures: A Comparative Analysis of Land and Resource Management Rights*, Australian Institutions for Aboriginal and Torres Strait Islander Studies, Canberra.

64 Section 35(i) of the *Canadian Constitution Act.*

65 IWGIA "Indigenous Poverty: an Issue of Rights and Needs" *Indigenous Affairs1/03*: 46.

66 *Ibid.*

67 *Ibid* at page 38.

68 *Ibid.*

69 *Ibid* at page 46.

CHAPTER 11

Bioprospecting and Biopiracy

MICHAEL BLAKENEY*

11.1 BIODIVERSITY CONSERVATION

A significant contribution has been made by the knowledge of indigenous peoples and traditional farmers in the development of new crop types and biodiversity conservation. These groups have been an important agency in the conservation of plant genetic resources and the transmission of these resources to seed companies, plant breeders and research institutions. They have not typically been paid for the value they have delivered, whereas breeders and seed companies have resorted to intellectual property rights to recover their development expenditures. On the other hand, farmers who utilise improved varieties are obliged to pay for them.

The economic value of biological diversity conserved by traditional farmers for agriculture is difficult to quantify.[1] It has recently been suggested that "the value of farmers' varieties is not directly dependent on their current use in conventional breeding, since the gene flow from landraces to privately marketed cultivars of major crops is very modest"[2] because "conventional breeding increasingly focuses on crosses among elite materials from the breeders own collections and advanced lines developed in public institutions." On the other hand, those collections and advanced breeding lines are often derived from germplasm contributed by traditional groups.

An increasingly significant economic value of biodiversity is the extent to which it provides a reservoir of species available for

* Professor, Queen Mary College, University of London; Director, Queen Mary Intellectual Property Research Institute.

domestication, as well as genetic resources available for the enhancement of domestic species. The modern biotechnological revolution has enabled the engineering of desirable genetic traits from useful local species. It is estimated that about 6.5 per cent of all genetic research undertaken in agriculture is focussed upon germplasm derived from wild species and land races.[3]

This paper examines a number of recent cases in which traditional agricultural knowledge has been converted into intellectual property rights and explores the possibilities for the protection of this knowledge within the context of the Convention on Biological Diversity (CBD) and the WTO Agreement on Trade Related Aspects of Intellectual Property Rights and the various national implementations of these international obligations. Finally, the paper considers proposals for regularising bioprospecting contracts.

11.2 THE CONSULTATIVE GROUP ON INTERNATIONAL AGRICULTURAL RESEARCH

The Consultative Group on International Agricultural Research (CGIAR), founded in 1971, is an informal association of public and private donors that supports an international network of 16 international agricultural research centres (IARCs), each with its own governing body. The major sponsors are the FAO, the World Bank, the Rockefeller and Ford Foundations, the United Nations Development Programme, the United Nations Environment Programme and the aid programmes of the EU and a number of individual countries. With a budget of some US$340 million per annum, the CGIAR oversees the largest agricultural research effort in the developing world.

This agricultural research commenced with the work of Norman Borlaug, an American plant breeder, who won the Nobel prize in 1970 for his work in developing high-yielding wheat varieties for Mexico. Borlaug, was the founding father of the Centro Internacional de Mejoramiento de Maiz y Trigo (CIMMYT), which became the first of the CGIAR centres. Following the establishment of CIMMYT, 15 other international agricultural research centres have been established, each focussing on crops and materials of interest to developing countries.[4] In addition to conducting research, the GGIAR, supports a collection of germplasm, which currently comprises over 600,000 accessions of more than 3,000 crop, forage and pasture species which are held at the research centres. These germplasm collections are held under the auspices of the FAO "in trust for the benefit of the international community, in particular the developing countries", include up to 40 per cent of all unique samples of major food crops held by gene banks worldwide. The FAO Commission on Genetic Resources for Food and Agriculture determines the policy under which the network of *ex-situ* collections operate.

In addition to the so-called "designated germplasm", which is held under the trust relationship with the FAO, the various CGIAR centres have developed "elite germplasm" and biological tools, such as isogenic lines, mutants and mapping populations, from the materials which have been deposited with them.

Since the late 1990s, difficult questions have been raised concerning the legal status of the germplasm collections of the agricultural research institutes which are members of the CGIAR. At the time of their establishment, the questions of ownership and intellectual property rights in the collections were very much subordinated to the mission to increase crop yields to feed a burgeoning world population. It has only been in recent years that ownership issues have become important, either as a bargaining counter in North-South negotiations or as a source of revenue.[5]

11.3 BIOPIRACY EPISODES

The status of the CGIAR collections was questioned in a series of so-called biopiracy episodes in which intellectual property rights were sought in relation to germplasm obtained from a number of CGIAR centres.

11.3.1 The 1998 Australian "biopiracy" episode

Germplasm ownership concerns were raised in 1998 as a consequence of Plant Breeder's Rights applications made in Australia by a number of agricultural research institutes in relation to a peavine and a lentil which had been bred from genetic stock obtained from the CGIAR gene bank: International Centre for Agricultural Research in the Dry Areas (ICARDA), located in Aleppo, Syria.[6] A charter for ICARDA had been established in November 1975 on the basis of an agreement between the World Bank, FAO and UNDP and the Canadian International Development Research Centre (IDRC), as the executing agency. Subsequently establishment agreements were negotiated by IDRC with

Syria (June 28, 1976), Lebanon (July 6, 1977) and Iran (July 20, 1976). These parallel agreements provide for the establishment of ICARDA in "the region" defined as the "Near East, North Africa and the Mediterranean region". ICARDA's headquarters were established in Aleppo, Syria. The agreements also provided for the Chairman of CGIAR to declare that ICARDA has been established as a legal entity allowing IDRC's role to lapse. This formal step does not appear to have been taken. The question of ownership of the ICARDA collection was raised in the context of whether its Director-General acted in breach of trust obligations, which he owed in relation to ICARDA genetic material, in permitting the Australian agricultural research institutes to seek intellectual property rights in applications of that material.[7]

The February 14, 1998 issue of *New Scientist* contained an editorial and leading article on the alleged biopiracy of two Australian agricultural agencies. The two agencies: Agriculture Western Australia and the Grains Research and Development Corporation (GRDC) had apparently applied for Plant Breeder's Rights (PBR) under the Australian Plant Breeder's Rights Act, 1994, in relation to two species of chickpea which had been bred from material which had been provided by the International Crop Research Institute for the Semi-Arid Tropics (ICRISAT). These PBR applications had to meet the statutory tests prescribed in s.43 of the Act that the new variety has a breeder, that it is distinct, uniform and stable and that it has not been or has only recently been exploited. The Australian Plant Breeder's Rights Office did not have an opportunity to make a determination on these matters because the furore caused by these applications led to their withdrawal, prior to determination.

The *New Scientist* editorialised that "it was hard to imagine what two Australian government agricultural agencies thought that they were up to when they applied for property rights on chickpeas grown by subsistence farmers in India and Iran."[8] A feature article in the *New Scientist* carried an accusation from a spokesperson from the South Asian Network on Food, Ecology and Culture which described the PBR applications as "blatant biopiracy" by "privatising seeds that belong to our farmers and selling them back to us."[9]

Research by RAFI[10] suggested that there were numerous other instances of "biopiracy" by other Australian agricultural research institutes. Reacting to the biopiracy controversy, CGIAR called for a moratorium on the granting of intellectual property rights over plant germplasm held in its centres. CGIAR Chairman, Dr Ismail Serageldin, explained the call for a moratorium as "the strongest signal the CGIAR can send governments to ensure that these issues be resolved and the materials in the CGIAR remain in the public domain."[11] In Australia, serious concerns were expressed about the implications which such a moratorium would have, particularly for its cultivation of cereals. Consequently, to prevent a recurrence of this incident, the operating regulations of the Australian Plant Breeders Rights Office were amended to oblige applicants for PBRs in relation to varieties derived from germplasm obtained from CGIAR Centres, to document that such applications were made with the permission of the relevant Centre.

Responding to concerns about the impact of intellectual property rights upon the operation of the CGIAR, it commissioned a report on the use of proprietary technologies by CGIAR Centres by the International Service for National Agriculture Research (ISNAR), which operates as its legal advisory body.[12] The report noted the burgeoning use of proprietary technologies by the centres and recommended that they undertake audits of their intellectual property management policies. ISNAR established a Central Advisory Service to provide legal counsel for the centres on intellectual property matters.

An issue which has not yet been addressed by the CGIAR or the FAO is the question of the rights, if any, of the indigenous and traditional communities from which seeds might have been collected by the various CGIAR institutes. That collection may have been informed by the knowledge of those communities, or may have occurred without the communication by the collector to those communities of the implications of the act of collection.

11.3.2 Blight-resistant rice

In the late 1970s a strain of rice from Mali, *Oryza longistaminata*, was identified by a researcher, working in Cuttack, North India, as being resistant to bacterial blight, a disease which particularly afflicts rice. In 1978 this resistant sample was taken to the International Rice Research Institute (IRRI) in Los Banos, Philippines for further investigation. Over a 15-year period, IRRI researchers developed through conventional breeding, a high-yielding, blight-resistant strain of rice. The IRRI researchers identified that this resistance was contributed by a single locus called Xa21. A post-doctoral research fellow, Dr Ronald, from the University of California at Davis, who was working at IRRI, was permitted with co-workers at Stanford University to map, sequence and clone the Xa21 gene. The molecular mapping process was facilitated by the construction of a BAC (Biologically Active Compounds) library utilising a biological tool provided by IRRI.

On June 7, 1995 the Regents of the University of California filed a patent application for "Nucleic acids, from *Oryza sativa*, which encode leucine-rich repeat polypeptides and enhance *Xanthomonas* resistance in plants." The inventors named in the application were Dr Ronald and her co-workers. The patent was granted by the United States Patents and Trademark Office on January 12, 1999 (US patent 5,859,339).

This patent generated some controversy in CGIAR circles because it was perceived to compromise IRRI's research efforts and those of its clients in the rice-producing regions of Asia. Bacterial blight is not a particular problem for US rice producers and a primary effect of the patent was to prevent the export of bacterial-blight resistant rice, utilising the patent to the USA. This patent also raised the question of equitable compensation, at least for the traditional farmers of Mali who had conserved *O. longistaminata*. UC Davis dealt with the issue of compensation by establishing a Genetic Resources Recognition Fund (GRRF) as a mechanism to share benefits arising from the commercial utilisation of its patent. It was also acknowledged that in the absence of this sort of mechanism, it would have been "more difficult for the university in the future to obtain research access to developing countries' national genetic materials."[13]

UC Davis also agreed to allow non-commercial researchers access to the gene, provided they did not develop commercial products based on that gene. The University also agreed that "IRRI would have full rights to develop new rice varieties incorporating cloned Xa21 and distribute this material as well as the clone to developing countries".[14]

The attempts by UC Davis to provide a mechanism for the sharing of benefits with traditional peoples to be derived from its patent on Xa21 were analysed in a case study by the World Intellectual Property Organization and the United Nations Environment Programme.[15] This study found that with one exception, the traditional peoples of Mali regarded *O. longistaminata* as a weed with a very low grain yield. It concluded that in designing benefit-sharing arrangements:

- The stakeholders are not limited to the formal scientific research institutions of the country of origin of the genetic resource;

- The ethnobotanical knowledge of local PGRFA is not necessarily and only held by local landowning farmers, but can also be held by local communities that are landless and subsist on mixed modes of income;
- The ethnobiological knowledge is not limited to indigenous communities.[16]

This case study illustrates a number of the practical problems with proposals for benefit-sharing under the CBD. First, the research into the blight-resistant properties of *O. longistaminata* commenced prior to the CBD coming into force; secondly, the local farming and indigenous communities were largely unaware of these properties; and thirdly, the itinerant poor community, which made use of the rice would be unlikely to enjoy any of the benefits which UC Davis could make available. It is for this reason that benefit-sharing norms are being developed by the international community.

11.3.3 Enola beans

On April 13, 1999 the US Patent and Trademarks Office granted patent no. 5,894,079 to Larry Proctor for an invention described in the patent grant as relating to "a new field bean variety that produces distinctly colored yellow seed which remain relatively unchanged by season." On May 28, 1999, Larry Proctor also obtained a US Plant Variety Protection Certificate on the bean variety.

Larry Proctor, was the president of a Colorado-based (USA) seed company, POD-NERS. Upon the grant of the patent, this company was reported to have written to all thc importers of Mexican beans in the United States, requiring the payment of a royalty of six cents per pound.[17] According to Miguel Tachna Felix, of the Agricultural Association of Rio Fuerte, this would have meant an immediate drop in export sales, over 90 per cent. POD-NERS was reported to have brought infringement actions against two companies that were selling Mexican yellow beans in the US. In January 2000, the Mexican government announced that it would challenge the US patent. Jose Antonio Mendoza Zazueta, Under-Secretary of Mexican Rural Development, declared that "We will do everything necessary, anything it takes, because the defense of our beans is a matter of national interest."[18] RAFI denounced the yellow bean patent as "Mexican bean biopiracy" and demanded that the patent be legally challenged and revoked. RAFI formally requested that FAO and the CGIAR investigate the patent as a likely violation of their 1994 Trust agreement.[19]

On December 20, 2000 the CIAT filed a formal request for re-examination of the US patent concerning the yellow bean, which was alleged to be the Mexican Enola bean.[20] CIAT's official request for re-examination of the patent stated that the claims for inventiveness contained in the patent failed to meet the statutory requirements of novelty and non-obviousness, and ignored the prior art widely available in the literature.[21] The challenge was particularly critical of the patent's claim of exclusive monopoly on any *Phaseolus vulgaris* (dry bean) having a seed color of a particular shade of yellow, pointing out that "it will make a mockery of the patent system to allow statutory protection of a color *per se*." Although, there was no evidence that the patent owner obtained his yellow beans from CIAT's gene bank, the patent challenge noted that CIAT maintained some 260 bean samples with yellow seeds, and six of the accessions were "substantially identical" to claims made in the patent.[22]

CIAT's patent challenge also asserted that the yellow bean was "misappropriated" from Mexico, and that this was in breach of Mexico's sovereign rights over its genetic resources, as recognised by the CBD. The USPTO is currently determining this challenge.

11.3.4 Yacon

In November 1999, five traditional Peruvian varieties of yacon held in the genebank at the International Potato Centre (CIP) in Peru, were distributed to the Peruvian Ministry of Agriculture, which passed them to researchers in Japan. Yacon (*Smallantus sonchifolius*) an ancient Andean crop, is eaten raw as a fruit in the Andes. It has a high fructose content with a high percentage of insulin, and the leaves was reported to have anti-diabetic properties.[23] CIP's Potato Germplasm Curator, Dr. Zozimo Huaman, alleged that this distribution of yacon by CIP was in breach of its trust obligations, particularly because the biosafety requirements of the Centre were apparently not followed.[24] Japanese researchers, in a seminar at CIP in September 2000, indicated that the area cultivated with yacon in Japan had been greatly increased in recent years and that it was utilised as a vegetable, pickles and juices. They also reported that the National Shikoku Agriculture Experiment Station had released the first commercial variety named "Sarada-Otome" on August 25, 2000. Dr Huaman expressed concern that, apparently because of plant breeders' rights, the Japanese researchers were not prepared to send germplasm of "Sarada-Otome" to be tested in Peruvian farmers' fields. He questioned the equity of denying to a source country, new derivatives of deposited germplasm.[25]

Upon learning of Dr. Huaman's allegation, CIP requested its Genetic Resources Policy Committee (GRPC) to determine if any violation of the FAO agreement had occurred. The GRPC, chaired by Dr. M. S. Swaminathan, was established by CIP as an independent advisory committee made up of internationally-known scientists as well as representatives of the NGO community, private sector, and developing and developed country governments. The committee concluded that CIP had no right to interfere in Peru's sovereign decision to send the germplasm to Japan and commended CIP for its proper management of its germplasm held "in-trust."[26]

As is discussed below, one impact of intellectual property issues upon the CGIAR has been calls for the limitation of the availability of intellectual property rights in relation to plant genetic resources. Another approach has been to embrace the new legal reality. Some CGIAR Centres perceive that CGIAR-generated intellectual property might be used as a bargaining chip, to be traded for biological tools patented by the private sector. For example the *Policy on Intellectual Property* of the International Maize and Wheat Improvement Centre (CIMMYT) envisages that intellectual property protection may be sought "to facilitate the negotiation and conclusion of agreements for access to proprietary technologies of use to CIMMYT's research and in furtherance of its mission."[27] This proprietisation of public sector agriculture research is questioned, particularly by those NGOs opposed to patenting in the life sciences.[28]

11.3.5 Nuna beans

On March 21, 2000 a patent was granted to a US corporation[29] in relation to a "bean-nut popping bean" apparently derived from crosses involving at least 33 Andean nuna bean varieties from Peru, Bolivia, Ecuador, and Colombia. RAFI reported that a meeting of a tribunal of Indigenous elders from six Andean communities that grow nuna beans met in February 2001 and condemned the patenting as biopiracy of their Andean heritage and demanded that CIAT—The International Centre for Tropical Agriculture, the CGIAR Centre based in Cali, Colombia—uphold its obligation under a United Nations "trust agreement" to keep farmer-bred bean varieties in the public domain.[30]

RAFI reported the views of a number of scientists working with nuna who were concerned that the patent would limit improvements in the crop to the prejudice of the traditional Andean peoples. In particular it was observed that toasting nunas used less fuel than boiling beans, a feature important to economic and environmental conditions in areas of the world where fuel is scarce. Additionally, RAFI reported that the US patent also prejudiced a stratagem to use popping beans grown in the Andes as a substitute for illicit crops.

The patent was described as "particularly offensive to Andean farmers and indigenous people" because it extended to crosses involving at least 33 Andean nuna varieties traditionally bred and developed over centuries in Peru, Bolivia, Ecuador, all of which were freely provided by Andean farming communities, "who allowed their bean varieties to be put into the public realm in order to ensure the continued maintenance of the world's seed biodiversity." Nine of these varieties were held in CIAT's international bean collection as designated in-trust accessions, all being farmers' varieties collected in Peru.

This case has been adopted by a number of NGOs as a test of the international intellectual property community's resolve to support the conservation and development of indigenous knowledge.

11.3.6 Peruvian maca

Indigenous peoples' and farmers' organisations from the Andes and the Amazon meeting at the Ecological Forum in Lima, on June 28 denounced US patents on maca, the high-altitude Andean plant (of the *Cruciferae* [mustard] family) that has been grown for centuries by indigenous peoples in the Puna highlands of Peru, both as a staple food crop and for medicinal purposes.

The US patents were issued in relation to the Viagra-like therapeutic aspects of Maca.[31] The Ecological Forum requested that CIP, as promoter and protector of maca seed, take action to prohibit intellectual property claims in relation to all Andean crop germplasm and their genetic components, and indigenous knowledge related to these genetic materials.[32]

11.4 CGIAR'S RESPONSE TO THE "BIOPIRACY" EPISODES

In 1992, in anticipation of the Rio Earth Summit, the CGIAR had adopted a "Working Document on Genetic Resources and Intellectual Property." This provided that:

- Material from the genebanks at the centres will continue to be freely available in accordance with the 1989 CGIAR Policy on Plant Genetic Resources;
- Centres do not seek intellectual property protection unless it is absolutely necessary to ensure access by developing countries to new technologies and products; and
- [a]ny IPR acquired by a centre are exercised without compromising in any manner whatsoever the fundamental position of the CGIAR regarding the free access by developing countries to knowledge, technology, materials and plant genetic resources.[33]

In order to implement these obligations under the FAO-CGIAR Agreements, the Centres which have signed Agreements with the FAO make samples of in-trust germplasm available to requestors under a standard Material Transfer Agreement (MTA). Under this contractual agreement, when the recipient accepts the shipment of germplasm they are deemed to accept the terms of the standard MTA, which include the obligation not to claim any ownership or IPRs over the material. The obligations of the recipient include the obligation to ensure that all subsequent parties to whom the material is transferred also honour the same conditions.

One consequence of the biopiracy episodes was the establishment of a Central Advisory Service on Intellectual Property to inform the IP management of Centres. Another approach has been to embrace the new legal reality. Some CGIAR Centres perceive that CGIAR-generated intellectual property might be used as a bargaining chip, to be traded for biological tools patented by the private sector.[34]

The International Treaty on Plant Genetic Resources for Food and Agriculture, which was approved by the FAO Conference in November 2001 calls upon the CGIAR Centers to sign agreements with the Governing Body of the Treaty with regard to their *ex-situ* collections according to which, *inter alia*, "plant genetic resources for food and agriculture listed in Annex I ... shall be made available in accordance with the provisions set out in Part IV. Plant genetic resources for food and agriculture other than those listed in Annex I and collected before its entry into force that are held by IARCs shall be made available in accordance with the provisions of the MTA currently in use pursuant to agreements between the Centres and the FAO."

A Multilateral System ("MLS") was established by the International Treaty to facilitate access to plant genetic resources and for the fair and equitable sharing of benefits arising from their use.

11.5 THE CONVENTION ON BIOLOGICAL DIVERSITY (CBD)

The Rio Earth Summit, which was convened in June 1992, promulgated the Convention on Biological Diversity (CBD), The Rio Declaration on Environment and Development and Agenda 21. The CBD represented an attempt to establish an international programme for the conservation and utilisation of the world's biological resources[35] and for the "fair and equitable sharing" of the benefits arising from the utilisation of genetic resources[36]. "The single most divisive issue in the negotiations was the relationship between intellectual property rights and access to genetic resources."[37] The developing countries of the South, generally speaking the most substantial source of genetic resources, sought to use the CBD as a means of bargaining access to those resources for royalties, technology and research data. Thus the CBD contains articles on access to genetic resources (Art. 15); access to and the transfer of technology (Art. 16); informed consent and the distribution of benefits of biotechnological innovations (Art. 19). The industrialised group of countries, obviously the principal source of biotechnological innovation, insisted that the CBD did not conflict with intellectual property rights. Thus for example, Art. 16 (2) contains the statement that "In the case of technology subject to patents and other intellectual property rights, such access and transfer shall be provided on terms which recognise and are consistent with the adequate and effective protection of intellectual property rights."

Reflecting the uncomfortable political deal which was struck in bringing the CBD to conclusion, the language of the Convention is unfortunately vague. The positive affirmation of principles in a number of areas is qualified by vague transcendental values. Thus the respect for intellectual property affirmed by Art. 16 (2) is counterbalanced by the phrase in the same provision that "access to and the transfer of technology ... shall be provided and/or facilitated under fair and most favourable terms ..." Similarly, Art. 15(4) provides that "access [to genetic resources] where granted shall be upon mutually agreed terms." Art. 19(2) provides that "access ... to the results and benefits arising from biotechnologies ... shall be on mutually agreed terms." Since mutuality is a precondition for an agreement of any sort, these provisions may be mere rhetoric. On the other hand, they may be a guarantee against unilateral expropriation.

11.5.1 Scope of the CBD access regime

Article 1 of the CBD envisages "appropriate access to genetic resources" and "the fair and equitable sharing of benefits arising out of the utilisation of genetic resources." "Genetic resources" are defined in Art. 2 as meaning "genetic material of actual or potential value." The term "genetic material" is then defined in Art. 2 to mean "any material of plant, animal, microbiological or other origin containing functional units of heredity." On a strict analysis of this definition, it is suggested that biochemical extracts which do not contain DNA or RNA would be outside the scope of the CBD.[38] Thus the Convention would apply to seeds and cuttings and DNA extracted from a plant, such as a chromosome, gene, plasmid or any part of these such as the promoter part of a gene.[39]

Article 9 deals with "the conservation of components of biological diversity outside their natural habitats," for example, in germplasm and seed banks, botanical gardens, museums, laboratories and agricultural research institutions. This article calls for national legislation to provide for the acquisition, conservation, storage and management of these *ex-situ* collections. The access and benefit-sharing provisions of the CBD do not apply to the genetic resources of a country which were collected prior to the entry of the CBD into force in that country.[40] Thus a country with a pre-existing collection of genetic material has the sovereign right to control access to that collection, but has no legal right to insist upon a share of any benefits derived from the use of that collection. Also, the CBD applies to those genetic resources which originate in the country of a contracting party.[41]

11.5.2 Sovereign rights over genetic resources (Art 15 (1))

Article 15(1) of the CBD affirms "the sovereign rights of States over their natural resources" and provides that "the authority to determine access to genetic resources rests with the national governments and is subject to national legislation." This provision, dealing as it does with access to genetic resources, does not refer to the question of the ownership of genetic resources. This leaves unanswered the ownership issues raised by the creation of the CGIAR germplasm collections.

11.5.3 Mutually agreed terms, prior informed consent and benefit-sharing

Article 15(4) of the CBD envisages that where access is granted it will be subject to mutually agreed terms. Currently the conventional form of access agreement is the Material Transfer Agreement (MTA).[42] A number of the provisions of the CBD refer to the equitable sharing of benefits arising from the utilisation of the genetic resources of a signatory. Article 15(7) requires each Contracting Party to "take legislative, administrative or policy measures, as appropriate" and in accordance with a number of specified provisions of the Convention, "with the aim of sharing in a fair and equitable way, the results of research and development and the benefits arising from the commercial and other utilisation of genetic resources with the Contracting Party providing such resources." Article 8(j) envisages the "equitable sharing" of benefits with indigenous and local communities, arising out of the use of the traditional knowledge, innovations and practices of those communities. Article 21 provides for the establishment of a "mechanism" for the provision of financial resources to developing country parties to the CBD.

Complementary to the equitable sharing of benefits, the CBD provides for the access of developing country signatories to technologies which may result from the utilisation of the genetic resources which they may provide. Article 16(1) recites the importance of access to biotechnologies to attain the objectives of the CBD and Art 16(2) provides for the access to technologies by developing countries on "fair and equitable terms, including on concessional and preferential terms." Article 19(1) requires parties to take appropriate measures to "provide for the effective participation in biotechnological research activities by those Contracting Parties, especially developing countries, which provide the genetic resources for such research." Article 19(2) requires parties to "take all practicable measures to promote and advance priority access on a fair and equitable basis ... especially developing countries, to the results and benefits arising from biotechnologies based upon genetic resources provided by those Contacting Parties" on mutually agreed terms.

At the second Conference of the Parties (COP), held in Jakarta, from 6 to 17 November 1995, a Report including "Possible elements of guidelines on mutually agreed terms" was tabled.[43] The possible elements which were suggested to Parties for inclusion in access and benefit-sharing arrangements included, *inter alia*, "agreeing on respective *intellectual property rights* over the genetic resources and technologies developed using them." The 4th COP decided in Decision IV/8 to establish a Panel of Experts with the mandate "to draw upon all relevant sources ... in the development of a common understanding of basic concepts and to explore all options for access and benefit-sharing on mutually agreed terms including guiding principles, guidelines, and codes of best practice for access and benefit-sharing arrangements."

The Panel of Experts on Access and Benefit-sharing, at its first meeting, held in San José, Costa Rica, from October 4–8, 1999, concluded that one of the "key lessons with respect to promoting mutually agreed terms in access and benefit-sharing arrangements" is that "Contractual agreements, for the moment, are the main mechanism for gaining access to genetic resources and delivering benefits."[44] Considering that transaction costs have a significant impact on actual use of genetic resources, the Panel identified "standardised Material Transfer Agreements" as one of the mechanisms to reduce transaction costs.[45]

The 5th COP in Decision V/26 decided, *inter alia*, to establish an *Ad Hoc* Open-Ended Working Group on Access and Benefit-sharing with "the mandate to develop guidelines and other approaches for submission to the Conference of the Parties and to assist Parties and stakeholders in addressing the following elements as relevant to access to genetic resources and benefit-sharing, *inter alia*, terms for prior informed consent and mutually agreed terms; roles, responsibilities and participation of stakeholders; relevant aspects relating to *in-situ* and *ex-situ* conservation and sustainable use; mechanisms for benefit-sharing, for example through technology transfer and joint research and development; and means to ensure the respect, preservation and maintenance of knowledge, innovations and practices of indigenous and local communities embodying traditional lifestyles relevant for the conservation and sustainable use of biological diversity, taking into account, *inter alia*, work by the World Intellectual Property Organization on intellectual property rights issues.

The second Meeting of the Panel of Experts on Access and Benefit-sharing, which met in Montreal, from March 19–22, 2001, considered a Note by the Executive Secretary which highlighted certain aspects of developing instruments to assist in the elaboration of fair and equitable contractual arrangements. These included:

- To reduce transaction costs, measures could include standard Material Transfer Agreements and Umbrella Agreements, under which repeat access under expedited arrangements can be made;
- Mutually agreed terms should also include provisions on user obligations;
- Different resources and uses require different contractual arrangements. Therefore, to the extent possible, commercial arrangements should be anticipated at the outset;
- Benefits are often generated from the commercialisation of derivatives that use genetic resources as a source of innovation, such as synthesised products. In these instances, for fair and equitable benefit-sharing, it is important that the scope of contracts include the full range of biotechnology applications in addition to biological resources accessed;
- In order to reflect the increasing role of intermediaries in contractual arrangements and access-permitting mechanisms, a flexible and simple approach to protect the interest of all parties should be elaborated;
- Parties should be aware of relevant agreements that may pre-date an agreement under development.[46]

In its Report the Expert Panel noted that intellectual property clauses played a fundamental role access and benefit-sharing contracts and that there was “a need for awareness and capacity-building at all levels, as well as a need to develop up-to-date model intellectual property right clauses.” and that WIPO might assist in this regard.[47]

11.5.4 Indigenous and local communities

The Rio Declaration in Principle 22 stated that "Indigenous peoples and their communities ... have a vital role in environmental management and development because of their knowledge and traditional practices." Chapter 26 of Agenda 21 detailed the relationship which conference participants recognised between indigenous peoples and their lands. The Agenda, at para. 26.3(a), required governments:

> to establish a process to empower indigenous peoples and their communities' through measures that include:
> - recognition of their values, traditional knowledge and resource management practices with a view to promoting environmentally sound and sustainable development;
> - enhancement of capacity-building for indigenous communities based on the adaptation and exchange of traditional experience, knowledge and resource-management practices, to ensure their sustainable development;
> - establishment, where appropriate, of arrangements to strengthen the active participation of indigenous peoples and their communities in the national formulation of policies, laws and programs relating to resource management and other development processes that may affect them.

The Preamble to the CBD recognised the

> ... close and traditional dependence of many Indigenous and local communities embodying traditional lifestyles on biological resources, and the desirability of sharing equitably arising from the use of traditional knowledge, innovations and practices relevant to the conservation of biological diversity and sustainable use of its components.

Article 8(j) of the Convention required each signatory

> ... subject to its national legislation, respect, preserve and maintain knowledge, innovations and practices of indigenous and local communities embodying traditional lifestyles relevant for the conservation and sustainable use of biological diversity and promote their wider application with the approval and

> involvement of the holders of such knowledge, innovations and practices and encourage the equitable sharing of the benefits arising from the utilisation of such knowledge, innovations and practices.

The provisions of Art. 8(j) require implementation through national legislation. It is expressed to be subject to national legislation, in order to preserve legislation on this subject which predates the CBD.[48]

11.6 REGIONAL AGREEMENTS ON ACCESS AND BENEFIT-SHARING

The implementation of CBD principles has been attempted in two draft regional framework agreements: (a) the draft ASEAN Framework Agreement on Access to Biological and Genetic Resources ("the draft ASEAN Framework Agreement"); and (b) Decision 391 on a Common System on Access to Genetic Resources of the Commission of the Cartagena Agreement.

These framework agreements have been developed by regional economic integration organisations in an endeavour to set minimum standards for determining access to genetic resources within a region; to ensure that national access regulations are uniform and consistent with the identified minimum standards; and to strengthen the negotiating capacity of the member countries to the framework agreement. These framework agreements mirror the negotiating strategy of the earlier framework agreements on intellectual property.[49]

Article 16 of Decision 391 provides in Chapter I that "[a]ll access procedures must include the presentation, admission, publication and approval of an application, signature of a contract, issue and publication of the corresponding resolution and a declaratory record of actions linked with such access."

Contractual agreements may be used to establish the specific terms and conditions for access and benefit-sharing in respect of individual genetic resources and associated subject matter, such as derivatives or biodiversity-related traditional knowledge. Typically, it is required that the terms of the access contract shall comply with the contents of the framework agreement and the national access legislation of the relevant member country of the framework agreement. The Framework Agreements may also include provisions or measures pertaining to intellectual property issues which may relate to the rights and obligations to be established in the access contracts stipulated by the framework agreement.

The standards established in framework agreements are typically implemented into national law through national access legislation for genetic resources. Additionally, model laws for access to genetic resources are being developed by regional integration organisations, such as the Organization of African Unity. These model laws also foresee as an implementing tool for national access legislation the use of contractual agreements between the National Competent Authority and the concerned local community or communities on the one hand and the applicant or collector on the other.[50]

11.7 NATIONAL ACCESS LEGISLATION

More than 30 countries had reportedly promulgated, or were in the process of developing, national legislation on access to genetic resources and benefit-sharing.

The pioneering national legislation was the Philippines Executive Order No. 247, "Prescribing a Regulatory Framework for the Prospecting of Biological and Genetic Resources, their By-products and Derivatives, for Scientific and Commercial Purposes, and for Other Purposes", which became law in 1995.

The purpose of EO 247 is identified in the Preamble as regulating "the prospecting of biological and genetic resources so that these resources are protected and conserved, are developed and put to the sustainable use and benefit of the national interest." This includes the identification and recognition of "the rights of indigenous cultural communities and other Philippine communities to their traditional knowledge and practices when this information is directly and indirectly put to commercial use."

The Preamble also asserts that "wildlife, flora and fauna, among others, are owned by the State and the disposition, development and utilisation thereof are under its full control and supervision". However, the State's resource rights are not absolute, in that prospecting is only permitted within "the ancestral lands and domains of indigenous cultural communities … with the prior informed consent of such communities; obtained in accordance with the customary laws of the concerned community." Permission for bioprospecting depends on a research agreement between the bioprospector and the government.

For an agreement to be granted, a research proposal must be submitted to the government, with a copy submitted to any community that may be affected. At a minimum, the agreement must inform the government and affected communities if a commercial product results from the research, with a provision for payment of royalties to the government and community if commercial use results from any biogenetic resources taken.

This pioneering legislation has been criticised for the complexity of the implementing regulations, with very few research permits being issued.[51]

11.8 WIPO AND ACCESS TO GENETIC RESOURCES.

WIPO's involvement with the issue of access to genetic resources commenced in 1999 with a study, commissioned jointly with the United Nations Environment Programme (UNEP), on the role of intellectual property rights in the sharing of benefits arising from the use of biological resources and associated traditional knowledge. These matters were taken up at the third session of the Standing Committee on the Law of Patents (SCP) in September 1999. The SCP requested the International Bureau to include the issue of protection of biological and genetic resources on the agenda of a Working Group on Biotechnological Inventions, to be convened at WIPO in November 1999. The Working Group, at its meeting, the following month, recommended the establishment of nine projects related to the protection of inventions in the field of biotechnology. The Working Group decided to establish a questionnaire for the purpose of gathering information about the protection of biotechnological inventions, including certain aspects regarding intellectual property and genetic resources, in the Member States of WIPO.

In response to the invitation issued by the SCP, WIPO organised a Meeting on Intellectual Property and Genetic Resources on April 17 and 18, 2000. The Meeting addressed issues that generally are raised in the context of access to, and *in-situ* preservation of, genetic resources in their direct or indirect relationship with intellectual property. The Chairman's Conclusions from the Meeting state that a consensus was reached that:

> WIPO should facilitate the continuation of consultations among Member States in coordination with the other concerned international organisations, through the conduct of appropriate legal and technical studies, and through the setting up of an appropriate forum within WIPO for future work.

At the third session of the WIPO Standing Committee on the Law of Patents in September 1999 the delegation of Colombia proposed the introduction into the Patent Law Treaty, proposed as a means of achieving some global harmonisation of patent registration procedures, an article which provided that:

1. All industrial protection shall guarantee the protection of the country's biological and genetic heritage. Consequently, the grant of patents or registrations that relate to elements of that heritage shall be subject to their having been acquired made legally.
2. Every document shall specify the registration number of the contract affording access to genetic resources and a copy thereof whereby the products or processes for which protection is sought have been manufactured or developed from genetic resources, or products thereof, of which one of the member countries is the country of origin.

The Diplomatic Conference, which commenced on May 11, 2000, became bogged down on the question of obliging the identification of source countries in biotechnological patent applications. To facilitate progress on the procedural aspects, the source country question was referred to an expert group for further consideration. In a press release issued on June 1, 2000, WIPO reported that it had also received a mandate to discuss this issue from the COP 5 meeting in Nairobi and that this request would be referred to its General Assembly in September 2000.

In a Note dated September 14, 2000, the Permanent Mission of the Dominican Republic to the United Nations in Geneva submitted two documents on behalf of the Group of Countries of Latin America and the Caribbean (GRULAC) as part of the debate on in the WIPO General Assembly on "Matters Concerning Intellectual Property and Genetic Resources, Traditional Knowledge and Folklore."[52] The central thrust of these documents was a request for the creation of a Standing

Committee on access to the genetic resources and traditional knowledge of local and indigenous communities. "The work of that Standing Committee would have to be directed towards defining internationally recognised practical methods of securing adequate protection for the intellectual property rights in traditional knowledge."[53]

The GRULAC documents suggested that questions concerning the use and exploitation of genetic resources and biodiversity and also traditional knowledge, could be divided into two groups depending on whether they are currently recognised or being addressed by intellectual property in the international environment. The first group includes problems whose solutions could in principle be found in known intellectual property regimes. In this group, the preferred remedy would be the broadening or clarification of existing intellectual property remedies.

It was suggested that the second group comprised those aspects, questions and problems the settlement of which calls for recognition and acceptance of the values and interests whose protection is sought, and the creation of new disciplines and provisions so that their protection may be established at the international level. The GRULAC documents envisaged that the Committee would examine the protection needs and expectations of sectors that possess traditional knowledge and to determine the manner in which they require an adjustment of existing intellectual property regimes or the creation of new ones. The Committee might also consider it necessary to ascertain whether some of the protection claims were not completely outside the present or prospective framework of intellectual property.

In order to clarify the future application of intellectual property to the use and exploitation of genetic resources and biodiversity and also traditional knowledge, it was suggested that the Committee could clarify: (a) the notions of public domain and private domain; (b) the appropriateness and feasibility of recognising rights in traditional works and knowledge currently in the public domain, and investigating machinery to limit and control certain kinds of unauthorised exploitation; (c) recognition of collective rights; (d) model provisions and model contracts with which to control the use and exploitation of genetic and biological resources, and machinery for the equitable distribution of profits in the event of a patentable product or process being developed from a given resource embodying the principles of prior informed consent and equitable distribution of profits in connection with the use, development and commercial exploitation of the material transferred and the inventions and technology resulting from it; (e) the protection of undisclosed traditional knowledge.

Finally, it was suggested that in concert with the secretariat of UPOV, the Committee could embark on the exploration of possible options for defining *sui generis* systems for the protection of genetic resources and biodiversity.

At the WIPO General Assembly the Member States agreed to the establishment of an Intergovernmental Committee on Intellectual Property and Genetic Resources, Traditional Knowledge and Folklore. Three interrelated themes were identified to inform the deliberations of the Committee: intellectual property issues that arise in the context of (i) access to genetic resources and benefit-sharing; (ii) protection of traditional knowledge, whether or not associated with those resources; and (iii) the protection of expressions of folklore.[54]

In November 2000, WIPO convened an Inter-regional Meeting on Intellectual Property and Traditional Knowledge at Chiangrai, Thailand to provide an opportunity for developing countries to contribute to the activities of the Intergovernmental Committee. The meeting recommended that governments identify, catalogue, record and document genetic resources and traditional knowledge and that national mechanisms be established to regulate access to and benefit-sharing in genetic resources and the protection of traditional knowledge and folklore.

At the first Session of the Intergovernmental Committee on Intellectual Property and Genetic Resources, Traditional Knowledge and Folklore ("IGC") held in Geneva from April 30, to May 3, 2001, the Member States determined the agenda of items on which work should proceed and prioritised certain tasks for the Committee. Principal among these was "the development of "guide contractual practices," guidelines, and model intellectual property clauses for contractual agreements on access to genetic resources and benefit-sharing."[55]

At its second session, held in Geneva from December 10–14, 2001, the IGC formulated "Operational Principles for Intellectual Property Clauses of Contractual Agreements Concerning Access to Genetic Resources and Benefit-Sharing," which suggested sample clauses for bioprospecting contracts.[56] Subsequent sessions have resulted in the formulation of "Operational Principles for Intellectual Property Clauses of Contractual Agreements Concerning Access to Genetic Resources and Benefit-Sharing", a tool-kit for the formulation bioprospecting contracts and the preparation of technical guides for patent offices in the protection of traditional knowledge in their search activities.[57]

11.9 THE TREATY ON PLANT GENETIC RESOURCES

The TRIPS Agreement is primarily concerned with Member nations' obligations to establish a legal infrastructure to permit the privatisation of intellectual property rights. Article 27.3(b) permits the extension of those private rights to genetic resources. The TRIPS Agreement is seen by some to be in tension with the Convention on Biological Diversity (CBD), which is concerned with conserving the "global genetic commons" for humankind. The Conference of the Parties (COP) to the CBD has reported that the value and benefit of genetic materials in the global biosphere may be realised and shared through intellectual property rights.[58] The COP Secretariat has also noted the importance in the relationship between trade and biological diversity of the interrelationship between the TRIPS Agreement and the CBD.[59] The COP Panel of Experts on Access and Benefit-Sharing concluded that IPRs were a significant influence upon benefit-sharing[60], but consensus has not been achieved within the COP on whether this influence has been positive or negative.

A significant recent development, which will have an important impact upon the negotiation of access to plant genetic resources, was the promulgation in November 2001 of the Treaty on Plant Genetic Resources. This Treaty was the enactment in a binding form of the International Undertaking on Plant Genetic Resources, which had been adopted by the 1983 the Conference of the FAO. The International Undertaking had originally been predicated on the principle that plant genetic resources for food and agriculture (PGRFA) should be freely exchanged as a "heritage of mankind" and should be preserved through international conservation efforts. In subsequent years the principle of free exchange was gradually narrowed by the impact of intellectual property rights upon agriculture. In November 1989 the 25th Session of the FAO Conference adopted two resolutions providing an "agreed interpretation" that plant breeders' rights were not incompatible with the Undertaking. The acknowledgment of plant variety rights obviously benefitted industrialised countries, which were active in seed production. In exchange for this concession, developing countries won endorsement of the concept of "farmers' rights".

Subsequent negotiations on the text of the International Undertaking sought to reconcile the proposition that PGFRA were the common heritage of mankind with the sovereignty of states over their plant genetic resources and the Treaty on Plant Genetic Resources represents an attempt to reconcile this tension in a formal instrument.

The objectives of the Treaty, are stated in Article 1 to be "the conservation and sustainable use of plant genetic resources for food and agriculture and the fair and equitable sharing of the benefits arising out of their use, in harmony with the Convention on Biological Diversity, for sustainable agriculture and food security".

Article 4 of the Treaty requires signatories "where appropriate" to "promote an integrated approach to the exploration, conservation and sustainable use of plant genetic resources for food and agriculture." Article 10.2 contains the agreement of the Contracting Parties to "establish a multilateral system, which is efficient, effective and transparent, both to facilitate access to [PGFRA] and to share, in a fair and equitable way, the benefits arising from the utilisation of these resources, on a complementary and mutually reinforcing basis." Facilitated access to PGFRA is to be provided in accordance with the conditions prescribed in Article 12.3. Paragraph (d) of this provision provides that the recipients "shall not claim any intellectual property or other rights that limit the facilitated access" to PGFRA, or their "genetic parts or components," in the form received from the Multilateral System. This, of course, does not prevent intellectual property rights being claimed in relation to germplasm which is modified by the recipient.

Article 13.1 recognises that benefits accruing from facilitated access to PGFRA shall be shared fairly and equitably under this Article. Article 13.2 envisages that this sharing of benefits include the exchange of technical information, access to technology, capacity building and the sharing of monetary benefits from commercialisation.

The Treaty has come into effect, following accession by the requisite number of countries, on June 29, 2004.[61]

11.10 FARMERS' RIGHTS

Article 9 of the International Treaty on Plant Genetic Resources for Food and Agriculture implements the proposal which was developed under the International Undertaking for the recognition of farmers' rights. The policy behind this recognition is stated in Article 9.1, namely that

> The Contracting Parties recognise the enormous contribution that the local and indigenous communities and farmers of all regions of the world, particularly those in the centres of origin and crop diversity, have made and will continue to make for the conservation and development of plant genetic resources which constitute the basis of food and agriculture production throughout the world.

Article 9.2 envisages that "the responsibility for realising Farmers' Rights, as they relate to Plant Genetic Resources for Food and Agriculture, rests with national governments" and that national legislation should include measures relating to:

(a) protection of traditional knowledge relevant to plant genetic resources for food and agriculture;
(b) the right to equitably participate in sharing benefits arising from the utilisation of plant genetic resources for food and agriculture;
(c) the right to participate in making decisions, at the national level, on matters related to the conservation and sustainable use of plant genetic resources for food and agriculture.

Finally, Article 9.3 provides that the Article shall not be interpreted "to limit any rights that farmers have to save, use, exchange and sell farm-saved seed/propagating material."

An assumption of Art. 9.1 is that the landraces used by traditional farmers are a dynamic genetic reservoir for the development of new varieties and for the transmission of desirable genetic traits. The traditional knowledge of local and indigenous communities is similarly perceived. As a means of remunerating these groups for their past contributions to the development of plant genetic resources for food and agriculture production, there can be little argument, except about the quantum and distribution of this remuneration.

Inevitably, any calculation of the equitable share, which traditional farmers and indigenous communities might enjoy under a Farmers' Rights, or Traditional Knowledge regime will be arbitrary. However the intellectual property system is no stranger to arbitrary calculations, thus the 20-year length of a patent term is intended to provide an opportunity for the compensation of all inventors, whatever the area of technology. Similarly the 25 years exclusivity which the UPOV Convention provides for new varieties of trees and vines, takes no account of variations in R&D costs between the different varieties.

The principal ways in which plant genetic resources are translated into food and agriculture production is through plant breeding and plant patenting. Standing at the heart of a Farmers' Rights regime is the concept of the equitable sharing of benefits with farmers for their contribution to innovations in plant breeding and plant patenting. It is estimated that about 6.5 per cent of all genetic research undertaken in agriculture is focussed upon germplasm derived from wild species and landraces[62]

Article 9.2 obliges the Contracting Parties to the Plant Genetic Resources Treaty "to take measures," subject to their national legislation to protect and promote Farmers' Rights. The content of these rights is defined in the balance of that provision and embraces the protection of traditional knowledge, equitable benefit-sharing and the right to participate in decision making. The Treaty leaves open the legal context within which Farmers' Rights are to be enacted.

National legislation on Farmers' Rights tends to combine one of the versions of UPOV with some of the access principles of the CBD. The African Model legislation for the Protection of the Rights of Local Communities, Farmers and Breeders, and for the Regulation of Access to Biological Resources, which was adopted by the OAU, Heads of States Summit at Ouagadougou in June 1998, adopts a *sui generis* regime based on UPOV 1991. However, most national statutes prefer access legislation combined with UPOV 1978 (e.g., Andean Community's Common System on Access to Genetic Resources, 1996; Costa Rica's Biodiversity Law 1998; India's Community Intellectual Property Rights Act 1999; Kenya's Seeds and Plant Varieties Act 1975).

11.11 ACCESS TO PGRFA AND THE DOHA NEGOTIATING AGENDA

In the same month that the International Treaty on Plant Genetic Resources for Food and Agriculture was concluded, the WTO Ministerial Meeting in Doha issued a Ministerial Declaration which set out the negotiating agenda for the next trade round of the WTO. Article 19 of the Declaration instructed the Council for TRIPS, in pursuing its work programme, "to examine, *inter alia*, the relationship between the TRIPS Agreement and the Convention on Biological Diversity, the protection of traditional knowledge and folklore, and other relevant new developments" raised by Members pursuant to a general review of the TRIPS Agreement.

The Doha Ministerial had set the deadline of December 2002 within which the review, referred to in Clause 19 of the Doha Declaration had referred, was to be finalised and reported to the Trade Negotiations Committee (TNC) "for appropriate action." However, after Doha, the discussions in the TRIPS Council were dominated by the consideration of the public health and patenting issue and the question of plant variety protection under Article 27.3(b) was somewhat neglected. However, in anticipation of the Cancun Ministerial, Morocco, on behalf of the African Group of countries made a Joint Communication to the Council for TRIPS, on June 26, 2003, in an endeavour to finalise the longstanding issues relating to the review of Article 27.3(b). The Joint Communication contained proposals (i) indicating the solutions that the African Group considered needed to be found; (ii) setting out possible areas of agreement on issues that have arisen; and (iii) providing suggestions on how to resolve issues on which members had not been able to reach a common understanding.[63]

The Joint Communication maintained that the requirement to protect plant varieties should be consistent with and supportive of the public policy goals of Member States relating to food security, nutrition, the elimination of rural poverty, and the integrity of local communities. Also asserted was the importance of preserving the system of seed saving and exchange, as well as selling among farmers, in which the legitimate rights of commercial plant breeders should be protected and but balanced against the needs of farmers and local communities, particularly in developing country Members. The Joint Communication urged the implementation of the TRIPS Agreement, the Convention on Biological Diversity and the International Treaty on Plant Genetic Resources in a mutually supportive and consistent manner, Members should retain the right to require, within their domestic laws, the disclosure of sources of any biological material that constitutes some input in the inventions claimed, and proof of benefit-sharing. Areas that were identified as those where delegations had not reached a common understanding concerned the possibility under Article 27.3(b) for members to grant patents on micro-organisms and on non-biological and micro-biological processes for the production of plants or animals. To deal with the issue of biopiracy, the African Group recommended a combination of access contracts to regulate the activities of researchers and other gatherers and the use of databases of traditional knowledge by patent offices, in examining patent claims to determine whether they meet the requirements of novelty, inventiveness and usefulness. Noting the slowness of progress, which was being made in WIPO, the Joint Communication suggested that the Council for TRIPS should consider adopting a Decision on Protecting Traditional Knowledge.

ENDNOTES

1 E.g., see S. Brush. 1994. *Providing Farmers' Rights Through In Situ Conservation of Crop Genetic Resources.* Berkeley, University of California.

2. C. Correa, *Options For The Implementation of Farmers' Rights at The National Level,* South Centre, Trade-Related Agenda, Development And Equity Working Papers, no. 8, December 2000. Citing Wright. 1998. Intellectual Property and Farmers' Rights. In *Agricultural Values of Plant Genetic Resources*. Edited by R. Evenson, D. Gollin and V. Santaniello. Wallingford, FAO/CEIS/CABI, 228.

3 McNeely. 2001. Biodiversity and Agricultural Development: The Crucial Institutional Issues. In *Tradeoffs or Synergies? Agricultural Intensification, Economic Development and the Environment.* Edited by D. R. Lee and C. B. Barrett. Wallingford, CABI, 399 at page 404.

4 These centres are: the Centro Internacional de Agricultura Tropical (CIAT), Centre for International Forestry Research (CIFOR), Centro Internacional de la Papa (CIP), International Centre for Agricultural Research in the Dry Areas (ICARDA); International Centre for Living Aquatic Resources Management (ICLARM), International Centre for Research in Agroforestry (ICRAF), International Crop Research Institute for the Semi-Arid Tropics (ICRISAT); International Livestock Research Institute (ILRI), International Institute of Tropical Agriculture (IITA), International Plant Genetic Resources Institute (IPGRI) International Rice Research Institute (IRRI) and the West Africa Rice Development Association (WARDA).

5 See Blakeney. 1997. Access to Genetic Resources: The View from the South. 3 *Bioscience Law Rev.* pp. 97–103.

6 "Editorial. Lest We Starve", no. 2121, *New Scientist*, February 14, 1998, 3; Edwards and Anderson, "Seeds of Wrath", *Ibid*, 14.

7 See Blakeney. 1998. Intellectual Property Rights in the Genetic Resources of International Agricultural Research Institutes—Some Recent Problems. 1 *Bioscience Law Rev.* pp. 3–11.

8 "Editorial. Lest We Starve", no. 2121, *New Scientist*, February 14, 1998, 3.

9 Edwards and Anderson, "Seeds of Wrath", *Ibid*, 14.

10 Editor's note: The Rural Advancement Foundation International is an international non-governmental organisation "dedicated to the

conservation and sustainable advancement of cultural and ecological diversity and human rights." It has been renamed the ETC Group (Action Group on Erosion, Technology and Concentration). Website: (http://www.etcgroup.org).

11 CGIAR Press Release "CGIAR Urges Halt to Granting of Intellectual Property Rights for Designated Plant Germplasm", February 11, 1998, available online: (http://www.cgiar.org:80/ germrel.htm).

12 J. Cohen, C. Falconi, J. Komen and M. Blakeney, *The Use of Proprietary Biotechnology*, Research Inputs at Selected CGIAR Centers. (The Hague: CGIAR, March 1998).

13 P. Ronald quoted in WIPO/UNEP, *The Role of Intellectual Property Rights in the Sharing of Benefits Arising from the Use of Biological Resources and Associated Traditional Knowledge. Selected Case Studies*, WIPO: Geneva, 2001, 13.

14 *Ibid.*, 14.

15 See n.17 supra.

16 *Ibid.*, at 24.

17 "Mexican Bean Biopiracy," Biotechnology Notice Board, posted by: PANUPS (panupdates@panna.org), January 24, 2000.

18 Quoted, *Ibid.*

19 "Mexican Bean Biopiracy," RAFI Geno-Types, January 15, 2000.

20 RAFI, "Enola Bean Patent Challenged", news release, January 5, 2001.Available online: (http://www.rafi.org/).

21 *Ibid.*

22 *Ibid.*

23 National Research Council. *Lost Crops of the Incas: Little Known Plants of the Andes with Promise for Worldwide Cultivation*. National Academy Press. Washington DC., 1989.

24 E.g., see Huaman, "Unethical distribution to Japan of Yacon held in trust by CIP." Circulated on the biodiv-conv listserver run by BIONET (http://www.bionet-us.org/), April 7, 2001.

25 *Ibid.*

26 Zandstra, "Potato Center Upholds Letter and Spirit of FAO Agreement," available online: (http://www.bionet-us.org/), April 9, 2001.

27 CIMMYT, *Policy on Intellectual Property*, Article III.4.v, available online: (http://www.cimmyt.org/resources/obtaining/seed/ip_policy/htm/ip-policy.htm).

28 E.g., see RAFI, "In Search of Higher Ground. The Intellectual Property Challenge to Public Agricultural Research and Human Rights and 28 Alternative Initiatives," *The Occasional Paper Series*, vol. 6, no. 1, September 2000.

29 US Patent No. 6,040,503; Patent Cooperation Treaty patent no.WO99/11115.

30 See note 28 above.

31 US Patent No. 6,093,421—Biotics Research Corporation / Issued: July 25, 2000 / Title: Maca and antler for augmenting testosterone levels; US Patent No. 6,267,995—Pure World Botanicals, Inc. / Issued: July 31, 2001 / Title: Extract of Lepidium meyenii roots for pharmaceutical applications. Applications pending in Australia, the European Patent Office, and at World Intellectual Property Organization (WIPO).

32 Available online: (http://www.etcgroup.org/), July 3, 2002.

33 "CGIAR Working Document on Genetic Resources and Intellectual Property," (1992). CGIAR Mid-term Meeting. In *Summary of Proceedings and Decisions*, Istanbul. World Bank, Washington DC.

34 See text above accompanying notes 26–28.

35 See F. McConnell. 1996. *The Biodiversity Convention. A Negotiating History*. London, The Hague, Boston: Kluwer.

36 CBD, Art. 1.

37 Chandler. 1993. The Biodiversity Convention: Selected Issues of Interest to the International Lawyer. 4 *Colo. J. Int'l Envl L & Policy* 141 at page 161.

38 See L. Glowka, F. Burhenne-Guilmin and H. Synge. 1994. *A Guide to the Convention on Biological Diversity*. Gland, IUCN, at page 3.

39 See L. Glowka. 1998. *A Guide to Designing Legal Frameworks to Determine Access to Genetic Resources*. Gland, IUCN, at page 4.

40 CBD, Art. 15(3) and see Yusuf, "International Law and Sustainable Development: The Convention on Biological Diversity," in A. A. Yusuf, (ed.) *African Yearbook of International Law*, vol. 2, The Hague, Boston and London, Kluwer, 1995, 109.

41 *Ibid.*

42 See J. I. Cohen, C. Falconi, J. Komen and M. Blakeney, *The Use of Proprietary Biotechnology Research Inputs at Selected CGIAR Centres*, International Service for National Agricultural Research (ISNAR), The Hague, 1998.

43 UNEP/CBD/COP/2/13, Section H, para. 90–92.

44 See UNEP/CBD/COP/5/8, para. 50 and 53.

45 *Ibid.*, para. 56(d).

46 UNEP/CBD/ABS-EP/2/2, para. 37(a)–(g).

47 UNEP/CBD/WG-ABS/1/2, para. 77(d).

48 See Chandler, above at note 37.

49 See Blakeney. 1998. The Role of Intellectual Property in Regional Commercial Unions. 4 *J. of World Intellectual Property* 691.

50 See, for example, Articles 7(2) and 8 of the Draft African Model Legislation for the Protection of the Rights of Local Communities, Farmers and Breeders and for the Regulation of Access to Biological Resources of the Organization of African Unity (OAU), as contained in Annex III of document OAU/AEC/TD/MIN/7(iii).

51 See G. Dutfield, *Developing and Implementing National Systems for Protecting Traditional Knowledge: A Review of Experiences in Selected Developing Countries*, UNCTAD, 2001.

52 WIPO Doc. WO/GA/26/9.

53 *Ibid.*, Annex I, 10.

54 See WIPO, "Matters Concerning Intellectual Property Genetic Resources Traditional Knowledge and Folklore", WIPO Doc, WO/GA/26/6, August 25, 2000.

55 See WIPO Doc, WIPO/GRTKF/IC/2/3, September 10, 2001, para. 1.

56 *Ibid.*

57 *Ibid.*

58 Conference of Parties, Convention on Biological Diversity (CBD). *The impact of intellectual property rights systems on the conservation and sustainable use of biological diversity and on the equitable sharing of benefits from its use.* ENEP/CBD/COP/3/22, September 22, 1996.

59 Conference of Parties, Convention on Biological Diversity (CBD), *The Convention on Biological Diversity and the Agreement on Trade Related Intellectual Property Rights: relationships and synergies.* UNEP/CBD/COP/3/23, October 5, 1996.

60 Conference of Parties, Convention on Biological Diversity (CBD), *Report of panel of Experts on access and benefit sharing*. UNEP/CBD/COP/5/8, November 2, 1999.

61 See Article 28 of the Treaty, the text of which is available online at the following website: (http://www.fao.org/ag/cgrfa/itpgr.htm).

62 See R. McNeely. 2001. Biodiversity and Agricultural Development: The Crucial Institutional Issues. In *Tradeoffs or Synergies? Agricultural Intensification, Economic Development and the Environment*. Edited by D. R. Lee and C. B. Barrett. Wallingford: CABI, pp. 399–408.

63 IP/C/W/404, "Taking Forward the Review of Article 27.3(b) of the TRIPS Agreement," June 26, 2003.

CHAPTER 12

Fitting Traditional Knowledge Protection and Biopiracy Claims into the Existing Intellectual Property and Unfair Competition Framework

CHARLES R. MCMANIS*

12.1 INTRODUCTION

In the growing international debate over the legal protection of traditional knowledge,[1] one frequently hears the view expressed that the traditional knowledge of indigenous peoples and local communities does not readily fit into the existing intellectual property regimes of the industrialised world,[2] that these regimes basically promote the interests of the industrialised world and encourage what has come to be called (and vilified as) "biopiracy,"[3] and that, accordingly, an entirely new, *sui generis* system of legal protection for traditional knowledge is urgently required.[4] In this chapter I will argue that, to the contrary, 1) existing intellectual

* Thomas & Karole Green Professor of Law, Washington University, St. Louis, U.S.A. The author gratefully acknowledges the valuable research assistance of Ms. Heather Megan Fuller, J. D., Washington University, 2004, and Dr. Natalie Lissy, J. D. Washington University, 2004, in preparing this article for publication.

property regimes (inclusive of the closely related law of unfair competition) and associated contractual mechanisms, can provide far more comprehensive legal protection for the traditional knowledge of indigenous peoples than critics generally acknowledge; 2) existing intellectual property regimes (either as they stand or with two relatively minor modifications described below) are not only capable of providing affirmative legal protection for the genetic resources of developing countries and associated traditional knowledge of indigenous and local communities therein but also of preventing authentic instances of biopiracy; and 3) creating an effective *sui generis* system of legal protection for the traditional knowledge of indigenous peoples, by contrast, is likely to be fraught with far more practical and theoretical difficulties than would be involved in modifying the current intellectual property system in two important respects—namely requiring disclosure of the origin of relevant genetic resources and evidence of prior informed consent of those providing such resources and/or any associated traditional knowledge as a condition for enforcing otherwise valid intellectual property rights. Thus, while by no means opposing the effort to develop effective *sui generis* legal systems for protecting traditional knowledge, the discussion in this chapter concludes that, at least in the short run (and perhaps in the long run as well), existing intellectual property regimes (inclusive of the law of unfair competition), together with associated contractual mechanisms, offer the most realistic avenue for securing effective legal protection for traditional knowledge holders, and that, if modified as suggested herein, existing intellectual property regimes can be made adequate to the task.

The underlying premise of the discussion in this chapter is that the interrelated problems of biodiversity loss, biopiracy, and inadequate legal protection for traditional knowledge can be traced, in a relatively straightforward manner, to a common root cause, and for that reason all three problems are likewise amenable to a relatively straightforward solution. The common root cause is the systematic under-valuation of biodiversity and associated traditional knowledge, not only as instrumental means to other ends, but also as ends unto themselves, valuable for their own sake.[5] Systematic under-valuation of biodiversity, if it continues unchecked, is likely to produce what biologists are calling the Sixth Great Extinction[6]—an extinction resulting, not from the impact of a meteor or other natural calamities, as with earlier epic extinctions, but rather from the impact of humankind itself on "this fragile earth, our island home."[7]

Meanwhile, social scientists are warning that the same forces driving biological extinctions are also producing rampant cultural homogenisation,[8] a phenomenon that has been called the "extinction of experience"—a "radical loss of direct contact and hands-on interaction with the surrounding environment that traditionally comes through subsistence and other daily life activities."[9] In a very real sense, the mounting protests over "biopiracy," and over globalisation more generally, represent a visceral populist reaction to this systematic biocultural devaluation. Accordingly, the evident solution is to develop international legal mechanisms that will more adequately recognise the utilitarian and intrinsic value of biocultural diversity. For that to occur, however, the legal mechanisms must grow out of an international negotiating process in which the bargaining power of the various stakeholders is more or less symmetrical, and the legal mechanisms chosen must be based on theoretically sound foundations and be capable of relatively low cost implementation and administration as a practical matter.

Fortunately, a growing international awareness of the link between the development of biotechnology and the preservation of genetic resources is creating precisely the necessary window of opportunity for such negotiations, as technology-rich industrialised countries, which are spearheading the development of biotechnology, are conversely discovering that they are relatively biodiversity-poor, while developing countries, although technology-poor, are beginning to realise that they are the stewards of the bulk of the earth's biodiversity. It is thus no coincidence that during the last decade of the 20th century two parallel rounds of international negotiations yielded two multilateral agreements designed to bolster the respective positions of the technology-rich industrialised world and the biodiversity-rich developing world, thus setting the stage for further international negotiations to hammer out a more comprehensive global bargain.

On the one hand, the long stalled Uruguay Round of multilateral trade negotiations eventually produced the Marrakesh Treaty of 1994, which established the World Trade Organization and adopted an accompanying bundle of international agreements, including the Agreement on Trade Related Aspects of Intellectual Property Rights (commonly called the TRIPS Agreement),[10] which seeks to impose on the developing world international minimum standards for intellectual property protection and enforcement. By January 1, 2005, all but the least-developed countries of the world must be into full compliance with

TRIPS, including its most controversial patent and plant variety protection provisions, contained in Article 27 of the TRIPS Agreement.[11] Disputes over compliance with TRIPS obligations are subject to resolution through the larger WTO dispute settlement process, and multilateral trade sanctions may be authorised to enforce compliance.

On the other hand, a second set of multilateral negotiations initiated by the developing world under the auspices of the United Nations Environmental Program succeeded in producing the Framework Convention on Climate Change[12] and the Convention on Biological Diversity (CBD)[13], both of which were opened for signature at the "Earth Summit" in Rio de Janeiro in 1992. The Climate Change Treaty requires countries in the industrialised world to limit net emissions of greenhouse gases and facilitate transfer of environmental technology to the developing world.[14] The CBD, in turn, obliges countries in the developing world to conserve, sustainably use, and guarantee access to genetic resources in return for a fair and equitable sharing of benefits arising out of the utilisation of these resources.[15] As a part of this larger objective, Article 8(j) of the CBD specifically calls upon its members to "respect, preserve and maintain knowledge, innovations and practices of indigenous and local communities embodying traditional lifestyles relevant for the conservation and sustainable use of biological diversity, and to promote their wider application with the approval and involvement of the holders of such knowledge, innovations and practices and encourage the sharing of benefits arising from the utilisation of such knowledge, innovations and practices ..."[16]

In contrast to the binding and enforceable provisions of the TRIPS Agreement, the CBD is essentially a toothless declaration of good intentions, as no enforcement mechanism is specified and much of the treaty language, including Article 8(j)'s recognition of the need to protect traditional knowledge, is hortatory rather than mandatory. Ironically, however, as the deadline for compliance with the most controversial provisions of the TRIPS Agreement draws near, the balance of negotiating power between the developing and industrialised worlds seems to be growing more symmetrical, rather than less, as both parts of the world have been forced to confront the unruly phenomenon of globalisation and its discontents.

Following the ballooning currency crisis of 1997 and the 1999 teargas-beclouded collapse of the Third WTO Ministerial Conference in Seattle, amidst violent anti-globalisation protests, the Doha WTO Ministerial Declaration of 2001 specifically sought to place the needs and interests of developing countries at the heart of the Work Programme adopted in that Declaration.[17] Specifically the Doha Declaration stressed the importance of implementing and interpreting the TRIPS Agreement in a manner supportive of public health, by promoting access to existing medicines and research and development into new medicines, as spelled out in a separate declaration acknowledging the gravity of the public health problems afflicting many developing and least developed countries, especially those resulting from HIV/AIDS, tuberculosis, malaria and other epidemics, and noting that TRIPS does not and should not prevent members from taking various enumerated measures to protect the public health.[18] In addition, the Doha Declaration specifically directed the TRIPS Council to examine the relationship between the TRIPS Agreement and the CBD, as well as the protection of traditional knowledge and folklore.[19]

Notwithstanding the subsequent deadlock at the Fifth WTO Ministerial Conference in Cancun, in September 2003 (this time over the industrialised world's reluctance to grant developing countries increased access to agricultural and textile markets and the concomitant refusal of developing countries to launch negotiations designed to promote greater international investment, competition, transparency in government procurement, and trade facilitation), negotiations are nevertheless proceeding, and the WTO continues to offer the most promise for the developing world to negotiate stronger legal protection for biodiversity and traditional knowledge, given the symmetrical advantages to be gained by developing and industrialised countries.[20] In return for the commitment on the part of developing countries to conserve, sustainably use, and ensure access to their genetic resources, and to strengthen legal protection and enforcement of intellectual property rights in the developing world, industrialised countries may find it necessary to adopt legal measures to ensure that developing countries and indigenous or local communities located therein will equitably share in the benefits arising out of the use of those genetic resources. However, for the developing world and its indigenous and local communities to take maximum advantage of this unique window of opportunity, they must develop a coherent strategy for ensuring that the intellectual property regime mandated by the TRIPS Agreement, as well as any *sui generis* systems adopted for the protection for traditional knowledge, are based on theoretically sound foundations and are capable of relatively low cost implementation and administration.

By way of suggesting what the salient features of that coherent strategy might be, the first section of this chapter will examine the various forms of traditional knowledge for which legal protection might be sought, thereby ascertaining the extent to which such traditional knowledge can qualify for the various existing forms of intellectual property and unfair competition protection that are mandated by the TRIPS Agreement. The next section, in turn, will clarify what does and does not constitute biopiracy and demonstrate how existing forms of intellectual property and unfair competition protection can be utilised defensively to prevent authentic instances of biopiracy. Finally, the last section will discuss how these same bodies of intellectual property and unfair competition law and associated contractual mechanisms can be utilised and/or modified to ensure adequate affirmative legal protection for traditional knowledge, explain the various theoretical and practical difficulties that must be overcome in creating an effective *sui generis* system of protection for traditional knowledge, and conclude that the enactment of relatively minor changes in existing forms of intellectual property law might provide a more workable alternative, at least in the short run.

12.2 TRADITIONAL KNOWLEDGE AND EXISTING FORMS OF INTELLECTUAL PROPERTY AND UNFAIR COMPETITION LAW

Any argument suggesting that existing forms of intellectual property protection and associated unfair competition law and contractual mechanisms might be adequate to protect traditional knowledge must withstand simultaneous assaults on two fronts. Many who are strong proponents of environmental protection and the rights of indigenous communities tend to be profoundly suspicious of the goals and social utility of intellectual property law and the workings of the market economy generally, and often display a rather superficial understanding (and occasionally a rather profound misunderstanding) of how intellectual property systems actually operate in practice to stimulate innovation in a market economy. Conversely, many proponents of a robust market economy and strong intellectual property rights as an essential element thereof tend to be profoundly suspicious of the economic justification for environmental protection, and often display a rather superficial understanding (and occasionally a rather profound misunderstanding) of the realities confronting the developing world generally, and indigenous and local communities in particular, as they struggle to preserve genetic resources and local cultural diversity in the face of the onslaught of globalisation.

On the specific question of traditional knowledge protection, environmentalists and advocates for the rights of indigenous and local communities tend to dismiss existing intellectual property rights as culturally biased against the developing world and traditional cultures, and utterly inadequate to their needs, inasmuch as the underlying ideological assumptions of conventional intellectual property law are said to be traceable to distinctively Western notions of individualism, economic progress, and social utility, that inevitably promote the commodification of culture in ways that are largely inimical to the survival of traditional communities in the developing world.[21] Conversely, proponents of strong intellectual property rights all too often seem to corroborate these suspicions, as they tend to dismiss efforts to create stronger legal protection for the traditional knowledge of indigenous communities as the laughable proposals of confused romantics, inasmuch as traditional knowledge is essentially static and non-new, thus having no legitimate claim to intellectual property protection and being of marginal utility at best in the innovative process.[22] The first section of this chapter will seek to explain why both critiques are fundamentally misguided, based as they are on profound misunderstandings as to the nature of intellectual property law and nature of traditional knowledge, respectively.

12.2.1 Traditional knowledge as innovation and a means of cultural identification

Well before the WTO Doha Declaration of 2001, the World Intellectual Property Organization (WIPO), a specialised UN agency responsible for the promotion of intellectual property worldwide, established in the fall of 2000 the WIPO Intergovernmental Committee on Intellectual Property and Genetic Resources, Traditional Knowledge and Folklore (hereinafter "Intergovernmental Committee" or IGC).[23] The mandate of the IGC is to facilitate discussion of intellectual property issues that arise in the context of: (i) access to genetic resources and benefit-sharing, (ii) protection of traditional knowledge, innovations and creativity, and (iii) protection of expressions of folklore, including handicrafts.[24]

In an initial overview document, the Intergovernmental Committee conceded that, given the highly diverse and dynamic nature of traditional knowledge, it might not be possible to develop a singular and exclusive definition of the term.[25] However, the IGC also concluded that such a definition may not be necessary in order to delimit the scope of subject matter for which protection has been sought, as neither of the two basic international intellectual property conventions administered by the WIPO—namely the Paris Convention for the Protection of Industrial Property, and the Berne Convention for the Protection of Literary and Artistic Works—contains exclusive definitions of what constitute "inventions," "industrial designs," or "literary and artistic works," respectively, and that national intellectual property systems likewise function perfectly satisfactorily without ironclad subject matter definitions for what constitutes an invention or a work of authorship, as the more important definitional and conceptual issues have to do with the substantive and procedural standards affecting the availability, acquisition, scope, maintenance and enforcement of intellectual property rights.[26]

Nevertheless, the Intergovernmental Committee has gleaned a number of useful definitions from documents accompanying various international agreements that make reference to traditional knowledge.[27] The Executive Secretary of the CBD, for example, has defined the term as "a body of knowledge built by a group of people through generations living in close contact with nature."[28] Such knowledge typically includes "a system of classification, a set of empirical observations about the local environment, and a system of self-management that governs resource use."[29] Contrary to popular misconception (embraced all too uncritically by proponents of strong legal protection for more conventional forms of intellectual property), traditional knowledge is not static and unchanging (i.e., non-new), but rather develops and changes over time, albeit by means of traditional or customary practices.[30] As the Executive Secretary of the CBD has noted, "*innovation* is a feature of indigenous and local communities whereby tradition acts as a filter through which innovation occurs."[31] Consequently, it is "traditional methods of research and application and not always particular pieces of knowledge that persist."[32]

Others, including Dr. Nuno Carvalho, Head of the Genetic Resources, Biotechnology and Associated Traditional Knowledge Section of the Traditional Knowledge Division of the WIPO, would add a further qualification.[33] Traditional knowledge—whether understood in the strict sense as encompassing knowledge and ideas as such or in a broader sense as extending to expressions of knowledge and ideas as well—commonly serves as a means of cultural identification, and thus must be understood "holistically" in the sense that both its spiritual and practical elements serve the same purpose of integrating the community with its environment.[34]

For purposes of determining which forms of existing intellectual property or unfair competition law might apply, traditional knowledge must be divided into that which is widely (i.e., publicly) known, that which is collectively known by a particular community but not widely known by society as a whole, and that which is known only by selected members of a particular community, culture, or society.[35] Again contrary to popular misconception (fostered by organisations purporting to speak for indigenous communities but all too often simply reading into traditional cultures their own ideological predispositions), traditional knowledge, particularly traditional medicinal knowledge, is just as likely to be closely held by selected members of a community as it is to be collectively known by the community as a whole.[36] Even collectively known traditional knowledge—such as collectively practiced agricultural knowledge—may or may not be widely known or readily accessible to the rest of humanity.[37]

To be sure, some traditional medicinal knowledge, such as traditional Chinese and Ayurvedic medicine, and much traditional agricultural knowledge, such as that embodied in the international germplasm collections of the Consultative Group on International Agricultural Research (CGIAR) that were placed under the auspices of the United Nations Food and Agriculture Organization (FAO) in 1994 to be held in trust for the benefit of humanity, are widely known and documented, and thus present distinctive (albeit not insurmountable) problems in the development of an international system for equitable benefit-sharing.[38] On the other hand, some collective knowledge of a community corresponds more closely to what in Western cultural and legal terms might be called corporate, proprietary, or closely held know-how, and would thus be capable of either being protected as proprietary know-how or shared with the rest of humanity, depending on the consensus (and cohesion) of the collectivity that possesses it.[39]

12.2.2 Fitting traditional knowledge into existing intellectual property and unfair competition law

In Western legal and philosophical terms, traditional knowledge (and for that matter, human knowledge generally) can be divided into what the United States Constitution speaks of as "Science" and "the useful Arts."[40] These terms are not to be understood in their modern sense, however, but as a distinctly 18th century effort on the part of the framers of the US Constitution to capture the Greek philosophic distinction between *theoria* (those things worthy of being known for their own sake) and *praxis* (those things worthy of being known as a useful means to some other end). It is in this anachronistic sense that the US Constitution is to be understood when it states that the constitutionally mandated purpose of statutory copyright and patent law in the United States is to "promote the Progress of Science and the Useful Arts."[41] Thus understood, this constitutional phrase appears sufficiently capacious to encompass essentially all types of traditional knowledge, be it "folklore" (i.e., expressions of the traditional beliefs, legends, and customs of a people, all of which are presumptively valuable for their own sake), handicrafts (which are capable of being valued both for their own sake and as useful means to other ends), or traditional medicinal or agricultural knowledge (the two main categories of traditional *praxis*, or useful knowledge).

This fundamental division of human knowledge into utilitarian "arts," or *praxis*, and philosophically valuable "Science," or *theoria*, respectively, is also reflected in the titles of the two "Great Conventions" adopted in the late 19th century for the more effective international protection of intellectual property—namely the 1883 Paris Convention for the Protection of Industrial Property[42] and the 1886 Berne Convention for the Protection of Literary and Artistic Works[43]. Industrial property includes any work of the human intellectual that might serve a useful function, while literary and artistic works include virtually any expression of those things worthy to be known for their own sake.

The Paris Convention declares that the protection of "industrial property" has as its object patents, utility models, industrial designs, trademarks, services marks, trade names, indications of source or appellations of origin and the repression of unfair competition.[44] It goes on to state that "industrial property" shall be understood in the broadest sense and shall apply not only to industry and commerce proper but likewise to agricultural and extractive industries and to all manufactured or natural products.[45] Likewise, the Berne Convention states that the term "literary and artistic works" shall include every production in the literary, scientific and artistic domain, whatever may be the mode or form of its expression.[46] Echoing this same broad division of human knowledge, the 1967 Convention Establishing the World Intellectual Property Organization (WIPO)—the United Nations agency that is today responsible for promoting the protection of intellectual property worldwide as well as administering the Paris and Berne Conventions—states that intellectual property includes not only the forms of intellectual property protection recognised in the two Great Conventions, but also "all other rights resulting from intellectual activity in the industrial, scientific, literary or artistic fields."[47]

The capaciousness of the foregoing constitutional and treaty terms makes it evident that they are designed to cover the entire spectrum of innovative human activity, inclusive of any innovative human activity that might be defined as "traditional knowledge." At the same time, the US Constitution makes it equally clear that the intellectual property protection authorised must serve an essentially utilitarian and public purpose—i.e., promoting "the Progress of Science and the useful Arts"—and must be limited not only in time but also in respect of the subject matter and persons eligible for protection—i.e., the Writings of Authors and Discoveries of Inventors (from which a constitutional copyright standard of originality and a constitutional patent standard of inventiveness have been deduced).

While the Paris Convention contains no analogous language, that is only because goals of the Paris Convention are more modest, as it merely obliges its members to offer "national [i.e., non-discriminatory] treatment" to the nationals of other member countries with respect to any industrial property protection that the member country chooses to provide for its citizens, and establishes an international priority system for the registration of industrial property.[48] The Berne Convention goes a step further, establishing certain minimum standards for copyright protection in addition to obliging its members to accord national treatment to the nationals of other member countries, but it is only in the TRIPS Agreement that international minimum standards for the protection and enforcement of intellectual property rights in general are prescribed, and in so doing the TRIPS Agreement states that the "protection and enforcement of intellectual property rights should contribute to the promotion of technological innovation and to the transfer and dissemination of technology, to the mutual advantage of producers and users of technological knowledge and in a manner conducive to social and economic welfare, and to a balance of rights and obligations."[49]

If the objective of intellectual property law is to provide a limited form of affirmative protection for industrial property and literary and artistic works, Article 10*bis* (2) of the Paris Convention makes it clear that the objective of unfair competition law is to provide defensive protection against "any act of competition contrary to honest practices in industrial or commercial matters."[50] While Article 10*bis* (3) of the Paris Convention states that various forms of deceptive commercial conduct injurious to competitors—i.e., passing off, trade disparagement, and deceptive advertising—are "in particular" to be prohibited, both the broad language of Article 10*bis*(2) and the complementary language of Article 39 of the TRIPS Agreement make it clear that all natural and legal persons, and not simply commercial competitors, are to be the beneficiaries of this protection.[51] Likewise, Article 40 of TRIPS recognises that because some contractual licensing practices or conditions pertaining to intellectual property rights which restrain competition may have adverse effects on trade and may impede the transfer and dissemination of technology, nothing in TRIPS prevents member countries from specifying licensing practices or conditions that constitute an abuse of intellectual property rights having an adverse effect on competition.[52]

With these general features of the scope and objectives of intellectual property and unfair competition law in mind, we turn now to how the specific forms of intellectual property protection specified in the TRIPS Agreement might be utilised to protect traditional knowledge.

12.2.2.1 Traditional knowledge as undisclosed information

Any traditional knowledge—whether it is embodied in particular expressions of literary or artistic works, or particular utilitarian products or processes—that is not widely known or readily accessible to humanity generally may (and indeed must) be protected pursuant to Article 39 of the TRIPS Agreement as undisclosed information. Article 39.2 specifies that "natural and legal persons" shall have the possibility of preventing information lawfully within their control from being disclosed to, acquired by, or used by others without their consent in a manner contrary to honest commercial practices[53] so long as such information:

(a) is secret in the sense that it is not, as a body or in the precise configuration and assembly of its components, generally know among or readily accessible to persons within circles that normally deal with the kind of information in question;
(b) has commercial value because it is secret; and
(c) has been subject to reasonable steps under the circumstances, by the person lawfully in control of the information, to keep it secret.[54]

Any traditional knowledge that meets these relatively minimal requirements for protection as undisclosed information thus qualifies for the legal protection mandated by Article 39 of the TRIPS Agreement, whether or not the information happens to be used in a conventional trade or business. Contrary to the misimpressions fostered by both proponent and opponents of intellectual property protection, know-how protection is not limited to those who are engaged in a trade or business, but extends to any natural person or legal entity possessed of information that is valuable because it is not generally known. In other words, the justification for know-how protection can be said to extend beyond mere economic concerns, as know-how protection promotes the self-determination of the knowledge holder as well.

Equally important for the protection of undisclosed traditional medicinal and agricultural knowledge, Article 39.3 goes on to specify that WTO members, when requiring, as a condition of approving the marketing of pharmaceutical or agricultural chemical products that utilise new chemical entities, the submission of undisclosed test *or other* data, the origination of which involves a considerable effort, shall protect such data against unfair commercial use.[55] The italicised language in this provision appears broad enough to cover any traditional knowledge that WTO members might require to be disclosed to a government agency as a condition of approving the marketing of pharmaceutical or agricultural products that utilise new chemical entities, regardless of the reason for the required disclosure of such information.

Any traditional knowledge that is or might become widely known, thus losing any claim to protection under Article 39 of TRIPS, may nevertheless qualify as one or more of the following forms of intellectual property for which legal protection is mandated by the TRIPS Agreement: 1) copyright and related rights; 2) trademarks; 3) geographical indications; 4) industrial designs; and/or 5) patents and plant varieties.

12.2.2.2 Expressions of traditional knowledge and folklore as literary or artistic works or industrial designs

Article 9 of the TRIPS Agreement specifies that copyright and related rights protection is to be made available by all WTO members in accordance with Articles 1–21 of the Berne Convention and the Appendix thereto, excepting only Article *6bis* of the Berne Convention, which deals with the moral rights of authors.[56] Notwithstanding the latter exception in TRIPS (a gap in protection which, in any event will be filled in any WTO member country that also happens to be a member of the Berne Convention), the subject matter that must be protected under the Berne Convention, as we have seen, is extremely broad. So, too, are the exclusive rights that the Berne Convention mandates, which include the right of 1) reproduction, 2) translation or any other adaptation, arrangement, or alteration of the work, 3) public performance of any dramatic, dramatico-musical and musical work, 4) broadcasting, rebroadcasting, wire communication, transmission by loudspeaker or any other analogous instrument of any literary or artistic work; and 5) public recitation or any other communication to the public of a recitation of any literary work.[57]

Pursuant to Article 5 of the Berne Convention, moreover, the enjoyment and exercise of the exclusive rights mandated under the Berne Convention are not to be subject to any formality, thus minimising the burden on those invoking the law's protection for any qualifying expressions of traditional knowledge.[58] Under Article 14*ter* of the Berne Convention, the exclusive right of artists, authors, and composers (and after their death the persons or institutions authorised by national legislation) to an interest in any sale of a work subsequent to the first transfer by the artist, composer, or author, is permitted, though not required.[59]

Although the Berne Convention itself does not attempt to define who constitutes an "author," and national legislation may vary in this regard, it is clear that a very low level of originality or creativity will suffice to meet the Berne requirement of authorship, and that member countries retain considerable discretion in defining what constitutes a protectible literary or artistic work. In the United States, at least, original authorship means little more than that a particular work owes its origin to the person or persons claiming protection, and is not a mere slavish copy of some pre-existing work.[60] The courts have emphasised that copyright protection is available so long as the author contributes something more than a trivial variation, something recognisably the author's own—though when it comes to enforcing the exclusive rights of those authors, the courts may (or may not) limit protection to those discrete elements that are distinctly recognisable as the author's own contribution.[61] The term of protection mandated by the TRIPS Agreement is to be either the life of the author plus 50 years or, in the case of anonymous or pseudonymous works 50 years after the work has been made available to the public or, if not published, its creation.[62]

All WTO member countries that are also Berne Convention members must ensure that independently of an author's economic rights, and even after the transfer of those rights, an author is to have the moral right to claim authorship of the work and to object to any distortion, mutilation or other modification of, or other derogatory acting in relations to the work, which would be prejudicial to the author's honour or reputation.[63] This means that when members of indigenous or local communities provide expressions of traditional knowledge or folklore to researchers, they must be recognised as the author of that work. TRIPS itself adopts Article 7*bis* of the Berne Convention, which explicitly recognises the concept of joint authorship by specifying that the term of copyright in such cases shall be calculated from the death of the last surviving author.[64] Increasingly, academic researchers, such as anthropologists and ethnobiologists, are realising that when they collaborate with particular members of indigenous or local communities, those individuals are entitled to be named as joint authors of any resulting published work. Article 10.2 of TRIPS also makes clear that compilations of data or other material, whether in machine readable or other form, which by reason of the selection or arrangement of their contents constitute intellectual creations, shall be protected as such.[65] Here, too, TRIPS suggests that a fairly low level of authorial originality will suffice to qualify works for copyright protection.

In any event, as long as expressions of traditional knowledge or folklore possess any elements of authorial originality, they are to that extent subject to protection against unauthorised reproduction, adaptation, or public performance pursuant to the requirements of the

Berne Convention. Those who argue that the copyright requirement of originality of authorship renders copyright law largely unsuitable to protect expressions of traditional knowledge and folklore, seem to be confusing the relatively low standard of authorial originality required by copyright law with the more exacting standards of novelty and inventive step (or non-obviousness) that set the threshold for patent protection, and also seem unaware of the protectibility of both works of joint authorship and derivative works (i.e., works based on pre-existing works). In reality, most expressions of traditional knowledge and folklore will be protectible as copyrightable literary or artistic works, thus giving the creators of those expressions of traditional knowledge and folklore the exclusive right to authorise reproductions, adaptations, and public performances of their works. In addition to the relatively low standard for copyright protection, the relatively lengthy term of protection specified for copyrighted works is another attractive feature of copyright protection, as Article 12 of TRIPS specifies that whenever the term of protection of a work other than a photographic work or work of applied art is calculated on a basis other than the life of a natural person, the term shall be no less than 50 years.[66]

Where expressions of traditional knowledge or folklore are embodied in useful articles (i.e., works of applied art), they may qualify for protection as industrial designs, whether or not they qualify for copyright protection. Article 25 of TRIPS specifies that members are to provide for the protection of independently created industrial designs that are new or original.[67] Members may (but are not required to) provide that designs are not new or original if they do not significantly differ from known designs or combinations of known designs. Likewise, members may (but are not required to) provide that such protection shall not extend to designs dictated essentially by technical or functional considerations.[68] Article 25 goes on to state that members shall ensure that requirements for securing protection for textile designs, in particular in regard to any cost, examination or publication, do not reasonably impair the opportunity to seek and obtain such protection.[69] Article 26, in turn, specifies that the owner of a protected industrial design shall have the right to prevent third parties not having the owner's consent from making, selling or importing articles bearing or embodying a design which is a copy, or substantially a copy, of the protected design, when such acts are undertaken for commercial purposes.[70] The duration of such protection is to amount to at least (but need not be limited to) 10 years.[71]

12.2.2.3 Expressions of traditional knowledge or folklore as trademarks, certification and collective marks, and/or geographical indications

Article 15 of TRIPS specifies that any combination of signs, capable of distinguishing the goods or services of one undertaking from those of other undertakings shall be capable of constituting a trademark.[72] While invoking this form of protection for particular expressions of traditional knowledge or folklore may seem to encourage or even require the "commodification" of culture as a condition of qualifying for protection, this is not necessarily the case. Indeed, two particular forms of protection made available in the United States for distinctive marks are particularly important for preventing others from making unauthorised commercial use of distinctive marks in such a way as to create the misimpression among the consuming public that an indigenous community or culture has commodified its traditional cultural symbols when in fact it has not. Section 4 of the Lanham Act specifies that collective and certification marks, including indications of geographical origin, shall be registrable in the same manner and with the same effect as trademarks, "by persons, and nations, States, municipalities *and the like*, exercising legitimate control over the use of the marks sought to be registered, even though not possessing an industrial or commercial establishment ..."[73] Indeed, the registration of a certification mark can be cancelled at any time if the registrant engages in the production or marketing of any goods or services to which the mark is applied or permits the use of the certification mark for purposes other than to certify.[74] Thus, any association or collectivity could register cultural symbols as certification or collective marks, thereby securing for the association or collectivity the exclusive right to authorise use of those certification or collective marks.

TRIPS itself requires, in Article 22, that WTO members protect any geographical indication that identifies a good as originating in a particular territory, region or locality of a member, where a given quality, reputation or other characteristic of the good is essentially attributable to its geographical origin.[75] In such a case, WTO members must provide a legal means for interested persons to prevent the use of any means in the designation or representation of a good that indicates or suggests that the good in question originates in a geographical area other than the true place of origin in a manner which misleads the public as to the geographical origin of the good or otherwise constitutes an act of unfair competition within the meaning of Article 10*bis* of the Paris Convention, which obliges members, in turn, to prohibit such practices as passing off, trade disparagement, and false or misleading advertising.[76]

Indeed, in response to demands by France and other wine producing countries, Article 23 of the TRIPS Agreement requires that additional protection be provided for geographical indications for wines and spirits, so as to prohibit any use of a geographical indication for any wines or spirits that do not in fact come from the designated locale, even where the true geographic origin is clearly specified,[77] and Article 24 goes on to require, as a "built-in" agenda item for the TRIPS Council, further international negotiations aimed at increasing the protection of individual geographical indications for wines and spirits.[78] This built-in agenda item, as well as the requirement for increased protection for geographical indications for wines and spirits, so obviously discriminates in favour of wines and spirits above other geographically identified products and services, such as agricultural products or expressions of folklore, that not even the most ideologically committed proponents of strong intellectual property rights can offer a principled justification for the distinction.[79] Thus, the developing world is now quite effectively using the very international negotiations that TRIPS calls for as a "bully pulpit" to demand equal protection for all geographical indications. Should this effort be successful, any geographical indication identifying particular products or services as originating in a particular geographic locale would be protectible against any use, whether or not misleading, on any products or services that do not in fact originate from that locale. While the social utility of granting such strong protection for geographical indications is highly debatable, such protection would certainly enhance the economic value of geographic indications and would give entities located within such locales a much greater degree of control over the unauthorised use of such geographical indications.

12.2.2.4 Traditional knowledge as protectible under the law of patents or plant variety protection

Finally, Article 27 of TRIPS specifies that, subject to a number of important exceptions, WTO members are to make patent protection available for any inventions, whether products or processes, in all fields of technology, provided that they are new, involve an inventive step and are capable of industrial application.[80] While one of the exceptions permits WTO members to exclude from patentability plants and animals other than micro-organisms, and essentially biological processes for the production of plants or animals other than non-biological or microbiological processes, a further proviso specifies that WTO member must provide for the protection of plant varieties either by patents or by an effective *sui generis* system or by any combination thereof.[81]

Both sides in the debate over traditional knowledge protection tend summarily to dismiss the availability of patent protection for traditional knowledge, and for remarkably similar reasons—namely because patent law is by definition limited to protection of individual inventors whose inventions meet the exacting standards of novelty, inventiveness, and utility, thereby altogether excluding any protection for collectively or incrementally developed traditional medicinal or agricultural knowledge of indigenous or local communities, however useful it may be, as it is by definition non-new and insufficiently inventive to qualify for patent protection. However, both ideological extremes base their conclusions on a rather superficial, even myopic, understanding of how, on the one hand, intellectual property law and related contractual mechanisms, and other the other hand, traditional medicinal and agricultural knowledge systems and related customary law, function in practice.

To begin with, it is important to understand that "novelty" in patent law means little more than that the claimed invention is not disclosed in the "prior art,"[82] however that legal term of art turns out to be defined under national law. What counts as prior art and how "novelty" is defined in various patent systems around the world is highly variable, and neither the Paris Convention nor the TRIPS Agreement prescribes a particular definition of either prior art or novelty. Some of the strongest advocates for the interests of the developing world in the continuing debates over international standards for intellectual property protection argue that the requirements of the TRIPS Agreement should be interpreted flexibly, so as to allow countries in different stages of economic development to define "novelty" in a manner that is consistent with their particular economic and social needs.[83] Developing countries may wish to define novelty, as do most patent systems around the world, as requiring absolute, worldwide novelty, but there is no requirement that they do so, if it happens to be in their interest to define it differently. On the other hand, there seems to be little advantage, and indeed a great risk of potential harm to developing country innovators, in demanding that patent systems in the industrialised world, such as the patent system in the United States, adopt a rule of absolute novelty. Indeed, as will be discussed in the next section of this chapter, the rather unique definition of novelty in US patent law, harking back to the days when the United States was itself a developing country, although at the root of many of the most highly publicised, albeit somewhat misguided, claims of biopiracy, may actually be highly beneficial to developing country innovators.

Likewise, the definition of the required "inventive step," or "non-obviousness," for patent protection varies considerably from country to country.[84] Here again, advocates for the interests of the developing world argue for a flexible definitional approach, as developing countries may initially have a stronger interest in promoting "petty patents" for the small, or low-tech, innovations of their own nationals than in restricting patentability to cutting edge high technology that is more likely to be owned by foreign nationals. Likewise, attempting to prevent alleged biopiracy by tightening up the inventive step, or non-obviousness, requirement in the patent systems of the industrialised world, thereby potentially excluding the patentability of much innovation originating in the developing world, risks doing far more damage to the development prospects of developing countries than the "biopiracy" that such a change is designed to prevent. Here again, insisting that industrialised countries tighten up patent requirements that might well benefit developing country innovators seems counterproductive.

Nor should the third and final substantive requirement for patentability—utility, or capacity for industrial application—be interpreted in a particularly rigorous manner. After all, the TRIPS Agreement merely states that patent protection shall be available for all inventions that are new, involve an inventive step and are capable of industrial application. It does not specifically foreclose the possibility that a WTO member might wish to extend patent protection to subject matter that is not new and non-obvious or for which there is no demonstrated utility. While there are strong economic arguments for not extending patent protection to non-new or obvious subject matter, the same cannot be said for the requirement of utility. In the United States, at least, both plant patent and design patent protection are made available without any requirement that utility be demonstrated, and it has been persuasively argued that the utility requirement is something of a extraneous requirement even for the grant of "utility" patents, as applicants are hardly likely to expend the time, effort and funds required to obtain patent protection for an essentially useless invention (though they may very well apply for patents where the specific utility of the disclosed invention is somewhat speculative).

More important than the substantive requirements for patent protection are the procedural disclosure requirements, as these ensure that the public, for its part, benefits from the patent "bargain." As we have seen, for example, the United States Constitution itself specifies that copyright and patent protection is to "promote the Progress of Science and the useful Arts," rather than simply rewarding authors and inventors the exclusive rights to the fruits of their intellectual labour.[85] That public purpose is also implicit in the constitutional requirement that these exclusive rights be awarded only for "limited Times." Also implicit in the grant of even these time delimited exclusive rights is an obligation on the part of the author or inventor, as a *quid pro quo* for the temporary grant of exclusive rights, to make full public disclosure of his or her writing or discovery so that the public can benefit from the product of that intellectual effort. Particularly in developing countries, the obligation to make full disclosure of the invention is of paramount importance, as it will serve to "teach" the art disclosed and temporarily protected.

Both in the United States and elsewhere, it is recognised that a certain tension exists between the policies underlying patent law and the policies underlying the grant of trade secret or know-how protection. Whereas patent law is designed to encourage full public disclosure in return for the grant of exclusive rights of limited duration, trade secret law is designed to ensure a minimum level of commercial privacy for an indeterminate time, which may be greater or less than the limited term of patent protection, depending on how vulnerable or resistant to reverse engineering the particular know-how is. In most cases this tension turns out to be more apparent than real, as can be deduced from the carefully delimited rights that trade secret law creates in non-publicly disclosed know-how. Unlike patent rights, these rights are not, strictly speaking, property rights, as they are not "rights against the world," in the same sense that patent rights and copyrights are. Rather, the rights in know-how are more properly understood as a facet of the law of unfair competition, as they merely prohibit the acquisition, use, or disclosure of another's know-how by certain, enumerated unfair means that are defined by the law of contracts and torts, respectively.[86] That TRIPS adopts this view of the protection of know-how is made clear both in the text of Article 39, which specifically identifies the protection of undisclosed information as a facet of protection against unfair competition within the meaning of Article 10*bis* of the Paris Convention, and in the accompanying footnote, which enumerates the various unfair means for which legal remedies must be made available, all of which turn out to be either tortious in nature or breaches of express or implied contracts.[87]

Still, there are specific points of tension in the protection of patents and know-how, and these arise most acutely in the articulation and administration of the disclosure requirements of patent law. The first point of tension arises in the patent application and examination process. It is in the public interest that an applicant for a patent be required to make full public disclosure as quickly as possible, not only in order to "teach" the disclosed art, but also to put on notice those who might contest the novelty and non-obviousness of the claimed invention. On the other hand, premature public disclosure of patent applications will undermine the incentive to seek patent protection, as at least some patented inventions may be capable of being protected as proprietary know-how for an indefinite period of time. Indeed, the very availability of legal protection for proprietary know-how clearly siphons off at least some potentially patentable innovation, notwithstanding the US Supreme Court's head-in-the-sand response to the problem.[88] Requiring a patent applicant to publicly disclose an invention before there is any assurance that patent protection will indeed be granted only adds to the disincentive to seek patent protection.

While most patent systems contain a "laying open" feature, by which patent applications must be published 18 months after filing, the US patent system for much of its existence did not.[89] Rather, patent applications remained confidential unless and until a patent actually issued.[90] While this provision was clearly not helpful for the efficient operation of the patent system, it was nevertheless justified as a necessary compromise, and is evidence of a strong federal policy of promoting both federal patent and essentially state law trade secret, or know-how, protection. Even today, as a result of the assiduous lobbying of independent inventors and small businesses, when the US found it in its interest to response to international pressure and adopt an 18-month laying open provision, any applicant for a US patent (including foreign applicants) may request upon filing, after certifying that the invention disclosed in the application has not and will not be the subject of an application filed in another country, or under a multilateral agreement, that requires publication of applications 18 months after filing, that his or her application not be published.[91] Just as this provision protects independent inventors and small businesses, so it would arguably protect developing country innovators who wish to seek US patent protection without giving up the option to fall back on trade secret, or know-how protection, should a patent not issue.

A second point of tension between the policies of patent and know-how protection arises when patent disclosure requirements include an obligation to disclose the best mode for carrying out the invention. While TRIPS does not require WTO members to adopt a best mode disclosure requirement, it explicitly indicates that such a requirement is permissible,[92] and developing countries would be well advised to adopt such a requirement in their own patent systems, even though it is not necessary under TRIPS, as the requirement will help ensure that the patent in fact "teaches" the art disclosed, by requiring the disclosure of any know-how associated with the best mode for carrying out the patented invention. On the other hand, there is no obligation to disclose know-how unless that know-how is indeed part and parcel of the best mode for carrying out the invention. Much undisclosed know-how that may in fact be involved in the research and development process leading to a patentable invention may not fall within the best mode disclosure requirement. Likewise, the invention may simply constitute a non-obvious way of combining or building on otherwise unpatentable know-how—be it know-how that is proprietary or freely available in the public domain. This is precisely where the vexed issue of biopiracy raises its ugly head. This volatile issue deserves separate and extended examination in the next section.

12.3 BIOPIRACY—WHAT IT IS AND WHAT IT IS NOT

Unfortunately, whether deployed by ideological proponents of strong intellectual property rights or by ideological opponents of neo-colonial forms of economic exploitation in developing countries, the rhetoric of "piracy" generally sheds more heat than light, as a claim of "piracy" assumes precisely what others might plausibly deny—namely that the particular subject matter in controversy is (or should be) legally recognised as capable of ownership of some sort, be it private, collective, or sovereign in nature. Thus, a standard defence to any allegation of piracy (other than piracy on the high seas, which is a universally recognised international crime) is that the thing said to have been pirated is or should be free for the taking, whether that thing turns out to be technology developed in the industrialised world or genetic resources and associated traditional knowledge used or maintained in the developing world.

For example, notwithstanding all of the blustering in the industrialised world in the 1980s about rampant intellectual property piracy in the developing world,[93] the more mundane reality was that, prior to the adoption of the TRIPS Agreement, the developing world was simply under no obligation to provide any particular level of intellectual property protection for industrialised world technology, and much of the developing world saw utterly no reason to create such protection, as the owners and beneficiaries would primarily be foreigners, while the local population would wind up footing the bill, at least in the short run. The resort to the rhetoric of piracy was particularly unfortunate, as it tended to plant a misconception in the developing world that intellectual property rights are somehow worldwide in scope, or in any event ought to be recognised as the product of some universal natural law, when in reality, prior to the adoption of the TRIPS Agreement, developing countries were entirely free, even if they were members of the Paris Convention, to decide for themselves whether and to what extent they would provide industrial property (inclusive of patent) protection, so long as they avoided discriminating against foreign nationals with respect to whatever industrial property protection they chose to make available to their own nationals.[94]

The more recent allegations of "biopiracy" have likewise tended to shed far more rhetorical heat than light. At the heart of much of the rhetoric of biopiracy is the logical fallacy of equivocation—a fallacy that is easily demonstrated by examining a proposed definition of "biopiracy" offered by the advocacy group that claims to have coined the term. The Action Group on Erosion, Technology and Concentration (ETC), formerly known as RAFI,[95] has defined biopiracy as "the appropriation of the knowledge and genetic resources of farming and indigenous communities by individuals or institutions seeking exclusive monopoly control (usually patents or plant breeders' rights) over these resources and knowledge."[96]

This proffered definition is both highly misleading and fundamentally ambiguous. It is misleading both because one cannot obtain patents or plant breeders rights covering the knowledge or genetic resources of farming and indigenous communities, as such, but only on inventions or plant varieties that may have been derived from such knowledge or genetic resources (though the line between these two can admittedly be exceedingly fine in some cases), and also because patents and plant breeders' rights do not necessarily endow holders of those rights with what economists would define as monopoly control (which would exist only if there are no fungible non-infringing substitutes for the subject matter protected). The definition is fundamentally ambiguous because these appropriations can hardly be condemned as "misappropriations" without implicitly asserting a legal claim of ownership in—or at the very least a legal claim as to the unfairness of the unauthorised use of—the knowledge or genetic resources of farming and indigenous communities.

In short, any serious discussion of "piracy" (whether of intellectual property, genetic resources, or the traditional knowledge of indigenous or local communities) must address a variety of foundational questions—namely, 1) what should and should not be capable of being owned, 2) who should and should not qualify as an owner, 3) what is the precise scope of the rights that owners should enjoy in that which is owned, 4) what, if any, rules should govern the relations among joint owners and the transfer of rights from one owner to another, 5) what should be protected by property rules and what should be protected only by the more limited liability rules of the law of unfair competition and contracts, and 6) what does and does not constitute unfair competition or an enforceable contract and breach thereof? As we have seen, during the final decade of the 20th century, a number of these questions were addressed, and to some extent resolved, in the TRIPS Agreement and the Convention on Biological Diversity (CBD). TRIPS categorically recognises certain minimum intellectual property standards that all WTO members must meet, and the CBD categorically declares that States have the sovereign right, in accordance with the Charter of the United Nations and the principles of international law, to exploit their own resources pursuant to their own environmental policies, and also the responsibility to ensure that activities within their jurisdiction or control do not cause damage to the environment of other States or of areas beyond the limits of national jurisdiction.[97]

On the other hand, the CBD is much more equivocal in its imposition of an obligation on the part of States to create private legal rights, notwithstanding its stated objectives to promote access to genetic resources, access to and transfer of technologies that are relevant to the conservation and sustainable use of biological diversity or make use of genetic resources, and to provide effective legal protection for the knowledge, innovations, or practices of indigenous and local communities. On these points, as we have seen, the CBD amounts to little more than a declaration of good intentions. For meaningful legal mechanisms to ensure access to and transfer of technology relevant to conservation or making use of biological diversity, or to ensure an equitable sharing of the benefits arising out of the use of genetic resources, or to protect the traditional knowledge of indigenous and local communities, interested parties will need to look, rather, to the intellectual property regime mandated by TRIPS, together with associated contractual mechanisms, as a starting point.

To get a better sense of what should and should not be legally protected, and what should and should not count as biopiracy, it will be useful to analyse some of the most highly publicised instances of alleged biopiracy a bit more carefully than has generally been the case, in an effort to separate, as it were, the wheat from the chaff. Virtually all of the most highly publicised controversies can be named after a plant that was at the heart of the biopiracy allegations—for example, the neem tree, ayahuasca, quinoa, basmati rice, turmeric, maca, Enola bean, and Hoodia cactus controversies—and, with the single exception of the Hoodia cactus controversy, all have involved US patents on plant products, plant varieties, or plant-related processes. These seven US patent controversies, in turn, illustrate some equally controversial, and to some extent unique, features of U.S. patent law.

12.3.1 Biopiracy Claims and US Patent Law

In examining the following seven US patent controversies, it is important first to identify the particular features of US patent law that are at the root of much of the furore that these patents have caused in the developing world. The most prominent of these features are the distinctive US novelty and priority rules. According to section 102(a) of the US patent law, a person is entitled to a patent unless the invention was known or used by others in this country, or patented or described in a printed publication in this or a foreign country, before the invention thereof by the applicant for the patent.[98] Thus US patents adopts a relative novelty rule, under which only foreign patents and printed publications, and not foreign knowledge or use, is disqualifying.

US patent law also gives priority to the applicant who is "first-to-invent" in the United States.[99] In 1999, the US priority rule was amended so as to allow an applicant for a patent to establish a date of invention by reference to knowledge or use thereof in a WTO member country.[100] In the absence of a priority dispute between two competing claimants, the only other limitation that section 102 places on an applicant's ability to obtain a US patent on subject matter known or used in other countries but not in the US is the further provision in section 102(f) that a person is not entitled to a patent where he or she did not "invent the subject matter sought to be patented."[101] This so-called "originality" requirement has been interpreted to mean only that a person cannot obtain a patent on an invention if the *complete* idea for the invention was obtained from another source.[102] In contrast to the novelty rule, the originality rule has been interpreted to bar a patent on an invention where the complete idea for the invention was derived from *any* source (foreign as well as domestic).[103] Where an idea derived from a foreign source is not a complete idea for the invention, that derivation may be sufficient to disqualify the invention as obvious if the idea, when combined with the relevant prior art and the ordinary level of skill in the art in the United States, renders the invention obvious, though neither the Supreme Court, the Court of Appeals for the Federal Circuit, nor the latter's two predecessor courts have explicitly so held.[104]

The rationale for the relative novelty rule is twofold. Adopted long before the era of telecommunications, globalisation, or the World Wide Web, the relative novelty rule was first of all designed to side step the substantial evidentiary difficulties that an absolute novelty rule would spawn. While this rationale is becoming increasingly implausible in the present world of instant communications and information overload, the relative novelty rule also embodies a deeper policy choice that arguably does have continuing relevance in today's world. At the time of the rule's enactment, after all, the United States was itself both a developing country and a country of immigrants. There were thus strong public policy reasons to adopt a patent novelty rule that would encourage the importation of technology and innovation into this rapidly developing country, while at the same time refusing to protect the work of foreign authors and inventors. Thus, while Congress and the American reading public politely ignored the pleas of the famous British novelist, Charles Dickens, who made two extended tours of the US in a vain effort to persuade the US citizenry to grant copyright protection for his works,[105] the US patent novelty rule was at the same time serving as a magnet to attract patent applications from among the burgeoning immigrant population who might have brought with them various technical skills and know-how that, if publicly disclosed, might help stimulate the rapid development of the country. As the current controversy over biopiracy backhandedly illustrates, the policy of encouraging the importation of innovation into the United States arguably has continuing relevance today, albeit for quite different reasons, for as will be explained in more detail below, the US relative novelty rule is arguably more beneficial to developing countries than an absolute novelty rule would be.

Among those who have thought seriously about the issue of biopiracy, it is generally recognised that allegations of biopiracy must be divided into two distinct types: 1) those arising out of the grant of a "bad" (i.e., invalid) patent or "bad" (i.e., overbroad) patent claims; and 2) those arising out of the grant of valid patents pursuant to patent standards that are either a) too low, or b) fail to incorporate proposed provisions requiring disclosure of the origin of any genetic resources or traditional knowledge utilised in the inventive process and evidence of prior informed consent by the relevant source countries and communities.[106] While the first type of biopiracy claim has a solid legal foundation under existing patent law, the second is more a political than a legal argument.[107] At the moment WTO members are under no obligation under the TRIPS Agreement to define the general patent standards of novelty, inventive step, and capability of industrial application in any particular way, and while the CBD states as a general principle that countries which provide genetic resources are entitled to have access to and the transfer of technology that makes use of those resources, it creates little in the way of specific binding legal obligations in that regard for its members, of which (lamentably) the United States is not yet one.[108]

The next section of this chapter will examine and compare those biopiracy claims arising out of the grant of "bad" (i.e., invalid) US patents or "bad" (i.e., overbroad) patent claims and those arising out of the grant of valid US patents based on patent standards that are arguably "too low." The last section will examine proposals to modify existing international patent law to require disclosure of origin of genetic resources or traditional knowledge utilised in the inventive process and evidence of prior informed consent by the relevant source countries and communities, as well as proposals to create a new, *sui generis* form of intellectual property protection for traditional knowledge.

12.3.2 Biopiracy: Granting "bad" US patents or "bad" patent claims vs. US patent standards that are "too low"

Biopiracy claims of the first type could be (and in fact have been) raised in administrative or judicial proceedings challenging the validity of a US patent granted on an invention deriving in some measure from genetic resources or traditional knowledge from a foreign country. As we have seen, the basis for such challenges could be either: 1) that the invention is not new (even under the "relative novelty" rule followed in the US); 2) that the applicant is not the original and first inventor under existing originality and priority rules; or 3) that the invention is obvious.

Even in clear-cut cases of patent invalidity, however, the moral and economic injustice of the biopiracy embodied an apparently invalid US patent must be balanced against the costs involved in challenging the validity of the patent, together probability (or improbability) that an unchallenged invalid US patent will actually do any economic harm to a developing country, or to indigenous or local communities, and/or individuals whose genetic resources or traditional knowledge were utilised. In reality, most patents, even clearly valid patents, are economically worthless to their owners and thus pose little risk of economic harm to anyone else. Developing country governments, as well as indigenous and local communities or NGOs acting in their behalf, would be well advised to mount such challenges only where the risk of potential economic harm from the invalid patent or patent claims and/or the intangible benefits (such as the assertion of cultural identity and the exercise of self-determination in particularly egregious cases of "bad" patents or overbroad patent claims) to be derived from the challenge are manifest and no other parties are likely to mount a challenge to the validity of the patent or overbroad claims.

If an invalid (but not yet invalidated) US patent poses any serious economic risk to developing countries or any indigenous or local communities therein, parties willing to challenge the patent's validity will probably not be lacking, for if the invalid patent has any economic value at all to its holder, it could only be for illegitimate use as a club to induce particularly vulnerable parties within the US or importers to the US to pay royalties rather than challenge to the patent's validity. However, because any attempt or threat to enforce an obviously invalid patent might very well give rise to a claim of attempted monopolisation in violation of

US antitrust laws, those parties vulnerable to such coercive tactics will have ample economic incentive to mount a challenge to the validity of the patent, coupled with an antitrust counter-claim for treble damages.[109] Indeed, where this kind of tactic is being used on parties whose genetic resources and/or traditional knowledge have been utilised in securing the patent, it would clearly make economic sense for those parties to file a challenge to the validity of the patent, accompanied by a claim for treble damages under US antitrust laws.[110]

With the foregoing points in mind, a detailed comparison of the most prominent biopiracy controversies involving US patents is in order. What this comparison will reveal is that, of the seven biopiracy controversies, four involved valid US patents (two of which were nevertheless essentially worthless) that were apparently challenged as a result of misunderstandings about the US relative novelty rule, one involved a clearly invalid (but essentially worthless) patent that was eventually invalidated but in any event posed little potential harm to anyone, one involved a combination of valid (but quite narrow) claims and other overbroad claims that could have potentially caused economic harm to developing countries but were duly narrowed upon re-examination, and only one (still pending) controversy involves a patent that may well be invalid and is posing a threat of actual harm to a developing country.

12.3.3 An analysis of prominent biopiracy controversies involving US patents

1. *The Neem Patents*—The mother of all biopiracy controversies is the one generated by the 1992 grant of a US patent (Patent No. 5,124,349) to W. R. Grace & Co. for a "storage stable azadirachtin formulation," the active ingredient of which is derived from the neem tree (*Azadirachta indica*), which is common in India but not in the US[111] In 1994, the US Environmental Protection Agency registered Neemix, Grace's stabilised solution for use on food crops.[112] This was the first product derived from the neem tree approved for such use in the United States.

The neem tree has been the subject of a considerable number of patents in the US and elsewhere in the world, virtually all of which appear to have utilised public domain traditional knowledge as a starting point.[113] W. R. Grace's timing, however, was spectacularly bad, as the patent issued just as the CBD was opened for signature and the Uruguay Round was producing the WTO and the TRIPS Agreement.[114]

In 1995, "a coalition of 225 agricultural, scientific and trade groups, as well as over 100,000 Indian farmers represented by the Foundation on Economic Trends," filed a petition to revoke the W. R. Grace US patent "on grounds that it lacked novelty and, in addition, was immoral."[115] "The coalition vowed that it would make the W. R. Grace patent a watershed in international intellectual property disputes, in which it would convince the world that the West was guilty of rampant intellectual piracy."[116] This campaign did not succeed in the US.[117] However, the coalition did manage to convince the European Patent Office to revoke a neem-related patent issued to W. R. Grace in Europe, but not the patent that was equivalent to 5,124,349.[118]

For all of the controversy generated by the grant of the US patent, it was not so much a legal controversy as a political one, generated by a fundamental misunderstanding of basic principles of patent law generally and the US relative novelty rule specifically.[119] Contrary to the impression created by some critics of this patent, the W. R. Grace patent was not to the neem seed itself,[120] nor to its use as a natural (and environmentally friendly) insect repellent, which is one of the customary uses made of the neem seed in India.[121] Rather, the patent was on a method of production and a resulting product consisting of a storage stable solution "containing azadirachtin" wherein the solution was "non-degrading to azadirachtin."[122] The result of this invention was an azadirachtin-containing solution with improved stability and longer shelf life[123] as compared to the natural product, which is highly unstable.[124] The claimed invention was thus an improvement on the natural product and had the effect of making the benefits of the active ingredient available even in areas where the neem tree itself will not grow and to which the active ingredient could not be shipped otherwise. Contrary to comments propagated by opponents of the Grace patent, anyone in the United States can use neem extract prepared in the traditionally known way or by any method besides the patented method; further, anyone anywhere outside of the United States, even in India, can continue to use neem extract and can even prepare the extract by the method described in the Grace patent because Grace's patent rights are limited to the United States only.[125]

While use of the neem seed as a natural insect repellent has apparently been widely known in India for generations,[126] the particular method and product claimed in the W. R. Grace patent were arguably new, at least in the United States[127] and perhaps in India itself.[128] Thus, claims that the invention was not "new" were in actuality either based on a misunderstanding of the US relative novelty rule[129] or a basic misunderstanding of patent law, which allows patents to be granted for inventions based on knowledge present in the public domain.[130] In this case, the US patent system functioned precisely as it was supposed to, by encouraging the public disclosure in the US of an invention that was based upon, but did not claim, traditional Indian knowledge that was widely known and thus in the public domain.[131]

Interestingly, following on the heels of the highly publicised W. R. Grace neem patent controversy, at least seven US neem-related patents were filed by Indian nationals, companies, or non-profit research institutions over the next six years.[132] Thus, the W. R. Grace neem patent controversy apparently had the salutary effect of stimulating the filing of US patents by Indian researchers—a development that arguably benefits, rather than harms, India, as it will give Indian researchers limited exclusive rights in their neem-related inventions in the U.S.[133]

2. The Ayahuasca Plant Patent—If the neem controversy is the mother of all biopiracy cases, the ayahuasca plant patent controversy has a legitimate claim to being an even more remote progenitor of existing US biopiracy controversies, as it traces back to a 1986 plant patent, No. 5,751, granted to one Loren Miller, an American, granting him exclusive rights in a variety of *Banisteriopsis caapi*, which he had called "Da Vine."[134] The patent description stated that the "plant was discovered growing in a domestic garden in the Amazon rainforest of South America."[135] The patentee claimed that Da Vine represented a new and distinct variety of *B. caapi*, primarily because of the flower colour.[136]

For generations, "shamans of indigenous tribes throughout the Amazon Basin have processed the bark of [*B.*] *caapi* to produce a ceremonial drink known as "ayahuasca," which is used "in religious and healing ceremonies to diagnose and treat illnesses, meet with spirits, and divine the future."[137] Upon learning about the US plant patent in 1994, the Coordinating Body of Indigenous Organizations of the Amazon Basin (COICA), an umbrella organisation representing over 400 indigenous groups, and the Amazon Coalition enlisted the Centre for International Environmental Law (CIEL) to file a request for re-examination of the patent.[138] CIEL argued that Da Vine was neither new nor distinct.[139]

They also argued that granting the patent would be contrary to the public policy and morality aspects of the patent statute because of the sacred nature of *B. caapi* throughout the Amazonian Basin.[140] Finally, CIEL introduced extensive new prior art,[141] which initially led the USPTO to reject the patent claim,[142] agreeing that Da Vine was not distinguishable from the prior art presented by CIEL, but after further arguments presented by the patentee reinstated the patent (which in any event was due to expire at the end of 2003).[143]

Generally overlooked in discussions of the Ayahuasca controversy is that the patent involved here was not a utility patent (i.e., a patent for an invention), but rather a form of patent protection that is virtually unique to the United States—namely, plant patent protection, which was first made available in 1930.[144] Plant patent protection differs from utility patent protection in a number of important respects. First, the subject matter of plant patent protection extends to any asexually reproduced plant (i.e., any plant that one has precisely genetically reproduced by a cutting or other asexual means), including any "cultivated sports, mutants, hybrids, and newly found seedlings, other than a tuber propagated plant or a plant found in an uncultivated state."[145] Because Miller claimed to have found the plant in a cultivated garden in the Amazonian rain forest, and was apparently able to asexually reproduce the plant by means of a cutting,[146] that plant variety would qualify for US plant patent protection, so long as it was new (in the same, relative-novelty sense that applies to utility patents), distinct (in the sense of being distinguishable from existing varieties of plants disclosed in the prior art), and non-obvious (in the same sense as is required for utility patents) in the United States.[147] While the utility requirement is replaced by the distinctness requirement for plant patent protection, thus distinguishing plant patents from utility patents,[148] there is both an asexual reproduction and a non-obviousness requirement,[149] thus distinguishing plant patent protection from *sui generis* plant variety protection.[150] As long as the patented plant variety is a distinct variety that is asexually reproducible and has in fact been asexually reproduced, is new in the relative sense that the variety is not disclosed in the relevant prior art—i.e., was not known or used in the US and was not the subject of a patent or printed publication in the US or elsewhere prior to the filing of the plant patent application—and was not obvious in light of what was disclosed in the prior art, the plant variety would be patentable under US plant patent law.[151]

As for the argument that a US patent on the plant variety should have been denied because of the sacred nature of the vine, which indigenous peoples in South America have characterised as a religious symbol analogous to the Christian cross or Eucharist, the very statement of the argument reveals the theoretical and practical difficulties implicit therein. To begin with, the morality exception in US patent law is a variation of the utility requirement—the theory being that antisocial inventions lack moral utility—and utility is not a requirement for plant patent protection.[152] Moreover, while it might very well be appropriate as a matter of sound public policy to deny intellectual property protection on moral grounds, a threshold question that must be resolved in such cases is whose moral standards should be relevant in making such a determination? Should the US Patent and Trademark Office entertain arguments that inventions involving the production of alcoholic beverages should be denied as contrary to Islamic law or that inventions involving the slaughter of animals for food should be denied as contrary to Hindu or Buddhist principles of vegetarianism? While Article 27.2 of TRIPS specifically permits WTO member countries to exclude from patentability any invention the commercial exploitation of which is contrary to *ordre public* or morality, that same provision makes it clear that the exclusions contemplated are those involving patents the commercial exploitation of which is both prohibited by law and in fact contrary to the *ordre public* or morality within the territory of the particular member country.[153]

Also overlooked in the furore over Loren Miller's plant patent is just how narrow the exclusive rights turn out to be. Unlike the exclusive rights in patented inventions, the exclusive rights conferred by a US plant patent are limited to "the right to exclude others from asexually reproducing the plant, and from using, offering for sale, or selling the plant so reproduced, or any of its parts, throughout the United States, or from importing the plant so reproduced, or any parts thereof, into the United States."[154] Thus, to infringe a plant patent, one must be shown to have asexually reproduced the particular variety that is protected. Plant patent protection is thus more analogous to copyright protection, in the sense that it merely protects against unauthorised reproduction of the protected variety, than to utility patent protection, which creates exclusive rights even against subsequent independent inventors of the invention.[155]

Indeed, the narrowness of this exclusive plant patent right is commonly cited as one of the principal reasons that plant innovators have continued to press for utility patent protection for newly developed varieties of plants, notwithstanding the enactment of plant patent 1930 and the later enactment of plant variety protection in 1970.[156] Both US plant patents and US plant variety protection are widely perceived as being of little value, as the US plant patent law requires too much (i.e., non-obviousness) for too little (i.e., an exclusive right to prevent reproduction),[157] while US plant variety protection undercuts the plant breeder's exclusive rights with a broad privilege on the part of other breeders to use protected varieties to create new varieties of their own and an equally broad farmer's privilege to replant saved seed of a protected variety.[158]

It is thus no accident that, whereas the W. R. Grace utility patent on the neem seed extract is numbered 5,124,349 (representing the number of US utility patents that had previously been granted since the US patent system was created in the late 18th century), Loren Miller's plant patent is numbered 5,751 (representing the number of US plant patents that had previously been granted since 1930). CIEL seems to have spent a substantial sum of money attacking a plant patent that: 1) may not have been all that valuable to Loren Miller (though the fact that Miller stoutly defended his patent against attacks on its validity indicates that Miller believed the plant patent to have had at least some economic value),[159] and 2) that could not conceivably cause any economic harm to indigenous communities in the Amazonian Basin unless some of those indigenous communities should eventually overcome any lurking religious scruples and decide to start importing into the United States any varieties of *B. caapi* that Loren Miller might argue were asexually reproduced from his US protected variety.[160] In short, for all of the sound and fury that went into challenging the validity of this plant patent, the challenge ultimately signified very little, other than illustrating the need to be more discriminating in mounting claims of biopiracy.

3. The Quinoa (and Basmati Rice) Patents—The quinoa and the later basmati rice patent controversies bear certain superficial similarities, but are quite distinct in other more important respects. Both the quinoa and basmati rice patents contained valid (but quite narrow) patent claims, but the two controversies are nevertheless distinguishable, in that 1) the quinoa patent eventually proved to be an entirely valid, but essentially worthless patent, while the basmati rice patent contained both valid claims and more troubling overbroad claims that were ultimately rejected upon re-examination; 2) these overbroad claims were challenged by the same organisation that successfully mounted a challenge in the intervening turmeric patent controversy that will be discussed in the next section; and 3) even after the overbroad claims in the basmati rice patent were rejected, the basmati rice controversy lived on as a geographical indication controversy, albeit one involving an admittedly weak geographic indication.[161] Accordingly, the principal focus of this section will be the quinoa patent controversy, while the basmati rice and turmeric patent controversies will be discussed in more detail in the section immediately following.

In 1994 a US patent (Patent No. 5,304,718) was granted to Sarah Ward and Duane Johnson, who were agronomists at Colorado State University, for "Cytoplasmic Male Sterile Quinoa."[162] The assignee named in the patent is Research Corporation Technologies, Inc., an independent technology company that works in partnership with universities and research institutions worldwide to commercialise their early-stage technologies.[163] Quinoa (*Chenopodium quinoa*) is described as "a highly nutritious drought-resistant food crop grown in the cold high-elevation regions of the Andean countries of South America."[164] "Indigenous communities ... have bred numerous varieties, including Apelawa, named after a village in Bolivia."[165] "In order for plant breeders to produce hybrids from self-pollinating quinoa plants, the male properties of one parent must be eliminated."[166] Use of male sterile plants can avoid the labour-intensive removal of anthers from individual plants.[167] The patent states that male sterile quinoa lines have been reported in technical literature but claims that a reliable system of cytoplasmic male sterile plants has not been "available for commercial production of quinoa hybrids."[168]

This particular patent attracted the ire of Rural Advancement Foundation International (RAFI; now the Action Group on Erosion, Technology and Concentration (ETC)): Rather than attacking the patent in the USPTO, however, RAFI/ETC chose to mount a media and political campaign against the two academics who filed the patent and their academic employer (a form of harassment that has become sufficiently common that academics now speak of it as "getting RAFI'd").[169] In the blizzard of misleading and inaccurate assertions and quotes it produced about the patent, RAFI/ETC did identify one potentially significant, albeit speculative, adverse impact that the patent could have on indigenous Andean farmers.[170] Apparently, consumption of quinoa in the US and Europe is growing, and most quinoa is currently imported from Bolivia, where it is grown by Bolivian campesinos.[171] In a 1996 Biopiracy Update, RAFI/ ETC warned that if a larger market for quinoa is developed in the US for high-yielding hybrids derived from a traditional Bolivian variety, it could displace Bolivia's current export market—though no evidence of any actual adverse impact of the patent on the Bolivian export market was cited.[172]

Having made this speculative point about the possible adverse effect of the patent on Bolivian farmers, the RAFI/ETC report went on to state that "[w]hether or not the patent has any direct impact on Bolivia's farmers ... there is no denying that they have effectively lost control of traditional quinoa seeds that were developed over centuries by indigenous peoples of the Andes."[173] The irony in this statement is that the loss of control that RAFI/ETC is concerned about is due to the fact that quinoa seeds have fallen into the public domain. If RAFI/ETC seriously wished to help Bolivian farmers retain control over quinoa varieties that they have developed, it would devote more of its efforts to ensuring that Bolivian farmers or non-profit agricultural research facilities were securing timely utility patent, plant patent, and/or plant variety protection in the US and Bolivia, rather than issuing broadside attacks on intellectual property law as the nemesis of indigenous communities and the developing world generally.[174] As it is, RAFI/ETC seems to be demanding the right of Bolivian farmers to control what others do with genetic materials that are in the public domain.[175] As we have seen, implicit in this rhetorically appealing claim is a breathtakingly broad assertion of a private right to control information in the public domain, in direct opposition to the oft-stated view of public research organisations, as well as many proponents of farmers' rights, that plant genetic resources should be freely available as "the common heritage of mankind."[176]

While RAFI/ETC subsequently claimed that the pressure of the Andean farmers had "forced Colorado State University ... to surrender" the quinoa patent[177] (a useful assertion for generating contributions, after all), the actual reason behind the decision not to pay the maintenance fee that would be necessary to prevent the patent from being abandoned was apparently more prosaic.[178] According to a listserve message by John A. Daly, a consultant on science, technology and development matters, which lambasted RAFI/ETC for "having gone overboard in the wrong direction on this patent," the trait developed by Ward and Johnson "could not be used for commercial production of hybrid quinoa seed because it has not been possible to find other necessary complementary germplasm in quinoa."[179] Thus, "it appears that the patent has no value because it will not lead to commercial hybrid quinoa."[180] The quinoa patent controversy aptly illustrates that there is generally no economic incentive to maintain worthless patents.

As one commentator has suggested, perhaps the most important lesson to be drawn from the quinoa patent controversy is the wisdom of requiring (where feasible) that patent applicants "disclose the origins of all source biological material from which the inventions they claim are derived,"[181] particularly where, as here, it would probably have been in the best interests of the patent applicants to make such a disclosure anyway, as it might have helped avoid the subsequent controversy.[182] The proposal to require disclosure of origin of genetic resources as a routine part of the patent application process will be discussed in the last section of this chapter.

4. The Turmeric and Basmati Rice Patents—In 1995, a US patent on "Use of Turmeric in Wound Healing" was awarded to two Indian nationals who had as a condition of employment assigned their patent rights to their employer, the University of Mississippi Medical Center,[183] as is customary practice among US research organisations. Whatever else might be said about this admittedly "bad" US patent, it does illustrate how the US relative novelty rule encourages the importation of technology into the US, as that is precisely what seems to have happened in this case.[184] Once the patent is issued, however, the Indian Council of Scientific and Industrial Research (CSIR)—the same organisation that would later challenge the basmati rice patent—requested re-examination of the patent, arguing that turmeric has been used for thousands of years for healing wounds and rashes and therefore its medicinal use was not novel.[185] The CSIR claim was supported by documentary evidence of traditional knowledge, including an ancient Sanskrit text and a paper published in 1953 in the Journal of the Indian Medical Association.[186] Based on this documentary evidence, the US Patent and Trademark Office revoked the patent.[187] The legal costs incurred by India to challenge the turmeric patent were calculated by the Indian Government to be about $10,000.[188]

The critical question is what CSIR got for its efforts in this case, beyond invalidating an admittedly "bad" US patent. According to news reports, CSIR challenged the turmeric patent partly for symbolic reasons and partly to acquire expertise in US patent re-examination procedures[189]—expertise that would later stand the CSIR in good stead when it filed for re-examination of the basmati rice patent, whose broad claims posed a far more serious risk of potential economic harm to India than the essentially worthless turmeric patent.[190]

For while the turmeric patent was disturbingly overbroad,[191] a broad patent is not necessarily a strong patent, as the outcomes of the turmeric and the basmati rice patent controversies both illustrate.[192] Indeed, the turmeric patent was even weaker than the broad product claims of the basmati rice patent, which encompassed any rice plant that possessed certain characteristics,[193] as the turmeric patent merely claimed a method of treatment. Because infringement of method patents is notoriously difficult to detect, particularly where the method involves a staple article of commerce such as turmeric (which has culinary as well as medicinal uses) and use of the method does not produce a publicly distributed product that will notify the patent holder that the method patent is indeed being infringed, method patents are generally far less valuable than product patents.[194]

Further, as a result of a 1999 amendment to US patent law, the prospective value of medical method patents (though not the turmeric patent itself, as the amendment does not apply to patents issued based on a filing date prior to September 30, 1996) was further diminished by section 287(c) of the US patent law, which states that "[w]ith respect to a medical practitioner's performance of a medical activity that constitutes an infringement ... the provisions of [the patent act providing the remedies of damages, injunction and the award of attorney fees] shall not apply against the medical practitioner or against a related health care entity with respect to such medical activity."[195] (Critics of this amendment, which was lobbied through by the politically powerful American Medical Association,[196] claim that the provision makes medical method patents essentially worthless, as it robs them of any practical method of enforcement.[197]) As a practical matter, if the turmeric patent was worth anything at all to the University of Mississippi Medical Center, it was primarily as a defensive patent filing, which would notify the medical research world that the patent holder was engaging in this kind of research, thereby precluding anyone else from filing a subsequent patent that might claim this subject matter.

Nor would the turmeric patent have likely had any potential adverse impact on the millions of Indian users of this traditional method of healing, as Article 27.3(a) of the TRIPS Agreement specifically permits

WTO members to exclude from patentability any "diagnostic, therapeutic and surgical methods for the treatment of humans or animals."[198] Thus, while the time and money CSIR spent to challenge the turmeric patent was probably well worth the effort, given the expertise that CSIR gained for later deployment in the far more important basmati rice patent controversy, the turmeric patent itself was an essentially worthless US patent that would have had no conceivable adverse effect on Indian nationals in either the US or India.

5. The Maca Patents—Flushed with its claim of victory in the quinoa patent controversy,[199] RAFI/ETC has more recently unleashed a similar media campaign against several patents on extracts from "maca, a high-altitude Andean plant (of the *Cruciferae* (mustard) family) that has been grown for centuries by indigenous peoples in the Puna highlands of Peru, both as a staple food crop and for medicinal purposes."[200] "Today, maca-based products are commonly promoted as natural enhancers of sexual function ('natural Viagra') and fertility."[201] While that has stimulated demand for maca-based product in the developed world, ETC claims that two recent US patents related to maca may actually foreclose opportunities for the "true innovators" of the Andean crop.[202]

Although the indigenous peoples' and farmers' organisations that gathered at the offices of the Ecological Forum in Lima, Peru to denounce "patents on maca,"[203] the patents in question are in fact for extracts of *Lepidium meyenii* roots for pharmaceutical applications[204] and a composition of maca and antler for augmenting testosterone levels.[205] "The coalition is also requesting that the Lima-based International Potato Center (CIP)," which is a member of the Consultative Group for International Agricultural Research (CGIAR), "as a promoter and protector of maca seed, take action to prohibit intellectual property claims—not just on seeds and genetic materials held in its gene bank, but on traditional knowledge of indigenous communities."[206] ETC suggests that CIP "follow the example of its sister institution in Columbia, the International Center for Tropical Agriculture (CIAT), which has formally challenged a US patent on Mexico's yellow bean" (see the Enola Bean controversy below).[207]

Without a trace of irony, ETC notes that "[t]wenty years ago agricultural experts declared that maca was in danger of extinction as a domesticated" crop.[208] While ETC admits that "increased demand for maca has created new markets and income for Peruvian farmers," it claims that the US patents "may ultimately foreclose opportunity for farmers and indigenous people who are the true innovators of the Andean crop."[209] ETC goes on to quote Alejandro Argumedo of the Quechua-Ayamara Association for Sustainable Livelihoods (ANDES) as saying "Ironically, now we are in danger of losing maca—not to extinction—but to predatory US patents."[210]

A moment's reflection, however, demonstrates that these are utterly fallacious arguments, as the US maca patents did little more than help create a market for a plant that was in danger of going extinct. The only way that the US patents on maca extracts and mixtures could adversely affect Peruvian farmers would be in barring imports of those particular extracts or mixtures.[211] The patents could not be used to bar the import of maca itself.[212] And one wonders where, other than the Andes, the holders of these "predatory" US patents might be expected to secure adequate supplies of maca, a high-altitude Andean plant that is apparently grown at elevations higher than all but the highest snow-capped peaks in the United States.[213] Yet, rather than critically examining any of these points, ETC is content to mass circulate this kind of disinformation on its website.[214] While perhaps useful in promoting its own ideological agenda, ETC is sadly doing a real disservice to indigenous farmers and communities in the Andes on whose behalf it purports to speak.[215]

6. The Enola Bean Patent—Of all the high-profile biopiracy controversies stimulated by US patents, the most serious is the one generated by Patent No. 5,894,079, a utility patent on a yellow bean derived (and apparently virtually indistinguishable) from a bean that Mexicans and other Latin Americans have been eating (and growing) for centuries.[216] Named the Enola Bean, based on the middle name of the patent holder's wife,[217] the bean was supposedly developed from a bag of dry beans that, according to the patent, were purchased and brought over from Mexico in 1994.[218] However, the patent holder's patent lawyer concedes that the date recited in the patent is "an unfortunate error, since the beans were actually brought over in 1991."[219] That error was indeed unfortunate, if it was indeed an error, as the patent holder apparently would not have been physically able to produce a new variety in the time specified in the patent.[220] Thus, many reputable academic and other public-sector research organisations, such as Centro Internacional de Agricultura Tropical (CIAT), and not simply ETC/RAFI, suspect that the patent holder may have simply given the bean a new name and gotten patent rights that the patent holder is now using to exclude imports of yellow beans from Mexico.[221] It is little wonder that CIAT has decided to challenge the Enola bean patent.[222]

But the patent holder may be playing an exceedingly dangerous game, as he is attempting, on the one hand, to argue (in order to defend the patent's validity) that his patented bean is distinguishable from Mexican yellow beans, but have nevertheless brought an infringement proceeding against importers of Mexican yellow beans.[223] To the suspicious eye, this looks like the patent holder is trying to have it both ways.[224] Together with the "unfortunate error" in the patent about the date the progenitor beans were supposedly brought over from Mexico, the behaviour of the patent holder begins to give off the unsavoury aroma of possible patent misuse or worse, particularly as Mexico has claimed that a process of "genetic fingerprinting shows that the Enola bean is the same as a bean registered in Sinaola, Mexico, in 1978."[225]

If it can be established in court that the patent holder did not, in fact, engage in any inventive activity, and is simply using an invalid patent to try to induce royalty payments, then the patent holder may find itself facing, not simply a challenge to the validity of its patent, but an antitrust counterclaim for treble damages in the infringement proceedings that the patent holder has brought against the importer of Mexican beans.[226] Thus, while the validity of this patent is open to serious challenge, and will clearly have an adverse impact on Mexican farmers if it is not challenged,[227] there seems to be no dearth of parties willing, indeed anxious, to mount a challenge to its validity. Again, the main lesson to be drawn from this case is the wisdom of requiring the disclosure of the origin of genetic resources as a routine part of the patent application process—a topic which will be addressed in more detail in the last section of this chapter.

12.3.4 General conclusions on the biopiracy episodes

In short, the foregoing biopiracy controversies stimulated by the issuance of US patents confirm that an important distinction must be drawn between those claims of biopiracy that are based on arguably "bad" patents (i.e., the basmati rice, turmeric, and Enola bean controversies), and those biopiracy claims that are, in effect, asserting that US patent standards are too low (i.e., the neem, ayahuasca, quinoa, and maca controversies). As we have seen, while the former have a sound legal basis in existing US patent, the latter claims are essentially making political policy arguments.

As for the first kind of claim, there may be occasions where it would be in the interest of a developing country or representatives of indigenous or local communities to challenge a "bad" US patent, but not every bad patent poses the same risk to developing countries, indigenous or local communities, and/or individuals whose genetic resources or traditional knowledge served as the starting point for such a patent, as the turmeric patent controversy illustrates. Arguably, only where the patent holds the potential for doing serious harm in a developing country that is the source of the genetic resources or traditional knowledge on which the patent is based should such a challenge be mounted. As the Enola bean patent controversy illustrates, however, those kinds of "bad" patents will probably not lack for challengers to the validity of the patent in any event.

By contrast, any developing-world effort to mount a challenge to US patent standards as too low would seem to be a spectacularly bad idea, for as we have already seen in the earlier part of this chapter, low US patent standards might in fact be significantly more beneficial to developing country innovators than would any hypothetical benefits (if any) that might accrue to developing countries from a general tightening up of US patent standards. The reality is that the issuance of valid patents under existing US patent standards that are arguably "too low" may well generate substantial benefits to developing country innovators who take advantage of the availability of US patent protection, while the benefits accruing to developing countries from a tightening up of those patent standards is highly speculative, and might indeed cause significant harm to developing countries, as their innovators might find themselves unable to market their innovations in the world's most lucrative single market for innovation.

If any patent standards need to be tightened, it is arguably the patent standards that are adopted by developing countries, now that the era of free riding on the innovative activity of the industrialised world is drawing to a close. Just because the United States chooses, for whatever policy reason, to set low patent standards for its system of patent protection does not mean that a developing country is under any international obligation to adopt the same standards or to automatically grant patent protection to inventions that have been patented in the United States. To the extent that the developing world is labouring under the erroneous impression that there is such an obligation, that misimpression is ironically a probable consequence of the rhetoric of "piracy" deployed by industrialised world intellectual property owners in their overzealous effort to advance the international negotiations that eventually produced the TRIPS Agreement. Having been the first to deploy the rhetoric of piracy, intellectual property owners in the industrialised world have only themselves to blame for the "biopiracy boomerang" that is now being used with such effect by the developing world in multilateral trade negotiations.

In actuality, however, as long as a developing country's patent standards are not manifestly inconsistent with the TRIPS Agreement and are not radically out of sync with customary patent practice in the few areas of patent law where widespread customs actually exist, each WTO member is free to choose its own patent standards. Apart from establishing an international priority date for any patents that might otherwise issue under a developing country's patent laws, the grant of a patent in the US is largely irrelevant to a developing country's grant or denial of a patent on the same invention, so long as the patent protection accorded in that country meets the general standards outlined in TRIPS.

Finally, while it may make sound policy sense to adopt an international requirement for patent applicants to disclose the origin of any relevant genetic resources and/or traditional knowledge relied upon in developing the claimed invention and evidence of the prior informed consent of the source countries, communities, and/or individuals involved, such proposals must either be consistent with the TRIPS Agreement as it currently stands or be formally proposed as a modification of TRIPS. Likewise, any proposal for a new form of *sui generis* legal protection for traditional knowledge, though clearly permissible under TRIPS (which after all specifies only minimum, not uniform, standards for intellectual property protection) must be based on theoretically sound foundations and be capable of easy implementation and administration. These two issues will be explored in the next, and final, section of this chapter.

12.4 MODIFYING EXISTING SYSTEMS OF INTELLECTUAL PROPERTY PROTECTION VS. CREATING A NEW *SUI GENERIS* SYSTEM OF LEGAL PROTECTION FOR TRADITIONAL KNOWLEDGE

Before considering any proposals for new, *sui generis* forms of protection for traditional knowledge, it would first behove the various international entities to explore some of the more modest proposals that have been made for modifying existing intellectual property regimes to provide more effective legal protection for traditional knowledge. For example, the WIPO or WTO (or both) might wish to explore how know-how licenses and material transfer agreements, as well as the concepts of joint authorship, inventorship and joint breeders' rights, can more effectively be utilised to channel traditional knowledge (and knowledge-holders) into one or more of the existing intellectual property regimes.

A specific issue that needs to be addressed is precisely how one might structure, consistent with the TRIPS Agreement, any proposal to modify patent and/or plant variety protection systems (or for that matter any other form of intellectual property protection) to require, as a condition of acquiring or enforcing patent, plant variety, or any other intellectual property rights, that the rights holder disclose the origin of any genetic resources and/or traditional knowledge relied upon in developing the intellectual property for which protection is sought and provide evidence of prior informed consent of the relevant source countries, communities and/or individuals. Only after considering how this relatively modest proposal might (or might not) work in practice, should one undertake the more ambitious project of creating an entirely new, *sui generis* system of legal protection for traditional knowledge—particularly, as the latter project is likely to be fraught with theoretical and practical difficulties of its own.

12.4.1 Required disclosures of origin and evidence of prior informed consent

At the third session of the World Intellectual Property Organization's Standing Committee on the Law of Patents in September 1999, the Delegation of Columbia proposed the introduction of a new article to the draft Patent Law Treaty that would recognise that all industrial property protection should guarantee the protection of a country's biological and genetic heritage, and specify that the grant of patents or registrations that relate to elements of that heritage are to be subject to their having been acquired legally.[228] In response to that proposal, the World Intellectual Property Organization (WIPO) eventually established an Intergovernmental Committee on Intellectual Property and Genetic Resources, Traditional Knowledge and Folklore (hereinafter Intergovernmental Committee or IGC), which has undertaken a comprehensive program of work related to the protection of genetic resources, traditional knowledge and folklore.[229] While the IGC has not yet addressed the issue raised by the Delegation of Columbia, it has issued a report entitled "Elements of a *Sui Generis* System for the Protection of Traditional Knowledge."[230]

Before the WIPO or any of its members pursue the *sui generis* option, however, it behoves the WIPO to address the merits of the proposal of the Delegation of Columbia, as well as various other proposals that have been made to modify existing patent systems to require disclosure of origin of genetic resources and/or traditional knowledge and evidence of prior informed consent of any source countries, communities, or individuals. While the WIPO has thus far been reticent on that question, one of its officials, Dr. Nuno Pires de Carvalho, by contrast, has addressed the issue in a series of published and soon-to-be published articles, including one published article aptly entitled "Requiring Disclosure of the Origin of Genetic Resources and Prior Informed Consent in Patent Applications Without Infringing the TRIPS Agreement: The Problem and the Solution,"[231] and a second soon-to-be published article entitled "From the Shaman's Hut to the Patent Office: A Road Under Construction."[232]

In these articles, Dr. Carvalho points out that requiring the disclosure of origin of genetic resources and evidence of prior informed consent as a condition for acquiring a patent is likely to be held inconsistent with the TRIPS Agreement as it currently stands. This is because Article 27.1 makes it quite clear that patents are to be made available for *any* inventions, whether products or processes, in all fields of technology, provided they are new, involve an inventive step and are capable of industrial application. Likewise, Article 62.1 makes it clear that procedures and formalities required as a condition of the acquisition or maintenance of intellectual property rights must be: 1) reasonable;

and 2) consistent with the provisions of the TRIPS Agreement.[233] Dr. Carvalho concludes that any conditions imposed on the acquisition of patents will be found inconsistent with TRIPS unless the conditions: a) help patent examiners assess the novelty, inventiveness and susceptibility of industrial application; b) help patent examiners determine inventorship and, consequently, ownership; or c) are aimed at evidencing the payment of fees. Requiring disclosure of origin and evidence of prior informed consent for any purpose other than for these limited goals would interfere, and thus inconsistent with, the goals embodied in TRIPS. As Dr. Carvalho puts it, "patents are not certificates of *good* behaviour."[234] Rather, they are certificates of *inventive* behaviour.[235]

On the other hand, Dr. Carvalho argues quite persuasively that a conflict with TRIPS can be avoided if the disclosure of origin and prior informed consent requirement is made a condition for enforcing the patent, drawing on established patent law doctrines of fraudulent procurement and unclean hands generally.[236] Thus, instead of imposing the requirement as a condition of patentability, he suggests making the *enforceability* of patent rights dependent on compliance with such a requirement.[237]

This proposal has three additional practical advantages over requiring the disclosure of origin of genetic resources and evidence of prior informed consent as condition for acquiring a patent. First, making the requirement a condition for enforcing the patent will avoid imposing on already overworked patent offices the crushing burden that would be entailed in examining thousands (or even millions) of patent applications involving genetic resources or traditional knowledge to ensure compliance with the disclosure requirement, irrespective of how valuable (or worthless) the patent, if issued, might turn out to be. Second, making the requirement a condition for enforcing a patent will serve to focus the inquiry into the adequacy of the disclosure of origin and evidence of prior informed consent on those few issued patents that are sufficiently valuable to give their owner an economic motivation to bring infringement proceedings in a court of law. One can equitably share economic benefits, after all, only where there are economic benefits to be shared. Third, the failure to comply with the disclosure requirements will not invalidate the patent—thereby killing the goose that would otherwise lay the golden egg—but, rather, will create a strong incentive on the part of the patent holder to retroactively strike a deal with those from whom prior informed consent should have been gotten in the first place, thereby giving those parties a measure of bargaining power to extract, and perhaps even a legal restitutionary claim to, an equitable share of the benefits accruing from the enforcement of the patent.[238]

But how would this disclosure requirement be administered, as a practical matter, and when would the disclosure occur, if not during the patent application process? The short answer is that the required disclosure *would* occur during the patent application process. It is just that the disclosure called for would not be administratively examined, nor would a failure to disclose during the patent application process have any bearing on the grant or denial, or the ultimate validity, of a patent. Relieving patent offices of the burden of examining such disclosures only makes sense, as it is highly unlikely that a patent examiner can ferret out a failure to disclose or an inadequate disclosure in any event. To paraphrase Dr. Carvalho, patent examiners are examiners of inventive behaviour, and have no particular training or expertise in ferreting out the bad behaviour of non-disclosing patent applicants, even when the non-disclosure goes to the validity of the patent claims.[239] Indeed, that is one of the reasons why so many issued patents turn out to be "bad" patents that are subsequently invalidated in infringement proceedings.[240]

By way of demonstrating the rationale for minimising the role of the patent office in administering any disclosure requirement with respect to genetic resources or traditional knowledge, an analogy can be drawn to the fairly perfunctory requirements in US patent law for establishing that an invention has the requisite utility (or, in European parlance, is susceptible of industrial application). As Professor Scott Kieff has pointed out, it is not clear that the patent system needs a separate utility requirement, as there is unlikely to be any harm to the public in granting useless patents.[241] After all, if a patented invention indeed turns out to be useless, who would want to practice it; and if no one would want to practice it, how is the public harmed by its issuance, so long as the patent holder pays all of the required filing and maintenance fees? Indeed, would rational patent holder continue to pay maintenance fees on an essentially useless patent?[242] Unlike patents that might be invalid for non-novelty or obviousness, a useless patent doesn't even confer any illicit bargaining power on its owner, as no one will be inclined to license, or even to infringe, a useless patent. To be sure, a seemingly useless patent may at some point prove to have utility, but if that turns out to be so, issuance of the patent may have aided in the search for utility, and as Professor Kieff points out, even an inherently useless patent imparts knowledge, if only knowledge of what *not* to do. For all of these reasons, the utility requirement in US patent law has played (and arguably should play) only a marginal role in the patent application or invalidation process.

Likewise, because the failure to disclose the origin of genetic resources and evidence of prior informed consent cannot play *any* role in the decision to deny or invalidate a patent, without simultaneously running afoul of the TRIPS Agreement, it makes all the more sense to reduce the role of the patent office to that of simply accepting the required disclosures and maintaining a record of them for future use in patent infringement litigation. In the event that a patent issues and patent infringement proceedings are initiated (or indeed merely threatened), the party accused of infringement will have ample motivation to examine the patent record to discover any basis for invalidating or otherwise avoiding enforcement of the patent.

In any event, just as infringement proceedings tend to shine the light of public scrutiny on the validity of patents, as well as on any inequitable behaviour on the part of the patent holder in the acquisition or enforcement of the patent, so those infringement proceedings will likely provide the best opportunity to examine whether the holder of an admittedly valuable patent has in fact made the required disclosure of origin and evidence of prior informed consent with respect to any genetic resources or traditional knowledge relied on in the inventive process. Even if an accused infringer, for whatever reason, has no particular incentive to blow the whistle on the patent holder for failing to comply with the disclosure of origin and evidence of prior informed consent requirements—the accused infringer, after all, may simply wish to attack the validity of the patent, but even so will be serving the interests of those who might otherwise have a claim to an equitable sharing of the benefits flowing from the patent—the infringement proceeding itself is likely to attract the attention of those source countries, communities or individuals who might have a claim to an equitable sharing of any benefits growing out of the recovery of damages or profits in patent infringement proceedings. Indeed, these parties need not wait until the patent holder contacts them in an effort to wash the patent holder's unclean hands. Violation of the disclosure of origin and evidence of prior informed consent requirement would appear to give these parties a restitutionary claim for unjust enrichment, thus enabling them to invoke the court's assistance in reaching an equitable agreement with the patent holder.[243] Moreover, because the value of genetic resources and/or traditional knowledge might be far more apparent once a patent is granted and infringed, than might have been the case when the patent holder initially acquired the genetic resources and/or traditional knowledge, there would be a strong incentive on the part of the recipient of those resources and/or knowledge to strike a bargain upfront, rather than face the prospect of restitutionary claims further down the line. At the same time, any temptation on the part of the source country, community, or individuals, to hold out for a better bargain could be minimised by terms that promise the providers a percentage of any royalties that any patent might eventually generate.

This brief summary of how a disclosure of origin and evidence of prior informed consent requirement, imposed as a condition for enforcing a patent, would operate in practice should suffice to demonstrate that the requirement would seem to create a strong incentive on the part of inventors to obtain either prior or retroactive informed consent to utilise genetic resources and/or traditional knowledge, thus enhancing both the value and the utility of know-how licenses and material transfer agreements as devices for channelling traditional knowledge (and knowledge holders) into one or more of the existing intellectual property regimes. The only remaining question is whether a new *sui generis* system of protection for traditional knowledge would ensure a more equitable and efficient sharing of the benefits. It is to this question that we now turn.

12.4.2 *Sui Generis* protection for traditional knowledge

While much attention and interest is currently being expressed in creating a new, *sui generis* form of protection for traditional knowledge, the history of previous efforts to develop other *sui generis* forms of intellectual property protection does not bode well for the success of any such effort, for two reasons.

First, proposals for new, *sui generis* forms of intellectual property protection generally tend to unleash a phenomenon that can best be described as the "politics of intellectual property law"—i.e., good old fashioned political logrolling—the outcome of which is more likely to turn on which of the various competing stakeholders have the most political clout than on what is actually in the public interest.[244] Even where those stakeholders interested in seeking more effective legal protection for traditional knowledge might have sufficient political clout to procure the enactment of strong *sui generis* protection in one or more countries, that protection may or may not promote the larger public interest in those countries, and even if it does, such protection may simply deflect bioprospecting activity to other, less protective countries, thus generating a proverbial "race to the bottom."[245]

Second, even where political and/or economic clout does not wholly determine the outcome or generate a race to the bottom in the protection of traditional knowledge, *sui generis* intellectual property schemes generally have an unfortunate history of failing to promote not only the public interest, but also the private interests of those the protection is supposed to promote because such *sui generis* schemes have been based on flawed theoretical foundations, both as a matter of law and as a matter of economics. If *sui generis* protection for traditional knowledge is to succeed, it cannot afford to ignore the lessons of the past.

As Professor J. H. Reichman has demonstrated in great detail elsewhere, the history of *sui generis* forms of intellectual property protection is largely a history of chronic states, or recurring cycles of under- or over-protection for the subject matter of that *sui generis* protection, neither of which succeeds in serving the public interest, as under-protection fails to generate an adequate incentive to innovate, while over-protection simply increases the social cost of any innovations that are generated.[246] The reason for this highly unsatisfactory state of affairs, according to Professor Reichman, is that *sui generis* schemes of intellectual property protection lack any coherent theoretical foundation, as they tend to be cobbled together hybrid systems of protection, randomly combining various elements of patent and copyright law in ways that do not adequately calibrate the cost of acquiring the rights with the value of the rights acquired.[247] Either the cost of acquiring protection is unduly high in light of the limited rights that are acquired (the current state of affairs with respect to US plant patent and plant variety protection)[248] or the minimal cost of acquiring protection yields far too much protection for far too little intellectual effort (as is the case with the protection mandated by the EU Database Directive, which Reichman characterises as a "legal monstrosity,"[249] for having endowed electronic database publishers with potentially perpetual exclusive rights in disembodied information and data structures, without analogous exceptions and limitations that typically safeguard the public interest in existing copyright law.)

What Reichman proposes, as an alternative to the proliferation of ad hoc *sui generis* forms of intellectual property protection for various types of "incremental innovation bearing know-how on its face,"[250] is a one-size-fits-all system of "constructive trade secret" or unfair competition protection of the sort recognised in the *INS v. AP*[251] news piracy case, for any innovation or investment of time, labour, and money that lacks sufficient natural lead time protection to incur the benefits of conventional trade secret protection. According to Reichman, however, this constructive trade secret protection should be for a strictly limited term of, say three to five years, after which the subject matter will fall into the public domain.[252]

Needless to say, those seeking to create a new *sui generis* form of protection for traditional knowledge have been far more attracted to the model of database protection that Reichman describes as a "legal monstrosity" than they have to Reichman's own proposals for a limited form of constructive trade secret protection for incremental innovation that lacks natural lead time protection. Indeed, Dr. Carvalho himself argues that the only effective way to document and formalise the protection of traditional knowledge is through collections, or inventories, or databases.[253] Yet, the creation of such protection for collections of data is no more theoretically sound when proposed as a means of protecting traditional knowledge than when proposed as a means of forcing users of databases, including developing country governments, academic and public sector researchers, as well as commercial users, to underwrite the social costs generated by granting overbroad database protection to commercial entities.

Quite apart from these underlying theoretical problems with existing *sui generis* forms of intellectual property protection, there are some very practical definitional problems with respect to how one should define: 1) the subject matter of protection, 2) the scope of the exclusive rights in that subject matter, 3) the standards for claiming ownership, and 4) the rules governing co-ownership and the resolution of disputes among co-owners. We have already seen how difficult it has been to define exactly what is meant by traditional knowledge, but that definitional dilemma is minor when compared with trying to define any of the foregoing basic elements necessary to create an operational intellectual property system.

For example, given that *sui generis* systems of intellectual property protection, such as that mandated by the European Database Directive for collections of data, are in effect hybrid systems of protection, combining elements of patent and copyright law, which rule with respect to the relationship of co-owners should apply to databases—those governing co-owners of patents or those governing co-owners of copyrights? Under US law, at least, the two are not the same. Under US patent law, each of the joint-owners of a patent may, in the absence of any contrary agreement, make, use, offer for sale, sell or license the patent without accounting to the other owners.[254] Under US copyright law, by contrast, while co-owners of a copyright are treated as having an undivided ownership in the entire work and can use or license the whole work as each wishes, there is a duty to account for profits to the other joint owners, and a joint owner cannot assign the work or grant an exclusive license in it without the written consent of the other co-owners.[255]

These differences in the relationship of co-owners of patents and copyrights reflect certain fundamental differences in the nature of patents and copyrights. Whereas the scope of patent rights are sufficiently broad that giving co-owners virtually free reign in the enjoyment of these rights is not thought to create any real risk that one co-owner will impair the value of the patent as a whole, the same is not true for copyrights, where the use of the work by one joint owner in this era of mass communications could potentially destroy, or at least deplete the residual value in the copyright that remains to be tapped by the non-using joint owner. Thus, the rule requiring that joint owners of copyright account to each other avoids a destructive race between those joint owners to be the first to exploit.

So, which rule should apply to joint-owners of *sui generis* forms of protection for traditional knowledge, other *sui generis* database rights, or for that matter, conventional trade secrets? Rights created by conventional trade secret law are arguably more analogous to copyrights in the sense that one joint-owner could essentially destroy the rights of the other co-owner by publicly disclosing the trade secret. Indeed, it could be argued that rights in conventional trade secrets are not property rights at all, but rather the product of a mélange of contract and tort doctrines, which largely finesse the problems associated with property ownership. The *sui generis* rights mandated by the EU Database Directive, by contrast, are arguably more robust than either copyrights or rights in trade secrets, and thus more analogous to patent rights, as the protection is not limited to originality in the selection and arrangement of the data, as it is in copyright law, or to undisclosed information, as it is in trade secret law, but extends legal protection to publicly disclosed collections of data as such.

While problems of joint-ownership are unlikely, as a practical matter to plague makers of conventional databases, as such makers are likely to be incorporated business entities that can assert sole ownership to rights in databases created by the collective effort of employees, as the database will amount to a work for hire, problems of joint ownership of traditional knowledge are likely to generate for more complex joint ownership problems, and the larger the collectivity of joint owners, the more complex the problems of joint ownership are likely to be. The WIPO report entitled "Elements of a *Sui Generis* System for the Protection of Traditional Knowledge" recognises that while conventional intellectual property rights are originally vested in the originators, who can then transfer their rights through contractual or legal arrangements, traditional knowledge is generally understood as being the creation of a collective originator.[256] To resolve such matters, the report stresses the importance of consulting the customary law of a given community, which may specify that knowledge held by an individual member of the community is nevertheless owned by the community as a whole.[257]

12.5 CONCLUSION

In short, creating new *sui generis* property rights in traditional knowledge is not problem-free. Nor is it certain that the establishment of such a system will in fact promote an equitable sharing of the benefits arising out of the use of that traditional knowledge, as it is not at all clear that such systems will in fact generate substantial economic benefits to rights holders at all, as there is no guarantee that these systems will function in the same way that patent and copyright systems do. The *sui generis* system of plant variety protection in the United States, for example, does not seem to have stimulated any significant amount of licensing (or at least any licensing that is visible to the public), as the privilege of plant breeders to use a protected variety of another breeder to create new and distinct varieties of their own, as well as the farmers' privilege to save seeds, vitiates most of the incentive to seek licenses.[258] Any system of protection that fails to generate licenses will in all likelihood fail to generate significant benefits to right holders.

Thus, before international agencies or national governments launch into yet another ambitious, yet dubious, experiment in trying to cobble together a new *sui generis* system of protection for traditional knowledge, it might be well to give more serious consideration to making modest, yet theoretically well-founded modifications in the existing intellectual property system, such as requiring the disclosure of origin of genetic resources and/or traditional knowledge relied on in the creative process and evidence of prior informed consent of the source countries, communities, and/or individuals. Such a modification has the virtue of being relatively easy to implement and administer, to say nothing of the potential it holds for actually generating economic benefits to be equitably shared with traditional knowledge holders.

ENDNOTES

1 For a discussion of what is meant by "traditional knowledge," see *infra* Part 12.2.1. For a summary of the unfolding debate over the legal protection of traditional knowledge, see e.g., Charles R. McManis, The Interface Between International Intellectual Property and Environmental Protection: Biodiversity and Biotechnology, 76 *Wash. U.L.Q.* 255 (1998) [hereinafter *Biodiversity and Biotechnology*] Charles R. McManis, Intellectual Property, Genetic Resources and Traditional Knowledge Protection: Thinking Globally, Acting Locally, 11 *Cardozo J. of Int'l & Comp. L.* 547 (2003) [hereinafter McManis, *Thinking Globally, Acting Locally*].

2 See, e.g. Darrell A. Posey & Graham Dutfield, *Beyond Intellectual Property: Toward Traditional Resource Rights for Indigenous Peoples and Local Communities* 92 (1996) [hereinafter Posey & Dutfield]: "IPR laws are generally inappropriate and inadequate for defending the rights and resources of local communities. IPR protection is purely economic, whereas the interests of indigenous peoples are only partly economic and linked to self-determination. Furthermore, cultural incompatibilities exist in that traditional knowledge is generally shared and, even when it is not, the holders of restricted knowledge probably still do not have the right to commercialise it for personal gain." But see *infra* notes 36–39 and accompanying text, note 41, text accompanying notes 72–74, and text notes 54 and 79, rebutting each of these assertions.

3 See, e.g., "Biopiracy refers to the appropriation of the knowledge and genetic resources of farming and indigenous communities by individuals or institutions seeking exclusive monopoly control (usually patents or plant breeders' rights) over these resources and knowledge," available online: (http.www.etcgroup.org/documents/Biopiracy+10Com.pdf) (accessed March 7, 2004). As for what does, and does not, constitute "biopiracy," see *infra* Part 12.3.

4 See, e.g., Posey & Dutfield, *supra* note 2, 94–100 (discussing, as possible alternatives to conventional IPRs, the concepts of traditional resource rights, community IPRs, and community intellectual rights, that "accommodate more adequately the concern of traditional communities to prevent others from privatising their knowledge and resources." *Ibid.* at 100).

5 See generally Gretchen C. Daily (ed.), Nature's Services: Societal Dependence on Natural Ecosystems (1997); Ursula Goodenough, The Sacred Depths of Nature (1998); Luisa Maffi (ed.), *On Biocultural Diversity: Linking Language, Knowledge, and the Environment* (2001) [hereinafter Maffi].

6 See, e.g., Stuart L. Pimm, & Thomas M. Brooks, The Sixth Extinction: How Large, Where, and When? in Peter H. Raven (ed.), *Nature and Human Society: The Quest for a Sustainable World* (1997).

7 The Book of Common Prayer 370 (1977).

8 See David Harmon, *On* the Meaning and Moral Imperative of Diversity, in *Maffi*, *supra* note 5, at page 61.

9 See Maffi, *supra* note 5. See *also* Luisa Maffi, *Linguistic and Biological Diversity: The Inextricable Link*, available online: (http://www.terralingua.org/DiscPapers/DiscPaper3.html) (accessed May 3, 2004).

10 Agreement on Trade-Related Aspects of Intellectual Property Rights, Including Trade in Counterfeit Goods, December 15, 1993), 33 I.L.M. 81 (1994) [hereinafter TRIPS Agreement], available online: (http://www.wto.int/) (accessed March 13, 2004).

11 See TRIPS Agreement Article 65 and Article 66.

12 Framework for Convention on Climate Change [hereinafter Climate Change Treaty], available online: (http://unfccc.int/) (accessed March 25, 2004).

13 Convention on Biological Diversity [hereinafter CBD], available online: (http://www.biodiv.org/default.aspx) (accessed March 25, 2004).

14 See Climate Change Information Kit, The Climate Change Convention Sheet 18, available online: (http://unfccc.int/resource/iuckit/infokit2001.html) (accessed March 25, 2004).

15 See CBD Article 1 available online: (http://www.biodiv.org/convention/articles.asp?lg=0&a=cbd-01) (accessed March 25, 2004).

16 Available online: (http://www.biodiv.org/convention/articles.asp?lg=0&a=cbd-08) (accessed March 25, 2004).

17 Doha Ministerial 2001: Ministerial Declaration, available online: (http://www.wto.org/english/thewto_e/minist_e/min01_e/mindecl_e.htm) (accessed March 25, 2004).

18 Doha Ministerial 2001: Ministerial Declaration, TRIPS, available online: (http://www.wto.org/english/thewto_e/minist_e/min01_e/mindecl_e.htm) (accessed March 25, 2004).

19 *Ibid.*

20 See Laurence Tubiana, Post Cancun WTO: Focus on the Objectives, Not the Means, *Bridges* Sep–Oct 2003; Eric Hazard, The Cotton Thread: Was

Cancun a Failure of Regulation or a Success for Deregulation? *Bridges* Sep–Oct 2003; Regional Integration Spurred and Complicated by Cancun, *Bridges* Sep–Oct 2003.

21 See *supra* notes 2 and 4.

22 For example, a prominent US federal appellate judge specialising in intellectual property matters has critiqued the author's own proposals to protect traditional knowledge as know-how or trade secrets as "laughable," while another equally prominent US federal appellate judge described the author as a "confused romantic," and went on to suggest that because traditional knowledge is essentially static and non-new it had no legitimate claim in intellectual property protection and was of marginal utility, at best, in the innovative process. But see *infra* text accompanying notes 30–32, and 38–39, responding to these critiques. For obvious reasons, the judges in question will remain nameless.

23 See online: (http://www.wipo.int/tk/en/igc/index.html) (accessed April 3, 2004). ("The WIPO Intergovernmental Committee on Intellectual Property and Genetic Resources, Traditional Knowledge and Folklore (the "IGC") was established by the WIPO General Assembly in October 2000 (document WO/GA/26/6) as an international forum for debate and dialogue concerning the interplay between intellectual property (IP), and traditional knowledge, genetic resources, and traditional cultural expressions (folklore).")

24 WIPO, Matters Concerning Intellectual Property and Genetic Resources, Traditional Knowledge, and Folklore—An Overview, WIPO/GRTKF/IC/1/3 (March 16, 2001).

25 Intergovernmental Committee on Intellectual Property and Genetic Resources, Traditional Knowledge and Folklore, WIPO/GRTKF/IC/3/9 (May 20, 2002).

26 *Ibid.*

27 *Ibid.*

28 Report on the Role of Intellectual Property Rights in the Implementation of Access and Benefit Sharing Arrangements, available online: (http://www.biodiv.org/doc/meetings/abs/abswg-01/official/abswg-01-04-en.pdf) (accessed April 3, 2004).

29 *Ibid.*

30 See Michael J. Balick, *Traditional Knowledge: Lessons from the Past, Lessons for the Future*, available online: (http://ls.wustl.edu/centeris/Confpapers/PDFWrdDoc/Balick.pdf) (accessed May 2, 2004).

31 Report on the Role of Intellectual Property Rights in the Implementation of Access and Benefit Sharing Arrangements, available online: (http://www.biodiv.org/doc/meetings/abs/abswg-01/official/abswg-01-04-en.pdf) (accessed April 3, 2004).

32 *Ibid.*

33 Nuno Pires de Carvalho, *From the Shaman's Hut to the Patent Office: In Search of Effective Protection for Traditional Knowledge*, available online: (http://www.law.wustl.edu/centeris/Confpapers/index.html) (accessed May 1, 2004).

34 *Ibid.*

35 See generally Stephen A. Hansen and Justin W. VanFleet, *Traditional Knowledge and Intellectual Property: A Handbook on Issues and Options for Traditional Knowledge Holders in Protecting their Intellectual Property and Maintaining Biological Diversity* (American Association for the Advancement of Science, 2003).

36 *Ibid.*

37 *Ibid.*

38 Available online: (http://www.cgiar.org/index.html) (accessed April 3, 2004).

39 See generally *supra* note 33.

40 See US Const. Article 1 §8 clause 8.

41 *Ibid.* While the US Constitution thus embraces a purely utilitarian and instrumental justification for intellectual property protection, intellectual property theorists have also sought to justify intellectual property rights as a necessary incident of self-determination. See, e.g., Margaret Jane Radin, Property and Personhood, 34 *Stanford L. Rev.* 957 (1982); Alfred Yen, Restoring the Natural Law: Copyright as Labour and Possession, 51 *Ohio St. L.J.* 517 (1990); Wendy J. Gordon, A Property Right in Self-Expression: Equality and Individualism in the Natural Law of Intellectual Property, 102 *Yale L.J.* 1533 (1993). Still other intellectual property theorists have challenged the notion of individual authorship, arguing that the concept of authorship is a "social construct," and that all creations are largely a product of communal forces. See, e.g., Martha Woodmansee & Peter Jaszi, eds., *The Construction of Authorship: Textual Appropriation in Law and Literature* (1994), discussed in Robert P. Merges, Peter S. Menell, & Mark A. Lemley, Intellectual Property in the New Technological Age 10 (3rd ed., 2003).

42 Available online: (http://www.wipo.int/edocs/trtdocs/en/wo/wo020en.htm) (accessed May 2, 2004) [hereinafter Paris Convention].

43 Available online: (http://www.wipo.int/clea/docs/en/wo/wo001en.htm) (accessed May 2, 2004) [hereinafter Berne Convention].

44 Paris Convention Article 1 clause 2, available online: (http://www.wipo.int/edocs/trtdocs/en/wo/wo020en.htm#P69_3843) (accessed May 2, 2004).

45 Paris Convention, Article 1 clause 3, available online: (http://www.wipo.int/edocs/trtdocs/en/wo/wo020en.htm#P69_3843) (accessed May 2, 2004).s

46 Berne Convention, Article 2 clause 1, available online: (http://www.wipo.int/clea/docs/en/wo/wo001en.htm) (accessed May 2, 2004).

47 Available online: (http://www.wipo.int/tk/en/glossary/index.html) (accessed May 3, 2004).

48 See Paris Convention, Article 3, available online: (http://www.wipo.int/edocs/trtdocs/en/wo/wo020en.htm#P79_6033) (accessed May 3, 2004).

49 TRIPS Agreement, Article 7, available online: (http://www.wto.org/english/docs_e/legal_e/27-trips_03_e.htm) (accessed April 4, 2004).

50 Available online: (http://www.wipo.int/edocs/trtdocs/en/wo/wo020en.htm#P69_3843 (accessed May 2, 2004).

51 Available online: (http://www.wto.org/english/docs_e/legal_e/27-trips_04d_e.htm#8) (accessed May 2, 2004).

52 *Ibid.*

53 See Article 39.2, fn. 10 which states "[f]or the purpose of this provision, 'a manner contrary to honest commercial practices' shall mean at least practices such as breach of contract, breach of confidence and inducement to breach, and includes the acquisition of undisclosed information by third parties who knew, or were grossly negligent in failing to know, that such practices were involved in the acquisition ... ." available at (http://www.wto.org/english/docs_e/legal_e/27-trips_04d_e.htm#Footnote10) (accessed May 2, 2004).

54 Available online: (http://www.wto.org/english/docs_e/legal_e/27-trips_04d_e.htm) (accessed April 4, 2004).

55 Article 39.3, available online: (http://www.wto.org/english/docs_e/legal_e/27-trips_04d_e.htm) (accessed April 4, 2004).

56 Article 9, available online: http://www.wto.org/english/docs_e/legal_e/27-trips_04_e.htm (last visited April 4, 2004).

57 Available online: (http://www.wipo.int/clea/docs/en/wo/wo001en.htm) (accessed April 5, 2004).

58 *Ibid.*

59 *Ibid.*

60 See *Feist Publications, Inc. v. Rural Telephone Service Co.*, 499 US 340 (1991).

61 *Ibid.*

62 See *infra* text accompanying note 66.

63 Available online: (http://www.wipo.int/clea/docs/en/wo/wo001en.htm) (last visited April 5, 2004).

64 See TRIPS Agreement, Article 9, available online: (http://www.wto.org/english/docs_e/legal_e/27-trips_04_e.htm#1) (last visited May 3, 2004).

65 Article 10.2, *id.*

66 Available online: (http://www.wto.org/english/docs_e/legal_e/27-trips_04_e.htm) (last visited April 4, 2004). ("Whenever the term of protection of a work, other than a photographic work or a work of applied art, is calculated on a basis other than the life of a natural person, such term shall be no less than 50 years from the end of the calendar year of authorised publication, or, failing such authorised publication within 50 years from the making of the work, 50 years from the end of the calendar year of making.")

67 Available online: (http://www.wto.org/english/docs_e/legal_e/27-trips_04b_e.htm) (last visited April 4, 2004).

68 See TRIPS Agreement, Article 25 clause 1, available online: (http://www.wto.org/english/docs_e/legal_e/27-trips_04b_e.htm) (accessed April 4, 2004).

69 See TRIPS Agreement, Article 25 clause 2, available online: (http://www.wto.org/english/docs_e/legal_e/27-trips_04b_e.htm) (accessed April 4, 2004).

70 See TRIPS Agreement, Article 26 clause 1, available online (http://www.wto.org/english/docs_e/legal_e/27-trips_04b_e.htm) (accessed April 4, 2004).

71 See TRIPS Agreement, Article 26 clause 3, available online (http://www.wto.org/english/docs_e/legal_e/27-trips_04b_e.htm) (accessed April 4, 2004).

72 Available online: (http://www.wto.org/english/docs_e/legal_e/27-trips_04_e.htm#6) (accessed April 4, 2004).

73 15 U.S.C. §1054 (2004) (emphasis added).

74 15 U.S.C. §1064 (2004).

75 Available online: (http://www.wto.org/english/docs_e/legal_e/27-trips_04b_e.htm) (accessed April 4, 2004).

76 *Ibid.* For a discussion of one of the more prominent biopiracy controversies involving an admittedly weak geographical indication, see *infra* notes discussing controversial US patents and trademarks related to Basmati rice.

77 *Ibid.*

78 *Ibid.*

79 On this point, the author is indebted to Dr. Tae-man Kim, J. S. D., Washington University, 2003, for the insights gained from Dr. Kim's dissertation, "International Standards for Protection of Geographical Indications: Focusing on Two Outstanding Issues" (2003) (on file at Washington University School of Law and with the author).

80 Available online: (http://www.wto.org/english/docs_e/legal_e/27-trips_04c_e.htm) (accessed April 4, 2004).

81 See Article 27 clause 3(b), available online: (http://www.wto.org/english/docs_e/legal_e/27-trips_04c_e.htm) (accessed April 4, 2004).

82 See Donald S. Chisum, 1-3 Chisum on Patents §3.01 (2003).

83 Carlos M. Correa, Intellectual Property Rights, the WTO and Developing Countries The Trips Agreement and Policy Options, 57–60 (Zed Books Ltd. 2000) [hereinafter Correa].

84 *Ibid.* at 60.

85 US Const. Article I § 8 clause 8.

86 See *supra* note 53.

87 Available online: (http://www.wto.org/english/docs_e/legal_e/27-trips_04d_e.htm (accessed April 4, 2004). See *also supra* note 53.

88 See *Kewanee Oil Co. v. Bicron Corp.*, 416 US 470 (1974) (holding that patent law did not pre-empt Ohio state trade secret law, even though the trade secret in issue was clearly patentable but in fact unpatented).

89 See online: (http://www.uspto.gov/web/offices/pac/doc/general/index.html#pub) (accessed May 3, 2004).

90 *Ibid.*

91 35 U.S.C. §122 (2004).

92 TRIPS Agreement, Article 29 clause 1, available online: (http://www.wto.org/english/docs_e/legal_e/27-trips_04c_e.htm#5) (accessed

April 4, 2004). ("Members shall require that an applicant for a patent shall disclose the invention in a manner sufficiently clear and complete for the invention to be carried out by a person skilled in the art and may require the applicant to indicate the best mode for carrying out the invention known to the inventor at the filing date or, where priority is claimed, at the priority date of the application.")

93 See Charles R. McManis, Taking TRIPS on the Information Super Highway International Intellectual Property Protection and Emerging Computer Technology, 41 *Vill. L. Rev.*, 207, 211 (1996).

94 See *supra* note 48.

95 ETC, under its previous incarnation as RAFI, is the same latter-day David that deployed the phrase "Terminator Technology" with such deadly rhetorical effect as to temporarily slay a proprietary biotechnology that, even though it happens to be the intellectual property of that agricultural Goliath called Monsanto (a.k.a. "Monsatan"), nevertheless holds as much promise as peril in the brave new world of genetically modified crops, as being able to shut down the reproductive capacity of genetic modified seeds may be the key to preventing inadvertent gene flow from GM crops to conventional crops or wild ancestors.

96 Available online: (http://www.etcgroup.org/text/txt_key_defs.asp) (accessed April 4, 2004). ("Biopiracy refers to the appropriation of the knowledge and genetic resources of farming and indigenous communities by individuals or institutions who seek exclusive monopoly control (patents or intellectual property) over these resources and knowledge. ETC group believes that intellectual property is predatory on the rights and knowledge of farming communities and indigenous peoples.")

97 CBD art. 14 available online: (http://www.biodiv.org/convention/articles.asp?lg=0&a=cbd-14) (accessed May 3, 2004).

98 35 U.S.C. §102(a) (2004).

99 35 U.S.C. §102(g) (2001).

100 35 U.S.C. §104 (2001).

101 35 U.S.C. §102(f) (2001).

102 See R. Carl Moy, 2 Moy's Walker on Patents §§8:1-8:10 (4th ed. 2003).

103 *Ibid.*

104 *Ibid.*

105 J. B. Priestley, Charles Dickens and His World, 48 (Thames and Hudson 1978).

106 Commission on Intellectual Property Rights, Final Report Ch. 4 (2002), available online: (http://www.iprcommission.org/graphic/documents/final_report.htm) (accessed May 3, 2004) [hereinafter CIPR Final Report]. For other thoughtful discussions of biopiracy, see Correa, *supra* note 83, and Philip Schuler, *Biopiracy and Commercialization of Ethnobotanical Knowledge* in J. Michael Finger & Philip Schuler, Poor People's Knowledge: Promoting Intellectual Property in Developing Countries 159-181 (2004)(discussing five of the seven biopiracy controversies discussed in Part II. C. of this paper) [hereinafter Schuler].

107 *Ibid.*

108 Although President Clinton eventually signed the CBD, Congress has not yet ratified it. See McManis, *Thinking Globally, Acting Locally, supra* note 1, at 548.

109 See *supra* note 82, §17.05[3].

110 See *Ibid.* §19.03[1][f]. For assistance and representation in mounting challenges to the validity of US patents, developing country governments and/or any indigenous or local communities located therein now have access to two public interest organisations recently established in the United States for this purpose. See Public Interest Intellectual Property Advisors, Inc., (http://www.piipa.org), and the Public Patent Foundation, available online: (http://www.pubpat.org/). For a recent example of such representation, see *infra* note 215.

111 U.S. Patent No. 5,124,349 (issued June 23, 1992). The patent claims both compositions that contain non-degrading azadirachtin extracted from neem seeds and also processes for the preparation for storage-stable azadirachtin-containing compositions. *Ibid.* See generally Schuler, *supra* note 106, at 161 (describing the neem controversy as "[e]veryone's favorite biopiracy story").

112 Emily Marden, *The Neem Tree Patent: International Conflict over the Commodification of Life*, 22 B.C. Int'l & Comp.L.Rev. 279, 284 (Spring 1999) [hereinafter Marden].

113 A March 22, 2004 search on the US Patent Office website, using the search query "spec/(neem) or (azadirachtin)" resulted in 530 patents that contained either the term neem or azadirachtin in their specification.

114 Interestingly, although the Grace patent generated considerable public outcry, 18 patents involving neem extract were issued prior to the 5,124,349 patent.

115 Marden, *supra* note 112, at 279, 286.

116 *Ibid.*

117 The US Patent Office issued a Re-examination Certificate confirming the validity of the nineteen claims of the 5,124,349 patent on October 20, 1998. Re-examination certificate available online: (http://lexisnexis.com/lawschool/), Utility Patent database (accessed March 29, 2004).

118 The European Patent Office issued a patent, EP 0436257, to the Grace Company on September 14, 1994. EP 0436257 available online: (http://www.lawschool.westlaw.com/), EPO database (accessed March 28, 2004). The patent was revoked on May 17, 2000. Ajay Phadke, *How the Neem patent fight was won* (May 17, 2000), available online: (http://home.intekom.com/tm_info/rw00518.htm) (accessed March 28, 2004).

Scholars have attributed the success of the Grace patent opponents at the European Patent Office and their failure at the US Patent Office to the difference in novelty standards in European and US patent law. See, e.g., Craig Allan Nard, *In Defence of Geographic Disparity*, 88 Minn. L. Rev. 222, 223 (Nov 2003); Shubha Ghosh, *Traditional Knowledge, Patents, and the New Mercantilism (Part II)*, 85 J. Pat. & Trademark Off. Soc'y 885 (Nov 2003); Shubha Ghosh, *Globalization, Patents, and Traditional*

Knowledge, 17 Colum. J. Asian L. 73 (Fall 2003); Shubha Ghosh, *The Traditional Terms of the Traditional Knowledge Debate*, 23 Nw. J. Int'l L. & Bus. 589 (Spring 2003); Margo Bagley, *Patently Unconstitutional: The Geographic Limitation on Prior Art in a Small World*, 87 Minn. L. Rev. 679 (Feb 2003). While the novelty requirements do differ between the two patent offices and can affect the patentability of inventions, this difference alone does not explain the different outcomes in the present controversy, as the inventions patented in the US and Europe were distinct. *Compare* US 5,124,349 *with* EP 0436257. US 5,124,349 contained both composition and process claims. The composition claims of the 5,124,349 patent pertain to "a neem seed extract solution *containing azadirachtin*" while the process of preparation claims pertain to preparing compositions *containing* "azadirachtin extract." (emphasis added). In contrast, EP 0436257 consists of only method claims pertaining to the use of "a hydrophobic neem oil which is *substantially free of azadirachtin*" to control fungi and prevent fungi infestation. (emphasis added). Thus, the subject matter of the two patents differed.

The US patent claims azadirachtin-containing solutions and methods of preparing such solutions. The European patent claims only a method (a method of using a neem extract as a fungicide) that is distinct from that of the US patent. This difference is patent subject matter likely contributed to the different outcomes in the two patent offices. The US patent disclosed the inventive steps of formulating storage-stable forms of azadirachtin and the methods to make such solutions. These inventions likely drew upon knowledge for chemical analysis and preparation that are available in the public domain and that were not being used by farmers in India. David R. Downes, *How Intellectual Property Could be a Tool to Protect Traditional Knowledge*, 25 Colum. J. Envtl. L. 253, 281 (2000) [hereinafter Downes]. The European patent disclosed methods of contacting an azadirachtin-free neem solution to fungi in order to control fungi and of contacting the neem solution to plants to prevent fungi infestation. The opponents of the neem patents demonstrated lack of novelty only with respect to these specific methods. Notice of opposition 1995-06-14 available online: (http://ofi.epoline.org/view/GetDossier/) (accessed March 30, 2004). The opponents, led by Magda Alvoet of the Green Group of the EPC, presented evidence that the use of a hydrophobic, substantially azadirachtin-free neem extract as a fungicide was known prior to the patent application. *Ibid.* Thus, the opponents presented evidence that this invention lacked novelty under article 54 of the European Patent Convention (EPC). *Ibid.* The opponents also presented evidence that the patent lacked an inventive step as required by article 56 of the EPC. *Ibid.* Interestingly, the opponents also presented additional arguments that the patent was invalid, including an argument that the patent was immoral under article 56(a) of EPC. *Ibid.* However, the European Patent Office revoked the patent on the bases of lack of novelty and lack of inventive step. Ajay Phadke, *How the Neem patent fight was won* (May 17, 2000), available online: (http://home.intekom.com/tm_info/rw00518.htm) (last visited March 28, 2004).

119 For the US relative novelty rule, see 35 U.S.C. § 102 (2001), and text following notes 98 and 104 *supra*. For a discussion of the political controversy surrounding the W. R. Grace neem patent, see McManis,

Biodiversity and Biotechnology, *supra* note 1, 257–259, and commentators cited *supra* notes 112 and 118.

120 US Patent No. 5,124,349 (issued June 23, 1992).

121 Marden, *supra* note 112, at pages 279, 283.

122 US Patent No. 5,124,349 issued June 23, 1999).

123 As stated in the patent specification, "the term 'storage stable' refers to formulations that have retained at least 80 per cent of their active ingredient content after one year at room temperature." *Ibid.*

124 Natural extracts are active for only eight days after exposure to sunlight, as compared to the patented extract, which, as discussed in note 123, is stable for a year. Panel on Neem, Neem: A Tree for Solving Global Problems 18 (National Academy Press 1992) [hereinafter Neem Panel].

125 See Downes, *supra* note 118, at 280 (stating that the patent will not interfere with "Indian farmers' traditional practices" and that "there is no patent on the neem tree"); Marden, *supra* note 112, at 285 (expressing doubt that the Grace patent will have any effects at all on Indian farmers); Neem Panel, *supra* note 124, at 290 (stating that activists fear that the patent will force Indian farmers to pay Grace for their own knowledge).

126 Marden, *supra* note 112, at 283.

127 The specification states the inventors discovered that certain solvents caused the degradation of azadirachtin, while the use of other solvents increased the stability of azadirachtin. US Patent No. 5,124,349 (issued June 23, 1992). The opponents of the patent did not show this to be previously known in the United States or in printed publication anywhere in the world.

128 The 5,124,349 patent was a continuation-in-part application, filed on October 31, 1990, based on an earlier patent application the company filed. This earlier application was filed on June 26, 1989 and issued on March 19, 1991 as US 5,001,146. A continuation-in-part application incorporates the material of the parent application and adds additional new matter. In the case of these two patents, the additional material added in the 5,124,349 patent led to an additional element of the composition claim as compared to the 5,001,146 patent. Claim 1 of the 5,001,146 patent reads, "A storage-stable pesticide composition comprising a neem seed extract solution containing azadirachtin wherein the solution is characterised as having at least 50 per cent by volume aprotic solvent and less than 15 per cent by volume water said solution being non-degrading to azadirachtin." Claim 1 of the 5,124,349 patent reads, "A storage-stable pesticide composition comprising a neem seed extract solution containing azadirachtin wherein the solution has at least 50 per cent by volume aprotic solvent, *at least about 1.0 per cent but less than 10 per cent surfactant*, and less than 15 per cent by volume water, said solution being non-degrading to azadirachtin." (emphasis added).

Interestingly, in June 1990, W. R. Grace filed an application and had a patent granted in August 1994 for the same invention in Europe. EP 0405291. The patent's application claimed priority to the application that eventually issued as the US 5,001,146 patent. Claim 1 of EP 0405291 reads, "A storage-stable pesticide composition comprising a neem seed extract solution containing azadirachtin wherein the solution is characterised as having at least 50 per cent by volume aprotic solvent and less than 15 per cent by volume water." This claim is virtually identical to claim 1 of the 5,001,146 patent. However, when critics of the Grace company speak on the matter of biopiracy, they focus on their success in revoking an unrelated patent, the EP 0436257 patent, and fail to mention that a European patent was issued on the same invention as US 5,001,146 and very similar to US 5,124,349. See commentators cited *supra* note 118.

The EP 0405291 patent was issued by the European Patent Office, which uses the absolute novelty requirement. Scholars continue to criticise United States patent law's relative novelty standard and blame this standard for the existence and validity of Grace's 5,001,146 and 5,124,349 patents. However, the *same subject matter* is the claimed invention in the European Patent Office. Perhaps these critics should accept the fact that W. R. Grace actually invented something new and pirated nothing. At a minimum, the critics should refrain from comparing apples to oranges and should not aim to further their cause by misrepresenting facts.

129 No evidence has been shown to demonstrate that people in the United States knew of the disclosed ways to improve stability or that a publication disclosing such information was in existence anywhere in the world at the time the patent was filed. Thus, the invention appears to be novel in the United States as required by the patent laws. 35 U.S.C. § 102.

130 See discussion above at section 12.3.1 of this chapter on "Biopiracy claims and US Patent Law".

131 The use of neem extract as an insecticide was known outside of India prior to filing of the Grace patent: In 1959, a German entomologist reported that the neem tree in India survived a locust infestation that devoured all other trees. Marden, *supra* note 112, at 283. Subsequently, researchers worldwide discovered that azadirachtin was the component in neem extract responsible for this property. *Ibid.* However, until the Grace patent, azadirachtin in neem extracts was highly unstable. *Ibid.*

132 Graham Dutfield, Intellectual Property Rights, Trade and Biodiversity 66, Case Study 5.5: The Neem Patents and Appendix 1 (Earthscan Publications 1999) [hereinafter Dutfield].

133 *Ibid.* at 66, Case Study 5.5.

134 US Patent No. Plant 5,751 (issued 17 June 1986). See generally Schuler, *supra* note 106, 169–171.

135 *Ibid.*

136 *Ibid.*

137 Downes, *supra* note 118, at 279.

138 Glenn M. Wiser, *PTO Rejection of the "Ayahuasca" Patent Claim*, available online: (http://www.ciel.org./Biodiversity/ptorejection.html) (accessed March 17, 2004) [hereinafter Wiser].

139 Request for Re-examination of U.S. Patent No. Plant 5,751 at 3, available online: (http://www.ciel.org./Biodiversity/ayahuascapatentcase.html) (accessed March 17, 2004) [hereinafter CIEL Request for Re-examination].

The "Da Vine" cultivar is neither distinct nor new, because the medicinal and morphological characteristics on which the claim is based are well within the normal range of variation for individual plants of the species, and both the species and the characteristics described in the patent are well-known, not only in the scientific literature, but also in the systems of traditional knowledge of indigenous groups throughout the Amazon.

Ibid. Arguments that an issued patent is not novel in light of prior art that the examiner had not seen while examining the patent are relevant. However, as United States patent law currently stands, the fact that a purported invention is known by indigenous peoples is irrelevant if the invention is not publicly known in the United States or not in published form anywhere in the world. 35 U.S.C. § 102 (2001). Also, the fact that the one specific type of *B. caapi*, "Da Vine" has some shared properties with other types of *B. caapi* does not mean that it is not unique. The plant can be unique for other reasons, not because of its potential medicinal properties.

140 *Ibid.* The Request claimed that "issuance of the Patent does not meet the public policy and morality aspects of the Patent Act, which preclude awarding a patent on a plant such as *Banisteriopsis caapi* that is sacred to indigenous peoples throughout the Amazon region and has been used and revered in their cultures for many generations." *Ibid.* at pages 3–4. However, the morality restriction on patentability is a narrow one: "A patent will be withheld only if the invention cannot be used for *any* honest and moral purpose. And the courts should not apply subjective ideas of honesty and morality." Chisum on Patents § 4.03, available at: (http://lexisnexis.com/lawschool), Patent Law database (last visited April 13, 2004) (emphasis added).

141 *Ibid.* at pages 1–2.

142 Wiser, *supra* note 138. The patent was rejected on November 3, 1999. *Ibid.* The basis for the rejection was on narrow grounds, specifically, that the patent was barred by 35 U.S.C. § 102(b): The invention sought to be patented was described in a printed publication more than one year prior to the date of the patent application. *Ibid.* The PTO did not acknowledge or comment on the public policy and morality arguments made by CIEL. *Ibid.* The prior art that the Request had brought to the examiner's attention included herbarium specimen sheets. *Ibid.* The sheets described *B. caapi* flowers that were the same colour as what the patent application claimed was the particularly characterising feature (but not the sole distinct feature) of "Da Vine": rose colour of flower petals that fade with age to near white. US Patent No. Plant 5,751.

143 On January 26, 2001, the PTO held that the patented invention was neither anticipated nor rendered obvious by the prior art. Notice of Intent to Issue Re-examination Certificate—Statement of Reasons for Patentability and/or Confirmation, available online: (http://www.ciel.org./Biodiversity/ayahuascapatentcase.html) (accessed March 17, 2004). The examiner stated that several distinctions existed between the prior art *B. caapi* and Da Vine. *Ibid.* These distinctions demonstrated that Da Vine was distinct as compared to the prior art. *Ibid.* The leaf size and shape differed, with the leaves of Da Vine having a "comparably greater length to width ratio,

while being slimmer and smaller in overall size, and the adult foliage having a more acuminate tip" than the prior art. *Ibid.* at 2. In its Notice, the PTO stated that "Patent Owner's continuing arguments relative to distinctness of flower colour remain unpersuasive in and of themselves." Notice of Intent to Issue Re-examination Certificate—Statement of Reasons for Patentability and/or Confirmation at 2. Thus, CIEL was correct that the colour was not novel or the distinguishing feature of Da Vine. In fact, this was the characteristic on which CIEL had based its arguments in its Request, *supra* note 139. However, an invention just has to be *distinct*, not *distinct in flower colour* in order to be patentable and the PTO found sufficient examples of distinctiveness in the present case. Notice of Intent to Issue Re-examination Certificate—Statement of Reasons for Patentability and/or Confirmation, available online: (http://www.ciel.org./Biodiversity/ayahuascapatentcase.html) (last visited March 17, 2004).

Subsequent to the patent's reinstatement, CIEL issued a harsh criticism of the PTO decision. See Wiser, *supra* note 138. CIEL reported that the PTO's revocation of the patent was based on the lack of difference in flower colour between Da Vine and the prior art and thus the patent should not have been reinstated. *Ibid.* at 3.

CIEL further stated that because leaf size and shape were not mentioned in the re-examination, this fact meant that the PTO held these alone to be insufficient to render Da Vine distinct. *Ibid.* However, just because the PTO did not mention these features does not mean the PTO disregarded the features. Since the Request had focused on flower colour, the PTO focused on flower colour in its initial revocation of the patent. The patent stated that the Da Vine was "particularly characterised" by its colour. US Patent No. Plant 5,751. The patent did not state that this was the only feature that distinguished Da Vine from other *B. caapi* plants. In fact, the patent contains a table comparing eight characters and showing how Da Vine differs from other *B. caapi* in these characteristics. US Patent No. Plant 5,751. Thus, even though the flower colour of Da Vine was not new and distinct, it was reasonable for the PTO to conclude that other features were in fact distinct and new and thus worthy of a patent since flower colour is not the only characteristic that can make a plant distinct and since the patent never claimed that colour was the sole distinct characteristic.

So long as there is at least one botanical characteristic of the plant which is distinguishing, or if the combination of characteristics is distinguishing, and so long as the plant is stable relative to expression of this and all other characteristics described and illustrated through asexual reproduction, the grant of Plant Patent protection under 35 U.S.C. 161 is proper.

Notice of Intent to Issue Re-examination Certificate- Statement of Reasons for Patentability and/or Confirmation, available online: (http://www.ciel.org./Biodiversity/ayahuascapatentcase.html) (accessed March 17, 2004).

Further, CIEL was extremely critical of the patent re-examination process. See Wiser, *supra* note 138. First, CIEL was very critical of the fact that once they made their initial request for re-examination, they were no longer allowed to participate in the re-examination process; specifically, they could not make counterarguments to the arguments Miller made in support of his patent. *Ibid.* at page 3. However, the law in operation at the time the patent was filed did not allow such involvement by CIEL or any third party. The PTO was not intentionally disadvantaging CIEL and the indigenous peoples CIEL was representing. In fact, the frustration experienced by CIEL in this re-examination was shared by many and eventually led to the enactment of the Optional Inter Partes Re-examination Procedure Act of 1999. Donald Chisum, *et al.*, *Principles of Patent Law* 155 (2nd ed. 2001). Thus, the PTO is responding to the needs of all parties concerned in the issuance of a patent and in the future, all interested third parties, including representatives of indigenous peoples, will be allowed to participate in each step of the re-examination process. It was improper and erroneous for CIEL to criticise the PTO for merely following the law and to assert a hidden agenda existed in the agency's actions.

Second, CIEL argues that the PTO violated the Code of Federal Regulations by allowing Miller to receive numerous extensions for replying to the re-examination and to present "new material and legal arguments" in defence of his patent after the rejection was made final. See Wiser, *supra* note 138. CIEL argues that, according to 37 C.F.R. § 1.113(a), once the rejection of a claim is made final, the "patent owner's reply is limited to appeal ... or amendment. The regulations contain no exceptions to this rule." *Ibid.* However, the next section of the regulation, § 1.114, demonstrates that the PTO procedure was proper and not in violation of the Regulations. 37 C.F.R. § 1.114 (2000). Specifically, § 1.113(a) reads in part, "[r]eply to a final rejection or action must comply with § 1.114." 37 C.F.R. § 1.113(a). Section 1.114(a) reads in part, "[a]n applicant may request continued examination of the application by filing a submission and the fee set forth ...." 37 C.F.R. § 1.114. Thus, Miller obeyed the rules when he applied for extensions and the PTO also followed the rules in granting them. Section 1.114(c) defines "submission" in § 1.114(a) as "an information disclosure statement, an amendment to the written description, claims, or drawings, *new arguments*, or *new evidence* in support of patentability." 37 C.F.R. § 1.114 (emphasis added). Again, it was not improper for the PTO to allow Miller to submit new arguments in support of the "Da Vine" patent. Indeed, the PTO would have been in violation of the law had it denied such requests for extensions and denied Miller the opportunity to introduce new arguments.

144 Codified in 35 U.S.C. §§ 161–164; see *also* Donald Chisum, *et al.*, Principles of Patent Law 290 (2nd ed. 2001).

145 35 U.S.C. § 161 (2001).

146 Indeed, the PTO stated that

> There are two steps of inventorship in a Plant Patent, the breeding or discovery of the plant (such discovery must be in a cultivated area and includes recognition and appreciation of the distinctive and novel characteristics of the plant (*Nicholson v. Bailey* 125 USPQ 157), and successful asexual reproduction (In re Kulis 70 USPQ 165). The patent clearly indicates that both of these requisite steps have been accomplished by the patent owner. The record in the

> patent file does not support requesters' allegation that 'Da Vine' is a "wild plant" and thus statutorily ineligible for Plant Patent Protection under 35 U.S.C. 161. Indeed, the record supports just the opposite.

Notice of Intent to Issue Re-examination Certificate—Statement of Reasons for Patentability and/or Confirmation.

147 35 U.S.C. §§ 161–162 (2001).

148 "Normally, the three requirements for patentability are novelty, utility, and obviousness. For plant patents, the requirement of distinctness replaces that of utility, and the additional requirement of asexual reproduction is introduced." *Yoder Brother, Inc. v. California-Florida Plant Corp.*, 537 F. 2d 1347, 1377 (5th Cir. 1976) (internal citations omitted).

149 35 U.S.C. § 161 states that, "the provisions of this title relating to patents for inventions shall apply to patents for plants, except as otherwise provided" and also adds the asexual reproduction requirement. § 162 relieves plant patents of the § 112 requirements that apply to utility patents. Case law has interpreted the § 101 utility requirement as the distinctiveness requirement. See *supra* note 38. Thus, plant patents must satisfy the §§ 102–103 requirements of novelty and non-obviousness, respectively.

150 7 U.S.C. § 2402 (2004).

151 35 U.S.C. §§ 161-162 (2001).

152 See *supra* note 38.

153 Article 27.2 of the TRIPS Agreement specifically permits WTO members to exclude from patentability any invention the commercial exploitation of which is contrary to the morals of that country:

> Members may exclude from patentability inventions, the *prevention within their territory* of the commercial exploitation of which is necessary to protect *ordre public* or morality, including to protect human, animal or plant life or health or to avoid serious prejudice to the environment, provided that such exclusion is not made merely because the exploitation is prohibited by their law.

Trade-Related Aspects of Intellectual Property Rights, full text available online: (http://www.wto.org/english/tratop_e/trips_e/t_agm0_e.htm) (accessed April 10, 2004).

154 35 U.S.C. § 163 (2001) (emphasis added).

155 Contrast 35 U.S.C. § 163 *and* 35 U.S.C. § 154(a)(1).

156 "Plant patents under the PPA [Plant Patent Act] thus have very limited coverage and less stringent requirements than § 101 utility patents." *J.E.M. Ag Supply Inc. v. Pioneer Hi-Bred Internat'l, Inc.*, 534 US 124, 133 (2001). "Because of the more stringent requirements, utility patent holders receive greater rights of exclusion than holders of a PVP [Plant Variety Protection] certificate." *Ibid.* at 144.

157 35 U.S.C. §§ 161-163 (2001).

158 7 U.S.C. § 2402 (2004). For a critique of US plant variety protection, see Mark D. Janis & Jay P. Kesan, US Plant Variety Protection: Sound and Fury...?, 39 *Houston L. Rev.* 727 (2002) [hereinafter Janis & Kesan].

159 Ironically, CIEL acknowledges and comments on this fact, stating,

> Miller's protracted legal efforts left him with a patent that is economically worthless ... The scope of protection offered by a U.S. plant patent is too narrow to give Miller anything of economic value. ... That protection extends only to the "single germplasm" contained in the patented plant and its asexually reproduced progeny.

Wiser, *supra* note 138.

CIEL further goes on to state, "the 'Da Vine' patent gives Miller exclusive rights over nothing more than his original plant and specimens grown from its cuttings—it does not give him rights over any other specimens of *B. caapi*, even specimens that may be identical in appearance to 'Da Vine'." *Ibid.*

160 Ironically again, CIEL also acknowledges the fact that Miller's patent on "Da Vine" does not threaten the indigenous peoples of the Amazon basin or their uses of ayahuasca and states, "the patent gives Miller no power whatsoever to control any of the qualities that make the ayahuasca vine important to indigenous peoples or possibly commercially attractive to US investors." *Ibid.* at 13.

Although CIEL acknowledges that the patent will not injure or prevent the use of ayahuasca by indigenous people of the Amazon basin, it claims that the issuance of this patent shows the problems that exist with the US patent system—the fact that it will not allow for the preservation of biological diversity and traditional knowledge of indigenous peoples. *Ibid.* However, as this "Da Vine" controversy demonstrates, the traditions of these peoples will not be threatened by the issuance of US patents. The rights granted by the patent are valid and enforceable only within the US Thus, if an invention or plant is known elsewhere, the US patent holder cannot assert his rights anywhere outside of the US. Thus, Miller cannot prevent the Amazon basin people from using ayahuasca. Likewise, the W. R. Grace Company cannot prevent Indian farmers from using neem extract or the neem tree in general. In addition, as discussed above, Miller's patent only protects the plant of the patent from asexual reproduction. Miller cannot prevent the use or importation of ayahuasca, other than of "Da Vine", into the US. He cannot prevent any products made from ayahuasca from being imported or even made in the US, as long as those products are not made from "Da Vine."

161 The quinoa patent claims were all limited to a specific variety of quinoa (ATCC accession no. 75154). In contrast, the basmati rice patent, US Patent No. 5,663,484 (issued September 2, 1997), originally contained 20 claims. Of these 20, only three claims pertained to specific varieties of rice that had been bred by the inventors and deposited at a public depository (ATCC accession nos. 75939, 75940, 75941). The Council for Scientific and Industrial Research (CSIR) filed a request for re-examination of the 5,663,484 patent. Shubha Ghosh, *Globalization, Patents, and Traditional Knowledge*, 17 Colum. J. Asian L. 73, 101 (Fall 2003). The PTO issued its Re-examination Certificate on January 29, 2002, Re-examination Certificate available online: (http://lexisnexis.com/lawschool/), Utility Patent database (accessed March 29, 2004), rejecting 15 of the original claims. These 15 claims were directed toward broad subject matter. For

example, claim 1 read, "A rice plant, which plant when cultivated in North, Central or South America, or Caribbean Islands a) has a mature height of about 80–140 cm; b) is substantially photoperiod insensitive; and c) produces rice grains having i) an average starch index of about 27–35, ii) an average 2-acetyl-1-pyrroline content of about 150–2,000 ppb, iii) an average length of about 6.2–8.0 mm, an average width of about 1.6–1.9 mm, and an average length-to-width ratio of about 3.5–4.5, iv) an average of about 41–67 per cent whole grains, and v) an average lengthwise increase of about 75–150 per cent when cooked." US Patent No. 5,663,484. Three of the claims, claims 8, 9, and 11, were confirmed to be valid because they were directed to specific varieties of rice that were deposited as accession nos. 75939, 75940, 75941, respectively. Re-examination Certificate available online: (http://lexisnexis.com/lawschool), Utility Patent database (accessed March 29, 2004). In addition, claim 12 was amended to be dependent on claims 8, 9, and 11. Claim 13 was amended to be dependent on claim 12. *Ibid.* Thus, the only basmati rice claims that were confirmed as valid and not cancelled were the claims that pertained to specific, deposited varieties (accession nos. 75939, 75940, 75941). The broad, generalised claims—which conceivably could have been used to bar imports of Pakistani or Indian basmati rice, should that rice fall within the scope of these broad claims, thus posing a risk of real economic harm to Pakistan and India—were cancelled. In contrast to the basmati patent, all of the claims of the quinoa patent pertain to the specific, deposited variety (accession no. 75154), thus posing little or no risk of economic harm to importers of other varieties of quinoa.

For a discussion of the geographical indication aspect of the basmati rice controversy, see Dutfield, *supra* note 132, at 87 (noting that "basmati" is not a geographical indication *per se* in either Pakistan or India and is understood in the US in a purely generic sense).

162 US Patent No. 5,304,718 (issued April 19, 1994).

163 *Ibid.* See *also* online: (http://www.rctech.com/index.htm) (accessed April 9, 2004).

164 Dutfield, *supra* note 132, at 66, Case Study 5.6: The Quinoa Patent.

165 *Ibid.*

166 *Ibid.*

167 *Ibid.*

168 US Patent No. 5,304,718 (issued April 19, 1994).

169 The expression "getting RAFI'd" is how academic researchers who have been the target of this form of attack have summarised their experience in personal communications with the author. For examples, see ETC, *Quinoa Patent Dropped: Andean Farmers Defeat US University*, available online: (http://www.etcgroup.org/article.asp?newsid=59) (accessed March 17, 2004) [hereinafter ETC, *Quinoa Patent Dropped*]; ETC, *Bolivian Farmers Demand Researchers Drop Patent on Andean Food Crop*, available online: (http://www.etcgroup.org/article.asp?newsid=75) (accessed March 17, 2004) [hereinafter ETC, *Bolivian Farmers Demand*]; ETC, *1996 Biopiracy Update*, available online: (http://www.etcgroup.org/article.asp?newsid=197) (accessed March 17, 2004) [hereinafter ETC, *1996 Biopiracy Update*]. In

such releases, for example, ETC makes highly misleading statements such as "[o]ur intellectual integrity has been violated by this patent. Quinoa has been developed by Andean farmers for millenia [sic] it was not 'invented' by researchers in North America." ETC, *Bolivian Farmers Demand, supra*. This statement is incorrect because the patent was not on quinoa; it was on a specific hybrid strain only. See *infra* notes 173 and 182. ETC also makes such inflammatory and misleading statements as "[this patent] is a clear threat to food security. The patenting of any food crop is morally offensive, and should not be allowed by governments" and "[t]here's something terribly wrong when patent offices grant monopoly patents on food crops—especially poor peoples' staple foods." ETC, *Bolivian Farmers Demand, supra*. To the contrary, there is no threat to food security as a result of the issuance of this patent. Farmers anywhere in the world, even in the United States, can continue to grow traditional strains or any strains of quinoa other than the one newly created hybrid variety (accession no. 75154) that is the subject of the patent. Also, farmers in the Andean mountain region can continue to grow their varieties of quinoa and even the patented strain if they somehow had possession of it since the rights granted in the patent are enforceable only in the United States.

170 ETC, *1996 Biopiracy Update, supra* note 169.

171 *Ibid.*

172 *Ibid.*

173 *Ibid.* This assertion is incorrect. The patent at issue pertains to one specific strain of quinoa; a deposit of which was made at the ATCC and was given accession number 75154. US Patent No. 5,304,718 (issued April 19, 1994). Thus, the patent does not give the patent assignee the right to prevent others from growing, using, offering to sell, selling, or importing into the United States any variety of quinoa other than this specific variety, 75154.

In addition, the patent rights that were granted are limited to the United States only. Thus, if a Bolivian or Peruvian farmer had the 75154 seed in his possession, he could grow, use, offer to sell, sell, and export the seed or plant or grain anywhere in the world other than the United States. The patent assignee has absolutely no rights whatsoever over the "traditional quinoa seeds" because those traditional seeds are not the subject matter of the patent. Further, such seeds would not be able to be the subject of a US patent for two reasons. First, the patent application would fail because the applicant, by just filing an application on seed he acquired elsewhere but did not manipulate in any way, would not have "invented" anything and thus would fail the requirement of § 102 of the patent laws which states, "A person shall be entitled to a patent unless ... (f) he himself did not invent the subject matter to be patented." 35 U.S.C. § 102 (2001). Second, if the applicant had done nothing more than slightly, insignificantly modify the seed, the invention would be unpatentable due to obviousness under § 103 of the patent laws. 35 U.S.C. § 103 (2001). This misconception of the rights a US patent confers is analogous to the misconception that occurred with the neem seed extract patent. See *supra* text accompanying notes 111–133.

174 Note, for example, that the neem seed patent controversy eventually stimulated Indian research organisations, companies, and individuals filed

for and obtained U.S. patents for their own neem-related inventions. See *supra* notes 132–133 and accompanying text.

175 For a discussion of the fundamental theoretical ambiguity underlying RAFI/ETC's position, see *supra* text following note 96.

176 See, e.g., International Undertaking on Plant Genetic Resources 1983, amended 1989, 1991, available online: (http://www.mtnforum.org/resources/library/iupgr91a.htm) (accessed April 13, 2004) ("The objective of this Undertaking is to ensure that plant genetic resources of economic and/or social interest, particularly for agriculture, will be explored, preserved, evaluated and made available for plant breeding and scientific purposes. This Undertaking is based on the universally accepted principle that plant genetic resources are a heritage of mankind and consequently should be available without restriction."). As an example, the Consultative Group on International Agricultural Research (CGIAR) is an association of public and private members working, *inter alia*, to protect biodiversity and to make food crops publicly available. See The Consultative Group on International Agricultural Research, available online: (http://www.cgiar.org/who/index.html) (last visited April 10, 2004). As stated on their website:

The CGIAR holds one of the world's largest *ex-situ* collections of plant genetic resources in trust for the world community. It contains over 500,000 accessions of more than 3,000 crop, forage, and agroforestry species. The collection includes farmers' varieties and improved varieties and, in substantial measure, the wild species from which those varieties were created.

The CGIAR has placed its collections under the auspices of FAO within the International Network of Ex-Situ Collections. *The terms of the agreements signed between the FAO and CGIAR Centres, stipulate that the germplasm within the in-trust collections will be made available without restriction to researchers around the world*, on the understanding that no intellectual property protection is to be applied to the material. Samples of the in-trust germplasm are thus made available by the individual Centres under a standard Material Transfer Agreement (MTA). *Ibid.* (emphasis added).

For a discussion of the new International Treaty on Plant Genetic Resources for Food and Agriculture that has superceded the International Undertaking and abandoned the "common heritage" language of the International Undertaking, see McManis, *Thinking Globally, Acting Locally*, *supra* note 1, 554–556.

177 ETC, *Quinoa Patent Dropped*, *supra* note 169.

178 ETC makes the assertion that "[w]e knew that the 'inventors' would have to make a major fee payment to the patent office … or the patent would be automatically lost." *Ibid.* Curiously, the "major fee payment" was only $830.00 (likely not a "major" sum to a technology company). See 37 C.F.R. § 1.20(e) (2000).

179 John Daly, *Re: Quinoa Patent Info Online*, available online: (http://library.wustl.edu/~listmgr/devel-1/Jul1997/0008.html) (accessed November 17, 2003).

180 *Ibid.*

181 Dutfield, *supra* note 132, at 66, Case Study 5.6: The Quinoa Patent.

182 The inventors of the 5,304,718 patent deposited a sample of the invention variety at the ATCC in order to satisfy the enablement requirement of 35 U.S.C. § 112. 37 C.F.R. § 1.802. The only rights conferred by the patent were the rights to exclude others from making, using, offering to sell, selling, or importing into the United States the specific strain, accession number 75154, claimed in the patent. 35 U.S.C. § 154. The patent does not allow the assignee to prevent others from making, using, offering to sell, selling, or importing into the United States any other variety of quinoa. Thus, RAFI/ETC was incorrect when it stated, "the patent covered a method of hybridizing quinoa that also subsumed 43 other traditional Andean quinoa varieties ...." ETC, *Quinoa Patent Dropped*, *supra* note 169. RAFI/ETC was also incorrect when it stated, "the US patent is not limited to a single hybrid variety, it claims any quinoa hybrid that is derived from Apelawa" and "[b]y slapping a patent on quinoa the US researchers have selfishly appropriated knowledge and genetic resources that belong to indigenous peoples of the Andes." ETC, *Bolivian Farmers Demand*, *supra* note 169. Finally, RAFI/ETC erred when it stated, "The US patent claim is not limited to a single hybrid variety, it claims any quinoa hybrid that is derived from Apelawa male sterile cytoplasm. According to the patent, this includes, but is not limited to, traditional Andean varieties such as: [list of varieties]. In accordance with patent requirements, seeds of the traditional Bolivian Apelawa variety are now on deposit." ETC, *1996 Biopiracy Update*, *supra* note 170.

An examination of the 5,304,718 patent claims shows that the subject matter of each claim pertains to and is limited to only the quinoa variety that was deposited as accession number 75154. The patent rights go no further. Although not clear from the face of the patent, the deposited variety is not a variety that is indigenous to the Andean mountain region. However, because of the deposit in a publicly accessible depository, additional description was not required, 37 C.F.R. § 1.801; see *also* Chisum on Patents § 1.05 Suppl., available online: (http://lexisnexis.com/lawschool), Patent Law database (accessed April 13, 2004) ("The description requirement for plants includes a deposit of biological material, for example, seeds, and mandates that such material be accessible to the public.") The variety patented is not native to the Andes because it is a cross between an Apelawa strain of quinoa and "a quinoa line of Chilean (Linares) origin which has undergone several cycles of cultivation in Colorado." US Patent No. 5,304,718; see *also* John Daly, *Re: Quinoa Patent Info Online*, available online: (http://library.wustl.edu/~listmgr/devel-1/Jul1997/0008.html) (accessed November 17, 2003) ("Ward/Johnson [the inventors] appear to have been the first to reduce to practice a method for the production of cytoplasmic male-sterile Apelawa quinoa which resulted from the inventor's [sic] research and development of germplasm that came from a cross of Andean quinoa and a related Colorado species."); Dutfield, *supra* note 132, at 66, Case Study 5.6: The Quinoa Patent (stating that inventor Ward said the male-sterile trait from the Apelawa quinoa was transferred to a quinoa strain that grew in the US and stating "[t]he cytoplasm ... does not exist in quinoa plants growing in South America but had been transferred naturally from a related weed species growing nearby in Colorado"). Thus, the inventors did in fact invent a new variety of quinoa. Dutfield argues that had the patent been more clear as to this cross between the Apelawa and Colorado varieties of quinoa, much of the controversy and rhetoric may have been avoided: "the failure to indicate the non-Bolivian provenance of the cytoplasm inducing male sterility or to refer to its discovery made it possible to interpret the patent very broadly in ways the inventors may not have intended". *Ibid*. However, if RAFI had read the patent claims and understood that all that a patent can cover is what is actually claimed and not everything that is disclosed or mentioned in the patent application, it would have seen that the patent claims themselves make clear that only one specific variety (accession no. 75154) is protected by the patent. Claim 1 of the 5,304,718 patent reads, "A quinoa seed of the variety Apelawa having male sterile cytoplasm and assigned ATCC accession no. 75154." US Patent No. 5,304,718 (issued April 19, 1994).

183 US Patent No. 5,401,504 (issued March 28, 1995).

184 For a discussion of the rationale underlying the US novelty rule, *see supra* text following note 104. For a general discussion of how traditional knowledge about turmeric has been transmitted from India to the U.S., see Schuler, *supra* note 106, at 168, who notes that there are presently almost 400 U.S. patents involving turmeric, the earliest of which was approved in 1974, and the assignee of one of which happens to be CSIR, the same organisation that mounted this challenge to the 5,401,504 turmeric patent. *Ibid.* at 169. For a discussion of the turmeric patent claim, see *infra* note 191. The incentives motivating the inventors to file the turmeric patent in this case were probably more academic than economic, given their status as university researchers and their pre-existing assignment of all patent rights to their employer.

185 For a more detailed discussion of the turmeric patent controversy, see Schuler, *supra* note 106, 166–1669; Downes, *supra* note 118, at 278. For the details of the CSIR challenge to the validity of the *basmati* rice patent, see *supra* note 161.

186 CIPR Final Report, *supra* note 106, at 76.

187 Re-examination Certificate available online: (http://lexisnexis.com/lawschool), Utility Patent database (accessed March 29, 2004). On April 21, 1998, the PTO cancelled all six claims of 5,401,504. *Ibid.*

188 CIPR Final Report, *supra* note 106, at 76.

189 See Schuler, *supra* note 106, at 168.

190 For a discussion of the specific basmati rice patent claims, the outcome of the CSIR petition for re-examination of these claims, and the potential risk of economic harm to India that the broad patent claims that were eventually rejected might have posed, see *supra* note 161. See *also* Schuler, *supra* note 106, at 171, pointing out that South Asian growers stand to suffer some competition in the marketplace from American-grown basmati—though it is important to distinguish between economic harm resulting from *competition* and economic harm resulting from use of a patent to *bar* competing imports of South Asian basmati rice.

By contrast, assertions by one commentator that had the turmeric patent not been challenged, Indian nationals in the US would "infringe this patent were they to rely on their own traditional knowledge to treat their children's wounds," and that, "if the University of Mississippi been awarded a similar patent in India, tens of millions of people would then have become patent infringers!" see Dutfield, *supra* note 132, at 65, are both misleading and naive. The first assertion is misleading because Indian nationals residing in the US and using traditional methods that have existed for thousands of years would not be infringing methods that were invented by the patent applicants. Although the US novelty standard is one of relative novelty, the § 102(f) requirement that the inventors actually invent what they seek to patent must still be satisfied. 35 U.S.C. § 102(f) (2001). It is true that if the applicants purported to invent something that was in fact traditional knowledge (as these applicants apparently did), then anyone who practiced the patented technique would technically be infringing until the patent was administratively rejected upon re-examination (as it eventually was) or judicially invalidated for failure to satisfy § 102(f). But the statement is also somewhat naïve because in order for an infringement proceeding to be brought, the infringer must first be identified, and as is noted *infra* in text accompanying note 194, identifying infringers of a method claim involving a staple article of commerce is notoriously difficult—so difficult, indeed, that it makes such a patent essentially worthless.

The second assertion is utterly fatuous as it is highly unlikely that diagnostic, therapeutic, or surgical methods have ever been or will ever be made patentable in India, there being no international obligation to do so, as is noted *infra* in text accompanying note 198. Even if such methods were patentable in India, the application for treating wounds with turmeric would probably be rejected because the use of turmeric for wound healing is not novel in India. Even if the particular method claimed happened not to be identical to traditional methods, the application would still likely fail for being obvious in light of the known traditional methods.

191 Claim 1 of the 5,401,504 patent read, "A method of promoting healing of a wound in a patient, which consists essentially of administering a wound-healing agent consisting of an effective amount of turmeric powder to said patient." This is extremely broad claim that was apparently not narrowed by any disclosures in the patent application.

192 While a broad patent "may be strong on offense because it covers more and therefore is more likely to be infringed ... it also is weak on defence because it may cover something in the prior art or fail to contain a sufficiently detailed disclosure and therefore it is more likely to be invalid." F. Scott Kieff, *Perusing Property Rights in DNA*, in F. Scott Kieff, ed. Perspectives on Properties of the Human Genome Project 139 (2003) [hereinafter Kieff] (citing and elaborating on the statement of the late Judge Giles S. Rich that "the stronger a patent, the weaker it is, and the weaker a patent, the stronger it is.").

The *basmati* rice patent likewise contained broad claims, but as with the turmeric patent, the broad claims of the basmati rice patent were ultimately rejected upon re-examination precisely because they were overbroad. See *supra* note 161 and accompanying text.

193 See *supra* note 161.

194 Chisum on Patents § 16.02, available online: (http://lexisnexis.com/lawschool), Patent Law database (accessed April 13, 2004) ("A process consists of one or more operative steps, and, accordingly, direct infringement by unauthorised use of a process consists of the performance of all the process's operative steps.").

195 35 U.S.C. § 287(c) (2001). However, § 287(c)(2)(A) defines "medical activity" so as to not include, *inter alia*, "the practice of a patented use of a composition of matter in violation of such patent." *Ibid.* It is not clear how broadly this phrase will be interpreted in biotechnology cases and whether a medical practitioner practicing the turmeric patented method would have been found liable for infringement under this section, had the law been in existence at that time.

196 Jeffrey I. D. Lewis, *Medical Process Patent Legislation Enacted*, available online: (http://www.pbwt.com/Resources/index-article.html) (accessed April 13, 2004).

197 See, e.g., Cynthia M. Ho, Patents, Patients, and Public Policy: An Incomplete Intersection at 35 U.S.C. § 287(c), 33 *U.C. Davis L. Rev.* 601, 669–70 (2000) (arguing that § 287 (c) is likely invalid under TRIPS).

198 Trade-Related Aspects of Intellectual Property Rights, full text available online: (http:.//www.wto.org/english/tratop_e/trips_e/t_agm0_e.htm) (accessed April 10, 2004).

199 See *supra* the discussion, in the immediately preceding section, on the Quinoa Patent.

200 ETC, *Peruvian Farmers and Indigenous People Denounce Maca Patents*, available online: (http://www.etcgroup.org/article.asp?newsid-353) (accessed April 11, 2004) [hereinafter ETC, *Maca Patents*].

201 *Ibid.*

202 *Ibid.* In fact, however, neither of the patents is a threat to Peruvian farmers because, like the neem patent, the patents do not claim any variety of maca plants, as such, but rather claim specific materials derived from maca. Therefore, Peruvian farmers can still export maca to the United States and the inventors can then use the maca to prepare the patented inventions. This situation is actually beneficial to the Peruvian farmers since they should enjoy an increased demand for their product. The first patent at issue is US Patent No. 6,267,995 (issued July 31, 2001), which is entitled "Extract of Lepidium Meyenii Roots for Pharmaceutical Applications." The existence of this patent does not foreclose opportunities to Peruvian farmers or any other indigenous peoples. First, the patent is valid only in the United States so others can continue to use maca however they wish, and can even practice the patented invention anywhere else in the world. Second, the patent provides only narrow, limited rights to the US patent holder. Although the claims are to an extract from maca, they pertain to an extract that is prepared by a very specific process and therefore do not prevent others from making an extract, even the exact same extract, by any other method in the United States. Claim 1, the sole independent claim, reads, "An isolated composition obtained by extracting *Lepidium meyenii* roots, said composition being substantially free of cellulose and

comprising: a) between about 5–9 per cent of benzyl isothiocyanate, b) between about 1–3 per cent of Lepidium sterol component, c) between about 20–30 per cent of Lepidium fatty acid component, and d) about 10 per cent or more of macamide component, *said composition being prepared by a process comprising*: i) contacting *Lepidium meyenii* roots with a first aqueous solvent comprising about 90 per cent volume percentage or more of water, ii) separating residual *Lepidium meyenii* root material from the first contacted aqueous solvent, iii) contacting the residual *Lepidium meyenii* root material with a second aqueous solvent comprising a mixture of an alcohol and water having about 90 per cent volume percentage alcohol or more to form a liquor, and iv) concentrating the liquor to obtain the composition." *Ibid.* (emphasis added).

The second patent at issue is US Patent No. 6,093,421 (issued July 25, 2000), which is entitled "Maca and Antler for Augmenting Testosterone Levels." *Ibid.* Again, this patent also does not cause problems for Peruvian indigenous peoples. First, the patent is valid only in the United States and therefore, anyone can practice the patented invention anywhere else in the world. Second, because this is a process patent, detecting infringement can be very difficult since every step of the patented process must be followed in order to infringe. Third, the patent is for a process of using maca and antler in combination. Claim 1 reads "A process of increasing testosterone levels in a man comprising: orally administering to a man in need of such treatment, an effective amount of a composition *containing maca and antler*." *Ibid.* Thus, to infringe, a composition of maca with antler must be administered. To avoid literal infringement, maca can be administered, followed by the step of antler being administered, to a man; or the steps can be reversed so that antler is first administered then maca is administered. As long as maca and antler are not in the same composition, there can be no literal infringement. (It is doubtful that infringement would be found under the doctrine of equivalents since both maca and antler separately are thought to increase testosterone levels so the combination of this patent is what makes it unique. Practicing the steps separately or in succession would likely not be equivalent to practicing the patent's combination)

ETC also was concerned about a filed patent application, US Patent Application No. 878,141 (filed June 8, 2001). The application has since been abandoned but a patent was granted on a continuation application: US Patent No. 6,552,206 (issued April 22, 2003). This patent is entitled "Compositions and Methods for Their Preparation from Lepidium." Again, this patent does not foreclose any opportunities to indigenous peoples. Although the patent title seems broad, the claims do not specifically use maca. Claim 1 reads, "A N-benzyl-16(R,S)-hydroxy-9-oxo-10E,12E,14E-octadecatrieneamide having a chemical formula C.sub25 H.sub.35 NO.sub.3." Claim 3, the other independent claim, reads, "A N-benzyl-9,16-dioxo-10E,12E,14E-octadecatrieneamide having a chemical formula C.sub.25 H.sub.35 Nosub.3." Neither of these claims specifies that these compounds are made or extracted from maca. In fact, the specification states that the compounds "can be synthetically prepared, or obtained from Lepidium plant material. ..." Thus, the inventors can make the compounds in their lab without ever using maca as a source.

A fourth patent on maca has been issued: US Patent No. 6,428,824 (issued August 6, 2002), entitled "Treatment of Sexual Dysfunction with an Extract of Lepidium meyenii Roots." Claim 1 reads, "A method of treating sexual dysfunction in an animal, comprising: administering a sexual dysfunction treating effective amount of an isolated composition derived from an aqueous solvent extract of *Lepidium* meyenii root to an animal in need of treatment for sexual dysfunction said isolated composition being substantially free of cellulose and comprising: a) between about 5–9 per cent of benzyl isothiocyanate, b) between about 1–3 per cent of Lepidium sterol component, c) between about 20–30 per cent of Lepidium fatty acid component, and d) about 10 per cent or more of macamide component." This claim is the method of use claim of the almost identical composition that was claimed in US Patent No. 6,267,995 and this patent application is in fact a divisional application of that patent's application. Although this patent uses essentially the same composition as US Patent No. 6,267,995, this patent's process claim is not limited to the composition being prepared in a specific manner as US Patent No. 6,267,995 was. Thus, this patent claim is broader in that regard. However, it is narrower in the sense that to infringe, the composition must used in a particular way and for a particular purpose—namely, to treat sexual dysfunction is an animal in need of such treatment.

203 *Ibid.* Such an assertion is incorrect because, as stated *supra* note 202, the two patents are not on maca, but on products *derived from* maca. In addition, a third patent's claimed composition can even be prepared synthetically and does not require the use of maca at all. US Patent No. 6,552,206 (issued April 22, 2003).

204 US Patent No. 6,267,995 (issued 31 July 2001); see *also supra* note 202.

205 US Patent No. 6,093,421 (issued 25 July 2000); see *also supra* note 202.

206 ETC, *Maca Patents*, *supra* note 200.

207 *Ibid.*

208 *Ibid.*

209 *Ibid.* As discussed in note 202, the patents are on products derived from maca, not on maca itself. Thus, no opportunities are being foreclosed. In fact, development of the patented compositions and processes may increase demand for maca and create a large export market for the growers of this crop.

210 *Ibid.* This statement is incorrect and nonsensical. As discussed in note 202, the patents are not on maca. Thus, the growers of maca can export maca to the United States because the patent is not on maca, and they can do whatever they wish with maca outside of the United States, even to the point of practicing the patented processes and making the patented compositions.

211 See *supra* notes 201–203.

212 *Ibid.*

213 Maca grows at altitudes "between 3,800 (12,500 feet) and 4,400 meters (14,450 feet) above the sea level." This and additional information about maca is available online: (http://www.intimaca.com/#description) (accessed April 13, 2004).

214 See ETC, *Maca Patents*, *supra* note 200. For a discussion of these inaccuracies, see *supra* notes 201–203.

215 Fortunately, despite ETC's campaign of misinformation, a more responsible international intellectual property nonprofit organisation, Public Interest Intellectual Property Advisors (PIIPA), has been retained to provide pro bono legal representation for the coalition representing the indigenous maca farmers, the Working Group on Maca. Alicia Upano, *D.C. Team Gets to the Root of the Problem*, Legal Times, Week of January 12, 2004, Vol. XXVII, No. 2. The Group is being represented by Sterne Kessler Goldstein & Fox of Washington DC. The managing partner of the firm, Jorge Goldstein, is quoted as saying that the Group has two legal options: "attempt to revoke existing patents through re-examination at the US Patent and Trademark Office or add an inventor to the patent—a method in which Goldstein says a tribe could share patent ownership with the [patent holder]." *Ibid.* Although the exact grounds for the re-examination are not apparent, this is a strategy that has succeeded in certain cases, such as the turmeric and basmati rice patent controversies, see *supra* notes 183–198 and accompanying text; but has failed in others, such as the US neem patent controversy, see *supra* notes 111–133 and accompanying text. The second option, to name additional inventors, suggests that the invention may have been derived from specific traditional knowledge holders and, if so, would offer support for one of the proposals currently being considered to assure that indigenous peoples are acknowledged for their contributions to the subject matter of patent applications filed in the US Patent Office. See *infra* section 12.4 of this chapter.

216 US Patent No. 5,894,079 (issued 13 April 1999). The inventor has also received a Plant Variety Protection Certificate from the Department of Agriculture for his plant. Plant Variety Protection Certificate No. 9700027 (issued May 28, 1999).

217 Timothy Pratt, *Patent on Small Yellow Bean Provokes Cry of Biopiracy*, New York Times, March 20, 2001, page F5, available online: (http://lexisnexis.com/lawschool), New York Times database (accessed April 14, 2004) [hereinafter Pratt].

218 US Patent No. 5,894,079 (issued April 13, 1999).

219 Pratt, *supra* note 217, at F5.

220 *Ibid.*

221 ETC, CIAT, and the Mexican government are seeking to have the patent revoked. ETC, *Mexican Bean Biopiracy*: US-Mexico Legal Battle Erupts over Patented "Enola" Bean, available online: (http://www.etcgroup.org/documents/geno_mexicanbean.pdf) (accessed April 14, 2004) [hereinafter ETC, *Mexican Bean Biopiracy*]. Apparently, the patent holder, Larry Proctor, is claiming that his patented Enola bean is not the same as the Mayacoba bean that importers claim to be importing, and that Mexican farmers are

in fact raising his Enola bean and selling them as Mayacoba beans. See Schuler, *supra* note 106, at 175.

Although the validity of this patent is indeed questionable, ETC weakens the credibility of its opposition to the patent by advancing several baseless arguments for why the patent should be revoked. For example, in support of its position, ETC quotes an academic, Professor James Kelly, a bean breeder at Michigan State University, as having said that the patent is "inappropriate, unjust and is not based on the scientific evidence or facts." ETC, *Mexican Bean Biopiracy*, *supra* note 221. However, conclusory assertions of this sort do not provide legal grounds for revocation of the patent. This same professor is quoted as saying, "I would challenge the *procedure* they used as not being unique ... this is a routine *procedure* used by bean breeders ... ." *Ibid.* (emphasis added). However, even if the procedure used by Proctor was known, he would still be able to invent a new composition, in this case a plant, with the known methods if the patent claims are to the composition and not to the method. In this case, 12 of the 15 patent claims are to compositions. Thus, this argument is wholly inapplicable to these claims and could not be used to invalidate them. Moreover, even though three of the claims are to methods, the methods claimed in the patent are in fact quite narrow. The three method claims are limited to using a specific bean plant for their execution. The specific bean plant used is the bean plant of the specific seed that was deposited at ATCC under accession number 209549 and thus the methods can go no further than to exclude others from using the deposited line in practicing the recited method.

222 CIAT filed a request for re-examination of the 5,894,079 patent through the law firm of Dodds & Associates on December 18, 2000. Request for Re-examination, available online: (http://www.ciat.cgiar.org/pdf/enola_legal_challenge.pdf) (accessed March 20, 2004) [hereinafter CIAT Request]. It was predicted that the PTO would reply to the request within three months. ETC, *Enola Bean Patent Challenged*, available online: (http://www.etcgroup.org/article.asp?newsid=96) (accessed March 17, 2004) [hereinafter ETC, *Enola Bean Patent Challenged*]. However, the patent holder, Larry Proctor, has since amended the original patent and filed 43 new claims, thereby delaying a decision from the PTO. ETC, *Proctor's Gamble:* Yellow Bean Patent Owner Sues 16 Farmers and Processors in US, available online: (http://www.etcgroup.org/documents/ProctorGamblefin.pdf) (accessed April 14, 2004) [hereinafter ETC, *Proctor's Gamble*].

The CIAT Request raises several interesting arguments pertaining to the patent's invalidity. However, the arguments are not on point and cannot support a revocation of the patent. First, the Request makes an argument based on the Convention for Biodiversity (CBD). CIAT Request, *supra*, at 2. The CIAT Request states, "The original starting materials from which this invention derives were brought into the United States without a required export permit from the country of origin of the material, which was Mexico. Under the terms of the [CBD] the original genetic material from which this invention was derived is sovereign property of the country of Origin [sic]." *Ibid.* The problem with this argument is that the U.S. has not ratified the CBD and its terms are therefore not enforceable here.

Next, the CIAT Request argues that the deposited seed should be destroyed because, "[t]his material was misappropriated from its true title holder, the country of Mexico. Furthermore, the plant health status of this material is unknown, it could contain seed-borne pathogens, poses [sic] a danger to American agriculture." *Ibid.* at pages 2–3. Two problems exist with this argument. First, Proctor claims to have legally bought a bag of beans in Mexico. Thus, he did not misappropriate the beans from the Mexican government. If the beans were in fact so important to Mexico, why were there no restrictions on the purchaser of the beans? There is no indication that the bag of beans was transferred subject to any restrictions on the use of the beans. Second, the beans are apparently not a danger to American agriculture. The deposited seeds had been allowed into the US and (assuming that was in 1991, not 1994, as claimed in the patent) the beans had been propagated for over two years before the patent application was filed. If the seeds posed any risk of harm, the harm has already been done. Also, if the seeds do pose a safety risk, the importers challenging the patent would not be allowed to import these beans into the US either, assuming that they are correct that the patented beans are no different from the beans that Mexicans have been exporting to the US for years.

Next, the CIAT Request claims that numerous pieces of prior art disclosing the beans exist. *Ibid.* at page 3. It states, "[w]e outline here a substantial body of prior art that relates to improvement of beans in general and to 'yellow beans' in particular." *Ibid.* Several problems arise. First, as discussed *supra*, note 221, it is inconsequential to the validity of the composition claims of the patent that the techniques used by Proctor were known in the art. In composition claims, the invented *product* of the technique is being patented. Such an argument applies only to the method claims, but as discussed in note 221, the method claims of the patent are limited to using the specific deposited variety of bean in practicing the method. Second, prior art pertaining to yellow beans may be of no consequence. With respect to the claims to the deposited variety of bean seed (accession number 209549), the deposited bean seed variety is said to possess several unique characteristics, in addition to the bean colour. As the patent specification stated, the patented, deposited seed is for a plant with "small leaves, good adherence of the pod to the branches of the plant, as well as resistance to pod shattering" in addition to the yellow colour. US Patent No. 5,894,079; see *also infra* note 223. Thus, prior art relating to yellow beans does not necessarily anticipate (i.e., make non-novel) the claims to the deposited seed that has several unique characteristics, the combination of which can be novel. With respect to the broader patent claims on beans of yellow colour, if the prior art beans are in fact the exact same shade, they may be anticipatory, as discussed *infra* note 223. If the yellow beans in the prior art are not the same, then the art cannot be anticipatory of the patented beans. CIAT Request, *supra*, at page 4 (claiming only that six accessions in CIAT's gene bank are the identical yellow colour as the patented beans).

Next, the Request reports that CIAT is a repository for genetic resources that "are held under a trust agreement between CIAT and the Food & Agriculture Organization (FAO) of the United Nations," asserts that "these collections are International Public Goods upon which no form of Intellectual Property protection is afforded," and then states that the beans at issue are "substantially identical" to beans in the CIAT collection. *Ibid.* If specimens deposited at CIAT are distributed to researchers, the researchers cannot seek intellectual property protection for the samples they received. However, this does not mean that independently acquired specimens that are identical to deposited specimens cannot be the subject of intellectual property rights. The Material Transfer Agreement (MTA) used by CIAT and CGIAR states, "[t]he material is held in trust under the terms of this agreement ,and the recipient has no rights to obtain Intellectual Property Rights (IPRs) on the material or related information ... The recipient, therefore, hereby agrees not to claim ownership over the material, nor to seek IPRs over that material, or its genetic parts or components, *in the form received*." MTA, available online: (http://www.cgiar.org/pdf/mta2003_en.pdf) (accessed April 16, 2004) (emphasis added). Thus, a party who obtains a specimen from the collection can obtain IPRs over any form of the specimen *other than* in the form received. Likewise, if a party did not obtain a sample from CIAT or CGIAR, it did not receive the specimen in *any* form from CGIAR or CIAT and thus is not precluded by the MTA from obtaining IPRs. The MTA cannot be enforced against a party that is not in a contractual relationship with CGIAR or CIAT. There is no evidence that Proctor received any specimen or was a party to any contract with CGIAR or CIAT; thus, the terms of CGIAR and CIAT's MTA do not apply to Proctor and cannot be used to challenge his patent.

223 Initially, Proctor brought suit against two importers: Tutuli Produce of Nogales, Arizona and Productos Verde Valle of Guadalajara, Jalisco, Mexico. ETC, *Mexican Bean Biopiracy*, *supra* note 221. Proctor has since brought suit for patent infringement against a total of 16 small seed companies and farmers in the United States. ETC, *Proctor's Gamble*, *supra* note 122. But if Proctor in fact invented a new variety of bean that was not previously known in the United States or Mexico, it is difficult to see how all of these importers and farmers can be infringing the patented bean unless they all somehow were able to purloin samples of Proctor's beans. Apparently, Proctor is claiming that the Mexican farmers did just that. See Schuler, *supra* note 106, at 175.

224 In order for the patent to be valid, it must be useful, novel, and non-obvious. Proctor claims that he has bred a new, uniform variety of yellow beans that is distinct from already-known beans. According to the patent, Proctor selected for and ultimately bred a bean plant that has "small leaves, good adherence of the pod to the branches of the plant, as well as resistance to pod shattering" and the seed of which has a distinctive yellow colour that "is present throughout the entire seed coat and remains uniform and stable season to season." US Patent No. 5,894,079. Proctor also deposited a sample of his Enola bean seed at the ATCC depository; the bean was assigned accession number 209549. *Ibid.* Thus, only if a homogenous,

uniform population of a bean with these characteristics did not exist or was not known before Proctor bred it would Proctor have in fact invented a new bean.

This raises two problems for Proctor. First, if all that he invented was a specific variety of yellow bean, then his patent claims can go no further and can be no broader than that deposited bean. This means that Proctor's right to exclude others can only go so far as to exclude others from using, making, offering to sell, and importing this *specific deposited* bean. 35 U.S.C. § 154. Regarding the claims of his patent, claim 1 appears to be valid if Proctor did in fact selectively breed this bean. Claim 1 reads "[a] Phaseolus vulgaris field bean seed designated Enola *as deposited* with the American Tissue Type Culture Collection under accession number 209549." US Patent No. 5,894,079 (emphasis added). In addition, the claims that are dependent on claim 1, claims 2 through 7, also appear to be valid because they are limited to and based on the specific deposited bean of claim 1. In contrast, the validity of claim 8 is doubtful. Claim 8 reads "[a] field bean variety of *Phaseolus vulgaris* that produces seed having a seed coat that is yellow in colour, wherein the yellow colour is from about 7.5 Y 8.5/4 to about 7.5 Y 8.5/6 in the Munsell Book of Colour when viewed in natural light." US Patent No. 5,894,079. This claim is broader than claim 1 and likely embraces bean varieties other than the bean variety that Proctor bred. If any of these bean varieties, having this same yellow colour, were publicly known in the United States (as they would be if they were being imported from Mexico or were being grown here) or published anywhere in the world, the claim is invalid. Since Proctor emphasised in the patent that he bred a specific bean, it is difficult to see how he could have invented or bred something broader than the specific deposited bean.

Second, if Proctor was in fact the first person to breed this bean and this bean was not known in the United States until he bred it, then it is highly unlikely that Mexicans are infringing by importing the patented beans into the United States, unless one credits his claim, see Schuler *supra* note 106, at 175, that Mexican farmers have somehow acquired his Enola bean and are selling them as Mayacoba beans. Without credible evidence to back up that assertion, Proctor cannot prevail in his infringement claims against Mexican importers and American farmers.

225 Pratt, *supra* note 217, at F5.

226 Chisum on Patents § 19.04, available online: (http://lexisnexis.com/lawschool), Patent Law database (accessed April 14, 2004) ("A patent owner may exploit a patent in an improper manner by violating the antitrust laws or extending the patent beyond its lawful scope.").

227 ETC, *Enola Bean Patent Challenged, supra* note 222. According to ETC, the spokesman for the Agricultural Association of Rio Fuerte in Sinaola, Mexico, export sales have dropped over 90 per cemt after Proctor received the patent and threatened bean importers in the United States with infringement suits. *Ibid.*

228 See WIPO, Matters Concerning Intellectual Property and Genetic Resources, Traditional Knowledge and Folklore, WO/GA/26/6 (August 25, 2000).

229 See WIPO, Matters Concerning Intellectual Property and Genetic Resources, Traditional Knowledge and Folklore—An Overview (March 16, 2001).

230 Available online: (http://www.wipo.int/tk/en/documents/html/igc3-17.html) (accessed May 3, 2004).

231 Nuno Pires de Carvalho, Requiring Disclosure of the Origin of Genetic Resources and Prior Informed Consent in Patent Applications Without Infringing The TRIPS Agreement: The Problem and The Solution, 2 *Wash. U. J. L.* & Pol'y 371 (2000), available online: (http://ls.wustl.edu/Journal/2/p371carvalho.pdf) (accessed May 3, 2004) [hereinafter Carvalho, The Problem & the Solution].

232 Available online: (http://law.wustl.edu/centeris/Confpapers/PDFWrdDoc/Fromshaman2.pdf) (accessed May 3, 2004) [hereinafter Carvalho, A Road Under Construction].

233 Available online: (http://www.wto.org/english/docs_e/legal_e/27-trips_06_e.htm) (accessed May 3, 2004).

234 See *supra* note 232, at page 34.

235 *Ibid.*

236 *Ibid.* at pages 70–73.

237 *Ibid.* at page 73.

238 See generally Carvalho, The Problem & the Solution, *supra* note 231.

239 See Carvalho, A Road Under Construction, *supra* note 232, at pages 21–27.

240 See, e.g., *supra* notes 183–198, discussing the turmeric patent controversy.

241 See Kieff, *supra* note 192, at page 141.

242 See, e.g., *supra* notes 178–180, and accompanying text, discussing why the quinoa patent was abandoned.

243 The author is indebted to Mr. Dale Ernst, IP LLM, 2004, for suggesting the possibility of a restitutionary claim under these circumstances. See generally Restatement of Restitution §§1–3 (1988).

244 See generally J. H. Reichman and Pamela Samuelson, Intellectual Property Rights in Data? 50 *Vand. L. Rev.* 51 (1997) (discussing the politics that drove the promulgation of the European Union Database Directive).

245 Joseph Henry Vogel, *From the "Tragedy of the Commons" to the "Tragedy of the Commonplace": Analysis and Synthesis through the lens of Economic Theory*, available online: (http://www.law.wustl.edu/centeris/Confpapers/index.html) (accessed May 3, 2004).

246 J. H. Reichman, Legal Hybrids Between the Patents and Copyright Paradigms, 94 *Colum. L. Rev.* 2432, 2443–2444 (1994) [hereinafter Reichman, *Legal Hybrids*].

247 *Id.*

248 See generally Mark D. Janis & Jay P. Kesan, U.S. Plant Variety Protection: Sound and Fury...?, 39 *Hous. L. Rev.* 727 (2002).

249 Reichman, *Legal Hybrids*, *supra* note 246, at page 2496 (1994).

250 *Ibid.* at page 2444.

251 *International News Service v. Associated Press*, 248 U.S. 215 (1918).

252 See *supra* Reichman, *Legal Hybrids*, *supra* note 246, 2475–2476 (citing with apparent approval the Japanese Unfair Competition Prevention Act, Law no. 47/1993, 19 May 1993, Section 2(3), which forbids slavish duplication of new industrial product configurations for a three-year time period from the time the relevant products become available to the public).

253 See Carvalho, A Road Under Construction, *supra* note 232, at page 19.

254 See 35 U.S.C. §262 (2004).

255 M. Nimmer & D. Nimmer, 1-6 Nimmer on Copyrights §6.12 (2004).

256 WIPO/GRTKF/IC/4/8 (October 30, 2002).

257 *Id.*

258 See generally Janis & Kesan, *supra* note 158.

Index

Other Titles on Law

Essays in Singapore Legal History
edited by Kevin Y L Tan
ISBN 981 210 349 X (Limp)
ISBN 981 210 389 9 (Hardcover)

Rebuilding Lives, Restoring Relationships: Juvenile Justice and the Community
edited by The Subordinate Courts of Singapore
ISBN 981 210 219 1 (Limp)
ISBN 981 210 269 8 (Hardback)

Private Ownership of Public Housing In Singapore
by Tan Sook Yee
ISBN 981 210 114 4

ASEAN: The Evolving Legal Framework for Economic Cooperation
by Paul J Davidson
ISBN 981 210 185 3